VIRGINIA WILLS, TRUSTS, & ESTATES:

Code, Cases, Commentary

James G. Dwyer

William & Mary School of Law

About the Author

James G. Dwyer is the Arthur B. Hanson Professor of Law at the Marshall-Wythe School of Law, College of William & Mary, where he has been on the faculty since 2000. He teaches Trusts & Estates and Family Law, as well as other subjects. Professor Dwyer is also the BarBri lecturer for Virginia Wills, Trusts, and Estates, and he serves as Reporter of Decisions for the Virginia Court of Appeals.

Pulbished by KAMSET Press – Legal Division

Printed in the United States of America

ISBN: 978-0-9978973-0-2

SUMMARY OF CONTENTS

CONTENTS

Introduction

This volume compiles and analyzes Virginia law governing what happens to people's property when they die. Increasingly in recent decades, the law of wills, trusts, and estates has become more uniform across the country, as most states have adopted all or part of various uniform acts promulgated by the National Conference of Commissioners on Uniform State Laws. Most significant for Virginia attorneys, Virginia is now among the majority of states that has adopted the Uniform Trust Act.[1] Virginia has also adopted several uniform codes of smaller scope but has not embraced the other major uniform law, the Uniform Probate Code. In any event, courts in each state inevitably shape the law in a unique way by interpreting necessarily broad language in statutes, so studying Virginia statutes specifically and our courts' interpretation of those statutes is essential in practice. Attorneys should also know that the General Assembly in 2012 accomplished a major reorganization of the law relating to disposition of decedent's estates and gratuitous wealth transfers more broadly, consolidating many disparate Code titles into a new Title 64.2. This makes it much easier to locate current statutory law relating to any aspect of estate planning, administration, and litigation, but more complicated to locate case law interpreting code language.

Lawyering relating to disposition of decedents' estates occurs both before people die, in the form of "estate planning," and after they die, in the form of "the probate process." "Estate" is a broad term than can encompass all of a person's property, regardless of how it is transferred before, at the time of, or after death. So estate planning is essentially long-term plannin Migration From Community Property States g for disposition of property one will not use during one's life for one's own benefit. "Probate" refers to transfer of persons' wealth after they die and through a court. "Probate property" is property that passes through the probate process and includes property directed to others by a will and property as to which the decedent made no plans (the decedent's "intestate estate").

There are several ways, however, to transfer one's property outside the probate process. Making gifts while you are still alive is an obvious example, but there are important other ways with which one must be familiar. Trusts are an increasingly common alternative way, so they receive their own chapter in this volume. Other common alternatives to probate are joint titling of property and the beneficiary designations people make on their bank accounts, investment accounts, and life insurance policies, which generally do not require the involvement of a lawyer.

As a general matter, an estate planning lawyer will try to steer clients toward these "non-probate" means of transferring property just mentioned, for several reasons:

---

[1] For analysis of the most salient differences between the UTC and prior Virginia trust law, see John E. Donaldson and Robert T. Danforth, The Virginia Uniform Trust Code, 40 U. Rich. L. Rev. 325 (2005).

- The court typically charges a fee based on the size of the probate estate, and the estate administrator is generally entitled to a fee for services that is a fixed percentage of the value of the probate estate.
- Non-probate transfers happen more or less instantly at death, so intended recipients do not need to wait for the probate process to run its course.
- The probate process is public, whereas non-probate transfers are not disclosed to anyone but the beneficiaries.
- Non-probate transfers are less susceptible to challenge by disgruntled relatives who did not receive them.

Nevertheless, most Americans end up transferring the bulk of their assets remaining at death by will or intestacy, so after an initial chapter explaining how you determine which property is in the probate estate, this book covers intestacy and wills before moving on to trusts and other non-probate devices. The final chapters give you the nuts and bolts of administering an estate, given that lawyers are often the ones who do that, a primer on the tax aspect of estate planning, and some accessory issues that estate planning lawyers discuss with clients, such as advance directives relating to medical care in case of incapacity and providing in non-financial ways for minor offspring.

In case you are still deciding whether you want to study or practice in this field as you read this introduction, here are a couple of points about the nature of trusts and estates law. First, if you are someone who enjoys learning a complex set of laws and deploying them without having to think much about policy or grand theories, trusts and estates is for you. For the most part, the subject has little to offer anyone interested in normative ethics—that is, anyone who likes to reason about fairness and public policy. State law governing trusts and estates is by and large aimed simply at effectuating the intent persons had when they died or when they executed a will or trust instrument, on the assumption that people are entitled to do whatever they want with their property regardless of whether it is fair or consistent with sound public policy. One could ask and debate the fundamental question of why that assumption pertains even as to disposition of one's property after death, when one can no longer benefit from or exercise judgment as to distribution of one's property. But otherwise the subject does not call for any question other than "What did the decedent likely intend?" Linguists or philosophers of mind might be able to inject some interesting theoretical arguments into the analysis of that monotonous question, but in practice their perspectives are absent, so this text does not attempt to channel them into the discussion.

Second, estate planning is a terrific area of practice, in terms of job satisfaction. It is generally work that is constructive and non-adversarial, at times even heartwarming. The estate planning lawyer helps clients provide for their loved ones, and no one else has any right to be part of the conversation. It is low-key, predictable, and easy to schedule as you wish, in contrast to litigation or work subject to external deadlines such as tax preparation. Estate administration is also typically laid-back, not involving stringent deadlines or confrontations. Estate litigation can be depressing, as it usually entails surviving family members battling viciously over wealth none of them have any right to, as every resentment developed in the course of the family's history rears its ugly head, but litigation is rare. And usually your fee will come out of your client's take from the estate, which is a windfall for the client, so if you are someone who finds it harder to charge individuals hourly rates similar to those for doctors (but without insurance coverage) than to charge corporations, you would find estate litigation weighs less on your conscience than, for example, a divorce practice. And the family dynamics can be fascinating to observe. So on the whole, it is a highly attractive specialization.

A couple of additional definitions before beginning:

A "personal representative" (designated as "PR" henceforth) is typically appointed to act as agent for the person who died, charged with managing the estate and distributing it to heirs and beneficiaries. The agent is called the "executor" if the appointment results from a designation in the decedent's will. If instead the court selects the agent, s/he is called the "administrator." The personal representative stands in the shoes of the decedent, distributing the estate in accordance with the decedent's wishes at the time of death, as reflected in a valid will or as presumed by law to the extent any probate property is not covered by a valid will.

Though people commonly use the term "heir" to apply to anyone who receives wealth from a decedent's estate, legally it refers only to those who take by intestate succession, the topic of Chapter Two. Those who take by will (testate succession) are called devisees (of real property), legatees (of personal property), or more generically will beneficiaries (real or personal property).

Chapter One
The Probate Estate

Before applying rules for intestate succession and disposition of property by will to a decedent's estate, one must identify what property is subject to either set of rules. Only "probate" property passes by will or intestate succession. Even if a will mentions some specific property that the decedent did own just before dying, such as a house or a car, if the decedent set up a non-probate transfer of that property – for example, by joint titling or by placing it in a revocable trust, the will cannot govern disposition of that property and that provision in the will is simply ineffective. Likewise, the property would not be governed by the intestacy rules presented in Chapter Two.

I.   How to determine what the decedent owned before dying

Anything of value can constitute property potentially in the probate estate, even intangibles like intellectual property and contractual rights. Here are some indicia of ownership:

Major tangible assets such as houses, cars, and boats must have a title by law, so appearance of the decedent's name on the title of such property is a fairly clear indication of an ownership interest. Importantly, however, if that interest is as a "joint tenant with rights of survivorship," it disappears at death and living joint tenants (survivors) become the sole owners, so the jointly titled property would not go in the probate estate.

Bank accounts, investment accounts, and insurance policies also have owners' names "on them." If the decedent was the sole named owner of any such account or policy, and if there is no payable-on-death (POD) designation, then the account or policy payout goes in the probate estate. However, if they do designate a beneficiary and the beneficiary is living and not disqualified (as discussed later in the chapter), then the interest does not go into the probate estate; it passes outside of probate.

The decedent might also have had rights to collect money from other people or businesses in the future – for example, lawyers' fees not yet collected, a business's accounts receivable, or tort claims. It would be unusual for those to have a beneficiary or backup recipient designated or to be in trust, so those are most likely going to be part of the probate estate, which is to say that the personal representative can enforce the rights and add the money received to the probate estate.

Lastly, most decedents have a large number of items of tangible personal property, most of which are of little value but some of which, such as jewelry, could be very valuable. Some of these could have been placed in a trust, and therefore would pass outside of probate, but ordinarily they are not set up for non-probate transfer and so will be part of the probate estate. The PR will most likely have to determine a value for each item of property, which might well be the most aggravating part of estate administration.

In addition, though, there could be dispute about which personal property belonged to the decedent. In a situation where a surviving spouse is to receive less than the entire estate, he or she might claim that certain valuable items never belonged to the decedent or were gifted by the decedent during life. The PR could ask for documentation of original purchase or acquisition or of donative intent, but if the survivor says no such documentation exists, the PR might be helpless to verify or disprove the survivor's claim.

In Walters v. Walters, 69 Va. Cir. 334 (2005), a circuit court analyzed a situation where the decedent had a large amount of cash in the house that testimony revealed he has been keeping for his spouse in the event of his death. The court needed to determine whether the decedent had already given the money to the wife as a lifetime gift, or if instead it was part of the estate and counted against the wife's statutory allowances as a surviving spouse.

> Around 1994, the decedent and the Respondent started saving large amounts of currency in a fruitcake tin. At time of the decedent's death, the Respondent said that she knew the tin was in the attic and that it contained around $20,000. After the decedent's death, the decedent's son (Respondent's stepson) asked the Respondent if she knew where the money was located in the attic. When she said that she did not, the son brought the fruitcake tin downstairs and gave it to her, apparently at the direction of the decedent. The Petitioner corroborated the Respondent's testimony, stating that "I knew Dad had cash in the house ... He had told me about it several times. And he always said that if something happened to him, to make sure that [the Respondent] got the money, because it would take care of her until the insurance policy came." ...

> The Court finds that the money in the fruitcake tin belongs to the Respondent by virtue of the Will, not as an inter vivos gift. The Respondent cannot satisfy the burden of proof to characterize the money as a completed gift under the applicable Virginia statute, Va.Code Ann. § 55–3:

>> No gift of any goods or chattels shall be valid unless by deed or will, or unless actual possession shall have come to and remained with the donee or some person claiming under him. If the donor and donee reside together at the time of the gift, possession at the place of their residence shall not be a sufficient possession within the meaning of this section.

> In Taylor v. Smith, … the Court stated that the intention to make a gift must be inconsistent with any other theory, and that delivery of the gift must "[divest] the owner of all dominion and control over the property

and [invest] it in donee." 199 Va. 871, 874, 102 S.E.2d 160 (1958). In *Taylor*, the decedent rented a safety deposit box in the name of the person claiming the inter vivos gift. See id. at 872, 102 S.E.2d 160. The decedent gave the donee the keys to the box and told her that the money belonged to her. However, he borrowed the keys from time to time and was in possession of the keys at the time of his death. The Court concluded that "[u]nder the proved facts and circumstances in this case, Taylor did not intend to part with title to the contents of the box, and the delivery of the keys to defendant by Taylor did not divest him of all dominion and control over the property." Id. at 875, 102 S.E.2d 160.

As in *Taylor*, the Respondent's testimony at the hearing was not consistent with the requirements for an inter vivos gift. The decedent did not relinquish dominion and control over the money in the fruitcake tin until his death—he directed his son to give the money to the Respondent after his death. Furthermore, the Respondent admitted that she was not aware of the exact location of the tin and relied upon her stepson to deliver the tin to her after the decedent's death. According to the statute, when the donor and donee reside in the same house, a higher standard of delivery and possession must be met. See Va.Code Ann. § 55–3. In this case, the Respondent has not satisfied the delivery requirements for an inter vivos gift. The Commissioner's factual findings on this point are consistent with the evidence. ...

II.   Non-probate transfers

There are innumerable ways by which you can transfer your wealth at your death without it being part of the probate estate. You might want to do this because non-probate transfers happen immediately, so the people you would wish to benefit do not need to wait for the probate process runs its course. Another reason to "avoid probate" is to maximize what the decedent's intended beneficiaries receive; the state imposes a probate tax based on the total probate estate value (albeit only .1%), the court charges additional fees, the PR for the probate estate is generally entitled to take a percentage of the value of the estate (as much as 5%), and the PR might consult an attorney whose fee will also be paid from the probate estate. In addition, probate is a matter of public record, so any member of the public can look at the PR's inventory of the probate property and at the will if there is one. You might prefer not to have these things revealed to the world. Where non-probate transfers reduce the probate estate to less than $50,000 in personal property, probate is not required at all, sparing the PR from a lot of paperwork. See Va. Stat. § 64.2-601.

One reason to request probate regardless of the estate's size is to secure a final settlement of all of the decedent's debts. Creditors' rights to state a claim against an estate terminate at the closure of the probate estate. Absent probate, they are likely to have a longer time to do so. So when the decedent had credit problems or was the subject of a lawsuit, terminating creditors' claims is desirable and might justify the costs noted above.

Here is a brief summary of the main types of non-probate transfer devices:

A. Trusts

Chapter Five is devoted in its lengthy entirety to trusts. Here note simply that *inter vivos* trusts are a means of transferring property at death outside of probate. A typical *inter vivos* trust confers a life estate on the person who creates it (the trust "settlor" or "grantor") and a remainder interest (what follows a life estate) on whomever the settlor wishes to receive the property at his or her death. The trust operates to effect the transfer rather than intestacy law or a will. Trusts can also be created by a will, in which case they are called "testamentary trusts," but testamentary trusts do *not* avoid probate as to the property they are intended to control. Property that a will designates for placement in trust is part of the probate estate, and the trust effectively becomes one of the will beneficiaries.

B. Joint Tenancy

If you own property that is titled, such as real estate and automobiles, you can effect a non-probate transfer by retitling them in two or more names – your own and whomever you would want to get it in the event of your death – as "joint tenants with survivorship." In many other states, conveying title to two or more people as "joint tenants" creates a true joint tenancy, rather than a severable tenancy in common, but Virginia law requires language of survivorship in order to create a true joint tenancy. Va. Code §§ 55-20, 55-20.1. People commonly do this with spouses or offspring. Upon the original owner's death, such retitling causes the property to become automatically owned entirely by the other person(s) on the title. For spouses and real estate, specifically, titling as "tenants by the entirety" also effects a true joint tenancy – that is, with survivorship. Va. Code § 55-20.2

An alternative way to transfer real property outside of probate is to convey a remainder interest to the intended beneficiary, retaining a life estate. Technically, this is a lifetime gift rather than a death-time transfer, but the effect is the same; the original owner has full use and control of the property during life, and at death fee simple in the property vests in the remainder person.

In recognition that state residents might wish to transfer real property outside of probate yet not want the potential lifetime complications of creating a joint tenancy (e.g., requiring the joint tenant's consent to management or sale of the property), or the irrevocability of conveying a remainder interest, the Virginia General Assembly has created a device called a "transfer on death deed" that operates outside of probate, conveys no interest to others during the original owner's life, and is revocable up until the moment of death.

CODE OF VIRGINIA
Title 64.2. Wills, Trusts, and Fiduciaries[2]
Subtitle II. Wills and Decedents' Estates
Chapter 6. Transfers Without Qualification
Article 5. Uniform Real Property Transfer on Death Act.

§ 64.2-624. Transfer on death deed authorized.

An individual may transfer property to one or more beneficiaries effective at the transferor's death by a transfer on death deed.

§ 64.2-625. Transfer on death deed revocable.

A transfer on death deed is revocable even if the deed or another instrument contains a contrary provision.

§ 64.2-626. Transfer on death deed nontestamentary.

A transfer on death deed is nontestamentary.

§ 64.2-627. Capacity of transferor.

The capacity required to make or revoke a transfer on death deed is the same as the capacity required to make a will.

§ 64.2-628. Requirements.

A transfer on death deed: …

2. Shall state that the transfer to the designated beneficiary is to occur at the transferor's death; …

6. For property owned by joint owners to be effective, shall be executed by all joint owners …

§ 64.2-631. Effect of transfer on death deed during transferor's life.

During a transferor's life, a transfer on death deed does not:

1. Affect an interest or right of the transferor or any other owner, including the right to transfer or encumber the property; …

3. Affect an interest or right of a secured or unsecured creditor or future creditor of the transferor, even if the creditor has actual or constructive notice of the deed; …

5. Create a legal or equitable interest in favor of the designated beneficiary; or

6. Subject the property to claims or process of a creditor of the designated beneficiary.

§ 64.2-632. Effect of transfer on death deed at transferor's death.

---

[2] All statutes in this volume are from Title 64.2 of the Code of Virginia unless otherwise indicated. These top two headings will therefore be omitted in the rest of the book.

A. ... [O]n the death of the transferor, the following rules apply to property that is the subject of a transfer on death deed and owned by the transferor at death:

  1. Subject to subdivision 2, the interest in the property is transferred to and vests in the designated beneficiary at the death of the transferor in accordance with the deed. ...

  3. Subject to subdivision 4, concurrent interests are transferred to the beneficiaries in equal and undivided shares with no right of survivorship. ...

B. ... [A] beneficiary takes the property subject to all conveyances, encumbrances, assignments, contracts, mortgages, liens, and other interests to which the property is subject at the transferor's death. ...

C. If a transferor is a joint owner and is:

  1. Survived by one or more other joint owners, the property that is the subject of a transfer on death deed belongs to the surviving joint owner or owners with right of survivorship but remains subject to the naming of the designated beneficiary in the transfer on death deed; or

  2. The last surviving joint owner, the transfer on death deed is effective.

Joint ownership can also be created in a bank account. Adding another person's name to an account, however, will not necessarily have this result. The law reflects a recognition that sometimes account owners add another person to the account solely for management purposes, so the other person can manage the money for the benefit of the original owner. Litigation therefore arises over what the owner's intent was.

Supreme Court of Virginia.
Zink v. Stafford
257 Va. 46, 509 S.E.2d 833 (1999)

COMPTON, Justice.

*48 ... Thomas J. Stafford, a widower, died intestate in 1984, survived by his only children, a son, appellee Thomas L. Stafford, and a daughter, appellant June S. Zink. In 1985, the daughter qualified as administrator of the decedent's estate. **834 In 1988, the son filed a bill of complaint, ... alleg[ing], inter alia, that four promissory notes were estate assets rather than assets that passed to the daughter individually by right of survivorship, as she claimed. ...

At the time of his death, the decedent resided in Chesterfield County, where he had been engaged in farming, and in the development of a residential subdivision upon a parcel of land that he owned. Prior to his death, he built four houses in the subdivision, each on an individual subdivided lot. He sold each of the lots with improvements and in each instance took back a purchase money note secured by a deed of trust from the purchaser for part of the purchase price.

These notes have been referred to throughout this prolonged litigation as the "Higgerson note," the "Wood note," the "Brockwell *49 note," and the "Ross note," so called because the names referred to the makers of the notes and the purchasers of the real estate. The Higgerson note originally was payable to the decedent's order and subsequently endorsed by him on the note, "Pay to the order of Thomas J. Stafford or June S. Zink, or the survivor." The payee on the other three notes in each instance was "Thomas J. Stafford and June S. Zink, or the survivor."

Proceeds from the notes were deposited into a "collection account" at a local bank. The account was maintained in the names of "Thomas J. Stafford and June S. Zink as joint tenants with right of survivorship." During the several years before his death, the decedent's health failed, he "couldn't write checks on his own," and he was legally blind. Funds from the account were used for the decedent's maintenance or otherwise spent as he directed. ...

Section § 55-21 creates an exception to § 55-20 (which abolished the common law right of survivorship between joint tenants) "when it manifestly appears from the tenor of the instrument that it was intended the part of the one dying should then belong to the others." See *Buck v. Jordan*, 256 Va. 535, 542, 508 S.E.2d 880, 883 (1998). In *Pitts v. United States*, 242 Va. 254, 260, 408 S.E.2d 901, 904 (1991), interpreting those statutes, we found "that they were intended to apply to joint tenancies and to tenancies by the entireties created by an 'instrument' of conveyance or devise." We said that the promissory notes in issue there were "not such instruments."

The daughter argues ...**835 ... that the Wood, Brockwell and Ross notes, "in their original form, were the instruments that created the joint form of ownership. They were therefore instruments of conveyance." Continuing, the daughter argues, "The Higgerson note could not, in its original form, be regarded as an instrument of conveyance." She says, "That note, like the notes in *Pitts*, was a memorial of a chose in action, meaning the right of Thomas J. Stafford to the *50 fund represented by the note. However, Mr. Stafford's endorsement of the Higgerson note so as to make it payable 'to the order of Thomas J. Stafford or June S. Zink, or the survivor' made the note, as indorsed, an instrument of conveyance" under § 55-21.

In response, the son ... argues, the broader question whether these notes create a survivorship interest is immaterial, because the notes did not vest any interest in the daughter during the decedent's lifetime. Before a survivorship interest in the daughter could have been created, the son contends, the father must have created a joint tenancy between himself and the daughter during his lifetime by conveying or giving her an interest in the notes that vested at the time of the gift. Without such a conveyance or gift, the son argues, a joint tenancy did not exist from which to create survivorship. We agree with the son. ...

In the present case, because the daughter did not purchase an interest in any of the notes, the only manner in which she could have become a joint tenant with her father was for him to have made a gift to her of an interest in the notes before his death.

To determine whether the decedent made a valid gift *inter vivos*, the trier of fact must look beyond the declarations on the instrument in question and consider the surrounding facts and circumstances. In Swan v. Swan's Ex'r, 136 Va. 496, 117 S.E. 858 (1923), a donor had retitled several shares of stock to include his wife's name. This Court said that the manner in which the shares of stock were retitled was technically sufficient to transfer title. But the Court further explained that "it is quite possible and often happens, for reasons of convenience or otherwise, that stock held in the name of one person really *51 belongs to another. In such a case the certificate, though prima facie evidence of ownership in the person to whom it has been issued, possesses no such magic or sacredness as to prevent an inquiry into the facts. Sometimes the transferee is merely a nominal holder or 'dummy,' and in that event, although the transfer may be perfectly regular and complete on its fac[e], the true ownership remains in the transferor, and that fact may be shown." Id. at 519, 117 S.E. at 865. …

When a donee claims title to personal property by virtue of a gift, the burden of proof rests upon the donee to show every fact and circumstance necessary to constitute a valid gift by clear and convincing evidence. One of the elements necessary to constitute a gift *inter vivos* is that title to the property must vest in the donee at the time of the gift. The gift "must be absolute, irrevocable and without any reference to its taking effect at some future period." Quesenberry v. Funk, 203 Va. 619, 623, 125 S.E.2d 869, 873 (1962). If a **836 purported gift is not to take effect until the donor's death, then there "is an abortive testamentary act and not a gift." Knight v. Mears, 156 Va. 676, 681, 159 S.E. 119, 120 (1931).

The evidence in the present case clearly shows that the decedent during his lifetime never divested himself of dominion and control over any portion of the promissory notes. Although the note proceeds were deposited into the joint "collection account" from which both the father and daughter could withdraw funds, she never deposited any of her own funds into the account during his lifetime. She admitted that during his lifetime she was on the account solely as a convenience to her father, and agreed in testimony that he was not making a gift of those proceeds to her during his lifetime. For example, when asked, "And you didn't consider one-half of those accounts yours while your father was alive?", she responded, "No, sir, I did not." Moreover, the daughter admitted she could not spend during his lifetime any monies in the account without his prior approval. Also, the evidence showed the interest earned on the account was reported as income on the father's tax returns and none of it was reported on her income tax returns.

Thus, the survivorship language on each note was an abortive testamentary act and not a gift. See Quesenberry, supra, 203 Va. at 623-24, 125 S.E.2d at 873 (gift *in praesenti* of interest in joint bank account naming father and daughter not shown when daughter *52 considered the money belonged to father during his lifetime); Wrenn v. Daniels, 200 Va. 419, 430, 106 S.E.2d 126, 133 (1958) (parol evidence showed decedent had not made valid gift *inter vivos* of interest in shares of stock and bank account titled jointly in name of decedent and his son).

In sum, because there was no valid gift to the daughter of any portion of the notes, she did not hold title with her father as a joint tenant. Thus, without the prerequisite of a joint tenancy, survivorship could not be created. Consequently, we hold that the trial court correctly determined that the promissory notes and their proceeds were estate assets and did not pass to the daughter individually. ...

Supreme Court of Appeals of Virginia.
Colley v. Cox, 209 Va. 811, 167 S.E.2d 317 (1969)

HARRISON, Justice.

Iris Burgess Cox, executrix and legatee under the will of Pearl Tate Colley, ... alleged... that the estate consisted, in part, of a $10,000 savings account in Colonial-American National Bank, Roanoke, Virginia, in the name of Pearl Tate Colley or James T. Colley. Dr. Colley answered, claiming ownership of the joint account. **318 ... *812 ...

Mrs. Colley died on January 16, 1965, and her will disposed of an estate consisting of real and personal property valued at approximately $30,000. She named her friend, Mrs. Cox, as executrix and bequeathed her the sum of $500. Various other bequests were made, including one in the amount of $1000 to Dr. Colley, who was also named in the residuary clause.

The decedent lived in the City of Roanoke and was estranged from her husband. She was survived by a son, Dr. Colley, of Rocky Mount, Virginia, and one daughter who resides out of the state. The sole bequest to this daughter was a bedroom suite of furniture...

Following a heart attack, and on or about August 26, 1962, the decedent decided to add the name of her son, Dr. Colley, on the $10,000 savings account. She attended to the transaction personally. Mrs. Alice F. Jones, who was then employed by the bank, testified that Mrs. Colley came into the bank and stated that '(s)he just wanted her son's name on the account, and that's what I did for her'. Mrs. Jones stated that she did not go into details with Mrs. Colley about the account but that she 'gathered from her it was for him (meaning Dr. Colley). Because she did not make it for convenience. She never used that account at all except to draw the interest, * * *'.

Sidney Elmore, Jr. had known Mrs. Colley for about 16 years prior to her death, and performed odd jobs for the decedent, such as purchasing groceries, paying bills, and depositing money in the bank. He stated that after Mrs. Colley had her bad heart attack, she mentioned to him 'that she ought to have her account at the Colonial-American Bank changed to James' name on it so that he would be able to get the money out of the bank.' This witness, when asked if she said under what circumstances would he be able to get it, responded, 'No, she told me that she was putting it in his name so that he could have the money. That's exactly what she said.' Elmore further testified that the decedent told him 'that she was going to notify Miss

Jones at the bank to mail her out a card so that she could have it set up in a joint account so that James, Dr. Colley, could get the money.' *813

Mrs. Cox testified that on several occasions after Dr. Colley's name was added, Mrs. Colley told her that she was sick and that she wanted to have her card changed at the bank; that she did not tell her how she wanted to have it fixed or anything, other than that she said she wanted to make other arrangements; and that she did not want his name on there.

The only other witness was Dr. Colley. He testified that he signed the joint savings account; that he did not look after any business for his mother and did not write any checks or pay any of her bills, other than her drug bill. Dr. Colley was not consulted by Mrs. Colley regarding the setting up of the joint account. He stated that to some extent he and his mother were estranged for the last year of her life.

Introduced in evidence was the savings account which is the subject of this controversy. The pertinent part is as follows:

SAVINGS

JOINT ACCOUNT

PEARL TATE COLLEY OR J. T. COLLEY

COLONIAL-AMERICAN NATIONAL BANK, Roanoke, Va. is hereby authorized to recognize either of the signatures below in the payment of funds or **319 the transaction of any other business. Either one or both or the survivor to sign. The signature of either one to be sufficient for withdrawal of all, or any part of the funds standing to the credit of the above account.

The account card was signed by Mrs. Colley and Dr. Colley, and the passbook remained in the possession of decedent. ... *814 ...

Admittedly the testimony relied upon by appellant would be persuasive were it necessary for him to rebut the presumption that the joint account was created for the convenience of Mrs. Colley. However, under the facts in this case the presumption never comes into play. The rights of the parties here must be determined by rules pertaining to the interpretation of contracts. We must search for and then give effect to the intention of the parties. It is for this reason that the provisions of the signature card become significant. The card constitutes the contract between the depositor of money, and the bank in which it is deposited, and it controls the terms and disposition of the account.

Relevant to our decision are the provisions of Code § 55-20 which abolish survivorship as between joint tenants, and Code § 55-21 which provides that § 55-20 shall not apply 'to an estate conveyed or devised to persons in their own right when it manifestly appears from the tenor of the instrument that it was intended the part of the one dying should then belong to the others.' The provisions of Code § 55-21 were held to apply to bank accounts in Johnson v. McCarty, 202 Va. 49, 56, 115 S.E.2d 915, 920 (1960).

An examination of the provisions of the savings account under review discloses it to be a 'joint account of Pearl Tate Colley or Dr. Colley'. The parties authorized the bank to permit either one or both or the survivor to withdraw all or any part of the funds therein. Obviously, the language was designed to provide the bank with the protection afforded it by Code § 6.1-72. Under this section, when a deposit is made in any bank under the names of two or more persons, payable to either, or to the survivor, such deposit may be paid to any such person whether the others be living or not, and the receipt of the person so paid constitutes a complete release and discharge of the bank for any payment made. In King v. Merryman, referring to this statute, the court said: *815

> It establishes no presumption as to the ownership of the money as between two persons named in a joint savings account, with or without an extended right of survivorship. It is manifestly for the protection of the bank and not declaratory of the rights of the depositors in the fund as between themselves. Each depositor is merely given the right to receive **320 payment out of the funds from the bank during his lifetime, and the survivor the right after the death of the other person. The bank is discharged from liability for any payment so made.'

For the joint account here to be held a survivorship account it must manifestly appear from the tenor of the instrument that it was intended the part of Mrs. Colley, the party dying, should then belong to Dr. Colley, the survivor.

Mrs. Jones testified regarding three types of accounts that one could have at the bank, and described them as an individual, a power of attorney, and a joint savings with survivorship. From her evidence it appears she regarded the joint account of Mrs. Colley or Dr. Colley as a joint account with survivorship. Without doubt, the parties and the bank could have, by appropriate language, created it as a joint account and provided that upon the death of either the survivor would become the sole owner thereof. But this was not done, and we cannot read into the language of the instrument such a manifest intention.

Our decision here is controlled by King v. Merryman, Supra. There the bank was authorized to change a savings account which then stood in the name of A. V. Dodson to a joint account of A. V. Dodson and Mrs. Lottie King (his daughter) and 'subject to the check of either of us or the survivor'. Referring to the form of the deposit, this court said:

> 'The deposit on May 24, 1949, in accordance with instructions of the deceased, was made in statutory form. It expressly authorized the bank to credit the funds to the joint account of himself and daughter, and that it be made 'subject to the check of either of us or the survivor.' That is all the deceased requested of the bank. His written instruction merely directed that either of the depositors or the survivor should be allowed to withdraw funds

in the account. It does not contain language from which a presumption of an intention to create a joint tenancy, with the incident *816 right of survivorship, might flow. It does not contain any language showing that it was his intention or understanding that his daughter should take title to the fund or any portion thereof at his death.'

In Quesenberry v. Funk, the deposit was in the name of a father and his daughter 'jointly, with right of survivorship'. We held the account to be the property of the father's estate for the testimony showed the account was opened by him as a matter of convenience.

In Stevens v. Sparks, the account was opened in the name of a patient and his nurse 'as joint tenants with right of survivorship, and not as tenants in common'. There the evidence showed a manifest intention on the part of the deceased patient that the surviving nurse have the sole ownership at his death, and we so held.

In Wrenn v. Daniels, supra, bank deposits and certificates of stock were in the name of a father and his son 'as joint tenants with right of survivorship and not as tenants in common'. We held the evidence as conclusively proving that the accounts and stock certificates were placed in joint names by the father for his convenience.

In Wilkinson v. Witherspoon, the deposit was in the name of an uncle and his niece 'as joint tenants with right of survivorship and not as tenants in common, and as tenants by the entirety'. In addition, the signature card was fully descriptive of the rights of the parties, and provided that '(i)t is agreed by the signatory parties with each other and by the parties with you that any funds placed in or added to the account by any one of the parties is and shall be conclusively intended to be a gift and delivery at that time of such funds to the other signatory party or parties to the extent of his or their pro rata **321 interest in the account.' We held that the circumstances, including particularly the provisions of the signature card, showed the uncle's intent that the funds pass to his niece rather than as a part of his estate.

In Deal's Administrator v. Merchants & Mechanic's Savings Bank, et al., it was found as a fact that the joint deposit was made with an express understanding with the bank that the balance thereof, not checked out during the joint lives of the two depositors, was to become the property of the survivor. We held, under the facts of that case, that the effect of the deposit was to create a contract relation between the bank and the two joint depositors under which *817 the amount to the credit of the account became the property of the claimant as a survivor of the decedent and herself.

In Haynes v. Hurt, Supra, the presumption of deposit for convenience was held inapplicable where two persons deposit their funds in a joint bank account.

Where there is a clear expression of an intention that the survivor should become the owner of the account upon the death of the depositor, we have upheld that intention. Where such an intention is not fully disclosed by the terms of the deposit, but clearly appears when the terms of the deposit are considered along with other evidence, the intention has been upheld. Where a contrary intention has been shown to exist, the court has excluded the alleged rights of the survivor. However, in every case, with the possible exception of Deal, the tenor of the language of the deposit has been consistent with and indicated the creation of an account that would be payable to and become the account of the survivor.

The language in the instant case does not indicate a survivorship account, or indicate anything other than a joint account from which either person named could make withdrawals and from which, if a survivor withdrew funds, the bank would be protected.

It should be observed that Dr. Colley neither solicited nor encouraged the joint deposit by his mother, and, in fact, had no knowledge of her intention until he was requested to sign the signature card. So far as the record discloses he had no further conversations with his mother regarding the account, and did not know its status, or the amount therein, until after her death.

Despite the belief of Mrs. Jones that Mrs. Colley was creating 'a survivorship account', she admitted that Mrs. Colley did not actually discuss with her what a joint account was. Nothing was said between the two as to 'what would happen on a survivorship account'.

It, therefore, is clear that all Mrs. Colley requested of the bank was a joint account, irrespective of any intention that she might have previously entertained or expressed to Sidney Elmore, Jr. The account that she created does not contain language from which a presumption of an intention to create a joint tenancy with the incident right of survivorship, might flow. The signature card does not contain any language showing that it was her intention or understanding that her son should take title to the fund or any portion thereof at her death. In the absence of such intention, manifestly appearing, either from the tenor of the instructions given to the bank at the time the deposit *818 was made, or in the form of the deposit, no survivorship account was created. ... **322 Accordingly ... the joint account is the property of the estate of Pearl Tate Colley.

C.   Payable On Death (POD) designations

Judicial hesitation to treat jointly titled accounts as true joint tenancies when only the decedent contributed funds receives support from the fact that today account owners can very easily provide for non-probate transfer of account assets by completing a Payable on Death form. Banks, investment companies, and life insurance companies today routinely ask account or policy holders to designate someone as beneficiary in the event of their death. Nearly all life insurance policies do in fact name someone as beneficiary, because generally the only reason to take out such a policy is to benefit specific individuals one has in mind. In contrast, people generally open bank and investment accounts for their own benefit, yet most people nevertheless designate someone to receive whatever is in the account should they die while the account still exists and has a positive balance.

When these beneficiary designations are effective, they result in a non-probate transfer. The account balance or insurance proceeds become immediately and automatically owned by the persons designated. So the decedent's PR would have no control over them. The beneficiaries can contact the financial institutions directly and request disbursement.

These accounts and policies are contracts between the owners and the financial institutions, so they are governed by contract law rather than estate law. Virginia Nat. Bank v. Harris, 220 Va. 336, 341, 257 S.E.2d 867, 870 (1979). However, there are provisions in Title 64.2 explicitly approving of them, because historically POD designations on financial accounts were regarded skeptically, as illicit attempt to avoid the requirements for testamentary disposition of wealth at death. Cf. Virginia Nat. Bank v. Harris, 220 Va. 336, 257 S.E.2d 867 (1979) (rejecting a claim by a surviving spouse that decedent's designation of someone else as payable-on-death beneficiary of decedent's bank account was an attempted testamentary disposition that did not satisfy the rules for formalities of will execution [the subject of Chapter Three], and holding that the statute of wills did not apply to the deposit; instead the designated beneficiary's right to the account balance was to be determined by rules pertaining to interpretation of contracts).

Subtitle II. Wills and Decedents' Estates
Chapter 6. Transfers Without Qualification
Article 3. Uniform Transfers on Death (Tod) Security Registration Act.

§ 64.2-612. Definitions.
…

"Beneficiary form" means a registration of a security that indicates the present owner of the security and the intention of the owner regarding the person who will become the owner of the security upon the death of the owner. …

"Register"… means to issue a certificate showing ownership of a certificated security ...

"Registering entity" means a person who originates or transfers a security title by registration, and includes a broker maintaining security accounts for customers and a transfer agent or other person acting for or as an issuer of securities.

"Security" means a share, participation, or other interest in property, in a business, or in an obligation of an enterprise or other issuer...

"Security account" means (i) a reinvestment account associated with a security, a securities account with a broker, a cash balance in a brokerage account, cash, interest, earnings, or dividends earned or declared on a security in an account, a reinvestment account, or a brokerage account…, or (ii) a cash balance or other property held for or due to the owner of a security as a replacement for or product of an account security...

§ 64.2-613. Registration in beneficiary form; sole or joint tenancy ownership; applicable law.

A. Only individuals whose registration of a security shows sole ownership by one individual or multiple ownership by two or more with right of survivorship, rather than as tenants in common, may obtain registration in beneficiary form. ...

§ 64.2-614. Origination of registration in beneficiary form.

A security, whether evidenced by certificate or account, is registered in beneficiary form when the registration includes a designation of a beneficiary to take the ownership at the death of the owner or the deaths of all multiple owners.

§ 64.2-615. Form of registration in beneficiary form; effect.

A. Registration in beneficiary form may be shown by the words "transfer on death" or the abbreviation "TOD," or by the words "pay on death" or the abbreviation "POD," after the name of the registered owner and before the name of the beneficiary.

B. The designation of a TOD beneficiary on a registration in beneficiary form has no effect on ownership until the owner's death. A registration of a security in beneficiary form may be canceled or changed at any time by the sole owner or all then surviving owners without the consent of the beneficiary.

§ 64.2-616. Ownership on death of owner.

On death of a sole owner or the last to die of all multiple owners, ownership of securities registered in beneficiary form passes to any beneficiaries who survive all owners. ... [M]ultiple beneficiaries surviving the death of all owners hold their interests as tenants in common. If no beneficiary survives the death of all owners, the security belongs to the estate of the deceased sole owner or the estate of the last to die of all multiple owners.

§ 64.2-618. Nontestamentary transfer on death.

A transfer on death resulting from a registration in beneficiary form is effective by reason of the contract regarding the registration between the owner and the registering entity and this article, and is not testamentary.

§ 64.2-619. Terms, conditions, and forms for registration; examples.

A. A registering entity... may establish the terms and conditions under which it will receive requests... for cancellation of previously registered TOD beneficiary designations and requests for reregistration to effect a change of beneficiary. The terms and conditions so established may provide for... designating primary and contingent beneficiaries, and substituting a named beneficiary's descendants to take in the place of the named beneficiary in the event of the beneficiary's death. Substitution may be indicated by appending to the name of the primary beneficiary the letters LDPS, standing for "lineal descendants per stirpes." ...

Article 4. Nonprobate Transfers on Death

§ 64.2-620. Nonprobate transfers on death

A. A provision for a nonprobate transfer on death in an insurance policy, contract of employment, bond, mortgage, promissory note, certificated or uncertificated security, account agreement, custodial agreement, deposit agreement, compensation plan, pension plan, individual retirement plan, employee benefit plan, trust, conveyance, deed of gift, marital property agreement, or other written instrument of a similar nature is nontestamentary. Nontestamentary transfers also include writings stating that (i) money or other benefits due to, controlled by, or owned by a decedent before death shall be paid after the decedent's death to a person whom the decedent designates either in the instrument or in a separate writing, including a will, executed either before or at the same time as the instrument, or later; ... or (iii) any property controlled by or owned by the decedent before death that is the subject of the instrument passes to a person the decedent designates either in the instrument or in a separate writing, including a will, executed either before or at the same time as the instrument, or later. ...

***

If the decedent had financial accounts or life insurance and failed to designate a POD beneficiary, or named someone but that designation is ineffective for one of the reasons discussed below, the assets or insurance proceeds do not vanish, but go into the probate estate.

III.   Ineffective Non-Probate Transfers

PODs, joint tenancies, and other non-probate devices for transfer of wealth at death might be ineffective because the person named as a beneficiary or joint tenant is practically or legally incapable of receiving the property interest. This could be because that person predeceased the decedent or is treated in law as if having predeceased even though still alive (for reasons discussed below). Sometimes beneficiaries of non-probate instruments choose not to receive the wealth the instruments would transfer, because they want someone else to receive it, for tax reasons, because a creditor would take it, or for other personal reasons. In the absence of an effective backup beneficiary designation or another joint tenant, this would result in the property being part of the probate estate after all.

A. Predeceased beneficiary or joint tenant

If a joint tenant predeceased, and there is no other joint tenant but the current decedent, then the property would have become solely that of the decedent immediately.

The Code article authorizing transfer on death deeds of real property includes this provision:

Chapter 6. Transfers Without Qualification
Article 5. Uniform Real Property Transfer on Death Act

§ 64.2-632. Effect of transfer on death deed at transferor's death.

A. ... 2. The interest of a designated beneficiary is contingent on the designated beneficiary surviving the transferor. The interest of a designated beneficiary that fails to survive the transferor lapses. ...

4. If the transferor has identified two or more designated beneficiaries to receive concurrent interests in the property, the share of one that lapses or fails for any reason is transferred to the other, or to the others in proportion to the interest of each in the remaining part of the property held concurrently.

***

When a POD beneficiary predeceases the current decedent, there is no effect on the property until the account owner dies. In neither case do the predeceased person's heirs or will beneficiaries take in the place of the predeceased person. Instead the property would go into the owner's probate estate at death and be distributed in accordance with a will or the rules for intestate succession. In any of these contexts, though – non-probate transfer, intestate succession, and probating of a will – there could arise the question of who predeceased whom when a decedent and his or her heir or beneficiary die in the same event or at about the same time. In an effort to minimize the number of cases in which courts have to decide the order of death based on extensive and painful evidence, states have adopted a uniform statute to govern such cases. The following Act applies to every topic in this book as to which survivorship is relevant.

Subtitle V. Provisions Applicable to Probate and Nonprobate Transfers
Chapter 22. Uniform Simultaneous Death Act

§ 64.2-2203. Co-owners with right of survivorship; requirement of survival by 120 hours.

Except as provided in § 64.2-2205 [allowing for the governing instrument to provide otherwise], if (i) it is not established by clear and convincing evidence that one of two co-owners with right of survivorship survived the other co-owner by 120 hours, one-half of the property passes as if one had survived by 120 hours and one-half as if the other had survived by 120 hours and (ii) there are more than two co-owners and it is not established by clear and convincing evidence that at least one of them survived the others by 120 hours, the property passes in the proportion that one bears to the whole number of co-owners.

§ 64.2-2202. Requirement of survival by 120 hours under donative dispositions in governing instruments.

Except as provided in § 64.2-2205 for purposes of a donative provision of a governing instrument, an individual who is not established by clear and convincing evidence to have survived an event, including the death of another individual, by 120 hours is deemed to have predeceased the event.

§ 64.2-2200. Definitions.

As used in this chapter:

"Co-owners with right of survivorship" includes parties to a joint account, joint tenants, tenants by the entireties, and other co-owners of property held under circumstances that entitle one or more to the whole of the property or account on the death of the other or others.

"Governing instrument" means a deed, will, trust, insurance or annuity policy, account with POD designation, security registered in beneficiary form (TOD), or pension, profit-sharing, retirement, or similar benefit plan; instrument creating or exercising a power of appointment or a power of attorney; or a donative, appointive, or nominative instrument of any other type.

"Payor" means a trustee, insurer, business entity, employer, government, governmental agency, subdivision, or instrumentality, or any other person authorized or obligated by law or a governing instrument to make payments.

B. Disclaimer

No one is ever forced to accept gratuitous transfers. One may "disclaim" any non-probate transfer. Thus, the Virginia Code contains:

Subtitle V. Provisions Applicable to Probate and Nonprobate Transfers
Chapter 26. Uniform Disclaimer of Property Interests Act.

§ 64.2-2603. Power to disclaim; general requirements; when irrevocable.

A. A person may disclaim in whole or in part, any interest in or power over property…

D. To be effective, a disclaimer shall be in writing or other record, declare the disclaimer, describe the interest or power disclaimed, be signed by the person making the disclaimer, and be delivered or filed in the manner provided in § 64.2-2610. ...

E. A partial disclaimer may be expressed as a fraction, percentage, monetary amount, term of years, limitation of power, or any other interest or estate in the property.

F. A disclaimer becomes irrevocable when it is delivered or filed pursuant to § 64.2-2610 or when it becomes effective as provided in §§ 64.2-2604 through 64.2-2609, whichever occurs later.

G. A disclaimer made under this chapter is not a transfer, assignment, or release.

§ 64.2-2604. Disclaimer of interest in property.

...

B. Except for a disclaimer governed by § 64.2-2605 or 64.2-2606...:

1. The disclaimer takes effect as of the time the instrument creating the interest becomes irrevocable or, if the interest arose under the law of intestate succession, as of the time of the intestate's death.

2. The disclaimed interest passes according to any provision in the instrument creating the interest providing for the disposition of the interest, should it be disclaimed, or of disclaimed interests in general.

3. If the instrument does not contain a provision described in subdivision 2, the following rules apply:

a. If the disclaimant is an individual, the disclaimed interest passes as if the disclaimant had died immediately before the time of distribution. However, if by law or under the instrument, the descendants of the disclaimant would share in the disclaimed interest by any method of representation had the disclaimant died before the time of distribution, the disclaimed interest passes only to the descendants of the disclaimant who survive at the time of distribution.

b. If the disclaimant is not an individual, the disclaimed interest passes as if the disclaimant did not exist.

4. Upon the disclaimer of a preceding interest, a future interest held by a person other than the disclaimant takes effect as if the disclaimant had died or ceased to exist immediately before the time of distribution, but a future interest held by the disclaimant is not accelerated in possession or enjoyment.

§ 64.2-2605. Disclaimer of rights of survivorship in jointly held property.

A. Upon the death of a holder of jointly held property, a surviving holder may disclaim, in whole or in part, the greater of (i) a fractional share of the property determined by dividing the number one by the number of joint holders alive immediately before the death of the holder to whose death the disclaimer relates or (ii) all of the property except that part of the value of the entire interest attributable to the contribution furnished by the disclaimant.

B. A disclaimer under subsection A takes effect as of the death of the holder of jointly held property to whose death the disclaimer relates.

C. An interest in jointly held property disclaimed by a surviving holder of the property passes as if the disclaimant predeceased the holder to whose death the disclaimer relates.

***

A.(ii) prevents joint tenants from divesting themselves of their interest in a property to the extent that they contributed their own resources to acquisition of the property. The legislative intent was likely to protect creditors. The effect of C, in a situation where there were only two joint tenants – the decedent and the disclaimant -- is that the disclaimer results in the entire property going into the decedent's probate estate. If there were more than two joint tenants, the result would be that the joint tenants other than the decedent and the disclaimant become the sole owner(s) of the property.

There is also a provision in the Code specifically for disclaimer as to transfer-on-death deeds of real property. § 64.2-633 states simply that the "beneficiary may disclaim all or part of the beneficiary's interest ..."

A would-be beneficiary might execute a disclaimer for tax reasons – for example, a widow who does not need the wealth, who would pass it on to her children at her death anyway, and who might be subject to federal estate taxes. Or a spouse heading toward divorce might want to avoid receiving gratuitous transfers that could cause him or her to receive a smaller share of marital property in equitable distribution, given that judges might take into account a spouse's ownership of substantial separate property, as indicative of less need, in determining equitable shares in Virginia. Another reason is to keep wealth in the family rather than have it taken by the would-be beneficiary's creditors. Does the law allow that?

Supreme Court of Virginia.
Abbott v. Willey
253 Va. 88, 479 S.E.2d 528 (1997)

HASSELL, Justice.

… Patrick Willey and Shannon Willey are the children of Kathleen Willey and her deceased husband, Edward E. Willey, Jr. Plaintiffs recovered a judgment in the sum of $274,495.22 plus interest and costs against Kathleen Willey based upon a note she had executed with her husband. Edward Willey, Jr. died shortly after the note was executed in November 1993. *90

A life insurance company had issued a life insurance policy on the life of Edward E. Willey, Jr., and Kathleen Willey was entitled to receive $350,845.92 plus interest from the date of his death. Patrick and Shannon Willey were entitled to receive an equal sum from the life insurance policy.

According to the plaintiffs' allegations, Kathleen Willey, "without consideration, fraudulently and voluntarily, with intent to hinder, delay, and defraud the [p]laintiffs, disclaimed the benefits due to her under the life insurance policy. Upon disclaiming her death benefit proceeds, the [d]efendant Kathleen Willey became insolvent." Kathleen Willey's children received the death benefits and used those funds to support their mother.

The plaintiffs asserted that Kathleen Willey's disclaimer constituted a fraudulent transfer or conveyance under Code § 55–80 and a void voluntary conveyance under Code § 55–81. The plaintiffs also contended that Patrick and Shannon Willey, with fraudulent intent, received funds in the amount of $274,495.22 as a result of Kathleen Willey's disclaimer, and that they have been unjustly enriched and, therefore, hold these funds constructively for the benefit of the plaintiffs.

Code § 64.1–191 states in relevant part that a "beneficiary under a nontestamentary instrument ... may disclaim in whole or in part the succession to any property, real or personal, or interest therein." Code § 64.1–192 prescribes the method of delivering or filing a disclaimer under a nontestamentary instrument. Code § 64.1–193, which governs our resolution of this appeal, states:

> Unless otherwise provided in the nontestamentary instrument, the property or part thereof or interest therein disclaimed and any future interest which is to take effect in possession or enjoyment at or after the termination of the interest disclaimed shall be distributed as if the disclaimant had died before the effective date of the nontestamentary instrument. The disclaimer shall relate back for all purposes to the effective date of the instrument. A person who has a present and a future interest in *91 property and disclaims his present interest in whole or in part, shall be deemed to have disclaimed his future interest to the same extent if such disclaimer of a present interest would cause the future interest to become a present interest. ... **530

Applying the plain language contained in Code § 64.1–193, we conclude that once Kathleen Willey disclaimed her interest in the insurance proceeds, those proceeds were required to be distributed to Patrick and Shannon Willey as if Kathleen Willey had died before the effective date of the insurance policy. Code § 64.1–193 makes it perfectly clear that the disclaimer relates back "for all purposes" to the effective date of the life insurance policy. The plaintiffs and defendants agree that the effective date of the insurance policy precedes *92 the events that gave rise to the plaintiffs' purported cause of action against the defendants.

Code § 64.1–193 does not contain an exception which permits creditors to contest a disclaimer on the basis of a fraudulent or voluntary conveyance, and we decline the plaintiffs' invitation to add such an exception to the statute. Therefore, we hold that Kathleen Willey had an absolute right under Code § 64.1–191 to disclaim any interest she may have had in the insurance policy, and as a result of such disclaimer, she acquired no interest in the insurance proceeds because the disclaimer related back to the effective date of the insurance policy.

We find no merit in the plaintiffs' contention that the trial court erred by holding that their claim for unjust enrichment against Patrick and Shannon Willey is barred. Code § 38.2–3122 states in relevant part:

> The assignee or lawful beneficiary of an insurance policy shall be entitled to its proceeds against any claims of the creditors or representatives of the insured or the person effecting the policy, except in cases of transfer with intent to defraud creditors....

Here, Kathleen Willey's disclaimer related back "for all purposes" to the effective date of the insurance policy and, thus, she acquired no property interest which could be transferred. ...

––––––––––––

Chapter Three presents a bankruptcy court decision holding that after a debtor files for bankruptcy, he or she cannot effectively disclaim an inheritance or gift to which the debtor became entitled within six months of filing, and this decision might extend to non-probate transfers as well.

C. Former spouses

Another situation probably not anticipated is that the holder forgot to remove a former spouse as beneficiary at the time of divorce. The statutory provision dealing with this is from the Domestic Relations Title of the Virginia Code:

§ 20-111.1. Revocation of death benefits by divorce or annulment

A. Except as otherwise provided under federal law or law of this Commonwealth, upon the entry of a decree of annulment or divorce from the bond of matrimony..., any revocable beneficiary designation contained in a then existing written contract owned by one party that provides for the payment of any death benefit to the other party is revoked. A death benefit prevented from passing to a former spouse by this section shall be paid as if the former spouse had predeceased the decedent. ...

C. This section shall not apply (i) to the extent a decree of annulment or divorce from the bond of matrimony, or a written agreement of the parties, provides for a contrary result as to specific death benefits, or (ii) to any trust or any death benefit payable to or under any trust. ...

***

As hinted by the first phrase of paragraph A, this rule might be preempted by federal laws governing particular types of accounts or policies. Thus, in *Maretta v. Hillman*, 283 Va. 34, 722 S.E.2d 32 (2012) aff'd, 133 S. Ct. 1943 (2013), the Virginia Supreme Court held that the Federal Employees' Group Life Insurance Act preempts this state statute insofar as it requires that proceeds from the life insurance policies it governs go to the named beneficiary, without exception. Thus, former wife Maretta received a federal-employee decedent's life insurance proceeds instead of Hillman, his wife at the time of death. The U.S. Supreme Court had previously reached the same conclusion as to beneficiary designations in the Servicemen's Group Life Insurance Act. Ridgway v. Ridgway, 454 U.S. 46 (1981).

In the absence of a preempting federal law, however, this statutory provision effectively revokes any designation of a spouse in a non-probate instrument other than a trust upon divorce from that spouse, absent a contrary directive in a divorce settlement agreement. The legislative assumption is that people generally do not want to make gratuitous transfers upon death to former spouses, so if an account or policy has retained a designation made before the divorce, it is most likely because of inadvertence, a simple oversight on the part of the decedent. And the legislative aim, as always, is to effectuate the intent of the decedent. Paragraph C, though, gives effect to an expression of intent or agreement that the divorce will not cause a revocation, which can create complications.

Supreme Court of Virginia.
Faulknier v. Shafer
264 Va. 210 563, S.E.2d 755 (2002)

KINSER, Justice.

... **757 ... *213 The marriage between Loretta W. Faulknier and the decedent was dissolved by a decree of divorce entered in June 1989. A separation agreement that Faulknier and the decedent had previously executed was filed with that decree.[2]

> [2] The decree of divorce did not "affirm, ratify and incorporate by reference" the separation agreement. Code § 20-109.1.

As pertinent to this appeal, the separation agreement provided that "[Faulknier] shall remain as beneficiary on [the decedent's] Civil Service Life Insurance [.]" However, in 1996, the decedent designated Linda D. Shafer as beneficiary of that policy.

After the decedent's death in 1997, Faulknier filed a claim for the proceeds of that life insurance policy. The Office of Federal Employees' Group Life Insurance denied the claim because "THE LATEST DESIGNATION OF BENEFICIARY ON FILE THAT WAS COMPLETED BY THE INSURED ON 02/20/96 NAME[D]

SOMEONE OTHER THAN [FAULKNIER] AS BENEFICIARY." Faulknier then filed a bill of complaint against Shafer to recover the proceeds of the decedent's life insurance policy. ... *214 ... **758 ...

ANALYSIS

... *215 ....

> Constructive trusts arise, *independently of the intention of the parties, by construction of law; being fastened upon the conscience* of him who has the legal estate, in order to prevent what otherwise *would be a fraud*. They occur not only where property has been acquired by fraud or improper means, but also where it has been fairly and properly acquired, but it is contrary to the principles of equity that it should be retained, at least for the acquirer's own benefit. Leonard v. Counts, 221 Va. 582, 589, 272 S.E.2d 190, 195 (1980).

Courts of equity may impose constructive trusts whenever necessary to prevent a failure of justice. Richardson v. Richardson, 242 Va. 242, 245, 409 S.E.2d 148, 150 (1991).

> When property is given or devised to a defendant in breach of a donor's or testator's contract with a plaintiff, equity will impose a constructive trust upon that property in the hands of the recipient even though (1) the transfer is not the result of breach of a fiduciary duty or an actual or constructive fraud practiced upon the plaintiff, and (2) the one or devisee had no knowledge of the wrongdoing or breach of contract. Jones v. Harrison, 250 Va. 64, 69, 458 S.E.2d 766, 769 (1995). *216

Shafer argues, however, as she did before the circuit court, that Faulknier has an adequate remedy at law because the decedent's estate is solvent and contains sufficient assets to satisfy Faulknier's claim. Relying on *Jones*, Shafer contends that Faulknier must therefore pursue her contractual claim against the estate pursuant to either Code § 64.1-144 or § 64.1-171 before she can seek **759 the equitable remedy of imposing a constructive trust on the life insurance proceeds. We are not persuaded...

This Court held in *Jones* that the provisions of a property settlement and support agreement entitled the children of a decedent's former marriage to a constructive trust on the proceeds of life insurance policies payable to the decedent's second wife, even though there was no evidence that the second wife had done anything improper, had participated in the decedent's breach of the support agreement, or had knowledge of that breach. 250 Va. at 69-70, 458 S.E.2d at 769-70. See also Richardson, 242 Va. at 246-47, 409 S.E.2d at 151 (constructive trust imposed where transferee, who had not engaged in any wrongdoing and had furnished no consideration for the transfer, was unjustly enriched). Thus, we concluded that "because the other elements necessary to establish a constructive trust [were] present, the [second wife's] gratuitous receipt of a portion of the insurance proceeds forms the basis for imposing a constructive trust on that property." Jones, 250 Va. at 70, 458 S.E.2d at 770. In a footnote, we explained that the children had a contractual claim against the decedent's estate, but because the estate was insolvent, the children could claim a constructive trust in a portion of the proceeds of the insurance policies. Id. at 70 n. 3, 458 S.E.2d 766, 458 S.E.2d at 770 n. 3.

The statement in that footnote forms the basis of Shafer's contention that Faulknier must first seek redress from the decedent's estate. However, we decided Jones by reviewing the findings of a commissioner in chancery who had heard evidence. Id. at 67, 458 S.E.2d at 768. In contrast, the present case comes to us on a judgment sustaining a demurrer. Shafer's assertion that the estate in the present case is solvent is based solely upon documents that she appended to her memorandum in support of the demurrer. Those documents were not mentioned in Faulknier's bill of complaint. Thus, we will not consider them in deciding whether the allegations *217 in the bill of complaint state a cause of action.

Relying on Overby v. White, 245 Va. 446, 449, 429 S.E.2d 17, 19 (1993), Shafer also argues that the imposition of a constructive trust is warranted only when the recipient of funds obtained them in some wrongful way. She asserts that she had no knowledge of the decedent's beneficiary designation or separation agreement before he died. Based on that assertion and because there is no allegation that she colluded with the decedent, induced him to change his beneficiary designation, or otherwise acted with the intention of depriving Faulknier of the insurance proceeds, Shafer contends that impressing a constructive trust in this case in inappropriate.

Our decision in Overby is not dispositive of the issue before us. There, the plaintiff sought to have the court impress a constructive trust on an interest in property that the defendant had properly acquired before the conduct warranting a constructive trust had occurred. In contrast, Shafer did not acquire the life insurance proceeds before the decedent breached the terms of his separation agreement with Faulknier. We noted this same distinction in our decision in Jones. 250 Va. at 69, 458 S.E.2d at 769. Furthermore, our decision in Overby was not premised solely on the fact that the defendant had not engaged in any wrongdoing. Overby, 245 Va. at 450, 429 S.E.2d at 19. We have repeatedly stated that constructive trusts can arise even when property has been acquired fairly and without any improper means. See, e.g., Jones, 250 Va. at 70, 458 S.E.2d at 770; Nedrich v. Jones, 245 Va. 465, 474, 429 S.E.2d 201, 206 (1993); Richardson, 242 Va. at 245, 409 S.E.2d at 150; Leonard, 221 Va. at 589, 272 S.E.2d at 195.

Thus,... Faulknier pled facts which, if taken as true, are sufficient to state a cause of action for the imposition of a constructive trust on the basis that Shafer has been unjustly enriched. "A constructive trust is appropriately imposed to avoid unjust enrichment of a party." **760 Cooper v. Cooper, 249 Va. 511, 517, 457 S.E.2d 88, 92 (1995). Issues such as whether the decedent's estate has sufficient assets to satisfy Faulknier's claim, and if so, whose share of the *218 estate would be depleted by such a payment;4 whether Shafer was a gratuitous recipient of the life insurance proceeds;5 when she learned about the decedent's beneficiary designation on his life insurance policy; and whether she knew about the terms of the separation agreement between the decedent and Faulknier are matters to be considered in determining whether, on remand, Faulknier establishes by clear and convincing evidence her entitlement to a constructive trust on the life insurance proceeds.6 See Cooper, 249 Va. at 517, 457 S.E.2d at 92 ("constructive trust must be established by clear and convincing evidence"). … [P]roof of these issues has a bearing on whether Shafer has been unjustly enriched and whether a constructive trust is appropriate...[7]

> [7] Neither party addressed whether any provision of federal law, including 5 C.F.R. §§ 870.801 or 870.802, affects the validity of the decedent's beneficiary designation for his life insurance proceeds or the imposition of a constructive trust on those proceeds.

The recently-enacted Code article authorizing transfer on death deeds of real property also provides for divorce:

§ 64.2-632. Effect of transfer on death deed at transferor's death.

A. … 5. If, after making a transfer on death deed, the transferor is divorced *a vinculo matrimonii* or his marriage is annulled, the divorce or annulment revokes any transfer to a former spouse as designated beneficiary unless the transfer on death deed expressly provides otherwise.

***

D. Murderers

**Subtitle V. Provisions Applicable to Probate and Nonprobate Transfers
Chapter 25. Acts Barring Property Rights**

§ 64.2-2503. Concurrent ownership with or without survivorship

A. The death of the decedent caused by the slayer results in the vesting of the slayer's interest in property held by the decedent and the slayer as tenants by the entirety or any other form of ownership with the right of survivorship in the estate of the decedent as though the slayer had predeceased the decedent.

B. The death of the decedent caused by the slayer results in the severance of the slayer's interest in property held by the decedent and the slayer as joint tenants, joint owners, or joint obligees without the right of survivorship and the share of the decedent passes as a part of his estate.

***

Paragraph A of this Code section effectively abrogates a 1980 decision of the Virginia Supreme Court that was based on the general common law rule that one should not profit by wrong-doing. In Sundin v. Klein, 221 Va. 232, 269 S.E.2d 787

(1980), husband and wife held an acre of land as tenants by the entirety with survivorship. When the husband was convicted of second degree murder for killing his wife, the beneficiaries of the residuary clause in her will sought to prevent him from becoming sole owner of the land by virtue of the right of survivorship. The court held that the husband should not profit by the murder but also should not be further penalized by disposition of the property, as would result from complete divestment. So the court impressed a constructive trust upon a one-half undivided interest in the property for the benefit of the wife's estate, to be disposed of according to the terms of her will, with the husband holding the other undivided one-half interest free of any trust. Under current § 64.2-2503, the entirety of the property would have gone into the wife's probate estate, for disposition under her will.

§ 64.2-2504. Reversions and vested remainders

Property in which the slayer holds a reversion or vested remainder and would have obtained the right of present possession upon the death of the decedent shall pass to the estate of the decedent, if the decedent held the particular estate, during the period of the life expectancy of the decedent, or if the particular estate is held by a third person and measured by the life of the decedent, it shall remain in the possession of the third person during the period of the life expectancy of the decedent.

§ 64.2-2508. Proceeds of insurance...

A. Insurance proceeds payable to the slayer as the beneficiary or assignee of any policy or certificate of insurance or bond or other contractual agreement on the life of the decedent or as the survivor of a joint life policy shall be paid to the estate of the decedent, unless the policy or certificate designates some person as an alternative beneficiary to the slayer.

The statutory definition of a "slayer" and court interpretation of it appear in Chapter Two. The Virginia Supreme Court applied a predecessor to the current slayer statute to life insurance proceeds in Peoples Sec. Life Ins. Co. v. Arrington, 243 Va. 89, 412 S.E.2d 705 (1992). Though the statutory definition of "slayer" did not include the specific allegation against the beneficiary wife -- namely, that she "procured, participated in or otherwise directed" the death of her husband, the court held that the predecessor to § 64.2-2508 could be applied nevertheless, because the General Assembly had stated in another code provision (which is now Va. Code § 64.2-2511), that the slayer statute "shall be construed broadly in order to effect the policy of the Commonwealth that no person shall be allowed to profit by his own wrong, wherever committed" and is "not intended to be exclusive and all common law rights and remedies that prevent one who has participated in the willful and unlawful killing of another from profiting by his wrong shall continue to exist in the Commonwealth."

E. Non-probate transfers effected by undue influence or fraud

Charges of undue influence and fraud are common in the will context; many testators
are elderly when they execute their final will, and anyone who would do much better
under the intestacy rules presented in Chapter Two would be informed of the content
of the will and would have a strong financial incentive to challenge the will. Absent
failure to comply with formalities, an allegation that someone overcame the will of
the testator with fraud or undue influence is the best bet. Virginia law also allows
challenges to non-probate transfers, and even to lifetime gifts, based on undue
influence or fraud. Such challenges are rare, however, even though they too can have
the effect of depriving would-be heirs of substantial wealth, primarily because there
is no public disclosure of non-probate transfers. This is the downside of the privacy
that non-probate transfers afford; family members who could provide protection from
fraud and undue influence after the fact, after an account or policy-owner has passed
away, are far less likely to learn about the non-probate transfer. But such challenges
do nevertheless occur.

Supreme Court of Virginia.
Ayers v. Shaffer
286 Va. 212, 748 S.E.2d 83 (2013)

Opinion by Senior Justice LAWRENCE L. KOONTZ, JR.

*216 ... This case was decided on demurrer. "A demurrer admits the truth of all
material facts properly pleaded. ...." "A demurrer tests the legal sufficiency of facts
alleged in the pleadings, but not the strength of proof. ..." ...

Shara Ayers and Ryan Riley, are the great grandchildren of Elsie R. Smith ("Elsie")
and legatees to one half of her residuary estate under a will dated August 3, 2004.
This will was admitted to probate following Elsie's death on March 22, 2010. The
defendants are Audrey Wingo ("Audrey"), Elsie's sister and legatee to the remaining
half of her residuary estate, Toni Lynn Shaffer ("Toni"), her husband Bruce Shaffer
("Bruce"), and their son Michael T. Shaffer ("Mike"). Elsie's will nominated Toni as
executrix, and she qualified as executrix of Elsie's estate on April 14, 2010.

Ayers and Riley acknowledge that Elsie had become estranged from their mother,
Elsie's only living grandchild and nearest living lineal descendent, and that they had
lived with their mother in Colorado *218 "for a number of years." During this time,
Elsie and her husband, Charles Smith ("Charles"), lived on their farm in Washington
County. In 2004, both Elsie and Charles were in poor health and no longer able to
care for themselves and manage their property and affairs without assistance.
Beginning April 1, 2004, Toni and Bruce, who lived nearby, began providing
assistance to the Smiths.

Charles died on April 23, 2004. Elsie, who was then 80 years old and suffered from
diabetes, dementia and other medical problems, suffered a rapid decline in her mental
and physical health following Charles' death. The Shaffers continued providing care

to Elsie, assisting her with the daily activities of living as well as managing her property and affairs.

On May 13, 2004, Elsie went to the office of attorney H.G. Peters where she executed a **87 durable power of attorney ("DPOA") naming Toni as her agent and attorney-in-fact and Bruce as alternate agent and attorney-in-fact. The amended complaint expressly alleges that "at least [from] the time when Toni Shaffer became [Elsie]'s agent under the DPOA, and until her death, [Elsie] lacked the mental and physical capacity ... to seek and obtain independent advice on her own; to fully understand the complexities and effects of most financial transactions." However, the amended complaint further alleges that this lack of capacity did not impair Elsie's ability "to decide whom she wished her assets to pass to upon her death, and to express those wishes in her Will."

On August 3, 2004, Elsie, Toni, and Bruce returned to Peters' office where Elsie executed her last will and testament. Article VI of the will references a "contract with Toni Shaffer and her husband, Bruce Shaffer" which was executed in Peters' office that day. The contract stated that Toni and Bruce would provide "needed care" for Elsie for which they would be paid $500 per week. Additionally, Toni and Bruce were to receive $8000 for the assistance given to Elsie and Charles since April 2004. The agreement further provided that Toni and Bruce would "be paid the monies owed by [Elsie] from [her] estate," rather than during her lifetime. Likewise, the will directed "payment of any and all sums due pursuant to [this] contractual agreement," but otherwise made no bequest to Toni or Bruce. The amended complaint expressly acknowledges that Toni and Bruce provided care under the agreement over the next three years, during which time Elsie became "increasingly disoriented, calling [Toni and Bruce] several times daily, and at nights." *219

On October 29, 2007, Elsie began residing in an assisted living facility in Bristol, Tennessee, where her daily needs became the responsibility of the staff. In July 2008, she was admitted to a local hospital and then moved to a nursing home, where she received round-the-clock care from the staff. During this time, under the authority of the DPOA, Toni sold Elsie's home and the farm. Accordingly, the amended complaint alleges that after October 2007 the need for any assistance from the Shaffers in caring for Elsie and managing her property and affairs was greatly diminished or eliminated entirely.

Following Elsie's death on March 22, 2010, an initial accounting of her estate filed by Toni in her capacity as executrix showed that at the time of her death Elsie had cash assets in excess of $1,000,000. However, as a result of certain inter vivos financial transactions which included survivorship or pay on death provisions, the probate estate was less than $600,000.

• On May 21, 2004, Elsie signed a customer access agreement for an account at Wachovia Bank. Sometime prior to March 2009, the account was redesignated as "Elsie R. Smith and Toni Shaffer, POA." Following Elsie's death, the final statement *220 of the account showed only Elsie as the owner and indicated that the balance of $83,467.89 was withdrawn from the account by a cashier's check **88 payable to Audrey [Elsie's sister] directly, rather than to Elsie's estate.

• On June 22, 2004, Elsie, accompanied by Toni and Audrey, transferred the balance of an account at First Tennessee Bank titled solely in her name into a certificate of deposit of $80,500.00 titled jointly with Toni and Audrey with right of survivorship. Toni and Audrey received the proceeds from this account following Elsie's death.

• On November 23, 2004, Elsie, accompanied by Toni and Audrey, transferred the balance of a certificate of deposit at Highlands Union Bank titled solely in her name into a certificate of deposit of $75,018.13 titled jointly with Toni and Audrey with right of survivorship. When the certificate matured in November 2008, Toni, acting as a joint holder of the account, received a cashier's check for $87,769.85, with which she opened a certificate of deposit at Wachovia Bank in the name of Elsie, herself, and Bruce and a pay on death designation in favor of Audrey and Benjamin Shaffer ("Benjamin"), the Shaffers' grandson. Following Elsie's death, Mike, Benjamin's father, received half the proceeds of the certificate as custodian for Benjamin, and Audrey received the remainder.

• On September 7, 2007, Toni redeemed certificates of deposit at TruPoint Bank and Wachovia Bank for $97,260.56 and $53,766.84 respectively and deposited these funds into an account at Wachovia Securities titled jointly with right of survivorship in Elsie's and her names. Following Elsie's death, Toni withdrew the account balance of $156,976.08 and deposited these funds into an account titled in her name only. This account was later retitled in the Shaffers' names jointly.

The amended complaint... seek[s] to set aside all transactions that directly or indirectly benefited Toni, Bruce and Audrey respectively in that they were "procured by undue influence" and to recover those funds for *221 inclusion in Elsie's estate. Counts 7 and 8 seek to remove Toni as executrix of Elsie's estate and to assess damages against her for waste of the estate's assets. ...

The defendants alleged that the amended complaint as a whole fails to state any cause of action because it asserts that Elsie had testamentary capacity [because Ayers and Riley would receive half of Elsie's residuary estate under the will]. They contended, therefore, that Elsie was likewise competent to undertake the financial transactions in which she personally participated. Moreover, they contended that since Elsie personally participated in these transactions, Toni's role as agent and attorney-in-fact are not relevant to establishing whether she had a confidential relationship with Elsie as to these transactions. ... **89 ... *222 ... *223 ... **90

DISCUSSION

We clearly and concisely stated the law of undue influence in the formation of contracts in Parfitt v. Parfitt, 277 Va. 333, 672 S.E.2d 827 (2009). ... *224

A court of equity will not set aside a contract because it is "rash, improvident or [a] hard bargain" but equity will act if the circumstances raise the inference that the contract was the result of imposition, deception, or undue influence. To set aside a deed or contract on the basis of undue influence requires a showing that the free agency of the contracting party has been destroyed. Because undue influence is a species of fraud, the person seeking to set aside the contract must prove undue influence by clear and convincing evidence.

Direct proof of undue influence is often difficult to produce. In the seminal case of Fishburne v. Furguson, 84 Va. 87, 111, 4 S.E. 575, 582 (1887), however this Court identified two situations which we considered sufficient to show that a contracting party's free agency was destroyed, and, once established, shift the burden of production to the proponent of the contract. The first involved the mental state of the contracting party and the amount of consideration:

> [W]here great weakness of mind concurs with gross inadequacy of consideration, or circumstances of suspicion, the transaction will be presumed to have been brought about by undue influence.

The second instance *Fishburne* identified arises when a confidential relationship exists between the grantor and proponent of the instrument:

> [W]here one person stands in a relationship of special confidence towards another, so as to acquire an habitual influence over him, he cannot accept from such person a personal benefit without exposing himself to the risk, in a degree proportioned to the nature of their connection, of having it set aside as unduly obtained.

277 Va. at 339–40, 672 S.E.2d at 829.

Thus, "the presumption of undue influence arises and the burden of going forward with the evidence shifts [to the defendant] when weakness of mind and grossly inadequate consideration or suspicious circumstances are shown or when a confidential relationship is established." *225 Friendly Ice Cream Corp. v. Beckner, 268 Va. 23, 33, 597 S.E.2d 34, 39 (2004). Such a confidential relationship is "not confined to any specific association of the parties; it is one wherein a party is bound to act for the benefit of another, and can take no advantage to himself. It appears when the circumstances make it certain the parties do not deal on equal terms, but, on the one side, there is an overmastering influence, or, on the other, weakness, dependence, or trust, justifiably reposed; in both an unfair advantage is possible." 268 Va. at 34, 597 S.E.2d at 39–40.

We have further explained that "[t]rust alone, however, is not sufficient. We trust most men with whom we deal. There must be something reciprocal in the relationship before the rule can be invoked. Before liability can be fastened upon one there must **91 have been something in the course of dealings for which he was in part responsible that induced another to lean upon him, and from which it can be inferred that the ordinary right to contract had been surrendered." 268 Va. at 34, 597 S.E.2d at 40.

"We have identified several particular classes of relationships that may give rise to a presumption of undue influence. Among them ... is when one person is an agent for the other." Parfitt, 277 Va. at 341, 672 S.E.2d at 830. Undeniably, one such relationship is that between a principal and a person authorized to act as her agent and attorney-in-fact. Grubb v. Grubb, 272 Va. 45, 53, 630 S.E.2d 746, 751 (2006). Importantly, in such cases, the presumption of undue influence will "arise[ ] independently of any evidence of actual fraud, or of any limitations of age or capacity in the other party to the confidential relationship, and is intended to protect the other party from the influence naturally present in such a confidential relationship." Id. at 54, 630 S.E.2d at 751 (emphasis added).

A confidential relationship "springs from any fiduciary relationship, and when such relationship is found to exist, any transaction to the benefit of the dominant party and to the detriment of the other is presumptively fraudulent." Nicholson v. Shockey, 192 Va. 270, 278, 64 S.E.2d 813, 817. (1951). Thus, whenever a fiduciary relationship exists between parties, the existence of one or more transactions which benefit the party who owes a fiduciary duty to the other shifts the burden of proving the bona fides of *226 the transaction to the party owing the duty. Id. at 277, 64 S.E.2d at 817. It is not necessary that the transaction be accomplished directly as a result of the fiduciary relationship, but rather, it is the fact that "a confidential relationship existed between the parties at the time of the transaction" that gives rise to the presumption and the shifting of the burden of going forward with the evidence. Diehl v. Butts, 255 Va. 482, 489, 499 S.E.2d 833, 838 (1998); Friendly Ice Cream Corp., 268 Va. at 33, 597 S.E.2d at 39.

From this summary of the law, it is clear that to survive a demurrer, a complaint seeking to set aside a contract or other transaction favorable to a defendant or her interests because of undue influence by the defendant must allege either that because of great weakness of mind of the other party the defendant obtained the bargain for grossly inadequate consideration or under some other circumstance of suspicion, or alternately that a confidential relationship existed between the parties at the time of a transaction beneficial to the defendant, even in the absence of other suspicious circumstances. Both allegations will support a finding of undue influence resulting in a fraudulent transaction, and may be pled independently or in the alternative. ...

Although the amended complaint in this case contains allegations that the defendants exercised undue influence over Elsie both through her diminished capacity and as a result of confidential relationships, it is clear that the circuit court's determination to grant the demurrer was premised only on its determination that there was no confidential relationship between Elsie and Toni. The court concluded *227 that because the transactions were conducted by Elsie personally, or by Toni as a joint account holder, no confidential relationship **92 between Elsie and Toni arose by virtue of the DPOA, which in the court's view precluded any presumption of undue influence. ... Contrary to the court's ruling..., it was not necessary... for Toni to have exercised her authority under the DPOA to accomplish the transactions that benefited her or others close to her for the presumption of undue influence to apply. ...

Code § 6.2–619(A) provides that "[p]arties to a joint account in a financial institution occupy the relation of principal and agent as to each other, with each standing as a principal in regard to *228 his ownership interest in the joint account and as agent in regard to the ownership interest of the other party." In *Parfitt* we explained that where, as in this case, a joint account is established between two parties under which all the assets are contributed by one party, the second party becomes "an agent with regard to the entire account. By statute, a confidential relationship was established creating a fiduciary duty [and] a presumption that the self-dealing transactions were unduly obtained." 277 Va. at 342, 672 S.E.2d at 830 (internal citations and quotation marks omitted). Under such circumstances, it need not be alleged or proven that the defendant procured the creation of the joint account by undue influence. Rather, the existence of the account itself imposes a fiduciary duty on the defendant and with regard to a subsequent transaction creates the presumption of undue influence which shifts to the defendant the burden of proving the bona fides of the transaction.

Because the amended complaint alleges that Audrey, Toni, and Bruce were each made co-owners of one or more accounts with Elsie for which Elsie provided all the funds, under Code § 6.2–619(A) a confidential relationship existed between each of the three and Elise as a matter of law with respect to those accounts, and the burden would fall upon each of them to rebut the presumption that the transactions were the result of undue influence. Accordingly, …**93 the circuit court erred...

Moreover, even without the *229 existence of the [joint accounts and the] DPOA, the amended complaint contains allegations that would support a finding that a confidential relationship developed between Elsie and Toni. Specifically, it is alleged that Elsie was "dependent on Toni ... for both physical and mental/intellectual assistance" calling upon her both day and night. Likewise, in Count 5, the complaint alleges that "… a confidential relationship existed between [Elsie] and ... Bruce ... because of the aid Mr. and Mrs. Smith needed and requested" from him.

A confidential relationship will not necessarily arise in every case where a person requests or receives regular aid from another. Nonetheless, when the amended complaint is viewed as a whole, it is clear that Elsie was alleged to have relied almost exclusively on Toni and Bruce to maintain her property and for most of her daily needs and activities ...

With respect to Audrey, the amended complaint alleges… that Audrey "collaborated with Toni Shaffer in the handling of [Elsie]'s financial affairs, and especially in the process of persuading [Elsie] to sign documents to accomplish many of the ... transactions which Toni Shaffer proposed, advised, or persuaded [Elsie] to participate in," and that when Elsie was accompanied by Audrey to the banks to conduct these transactions, "[s]he was completely under the influence of, and dependent upon Toni Shaffer and/or her sister, Audrey Wingo. This was especially true in regard to the management of her financial affairs." Additionally, there are allegations that the familial relationship between Elsie and Audrey was of a confidential nature "especially after certain events caused [Elsie] to distrust her granddaughter (Plaintiffs' mother)." While these allegations are less specific than those concerning

Toni and Bruce, they nonetheless constitute facts and reasonable inferences which, taken as true, give rise to the existence of a confidential relationship and the consequent presumption of undue influence upon Elsie in those transactions that benefited Audrey. *230 …

For these reasons, we will … reverse… and remand the case to the circuit court for further proceedings consistent with the views expressed in this opinion.

In Economopoulos v. Kolaitis, 259 Va. 806, 812-13, 528 S.E.2d 714, 718 (2000), the Supreme Court stated, in the context of lifetime wealth transfers:

> A parent-child relationship, standing alone, is insufficient to create a confidential or fiduciary relationship. On the other hand, we have found a confidential relationship to exist in a familial relationship that is accompanied by an attorney-client relationship, or by a principal-agent relationship. We also have recognized a confidential relationship where one family member provides financial advice to or handles the finances of another family member.

F.   Creditors' Claims

The law facilitates non-probate transfers in order to simplify lawful transfer of property at death to intended beneficiaries. It does not do so in order to assist people in evading their debts or the rights of surviving spouses. Various code provisions aim specifically to avoid that result, while at the same time giving non-probate transfers priority over probate transfers. These are presented in Chapter Three, in the context of abatement of will bequests to satisfy debts.

As to transfer on death deeds of real property:

§ 64.2-634. Liability for creditor claims and statutory allowances.

A. After the death of the transferor, and subject to the transferor's right to direct the source from which liabilities will be paid, property transferred at the transferor's death by a transfer on death deed is subject to claims of the transferor's creditors, costs of administration of the transferor's estate, the expenses of the transferor's funeral and disposal of remains, and statutory allowances to a surviving spouse and children of the transferor including the family allowance, the right to exempt property, and the homestead allowance to the extent the transferor's probate estate is inadequate to satisfy those claims, costs, expenses, and allowances.

B. If more than one property is transferred by one or more transfer on death deeds, the liability under subsection A is apportioned among the properties in proportion to their net values at the transferor's death. ...

***

Obligations the decedent owed to dependent family members (spouses or children) at death or before a divorce, including alimony and child support, generally receive greater protection than do debts owed to commercial entities. The spousal protections discussed in Chapter Four operate against not only provisions in a will but also against non-probate transfers the decedent set up. Chapter Five addresses protection of trust settlor's creditors, including family "creditors."

IV.   Migration From Community Property States

As to spouses' ownership of property, Virginia is a "common law property" state. That means each spouse owns separately and absolutely all property that he or she acquires by any means on his or her own so long as he or she does not retitle it with an intent to gift it to the marital estate. For example, a husband's income from employment is, upon his receipt of it, absolutely his to do with as he pleases; he can gamble or give it away if he chooses, and the other spouse would have no recourse. If and when a married couple divorces, the other spouse would have some claim to wealth acquired by labor during the marriage, but we are here considering the situation of a decedent still married at the time of death. When retitling of separate property causes its transmutation into jointly-owned property is a topic for a domestic relations text. For present purposes, just be aware that retitling – for example, by putting one's salary into a joint bank account – or using separate property to purchase an asset (e.g., a car) that will be jointly titled or to pay off debt on an asset that is jointly titled (e.g., the family residence) does not necessarily change the character of the separate property into jointly-owned property. Actual intent matters. The PR might therefore have to do more digging when there are jointly-titled assets.

Nine U.S. states, however, are community property states: Arizona, California, Idaho, Louisiana, Nevada, New Mexico, Texas, Washington and Wisconsin. In those states, wealth acquired by labor during marriage is automatically and immediately jointly owned. Thus, even if a married person puts all her income into a bank account bearing only her name, her spouse has a 50% ownership interest in it. Why would a lawyer in Virginia need to know this? Because people move from state to state all the time. Estate planning clients might be planning to move from Virginia to a community property state and wonder whether property they currently hold as separate property would remain such and whether the community property nature of income in the new state changes any calculation about how to distribute an estate or how to avoid estate taxes. Conversely, a decedent might have lived and worked with a spouse in one of the community property states before moving to Virginia. The decedent's PR would need to know whether some assets nominally in the decedent's name, or of which the decedent had had sole possession and use, were actually half-owned by the surviving spouse, such that only half the value should be attributed to the decedent's estate. You would need to know whether property acquired by labor in, for example, Wisconsin, retained its community property status when a couple retired to Virginia. Virginia has adopted this uniform law to govern such cases.

Subtitle II, Chapter 3. Rights of Married Persons
Article 3. Uniform Disposition of Community Property Rights at Death Act

§ 64.2-317. Disposition upon death.

Upon death of a married person, one-half of the property to which this article applies is the property of the surviving spouse and is not subject to testamentary disposition by the decedent or distribution under the laws of intestate succession of the Commonwealth. One-half of that property is the property of the decedent and is subject to testamentary disposition or distribution under the laws of intestate succession of the Commonwealth. With respect to property to which this article applies, the decedent's one-half of the property is not subject to the surviving spouse's right to an elective share... [See Chapter Four]

§ 64.2-315. Application.

This article applies to the disposition at death of the following property acquired by a married person:

1. All personal property, wherever situated:

   a. Which was acquired as or became, and remained, community property under the laws of another jurisdiction;

   b. Which... was acquired with the rents, issues, or income of, or the proceeds from, or in exchange for, that community property; or

   c. Which is traceable to that community property;

2. All or the proportionate part of any real property situated in the Commonwealth which was acquired with the rents, issues or income of, the proceeds from, or in exchange for, property acquired as, or which became and remained, community property under the laws of another jurisdiction, or property traceable to that community property.

§ 64.2-316. Presumptions.

In determining whether this article applies to specific property, the following rebuttable presumptions apply:

1. Property acquired during marriage by a spouse of that marriage while domiciled in a jurisdiction under whose laws property could then be acquired as community property is presumed to have been acquired as, or to have become and remained, property to which this article applies; and

2. Real property situated in the Commonwealth and personal property wherever situated acquired by a married person while domiciled in a jurisdiction under whose laws property could not then be acquired as community property, title to which was taken in a form which created rights of survivorship, is presumed not to be property to which this article applies.

§ 64.2-322. Acts of married persons.

The provisions of this article do not prevent married persons from severing or altering their interests in property to which this article applies.

* * *

V.   Subtractions From the Probate Estate

Once the PA has determined what property is in the probate estate, the next step is to pay everyone other than heirs or will beneficiaries who has a claim upon the estate – debtors, tax authorities, etc.. The following statutory provision, indicating priority of estate obligations in the event the estate is not large enough to pay all, shows the full range of deductions the PA will make before distributing anything to heirs or will beneficiaries. At the top of the list is costs of administration, which includes the PA's commission and fees for any attorney the PA hires; the lawyers always get paid first.

Subtitle II, Chapter 5. Personal Representatives and Administration of Estates
Article 5. Liability of Personal Estate to Debts

§ 64.2-528. Order in which debts and demands of decedents to be paid

When the assets of the decedent in his personal representative's possession are not sufficient to satisfy all debts and demands against him, they shall be applied to the payment of such debts and demands in the following order:

1. Costs and expenses of administration;

2. The allowances provided in Article 2 (§ 64.2-309 et seq.) of Chapter 3 [for surviving spouse];

3. Funeral expenses not to exceed $4,000;

4. Debts and taxes with preference under federal law;

5. Medical and hospital expenses of the last illness of the decedent, including compensation of persons attending him not to exceed $2,150 for each hospital and nursing home and $425 for each person furnishing services or goods;

6. Debts and taxes due the Commonwealth;

7. Debts due as trustee for persons under disabilities; as receiver or commissioner under decree of court of the Commonwealth; as personal

representative, guardian, conservator, or committee when the qualification was in the Commonwealth; and for moneys collected by anyone to the credit of another and not paid over, regardless of whether or not a bond has been executed for the faithful performance of the duties of the party so collecting such funds;

8. Debts and taxes due localities and municipal corporations of the Commonwealth; and

9. All other claims.

No preference shall be given in the payment of any claim over any other claim of the same class, and a claim due and payable shall not be entitled to a preference over a claim not due.

***

Although this provision sets maximum amounts for funeral and medical expenses, those limits only apply in this context when estate assets are insufficient to cover all debts and expenses. When that is not the case, the PA is limited only by a 'reasonableness' standard.

§ 64.2-512. Funeral expenses

[R]easonable funeral and burial expenses of a decedent shall be considered an obligation of the decedent's estate, which shall be liable for such expenses to (i) the funeral establishment, (ii) the cemetery, (iii) any third-party creditor who finances the payment of such expenses, or (iv) any person authorized to make arrangements for the funeral of the decedent who has paid such expenses. ...

***

In Scott Funeral Home, Inc. v. First Nat. Bank of Danville, 211 Va. 128, 130-31, 176 S.E.2d 335, 337 (1970), the Supreme Court elaborated that reasonable expsnes "'correspond with decedent's station in life and matters in relation thereto, and with the value of the estate.'"

The statutory provision authorizing a commission for the PA also uses a 'reasonable' standard. See Chapter Six.

VI.   Small Estates

Before launching into study of wealth transmission through the probate process, note that for sake of efficiency the Code eliminates the need for appointment of a PR, and in absence of a will even for any court involvement, as to probate estates too small to warrant those expenses.

Chapter 6. Transfers Without Qualification.
Article 1. Virginia Small Estate Act.

§ 64.2-600. Definitions.

… "Small asset" means any indebtedness owed to or any asset belonging or presently distributable to the decedent, other than real property, having a value, on the date of the decedent's death, of no more than $50,000. A small asset includes any bank account, savings institution account, credit union account, brokerage account, security, deposit, tax refund, overpayment, item of tangible personal property, or an instrument evidencing a debt, obligation, stock, or chose in action.

"Successor" means any person, other than a creditor, who is entitled under the decedent's will or the laws of intestacy to part or all of a small asset.

§ 64.2-601. Payment or delivery of small asset by affidavit.

A. Any person having possession of a small asset shall pay or deliver the small asset to the designated successor of the decedent upon being presented an affidavit made by all of the known successors stating:

1. That the value of the decedent's entire personal probate estate as of the date of the decedent's death, wherever located, does not exceed $50,000;

2. That at least 60 days have elapsed since the decedent's death;

3. That no application for the appointment of a personal representative is pending or has been granted in any jurisdiction;

4. That the decedent's will, if any, was duly probated;

5. That the claiming successor is entitled to payment or delivery of the small asset, and the basis upon which such entitlement is claimed;

6. The names and addresses of all successors, to the extent known;

7. The name of each successor designated to receive payment or delivery of the small asset on behalf of all successors; and

8. That the designated successor shall have a fiduciary duty to safeguard and promptly pay or deliver the small asset as required by the laws of the Commonwealth. …

§ 64.2-602. Payment or delivery of small asset valued at $25,000 or less without affidavit.

A. Notwithstanding… § 64.2-601, any person having possession of a small asset valued at $25,000 or less may pay or deliver the small asset to any successor provided that:

1. At least 60 days have elapsed since the decedent's death; and

2. No application for the appointment of a personal representative is pending or has been granted in any jurisdiction.

B. The designated successor shall have a fiduciary duty to safeguard and promptly pay or deliver the small asset as required by the laws of the Commonwealth to the other successors, if any.

§ 64.2-603. Discharge and release of payor.

Any person paying or delivering a small asset pursuant to § 64.2-601 or 64.2-602 is discharged and released to the same extent as if that person dealt with the personal representative of the decedent. Such person is not required to see the application of the small asset or to inquire into the truth of any statement in any affidavit... Any person to whom payment or delivery of a small asset has been made is answerable and accountable therefor to any personal representative of the decedent's estate or to any other successor having an equal or superior right.

§ 64.2-604. Payment or delivery of small asset; funeral expenses.

Thirty days after the death of a decedent upon whose estate there shall have been no application for the appointment of a personal representative pending or granted in any jurisdiction, any person holding a small asset belonging to the decedent may, at the request of a successor, pay or deliver so much of the small asset as does not exceed [$4000] to the undertaker or mortuary handling the funeral of the decedent, and a receipt of the payee shall be a full and final release of the payor as to such sum.

Chapter Two
Intestate Succession

We first consider situations in which decedents leave no valid will (intestacy as to all probate property) or failed to include all their probate property in a valid will (partial intestacy). "Intestate" means 'not testamentary' – that is, not governed by a "Last Will and Testament."

As to any probate property not disposed of by will, state law dictates to whom it will go.[3] These people are called "heirs."

I.   Priority Among Heirs

The core rule for intestate succession sets forth the priority among legal and biological relatives for receiving intestate property. The priority is based on state legislators' assumptions about what a decedent *most likely would have wanted* in a particular family situation. The sole objective of intestacy rules is effectuating *presumed* intent, in the absence of expressed actual intent (i.e. a will), *not* fairness to those left behind nor any public purpose. Apart from certain protections for surviving spouses, people are deemed entitled to dispose of their property at death however they choose, regardless of whether it is fair to others or consistent with public policy. At the same time, intestate succession is generally not open to dispute based on evidence of individual circumstances that would ordinarily lead a 'reasonable decedent' to intend something other than the default rules; an underlying assumption is that if the decedent wanted to effect a non-standard distribution because of individual circumstances, she or he would have executed a will to do that.

Virginia complicates things by having separate statutory provisions for real property and personal property, but the list of priorities is the same; the purpose of treating them separately seems solely to be to indicate that certain expenses should be paid for with personal property rather than by liquidating real estate.

Subtitle II. Wills and Decedents' Estates
Chapter 2. Descent and Distribution.

§ 64.2-200. Course of descents generally; right of Commonwealth if no other heir.

A. The real estate of any decedent not effectively disposed of by will descends and passes by intestate succession in the following course:

---

[3] For the wealthiest 1% of decedents, federal estate tax law might require subtracting some of the value of the property the decedent owned just before dying. Virginia does not have an estate or inheritance tax.

1. To the surviving spouse of the decedent, unless the decedent is survived by children or their descendants, one or more of whom are not children or their descendants of the surviving spouse, in which case, two-thirds of the estate descends and passes to the decedent's children and their descendants, and one-third of the estate descends and passes to the surviving spouse.

2. If there is no surviving spouse, then the estate descends and passes to the decedent's children and their descendants.

3. If there is none of the foregoing, then to the decedent's parents, or to the surviving parent.

4. If there is none of the foregoing, then to the decedent's brothers and sisters, and their descendants.

5. If there is none of the foregoing, then one-half of the estate descends and passes to the paternal kindred and one-half descends and passes to the maternal kindred of the decedent in the following course:

   a. To the decedent's grandparents, or to the surviving grandparent.

   b. If there is none of the foregoing, then to the decedent's uncles and aunts, and their descendants.

   c. If there is none of the foregoing, then to the decedent's great-grandparents.

   d. If there is none of the foregoing, then to the brothers and sisters of the decedent's grandparents, and their descendants.

   e. And so on, in other cases, without end, passing to the nearest lineal ancestors, and the descendants of such ancestors.

B. If there are either no surviving paternal kindred or no surviving maternal kindred, the whole estate descends and passes to the paternal or maternal kindred who survive the decedent. If there are neither maternal nor paternal kindred, the whole estate descends and passes to the kindred of the decedent's most recent spouse, if any, provided that the decedent and the spouse were married at the time of the spouse's death, as if such spouse had died intestate and entitled to the estate.

C. If there is no other heir of a decedent's real estate, such real estate is subject to escheat to the Commonwealth...

§ 64.2-201. Distribution of personal estate...

A. The surplus of the personal estate..., after payment of funeral expenses, charges of administration, and debts, and subject to [Exempt Property and Allowances for surviving spouses and minor children], not effectively disposed of by will passes by intestate succession and is distributed to the same persons, and in the same proportions, as real estate descends pursuant to § 64.2-200.

B. If there is no other distributee of a decedent's personal estate, such personal estate shall accrue to the Commonwealth.

———————————

Narrative explanation:

If the decedent was married at time of death and either childless or having had children only with that surviving spouse, then the spouse takes everything. Though decedents generally want to provide for their children (and all of them), the law assumes that a surviving spouse who is also a parent to those children will, while living, use the inheritance at least in part to provide for the children if they are dependent and will, at death, pass whatever wealth is left to the offspring.

If, however, there is a surviving spouse but the decedent was a parent to one or more children who are *not* offspring of the surviving spouse – that is, from another relationship (marital or not; it does not matter), the law divides the estate, because it assumes the decedent would have wanted to benefit the children not of the marriage directly. The law assumes surviving spouses are less disposed to benefit step-children than they are to benefit their own children but that all the children were equally dear to the decedent. In fact, the decedent might not have had *any* children with the surviving spouse – for example, if the surviving spouse was the decedent's second spouse and they married later in life. The fractions in this case are one-third to the surviving spouse and two-thirds to be split among all the decedent's children. Certainly there will be cases in which this rule produces a result the decedent would not have wanted – for example, where the decedent had only one offspring, who is from a prior relationship and who was estranged from the decedent for decades, whereas the surviving spouse was married to decedent for decades and dependent on the decedent. But the rules aim at what most people would want in most situations and to keep things simple, avoiding litigation aimed at establishing the nature of the actual relationship between people, while leaving people free to execute a will if they want something different from the default rules embodied in intestacy law.

You might suppose there should also be a special rule for when the surviving spouse has offspring who are not offspring of the decedent – that is, where the decedent had step-children. But there is not. You might think there should be because the surviving spouse is likely to pass on some of the inherited wealth to all his/her offspring equally, yet the decedent likely would not have wanted to benefit step-children, at least not as much as the decedent's own offspring. In some cases, the absence of a special rule might seem innocuous. For example, if the decedent and surviving spouse had no children of their own, then even if the decedent had executed a will, s/he likely would have left everything to the spouse despite knowing some of it would eventually go to a step-child, simply because there is no other obvious person to give the wealth to and people are not likely to deprive their surviving spouse simply because s/he happens to have an offspring. In other cases, though, the absence of a special rule is more perplexing. For example, if the decedent and surviving spouse had two children, both now self-sufficient adults, and the surviving spouse also has an offspring from a pre-marital relationship (so older than the marital children but perhaps not doing well in life), the spouse would take the entire estate and then likely pass on any remainder to all three offspring in equal shares, and so in effect the current decedent's estate would equally benefit children and step-child, contrary to likely intent. But that is the way Virginia law is.

The next scenario is true of roughly half of all decedents – namely, they have no surviving spouse, but they have offspring. All the intestate property goes to the offspring and their descendants. The law presumes parents prefer benefiting their offspring and grandchildren over benefitting their native family (i.e., parents, siblings, etc.).

If, however, there is neither surviving spouse nor surviving offspring, then the property goes upstream to parents of the decedent. This is most likely with unusually young decedents, as it requires both that parents still be alive and that the decedent has not formed a family. Why not favor a decedent's siblings over parents, given that the former might be more likely to have need? One possible explanation is that the law assumes the parents will eventually pass on at least some of the property to the decedent's siblings anyway.

If the parents predeceased the decedent, then the intestacy rule directs property to the decedent's siblings and their descendants (i.e., the decedent's nieces and nephews).

It is fairly rare that paragraph 5 of § 64.2-200 applies, because few people die with no surviving spouse, child, grandchild, parent, sibling, niece, or nephew. Paragraph 5 says that in such a situation, the intestate property should be divided in half, and one half should go to the decedent's more distant relatives ("laughing heirs") on the paternal side and the other half to those on the maternal side. The rule says to look first for grandparents, and then for aunts and uncles of the decedent, but mostly likely the property is going to go to the decedent's first cousins in such a case – that is, to the offspring of the decedent's aunts and uncles. If on either side there is no grandparent, uncle/aunt, or first cousin, the next move is to second cousins (descendants of the brothers and sisters of the decedent's grandparents).

Virginia law goes to even further lengths to avoid "escheat to the state," looking without limit for cousins of any degree (consult a Table of Consanguinity to determine priority among laughing heirs). Moreover, if there still is no taker then the law looks even to heirs of a predeceased spouse! The analysis in the remainder of this Chapter will, however, largely stick to cases where there is some heir at least as close as a second cousin. Because there are plenty of other complicating sub-rules to worry about.

II.   Who is a spouse?

A spouse for inheritance purposes is someone who is a spouse by law, not simply "spiritually united" to the decedent or religiously married (as polygamists might do, for example). In forty U.S. states, including Virginia, legal marriage can arise only by state issuance of a marriage license and then a marriage certificate. The fact of marriage is thus established clearly at the time it arises.

In the other ten states (Alabama, Colorado, Iowa, Kansas, Montana, New Hampshire, Rhode Island, South Carolina, Texas, and Utah) and in the District of Columbia,[4] however, a "common law marriage" or informal marriage is possible. And even states that do not themselves allow for common law marriages to arise within their borders will recognize common law marriages that have arisen elsewhere. Thus, someone who dies a resident of Virginia might never have had a formal marriage to anyone, so there is no marriage certificate to prove that he or she was married at time of death, yet Virginia law will treat the decedent as married if he or she had entered into a common law marriage while domiciled in one of the jurisdictions that does authorize it, before moving to Virginia, and was never divorced.

Existence of a common law marriage might in fact be officially established only at the time of one spouse's death, when someone claiming to be the decedent's spouse wishes to inherit as such. To establish that a common law marriage existed, the person alleging it must demonstrate that, while residing in a common-law marriage state, the couple intended for a legal marriage to arise between them without a ceremony or state marriage certificate, believed that this actually occurred, lived like a married couple, and held themselves out to their community as legally married. In no state are two people legally married if they simply cohabit; cohabitation is a necessary but not sufficient condition in common-law marriage states.

Once two people are legally married, they remain such unless and until a court enters a divorce decree. Even marriages that arise informally in common-law marriage states are dissolved only by court decree; there is no such thing as "common law divorce" or informal divorce. Moreover, in Virginia, as in most other states, even during a period of physical separation that is a prelude to divorce they remain legally spouses to each other for inheritance purposes, though the separation could, along with other circumstances, support a finding of abandonment, as discussed below under "Bars to Succession." Spouses who are separating can, however, include in a separation agreement a waiver of any claims on the estate of the other.

III.   Who are the decedents' children?

The term "children" in Section 64.2-200 means "legal children" or persons whom the law treats as the decedents' children. It therefore includes adopted children, as

---

[4] There are an additional few states that previously allowed common law marriage to arise and that still recognize any common law marriages that arose before legislation was passed to eliminate the practice going forward.

discussed below. It can also result in exclusion of some biological offspring of a decedent, either because of an adoption by someone else that severs the connection between biological parent and children or because a biological father's paternity is never established.

"Illegitimacy" per se does not exclude a child from inheritance. The law today does not, and constitutionally may not, treat non-marital children worse than marital children. So if the decedent had some children with a surviving spouse and one or more by a prior non-marital relationship, or had one child with an unmarried partner and then more children after marrying that partner, all the children are treated the same in law, so long as the legal parent-child relationship is established.

When a legal-parent child relationship is established during the parent's life, that is typically recorded on the child's birth certificate, and that birth certificate – in the absence of a challenge to its accuracy – is all that is needed to prove the relationship for inheritance purposes. The ways by which the legal parent-child relationship is established during a parent's life are covered in a course on family law and appear in the Domestic Relations title of the Virginia Code. To state the main ones briefly: With respect to mothers, the mother-child relationship is established by proof of her having given birth or by legal adoption. Men also become legal parents by adoption, but otherwise legal fatherhood is more complicated. In the case of children born during marriage, there is a marital presumption that the husband is the biological and therefore legal father. This is subject to rebuttal, but someone would have to act affirmatively to overcome the presumption. Children born while their mother was not married are the child of a male decedent if the man and the mother executed an acknowledgement of paternity or if a court declared paternity. In *Hupp v. Hupp*, 239 Va. 494, 499, 391 S.E.2d 329, 332 (1990), the Virginia Supreme Court held that decisions of courts of other states that directly or implicitly determine the paternity of a child suffice to establish parentage for inheritance purposes in Virginia probate proceedings. In that case, an order for support of an illegitimate child issued by a Pennsylvania court "'necessarily determine[d] the issue of paternity'" as a matter of law, even though no genetic testing was done to prove biological connection.

A. Posthumous Determination

It is possible, in addition, for parentage to be established after an alleged parent's death, for the purpose of claiming inheritance or inclusion in any will bequest to "my children." This possibility gives rise to a lot of litigation; there are many biological fathers whose paternity is never established during their lives, but whose offspring seek a share of their estates when they die. Unsurprisingly, those who stand to lose all or part of an inheritance if such establishment occurs typically resist the alleged offspring's efforts. To establish paternity posthumously, the person claiming to be an offspring, or an agent for that person, would have to file a petition for adjudication of parenthood in the appropriate circuit court within one year of the decedent's death. The claimant must establish paternity by clear and convincing evidence, which can be genetic testing or various indicia that the decedent regarded and treated the child as his, such as living with the claimant's mother and "holding out" the claimant as his child in the community, on tax returns, etc.. Va. Code § 64.2-103. There is an asymmetry in inheritance law, however, as between child inheriting from parent and parent inheriting from child; Va. Code § 64.2-102 states that "paternity established pursuant to this subdivision is ineffective to qualify the father or his kindred to inherit from or through the child unless the father has openly treated the child as his and has not refused to support the child."

Supreme Court of Virginia.
Jones v. Eley
256 Va. 198, 501 S.E.2d 405 (1998)

STEPHENSON, Senior Justice.

… **406 On June 15, 1995, the Eleys filed a petition, pursuant to Code § 64.1–5.1, to establish that Bobby Julius Jones, who died February 24, 1995, was their biological father. Daniel Jones, Charles C. Jones, and David L. Jones, co-administrators of Bobby Jones' estate (the *200 co-administrators), contested the paternity claim. The co-administrators are Bobby Jones' brothers and claim to be his sole heirs at law. …

In 1957, Alice Eley and Bobby Jones began dating each other. Although they never married, they continued to maintain a close relationship. Bobby and Alice lived together continuously during the seven years preceding Bobby's death.

Alice Eley is the biological mother of Sheila Eley, born in November 1958, and Nathan Eley, born in December 1960. Alice testified that Bobby was the children's biological father.[2]

> [2] DNA testing was also undertaken. Two laboratories, however, were unable to perform the test on Bobby's DNA sample.

According to Alice, Bobby assumed financial responsibility for the Eleys until they became adults. Bobby gave Alice money "every week" for their support, and he provided extra money when needed. Bobby also sat for a "family portrait," and he and Alice took pictures "throughout the lifetimes with the kids."

Bobby acknowledged to a number of family members and friends that the Eleys were his children. During his last illness and shortly before his death, Bobby acknowledged to his attending physician that the Eleys were his children, and the physician testified that Nathan was Bobby's "spitting image."

The Eleys testified that their relationship with Bobby was that of parent and children. They recounted how Bobby often would "pick [them] up" and take them to various places such as parks and movie theaters. On several occasions, Bobby took them to Jones family reunions and gatherings in North Carolina. Bobby bought them clothes, and he "always" took Nathan to the barbershop. He often *201 attended high school and college basketball games in which Nathan participated. After Sheila had children,

Bobby had a close relationship with his grandchildren, whom he affectionately referred to as his "grandboys."

On December 13, 1974, Bobby signed an insurance beneficiary designation form on which he stated that Sheila Eley was his daughter and Nathan Eley was his son. Sheila received $12,000 as the named beneficiary of Bobby's certificate of deposit with his employer's credit union. She also received insurance proceeds of approximately $25,000 as the named beneficiary of Bobby's life insurance policies. Bobby named Nathan the beneficiary of approximately 160 bonds having a value "well over $10,000."

When Bobby died, the Eleys, along with Daniel Jones, made the funeral arrangements. Sheila had Bobby's mail forwarded to her home so she could pay his outstanding debts. The Eleys paid Bobby's hospital bill, doctor bills, funeral and burial expenses, and property tax.

III

... **407 ... Code § 64.1–5.2 provides that "evidence that a man is the father of a child born out of wedlock shall be clear and convincing." The section also provides that the evidence "may include, but shall not be limited to" eight enumerated items.[3]

[3] The enumerated items in Code § 64.1–5.2 are as follows:

1. That he cohabited openly with the mother during all of the ten months immediately prior to the time the child was born;

2. That he gave consent to a physician or other person, not including the mother, charged with the responsibility of securing information for the preparation of a birth record that his name be used as the father of the child upon the birth records of the child;

3. That he allowed by a general course of conduct the common use of his surname by the child;

4. That he claimed the child as his child on any statement, tax return or other document filed and signed by him with any local, state or federal government or any agency thereof;

5. That he admitted before any court having jurisdiction to try and dispose of the same that he is the father of the child;

6. That he voluntarily admitted paternity in writing, under oath;

7. The results of medically reliable genetic blood grouping tests weighted with all the evidence; or

8. Medical or anthropological evidence relating to the alleged parentage of the child based on tests performed by experts.

*202 ... While it is true that none of the eight items were proved, the statute, as previously noted, expressly provides that the evidence relating to paternity "shall not be limited to" those items. ...

The evidence shows that Bobby acknowledged his paternity to a number of people, one of whom was his treating physician during his last illness. This disinterested witness testified not only that Bobby acknowledged to him that the Eleys were his children, but also that Nathan Eley was Bobby's "spitting image."

The evidence also reveals that Bobby's interaction with the Eleys was indicative of a father and children relationship. ... Most significantly, Bobby completed and signed an insurance beneficiary designation form on which he stated that Nathan Eley was his son and Sheila Eley was his daughter. ...

*203 Finally, the co-administrators contend that the evidence should fail because, on one occasion, Alice unsuccessfully petitioned a juvenile and domestic relations district court to order Bobby to pay support for the Eleys. ... Code § 64.1–5.1(3)(b)...states that a person born out of wedlock is the child of a man if the paternity is established by clear and convincing evidence; "provided, however, that the paternity establishment ... shall be ineffective to qualify the father or his kindred to inherit from or through the child unless the father has openly treated the child as his and has not refused to support the child." The co-administrators assert that "it is apparent that BobbyJones **408 was refusing to support the children when he went to court and the child support case was dismissed." We do not agree.

The record is silent with respect to the basis for the dismissal of the petition. Alice testified, however, that, although Bobby always supported the Eleys, she "took him to court ... to get more money because [she] didn't feel that [Bobby] was giving [her] enough at that particular time." ... [W]e do not think the record supports the contention that Bobby ever refused to support them.

Moreover, we think the co-administrators' reliance upon the quoted clause in Code § 64.1–5.1(3)(b) is misplaced. The clause deals with the right of a father or his kindred to inherit from or through a child born out of wedlock, not with the establishment of paternity.

We recognize... that the General Assembly, in enacting Code § 64.1–5.1, has placed a heavy burden on people who undertake to prove that they are the paternal children of a decedent. ... Nevertheless, ... we conclude that the finding is fully supported by the evidence. ...

For purposes of genetic testing, persons claiming to be offspring can request exhumation.

Supreme Court of Virginia
Martin v. Howard
273 Va. 722, 643 S.E.2d 229 (2007)

OPINION BY Senior Justice ROSCOE B. STEPHENSON, JR.

… Tracey Myers Howard (the Plaintiff) filed suit against Janet Martin (the Defendant), seeking, pursuant to Code § 32.1–286(C), the *724 exhumation of the body of Palmer D. Martin (Palmer) to obtain a tissue sample for DNA testing. Howard claimed that she is Palmer's illegitimate daughter. The Defendant, who is Palmer's widow and the administratrix of his estate, filed an answer opposing exhumation. …

Palmer died intestate on June 19, 2005, in Russell County. He was survived by his spouse, Janet Martin, and two children by Janet. … Palmer was born in Virginia, but he lived in Ohio as a teenager and young man. In the mid–1970's, he returned to Virginia, where he resided until his death.

Howard's evidence at trial was that, while in Ohio, Palmer dated the Plaintiff's mother, Mary Jean Myers Shelt, for approximately three years, ending in 1972. During that time, Palmer and the Plaintiff's mother engaged in an exclusive, intimate sexual relationship. The Plaintiff was conceived and born on October 10, 1972, in Ohio. Palmer proposed marriage to Shelt and requested that she move with him to Virginia. Shelt declined the proposal and remained in Ohio.

Howard's evidence further showed that, during the Plaintiff's childhood, Palmer regularly kept in touch with her. He provided support and assistance to the Plaintiff and Shelt. He took them on trips and vacations and brought gifts to the Plaintiff. When the Plaintiff was older, Palmer gave her two motor vehicles and the down payment on her house. He paid for her wedding and joined her for the father-daughter dance at the reception. Through the years, Palmer acknowledged to family members and many others that he was the Plaintiff's father. At one time, the Plaintiff asked Palmer if he would submit to a blood test to corroborate his paternity. Palmer responded that he did not need a blood test because he knew the Plaintiff was his child.

In opposing the exhumation request, the Defendant testified that the exhumation would be painful for her and her children.

*725 Prior to the enactment of subsection C of Code § 32.1–286, there was no provision in the law allowing a person to seek exhumation of a body in order to obtain a sample for genetic testing to establish parentage. … **231 In 1997, … the General Assembly amended the exhumation statute by adding subsection C … Code § 32.1–286(C), as it existed when the present litigation was filed and as it currently exists, reads as follows:

> Upon the petition of a party attempting to prove, in accordance with the provisions of §§ 64.1–5.1 and 64.1–5.2, that he *726 is the issue of a person dead and buried, a court may order the exhumation of the body of a

dead person for the conduct of scientifically reliable genetic tests, including DNA tests, to prove a biological relationship. The costs of exhumation, testing, and reinterment shall be paid by the petitioner unless, for good cause shown, the court orders such costs paid from the estate of the exhumed deceased. This provision is intended to provide a procedural mechanism for obtaining posthumous samples for reliable genetic testing and shall not require substantive proof of parentage to obtain the exhumation order.

... In enacting Code § 32.1–286(C), the General Assembly expressly provided that the need of a qualified illegitimate child to prove parentage for the purpose of inheritance is sufficient cause for exhumation. No other cause need be shown. ... **232 ...*727 C

The Defendant further contends that, under the statute, a trial court "may, but is not required to, grant a request for exhumation for DNA testing" and that "[w]hether to grant or deny the request is left to the sound discretion of the court." We do not agree. While use of the word "may" ordinarily imports permission, it will be construed to be mandatory when it is necessary to accomplish the manifest purpose of the legislature.

In the present case, the use of the word "may" is jurisdictional and directional, rather than discretionary, and vests in the trial court the authority to order the exhumation. There is nothing in the statute to suggest that the court has the discretion to deny exhumation to a person who meets its stated requirements. The court's only discretion is limited to determining whether the petitioner is a "party attempting to prove" parentage for inheritance purposes...

There are cases where those hoping to establish paternity are not descendants but rather the putative father or his relatives. The following decision is based on a predecessor to Va. Code § 64.2-102 that had a more categorical exclusion of unwed fathers, but the result would be the same under current law.

Supreme Court of Virginia.
King v. Commonwealth
221 Va. 251, 269 S.E.2d 793 (1980)

HARRISON, Justice.

... The decedent, who died intestate on June 5, 1975, was the illegitimate daughter of Martha Golden and John Lawson. It was determined that her only possible heir was William Lawson, her putative father's brother. The appellants here are the heirs of William Lawson who died during the pendency of this proceeding. The escheator of the City of Fredericksburg filed a bill in chancery, seeking the escheat of Golden's estate. ...*253 ... The question before us is whether the relatives of a putative father who never legitimated his child pursuant to statute, and who was never determined to be the father in any judicial proceeding during the lifetime of either, may nevertheless take by intestacy from the illegitimate child. ...

In *Trimble* [v. Gordon, 430 U.S. 762 (1977) (invalidating on equal protection grounds an Illinois statute allowing children born out of wedlock to inherit by intestate succession only from their mothers, whereas children born in wedlock could inherit by intestate succession from both their mothers and their fathers] the overriding concern of the Court was the condemnation and statutory disability visited on the innocent illegitimate children of those who engage in a meretricious relationship. ... Here the disability being inflicted is not on the innocent illegitimate at all, but upon the putative father of the illegitimate and those claiming through him. It occurs only in *254 cases where the putative father fails to legitimate his child in the mode and manner prescribed by law. **795

... In Trimble the classification of potential heirs was legitimate children and illegitimate children, and the Supreme Court declined to sanction different treatment for these two groups. However, in the course of its opinion, the Court did state: "The more serious problems of proving paternity might justify a more demanding standard for illegitimate children claiming under their fathers' estates than that required either for illegitimate children claiming under their mothers' estates or for legitimate children generally."

In the instant case the classification of potential heirs involves maternal relatives of illegitimate children and paternal relatives of illegitimate children. ... We do not regard this classification as suspect, and the Commonwealth need only show a rational basis for the disparate treatment. ...

State intestacy laws apply only when a deceased leaves no will. These laws represent an effort by the legislature to express the presumed intentions of an intestate deceased. It is reasonable to assume that an illegitimate child would probably bear no affection for a putative father who had never bothered to legitimate him or her. If the child desired to rebut this assumption a will could be executed. Further, it is the mother of an illegitimate child who customarily assumes a disproportionate **796 share of the responsibilities and obligations of raising the child. Unless a father voluntarily supports his offspring, or is compelled by court action to do so, the mother must bear the entire burden, or call upon her own family for aid and assistance. This is but another reason why the General Assembly accords the maternal line of an illegitimate child different treatment from that accorded the putative paternal side in matters of intestate succession. ...*256 ... *257 ... 797 ...

[T]he decree of the court below, escheating the estate of Carrie M. Golden, deceased, was not directed at this illegitimate decedent, or designed as a punishment for the conduct of her parents, Martha Golden and John Lawson. ... We find no federal or state constitutional infirmity or statutory impediment in precluding inheritance by the paternal kindred of an illegitimate. ...

B. Effects of Termination of Parental Rights (TPR) and Adoption

A court can terminate a person's legal parent status in adjudication of a petition for TPR filed by a child protection agency. This might occur even when there is no corresponding or subsequent adoption, if only one of two legal parents is terminated or if permanent foster care is the plan for the child. In that case, the terminated parent(s) thenceforth may not inherit from the child, but the child can still inherit from the terminated parent(s) or through the terminated parent(s) from extended family. Va. Code § 64.2-102(5). This asymmetry resembles that in situations in which a biological father never established paternity as to, nor provided support for, an offspring while both were alive.

In most instances, though, a child protection agency will petition for TPR only when it anticipates an adoption. In addition, biological parents' rights can also be terminated in an adoption proceeding initiated by private parties wishing to adopt. What effect does an adoption have on inheritance? Virginia law treats differently a step-parent adoption and what might be called a "new family adoption," in which one or more adopters completely replace birth parents, whose status has previously been terminated or is terminated through the adoption proceeding.

Subtitle I. General Provisions
Chapter 1, Article 2. General Provisions

§ 64.2-102. Meaning of child and related terms

If, for purposes of this title or for determining rights in and to property pursuant to any deed, will, trust or other instrument, a relationship of parent and child must be established to determine succession or a taking by, through, or from a person:

> 1. An adopted person is the child of an adopting parent and not of the biological parents, except that adoption of a child by the spouse of a biological parent has no effect on the relationship between the child and either biological parent.

***

Thus, following a new-family adoption, the child can inherit from the adoptive parents and their kin but not from either birth parent or either birth parent's kin. A child who is the subject of a step-parent adoption, though, ends up with three parents for inheritance purposes. The child can still inherit from and through birth parents, and in addition now can inherit from and through the adoptive parent. There appears to be only one reported Virginia court decision analyzing the meaning and applicability of this provision regarding adoption, and it addressed the unusual situation of an adult adoption.

Supreme Court of Virginia.
Kummer v. Donak
282 Va. 301, 715 S.E.2d 7 (2011)

Opinion by Justice WILLIAM C. MIMS.

*303 ... Justine Critzer ("Critzer"), a Virginia resident, died intestate on March 31, 2006. No spouse, siblings, children, or parents survived her. Nancy Donak ("Donak") was appointed administratrix of her estate. Donak could not locate a will. Initially she believed Critzer's only heirs were distant cousins. Donak petitioned the Circuit Court of Warren County to serve notice on fifty-three individuals with possible claims, including Richard Kummer, Charles Kummer III, and Jane Kummer Stolte ("Kummer children"), the appellants. Donak subsequently discovered that the Kummer children's deceased mother, Mary Frances Kummer ("Mrs. Kummer"), was the biological sister of Critzer. Consequently, they were the niece and nephews of Critzer and apparently were her closest surviving heirs.

Donak then moved the circuit court in November 2007 for leave to file an amended list of heirs that named the Kummer children as "the only necessary parties to these probate proceedings, the only beneficiaries of the estate and the only persons to whom distribution should be made." The court granted the motion in December 2007 and ordered Donak to distribute Critzer's estate accordingly.

Shortly thereafter, Donak and the Kummer children began to administer the estate. They sold, with approval by court order, two properties: a seventeen-acre property worth $272,000 in March 2008 and a thirty-three acre property worth $405,000 in June 2008.

In October 2009, Donak filed a petition for aid and direction and motion for rule to show cause against distribution in the circuit court, based upon the fact that Mrs. Kummer had been adopted in 1981, at the age of 53, by her aunt by marriage, Arietta Henry Kaleta. ... *304 **9

II. ANALYSIS

... Code § 64.1–5.1 [now § 64.2-102, above] defines a child for purposes of Code § 64.1–1... The Kummer children ... assert that Code § 64.1–5.1 does not apply in this case because no parent-child relationship need be established, but rather it only requires proof of the relationship of two sisters. They also contend that the public policy behind intestate succession supports allowing property to descend to the closest blood relative and disfavors allowing the adoption of a person to sever the inheritance rights of her descendants.

Contrary to the Kummer children's assertion, this case unquestionably requires the establishment of a parent-child relationship *305 to determine whether they can inherit through their mother. ... To inherit as descendants of Critzer's sister, they must first establish that Mrs. Kummer was Critzer's sister for purposes of the statutory scheme. That cannot be done unless a relationship of parent and child is established to show a common parent of Mrs. Kummer and Critzer. Applying the unambiguous language of Code § 64.1–5.1, Mrs. Kummer became the child of her adopting parent and no longer was the child of her biological parents. Consequently, Critzer and Mrs. Kummer, while biologically sisters, were not legally sisters for purposes of intestate succession under Code § 64.1–1. ...

The Kummer children contend that the legislature never intended to divest an adopted child of inheritance rights from her biological family, because Code § 63.2–1215 [in the Social Welfare title of the Virginia Code], which delineates the legal effects of adoption, does not specifically address intestate succession.[5]

> [5] The Kummer children assert that, in removing former Code § 63.1–234 (1973 & Supp.1978), a descent and distribution provision in the adoption statute that barred inheritance from the biological family, the General Assembly intended to allow such inheritance because the provision was not replaced. Because Code § 64.1–5.1 is unambiguous, this Court will not consider the Kummer children's argument regarding legislative history.

Code § 63.2–1215 states:

> The birth parents ... shall ... be divested of all legal rights and obligations in respect to the child including the right to petition any court for visitation with the child.... Except [in cases of stepparent **10 adoption], any person whose interest in the child derives from or through the birth parent ... including but not limited to grandparents, stepparents, former stepparents, blood relatives and family members shall ... be divested of all legal rights and obligations in respect to the child including the right to petition any court for visitation with the child. In all cases the child shall be free from all legal obligations of obedience and maintenance in respect to such persons divested of legal rights. Any child adopted under the provisions of this chapter shall ... be, to all intents and purposes, the child of the person or persons so adopting him, and ... shall be entitled to all the rights and privileges, and subject to all the obligations, *306 of a child of such person or persons born in lawful wedlock.

This provision is consistent with Code § 64.1–5.1, as it declares that the adopted child becomes for "all intents and purposes" the child of the adopting parent. The child is then placed on equal footing in her adopting family as a child "born in lawful wedlock" to the adopting parents. This provision divested Mrs. Kummer's biological parents of their legal rights with respect to Mrs. Kummer. Such divestiture extends to collateral relatives whose interest derives through the parents, which includes Critzer. ...

[C]onsanguinity ceases to be paramount where the legislature expresses an intention to the contrary. Because there is no ambiguity in the applicable statutes, the Kummer children's public policy argument must fail.

The Kummer children assert that the adoption of an adult is not the same as the adoption of a minor, because it is motivated primarily by financial considerations.

Therefore, Mrs. Kummer's adoption should not be treated as having the same legal effect as a child adoption. We disagree.

Code § 63.2–1243, the adult adoption statute, provides that adoption of an adult shall have the same effect as adoption of a child:

> Any interlocutory or final order issued in any case under this section shall have the same effect as other orders issued under this chapter; and in any such case, the word "child" in any *307 other section of this chapter shall be construed to refer to the person whose adoption is petitioned for under this section.

Code § 64.1–5.1 has the same effect, as it refers to any "adopted person" rather than distinguishing between minor and adult. The plain language of these statutes evinces the intention of the legislature to treat minor and adult adoptees the same.

Thus, the Kummer children's inheritance rights do not change based on Mrs. Kummer's adoption as an adult rather than as a child. The effect of Mrs. Kummer's adoption as an adult divested her and her descendants of inheritance rights running from her biological family. The Kummer children are not Critzer's heirs-at-law and cannot inherit from her estate. ...

———————

The court's interpretation § 63.2–1215 here is flawed. That provision's declaration "that the adopted child becomes for 'all intents and purposes' the child of the adopting parent" is not equivalent to declaring and does not logically entail that the child is divested of the ability to inherit from or through her biological parents. The court could, however, simply have dismissed the Kummer children's appeal to that statutory provision on the grounds that § 64.1–5.1 is a more specific provision applicable only to intestate succession, invoking the *generalia specialibus non derogant* ("the general does not detract from the specific") canon of statutory interpretation. See Virginia Dep't of Health v. Kepa, Inc., 289 Va. 131, 142, 766 S.E.2d 884, 890 (2015) ("[W]hen one statute speaks to a subject in a general way and another deals with a part of the same subject in a more specific manner, the two should be harmonized, if possible, and where they conflict, the latter prevails.").

"Undue influence" is a concept closely associated with will execution in the field of trusts and estates, but it can also arise in the context of adult adoption. In re Adoption of Moore, 77 Va. Cir. 408 (Hanover County, 2009) involved an objection by a nephew of the renowned Doctor Bruce Vaughan English to treatment of one Frances Moore as the Doctor's adopted daughter and, as a result, sole heir. The Doctor died just three weeks after the adoption occurred. The nephew asserted that "Doctor English did not know Respondent for the required year before adoption and that the adoption was the product of Respondent's undue influence." The only aspect of the case decided in a published report was standing. The court held, consistent with rulings of appellate courts in six other states, that the nephew did have standing to challenge the adoption, despite having no interest in or party status with respect to the adoption per se, reasoning:

> Where, as here, it is alleged that the adoptee used undue influence to obtain the adoption for the sole purpose of becoming an heir, standing to protect the estate may be derived by collateral heirs or next of kin from the rights of the deceased as if he were alive. Such standing is further mandated by public policy. Were collateral heirs or next of kin denied standing to attack an adult adoption allegedly obtained by fraud or undue influence, the adoptee would be effectively immune. Fraud in such a manner, with its consequent deprivation of rightful heirs, would be without remedy. The Court is unwilling to accept such a loophole.

C. After-born heirs

What if a man dies while his wife is pregnant? Or if a couple freezes their eggs, sperm, or embryos and these are used to produce a child after one of them has died? These things do not happen often, but they happen. The law treats them just like offspring born before the decedent's death. § 64.2-204 of the Virginia Code states: "Relatives of the decedent conceived before his death but born thereafter, and children resulting from assisted conception born after the decedent's death who are determined to be relatives of the decedent as provided in [the statutory rules governing parentage in cases of assisted reproduction – in particular, Va. Code § 20-158] shall inherit as if they had been born during the lifetime of the decedent."

IV.   Predeceased family members

What if the decedent had been married but the spouse predeceased? Then the spouse is entirely out of the picture; nothing passes through predeceased spouses to their native family members.

What if the decedent had offspring but some or all of them predeceased? This is a different story. In that case, intestate property will pass through predeceased offspring to *their* offspring if they had any – that is, to the decedent's grandchildren. But by what fractions?

If there was only ever one offspring, it is a simple matter; all goes to that offspring's offspring in equal shares (assuming all still live). But things are usually not so simple. More often, there was more than one offspring and one or more is predeceased but not others. Virginia has a special provision to govern such cases:

Chapter 2. Descent and Distribution

§ 64.2-202. When persons take per capita and when per stirpes.

A. A decedent's estate... shall... be divided into as many equal shares as there are (i) heirs and distributees who are in the closest degree of kinship to the decedent and (ii) deceased persons, if any, in the same degree of kinship to the decedent who, if living, would have been heirs and distributees and who left descendants surviving at the time of the decedent's death. One share of the estate... shall descend and pass to each such heir and distributee and one share shall descend and pass per stirpes to such descendants.

That is not a well-crafted statute. What it is meant to say is this:

> *Figure out which category of heirs highest on the list of priority has a member living at the time of the decedent's death. Divide the estate into fractions based on the total number of persons in that category who are either a) still alive or b) predeceased but survived by one or more descendants. As to any predeceased members of that class who have a living descendant, give that person's share to his descendants.*

For example:

> At Mother's death, two of her five children (A and B) are still alive. C died seven years earlier, leaving behind a spouse but no children or other descendents. D died five years earlier, leaving behind five children. E died three years earlier, leaving one child.

> The surviving spouse of a predeceased heir never takes in place of that heir, so no portion of the estate passes through C. D and E have surviving descendants, however, so the estate is initially divided into four parts, one for each of Mother's children who survived or left descendants. Thus, A and B receive 25% each of the estate. D's children divide D's one-fourth share, so each receives 5% of the estate. E's child receives E's one-fourth, or 25% of the estate.

Now amend that hypo so A and B also predeceased mother, never having had any children, so Mother was survived by no children but by the six grandchildren. Then the estate is divided at the level of grandchildren, and so each grandchild would receive 1/6 of the estate.

Another example:

> Rock star Jim dies of a drug overdose at age 22, never having had any children. His parents' parental rights were terminated when he was 14 and he aged out of foster care, becoming an adult with no legal parents. He has two living sisters and a predeceased brother. The brother left behind one illegitimate daughter. Jim's sisters get one-third of the estate each, and Jim's niece gets one third.

What exactly does predeceased mean? And conversely, who is a "surviving" spouse or blood relative? What if a would-be heir died immediately after the decedent, because they were involved in the same fatal event, such as a car crash? The rule for "simultaneous death" in the intestate succession context is the same as the one you read for non-probate transfers in Chapter One. Here you get some more detail about how the law establishes the timing of deaths.

Subtitle V. Provisions Applicable to Probate and Nonprobate Transfers. Chapter 22. Uniform Simultaneous Death Act.

§ 64.2-2201. Requirement of survival by 120 hours for statutory rights.

Except as provided in § 64.2-2205, if the (i) title to property, (ii) devolution of property, or (iii) right to elect an interest in property, an augmented estate share or exempt property, or homestead or family allowance depends upon an individual surviving another, an individual who is not established by clear and convincing evidence to have survived the other individual by 120 hours is deemed to have predeceased the other. However, this section does not apply if its application would result in a taking of an intestate estate by the Commonwealth.

§ 64.2-2204. Evidence of death or status.

In addition to otherwise applicable rules of evidence, the following rules relating to a determination of death and status shall apply:

> 1. Death occurs when an individual is determined to be dead in accordance with the provisions of § 54.1-2972 [basing death on "absence of spontaneous respiratory and spontaneous cardiac functions" and a physician's conclusion that "attempts at resuscitation would not... be successful in restoring spontaneous life-sustaining functions"], or Chapter 23 (§ 64.2-2300 et seq.). ...

§ 64.2-2205. Exceptions.

Survival by 120 hours is not required if:

> 1. The governing instrument contains language dealing explicitly with (i) simultaneous deaths or deaths in a common disaster and that language is operable under the facts of the case, (ii) deaths under circumstances where the order of death cannot be established by proof, or (iii) the marital deduction, or the governing instrument contains a provision to or for the benefit of the decedent's spouse where it is the decedent's intent, as manifested from the governing instrument or external evidence, that the decedent's estate receive the benefit of the federal estate tax marital deduction;

2. The governing instrument expressly indicates that an individual is not required to survive an event, including the death of another individual, by any specified period or expressly requires the individual to survive the event, including the death of another individual, for a specified period; but survival of the event, another individual, or the specified period shall be established by clear and convincing evidence; ...

Chapter 23. Persons Presumed Dead.

§ 64.2-2300. Presumption of death from absence or disappearance.

A. 1. Any person who is a resident of the Commonwealth shall be presumed to be dead if such person:

a. Leaves and does not return to the Commonwealth for seven successive years and is not heard from;

b. Disappears for seven successive years and is not heard from; or

c. Disappears in a foreign country, his body has not been found, and he is not known to be alive, and a report of presumptive death by the Department of State of the United States has been issued.

2. Any person who is not a resident of the Commonwealth, but who owns real or personal property located within the Commonwealth, shall be presumed to be dead if such person disappears for seven successive years from the place of his residence outside of the Commonwealth and is not heard from.

3. The presumption created by this subsection shall be applicable in any action where the person's death is in question, unless proof is offered that the person was alive within the time specified or, in the case of a presumed death in a foreign country, at any time following the person's disappearance, whether before or after the report of presumptive death was issued.

B. The fact that any person was exposed to a specific peril of death may be a sufficient basis for determining at any time after the exposure that the person is presumed to have died less than seven years after the person was last heard from.

C. Any person on board any ship or vessel underway on the high seas who disappears from such ship or vessel, or any person on board an aircraft that disappears at sea, who is not known to be alive and whose body has not been found or identified prior to a hearing of a board of inquiry as to such disappearance, shall be presumed to be dead upon the findings of a board of inquiry that the person is presumed dead, or six months after the date of such disappearance, whichever occurs first. ...

§ 64.2-2301. Distribution of fund when presumption of death not applicable.

A. In any civil action wherein any estate or fund is to be distributed, if the interest of any person to the estate or fund depends upon his having been alive at a particular time and it is not known and cannot be shown by the exercise of reasonable diligence whether such person was alive at that time, and if the legal presumption of death does not apply, the court may enter an order distributing the estate or fund to those who would be otherwise entitled thereto if it were shown that such person was dead at such particular time.

B. Before any distribution is made pursuant to subsection A, the court shall require that... the heir at law, devisee, next of kin, legatee, beneficiary, survivor, or other successor in interest shall give a refunding bond with surety
...

§ 64.2-2306. Distribution of property; refunding bond.

Before any distribution of the proceeds of the estate of a person determined to be dead pursuant to this chapter or the payment or transfer of any of his other property is made, and before the sale of any real or personal property passing in kind by persons claiming such property..., the persons entitled to receive such proceeds or property in kind shall give a refunding bond without surety upon condition that if the person determined to be dead is in fact alive at that time, they will respectively refund to such person the proceeds or property... on demand, without interest thereon.

V.   Half relations

In this day of blended families, you are likely familiar with the terms "half-sister" and "half-brother." These are siblings with one but only one parent in common. So if mom has two children by two different fathers (regardless of whether mom married either man), these children are half-siblings with respect to each other. Likewise, if dad has a child with one woman and then another child with another woman, the children are half-siblings (again, without regard to the marital status at any time of the common parent). Are half-siblings treated the same in intestacy law? It depends on who the decedent is. If it is the common parent that dies, then they are treated equally. There is no such thing as a half-child. One is either the offspring of the decedent or one is not. If, however, the decedent is one of the siblings, then a special rule as to "half bloods" applies. Section 64.2-202 of the Virginia Codes states that "collaterals of the half blood shall inherit only half as much as those of the whole blood." This means that if the first-in-line heirs are siblings of the decedent (because the decedent had no surviving spouse, children or other descendants, or parents), then it matters whether the surviving siblings are all whole-siblings, all halves, or a mix of wholes and halves. If they are all wholes, they all take an equal fraction. Likewise, if they are all halves, they all take an equal fraction. This rule is relevant when there is a mix. In that case, you need to do some algebra. You need to figure out how to divide the estate so that each whole-sibling ends up with twice as much as each half-sibling. The formula for determining the denominator of the fraction is $2x + y$, where $x =$ number of whole siblings and $y =$ number of half-siblings. And the numerator for halves is 1, whereas the numerator for wholes is 2. Example:

> Dad has two children with his first wife, then three children with his second wife. His second wife also has a child from a prior relationship. So there are six children altogether, and they are all grown up when one child from the second marriage dies. Dad and second wife were already dead when this happened. The deceased offspring never had children of her own, so the decedent's heirs are the five siblings. Three of these siblings are half-siblings, two from Dad's first marriage and one from mom's pre-marital relationship. And two of these siblings are whole siblings; both of their parents were parents to the decedent also. So the denominator of the fraction to be applied is $(2 \times 2) + 3$, which $= 7$. Each whole sibling therefore takes 2/7 and each half-sibling takes 1/7 of the estate. There are two whole siblings, so their combined share is 4/7. And the combined shares of the half-siblings is 3/7, so it all adds up.

The rule for half-bloods could also apply when the heirs are cousins, nephews and nieces, or aunts and uncles. "Collateral relatives" are any relatives that are not ancestors or descendants.

> So suppose the children in the hypothetical above all have children of their own. The children of the children of Dad's first marriage are half-first cousins in relation to the children of the children of dad's second marriage. In other words, if you have a half-sibling, your children will be half-first-cousins *vis a vis* your half-sibling's children. So in the rare event that a decedent's estate is going to first cousins, you would examine the relationship among the people in the generation above them to see if the decedent's parent was a whole or a half sibling as to the blood-related parent of the first cousins. If there is a mix of whole- and half- first cousins, you need to ensure each whole takes twice as much as each half, using the same formula.

However, note that collaterals who are not siblings or descendants of siblings (i.e., aunts, uncles, and cousins) take only under paragraph A.5 of § 64.2-200, after the decedent's estate has been divided into halves ("moieties"), with one half going to the decedent's family on the paternal side and the other half going to the decedent's family on the maternal side. What if one of the collateral heirs on one side is related 'by the half blood' rather than 'by the whole blood'?

Supreme Court of Virginia.
Sheppard v. Junes
287 Va. 397, 756 S.E.2d 409 (2014)

Opinion by Justice LEROY F. MILLETTE, JR.

*401 In this appeal we consider the impact of a half-blood relative on the distribution of the paternal side of an intestate estate when all of the heirs are collaterals and the estate must be separated into paternal and maternal parts.

I. Facts and Proceedings

John Warren Shepperd died without having executed a will. In life, John never married and had no children. At the time of his death, John's parents and older sister had predeceased him. John's older sister had no children.

Linda Junes was appointed administrator of John's estate. Linda identified fourteen second cousins from John's maternal side, including Linda herself, who survived John's death. These fourteen second cousins stand **411 in equal relation to John, and they do not dispute that, *402 among themselves, they are entitled to equal 1/14 shares of whatever interest they collectively have in John's estate. After certification by a genealogical research firm, Linda also accepted Jason H. Sheppard, Jr., as John's half-uncle from John's paternal side who survived John's death.

Linda, in her capacity as administrator, filed a motion for aid and direction in the Circuit Court of Arlington County. Linda sought judicial assistance to determine the proper distribution proportions of John's estate according to Virginia's statutory scheme governing intestate succession because Jason's half-blood status complicated the task. In particular, Linda sought assistance to determine whether either (1) Jason could take the entirety of John's estate that was to pass to John's paternal side, because Jason was the only relative on John's paternal side, or (2) Jason could only take one-half of John's estate that was to pass to John's paternal side, and the remainder was to be distributed to the fourteen second cousins, because half-bloods can only take half of the inheritance of whole-bloods. ... *403

II. Discussion ... **412

1. Code § 64.2–200

... Code § 64.2–200 provides a sequential list of hierarchical classes of people to whom the decedent's estate may pass, set up by the General Assembly in descending priority. Each class on the list is defined by that class's relationship with the decedent, and the further down the list one goes the more distant the relation becomes. It is clear from the sequential nature of Code § 64.2–200's plain language that each subsection of that statute must be assessed in the order listed. Only if a subsection does not apply because no person qualifies as a member of that particular class may the next subsection be considered. Accordingly, because John had no surviving spouse, no children, no surviving parents, and neither a surviving brother or sister nor a brother or sister who had descendants, the first subsection of the statute applicable to John's estate is Code § 64.2–200(A)(5).

The preamble to Code § 64.2–200(A)(5) states that "[i]f there is none of the foregoing, then one-half of the estate descends and passes to the paternal kindred and one-half descends and passes to the maternal kindred of the decedent in the following course." ...We have previously explained... what effect this separation has on the distribution of a decedent's estate:

> [After a decedent's estate is separated into moieties], each moiety goes to the proper kindred as a class, on the paternal and maternal side respectively, and there is no further division into moieties as between the branches of paternal and maternal kindred. And each moiety keeps on its own side, regardless of the other, so long as there are any kindred, however remote, on that side. Williams v. Knowles, 178 Va. 84, 99 (1941).

... John's estate must be divided into two different, but equally valued, *405 moieties. One moiety passes to John's paternal kindred and the other moiety passes to John's maternal kindred. These moieties are treated as entirely separate so long as each passes to statutorily-identified kindred. ... For each moiety, the statutory provisions in Code § 64.2–200(A)(5)(a) through (e) are applied separately and independently.

John's paternal side moiety does not pass under Code § 64.2–200(A)(5)(a) because John had no surviving grandparent on his paternal side. Code § 64.2–200(A)(5)(b) states that "[i]f there is none of the foregoing, then to the decedent's uncles and aunts, and their descendants." Jason was an uncle on John's paternal side, and therefore John's paternal side moiety passes to Jason pursuant to Code § 64.2–200(A)(5)(b). ...

2. Code § 64.2–202

*406 ... [U]nder Code § 64.2–202(A) the decedent's estate must be divided into equal shares based on the number of "heirs and distributees" who qualify as part of the relevant class, so long as such persons either survive the decedent's death, or, if they did not survive the decedent's death, such persons left descendants who did survive the decedent's death. Once the number of shares is calculated, one share is distributed to each "such heir and distributee" on a per capita basis and to "such descendants" on a per stirpes basis. See also Ball v. Ball, 68 Va. (27 Gratt.) 325, 327 (1876) ("Whenever those entitled to partition are in the same degree of kindred to the intestate, they shall take per capita or by persons; and where a part of them being dead and a part living, the issue of those dead shall take per stirpes.").

Code § 64.2–202(A) states clearly that this division of the estate among equally positioned relatives applies either to the decedent's entire estate, or to "each half portion of such estate when division is required by subdivision A 5 of § 64.2–200." Therefore, the provisions of Code § 64.2–202(A) independently apply to each moiety of John's estate created pursuant to Code § 64.2–200(A)(5). *407 Jason, who is the only member of the class to which John's paternal side moiety passes under Code § 64.2–200, takes the entirety of John's paternal side moiety. ... Jason takes one-half of John's estate. ... **414 ...

Citing Code § 64.2–202(B), Linda argues that, because Jason is a half-blood collateral, he can only take half of John's paternal side moiety that he would otherwise be entitled to receive. Citing Code § 64.2–200(B), Linda argues that the portion of John's paternal side moiety that Jason is deprived of should instead pass to the maternal heirs. We disagree.

a. Code § 64.2–200(B)

Code § 64.2–200(B) applies if "there are either no surviving paternal kindred or no surviving maternal kindred, [or] there are neither maternal nor paternal kindred." ... When reviewing the Code § 64.2–200 categories in sequential order, if a subsection applies because a member of the identified class exists, a court must conclude its analysis at that point in applying Code § 64.2–200. ... Code § 64.2–200(B) is listed subsequent to Code § 64.2–200(A)(5)(a) through (e) and, by its terms, only applies if Code § 64.2–200(A)(5)(a) through (e) are inapplicable to either or both moieties. Thus, Code § 64.2–200(B) does not apply and cannot *408 affect distribution of John's paternal side moiety under Code § 64.2–202(A).

b. Code § 64.2–202(B)

Code § 64.2–202(B) provides that "collaterals of the half blood shall inherit only half as much as those of the whole blood." Code § 64.2–202(B) begins with the phrase "[n]otwithstanding the provisions of subsection A." This phrase indicates that the half-blood rule of Code § 64.2–202(B) operates to modify only the application of Code § 64.2–202(A). Moreover, by its terms, Code § 64.2–202(B) does not alter the division of the moieties required by Code § 64.2–200(A)(5). Thus, once the application of Code § 64.2–202(A) to each moiety is separately established, the extent to which Code § 64.2–202(B) modifies the Code § 64.2–202(A) distribution of John's paternal side moiety must be determined.

It is clear that Code § 64.2–202(B) does not modify the Code § 64.2–202(A) distribution in this case. John's paternal side moiety passes to a class comprised of only one heir: Jason. Even though Jason is a half-blood collateral heir, no whole-blood collateral heir exists as part of that class to which John's paternal side moiety passes. Without such a whole-blood collateral, no whole-blood inheritance exists to provide a statutory basis for applying Code § 64.2–202(B) to reduce John's inheritance. Thus, Code § 64.2–202(B) does not affect distribution of John's paternal side moiety as provided under Code § 64.2–202(A).

Moreover, it is of no consequence that John's fourteen second cousins are whole-blood collaterals. These fourteen second cousins take pursuant to John's maternal side moiety, and have no interest in John's paternal side moiety. Code § 64.2–200(A)(5). Their existence does not affect the class to which John's paternal side moiety passes, they are not a part of that class, and they do not alter the distribution of shares among the heirs within that class. ... *409 ... **415

.... We will therefore reverse ... enter final judgment in favor of Jason.

VI. Disclaimer

As with non-probate transfers, any probate transfers can be refused, in which case the heir is treated as having predeceased the decedent. As presented in Chapter One, Va. Code § 64.2-2603 states that "[a] person may disclaim in whole or in part, any interest in or power over property." When an heir is a minor, a "custodial parent of a minor for whom no guardian of the property has been appointed may disclaim, in whole or in part, an interest in or power over property... that, but for the custodial parent's disclaimer, would have passed to the minor as the result of another disclaimer." A minor generally would not inherit via intestacy laws unless one of the child's parent disclaimed an inheritance or the child is inheriting from or through a deceased parent.

§ 64.2-2603 allows for partial rather than complete disclaimer of an intestate share, so someone entitled to the entire estate, such as a surviving spouse, might choose to disclaim as to only half of the estate, allowing the other half to pass to those next in line, such as the disclaimant's children. The spouse might do this seeing no need to have it all her/himself, thinking the offspring could benefit more from having the assets, wanting to qualify for Medicaid payment of nursing home costs sooner rather than later, or for other reasons.

§ 64.2-2604 provides that the disclaimer of an intestate share "takes effect ... as of the time of the intestate's death." § 64.2-2610 requires the disclaimant to deliver a written disclaimer to "the personal representative of the decedent's estate or if no personal representative is then serving... with a court having jurisdiction to appoint the personal representative."

§ 64.2-2603 also states that a disclaimer of inheritance "is not a transfer, assignment, or release," which is relevant to state statutory protections for creditors or rules governing qualification for Medicaid or other state assistance that effectively penalize someone for alienating their assets to the detriment of others. Because an inheritance is not something to which one has a right, disclaiming it is treated as not equivalent to giving away one's property for such purposes. This rule is also supported by the overriding aim of intestacy law to replicate what the decedent would have chosen, and it is plausible to assume benefactors would be less inclined to direct assets to a family member deep in debt, if it would mean that family member cannot actually benefit from the gift because it goes immediately to creditors. § 64.2-2611, however, provides that a disclaimer is ineffective if, before executing it, the disclaimant exercised dominion over the expected inheritance in certain ways.

VII. Advancements

What if a decedent with no surviving spouse had, before dying, given a large gift to one of his or her offspring. The other offspring might contend that the decedent did not intend for the offspring receiving the gift to get more of the estate in the long run than the rest of them, to "double dip" so to speak. No, they say, the decedent was simply responding to the fact that that offspring needed the wealth immediately and could not wait till the decedent died, so was giving that offspring an advance payment of the expected inheritance. Virginia law reflects an acceptance of this contention when the other offspring can actually show this was the intent:

Chapter 2. Descent and Distribution

§ 64.2-206 Advancements brought into hotchpot.

When the descendant of a decedent receives any property as an advancement from the decedent during the decedent's lifetime or under the decedent's will, and the descendant, or any descendant of his, is also to receive a distribution of any portion of the decedent's intestate estate, real or personal, the advancement shall be brought into hotchpot with the intestate estate and the descendant is itled to his proper portion of the entire intestate estate, including such advancement.

***

This provision does not explain how a court is to determine that a gift was an advancement. Some early decisions of the Supreme Court provide guidance.

Supreme Court of Appeals of Virginia.
Rowe v. Rowe
144 Va. 816, 130 S.E. 771 (1925)

CHRISTIAN, J., delivered the opinion of the court.

This is a suit for partition brought by the seven adult children of H. C. Rowe against his widow, Lula B. Rowe, who was his second wife, and their infant son, Barnes Rowe, for the purpose of assigning the widow her dower, and dividing the real estate, of which H. C. Rowe died seized, among his children. ... *819 ...

H. C. Rowe in his lifetime had made substantial gifts to each of his seven children by his first marriage, as advancements, and by virtue of section 5278 Virginia Code, 1919 [predecessor of § 64.2-206], before they could come into partition and distribution of his estate, they must bring said advancements into hotchpot. The plaintiffs answered the cross-bill and exceptions, claiming that their respective gifts were made as absolute gifts and not as advancements. ...

The intent of section 5278 is to bring about as nearly as may be an equal division of the estate of a decedent among his children or other descendants, except so far as he may have himself intentionally distributed his estate unequally. Where the gift is substantial in amount, the law attaches the presumption to every gift by an ancestor to a descendant, that it is a gift by way of advancement, and this presumption is one of law and is based upon the supposed intention or desire of the ancestor that any inequalities in the division of his whole estate among his heirs-at-law and distributees shall be corrected as far as practicable. But this presumption may be rebutted by affirmative proof, and for the purpose of showing the real intention of the ancestor, his declarations *820 or statements made at the time of the gift, or subsequently, are competent evidence, as well as the circumstances of the ancestor **772 and relations existing between him and the child. Payne v. Payne, 128 Va. 33, 104 S.E. 712; Poff v. Poff, 128 Va. 62, 104 S.E. 719.

The evidence shows that H. C. Rowe died in the month of ___, 1922. In 1906 he gave Ira B. ('Burke') Rowe $300.00 and in 1920 he gave him an additional $1,000.00. On the 4th day of March, 1909, H. C. Rowe executed and delivered to each of four other children deeds conveying certain real estate to them respectively as and for homes. This was prior to his second marriage. On the 8th day of December, 1910, he conveyed to the daughter certain real estate. On August 2, 1915, he executed a deed to real estate to his son, Morris M. Rowe. Thus it is established without controversy that H. C. Rowe, during his life, gave to each of his children substantial gifts to which the law attaches the presumption that each was a gift by way of advancement, and casts upon each donee the burden of rebutting that presumption by affirmative proof. ...

They have proven that their father started life without means and that by hard work and frugality *821 he accumulated his estate, and to a greater or less extent they worked with and for him, thus aiding in the building up of his fortune. These circumstances and relations between their father and themselves cannot have any bearing upon this case, as there is no implied obligation upon the part of the father to remunerate his children for services; besides, the gifts to each of them was entirely voluntary.

It is also proven that H. C. Rowe declared that his wife would get her part of his estate upon his death, which would be more than what he had given his other children, and at her death it would go to her son. Advancements to children are not brought into hotchpot for the benefit of the widow; she is only entitled to share in the estate of the intestate of which he died possessed. [Ed: This is not entirely true today.] The purpose of the statute is equality among the children, subject to her distributive share in the personalty and dower interest in the real estate for her support and maintenance.

Nor does the age and dependence of the infant, coupled with the fact that they worked for and with their father in accumulating his estate, evidence any intention to discriminate against the infant, especially when the older children are men and women of mature years and established in life. The necessities of the infant for maintenance and education would naturally call for greater consideration from the parent.

The circumstances and relations of the father and children do not rebut the presumption of law that the gifts were made by way of advancements.

This brings us to the discussion of the declarations of H. C. Rowe. At the time of the respective gifts nothing was said, except two of the sons testified that he said 'he gave it without strings tied to it' and *822 another testified his father said 'he made the gift to be relieved of taxes and wanted them to enjoy the property in his lifetime.'

Giving to these declarations the most liberal construction, there is nothing incompatible with the presumption that the gifts were unconditional and irrevocable, thus answering the requirement of law that in order to be an advancement the parent must have irrevocably parted from his title in the subject advanced.

Subsequent to the gifts to his children, several witnesses testify that H. C. Rowe told them he had given all of his children homes except Burke, and he was going to give him money, and that when he died he wanted the rest of his property to be divided equally among all his children. The above declarations, while merely hearsay evidence, therefore unsatisfactory, because of the possibility of mistake or failure of memory, if standing alone, might be sufficient to establish an intention to divide his property unequally, but its effect is very much weakened if not destroyed by testimony of various witnesses that they had heard H. C. Rowe say, on different occasions, one while in his last sickness, that he had given all of his children homes but Burke who he gave money, and that he was going to give or wanted Barnes (the infant) to have the 'Betts place.' A presumption of law cannot be said to be rebutted where the evidence of equally credible witnesses for and against the presumption is equally balanced. ...

But the evidence of E. Hugh Smith, an attorney-at-law, and friend of H. C. Rowe, when he went to consult about making a will, establishes conclusively his real *823 intention that the gifts should be brought into hotchpot. After Smith had explained to him the rights of his wife in his property, and how any property he might give his infant son would go in event of his death without issue. Smith told him in event of his death, intestate, the gifts he had made his children **773 would be treated as advancements unless he expressed a contrary desire in writing. After some further conversation Rowe said: 'Well, I don't know but that the law makes as good a will as I could make.' With this knowledge of the law Rowe died without making any will or declaration about the gifts to his children.

Therefore, considering the circumstances of Rowe, his relations to his children, the conflicting declarations made about the division of his estate, and his knowledge of the law in regard to advancements, it is conclusively established that his real intention was that his estate should be equally divided as provided by law after his adult children had brought their gifts into hotchpot.

Two years after *Rowe*, the Supreme Court, in Trotman v. Trotman, 148 Va. 860, 139 S.E. 490 (1927), placed significant, though not determinative, weight on just the sort of family history – namely, sons having helped their father to develop a business – that the *Rowe* court thought "cannot have any bearing upon this case, as there is no implied obligation upon the part of the father to remunerate his children for services." The *Trotman* court said:

> Here was a man advanced in years, and with grown sons, possessed of a large estate to the accumulation of which they had contributed in a considerable measure and without stated compensation. In short, they

had worked for him all their lives. He was about to contract a second marriage. It is reasonable to assume that while yet free to act he desired to make some compensation for all that they had done, nor did it seem equitable to permit children who might thereafter be born to share equally in an estate which they had no part in accumulating. 148 Va. at 873-74.

What does it mean to bring the advancement "into hotchpot"? Basically, figure out what the value of the estate and each heir's share would have been if the gift had not been made, and then give the heirs other than the gift recipient what they would have gotten, if possible. In other words, aim to ensure that the other heirs do not lose out because of the lifetime gift, and count the lifetime gift as part of the recipient's share of the estate. So, the estate administrator would first calculate the value of the actual probate estate, then add to that the value (at the time given, see Ratliff v. Meade, 184 Va. 328, 334, 35 S.E.2d 114, 117 (1945)) of the lifetime gift that one offspring received (after this is determined, in fact, to have been intended as an advancement), and divide this sum (an artificial valuation of a hypothetical estate that still included the gifted property) by the number of offspring, to determine how much each would have received if the gifted property were still in the estate. And then the offspring who received the lifetime gift would only receive from the actual probate estate the difference between the value of the lifetime gift and (if it is larger) the value of what that offspring would have received from the probate estate if the gifted property were still in it. Then the other offspring would get from the actual probate estate property equal in value to their share of the hypothetical probate estate with the gifted property in it. Example:

> Mom is a widow with three adult children: X, Y, and Z. X and Y are doing fine, but Z had a business venture collapse and is left with nothing. Mom gives Z $100,000 to get back on his feet financially. Soon thereafter, Mom dies and her probate estate is worth $650,000. X and Y prove that Mom intended the $100,000 gift to Z as an advance inheritance. The estate administrator would distribute $150,000 to Z, $250,000 to X, and $250,000 to Y.

If an advancement exceeds what the recipient's share of the estate would have been, then the overall distribution cannot be equalized, because the probate court has no power to order the recipient to return any of the advancement or to reimburse the estate at all. See McCoy v. McCoy, 105 Va. 829, 54 S.E. 995, 999 (1906) ("While a child receiving an advancement from a parent may bring such advancement into hotchpot and share in the division or distribution of the estate of the parent after his death, he cannot be required to pay back to the estate any part of the advancement, and if it turns out that he has received, by way of an advancement an equal share with the others of the estate, or more than his share, he can only be excluded from participation in the division or distribution of the estate.").

Note that the rule of advancement also applies to grandchildren (and further descendants) who received a lifetime gift from the decedent, and that it also affects the share taken by descendants of someone who received an advancement. So if you change the example above so that it is a grandmother with three grandchildren who stand to take equally, you get the same result. Or if you change the example so that X received the lifetime gift as an advancement but then predeceased Mom, leaving children of his own who would subsequently take from Mom's estate by representation, then X's children would split $150,000.

VIII.   Bars to Succession

The intestacy rules are designed to effect presumed intent, based on what most people do. They do not aim to do this with great precision, changing distribution based on nuances in family relationships; they are based on what most people do when certain types of relationships exist. There are circumstances, though, in which the law attributes to decedents an intent to deviate from the default rules even though the decedents did not execute a will. They might be described as ones in which a) someone who ordinarily would be an heir is especially undeserving and b) the decedent might not have had an opportunity to draft an execute a will.

A.   Abandonment

Someone who abandons a spouse or child, deviating radically from normal expectations for that family relationship, might be judged morally undeserving of an inheritance from the person abandoned. In addition, a "minor or incapacitated child" (see statute below) would generally be incapable of executing a will, and the concept of "abandonment" with respect to a spouse generally entails leaving one's spouse bereft in either a financial or emotional sense, which could also inhibit someone from executing a will. Thus:

Chapter 3. Rights of Married Persons
Article 1.1., Elective Share of Surviving Spouse.

§ 64.2–308.14. Waiver of right to elect and of other rights; defenses

…

E. If a spouse willfully deserts or abandons the other spouse and such desertion or abandonment continues until the death of the other spouse, the party who deserted or abandoned the deceased spouse shall be barred of all interest in the decedent's estate by intestate succession...

§ 64.2–308.17. Statutory rights barred by desertion or abandonment

If a parent willfully deserts or abandons his minor or incapacitated child and such desertion or abandonment continues until the death of the child, the parent shall be barred of all interest in the child's estate by intestate succession.

* * *

"Abandonment" is an indefinite term, and so Virginia courts have had to make judgments as to when it has occurred, based on the facts of particular cases.

Supreme Court of Virginia.
Purce v. Patterson
275 Va. 190, 654 S.E.2d 885 (2008)

OPINION BY Senior Justice ELIZABETH B. LACY.

**886 *192 In this appeal, Marrill W. Purce asks us to reverse the judgment of the trial court holding that he willfully abandoned his wife, Dorothy M. Purce, who died on January 19, 2005, and therefore, under Code § 64.1–16.3 [predecessor to § 64.2-308}, was not entitled to an elective share of her augmented estate. *193

FACTS

… Dorothy and Marrill were married in July 1988. Dorothy had many health problems throughout the marriage and, while the couple lived together, friends and neighbors often took Dorothy to doctors' appointments, cleaned the home, and cooked meals. Dorothy's daughter, Vanessa C. Patterson, testified that Marrill did not visit Dorothy in the hospital during her illnesses and did not take care of her when she returned home.

Marrill and Dorothy had a tumultuous marriage. Dorothy complained to her daughter and friends of Marrill's treatment of her. In April 1997, Dorothy obtained a protective order against Marrill based on his physical abuse of her, and she renewed the order a few months later. The protective order expired in June 1998, and the parties resumed cohabitation. In October of 1998, Dorothy sought another protective order, claiming she was under severe stress because Marrill's girlfriend was harassing her, Marrill was drinking and staying out late every night, and she was afraid that she might have a stroke. The court denied the protective order.

In June 2000, Dorothy and Marrill agreed that Dorothy would leave the marital residence. After the separation, in August 2000, Dorothy sought a third protective order, claiming Marrill had threatened to kill her; the petition was denied. Dorothy filed a fourth petition for a protective order in June 2002, claiming among other things that Marrill hurt her arm and threatened her; however, she withdrew this petition.

Dorothy filed for a divorce in January 2003, identifying the grounds for the divorce as living separate and apart for more than one year. The divorce decree was never issued, and the parties remained legally married at the time of Dorothy's death.

Dorothy brought into the marriage rental properties she owned. Marrill, on the other hand, was retired during most of the marriage. Marrill did not participate in the management of the rental properties, and he did not provide any financial support to

Dorothy after the separation. During her last illness, Dorothy lived with her daughter in New Jersey. Marrill did not know Dorothy was in New Jersey, nor did he visit, call, or otherwise communicate with her. *194

DISCUSSION

...Marrill argues that post-separation conduct is not relevant to whether one spouse abandoned the other. We disagree. Code § 64.1–16.3(A) specifically addresses the period of abandonment that is relevant ... The clear language of this Code section requires a court to determine whether the willful desertion or abandonment continued "until the death of the spouse" and that determination is not limited to consideration of actions occurring prior to a separation, should one have occurred. ... **887

Marrill's remaining four assignments of error challenge the sufficiency of the evidence to support a finding of abandonment. Whether Marrill abandoned Dorothy is a mixed question of law and fact. ... The term "abandonment" is not defined in the statutes governing elective share claims. We agree with the parties that principles *195 developed in domestic relations law relating to abandonment are helpful in determining the issue of abandonment under Code § 64.1–16.3.

In the domestic relations context, "abandonment" is generally used synonymously with "desertion." This Court has defined desertion as "a breach of matrimonial duty—an actual breaking off of the matrimonial cohabitation coupled with an intent to desert in the mind of the deserting party." Domestic relations cases have considered "matrimonial duty" to include cooking, cleaning, support, and contributing to the well-being of the family. Mindful of these domestic relations cases, in resolving the issue in this case we will use the word "abandonment" to mean a termination of the normal indicia of a marital relationship combined with an intent to abandon the marital relationship.

While the term "abandonment" is similarly defined for purposes of domestic relations and elective share matters, there are significant differences in the analysis of the evidence when resolving the issue in the domestic relations and elective share contexts. For example, as we have noted, the relevant time period for determining abandonment for purposes of Code § 64.1–16.3 extends to the time of the deceased spouse's death and is not limited to the moment of separation, or the filing of a petition for divorce, as it is when abandonment is the ground upon which a divorce is sought. Compare ... Hudgins v. Hudgins, 181 Va. 81, 87, 23 S.E.2d 774, 777 (1943) ("[T]he absenting of one spouse from the other after the institution and during the pendency of a suit for divorce ... is not desertion in law."), with Code § 64.1–16.3.

A second distinction is the effect of the parties' agreement to separate or to seek a divorce. In an elective share analysis, an agreed separation or petition for divorce is relevant evidence of the termination of cohabitation, but is not evidence which defeats a finding of willful abandonment. In contrast, such an agreed separation or divorce petition may preclude a claim *196 of abandonment in a divorce action because a finding of abandonment in that context is based on fault which is inconsistent with parties agreeing to terminate cohabitation or to seek a divorce. With these distinctions in mind, we now turn to the evidence in this case.

In this case, the mutual decision to cease cohabitation and Dorothy's divorce petition based on living separately for more than a year implies that the termination of the marital relationship was not the product of willful abandonment but rather an agreement between the parties. As discussed above, however, this evidence is not dispositive in the context of an elective share claim. The relevant evidence is Marrill's conduct and his intent. Here, the record shows that both before and after Dorothy and Marrill agreed to separate, Marrill's conduct showed a lack of support for Dorothy and the marital relationship. While living together or apart, **888 Marrill provided Dorothy with little or no support or care during her illnesses and recoveries. Financially, Dorothy brought her rental properties into the marriage and managed the properties alone while living with Marrill. Marrill did not contribute to Dorothy's support in this regard.

After the separation, Marrill apparently did not communicate with Dorothy in any meaningful way because he did not even know she was living in New Jersey and did not acknowledge her final illness in any way. He did not support Dorothy financially, emotionally, or physically. Although he testified that he did not want the marriage to end, the trier of fact was not required to believe this testimony; indeed, the trial court found Marrill's testimony incredible. Nothing in the record showed Marrill tried or intended to reconcile with Dorothy. At the time of Dorothy's death, Marrill had ceased to perform any marital duties. Therefore, we conclude that the evidence is sufficient to support the trial court's holding that Marrill abandoned Dorothy prior to and continuing until the time of her death under Code § 64.1–16.3. ... Affirmed.

B.   The decedent's murderer

If disregard for a spouse can cause one to be barred from inheritance, then naturally killing your spouse has the same effect. Murder presumptively makes one undeserving, and it also prevents the victim from executing a will in reaction to the would-be heir's wrongdoing. Unlike the abandonment rule, which is limited to spouses and parents, the bar on inheritance by "slayers" is universal, applying regardless of the slayer's relationship to the decedent.

**Subtitle V. Provisions Applicable to Probate and Nonprobate Transfers
Chapter 25. Acts Barring Property Rights**

§ 64.2-2501. Slayer not to acquire property as result of slaying

A slayer, or any transferee, assignee, or other person claiming through the slayer, shall not in any way acquire any property or receive any benefits as the result of the death of the decedent, but such property or benefits shall pass as provided in this chapter.

§ 64.2-2502. Property passing by will or intestate succession

A. The slayer shall be deemed to have predeceased the decedent as to property that would have passed from the estate of the decedent to the slayer by intestate succession or that the slayer would have acquired by statutory right as the decedent's surviving spouse. An heir or distributee who establishes his kinship to the decedent by way of his kinship to a slayer shall be deemed to be claiming from the decedent and not through the slayer.

§ 64.2-2500. Definitions

As used in this chapter: …

"Slayer" means any person (i) who is convicted of the murder or voluntary manslaughter of the decedent or, (ii) in the absence of such conviction, who is determined, whether before or after his death, by a court of appropriate jurisdiction by a preponderance of the evidence to have committed one of the offenses listed in clause (i) resulting in the death of the decedent. For the purposes of clause (ii), the party seeking to establish that a decedent was slain by such person shall have the burden of proof.

§ 64.2-2510. Admissibility of judicial record determining slayer

The record of the judicial proceeding in which a person is determined to be a slayer shall be admissible in evidence for or against a claimant of property in any civil action arising under this chapter. A conviction shall be conclusive evidence of the guilt of the slayer.

***

Supreme Court of Virginia.
Osman v. Osman
285 Va. 384, 737 S.E.2d 876 (2013)

OPINION BY Justice DONALD W. LEMONS.

… Louis Moss Osman and Wanda M. Austin ("Executors"), co-executors of the estate of Carolyn Goldman Osman, and co-trustees of the Carolyn Goldman Osman Revocable Trust, Osman Family Trust and Goldman Family Trust fbo Carolyn Goldman Osman, filed a complaint and request for declaratory judgment in the circuit court, asking the court to declare that Michael Jeffrey Osman was a "slayer" under Code § 55–401 [predecessor of, and identical to the definition of slayer in § 64.2-2500 above]. …

The facts in this case are not in dispute. Carolyn Goldman Osman ("Carolyn") had three sons, Bradley Alan Osman, Louis Moss Osman, and Osman, all of whom were the beneficiaries of Carolyn's estate and various trusts. On December 7, 2009, Carolyn died as a result of Osman's actions. Her cause of death was strangulation and blunt force trauma to the head. Osman was charged with first-degree murder, but pled not guilty by reason of insanity.

Osman signed a stipulation of the Commonwealth's evidence, admitting that the Commonwealth would have established that on the morning of December 7, 2009, Carolyn came to Osman's house to drive him to traffic court. Osman strangled Carolyn and struck her head against the ground until she died. He fled the scene in Carolyn's car. A police officer stopped him shortly thereafter, and Osman admitted that he had killed his mother. Osman has a very long history of mental illness, and had been previously diagnosed with paranoid schizophrenia. He had become severely delusional and thought everyone, including his mother, meant to harm him. The Commonwealth agreed that Osman was insane at the time he killed his mother, and the trial court found him not guilty by reason of insanity.

Subsequently, ... Osman argued that the slayer statute only prevents someone from benefitting from an intentional wrongful act, and because he was insane at the time of the killing, he did not intend to kill her. ...

II. Analysis

*879 ... B. Code §§ 55–401 and 55–414

... Code § 55–401(1)(ii) provides that a person can be determined to be a slayer if a court determines, by a preponderance of evidence, that the person committed the "offense" of murder or voluntary manslaughter. Of course, proof of criminal "offenses" requires an evidentiary standard of "beyond a reasonable doubt." Read literally, the statute is internally inconsistent. ...

Code § 55–414, entitled "Construction"... states that this chapter "shall be construed broadly in order to effect the policy of this Commonwealth that no person shall be allowed to profit by his wrong, wherever committed." This statute further states that the purpose of this chapter is to "prevent one who has participated in the willful and unlawful killing of another from profiting by his wrong...." Giving effect to legislative intention, we have no difficulty interpreting Code § 55–401(ii) as requiring proof by preponderance of the evidence of the remaining elements of either murder or voluntary manslaughter. Preponderance of evidence is the burden of proof used in most civil actions. ...

Murder is the unlawful killing of another with malice. Malice, in a legal sense, means any wrongful act done willfully or purposely. In Virginia, all murder other than capital murder and murder in the first degree is murder of the second degree. To be found guilty of murder, a person must have acted maliciously; in other words, he must possess *880 the necessary mens rea. Mens rea is defined as "criminal intent." It is often referred to as "guilty mind."

However, in considering whether Osman is a slayer under Code § 55–401, we do not consider criminal intent ("mens rea"), we consider civil intent. Intent in a civil context only requires that a person intended his actions; there is no requirement that the person have knowledge that his actions were wrongful. When discussing intent and the differences between the term "willful" in a criminal context versus a civil one, the United States Supreme Court explained:

> [W]e have consistently held that a defendant cannot harbor such criminal intent unless he acted with knowledge that his conduct was unlawful. Civil use of the term [willful], however, typically presents neither the textual nor the substantive reasons for pegging the threshold of liability at knowledge of wrongdoing. Safeco Ins. Co. v. Burr, 551 U.S. 47, 57–58 n. 9 (2007).

In Johnson v. Insurance Co. of North America, 232 Va. 340, 350 S.E.2d 616 (1986), we ... held that an intentional injury exclusion clause in a homeowners policy precluded coverage for an insured who, while mentally ill, shot and injured a friend. The insured had avoided criminal liability because he was found not guilty by reason of insanity. However, in a subsequent action for personal injury we held that the insured's actions were intentional. He was excused from criminal sanctions because he did not know that his actions were wrongful. Nonetheless, he intended his actions; and, in a civil action for personal injury, the intentional injury exclusion clause applied. ...

In this case, the stipulated evidence presented at Osman's trial for murder clearly demonstrated that Osman intended to kill his mother... and we hold that, under the civil burden of proof of preponderance of the evidence, the evidence is sufficient to prove the elements of murder. This holding is consistent with the direction found in Code § 55–414 that we must interpret Code § 55–401 to effect the policy of this Commonwealth that no person should be allowed to profit from his wrong.

In Avent v. Commonwealth, we stated that "'[k]illing in self-defense may be either justifiable or excusable homicide. Justifiable homicide in self-defense occurs [when] a person, without any fault on his part in provoking or bringing on the difficulty, kills another under reasonable apprehension of death or great bodily harm to himself.'" Excusable homicide in self-defense occurs when the accused, although in some fault in the first instance in provoking or bringing on the difficulty, when attacked retreats as far as possible, announces his desire for peace, and kills his adversary from a reasonably apparent necessity to preserve his own life or save himself from great bodily harm. It is instructive to point out that a person who has committed a justifiable homicide *881 is not a person who has committed a "wrong," as anticipated by Code § 55–414. A person who committed an excusable homicide, however, may have committed a wrong in the initial provocation. The issue whether a person who kills in self-defense is a slayer is a question left for another day.

We hold that the circuit court did not err in holding that Osman is a slayer under Code § 55–401, and that as a result he cannot inherit his share of his mother's estate. ...

Justice McCLANAHAN, concurring.

... There is nothing in the language of Code § 55–401 indicating that it dispenses with the requirement of proving malice for one seeking to establish that an alleged slayer, though not "convicted" of murder, nevertheless "committed" murder. The statute simply reduces the burden for such proof from the beyond a reasonable doubt standard for criminal conviction to the civil preponderance of the evidence standard. Here, however, Osman's successful insanity defense established the basis for an exception to the requirement of proving malice as an element of murder: Osman's insanity negated consideration of whether he possessed malice at the time he killed his mother. A finding of not guilty by reason of insanity under Virginia law is predicated upon *882 findings that (a) the defendant "committed" the criminal offense charged, but (b) he was insane at the time of its commission. Code § 19.2–182.2 provides in relevant part that, "[w]hen the defense is insanity of the defendant at the time the offense was committed, the jurors shall be instructed, if they acquit him on that ground, to state the fact with their verdict." Indeed, absent a finding that the defendant committed the offense, his insanity defense would be irrelevant to the consideration of guilt; and he would be entitled to a finding of not guilty. ...

A finding of not guilty by reason of insanity, in turn, triggers the requirement under Code § 19.2–182.2 that the defendant shall be civilly committed at least temporarily, which can then lead to an indeterminate period of involuntary civil commitment. Consequently, "a person found not guilty by reason of insanity is not discharged from the constraints imposed upon him by law as a result of his criminal act. He is not free to resume his life in the community as he would be if he had been acquitted in the usual sense."

As to the mens rea element of a crime relative to the insanity defense, under Virginia law the finding of insanity necessarily supersedes any specific consideration of that element by the factfinder. In other words, evidence showing insanity trumps mens rea. *883 Accordingly, the finding that the defendant committed the criminal act (i.e., the actus reus), along with the finding that he was insane at the time of its commission, ends the inquiry. The defendant is nevertheless held accountable for his criminal act; his successful insanity defense excuses him from criminal punishment but subjects him to the constraints of involuntary civil commitment. ...

Justice POWELL, concurring.

*884 ... I am compelled to point out the unintentional consequences of the majority's interpretation of Code § 55–401(ii). By replacing the *mens rea* element with a civil intent element, I believe that the majority has unintentionally expanded the definition of "slayer" to include anyone who intentionally kills another, regardless of the circumstances. Thus, a person who kills another in self-defense, or as a result of some other form of justifiable homicide, would be, according to the majority, a slayer. Indeed, by arguing self-defense "a defendant implicitly admits the killing was intentional."

Consider, for example, a wife who kills her abusive husband while defending herself from his attacks. Under the majority's "civil intent" approach, the wife would be considered a slayer. She would thus be prohibited from inheriting or receiving any property or benefits resulting from the husband's death. Nor would she be entitled to any property that she would have acquired by statutory right as the surviving spouse. She would also effectively forfeit any property she owned as a tenant by the entirety or with right of survivorship with the husband. I do not read Code § 55–401 et seq. to warrant such a result.

In my opinion, the proper approach is to look at the elements of murder and determine whether the evidence is sufficient to prove by a preponderance of the evidence that Osman committed murder. As the majority has stated, murder is the unlawful killing of another with malice. "Malice may be either express or implied by conduct." "Implied malice exists when any purposeful, cruel act is committed by one individual against another without any, or without great provocation." ... This Court has recognized that a successful insanity defense does not serve to negate mens rea. ... *885 [It] excuse[s] a defendant from customary criminal responsibility, even if the prosecution has otherwise overcome the presumption of innocence by convincing the factfinder of all the elements charged beyond a reasonable doubt. ... Indeed, as Justice Rehnquist recognized in his concurrence in Mullaney v. Wilbur, 421 U.S. 684, 705–06 (1975):

> Although ... evidence relevant to insanity as defined by state law may also be relevant to whether the required mens rea was present, the existence or nonexistence of legal insanity bears no necessary relationship to the existence or nonexistence of the required mental elements of the crime.

Notably, Virginia has never allowed evidence of mental illness to rebut the mens rea element of a crime. The evidence demonstrates that Osman's mental illness only affected his motive for killing his mother, not his intent in doing so. Indeed, the stipulated evidence clearly demonstrated that Osman committed a purposeful, cruel act against his mother with no provocation that resulted in her death. Osman admitted that he intended his actions, and I would hold that the estate representatives have proved by a preponderance of the evidence that Osman committed murder and is therefore a slayer within the meaning of Code § 55–401. ...

*		*		*

Chapter Three
Wills

A "Last Will and Testament" disposes of all or part of the probate estate. Recall that, like intestacy rules, a will can have no effect on property that passes via non-probate transfer. Conceptually, non-probate transfers occur at the moment of death, whereas intestacy rules or a will operate at the moment after death.

The primary purpose of a will is to deviate from the default rules – that is, to effectuate some result as to disposition of one's property upon one's death different from what would occur by application of intestacy rules. (Although many people do execute wills that replicate the intestacy rules, perhaps in order to leave no doubt as to intentions regarding property or to designate an executor.) Therefore, when someone produces a document as the will of a person who just died, some or all of that person's intestate heirs might feel aggrieved by the document's provisions and so challenge the purported will. There are many grounds for such a challenge and a great deal of actual litigation that arises with respect to wills, making it especially important for estate planning attorneys to be meticulous in orchestrating will execution for clients. This Chapter addresses:

I.   Establishing the existence of a will

II.   Establishing the validity of the will

III. Establishing the contents of the will

IV.   Revocation and revival of wills

I.   Establishing the Existence of a Will

For a court to "probate" (i.e., approve) a document as a will, the proponent must prove that it is a will, and specifically the will of the decedent. For a document to constitute a will, rather than a non-testamentary writing (e.g., an inventory of property owned or an expression of intent to make a lifetime gift), it must

> ➤ have been created by someone with capacity to execute a will

> ➤ manifest testamentary intent – that is, an intent as to distribution of one's property at death ("*animus testandi*")

A. Capacity

Chapter 4. Wills.
Article 1. Requisites and Execution.

§ 64.2-401. Who may make a will; what estate may be disposed of.

A. Except as provided in subsection B, any individual may make a will to dispose of all or part of his estate at his death ... including any estate, right, or interest that the testator may subsequently become entitled to after the execution of the will.

B. An individual is not capable of making a will if he is (i) of unsound mind or (ii) an unemancipated minor.

***

Whether a decedent was an unemancipated minor is typically easy to establish, so that part of the rule does not give rise to litigation. There are many "will contests," though, that rest on a claim that the decedent was of unsound mind when he or she wrote the document proffered as a will.

The test Virginia courts have developed for capacity to make a will is less demanding than the test for capacity in most other legal contexts. It requires that *at time of execution*, the testator (person who is said to have executed the will) was *able to*:

(i)   understand the nature of the act (i.e., will execution)

(ii) recollect the nature and value (roughly) of his or her property

(iii) recollect the "natural objects of his or her bounty"

(iv) interrelate the above three things

Supreme Court of Virginia.
Parish v. Parish
281 Va. 191, 704 S.E.2d 99 (2011)

OPINION BY Justice WILLIAM C. MIMS.

*194 ... The decedent, Eugene Neal Parish ("Eugene"), suffered a head and spinal cord injury in 1982 due to being struck in the head with a metal pipe while at a bar. The injury left him paralyzed in his legs and right arm. Eugene sued the bar and the person who attacked him and recovered $3.5 million. At the time of his injury, Eugene's only child, David M. Parish ("David"), was eleven months old.

In 1983, Eugene was declared incompetent in Florida due to encephalopathy.[1]

[1]   Encephalopathy is "[g]eneralized brain dysfunction marked by varying degrees of impairment of speech, cognition, orientation, and arousal. In mild instances, brain dysfunction may be evident only during specialized neuropsychiatric testing; in severe instances, ... the patient may be

unresponsive even to unpleasant stimuli." Taber's Cyclopedic Medical Dictionary 761 (2009).

His wife was appointed as guardian. ... *195 Later, Eugene's mother assumed the duties as his guardian.

In 1989, Eugene moved to Tennessee and resided at a nursing facility near Memphis. David Wayne Parish ("David Wayne"), Eugene's brother, lived approximately 40 to 50 miles from Eugene's nursing facility. Diane E. Parish ("Diane") and David Wayne were married in 1998. Eugene's mother, who had acted as his conservator, remained in Florida. She agreed to transfer the conservatorship to David Wayne and Diane in Tennessee.

In 2000, David Wayne and Diane petitioned to be appointed as Eugene's co-conservators in Tennessee. ... **102 The Tennessee court granted the petition...

In the fall of 2002, David Wayne assisted Eugene in preparing a Last Will and Testament (the "will"). David Wayne testified at trial that Eugene had informed him "out of the blue" that he wanted a will. During Eugene's meeting with the paralegal who drafted the will, David Wayne acted as a translator because Eugene, who spoke through a voice box due to a tracheotomy, was difficult to understand. David Wayne was present in the room with the witnesses and the notary when the will was executed and witnessed on October 2, 2002.

In the will, Eugene bequeathed 25% of his estate to David Wayne, 25% to Diane, 25% to David, and 25% to other family members. *196 [3]

> [3] In the absence of a will, Eugene's entire estate would pass to his son David under Virginia's law of intestacy.

Eugene's will appointed David Wayne as executor and Diane as substitute executor. Neither David Wayne nor Diane informed David that Eugene had executed a will.

In 2003, David Wayne and Diane executed a statement of fiduciary in the probate court of Tennessee... The statement averred that Eugene continued to need conservators because his "condition remains [the] same—encephalopathy."

In 2004 David Wayne and Diane requested that David and his wife Jessika Parish take over as guardians and conservators of Eugene. David and Jessika, who lived in Virginia Beach, petitioned the local circuit court in Virginia to adjudicate Eugene incompetent and appoint them as guardians and conservators.

The circuit court appointed a guardian ad litem ("GAL"), who reported that Eugene required a guardian and conservator. Specifically, the GAL reported that Eugene "had difficulty speaking but was communicative and obviously could understand your guardian ad litem's questions and was able to respond." In response to one of the GAL's questions, Eugene "indicated that he was aware of the guardian/conservator proceeding, and even pointed out that his son's name was incorrect in the original Petition." The GAL further stated that Eugene's "understanding of his finances, however, seemed to be somewhat impaired in that he indicated that he presently had $3.5 million in the bank, obviously not recognizing the fact that his funds have been expended over the last twenty years in caring for him."

The Virginia circuit court granted the petition. The 2004 order appointing a temporary conservator found that Eugene "is incapacitated to such an extent that he is unable to care for himself, make medical decisions, manage his estate or understand his debts as they come due."

Eugene died in 2006. David qualified as his administrator. Diane then petitioned the circuit court to have David removed as administrator and herself appointed as executor pursuant to Eugene's will.[4]

[4] Diane averred that David Wayne had declined to serve as executor.

David filed a counterclaim to impeach the will. David claimed that Eugene lacked testamentary capacity to execute a will due to encephalopathy. He further claimed that David Wayne and Diane *197 subjected Eugene to undue influence. ... **103

A. EFFECT OF ADJUDICATIONS OF INCOMPETENCE

… Western State Hospital v. Wininger, 196 Va. 300, 311-12; 83 S.E.2d 446, 452-53 (1954), … required clear and convincing proof of capacity to overcome a presumption of insanity when the testator previously was adjudicated insane. However, we previously have held that "the mere fact that one is under a guardianship does not deprive him of the power to make a will." Gilmer v. Brown, 186 Va. 630, 637, 44 S.E.2d 16, 19 (1947). See also Gibbs v. Gibbs, 239 Va. 197, 202, 387 S.E.2d 499, 502 (1990) ("the appointment of a guardian cannot be regarded as prima facie evidence of mental incapacity"). *198

In *Gilmer*, we explained:

> Mental weakness is not inconsistent with testamentary capacity. A less degree of capacity is requisite for the execution of a will than for the execution of contracts and the transaction of ordinary business. One may be capable of making a will yet incapable of disposing of his property by contract or of managing his estate. Mental strength to compete with an antagonist and understanding to protect his own interest are essential in the transaction of ordinary business, while it is sufficient for the making of a will that the testator understands the business in which he is engaged, his property, the natural objects of his bounty, and the disposition he desires to make of his property. The condition of being unable, by reason of weakness of mind, to manage and care for an estate, is not inconsistent with capacity to make a will.
>
> 186 Va. at 637, 44 S.E.2d at 19.

In Thomason v. Carlton, 221 Va. 845, 276 S.E.2d 171 (1981), we revisited this issue:

> Neither sickness nor impaired intellect is sufficient, standing alone, to render a will invalid. If at the time of its execution the testatrix was

capable of recollecting her property, the natural objects of her bounty and their claims upon her, knew the business about which she was engaged and how she wished to dispose of her property, that is sufficient. Id. at 852, 276 S.E.2d at 175.

The mere fact that one is under a conservatorship is not an adjudication of insanity and does not create a presumption of incapacity. The conservator statutes at issue here are instructive. Florida law required that Eugene be shown "incapable of caring for himself or managing his property or ... likely to dissipate or lose his property or inflict harm on himself or others." Former Fla. Stat. § 744.331. Similarly, Tennessee law required a showing that Eugene was "in need of partial or full supervision, protection and assistance by reason of mental illness, physical illness or injury, developmental disability or other mental or physical incapacity." *199 Tenn.Code Ann. § 34–1–101(7). Virginia's statute requires showing that the respondent is "incapable of receiving and evaluating information effectively ... to such an extent that the individual lacks the capacity to ... manage property or financial affairs or provide for his support ... without the assistance or protection of a conservator." Code § 37.2–1000. **104

None of these statutes required a specific factual finding that Eugene was incompetent to such an extent that he could not execute a will under the standard we articulated in *Gilmer* and *Thomason*. Accordingly, the circuit court correctly ruled that Eugene's adjudications of incompetence due to encephalopathy and the attendant appointments of conservators did not create a presumption of incapacity.

B. CAPACITY

In the absence of a presumption of incapacity, "[t]he proponent of the will bears the burden of proving the existence of testamentary capacity by a preponderance of evidence and retains that burden throughout the proceeding." Gibbs, 239 Va. at 199, 387 S.E.2d at 500.5 In Gibbs, we further explained that

> the proponent of the will is entitled to a presumption that testamentary capacity existed by proving compliance with all statutory requirements for the valid execution of the will. Once the presumption exists, the contestant then bears the burden of going forward with evidence to overcome this presumption, although the burden of persuasion remains with the proponent. Id. at 200, 387 S.E.2d at 501.

To overcome the presumption of capacity, we do not require clear and convincing proof; rather "the contestants need only go forward with evidence sufficient to rebut the presumption." Id. at 201, 387 S.E.2d at 501.

David does not dispute that the will was duly executed according to Tennessee law; consequently the presumption of testamentary capacity applies and the burden of producing evidence shifted to David, the contestant of the will. *200

David testified that Eugene mistook him for David Wayne during a visit in December 2002. Eugene told David that he had a sister, but "[i]t was one of those things where he would send 29 cents a day to like Somalia or something like that.... He thought he had adopted a kid." Eugene constantly forgot things, and had short-term memory problems. They had discussions about a trust fund, when actually there was no such trust.

Jessika also testified that during the December 2002 visit Eugene mistook David for David Wayne. David had to explain "that he was little David all grown up." She described Eugene as "not all there." She described his difficulty comprehending the value of money: "[A]t Christmas time, when he was in the nursing home, he wanted to buy every employee at the nursing home either a fur coat or car, and almost couldn't be talked down from the idea."

David also presented the expert testimony of Dr. Eric Goldberg, a board certified neurologist who treated Eugene on three occasions from November 2004 through June 2005. Dr. Goldberg testified that the condition of a person with a traumatic brain injury, such as that suffered by Eugene, is "static," becoming neither better nor worse over time. He testified that Eugene "could follow a two-part command," that he "was not oriented to person, place or time," and that he had "no short term-memory." In Dr. Goldberg's opinion, Eugene was not able to understand and know the value of his estate or to remember all of his family members. He concluded that Eugene easily could be influenced and was not competent to execute a will.

We will assume without deciding that the testimony of David, Jessika, and Dr. Goldberg was sufficient to overcome the presumption of capacity. Therefore, the burden to produce evidence of capacity shifted back to David Wayne, the proponent of the will. Gibbs, 239 Va. at 200, 387 S.E.2d at 501.

"[I]t is the time of execution of the will that is the critical time for determining testamentary capacity." Thomason, 221 Va. at 853, 276 S.E.2d at 175. "[T]he testimony of those present at the factum—when the will is executed—is entitled to the greatest consideration." **105 Id. "[I]n determining the mental capacity of a testator, great weight is to be attached to the testimony of the draftsman of the will, of the attesting witnesses, and of attending physicians." Hall v. Hall, 181 Va. 67, 76, 23 S.E.2d 810, 814 (1943).

Leonard Kyles was the paralegal who assisted Eugene in drafting the will and was a witness to its execution. Kyles testified that he *201 was satisfied that Eugene knew what he was doing when he signed the will. Cheryl Campbell witnessed the execution of the will to notarize Eugene's signature. She testified that Eugene, when asked what the document was, replied it was his last will and testament. Eugene did not do or say anything to cause her concern as to his understanding of what was happening.

Dr. Elbert Hines, Eugene's treating physician at the nursing facility in Tennessee, testified that he saw Eugene at least once every 60 days, beginning in the fall of 2000. He assessed Eugene in September 2002 and testified with a reasonable degree of medical probability that Eugene was not confused in any way, that he knew what it was he was doing and who his relatives were at that time. Dr. Hines saw Eugene again in October and December 2002, and testified that he was alert and oriented to self and place and that he had not deteriorated since the September visit. Dr. Hines concluded with a reasonable degree of medical probability that Eugene could understand what property he owned and to whom he was giving it.

Additionally, David Wayne testified that on the day he took Eugene to sign his will, his mental condition was "just regular[,] just a regular guy." He further testified that Eugene was not confused and that he knew who all his family members were. Diane testified that Eugene's mental condition "was great," and that she conversed with him about family, politics, and baseball. Arnold Lindseth, Eugene's attorney in the Tennessee conservatorship, testified that in January 2003 he spent approximately two hours with Eugene at a bank setting up accounts and Eugene "seemed lucid [the] whole time" and "aware of what was going on."

Catherine Logan was Eugene's social worker at the nursing facility. She testified that Eugene understood who he was and who his relatives were. She testified that he suffered no cognitive impairment, "just short-term memory [problems]." However, she did testify that Eugene, who enjoyed feeding the pigeons outside the facility, sometimes thought he was feeding pigeons when he actually was feeding rats. Additionally, she stated that on the day Eugene signed the will he told her he was leaving half of his estate to "Little David," his son, when in fact he left only 25% to him.

We review the circuit court's finding of capacity for sufficient evidence. Eason v. Eason, 203 Va. 246, 253, 123 S.E.2d 361, 366 (1962) ("where the case has been fairly presented and there is credible evidence to support the conclusion" of the fact-finder, this *202 court will not disturb the verdict).

This evidence is sufficient to support the circuit court's ruling that Diane proved Eugene's testamentary capacity.[6] ...

> [6]   The circuit court ruled that that Diane proved Eugene's testamentary capacity by clear and convincing evidence. However, only a preponderance of the evidence was required. Gibbs, 239 Va. at 199, 387 S.E.2d at 500.

The Supreme Court's most recent decision regarding testamentary capacity principally addresses burdens of proof issues in challenges to testamentary capacity.

Supreme Court of Virginia.
Kiddell v. Labowitz
284 Va. 611, 733 S.E.2d 622 (2012)

Opinion by Justice CLEO E. POWELL.

... *616 Louise Bradford Judsen executed a will on April 19, 2010, ("the April will"), naming her beneficiaries: Judsen's cousin, Laurie Kiddell ("Laurie"); Laurie's husband, Lee Kiddell ("Lee"); their daughter, LeAnn Kiddell ("LeAnn"); two other first cousins; and the "American Cancer Association." The April will was prepared by Laurie from an online template.

On June 15, 2010, Judsen executed another will ("the June will"), naming Kenneth E. Labowitz, an attorney, as the executor of her estate. In the June will, Judsen bequeathed her dog and a cash gift for the dog's care to Laurie. Judsen bequeathed one-third of her residuary estate to the "Leukemia & Lymphoma Society Inc.," one-third to the "American Cancer Society Inc.," and one-third to a "Head Trauma Research Center" to be chosen in the sole discretion of her executor.

Judsen died on June 18, 2010, and the June will was admitted to probate. Laurie and LeAnn (hereinafter referred to collectively as "Kiddell") filed a "Complaint to Impeach Will" ... [and] alleged that Judsen lacked testamentary capacity when **625 she executed the June will. ....

Judsen was diagnosed with a terminal illness in February 2010. On May 13, 2010, Judsen's health had deteriorated and she was admitted to a hospital. At the request of Laurie, who lived in Illinois, Labowitz contacted Judsen in the hospital because Laurie wanted him to assist Judsen with her financial matters. Specifically, Laurie wanted Labowitz to be authorized to act under Judsen's power of attorney instead of Laurie. According to Labowitz, Judsen became "upset" with Laurie for sending Labowitz "to [perform duties under] the new power of attorney." Despite her anger, Judsen executed a new power of attorney naming Labowitz as her attorney in fact. Labowitz testified that, during the meetings that he had with Judsen, she was insistent *617 on returning home, concerned about her dog, and aware that she had only a small amount of cash among her assets.

According to Labowitz, Judsen also told him she wanted to execute a new will. Consequently, Labowitz contacted Sean Dunston, an attorney practicing primarily in the area of wills, trusts, and estates, to assist Judsen with her new will. Although Laurie sent the April will to Labowitz, Labowitz did not give Dunston the April will because Labowitz had previously filed it with the Fairfax County Circuit Court. Labowitz did not believe that he told Dunston about this will.

Dunston met with Judsen at the hospital on multiple occasions concerning the preparation of her will. According to Dunston, during a meeting with Judsen on June 3, she explained that she wanted to dispose of her estate by providing for the care of her dog and leaving the residue of her estate to three specific charities. On June 14, Dunston reviewed a draft will with Judsen. Judsen indicated that there was an error in the paragraph stating that she was "not unmarried." She advised Dunston that she was divorced. When Dunston asked if she wished to include any family members as beneficiaries, Judsen answered "no." However, she told Dunston that she wanted Laurie to take care of her dog. Dunston specifically reviewed with Judsen the clause that bequeathed her residuary estate to three charities.

Dunston finalized Judsen's will and returned to the hospital on June 15 with two paralegals from his office. After Dunston read all the provisions of the will aloud to Judsen, she confirmed that the will expressed her wishes, that she was of sound and disposing mind, and that she was signing the document freely and voluntarily. Judsen then executed the will. Dunston and one of the paralegals from his office witnessed the testator's execution of her will, and the other paralegal served as the notary public in accordance with the provisions of Code § 64.1–49. According to Dunston, there was no question in his mind that when Judsen executed the June will, she knew her property and the natural objects of her bounty. She understood that she was executing a will and knew how she wished to dispose of her property. The two paralegals also confirmed that although the testator seemed tired, she was coherent and able to respond to Dunston's questions. Neither paralegal had any concerns about the testator's ability to execute the will. One of them testified that the testator "fully underst[ood]" the document she was executing. *618

Laurie testified that she and Judsen were "very close" when they were growing up. Since 2005, when Judsen became involved in Laurie's business, they spoke several times each week. Laurie also testified that at some point, she talked with Judsen about drafting a will, and according to Laurie, Judsen stated that she wished to leave her estate to Laurie, her husband and daughter. Nevertheless, Laurie admitted that Judsen became angry with her when she contacted Labowitz to assist with Judsen's financial matters. Laurie believed that Judsen was **626 being "spiteful" when she executed the June will with terms that were dramatically different than the terms of the April will.

James Carlton, a tenant in Judsen's home and a witness to the April will, testified that when he visited Judsen at the hospital on June 14, she did not maintain eye contact with him and responded "yes" to every question he asked her. Carlton did not, however, see Judsen on the day she executed the June will. He also stated that Judsen had a tendency to "get mad at anybody who didn't do what she wanted when she wanted."

Dr. Abdulkadir Salhan, one of Judsen's attending physicians, testified that he completed a report on June 15, 2010, for the purpose of evaluating her competency. In that report, he opined that Judsen was "not competent" and "ha[d] a disability that prevent[ed] [her] from making or communicating any responsible decisions concerning [her] property." Dr. Salhan, however, conceded that medical record notations dated June 15 stated that Judsen understood "her disease, her diagnosis, stage, and prognosis." Dr. Salhan also admitted that he did not question Judsen concerning her property, finances, or family, and that he did not specifically assess her capacity to execute a will.

Dr. Thomas Hyde, who testified at trial as an expert in the field of neurology, reviewed Judsen's medical records, treatment plan, and medications. He opined that Judsen's cognitive abilities were markedly impaired on June 15, 2010, such that she would have been precluded from fully understanding the nature and extent of her property, the members of her family and "to whom she was giving property and in what manner." Dr. Hyde further opined that Judsen would have known that she was signing a paper but would not have known what was on it. … *619 …

In submitting the case to the jury, the parties agreed on two jury instructions, Instructions 5 and 6, related to this appeal. Jury Instruction 5 stated:

> ... The only question in this case is whether this writing is the last will of Louise Judsen. In deciding this question, you will have to consider this issue: Did Louise Judsen have testamentary capacity when she signed it? On this issue, the proponents of the will have the burden of proof by the greater weight of the evidence. ...

The instruction that followed, Jury Instruction 6, stated:

> You shall find the writing dated June 15, 2010 to be the last will [of] Louise Judsen if the proponent proved by the greater weight of the evidence that:
>
> (A) Louise Judsen was capable of making a will at the time she executed the writing.
>
> You shall find that the writing dated June 15, 2010 was not the last will [of] Louise Judsen if the proponent failed to prove the element above.

The circuit court also granted two jury instructions over Kiddell's objection... Instruction 8 stated:

> *620 ...The only question in this case is whether the writing of June 15, 2010, is the last will of Louise Bradford Judsen. In deciding this question you will have to consider these issues:
>
> **627 (1) The proponent of the will, the defendant Mr. Labowitz is entitled to a presumption that Ms. Judsen had testamentary capacity on June 15, 2010, at the time she executed the writing.
>
> (2) The opponents of the will, Laurie A. Kiddell and Leann M. Kiddell, must introduce evidence sufficient to rebut the presumption of testamentary capacity.
>
> (3) If you find that the opponents of the will have introduced evidence sufficient to rebut the presumption, the burden rests upon the proponent of the will to prove by the greater weight of the evidence that Ms. Judsen had testamentary capacity at the time of the execution of the June 15, 2010, writing.

Similarly, Instruction 9 stated:

> You shall find your verdict in favor of complainants, Laurie A. Kiddell and Leann M. Kiddell, if you find that they have introduced evidence sufficient to rebut the presumption of testamentary capacity and defendant, Mr. Labowitz, has failed to prove by the greater weight of the evidence that Ms. Judsen had testamentary capacity at the time of the execution of the writing.

You shall find your verdict in favor of the defendant, Mr. Labowitz, if the complainants have failed to present evidence sufficient to overcome the presumption of testamentary capacity or defendant, Mr. Labowitz, has proved testamentary capacity at the time of execution by the greater weight of the evidence.

... *621 ... We awarded Kiddell this appeal on ... whether the circuit court erred by granting Instructions 8 and 9...

II. ANALYSIS

... **628 ... *622 ... In a will contest, "the proponent of the will is entitled to a presumption that testamentary capacity existed by proving compliance with all statutory requirements for the valid execution of the will." Gibbs v. Gibbs, 239 Va. 197, 200, 387 S.E.2d 499, 501 (1990). ... *623 The burden of persuasion always remains with the proponent of the will, but once the proponent has proven compliance with statutory requirements for a valid will, the burden of production shifts to the opponent to "go forward with evidence sufficient to rebut the presumption." Gibbs, 239 Va. at 200–01, 387 S.E.2d at 501. ...

Where, however, the sanity of the testator is put in issue by the evidence of the contestant, the *onus probandi* lies upon the proponent to satisfy the court or jury **629 that the writing propounded is the will of a capable testator. Yet, upon the trial of that issue, there is an existent presumption in favor of the testator's sanity. ... *624 Hopkins, 108 Va. at 707, 62 S.E. at 927. A few years later, this Court approved the following instruction based on its holding in Hopkins:

> While the burden of proof is upon those offering a will for probate, to show testamentary capacity on the part of the testator at the time the will was executed to the satisfaction of the jury, yet the court tells the jury that there is in all cases an existing presumption in favor of the testator's sanity and capacity, which is to be taken into consideration by the jury in determining the question of competency.

Huff, 115 Va. at 76, 86, 78 S.E. at 575, 578.4 For the next hundred years, the Court addressed and approved the exact same instruction or a close variant. See Tate, 190 Va. at 500–01, 57 S.E.2d at 160–61; Jenkins, 152 Va. at 440, 147 S.E. at 260; Rust, 124 Va. at 26, 97 S.E. at 331. ... In *Rust*, ... [an] objecting party contended that the latter part of the instruction conflicted with the first part. Rejecting that argument, this Court first explained that when the proponent of a will shows compliance with all the statutory requirements for due execution, "the legal presumption of sanity comes to his relief and dispenses with any evidence to the contrary." Id. at 25, 97 S.E. at 331. ...**630 ...

Kiddell's contention that the presumption of *626 testamentary capacity disappears in the face of any evidence presented to the contrary is incorrect. A presumption of law cannot be said to be rebutted where the evidence of equally credible witnesses for and against the presumption is equally balanced. The rebutter has not carried the burden imposed upon him by law. Where the evidence for and against the presumption are equal the presumption will prevail. ...

Kiddell's argument not only ignores the fact that the trial court did not actually rule that the presumption was rebutted, but also, in persisting in her argument, Kiddell ignores the trial court's ultimate role in ruling on a motion to strike. "In ruling on a motion to strike, trial courts should not undertake to determine the truth or falsity of testimony or to measure its weight." Williams v. Vaughan, 214 Va. 307, 310, 199 S.E.2d 515, 517–18 (1973). "The credibility of witnesses and the weight to be given their testimony are matters peculiarly within the province of the jury." Id. at 310, 199 S.E.2d at 517. ... *627 ... The existence of the presumption of testamentary capacity is a matter of law, but whether the presumption has been sufficiently rebutted is a question of fact. ... [T]he presumption does **631 not disappear unless, as a matter of law, no rational finder of fact could find that the presumption had not been rebutted.

Unlike in some other jurisdictions, in Virginia a presumption disappears only if rebutted by ascertained or established facts or by substantial evidence "showing the true facts to be to the contrary." Kavanaugh, 175 Va. at 113, 7 S.E.2d at 128. Once Labowitz presented evidence that the June will was executed in compliance with statutory requirements, there was a presumption that Judsen had testamentary capacity at the time she executed that will. That presumption could be rebutted by evidence that Judsen was not competent at that time. However, even when the opponent of a will produces evidence that, if believed, *628 could ascertain or establish facts sufficient to rebut the presumption of the testator's capacity, the determination of whether the presumption has been rebutted is to be determined by the jury, unless the opponent has rebutted the presumption as a matter of law. The evidence presented by Kiddell, while potentially sufficient to rebut the presumption of capacity if believed, did not, as a matter of law, ascertain or establish Judsen's incapacity as a true fact. Thus, it was not sufficient to rebut the presumption as a matter of law. The circuit court did not err in ruling that the presumption had not been rebutted or in sending the evidence to the jury.

When the proponent of a will enjoys the presumption of testamentary capacity, the jury must be instructed as to this presumption. Where the evidence is in equipoise, the presumption comes to the proponent's rescue, allowing him to prevail. Indeed, if the jury is not advised of the presumption, the proponent is deprived of this benefit and, in the face of equal evidence, would be found to have not carried his burden even though the law is otherwise. For this reason, we hold that the presumption of testamentary capacity does not disappear, unless the circuit court rules that the presumption was rebutted as a matter of law because no rational fact finder could find that the presumption had not been rebutted. In this case, the circuit court did not err in instructing the jury as to the existence of the presumption. ...

Kiddell does not challenge the sufficiency of the evidence to sustain the jury verdict. Instead, ... Kiddell contends that Labowitz failed to establish a prima facie case of testamentary *629 capacity because he failed to prove that Judsen knew the natural objects of her bounty. … Generally, … capacity exists, if at the time a will is executed, the testator is "'capable of recollecting her property, the natural objects of her bounty and their claims upon her, knew the business about which she was engaged and how she wished to dispose of the property.'" Weedon, 283 Va. at 252, 720 S.E.2d at 558 (2012) (quoting Tabb v. Willis, 155 Va. 836, 859, 156 S.E. 556, 564 (1931)). The time of a will's execution "is the critical time for determining testamentary capacity." Thomason v. Carlton, 221 Va. 845, 853, 276 S.E.2d 171, 175 (1981). The testimony of witnesses present at the time of execution is entitled to "the greatest consideration" on the issue of a testator's mental capacity. "[I]n determining the mental capacity of a testator, great weight is to be attached to the testimony of the draftsman of the will, of the attesting witnesses, and of attending physicians." Hall v. Hall, 181 Va. 67, 76, 23 S.E.2d 810, 814 (1943); accord Parish, 281 Va. at 200, 704 S.E.2d at 105.

According to Dunston, who drafted the June will and witnessed its execution, Judsen fully understood that she was executing a will. He described Judsen as knowing her property, the natural objects of her bounty, and her wishes for the disposal of her assets. The two paralegals from his office, one who served as a witness to the execution of the June will and the other who served as the notary public, agreed. Both testified that they would not have witnessed or notarized the will if they had doubted that Judsen understood what she was doing or if she had seemed confused. *630 Furthermore, Dunston testified that he asked Judsen if she wished to include any family members as beneficiaries and she responded "no." She did, however, leave a cash gift and her dog to Laurie, and she requested that the bequest to the "Leukemia & Lymphoma Society Inc." be made in the name of her mother. Moreover, both Laurie and Labowitz testified that Judsen became angry with Laurie when she asked Labowitz to have Judsen substitute him for her as Judsen's attorney in fact.

This evidence, however, was in conflict with the testimony of Dr. Salhan and Dr. Hyde. Both opined that on June 15, 2010, Judsen was not capable of making decisions about her property. When a conflict exists in the "testimony on a material point, or if reasonably fair-minded [persons] may differ as to the conclusions of fact to be drawn from the evidence, or if the conclusion is dependent on the weight to be given the testimony," a jury issue exists. Thus, the circuit court did not err by refusing to strike Labowitz' evidence and, instead, allowing the issue of testamentary capacity to be decided by the jury. … **633

Chief Justice KINSER, with whom Justice LEMONS and Justice MIMS join, concurring in part and dissenting in part.

In Kavanaugh v. Wheeling, 175 Va. 105, 7 S.E.2d 125 (1940), this Court held that if a presumption "is rebutted or overcome by substantial evidence showing the true facts to be to the contrary, the presumption disappears." Id. at 113, 7 S.E.2d at 128. … Under the majority's construct, the presumption remains in the case as positive evidence to be weighed in determining whether the proponent has carried the ultimate burden of proving testamentary capacity by a preponderance of the evidence unless the opponent has established testamentary incapacity as a matter of law. In my view, that test for determining when the presumption of testamentary capacity disappears is inconsistent with the principle stated in *Kavanaugh*. Moreover, a finding that the opponent of a will has proven testamentary incapacity as a matter of law means that no rational fact finder could find the existence of testamentary capacity when the will was executed and judgment must therefore be entered in favor of the opponent. Furthermore, assuming the majority is correct in its conclusion that, unless the opponent establishes testamentary incapacity as a matter of law, the presumption of testamentary capacity remains as evidence in the case and aids the proponent in carrying the ultimate burden of persuasion, Instructions 8 and 9 did not instruct the jury accordingly. The majority, nevertheless, holds that the circuit court did not err by giving Instructions 8 and 9.

Unlike the majority, I believe that the presumption of testamentary capacity disappears when an opponent goes forward with evidence sufficient to rebut the presumption. In my view, the presumption is not evidence for a jury to consider. … *632 … *633 … "'Presumptions are indulged in to supply the place of facts; they are never allowed against ascertained and established facts. When these appear, presumptions disappear.'" Schmitt v. Redd, 151 Va. 333, 344, 143 S.E. 884, 887 (1928) …*634 … **635 … Not one of [our prior] cases even tangentially involved the question whether the presumption of testamentary capacity disappears when rebutted by sufficient evidence of incapacity. The majority does not claim otherwise, nor can it. Thus, the mere fact that the instructions were given and quoted with approval is not dispositive in the instant case. … Moreover, Instructions 8 and 9 are different from those given in Tate, Jenkins, Rust, and Huff. Those instructions told the jury to consider the presumption when determining the question of competency. … *635 … Furthermore, contrary to the majority's construct of the role the presumption plays, Instructions 8 and 9 did not tell the jury that if the evidence is in equipoise, the presumption tips the scales in favor of Labowitz and permits a finding that he proved testamentary capacity by a preponderance of the evidence. Yet, this is one of the reasons offered by the majority to explain why a jury must be instructed about the presumption of testamentary capacity. …

*636 … Finally, I point out that, under the majority's decision today, …*637 … each jury in a will contest will have to decide what is meant by "evidence sufficient to rebut the presumption of testamentary capacity." I fear that different juries will use varying definitions. Even the circuit court in ruling on Labowitz's motion to strike noted the absence in our jurisprudence of a definable evidentiary standard to employ in deciding if the opponent of a will has rebutted the presumption of testamentary capacity. Perhaps the absence of such guidance is indicative of the fact that a jury in such a case does not decide whether a presumption, operating as a rule of law, has **637 been rebutted. See Martin v. Phillips, 235 Va. 523, 526, 369 S.E.2d 397, 399 (1988) ("A presumption is a rule of law…."). …

———————————

An earlier decision of the court, Fields v. Fields (1998), rested on the principle that focus should be on evidence as to the testator's condition at the time of execution, because a person's capacity might wax and wane over time:

> The respondents presented evidence from numerous lay witnesses concerning the general mental and physical capacity of the testator between 1975 and 1988. In sum, that evidence shows that the testator was of declining health, that he was increasingly confused, and that he occasionally engaged in inappropriate behavior. Several witnesses testified that at times the testator would not recognize family members, could not discuss current affairs, and could not understand a legal document. On cross-examination, several of the witnesses conceded, however, that the testator could recognize family members and discuss family matters on occasion. Although all of these witnesses had regular contact with the testator, none testified concerning specific events reflecting his testamentary incapacity on November 1, 1988. ...

> In clarifying the degree of mental competence required for a person to have testamentary capacity, we have held that a testator need not "retain all the force of intellect which he may have had at a former period," Wooddy v. Taylor, 114 Va. 737, 741, 77 S.E. 498, 500 (1913), and under certain circumstances may even be legally incompetent to transact other business. See Tate v. Chumbley, 190 Va. 480, 493, 57 S.E.2d 151, 157 (1950). ... "[T]he time of execution of the will ... is the critical time for determining testamentary capacity. The testimony of witnesses as to the mental capacity of the testat[or] at this time carries great weight." Thomason v. Carlton, 221 Va. 845, 853, 276 S.E.2d 171, 175 (1981). Evidence of sickness or impaired intellect at other times is insufficient, standing alone, to render a will invalid. See also Tate, 190 Va. at 495, 57 S.E.2d at 158 (testatrix on furlough from mental institution was not per se incompetent to execute will).

255 Va. 546, 549-50; 499 S.E.2d 826, 827-28.

B.   Testamentary intent

To be probated as a will or codicil (amendment to a will), a document's language must manifest an intent that the document be effective affirmatively to dispose of some or all of the author's property at his or her death. One common contrasting case is one in which a decedent had written a letter to an attorney, expected executor, or intended beneficiary discussing what is to be done with property but in a way that suggests the author did not believe the letter itself would constitute a will or codicil.

Supreme Court of Virginia.
Wolfe v. Wolfe
248 Va. 359, 448 S.E.2d 408 (1994)

LACY, Justice.

**409 ... In 1982, Jared D. Wolfe executed a will disposing of his property. Ten years later, on April 29, 1992, he wrote a letter in which he stated "I want my daughters to share ⅓, ⅓, ⅓." On May 14, 1992, Jared committed suicide. Kathleen Wolfe, Jared's former wife and executor of his estate, submitted the will for probate but declined to offer the letter for probate. ...

To qualify a writing as a valid codicil to a will, the proponent of the writing must show more than an expression of how a testator wants his property distributed. The proponent of the proposed codicil must show that the writing itself was executed by the testator with the intent that it have testamentary effect. Without such intent, no document can be considered as effectively disposing of the author's property. Testamentary intent is determined by looking at the document itself, not from extrinsic evidence. Whether a particular writing evidences testamentary intent must be determined on a case-by-case basis.

The 1992 letter in issue in this case consists of three pages. It is addressed to Kathleen Wolfe as Jared's "Ex-wife" and "Executor *361 of my will" and was written on a day Jared unsuccessfully attempted to commit suicide. In the letter, Jared identifies the status of his tax matters, life insurance policies, and government payments to which one daughter was entitled. The letter also describes Jared's mental illness and his despair in coping with his illness. He signed the letter "Jared/Dad." The language at issue appears on the second page of the letter:

> As executor, I am asking you to do much for me and the girls, perhaps Gordon can help. God bless you, I know you will do your best. My will is out of date, but I think it will still stand up. I want my daughters to share ⅓, ⅓, ⅓.

The final sentence quoted above expresses Jared's intention that his property be equally divided among his three daughters. To qualify as a valid codicil, however, the letter must also reflect Jared's intent that it take effect as a testamentary document.

Jared did not expect his letter to revoke or supersede his existing will in its entirety because he addressed the letter to the "Executor of my will" and specifically stated his belief that the 1982 will would "stand up." While a will may be modified in part, Jared's letter contains no express language of partial revocation or amendment. See Code § 64.1-58.1. Even assuming that the language expressing Jared's desire that his daughters share equally contradicts the disposition in the will, an effective partial revocation exists only if such a contradiction is accompanied by an intent to effect a testamentary disposition. Such an intent cannot be found in this letter. Jared did not refer to the letter as a codicil or a will, or indicate in any affirmative way that the letter was to be given testamentary effect. To the contrary, Jared's statement "it will stand up" is not limited to selected portions of his will, but references the entire will.

Furthermore, the expression in the letter of Jared's desire that his daughters share equally is not necessarily inconsistent with the disposition of property under the will. In his will, Jared devised specific pieces of real property to two of the three daughters. The third daughter was to receive a grandfather's clock and the residue of the estate, **410 subject to the condition that if the property devised to the other two daughters was not part of Jared's estate at the time of his death, those daughters were to each receive one- *362 third of the residue of Jared's estate. Such disposition is to some extent consistent with the intent reflected in Jared's 1992 letter.*

The language of the 1992 letter, while showing Jared's desire that his daughters share equally in his estate, does not contain any evidence that he intended that letter to operate as his last will or as a codicil to his will. Rather, the evidence shows that Jared characterized his will as "out of date" but believed that it would be effective. Under these facts, we cannot conclude that the April 1992 letter demonstrates the testamentary intent to revoke portions of the 1982 will and to substitute a different disposition of the testator's property. ...

WHITING, Justice, dissenting.

... The letter reviews the status of Wolfe's affairs, expresses his intent to commit suicide, gives instructions to the executor regarding his estate, refers to his will, and then provides: "I want my daughters to share ⅓, ⅓, ⅓." Wolfe's 1982 will bequeathed a grandfather clock to one daughter, devised specific real properties to two of his daughters, and left the residue of his estate to a third daughter, with a provision that if either of the real properties were sold, the devisee of that particular property would receive one-third of the residue of his estate.

In my opinion, Wolfe clearly intended to avoid any disparities in the value of each daughter's share of his estate when he wrote the letter addressed to his executor. Given the person to whom the letter was written, the circumstances under which the letter was written (fully described therein), and the clear language of disposition quoted above, I think this particular writing bears the necessary "stamp of testamentary intent" within the document itself. ... *363...

Can you write your will on a napkin? Sure. Or scratch it on the headboard of a bed or the cinderblock of a prison cell. The medium on which writing appears can be relevant to determining whether there was testamentary intent, but there is no categorical rule that testamentary writing must be on paper designed for writing. The following case probating a sales receipt identifies additional factors for determining testamentary intent.

Supreme Court of Virginia
Bailey v. Kerns
246 Va. 158, 431 S.E.2d 312 (1993)

KEENAN, Justice.

... Edith M. Kerns, also known as Edith B. Kerns (Edith), died on July 6, 1988. When no will was found at the time of her death, her son, George F. Kerns, qualified as administrator of her estate. Less than seven months later, Edith's sister, Gertrude Bean, passed away. Among Bean's possessions was a hardware store receipt dated November 25, 1985. On the back of the receipt was an undated writing made in Edith's handwriting. **314 ... Wallace M. Bailey, also a son of Edith, appealed the order admitting the instrument to probate.

The writing, which was made entirely in the handwriting of Edith and was addressed to her son, George, states: *161

> George Kerns
> When this property is sold I want this
> Tommy Kerns $10,000
> Shelly Guidara $10,000
> David Penny $5,000
> Jamie Penny $5,000
> The rest goes to you and your family.
> Of course all my Bills are to be paid.
> Love you even if I haven't been much of a Mom-Edith B. Kerns

... At trial, David Penny testified that he had lived with Edith for several years and that he thought of her as his mother. Penny, his wife, and their two children, David and Jamie, who are named in the instrument, visited Edith once a week until the time of her death. Penny also testified that, at the time of her death, Edith still had several foster children living with her and that she was constantly fixing up her house and had expressed no desire to sell it.

Edith's sister, Charlotte Compton, testified by deposition that Edith had lived in the same house for over twenty years and that she seemed happy there. Compton also testified that Edith was very fond of David Penny, one of her foster children, and that she would not be surprised if Edith had made a gift to Penny's sons in her will.

George Kerns testified that his mother owned a 60% interest in the property in question, which consisted of four acres of land, the house in which she lived, and a house trailer. Kerns further testified that his mother had no other significant assets and that, approximately 15 years prior to her death, she told him that she had made a will.

David T. Kerns, Jr., Edith's grandson, testified ... that he had lived in Edith's house since 1979 and that he was still living there at the time of her death. David Kerns testified that Edith kept her personal papers either in a box on top of the refrigerator or in a small basket by her bed. He further testified that he had seen Edith place sealed envelopes in a safety deposit box at the bank. He also testified that Edith had indicated that she would like to live by the water. *162

George Kerns ... testified that his mother never mentioned any desire to live by the water. He also testified that the only time she mentioned selling the property was when she refused an unsolicited offer on the house. ...

The jury found that the holographic writing was the will of Edith B. Kerns. ...

The word "testamentary" means "applicable or related to death; having to do with dispositions or arrangements effective upon the happening of that event." Poindexter v. Jones, 200 Va. 372, 376, 106 S.E.2d 144, 146 (1958). Some evidence of testamentary intent must be found on the face of a writing before it can be held to be a valid will. **315 The determination whether the face of an instrument contains evidence of testamentary intent is a matter of law to be decided by the trial court. If the trial court determines that there is no evidence of testamentary intent within the four corners of the instrument, as a matter of law, that instrument is not a valid will.

When, as here, the decedent has not included in the instrument an express statement of her testamentary intention, the determination whether such intent appears on the face of the instrument is made by examining all its parts. Therefore, we shall consider the instrument before us as a whole in determining whether the trial court erred in ruling that it contained evidence of testamentary intent on its face.

We first observe that the instrument contains several elements commonly associated with wills. Edith allocated specific amounts of money to named individuals and then disposed of the balance of *163 the money from the sale of the property to George Kerns and his family, with the requirement that "Of course all my Bills are to be paid." Lastly, Edith gave a closing statement of affection and signed her name.

The instrument was addressed to Edith's son, instructing him what she wanted done "[w]hen this property is sold." This language is evidence that Edith did not intend to be the seller of the property and that she did not expect to be able to express her wishes at the time of the sale. Edith's direction that all her bills be paid is also evidence of testamentary intent because one does not ordinarily direct the payment of every existing debt out of a sale to take place during one's lifetime. In addition, Edith signed her full name at the end of the instrument, which was addressed to her son. This full signature is evidence suggesting that she intended the document to be more formal than a letter to her son.

We hold that these elements, appearing together, constitute evidence of testamentary intent on the face of the instrument. Our conclusion here is supported by Grimes v. Crouch, 175 Va. 126, 132-34; 7 S.E.2d 115, 117-18 (1940), in which this Court found evidence of testamentary intent on the face of a holographic writing that contained less language probative of testamentary intent. The writing in Grimes provided: "Ever thing left to sister for life times." "C.A. Grimes." This Court held that the word "left" was evidence of testamentary intent on the face of the instrument and, therefore, that the trial court had not erred in allowing the presentation of extrinsic evidence of testamentary intent and in submitting the case for the jury's consideration. ... This Court has stated that

> [i]t is a settled rule in this country and in England that in determining whether the instrument propounded was intended *164 to be testamentary, reference will be had to the surrounding circumstances, and the language will be construed in the light of those circumstances; and that if it shall appear under all the circumstances that the instrument was intended to be testamentary, the court will give effect to the intention, if it can be done consistently with the language of the instrument. But while the courts have **316 gone far in construing almost any form of instrument to be a will, we have been unable to find a case in which a paper with nothing on its face to indicate that it was intended to be testamentary was held to be entitled to probate as a holograph will.

Smith v. Smith, 112 Va. 205, 208, 70 S.E. 491, 492 (1911). Thus, in *Smith*, this Court applied the rule that when there is no evidence of testamentary intent on the face of an instrument, it cannot be admitted to probate as a will. However, when the face of the instrument contains some evidence of testamentary intent, extrinsic evidence may be admitted to determine whether the instrument is testamentary in nature. Grimes, 175 Va. at 132-34, 7 S.E.2d at 117-18. ... *165 ...

In the present case, ... Charlotte Compton's testimony that she would not be surprised if Edith had left something to David Penny's children... was made within the context of Compton's description of the close relationship between Edith and David Penny. Such evidence, relating to Edith's family circumstances and her relationship with persons named in the instrument, was admissible on the issue of testamentary intent. ... Compton's testimony that Edith seemed happy in her home... was probative as to whether Edith had any intent to sell her home in her lifetime. Therefore, we conclude that this **317 evidence was properly admitted. ... *166 ...

[T]his Court previously has stated that the word "beloved" was not evidence of testamentary intent. See Poindexter, 200 Va. at 378, 106 S.E.2d at 147. ... Poindexter, in which the Court considered a one-sentence instrument, does not reject the probative value of all statements of affection. When considered in context, statements of affection may be relevant to the issue of testamentary intent. Here, the statement of affection came at the conclusion of a document that contained specific **318 and residual dispositions of property, as well as a provision for the payment of all debts. In this context, we hold that Edith's statement of affection was probative of testamentary intent...

Another example of informal writing being probated as a will is found in *Henderson v. Henderson*, 183 Va. 663, 33 S.E.2d 181 (1945), where the Virginia Supreme Court found sufficient testamentary intent in this letter:

My dear Roy:

I will now have to make a change in my will. The bequest to Cora I now want to go to you and just keep this for business like transfer. I will have Abbot take up the matter with me if I am spared to get to Virginia. Another matter is in regard to dear Ernest. I also want you to have what I planned for him; if he should be living you are to have it just the same, as he is provided for as long as he lives by the arrangement made by Mr. McClay. I want you and yours to have what I planned to give Cora and Ernest. Just hold this little piece of paper in case there should be trouble. I have planned for Brother also for the Ripple boys and the McClay children. Mr. McClay asked me to leave them nothing but I cannot do that after all their kindness to me. Mr. McClay said he had an abundance for them. This is a private note for you. I do not want it known in Hancock. I of course will come to Ernest's aid if Raymond should not have sufficient to make him comfortable. *667 Raymond told me he had sufficient. I am so anxious for you, Annie and your family to be cared for in your old age.

Sister Ella.

The court quoted *McBride v. McBride*, 26 Gratt. (67 Va.) 476, 480 (1875), for the rule that:

[I]t is not necessary to the validity of a will that it should have a testamentary form, or that the decedent should know that he had performed a testamentary act, or that he should intend to perform such act. A deed poll, or an indenture, a bond, a marriage settlement, a letter, a promissory note, and the like, have been valid as a will. If the paper contains a disposition of the property, to take effect after the death of the testator, though it was not intended to be a will, but an instrument of a different shape, yet if it cannot operate in the character in which it was intended, it may operate as a testamentary act. It is not necessary that the paper should be the identical one intended by the testator for his last will and testament. If the instrument has once received the sanction of the testator as the final disposition of his property, it will so remain until revoked or cancelled in some one of the modes required by the statute. He may have always intended to make another will, but until that intention is consummated by the execution of a posterior instrument, the first will stand as the last will and testament, however little it may reflect the wishes of the testator.

And on 68 C.J. 645 for further elaboration:

The courts entertain liberal views as to the form and contents of codicils, and hold that an instrument, executed with a testamentary purpose and the requisite formalities, may operate as a codicil, although it is partly or wholly in the form of a letter, power of attorney, or deed, or although its only provision is one naming an executor.

The court then explained:

It is apparent from the sentence, 'I will now have to make a change in my will,' that the testatrix recognized the existence of the will formerly executed and by the use of the word 'now' she clearly indicated that she had a present intent to change her will. Also, that she clearly intended to change the former disposition of her property is shown by the language: 'The bequest to Cora I now want to go to you and just keep this for business like transfer.' The language also clearly indicates that the letter was not merely meant as a social epistle, but had reference to a matter of 'business like transfer.' This view is further fortified by the injunction to keep the letter intact. Then, too, the reference to 'dear Ernest' is followed by the language which indicates testatrix intended to devise to appellee the property theretofore devised to Ernest; and, again, the injunction, 'Just hold this little piece of paper in case there should be trouble.' ... While the following statement in the McBride Case, supra, is true, 'But when an attempt is made to establish a mere letter as a testamentary act, a request of the writer to destroy the letter leads irresistibly to the conclusion, his purpose was that that paper at least should not be his will,' it follows, by the same token, that when the writer of the letter twice emphasizes the importance of preserving the letter in order to avoid trouble, she intends the letter as a codicil to her will then in existence.

As a more recent example from a circuit court, the Circuit Court for Amherst County, in Eubank v. Eubank, 68 Va. Cir. 33 (2005), had no difficulty finding testamentary intent in a handwritten document that did not say anything like "this is my will" but said in the second paragraph "at my death I want my farm Walnut Hill 266A to go to my...." and was signed at the end. The court stated:

Under Virginia law, testamentary intent must be found on the face of the will or codicil, and not from extrinsic evidence. Quesenberry v. Funk, 203 Va. 619, 624, 125 S.E.2d 869 (1962). The word "testamentary" means "applicable or related to death." Poindexter v. Jones, 200 Va. 372, 276 (1958). The words "[A]t my death" clearly indicate that the codicil is related to death.

By way of bookending, the following two decisions rejected holographic writings as non-testamentary:

Supreme Court of Virginia.
McCutchan v. Heizer
217 Va. 938, 234 S.E.2d 275 (1977)

HARMAN, Justice.

... Emily McCutchan Beard, a resident of the City of Staunton, died on March 10, 1974. A will dated July 14, 1967, and a codicil dated April 8, 1971, both of which had been prepared by her attorney, were found in her safe deposit box at a Staunton bank. The parties agree these documents are valid testamentary instruments. *939

A holographic [handwritten] paper dated June 3, 1971, which is at issue here, was found among the deceased's personal effects in the drawer of a desk at her residence. The three pages of the holograph were still attached to a writing tablet. The holograph reads as follows:

> This to Frank
>
> My will is in the bank. Bob Hanger can get will his name is with bank National Valley, Bob and Campbell Heizer my executor of will. All I ask of the farm is to pay my bequests, you buy farm not paying over Twenty thousand.

**276 *940 In her 1967 will, the testatrix directed the payment of her just debts and expressed a desire concerning her place of burial and the manner in which her grave was to be marked. This will directed that the "McCutchan family lot at Bethel Presbyterian Church . . . be placed under perpetual care" and directed that all taxes, including death and succession taxes, be paid out of the residue of the estate. The will contained bequests ranging from $200 to $6000 to or for the benefit of eight individuals. Each of these bequests lapsed if the beneficiary died before the testatrix. The will also left the sum of $2,000 "to the Treasurer of Bethel Presbyterian Church . . . to be used for the work and purposes of the Church." The testatrix devised a two and one-half acre parcel of land, a part of her farm, to Charles Mason Thompson and directed her executors "to have the same surveyed and make conveyance of the same to the devisee."

Clause Tenth of the will provides:

> TENTH : I desire that certain items of personal property, consisting largely of household furniture and furnishings, be distributed as indicated in a memorandum written in my handwriting and to be filed along with this Will, but not to be recorded as a part thereof.

The residuary clause in the will provides:

> ELEVENTH : I direct the remainder of my property, real and personal, be converted into cash by my Executors, and that the proceeds therefrom, together with any lapsed or void legacies, together with such cash as may be a part of my estate, after payment of all debts, bequests,

taxes, costs of administration, etc., shall be paid in equal shares to: (1) Charles Mason Thompson, if he survive me; (2) Vallie D. Baylor, if she survive me; (3) Jane Thompson Clements, if she survive me; and (4) the Trustees of Bethel Presbyterian Church of Augusta County, Virginia, which gift to the said Church is made as a memorial to my father and mother, namely, James B. McCutchan and Susan Finley McCutchan, and the nature and recognition of this memorial, as well as the use of the funds, shall be determined within the discretion of the proper officers of the Church.

Vallie D. Baylor, who was a residuary beneficiary of the will and the legatee of a specific bequest of $6,000, contingent upon her surviving the testatrix, died on October 24, 1970. On April 8, *941 1971, the testatrix had her attorney prepare and she executed a codicil which revoked the specific bequest to Vallie D. Baylor and substituted the following clause in lieu thereof:

FOURTH : I give and bequeath to my cousin, Henry D. Baylor, of 322 College Park Drive, Staunton, Virginia, if he survives **277 me, the sum of Three Thousand Dollars ($3,000.00).

The codicil further provides:

In all other respects I do confirm and affirm my said Will of July 14, 1967.

Here, as in the trial court, the crucial question is whether the holograph shows on its face the testamentary intent (*animus testandi*) required to make it a testamentary document.

The appellant argues that it is not necessary that he show the deceased "intended to perform a testamentary act or make a formal codicil, but only to show that the writing contemplates a final disposition of property to take effect posthumously and to be revocable until the time of death." ... The rule applicable here was recently restated in Mumaw v. Mumaw, 214 Va. 573, 576-577, 203 S.E.2d 136, 138-139 (1974), where we pointed out:

Although it is true, as argued, that a letter can constitute a will, '(i)t must satisfactorily appear that he (the letter writer) intended the very paper to be his will.' [citations omitted] In addition, for such a writing to be valid will in Virginia, testamentary intent must be found on its face, not from extrinsic evidence. [citations omitted]

... *942 ... Clearly the deceased was mindful of the will which she had executed for she referred to "my will", "will" and "executor of will" in the holograph. That she attached great importance and significance to this document is evidenced by her recitation in the holograph of the location of the will and her suggestion as to how it could best be obtained. In the holograph she refers to "bequests", which could only refer to the words "give and bequeath" which appear no less than seven times in her will and the April 8, 1971, codicil. We attach significance to the fact that nowhere else in the holograph does the word "bequest" appear. Nowhere in the holograph does she either expressly or impliedly attempt to amend, revoke or modify what she referred to in the holograph as "her will". The two sentences, "All I ask of the farm is to pay my bequests. You buy farm not paying over twenty thousand.", are not words of gift or devise, but words of counsel and advice to "Frank", Frank McCutchan, Jr., the appellant here.

We hold, therefore, that the holographic writing fails to show on its face the required *animus testandi* to make it a testamentary document.

Supreme Court of Appeals of Virginia
Thompkins v. Randall
153 Va. 530, 150 S.E. 249 (1929)

CHICHESTER, J., delivered the opinion of the court.

... J. M. Randall lived in the city of Harrisonburg, Va., and was twice married. His first wife, Alice Randall, was the mother of Ida Thompkins and the grandmother of Mary Randall... She was quite industrious and with the help of the plaintiffs accumulated the funds with which the property, referred to in the record as 138 Wolfe Street, Harrisonburg, Virginia, was purchased. Title was taken in the name of J. M. Randall.

When J. M. Randall married Alice, she had a small daughter about nine years of age, whose name was Ida, she being now Ida Thompkins... Ida lived with her mother and her stepfather as a member of the family until she was about seventeen years of age, when she went to Pittsburg and secured employment. The other plaintiff, Mary Randall, is the child of Ida, and when she was two years old she was left at the home of J. M. Randall with her grandmother, Alice Randall, while her mother... sought work in Pittsburg. Mary Randall grew up in the J. M. Randall home where she was well cared for and was the object of the love and affection of both J. M. Randall and Alice Randall. Alice Randall died in 1913 and J. M. *533 Randall was married the second time in 1917. He died in 1927 and left no last will and testament unless the two letters, one to Ida Thompkins and the other to Mary Randall are construed to be testamentary. The letter to Ida Thompkins was written March 18, 1919, and was as follows:

HARRISONBURG, VA.,

March 18, 1919.

138 East Wolfe st.

Affirmed.

DEAR IDA:

Your letter Was gladly received today. I am glad to hear that you are
well it has been a long time since We have heard of each orther I lost
your address and I Would put it of from time to time of giting the
address from Mary. But I am Just the Same. I told you and Mary that
this House & lot and Every thing is to be long to you and Mary Ida I
mean What I say I am Sorry you do not beleave me. you must not think
Because I have Married I Will Make the place over to My Wife. I could
not do that and go before god in peace. I thought that Was Settle in your
mine Now the reason I did not Send Mary, any thing Christmas after
going to Richmond in october 1th 1918 to Bury my Brother Major I
came home and was down With Rheumatism I have it yet but not so bad
as I have had it and after Seeing Condishion of thing **250 down
home I mean Richmond. I give what I could to help my nices. 5 little
children Whose mother and Farther, had died, & left them. I hope you &
Mary Will Come home this Summer & know that this is home Every
thing is Just as it was when your mother live I am the Same to wards
you & Mary & Will be so untell I die. Every thing is the Trunk Just as
yourall left then you must pray more and drive the Evel thoughts from
you mine My god Bless you pray for me

(Signed) J. M. RANDALL. **534**

p s Ben Tolliver. Was Just hear he Send love to you'

He wrote the following letter to Mary Randall -

HARRISONBURG, VA., Feb. 25, 1925.

 138. east Wolfe st.

DEAR MARY:

It has been a long time since I Wrote to you. I am a shame. Just a few
lines to let you and Ida know that I am yet a live I suppose you think I
have forgoting you all but it is not true I love you all Just the same I
hope you Will Excuse me for not answering your sweet letter I received
Some time a go I have been sick with the Faiceal Neuralgia for over two
months not able to bee out doos, but is better now. I also received a
letter from Ida. Will answer it soon. give love to Ida Mary. I Want you
and Ida to know that this Home is for you and Ida & No body Else I
would not do other Wise I hope you all Will have Faith in me also glad
to know that you all have Bought Home up there. I can not Write this
morning I am nervis. Martha, sends much love to you & Ida Write soon
I am yours

(Signed) J. M. RANDALL

p s please give me Ida address I could not under it Wether it Was 228 N
N 9th st or 228 5th st.'

... ***535** ... All the authorities hold, indeed it is very clear, that it is not necessary to the validity of a will that it should have a testamentary form. ... ***536** ... ****251** ... ***537** ... 'It is necessary, however, that the writing, whatever it be, should have been designed by him as an actual disposition of property, to take effect after his death, not as a mere expression of what he intended or expected to do.' ... ***538** ...

[T]he letters which the plaintiffs seek to have probated do not show the testamentary intention with sufficient clearness, at the time the letters were written, to dispose of the property by the letters themselves. 'Heirs are favored in law, and get the benefit of any doubt affecting their rights.' The defendants here are the heirs at law of the writer of these letters and it certainly does not appear with sufficient clearness that the writer intended to dispose of his property by these letters. There is a promise, it is true, to leave the property to the plaintiffs here, at some future time, but the idea of disposing of his property by these letters is by no means clear, and when this is the case the heirs are to be favored and to get the benefit of any doubt affecting their rights. The promise in the letter of March 18, 1919: 'I told you and Mary that this House & lot and everything is to belong to you and Mary Ida, I mean What I say. I am sorry you do not beleave me,' and in the letter of February 25, 1925: 'I want you and Ida to know that this home is for you and Ida and nobody else,' are to be construed, we think, as promises to make a will in the future in favor of the addressees of those letters. If this were not true such expressions as these, or a promise to make a will, would be a will without the writer knowing or intending it to be such, and would take effect as a will though the writer might subsequently change his mind. Testamentary intent, we take it, means that the writing offered for probate must have been executed by the testator with the intent that such writing take effect as his last will. ***539** The letters offered for probate in this case show an absence of testamentary intent at the time they were written. To construe such letters as testamentary would be to make social correspondence a risky pastime. ...

See also Smith v. Smith, 112 Va. 205 (1911) (not finding testamentary intent in a dated and signed statement "Everything is Lous," where Lou was the writer's wife, because the language could be interpreted as stating an existing fact, not even carrying the connotation of a gift); and Poindexter v. Jones, 200 Va. 372 (1958) (not finding testamentary intent in a signed paper by her setting out city, state, and date and providing "I give all that I possess to my beloved nephew Hendley Jones," because "give" and "beloved" considered individually or together or with the other words in the writing had "no relation to death nor do they indicate testamentary intent").

More recent decisions of Circuit Courts in Virginia offer additional examples of contested cases, though not constituting binding precedent:

In Estate of McKagen, 90 Va. Cir. 118 (2015), a decedent had executed a will and then six years later wrote two notes addressed to the person she had names as executor. The court denied probate to the first note, which said: "3–2–12. I would like Ian to have $50,000.00. His address is in address book near telephone [sic] in living room. Ian Kustchatka. Signed Helen W. McKagen." The note made no reference to the author's estate nor to her death. The court admitted to probate, as a holographic codicil, the second note, which said: "Branden—If my assets are over $750,000 at the time of my demise, I would like Ian to have $50,000.00. It's not in the will but I trust you. That is my wish. Thanks, Helen. 12–7–12." That note referred both to the author's estate and to her death.

In Estate of Roland B. Baker, 4 Va. Cir. 276, 1985 WL 306773, the Frederick County Circuit Court this letter:

> To whom it may concern
>
> I hear by request our property everything we own be divided between the following
>
> John H. Rinker & Family
> Mr. & Mrs. Lewis Strosnider & Family
> Miss Kim Grow & May Walker
> Miss Chris Barcol) these in trust so mother
> Miss Tonya Barcol) can't spend
> $1.00 to Daisy Richard
>
> Roland B. Baker
>
> Bessie M. Baker

The court determined that Roland had written the entire document, so by inference Bessie herself had not signed it, so it could not constitute her will absent evidence she directed Roland to sign for her in her presence. It went on to hold it was also not Roland's will, because not a will at all:

> There is nothing in it that definitely indicates disposition at or after death. There is nothing in the four corners referring to the paper as a will or the event of death. The verbs "request" and "own" are in the present tense; the passive verb "be divided" without the addition of "shall" is as likely present tense as future, and perhaps more likely the former. The request is directed non-specifically and particularly is not to an executor. There is no reference to any other paper which might be of a testamentary character. Though not required and perhaps of only moderate significance it bears no date. There is no testamentary intent showing any of the generally accepted testamentary purposes: Positive disposition of property, revocation of some testamentary act previously made, revival of a testamentary paper previously revoked and appointment of an executor or guardian; consequently, "In the absence of a testamentary intent there can be no will."

And in Alexander v. Jones, 16 Va. Cir. 489, 1980 WL 342904, the Circuit Court for Henrico County refused to probate a letter the decedent had written to his lawyer that listed the decedent's assets, referred to "our recent conversation about my will," stated "I desire to have codicils added to my will " and "I wish to create a trust," and confirmed plans to meet at the lawyer's office. The court explained: "Nowhere in this writing does the decedent employ such terms as 'give,' 'bequeath,' or 'devise.'" Thus, "the decedent's expressions are precatory and merely tentative," suggesting an intention to execute a will at a later date at the lawyer's office, not an intention that the letter itself should constitute a will.

Another common contrasting case is a document that expresses a desire to disinherit a certain person but does not indicate to whom the author's probate estate should go instead. Courts will not give effect to language that manifests merely an intent that certain people should not receive anything. In other words, one cannot expressly disinherit people; to deprive intestate heirs, one must execute a will making an affirmative disposition of one's property to others.

Supreme Court of Appeals of Virginia
Delly v. Seaboard Citizens National Bank of Norfolk
202 Va. 764, 120 S.E.2d 45 (1961)

SPRATLEY, J., delivered the opinion of the court.

*765 ... Marie Elizabeth Purnell died on October 31, 1959, leaving three paper writings relating to her estate. One was a last will and testament dated April 22, 1952; the second was a last will and testament dated February 24, 1953; and the third was a paper writing dated August 14, 1959. Each writing was duly executed by the deceased, and witnessed and attested by competent witnesses.

Under the 1952 writing the testatrix bequeathed and devised to each of her two sons, John Wesley Purnell and Joseph Hugh Purnell the sum of $1,000.00; established a trust fund of $3,000.00 for her incompetent daughter, Margaret N. Purnell; and bequeathed the residue of her property to her daughter, Thelma Purnell Delly, the appellant.

Under the terms of the 1953 will, the testatrix expressly revoked all prior 'wills and codicils,' and then bequeathed and devised one-fourth of her estate to each of her two sons, John Wesley Purnell and Joseph Hugh Purnell; one-fourth to her daughter, Thelma Purnell Delly; and the remaining one-fourth to her incompetent daughter, Margaret N. Purnell.

The writing dated August 14, 1959, typed on stationery bearing the printed inscription 'Last Will and Testament,' reads, so far as is material, as follows:

> WHEREAS, I MARIE ELIZABETH PURNELL did on the 22nd day of April, 1952, make my last Will and Testament in writing, and whereas I desire to make an affirmative declaration concerning Mrs. Ida Purnell

O'Shura, I do now make **458 this codicil thereto, to be taken as part thereof.

I wish it to be clearly understood that under no circumstances is the aforesaid Ida Purnell O'Shura to receive anything from my estate. I have been advised that under my Will she will receive nothing, however, being fully acquainted of her vicious trouble-making character, I deem it advisable to make this declaration.

While I lived, she made false accusations against my character and conducted a general course of action which caused me ill health and largely contributed to my illness and death.

The 1953 instrument was admitted to probate by the Clerk of *766 the Circuit Court of the City of Norfolk on November 6, 1959, and the Seaboard Citizens National Bank of Norfolk qualified as administrator c.t.a. ... Thelma Purnell Delly ... contends that the writing of August 14, 1959, is a valid codicil executed with the intention of the decedent to revive her revoked will of April 22, 1952.

A 'will' or a 'testament' is generally defined as an act by which a person makes a disposition of his property after his death according to his own desires and wishes. There is also authority that: 'The word 'testamentary' in this connection may be taken to mean applicable or related to death; having to do with dispositions or arrangements effective upon the happening of that event;' as when the paper writing changes the executor of a will, or adds a co-executor. Lamb, Virginia Probate Practice, 1957, § 33, page 66.

In Coffman v. Coffman, et al., 85 Va. 459, 8 S.E. 672, 2 L.R.A. 848, 17 Am.St.Rep. 69, we held that an instrument, although sufficiently executed to constitute a will, was not entitled to probate where it made no affirmative disposition of the property of the testator, but attempted merely to exclude an heir of the testator from participation in the estate. Nor did a statement therein which purported to explain the exclusion of the heir make it a will.

The word 'will' is construed by statute in Virginia to 'extend to a testament, and to a codicil,' and also to 'any other testamentary disposition.' Code, § 64-47. In Fenton v. Davis, 187 Va. 463, 471, 47 S.E.2d 372, we approved the definition of a 'codicil' as 'an instrument made subsequent to a will and modifying it in some respects - and forming part of it, superseding it so far as inconsistent with it.' In Senger v. Senger, 181 Va. 786, 789, 27 S.E.2d 195, we said: 'The function of a codicil is to add to, supplement or alter the provisions of a will.' *767 'A 'codicil' is a supplement to, or addition to or qualification of, an existing will made by the testator to alter, enlarge, or restrain the provisions of the will.' 94 C.J.S., Wills, § 1, page 678. ... **459 ...

In Poindexter v. Jones, 200 Va. 372, 376, 106 S.E.2d 144, we quoted with approval the following statement from Judge Lamb's book on 'Virginia Probate Practice, 1957,' that: "At any rate it is just as important that *animus testandi* appear – and appear from the face of the paper itself, unaided by evidence *aliunde* – as that the formalities of execution required by the statute of wills be complied with." ... The above requirement and the regulations which apply to the probate of a will extend with like force and effect to the probate of a codicil.

The will of 1952 having been expressly revoked, Code of Virginia, 1950, § 64-59, it could not be revived except in the manner provided by Code, § 64-60. The latter section provides that: 'No will or codicil, or any part thereof, which shall be in any manner revoked, shall, after being revoked, be revived otherwise than by the re-execution thereof, or by a codicil executed in the manner hereinbefore required, and then only to the extent to which an intention to revive the same is shown.' (Emphasis added.)

Tested by the foregoing rules, the writing on August 14, 1959, does not meet the requirements of a will or a codicil. It makes no disposition of decedent's estate. No *animus testandi* is found therein. It does not modify any former will, nor is it inconsistent therewith. It is singularly bare of any expression of an intention to revive the revoked will of 1952. It does not incorporate therein any provisions of that will. The decedent wanted to make sure that Mrs. O'Shura should not, under any circumstances, receive anything from her estate. It was nothing more than a reference to the 1952 will, the decedent's interpretation of that instrument, and her reason for executing *768 the paper writing of 1959. Whether called a codicil or not, it did not make any change in the disposition theretofore made of her property, did not provide for a change of executor, nor supersede any provision of the will referred to.

The writing of August 14, 1959, was not entitled to be admitted to probate. This conclusion makes it unnecessary to further discuss appellant's contention that the 1959 writing, by referring to the will of 1952, operated to revive the will of 1952. Not being entitled to probate, it has no effect whatever on any previous will.

Prior decisions of the Virginia Supreme Court likewise emphasized that a document must contain an affirmative disposition of property, not merely an expression of intent to exclude certain persons, in order to have the testamentary intent required for probate. Thus, in *Boisseau v. Aldridges*, 5 Leigh, 222 (1834), the court denied probate of a written instrument with the heading -- "Memorandum. To prevent Burnett Aldridge and Burwell Aldridge from having any part of my estate that each might claim in right of their wives, without a will made by me" and stating:

> Not having made any will so as to dispose of my property, and two of my sisters marrying contrary to my wish, should I not make one I wish this instrument to prevent either of their husbands from having one cent of my estate,-say the husbands of my two sisters Martha Aldridge and Dorothy Aldridge,-nor either of them to have one cent, unless they should survive their husbands; in that case, I leave them to be paid out of the collection of any of my moneys 500 dollars each. Given under my hand and seal.

In *Coffman v. Coffman*, 85 Va. 459, 8 S.E. 672, 674-75 (1888), the court held that the following document was effective to revoke all prior wills but not effective to alter the distribution of his property dictated by intestacy laws (which would direct part of the estate to the author's son):

> I, Hiram Coffman, of Rockingham county and state of Virginia, do make and ordain this to be my last will and testament; hereby revoking all other wills heretofore by me made. It is my will that my son William H. Coffman be excluded from all of my estate at my death, and have no heirship in the same, he having become the heir to his mother's interest in her father's estate; and I, his guardian, have paid him, and am now about to make a final settlement with him, which will make as much to him, and probably more, than my estate will pay to each of my other legal heirs. In witness of this being my last will and testament, I hereunto set my hand, and annex my seal, this, the 10th day of March, 1877. HIRAM COFFMAN.

A Circuit Court has also held that a document naming an executor but making no provision as to property also cannot be treated as a will. Estate of Potts, 34 Va. Cir. 520 (Richmond) (1975). We will see below, however, that such a document can be effective as a codicil to a pre-existing will and serve to update or revive a prior will.

II.   Validity of a Will

If a document presented for probate as the will of a decedent is found to manifest testamentary intent, and if it is shown or assumed that the decedent was age 18 or older and of sound mind when the document was created, it is necessary to show that the document actually embodies the intentions of the decedent rather than someone else. Anyone could present a document after someone has died and claim that it is the decedent's Last Will and Testament, and people often try to coerce physically or mentally weakened individuals into writing a will in a particular way. To establish the validity of the testamentary document, its proponents must (A) show that the decedent signed it knowing its contents and (B) defeat any challenges alleging that undue influence or fraud on the part of someone other than the decedent caused the decedent to execute the will.

A. Formalities of Execution

To prove that the proffered document reflects the deliberate (rather than impulsive) testamentary intentions of the decedent (rather than someone else), will proponents must show compliance by the decedent with statutorily prescribed formalities of execution.

Subtitle II. Wills and Decedents' Estates
Chapter 4. Wills
Article 1. Requisites and Execution

§ 64.2-403. Execution of wills; requirements.

A. No will shall be valid unless it is in writing and signed by the testator, or by some other person in the testator's presence and by his direction, in such a manner as to make it manifest that the name is intended as a signature.

B. A will wholly in the testator's handwriting is valid without further requirements, provided that the fact that a will is wholly in the testator's handwriting and signed by the testator is proved by at least two disinterested witnesses.

C. A will not wholly in the testator's handwriting is not valid unless the signature of the testator is made, or the will is acknowledged by the testator, in the presence of at least two competent witnesses who are present at the same time and who subscribe the will in the presence of the testator. No [particular] form of attestation of the witnesses shall be necessary.

***

§ 64.2-403 suggests two forms a will can take, with different execution requirements for each: (1) a holographic (wholly in the decedent's handwriting) will and (2) a non-holographic (typed or handwritten by someone other than the decedent) will. The rules for the latter are much more stringent. The distinction between the two, though, has been blurred to some extent by fill-in-the-blank wills, which might be accepted as holographic if the portions that are handwritten themselves manifest testamentary intent.

In addition, Virginia recently adopted what might be called an 'informality forgiveness' statute, authorizing probate of a will despite failure of full compliance with § 64.2-403. Note, though, that except in very limited circumstances signature by the decedent – directly or by supervised proxy – is an absolute requirement.

§ 64.2-404. Writings intended as wills.

A. Although a document, or a writing added upon a document, was not executed in compliance with § 64.2-403, the document or writing shall be treated as if it had been executed in compliance with § 64.2-403 if the proponent of the document or writing establishes by clear and convincing evidence that the decedent intended the document or writing to constitute (i) the decedent's will, (ii) a partial or complete revocation of the will, (iii) an addition to or an alteration of the will, or (iv) a partial or complete revival of his formerly revoked will or of a formerly revoked portion of the will.

B. The remedy granted by this section (i) may not be used to excuse compliance with any requirement for a testator's signature, except in circumstances where two persons mistakenly sign each other's will, or a person signs the self-proving certificate to a will instead of signing the will itself and (ii) is available only in proceedings… filed within one year from the decedent's date of death and in which all interested persons are made parties.

***

As suggested by § 64.2-403, the process for proving that a will complies with requirements for execution differs for the two types of wills, holographic and non-holographic. There are some common elements, however – in particular, that the will be in writing and that there be a signature. The first section below addresses these common elements, and subsequent sections address the particular requirements for a holographic will and for a non-holographic will. Each section below first presents case law applying the requirements as stated in § 64.2-403 and then addresses when § 64.2-404 might excuse non-compliance. As will be seen, even before first enactment of an informality forgiveness statute in 2007, Virginia courts manifested some leniency regarding deviations from the requirements.

1. Common elements – writing and signature

To be probated, a will must be in writing and signed by the testator. Both these requirements connect with the law's aim of ensuring that a document treated as a will was intended by the decedent to be a will (rather than, for example, preliminary notes about disposing of one's property, or a plan for lifetime gifts); reflects the serious, deliberate intentions of a decedent, rather than a whim; and was finished rather than a first draft.

a. No oral wills

Thus, Virginia law does not recognize oral wills. This rule is clear-cut and of long-standing, so rarely needs to be stated by the higher courts in the state. Occasionally, though, would-be beneficiaries argue in the circuit courts that the court should give effect to intentions as to estate disposition that a decedent expressed verbally while alive, without avail. For example, in *Estate of Doughtie*, 70 Va. Cir. 329, 2006 WL 933372, the decedent had struck the name of one of three residuary beneficiaries in her will, because that person had died, and a half dozen people testified consistently that the decedent had stated what her plan was for that third of the residuary. The Circuit Court for the City of Roanoke accepted that testimony as probative of the decedent's actual statements and intentions at the time so expressed, but wasted no time concluding that this was irrelevant, because those intentions were never committed to writing.

b. No unsigned wills

The signature requirement is absolute but how it can be satisfied is less clear-cut, because (a) people come up with all sorts of ways of identifying themselves on a document and (b) some people executing wills put their names in places on the document different from what is normal – that is, at the end of the will and before any attachments. Virginia courts have always been fairly liberal about tolerating variance from the norm in both respects.

i.   What constitutes a signature?

At least since the mid-nineteenth century, a person's mark has been acceptable as a signature. *Rosser v. Franklin*, 47 Va. 1, 11 (1849) ("But whether the signing be by mark or by name only, in order to be a valid signing under the statute, it must, in the language of Judge Allen in Waller v. Waller, 1 Gratt. 454, 481, "be such as upon the face, and from the frame of the instrument, appears to have been intended, to give it authenticity. It must appear that the name so written was regarded as a signature, that the instrument was regarded as complete without further signature: and the paper itself must shew this."). The Virginia Supreme Court reaffirmed this a century later in *Ferguson v. Ferguson*, 187 Va. 581, 47 S.E.2d 346 (1948).

What if a testator is literate, but does not sign his or her full formal name? In *Pilcher v. Pilcher*, 117 Va. 356, 366 (1915), the Supreme Court found that the testator's initials were sufficient to meet the statutory requirements of a signature. Very recently, the Circuit Court for Fairfax County concluded in a letter opinion that "a testamentary document signed with only the first name of the testator meets the requirement of a signature" so long as the document is "signed in such a manner as to make it clear that the name was intended as a signature." *Estate of McKagen*, 90 Va. Cir. 118, 2015 WL 10376068. The court in that case found such intention "evidenced by the use of 'Thanks' prior to signing her name, and the fact that the name is written at the conclusion of the note."

ii.   Does location matter?

A signature is indicative of both testamentary intent and finality. The law assumes everyone knows that a will is a serious, solemn document requiring a signature, so although the presence of signature is not dispositive of testamentary intent (given that there are also many other kinds of documents that people routinely sign), the absence of one altogether strongly suggests that the author of the document either did not view it as a serious and solemn instrument or was not done with it. Signing is also typically the last thing people do with a will; they first sit down and start writing administrative and dispositive provisions as they think through their preferences, and only after they have decided that they are done and the will says exactly what they want it to say do they sign it. Yet Virginia law does not absolutely require that the signature be at the end of the document, and so courts have had to make subjective judgments about whether the testator intended a mark or writing of a name to constitute a will signature.

Supreme Court of Virginia.
Kidd v. Gunter
262 Va. 442, 551 S.E.2d 646 (2001)

KINSER, Justice.

*444 The plaintiffs, Margaret R. Kidd, Bernard G. Ragland, Sr., and Graham K. Ragland, the surviving whole blood siblings of Frances R. Fore (Fore), who died in March 2000, instituted suit in the circuit court, offering for probate as the holographic will of the decedent a handwritten journal prepared by Fore during her lifetime. The named defendants in the suit are the children of Fore's two deceased whole blood siblings, Fore's surviving half blood sibling, and the children of Fore's deceased half blood sibling. ...

The journal at issue is bound and contains many pages, most of which are blank. On the inside cover in a pre-printed box, the decedent wrote her name, "Frances R. Fore," and her address, "6602 Rollingridge Lane [,] Chesterfield, Va 23832." After the pre-printed word "Date," which appears in the box, Fore wrote the words "Started July 1994." On the first few pages of the journal, Fore listed some of her assets and then consecutively numbered the next twelve pages of the journal. On the page numbered 1, Fore wrote: "This journal has been set up to eliminate problems for my family at the time of my death." After then setting out specific funeral and burial instructions, Fore stated: "The next few pages will instruct you as to what happens to a lot of my personal belongings. All my money & other assets should be divided equally among Jimmy, Henry, Margaret, Bernard, & Graham, [Fore's whole blood siblings] if they are living at the time of my death." On the pages numbered 2 through 12, Fore made specific bequests of personal property to various individuals. Nothing appears on page 12 after the bequest listed there. Extraneous information is found on the next two unnumbered pages, which are then followed by many blank pages. Finally, several *445 pages at the end of the journal contain a list of Fore's insurance policies and bonds. ... A witness who qualified as an expert in document examination ... explained that Fore wrote some of the passages in different inks and that she did not write all the pages of the journal offered as her last will and testament at the same time. ... **648 ...

Although Code § 64.1–49 requires that a testator sign a will, the statute does not specify where the signature is to appear in a writing intended as a will. A testator's signature at the conclusion of the instrument may be the best method of executing a will in accordance with Code § 64.1–49, but this Court has repeatedly held that the signature need not appear at the foot or end of the instrument. [citations omitted] "[H]owever, it must appear unequivocally from the face of the writing" that the person's name therein is intended as a signature. Slate v. Titmus, 238 Va. 557, 560, 385 S.E.2d 590, 591 (1989). And, when a testator's name is in the opening clause or at the beginning of the writing, "such insertion of the name [is] 'an equivocal act', and in the absence of any affirmative evidence on the face of the paper, it [is] not manifest that the name was intended as a signature to the paper." McElroy v. Rolston, 184 Va. 77, 82, 34 S.E.2d 241, 243, (1945). In other words, "there must be a concurrence of *446 the *animus testandi* and the *animus signandi*—that is, the intention to make a will and the intention to sign the instrument as and for a will." Hamlet v. Hamlet, 183 Va. 453, 462, 32 S.E.2d 729, 732 (1945).

Although the circuit court found that Fore prepared the journal with testamentary intent, such intent alone is not sufficient to satisfy the signature requirement. This Court held in Meany v. Priddy, 127 Va. 84, 85, 102 S.E. 470, 470 (1920) that

> [no] mere intention or effort to dispose of property by will, however clearly and definitely expressed in writing, is sufficient; such purpose must be executed in the only manner authorized by the statute, that is, the writing itself must be authenticated by the signature of the decedent. It is not sufficient to raise a doubt as to whether his name is intended to authenticate the paper which is propounded as a will, for, to use the explicit language of the statute, it must be signed "in such manner as to make it manifest that the name is intended as his signature," and unless so signed it is not valid.

The plaintiffs... contend that Fore's signature on the inside cover of the journal satisfies the provisions of Code § 64.1–49. ... We do not agree.

In Hall v. Brigstocke, 190 Va. 459, 58 S.E.2d 529 (1950), the document in question, written wholly in the handwriting of the alleged testatrix, began within the phrase: "Roberta Leckie Rittenhouse Written by myself October 13th 1946 My Will[.]" After making specific monetary bequests and including two residuary clauses, one regarding the remainder of her money and the other disposing of any remaining property, the testatrix concluded the writing by stating: "This is My last Will and Testament." This Court concluded that

> *447 [t]he will itself is sufficient to show that the name was manifestly intended as a signature. It shows upon its face the finality of the instrument and the intent of the testatrix to make a will, and ... to sign as required by the statute. It is a complete **649 document which disposes of all of the testatrix's property and contains no blanks or anything that would indicate that it was not her last will and testament.... When the last sentence of the will ... is considered with the first paragraph, it is manifest that she intended her name as a signature to her will.

> Id. at 466–67, 58 S.E.2d at 533.

Similarly, in *Slate*, the writing showed the finality of the instrument and the testator's intent to make a will. The document, entirely in the decedent's handwriting, began: "I, Garland B. Slate, ... do hereby declare this to be my last will and testament." After disposing of his entire estate, Slate then wrote: "Given under my hand this 25th day of October 1986." This Court concluded that Slate, by including this final statement, "adopted his name in the exordium clause as his signature, thereby authenticating all that followed it." 238 Va. at 561, 385 S.E.2d at 592. That final phrase was the "other evidence" on the face of the writing that demonstrated that the signature was for the purpose of ratifying and authenticating the contents of the instrument. ...

Unlike the writings at issue in those cases, Fore's journal does not contain any statement or clause to denote finality to the document, i.e., there is nothing after the specific bequest on page 12 to indicate that Fore had finished her "will" and wished to adopt and authenticate the writing as her complete testamentary act. With regard to the lack of finality, it is also significant that there was undisputed evidence that Fore wrote the passages in different inks and at different times.

In *McElroy*, a case factually similar to the present one, the alleged testatrix included her name at the beginning of the writing, and ended the document with a residuary clause and statement naming a person to settle the estate. Concluding that there was nothing on the face of the instrument to indicate that the testatrix intended her name at the top of the page to be her signature to the will or to denote that she had finished the act of disposing of her property after her death, this Court stated that

> *448 [t]he name of a person at the top of a written instrument, without any reference whatever to it in the body of the instrument, manifests no clearer intention of the signer that it is intended as his signature to the instrument than his name appearing in the opening clause thereof, or elsewhere in its body, without evidence or explanation on the face of the paper showing that such name was signed there for the purpose of ratifying and authenticating its contents. It connects the writer with the paper, but it does not show a finality and completion of testamentary intent.

184 Va. at 83-84, 34 S.E.2d at 243-44.

In the present case, Fore placed her signature in a pre-printed box on the inside cover of the journal. That space is typically used to denote ownership of a journal rather than to ratify and authenticate the contents of the journal. As we said in *McElroy*, insertion of the decedent's name at the beginning of a writing is an "equivocal act." No affirmative evidence on the face of the journal demonstrates that Fore intended her signature in that box to be her signature to the will. Nor, as we said previously, is there evidence that she had completed the testamentary disposition of her property. Therefore, even though Fore clearly had testamentary intent, we conclude that she did not sign her journal "in such manner as to make it manifest" that her name on the inside cover was intended as a signature to the writing. Code § 64.1–49.

It is worthwhile to read the *Slate* decision as well, because it suggests the Justices are either inclined to treat a date as sufficient evidence of finality in the absence of a true signature or influenced by evidence extrinsic to the will, including writing on other documents connected to the will (in Slate, an envelope) and statements the testator supposedly made before dying. Slate also describes the factual scenarios in other prior cases where the Supreme Court effectively excused the absence of a true signature.

Supreme Court of Virginia
Slate v. Titmus
238 Va. 557, 385 S.E.2d 590 (1989)

STEPHENSON, Justice.

In October 1987, Garland B. Slate told his nephew-in-law, Edward B. Titmus, **591 where Titmus could find Slate's will if anything happened to Slate. Slate died on December 25, 1987. Several days later, Titmus found a sealed envelope at the place Slate had described. On the front of the envelope, in Slate's handwriting, was the following:

> Will of Garland B. Slate
> Atten: Edward B. Titmus

Within the envelope was a document, entirely in Slate's handwriting, that reads as follows:

> I, Garland B. Slate, Route 3-Box 456 Petersburg, Va. do hereby declare this to be my last will and testament.*559
>
> > I. I give and devise and bequeath to Edward B. Titmus all of my estate, both real and personal where ever situated.
> >
> > II. I appoint Edward B. Titmus the executor of this my last will and testament, and desire that no security be required of him as such.
>
> Given under my hand this 25th day of October 1986.

… *560 … To meet the statute's requirement, … it must appear unequivocally from the face of the writing that the person who writes his name therein intends it as his signature. Indeed, in Ramsey v. Ramsey, 54 Va. (13 Gratt.) 664, 670 (1857), the first case in which we construed the statute, we said that the statute "recognizes no will as sufficiently signed unless it appears affirmatively from the position of the signature, as at the foot or end, or from some other internal evidence equally convincing, that the testator designed by the use of the signature to authenticate the instrument."

Slate's heirs-at-law primarily rely upon Payne v. Rice, 210 Va. 514, 171 S.E.2d 826 (1970); McElroy v. Rolston, 184 Va. 77, 34 S.E.2d 241 *560 (1945); Hamlet v. Hamlet, 183 Va. 453, 32 S.E.2d 729 (1945); Warwick v. Warwick, 86 Va. 596, 10 S.E. 843 (1890), and *Ramsey* for the proposition that Slate's writing is not a valid will. The writings at issue in each of these cases, however, clearly lacked sufficient internal evidence to manifest that the testator intended his name as his signature. Moreover, most were incomplete and lacked the finality required of a valid will. **592 The writing in the present case… is more akin to those in Hall v. Brigstocke, 190 Va. 459, 58 S.E.2d 529 (1950) and Dinning v. Dinning, 102 Va. 467, 46 S.E. 473 (1904); *Dinning*. In *Hall*, the holograph in question began:

Roberta Leckie Rittenhouse

Written by myself October 13th 1946

My Will

After five pecuniary gifts, two specific bequests, and a residuary clause, the holograph concluded, "This is My last Will and Testament[.]"In upholding the writing as a valid will, we stated that the writing itself showed the finality of the instrument and the testatrix's intent to make a will. 190 Va. at 466, 58 S.E.2d at 533. We noted that the instrument was a complete document, disposing of the entire estate and containing no blanks. Finally, we said that the language of the will clearly showed that the name at the top was intended as testatrix's signature. The last sentence of the will, when considered with the first three lines, showed the manifest *561 intent of the testatrix that her name serve as her signature. Id. at 466-67, 58 S.E.2d at 533.

In *Dinning*, the holograph offered for probate as the will of William Dinning began with language naming an executor and directing payment of debts. After an orderly and complete disposition of testator's property, the will concluded, "I, William Dinning, say this is my last will and testament." In reversing the trial court's denial of probate, we held that the eight words following the signature constituted an "emphatic declaration" that the signature was intended to authenticate all that preceded it. 102 Va. at 470, 46 S.E. at 474. It served as the final consummation of the testator's purpose.

The purported will in the present case is a complete document; it disposes of Slate's entire estate and contains no blanks. The writing itself shows the finality of the instrument and Slate's intention to make a will. Slate's will begins, "I, Garland B. Slate, ... do hereby declare this to be my last will and testament." After disposing of his entire estate, Slate wrote, "Given under my hand this 25th day of October 1986." One definition of "hand" is "[a] person's signature." Black's Law Dictionary 644 (5th ed. 1979). Moreover, the phrase, "under the hand of," means "authenticated by the ... signature of." Webster's Third New International Dictionary 1026 (1981).

From a reading of the instrument as a whole, and paying particular attention to the phrase, "Given under my hand," we conclude that Slate intended his name, as written in the exordium clause, to be his signature to the will. By using the phrase, Slate adopted his name in the exordium clause as his signature, thereby authenticating all that followed it. Indeed, the phrase is just such "internal evidence" as was contemplated in Ramsey and its progeny. ...

LACY, C.J., with whom CARRICO, C.J., joins, dissenting.

There is no question that the author of the writing at issue intended it as his will. It is a complete document, disposing of the author's entire estate and shows the finality of the instrument. The only ingredient needed to transform a writing with these characteristics into a valid will is the name of the author appearing in *562 such a manner "as to make it manifest that the name is intended as a signature." Code § 64.1-49.

We must therefore determine the intent of the author when he wrote his name. The majority gleaned this intent from the authors of dictionaries, rather than from the normal and common understanding more probably used by the author of this writing. Under a plain reading of the document, I can only conclude that the author's name as it appeared in the document, "I, Garland B. Slate, Route 3-Box 456 Petersburg, Va." was used to identify himself as the testator in the declarant clause. Similarly, the closing phrase "Given under **593 my hand", implies that the writer actually wrote the document, a phrase of particular significance in a holographic will. The fact that the phrase may be defined as "authenticated by signature" without more, does not indicate that a person's name written in the preceding lines was that authenticating signature.

Furthermore, I am unable to distinguish this case from the *Warwick* and *Ramsey* cases cited by the majority. The majority has moved from "the manifest intent of the writer" to "under any construction or circumstances", as the test under § 64.1-49 for determining the existence of a signature and, therefore, a valid will. I therefore, must respectfully dissent.

The majority emphasized "Given under my hand," and perhaps it would have found that sufficiently indicative of finality even if there were no date, but it is difficult to imagine the court having reached the same decision if that phrase were followed by blank spaces for the date (i.e., "Given under my hand this ___ day of _____."

Among the precedents the Justices cited but did not describe:

Payne v. Rice (1970) rejected as lacking a signature a three-page document, entirely in the decedent's handwriting, stating:

> Last Will & testament of Clara Ellen Rice
>
> I Clara Ellen Rice residing in Arlington County Va, being of sound mind & body do hereby make this my last will and testament. First I direct all of my just debts and funeral expenses to be paid as soon as possible after my death. There is a saving account in the Old Dominion Bank at Ballston Va for this purpose.
>
> Second my house and 125 foot lot to my niece Alva W. Rice all silver, glassware and furniture in the house unless otherwise listed.
>
> To my beloved niece Adelaide Dove 748 Kern Rd Annandale Va. all my personal belongings, Jewelry and linens.
>
> To Ellen My bloodstone ring and sewing machine (portable) The upright machine belongs to Adelaide Dove.

To my very good friend and cousin Elsie Daniels, my rocking chair and large picture in living room

To my good & faithful friend Helen Hoffman, my set of Honeysuckle pattern China and fix irridescent sherberts.

To my nephew James R Rice I leave 500.00

The remainder of my land 182 feet is to go to my niece & her husband Billie & Bill Weeks.

I want each of my friends Lynda Clark, Mary Lee Feldman & Barbara Elmore to have 500.00

Also my very loyal friend Charles Haskins, I leave the sum of 1000 dollars.

If there is not enough cash left, please reduce these sums in proportion' (quotation marks supplied)

The court explained:

The document itself was still attached to a writing tablet, a fact which denotes a lack of finality. The paper ends without punctuation, which also shows a lack of finality in that it would indicate an incompetent document with something to be added. There was no disposition of the residue of the estate, this being another indication of a lack of finality.The record indicates that the testatrix was a woman of average education. She was possessed of a modest amount of property and had accounts in at least two banks. She had in her possession three will forms which were found in the same box with the holographic paper offered for probate. She had carried on correspondence with at least two of the witnesses who testified. She always signed these letters and cards at the bottom or end, as is the custom. She signed her checks at the end in the customary manner. Here the name of the decedent appears in the caption of the will and again in the exordium clause. The caption identifies the document and the name appearing therein, in the absence of the manifest intent to sign as required by statute, is not a signature. [citation omitted] The exordium clause identifies the person and the name appearing therein, in the absence of the manifest intent to sign as required by statute, is not a signature. [citations omitted]

210 Va. 514, 518, 171 S.E.2d 826, 829 (1970)

McElroy v. Rolston, 184 Va. 77, 83, 34 S.E.2d 241, 243 *560 (1945) rejected as lacking a signature a paper with only the decedent's handwriting on it stating:

June 6 1926 Alice Wright Mt Clinton Va This satment is writen buy my hand and it is as what I wont done with My Estate after my death first of all Dets shall be paid and also ever one that renders enny help in enny way I wont them two be paid And wont a nice Coffen & a good wood

Box and have the Furnel at the house and I wont Paul Paid full wages for all work done that I have not Paid him for. and I wont sister Anna two have $10.00 ten dolors Monney and all of the reste of my Property Two Go Two the Memorel Hospile I name John Rolston for for the Man Two setle my Estate'

The court explained:

> [T]here is not a word or explanation in the paper before us which in any way indicates that Alice Wright intended her name at the top of the page to be her signature to the will or that it was her concluded act in the disposal of her property after her death. Her name so placed is aided by no evidence or explanation on the face of the paper showing that it was used for the purpose of ratifying and authenticating the contents of the instrument, or that it imported a finality of her testamentary intent. Although it is apparent that Alice Wright was an uneducated person, it may be reasonably assumed that she was familiar with the ordinary custom of signing letters at the end, and we can but speculate as to any one of a number of reasons which impelled her to write her name at the top of the page of the writing in question. In such a situation speculation makes for a doubtful conclusion as to her real intention. The doubt thus raised prevents us from reaching the conclusion that it is manifest that her name as written was, under the circumstances mentioned, manifestly intended as her signature.
>
> 184 Va. 77, 84, 34 S.E.2d 241, 244 (1945)

Hamlet v. Hamlet (1945) rejected as lacking a signature a paper, one of three testamentary documents found in an envelope on the outside of which appeared in the decedent's handwriting, on one side "My last Will is enclosed here, written with Pencil, on Nov. 13th — 1941" and on the other side "My Will" written four times. The document in question said:

> Having had my other Wills examined by a Lawyer who stated that they contained some flaws, & at his suggestion & advice I am hereby writing this one in my own handwriting, that is my wish and Will to be carried out, on this Thirteenth (13th) day of November 1941.
>
> I, Dr. Robert, Edward Hamlet, now of Pamplin, Va. being of sound & disposing mind do hereby make, Publish & declare this to be my last Will & Testament, hereby Revoking any other Will, by me at any time made.
>
> [provisions for debts and disposition of property among family and friends]
>
> This Will is in my own handwriting, done by me of Good & Sound mind, on this 13th day of November 1941. I appoint John Hamlet Jr. as Administrator without Bond.

The court explained:

> It is true that we have held that the signature need not appear at the foot or end of the instrument, provided the paper shows on its face that the name placed in the writing was intended as a signature. ... But... it must be signed 'in such manner as to make it manifest that the name is intended as his signature,' and unless so signed it is not valid.' The appellants... stress the fact that the name is in the second and not in the opening paragraph. We are not impressed with this argument. The first paragraph is merely the author's explanation for rewriting his will. The second paragraph, in which the name is inserted, is that usually employed in the commencement of a will, and we have several times held that the placing of the name there does not of itself indicate that it was intended as a signature. It is next said that the insertion of the name in the second paragraph was intended as a signature because the writing consumes the entire second page, leaving insufficient space for a signature. This argument would have been more appropriate if there had been a signature on the back of the second page, or on a third detached page.

> The next to the last sentence of the writing is: 'This Will is in my own handwriting, done by me of Good & Sound mind, on this 13th day of November 1941.' It is argued that the word 'done' means concluded or ended, and denotes a finality to the writing even though there be no signature at the end. In our opinion it is more likely that what the author meant was that the act of reducing his testamentary wishes to writing was 'done' — that is, carried out or performed by him — while he was in 'Good & Sound mind.' In other words, his purpose was to declare his soundness of mind rather than his intent to authenticate or sign the instrument. ...

> Except for the change of his place of residence from Farmville to Pamplin, the language used in the second paragraph, in which the appellants say the name was intended as a signature, is the same as that employed in the opening paragraph of the typewritten will, which Dr. Hamlet knew must be signed and which he in fact did sign at the end. Again, in the opening paragraph he states that his 'other Wills' had been 'examined by a Lawyer who stated that they contained some flaws, & at his suggestion & advice I am hereby writing this one in my own handwriting...' As the trial court, in its written opinion, aptly said: 'Certainly no attorney would advise him to sign a will in that manner. 'Then, too, the fact that he was careful to sign the writings of June 1 and September 4, 1943, although they were in his own handwriting, would indicate that he appreciated the necessity for his signature.

> Furthermore, the writing indicates that the author was a man of business experience, and one who had accumulated considerable real and

personal property. He disposes of his 'farms in Prince Edward County,' his 'two houses & lots on Pine Street' in Farmville, and his 'Real Estate at Pamplin, Va.' He is bound to have known that the instruments by which he acquired these various properties were signed at the end in each instance by the former owner. It is hardly likely that he would have thought that an instrument such as a will, in which he was disposing of all of these properties, should have been executed in a less formal and entirely dissimilar manner.

In our opinion, ... [w]hile the animus testandi (the intention to make a will) is clear, the necessary animus signandi (the intention to sign) the instrument relied on is lacking.

183 Va. 453, 461-64, 32 S.E.2d 729, 732-33 (1945)

Warwick v. Warwick (1890) rejected as unsigned a holographic writing that began 'I, Abraham Warwick, Jr., of the county of Henrico, declare this to be my last will and testament' but otherwise did not contain the decedent's name, yet was found enclosed in an envelope marked in the decedent's handwriting: 'My Will — Abraham Warwick, Jr.' The court deemed the writing of the name at the beginning of the will "an equivocal act." It deemed the signature on the back of the envelope to be not part of the will but rather "extrinsic evidence," which is not admissible to prove or disprove the finality of a testamentary writing; "The finality of the testamentary intent must be ascertained from the face of the paper." 86 Va. 596, 10 S.E. 843, 845.

Finally, *Ramsey v. Ramsey* (1857) rejected a holographic paper that began: 'I, thomas Ramsey of Charlotte, do hereby make my last will and testament in manner and form following:', then directed payment of debts and disposition of the author's estate, and concluded by appointing an executor and stating the intention of 'hereby revoking all other and former wills or testaments by me heretofore made, this sixteenth of July, 1855.' The court found there was nothing in this document to support an inference that the decedent had intended the writing of his name at the outset to be "for the purpose of ratifying and authenticating the contents of the instrument." 54 Va. (13 Gratt.) 664, 670.

Placement of a signature anywhere other than at the end can also cause confusion about which portions of the writing that a document contains should be included in the will. In the following case, there was no real doubt that the decedent had signed her holographic will, but dispute about some writing that followed it.

Fenton v. Davis
187 Va. 463, 47 S.E.2d 372 (1948)

HUDGINS, C.J., delivered the opinion of the court.

This writ of error is to an order probating the following paper writing as the holograph will of Cortelyou H. Warren.

> 1-31-47
>
> To whom it may concern —
>
> Being of sound mind & body —
>
> I will.
>
> All of my personal property and insurance to my mother Corra Lee Warren 9016 Cottage Toll Road
>
> Norfolk Va. —
>
> CORTELYOU H. WARREN
>
> P.S. — Real estate & Government retirement — Insurance I.B.E.W.'

...

Elmer E. Davis qualified as administrator c.t.a. of decedent's estate. Mrs. Norva Fenton, only child of decedent, contended in the lower court and contends here... that the writing after the signature — 'P.S. — Real estate & Government retirement — Insurance I.B.E.W.' — was not authenticated and should not have been admitted to probate as a part of the will.... *466 ...**374

Proponents contend that that part of the writing which appears after the signature of the testator is nothing more than a change, alteration, or interlineation of the instrument which appears above the signature, and therefore it should be considered an integral part of the original will.

In Triplett v. Triplett, 161 Va. 906, 172 S.E. 162, it was held that a holograph will containing erasures and interlineations in the handwriting of the testator made after it was signed and witnessed could not be probated as an attested will, but could be probated as a holograph will if the erasures and alterations were made in the writing of the testator and if his name remained '* * * in such manner as to manifest that it was intended as a signature. The will then becomes re-executed with all the changes as valid and subsisting parts of the new will.'

The rule in Virginia is that '* * * the finality of testamentary intent must be ascertained from the face of *468 the paper, and extrinsic evidence is not admissible either to prove or disprove it.' Hamlet v. Hamlet, 183 Va. 453, 461, 32 S.E.(2d) 729.

The only logical conclusion to be drawn from interlineations and additions in a holorgaph will which are in the handwriting of the testator above the signature is that the testator intended for his original signature to be a re-execution of the will with interlineations and additions included. But when it appears from the face of the will that there is a testamentary disposition of all or part of testator's estate **375 appearing after the signature and nothing more, no logical inference of re-execution or re-authentication can be drawn. ...

The statute in Virginia does not designate the place of signature. ... *469 ... *470 ...**376 In Dinning v. Dinning, 102 Va. 467, 46 S.E. 473, the holograph will concluded with the clause, 'I, William Dinning, say this is my last will and testament.' The signature was at the end of the disposing part of the will but there were additional words after the signature as indicated. It was held that the words after the signature did not destroy the manifest intent appearing on the face of the will, that the name was intended as a signature to it.

The only logical deduction from the principles enumerated in the prior decisions of this court is that the name is not to be considered a signature to a will unless it is apparent on the face of the instrument that it was intended as such, and then the signature is only an authentication as to so much of the writing as it was designed to authenticate. There is nothing apparent on the face of the instrument in this case to indicate that the testator intended to authenticate anything that appeared after his signature.

Proponents contend that the letters 'P.S.' have great significance. It is a matter of common knowledge that P.S. is an abbreviation for 'postscript,' which according to Webster's Dictionary when used as a noun means 'a note or series of notes appended to a completed letter, book, or the like, usually giving an afterthought or additional information.' When used as a verb it means 'to add to.' Changes or additions to a will are usually made by a codicil. The same authority defines *471 'codicil' as 'an instrument made subsequent to a will and modifying it in some respects — and forming a part of it, superseding it so far as inconsistent with it.'

The writing on the instrument appearing after the signature in this case, standing alone, conveys no meaning. If, as contended by proponents, the testator intended to make a testamentary disposition of his real estate, government retirement, insurance I.B.E.W., then testator began a codicil which he did not complete. It is impossible to look at the writing after the signature and determine what disposition, if any, the testator intended to make. If he did intend to make an addition or change in his will, then he attempted to write a codicil which is not properly executed. Code, section 5226 ... [and] 5229 require the same formalities in the execution of a codicil as in the execution of the will itself. The abbreviation 'P.S.' and the writing appearing after the signature indicate, on the face of the instrument offered for probate, that they were written after the signature was made and there is nothing on the face of the paper which makes it manifest that the signature authenticated the words appearing after it. ...

The soundness of the rule in Virginia excluding parol evidence tending to show testamentary intent is apparent from the record in this case. The beneficiary stated in one part of her testimony that after the testator had completed his will and added the P.S. he said to her, 'Mother, this is my will, and if you live longer than I do *472 I want you to have everything I have.' 'He turned and * * * walked out.' In another part of her testimony she said, 'He never got up from the table. He said, 'I am sorry about this, but I will fix this for you Monday right. I will get a regular form and fix this right for you Monday.' 'That is the last words he said about it' The two statements are inconsistent and neither is pertinent to establish the testamentary intent. ...**377 ...

The incomplete sentence appearing on the instrument after the signature does not affect the validity of the disposition of the property named and described in the will above the signature. In other words, if a codicil is not properly executed, it is invalid, but its invalidity does not affect the validity of a will which has been executed in the manner prescribed by statute. 1 Page on Wills, Life Time Ed. 560; Parrott v. Parrott, 270 Ky. 544, 110 S.W.(2d) 272; Wikoff's Appeal, 15 Pa. 281, 53 Am.Dec. 597; Taylor's Estate, 230 Pa. 346, 79 A. 632, 36 L.R.A.(N.S.) 66.

The order of the trial court is modified by eliminating from probate all words appearing on the instrument after the signature. So modified, the order of the trial court is affirmed.

A final question that arises with some frequency is whether every page of a multi-page will must be signed. It is good attorney practice today to have a testator at least initial each page, but people who execute a will without good legal counsel might not think to take steps to ensure all pages are understood to be part of the will.

Supreme Court of Appeals of Virginia
Presbyterian Orphans' Home v. Bowman
165 Va. 484, 182 S.E. 551 (1935)

HOLT, J., delivered the opinion of the court.

*484 A writing which purports to be the last will and testament of Catherine Bowman was offered for probate to the clerk of the Circuit Court of Rockingham County... When this will was executed Catherine Bowman was ninety-two years old, but of sound mind and disposing memory. On or about October 6, 1933, she asked O. L. Burtner, a neighbor and life-long friend, to prepare for her such a paper. This he did, and took his draft to his home where it was copied in longhand by his daughter Helen. It and the attestation clause are wholly in her handwriting, with the exception of the figure '6th,' written *486 into the date line by Mr. Burtner himself. This new draft he took back to Miss Bowman, intending to have it in final form typewritten, but she said it was just what she wanted and insisted that it be executed then and there. She did then, in a manner hereafter noted, sign and her signature was properly witnessed. There is no suggestion of fraud or undue influence. If the subscription by the testatrix of her signature complied with the statute, then this will which embodies her wishes must be received.

It is made up of four sheets of paper, all uniform in texture, finish and appearance. Disposition of the entire estate is made on the first pages of the second and third sheets. Nothing is written upon the first sheet. This is the first paragraph on sheet two:

I, Catherine Bowman of Mt. Clinton, Virginia, being of sound and disposing mind, do hereby make, publish and declare this to be my last will and testament, hereby revoking all wills by me at any time heretofore made.

This residuary clause appears at the end of the first page of sheet three:

Ninth, I give and bequeath to Lynchburg Orphanage all the remainder of my property, both Real and Personal.

Given under my hand this 6th day of October, 1933.

There is room at the bottom of this page for the signature of the testatrix, but not for the certificate of the subscribing witnesses. All of this appears in this form about the middle of the first page of sheet four:

Subscribed by the testator and by us in her presence and in the presence of each other on the above mentioned date.

Catherine Bowman

O. L. Burtner, Witness

Roy L. Frank, Witness

This attestation clause and the words 'witness' is in the handwriting of Helen Burtner.

Burtner then took it with him to his home and kept it until after Miss Bowman's death, when he produced it for probate on November 20th and in the supervisor's room *487 read it to Mark Bowman, a nephew of the testatrix, and to L. W. Swank, his brother-in-law. Mr. Bowman said that the sheets which went to make up the will were not then pasted together and that he remembered this because Mr. Burtner, as he read it to them put one page behind the other until he had finished. Mr. Swank also said that these pages were not pasted together.

When this evidence was introduced Mr. Burtner was recalled and testified as follows:

3Q. Something was also said about the method of this paper's attachment, or the attachment of the several sheets. I will ask you first, whether all of these sheets were together at the time the will was read to Catherine Bowman?

A. They were, and were attached together.

4Q. Do you recall how they were attached together at that time?

A. I think they were attached with a clasp. I don't remember now, but I think I had a clasp on them and they were clasped together when I handed them to the clerk of the court. I remember I saw him leaf them over.

5Q. You say clasp. Do you recall what kind of clasp was used? **553

A. They were clasped at that time - I made the confession a while ago that this was not the will or document that I intended for Miss Bowman to sign. I wanted to have it typewritten; and when she insisted on signing the paper, I took the precaution to paste the will together.

MR. HARRIS: You did it when?

WITNESS: Pasted the leaves together?

6Q. Afterward, after it was signed. Now as I understand you, the paper was attached in some method, you don't recall just how, whether it was a clasp, or pin or how it was at the time she signed it?

A. Absolutely so.

7Q. And after it was done, you, thinking to make it more secure, pasted it together.

A. Pasted it together. I will make this further statement. *488 That this is absolutely the will of this testator, nothing added, or nothing subtracted. I make this statement on my sacred oath.

8Q. Mr. Burtner, you stated that you didn't remember how it was attached. I notice here on this paper, two holes. Do you know anything about when the holes were made in there?

A. It may be I had fastened it with a pin. I am not sure. But I am sure that the papers were fastened together.'

These sheets are now pasted together and in their upper left-hand corner are pin holes, one over the other, which seem to indicate that they were once pinned together. Burtner read the will to Swank and Bowman in the supervisor's office in Harrisonburg on the 20th of November, and said if there was no objection he would then offer it for probate. There was no objection and it was then and there presented to the clerk and accepted.

Bowman and Swank, testifying in the utmost faith, may have been mistaken. As Burtner read each page of the will, it would have been natural for him to fold over each sheet behind the unread pages. On the other hand, Burtner cannot be mistaken in saying that he did paste these sheets together when Catherine Bowman insisted on executing the will in its manuscript form. He has either told the truth or has perjured himself. He has no interest in the result of this litigation. He was long known to the testatrix and was trusted by her. There is every reason to believe that he is a man of good character. Moreover, these sheets are now pasted together. That in all probability would not have been done after the will was left in the custody of the clerk, and so if Swank and Bowman are correct this pasting was done after the paper was read to them and before it was taken to him. We think it fair to conclude that these sheets were in some manner fastened together when Burtner took them to Miss Bowman and that the pasting was done at the time the will was executed. *489

The residuary clause at the bottom of page three makes it plain that we are dealing with a completed will. The certificate of the attesting witnesses is written by the hand that wrote the will and written with the same ink. The writer, Helen Burtner, when she spoke of the above mentioned date, must have had in mind the date which she had written on the preceding sheet, and the testatrix when she wrote her name under this inscription, 'Subscribed by the testator,' must have intended to sign in that capacity. Moreover, 'in attested wills the connection between the testator and instrument is shown by the signing.' Waller v. Waller, 1 Gratt. (42 Va.) 454, 465, 42 Am.Dec. 564. All of this is to be taken in connection with the conclusion which we have reached, namely, that these several sheets at that time were in some manner fastened together.

In the Waller Case it was said: 'The attestation must be annexed or subscribed to a complete instrument, and to which, when so subscribed, no additions can be made.' The will itself must appear to be a complete instrument. This will does present that appearance. Its ninth and last article gives to the Lynchburg Orphanage 'all of the remainder of my property both real and personal' Nothing follows but the signatures and the attestation clause. When it is said that this signature must be attached in such manner that 'no additions can be made,' we have a statement which if literally applied is unworkable. It probably has never occurred to a testator that his signature must be so attached as to prevent the insertion of a line between it and the testimonium.

In Murguiondo v. Nowlan's Ex'r, 115 Va. 160, 78 S.E. 600, the signature was on the margin of a will's last sheet and not at its end. In Forrest v. Turner, 146 Va. 734, 133 S.E. 69, 72, the testator wrote his name on the back of a page on which his will appeared, **554 near the top line and not under anything. In re Morrow's Estate, 204 Pa. 479, 54 Atl. 313, 314, the court said: 'While leaving a blank at the foot of the first page was imprudent, in that it afforded an opportunity for fraudulent practice, it certainly would not of itself invalidate the will.' Note, 17 L.R.A.(N.S.) p. 354. The attestation clause is no part of the will, and so the fact that the testator's signature appears after it is unimportant. All that is necessary is that it must appear on the face of the document that the parties signing did in fact intend to sign in the capacity of testator. This does appear in the attestation clause under which Miss Bowman's name is written.

A will may be written on more than one sheet of paper, and it is good practice to have the testator identify each sheet, but it is not necessary, and it is not necessary that the attesting witnesses sign each sheet or acquaint themselves with the contents of the will. Dearing v. Dearing, 132 Va. 178, 111 S.E. 286 (1922). In Savage v. Bowen, 103 Va. 540, 49 S.E. 668, 671, Judge Harrison said: 'In the matter of executing a will, the statutory requirements must be complied with, but substance must not be sacrificed to form, and the end of the law to the means used for attaining it.'

It is perfectly true that some fraudulent provision might have been inserted above the attestation clause. It is still more certain that it has not been done. Judge Crump in Forrest v. Turner, supra, said: 'We should not seek to defeat the testamentary disposition of his (testator's) property, which a person plainly intended should take effect.' He then quotes with approval this statement of the law from In re Field's Will, 204 N.Y. 448, 97 N.E. 881, 39 L.R.A.(N.S.) 1060, Ann. Cas. 1913C, 842: 'The *491 evil of fraudulent changes in wills is rare, while the evil of defeating wills altogether in the manner suggested is common. Hence we think we have gone far enough, in the direction of rigid construction, and that the doctrine of certain authorities should not be extended, lest in the effort to prevent wrong we do more harm than good.' The patient is not helped by a remedy which carries him off.

Of course it must be manifest that the signature was intended as a signature. ... Testatrix's purpose has been made plain beyond all question. ....

---

2. Holographic wills

To ensure a document proffered as a decedent's will is not fraudulent, the law requires assurance that the document was actually written by or at the request of the decedent and reflects the decedent's intentions, rather than having been forged by someone else. One way to do this is to require witnesses to execution of the will. But the law allows as an alternative means of assurance that the document was handwritten by the decedent, it being very difficult for anyone adequately to imitate another person's handwriting throughout an entire document. § 64.2-403 ostensibly requires that the document be "wholly in the testator's handwriting," but what that means exactly, or whether it should be applied rigidly, has been the subject of much judicial analysis, as discussed below.

Proof that a will is wholly in the handwriting of, and signed by, the decedent is by the means indicated in § 64.2-403(B). Two disinterested witnesses (i.e., people who would not gain financially by the court's probating the will) must affirm that the handwriting and signature on the document are those of the decedent. These could be handwriting experts who match the will with other things known to have been written or signed by the decedent, or they could be family members or friends sufficiently familiar with the decedent's handwriting and signature. Dispute about whether handwriting on a document was that of the decedent is rare, but will proponents need to think through how they are going to prove that any other documents used for comparison were written by the decedent or that their witnesses could recognize the decedent's handwriting.

Supreme Court of Virginia
Bowers v. Huddleston
241 Va. 83, 399 S.E.2d 811 (1991)

RUSSELL, Justice.

... **812 ... Anne S. Brody, a resident of the City of Hampton, died on May 3, 1989. In December 1983, she had mailed to Frank C. Bowers, Jr., an attorney in Carmel, New York, (the proponent) a handwritten letter which reads as follows:

Dec 1, 1983

Dear Frank Bowers, Jr.

Attorney and Counseler [sic] at Law

I want you & my Sister Helen Huddleston of 705 Modesto *85 Street
Santa Cruz Ca. 95060 to be my Legal Heirs

God Bless you both.

Yours Truly Mrs Anna Brody

... The proponent presented the testimony of Terrence Martin, an attorney practicing in Newport News, who had represented Mrs. Brody in her last years. Mr. Martin testified that he had several documents in his file upon which to base a familiarity with Mrs. Brody's handwriting and that the purported will appeared to be in her handwriting. Mr. Martin had no interest in the outcome of the case.

The only other disinterested witness to testify with respect to the handwriting of the purported will was Lawrence M. Farmer, an examiner of questioned documents who had been employed as a special agent for the United States Secret Service for 23 years as an expert in the comparison of handwriting. The contestants made no objection to his qualification as an expert witness. Counsel for the proponent had furnished Mr. Farmer with the original purported will and with a series of handwritten letters from Mrs. Brody to the proponent (the exemplars).

The expert's opinion was that the purported will and the exemplars were written by the same hand. He had never met Mrs. Brody and had no personal familiarity with her handwriting. His knowledge of the authenticity of the exemplars was based entirely on the representations made to him by counsel for the proponent. No disinterested witness testified that the exemplars were in Mrs. Brody's handwriting. The proponent testified that he had received the letters in the mail and Mr. Farmer testified that he had received them from counsel and had compared them with the purported will. Although they were marked for identification and are included in the record, they were not received in evidence. *86

...The sole question presented on appeal is whether the proponent's evidence met the statutory requirement. Mr. Martin was a disinterested witness whose testimony tended to prove the fact in issue, but the two beneficiaries named in the purported will failed to meet the statutory criterion. We must focus, therefore, on the expert testimony. In ruling on the motion to strike, the trial court observed: "Mr. Farmer, **813 though he testified that the documents ... seemed to have been written by the same hand, he was not in the position to say whose hand it was." ...

Expert opinion testimony is frequently based on hearsay factual information, and that is no bar to admission of the expert opinion in a civil case. That fact, however, does not "relieve the court from its responsibility, when proper objection is made, to determine whether the factors required to be included in formulating the opinion were actually utilized." Swiney, 237 Va. at 233, 377 S.E.2d at 374. In the circumstances of this case, the expert testimony did nothing to accomplish the statutory requirement of proof, by a second disinterested witness, that the purported will was in the decedent's handwriting.

The proponent argues on brief that "this ruling, if allowed to stand, means that handwriting experts cannot be used to identify holographic wills except in the exceedingly rare case where the expert knew the testator prior to death and had seen him write." We do not share that concern. For example, where two disinterested witnesses, familiar with the testator's handwriting, are not available to identify the handwriting in a holographic will, a disinterested witness might still be able to identify... other documents known by him to be written by the testator. Those documents, introduced in evidence, could be utilized by an expert as exemplars for comparison with the purported will. Although a witness might be incapable of making an expert comparison between two questioned documents, the statute does not require such expertise. The witness might still be able to authenticate exemplars of the testator's handwriting, based upon first-hand knowledge of circumstances tending to prove that they had emanated from the hand of the testator. If such exemplars were then compared to a holographic will by satisfactory expert testimony, the resulting chain of circumstantial proof could, in our view, meet the statutory requirement. Because the expert testimony in the present case lacked such a factual basis, a link in the requisite chain of proof was absent and the chancellor correctly granted the contestants' motion to strike the evidence.

The *Fenton v. Davis* case presented above in the first subsection raised the issue whether non-expert testimony adequately demonstrated that a handwritten note was that of the decedent, and the court's analysis illustrates how dispute over handwriting could play out.

Fenton v. Davis
187 Va. 463, 47 S.E.2d 372 (1948)

*466 Eight witnesses testified as to the handwriting of decedent — five for proponents and three for contestant. Contestant contends that three of the five witnesses, namely, Carra Lee Warren and J. H. Warren, parents of decedent, and J. Carlton Hudson, one of attorneys for proponents, were not disinterested witnesses within the meaning of the statute. It is unnecessary to decide or even discuss **374 this question because the decision of the trial court is supported by the testimony of C. A. Weakley and Jack Dollar, two disinterested witnesses.

C. A. Weakley testified that he was an employee of the Southern Bank of Norfolk and that he was familiar with the handwriting of the testator. When first shown the alleged will he said it was similar but not well written according to the signature on file at his bank. He asked permission to leave the stand and make a further study and comparison of the writing with the acknowledged signature of testator in his possession. His testimony while he was on the stand the second time was neither positive nor convincing. He seemed undecided in his own mind whether or not the paper offered was in the handwriting of the testator; but after leaving the stand the second time he had access to different authenticated papers written by the testator, and, after studying them alone, he asked permission to go back on the witness stand and said:

> 'A. I have given it some more consideration and looked at it further, and I find his writing — it is his writing, only it was written in a different feeling. He was not feeling just right when he was writing it. In other words, He was — well, his spirits were low. In other words, he didn't put full pressure on the paper.
>
> 'Q. Is that paper, the will, in the handwriting of Mr. Warren, or not?
>
> 'A. I would say yes.
>
> 'Q. You haven't had any conversation with either of us since you got off the stand?
>
> 'A. No.'

Jack Dollar testified that he was an electrician and had *467 worked with testator for four or five years; that he had received a number of orders written by the testator; that he was familiar with testator's handwriting and that the paper writing offered for probate was in the handwriting of the testator. He first said that he could not make out the first word on the second line and he was not certain that it was in the handwriting of decedent. Later he was asked by the court:

> 'Q. Is it your opinion that the paper offered as a will is written entirely by Mr. Warren?
>
> 'A. I would say that it was, yes.'

In addition to the testimony of these two witnesses and the three alleged interested witnesses, the trial court compared duly authenticated documents written by decedent with the will. Hence, if we exclude from our consideration the entire testimony of the three alleged interested witnesses, there is ample evidence to sustain the decision of the trial court on the issue that the paper was wholly in the handwriting of the testator and that part which appears above the signature was a holograph will, executed as required by Code...

Most litigation regarding the validity of holographic wills, though, arises from documents containing additional writing that is not the handwriting of the decedent. It is in the nature of holographic will making that testators are on average less attentive to niceties and formalities. A trend toward laxity in this requirement – which could be viewed either as offering a narrow interpretation of what constitutes "the will" (excluding other writing on a page as not being part of the will) or as interpreting "wholly" to mean something like "sufficiently" -- began with cases in which persons penned an expression of testamentary intent on paper with a watermark or letterhead – that is, paper with some typed words that no one could confuse with the text of a will. It seemed silly to reject a clear expression of intent to create a will simply because there were some extraneous words on the same page, words that could in no way be part of a scheme to fabricate a will or deceive a testator. In recent decades, movement in society and the legal system to make it easier for people who cannot afford to hire an attorney to handle their own legal affairs has included sale and acceptance of pre-printed will forms. Those forms are designed to induce people to comply with the requirements for non-holographic wills, with lines for witnesses and a self-proving affidavit, but many people fail to complete those after they have written in by hand substantive provisions about disposition of their property. Many legal disputes have therefore arisen about whether such a document, which contains some typed words that are clearly meant to be part of a will but also some handwriting, can be probated with the attestation of witnesses. Generally, courts will entertain the possibility that such a document could be a holographic will, and simply examine the handwritten portions to see if they manifest the necessary testamentary intent and make a clear disposition of probate property.

More difficult, perhaps, are cases in which the paper on which the decedent's handwriting appears was originally a partial or complete draft of a will. What if a testator or the testator's lawyer initiated the drafting on a typrwriter or computer, but then the testator completed or made changes to it by hand, and the document has the testator's signature but does not have the necessary witness attestation?

Supreme Court of Virginia
Berry v. Trible
271 Va. 289, 626 S.E.2d 440 (2006)

OPINION BY Justice BARBARA MILANO KEENAN.

*293 … This issue arises out of a will contest between a niece and a sister of the decedent, Louise Trible St. Martin (Louise). Tamara Mowbray Berry (Tamara), Louise's niece, claimed that an attested document executed in 1993 (the 1993 will), which ultimately resulted in Tamara being the executor and sole beneficiary of Louise's estate, was Louise's last will and testament. Louise's sister, Esther Maddox Trible (Esther), asserted that Louise had executed a holographic will in 1997 leaving her entire estate to Esther. The alleged holographic will began with a handwritten phrase, "I Give and bequeath all," which appeared near the top of one page of a seven-page typewritten draft of a will drawn by Louise's attorney (the 1997 document). This phrase purportedly was connected by an arrow to the handwritten notation "Esther Maddox Trible" near the middle of the same page and signed "Louise Trible St. Martin" at the bottom of that page. Esther argued that the combined words, "I Give and bequeath all [arrow] Esther Maddox **442 Trible [signed] Louise Trible St. Martin," was Louise's last will and testament.

Louise died in March 2002. A few months later, Tamara submitted the 1993 will for probate in the circuit court. Esther, in turn, filed a bill of complaint to establish a lost will, presenting a facsimile copy of the single page of the 1997 document described above. This copy has been reproduced and is appended to this opinion. … *294 …

[I]n her 1993 will, Louise left her entire estate to her husband, Robert Louis St. Martin (Robert), and if he predeceased her, to Tamara. Robert died in June 1997. For many years, Louise had enjoyed a close relationship with Tamara that began during Tamara's childhood. After Robert's death, Tamara visited Louise often, helping her care for her pets and delivering groceries and medications to her.

Tamara grew worried about Louise's health and became concerned about her behavior, which Tamara considered "erratic." Louise and Tamara had several bitter arguments concerning Louise's ability to care for herself, which caused their personal relationship to deteriorate. Louise later confronted Tamara and told her to stop involving herself in Louise's affairs.

In September 1997, Louise became ill and was admitted to a hospital. While in the hospital, Louise telephoned her lawyer, Mildred F. Slater, who had prepared Louise's 1993 will. Louise informed Slater that Robert had passed away and asked Slater to draft a new will. According to Slater, Louise stated that she wanted to leave her entire estate to Esther and, if Esther predeceased Louise, to have her estate divided among all Louise's nieces and nephews. Slater also testified that Louise said she wanted Tamara stricken from the will. Slater prepared the requested document and sent a facsimile copy of the typewritten draft will to Louise's attending nurse at the hospital.

A few weeks later, Louise's nurse sent Slater a facsimile copy of the typewritten draft that had been altered to include several handwritten changes and additions on each page. The facsimile copy Slater received was missing a page from Slater's original draft. Additionally, section headings were renumbered and pages were rearranged.

The handwritten portions of the document were in both printed and cursive form. The handwritten entries included stricken portions *295 of typewritten text, additions, and arrows apparently connecting some of the handwritten notations to parts of the typewritten draft. Louise's living nieces and nephews, including Tamara, also were listed in the handwritten entries. Additionally, the portion of the document naming Slater as Louise's executor was struck, and Esther's name was handwritten in its place. Further, at the bottom of each page appeared the signature, "Louise Trible St. Martin."

The greatest number of handwritten changes in the reorganized document appeared on page seven, which originally was the second page of the typewritten draft prepared by Slater.

At the top of that page were the handwritten words, "Article # Two." Printed beneath and to the right of that notation was the phrase "I Give and bequeath all." Under the "d" in the word "and" was the tip of an arrow. The tail of **443 the arrow was about an inch lower and ended both next to the handwritten words "Esther Maddox Trible" and immediately above the first letter of the typed phrase that began "my property, real and personal, tangible and intangible ...."

There were other handwritten changes made to this page of the document. A provision leaving tangible personal property to Irene Trible, the former wife of one of

Louise's nephews, was struck. The handwritten phrase "want everything sold at auction" was written next to a typed sentence of the draft describing the disposition of Louise's estate should Esther predecease Louise. Addresses of nieces and nephews were written in the margins and connected to typed portions of the document by numerous arrows.

Because Slater had difficulty reading the handwritten entries on the document transmitted to her, she contacted Louise by telephone and also wrote her a letter asking for her assistance in making the corrections so that the will could be redrafted and executed. Louise refused to allow Slater to make any changes to the document during their conversation and did not respond to Slater's letter. Slater had no further contact with Louise

Louise's relationship with Tamara deteriorated further after Louise was released from the hospital. In September 1999, Tamara accepted a job transfer and moved with her family to North Carolina. Tamara and Louise stayed in occasional contact but never saw each other again.

After Louise's death, some friends and family members, including Esther and Tamara, went to Louise's home to help clean the house, which was in complete disarray. Despite a thorough search of *296 the home, they did not find either the 1993 will or the 1997 document.

Because a will could not be located, Esther asked Marshall National Bank to serve as the administrator of Louise's estate. The Bank qualified as administrator and sent a trust officer to Louise's home to search for evidence of Louise's assets. While examining boxes containing Louise's papers, the trust officer found an envelope containing the original 1993 will. Although the original 1997 document was not found, Esther eventually obtained the facsimile copy from Slater, who had retained it among her records. ... *297 **444 ...

Tamara argues that the handwritten phrase, "I Give and bequeath all [arrow] Esther Maddox Trible [signed] Louise Trible St. Martin," proffered by Esther as Louise's last will and testament, does not meet the requirements for a valid holographic will. Tamara asserts that these handwritten notations cannot be fully understood without considering the typewritten text and the other substantive handwritten entries appearing on the draft.

Tamara also observes that Louise signed each page of the 1997 document, not just the page on which the proffered handwriting appears, indicating that she intended the contents of the entire document to be her will. Thus, Tamara maintains that the face of the 1997 document shows that Louise was merely attempting to edit a typewritten draft, which could not qualify as a valid will because it was not wholly in Louise's handwriting and was not attested. ...

A holographic will must be made wholly in the testator's handwriting, and two disinterested witnesses must identify the handwriting as that of the testator. The testator must sign the will or have someone in her presence sign the instrument at her direction. The signed name must appear on the face of the document in a manner showing that the name is intended as a signature.

These statutory requirements are not intended to limit the power of a testator but to protect the testator's exercise of that power. In establishing *298 these requirements, the statute is designed to prevent mistakes, imposition, fraud, and deception. However, the safeguards of the statute are not designed to make the execution of wills a trap for the testator. Therefore, we give the statute "a sound and fair construction" with uniform insistence on "substantial compliance" with the statutory requirements.

A holographic will, like any will, must manifest the testator's intent of making a last and final disposition of her property. This testamentary intent need not be expressed in formal language in the will, provided that the face of the instrument establishes such intent.

In requiring that a holographic will be "wholly in the handwriting of the testator," the General Assembly did not contemplate that the word "wholly" should be applied in its absolute sense. We illustrated this point in *Bell [v. Timmins]* when considering a proffered will that was wholly in the testator's handwriting except for certain changes in spelling, punctuation, and phrasing that did not affect the content of the document and were made with the consent of the testator. 190 Va. at 652, 58 S.E.2d at 57. We confirmed the will's validity, holding that alterations to a handwritten will that do not affect the substance of the will, and have no impact on the will's testamentary intent, do not invalidate a testator's **445 holograph. Id. at 662-64, 58 S.E.2d at 62-63. In contrast to the facts in *Bell*, we are presented here with a proffered holographic writing containing only a portion of the testator's handwritten entries, which were made on the face of a typewritten document.

In resolving whether this selected handwritten phrase and notation constitute a valid will, we find that our decision in *Moon [v. Norvell]* is particularly instructive. There, the testator wrote a holographic will on the reverse side of a typewritten will that had been superseded by another duly attested will. The testator struck through all the printed material in the body of the superseded typewritten will except for an article dealing with payment of funeral expenses and debts. 184 Va. at 846-47, 36 S.E.2d at 633-34. On the reverse side of this former will, the testator wrote in her own hand another will. *299

We held that the presence of typewritten material on paper used to draft a holographic instrument does not destroy the effect of the holographic instrument as a will, provided that the typewritten material is not part of the handwritten instrument and is not referenced directly or indirectly in the handwritten instrument. Id. at 850-51, 36 S.E.2d at 635. We confirmed the holographic entries as the testator's last will and disregarded the typewritten material on the other side of the document in its entirety. We noted that in the holographic entries, the testator disposed of her entire estate and named the parties and the amount of property she wanted each to receive. We held that her writing left no uncertainty concerning her "dispositive intentions." Id. at 849, 36 S.E.2d at 635. In further support of our holding, we observed that the handwritten manuscript was not interwoven with the typewritten language and did not directly follow the typewriting, but appeared on the reverse side of the typewritten document. Id. at 851, 36 S.E.2d at 635-36. We also noted that the content of the handwritten instrument did not suggest that it was a continuation of any portion of the typewritten document. Id. at 852, 36 S.E.2d at 636.

In two other decisions, we confirmed the validity of holographic instruments that consisted of only a few words followed by a signature. In *Grimes v. Crouch*, 175 Va. 126, 129, 7 S.E.2d 115, 116 (1940), the deceased wrote in his own hand, "Ever thing left to sister for life times." His signature appeared immediately below this text. In *Gooch v. Gooch*, 134 Va. 21, 29, 113 S.E. 873, 876 (1922), we confirmed a decree admitting to probate a codicil written in the deceased's handwriting and signed by him directly below the following handwritten words: "My will is made in favor of my wife, Loulie M. Gooch ...." This handwritten entry appeared on a printed will form provided by the decedent's fraternal organization. Id. at 25-27, 113 S.E. at 874-75. Although these handwritten entries in *Grimes* and *Gooch* were very brief, they constituted all the handwriting of the testator that appeared on the documents under review. Further, the handwritten *300 language was self-contained and could be understood without reference to the typewritten text. Thus, our holdings that these holographic entries were valid instruments in and of themselves did not result from the exclusion of any other handwritten entries made by the testator.

We also have confirmed the validity of a holographic will written on the reverse side of a hardware store receipt. In that case, Bailey v. Kerns, 246 Va. 158, 160-63, 431 S.E.2d 312, 313-15 (1993), the printed material on the receipt was not a factor in our analysis of the proffered will because the content of the receipt bore no relationship to the handwritten entries, which we considered in their entirety. **446

Two fundamental principles characterize our holdings regarding the holographic wills approved in the above decisions. First, in each of those decisions, we considered all the holographic entries made by the testator, rather than only selected portions of those writings advanced by the will's proponent. Second, as exemplified by our analysis in *Moon*, we were not required to consider the printed material on those documents as part of the will because the handwritten entries were "not interwoven with the typewriting," and did not continue from the typewriting in physical form, by reference, or in sequence of thought. 184 Va. at 851-52, 36 S.E.2d at 635-36.

These distinctions are critical to our analysis of the present case. Here, Esther asks us to disregard many of Louise's substantive handwritten entries that are plainly related to the typewritten text. At the top of the page on which the proffered holograph appears, Louise wrote "Article # Two," thereby suggesting that both the handwritten and typewritten material below were part of a larger document. On that same page, Louise connected to the typewritten text, by lines and arrows, other handwriting supplementing the substantive typewritten provisions for contingent beneficiaries, as well as a direction that she "want[ed] everything sold at auction."

We also observe that the three portions of text that form the proffered holographic will are selected from three separate locations on the one page. Louise's signature, however, appears at the bottom of that page, which contains other substantive portions of handwritten and typewritten text. Thus, we perceive no basis for concluding that Louise intended that her signature on this page apply only to the isolated phrase propounded by Esther.

Esther also asks us to disregard the five other pages of typewritten text that Louise returned to Mildred Slater. We are unable *301 to do so, however, because Louise signed the bottom of each page and made substantive changes to the typewritten text on several of those pages. Louise's signature at the bottom of each page also leaves unresolved whether she intended that her signatures validate all the typed and handwritten material appearing above each signature, or whether she intended that the signatures merely verify her changes to the document that she contemplated her attorney would redraft. In addition, Louise's signature at the end of the document, which appears immediately after a typewritten reference to a will "consisting of seven (7) typewritten pages," is not consistent with Esther's contention that the proffered holograph alone was Louise's last will.

Acceptance of Esther's argument would require us to discard the two principles discussed above that have guided so many of our decisions on holographic wills. We are unwilling to do so and, instead, take this opportunity to reaffirm those basic principles.

We hold that a holographic will may only be established upon consideration of all handwritten entries made by the testator on a document, not upon consideration of only portions of those handwritten entries selected by the will's proponent. We articulate this principle because a contrary conclusion would allow a proponent to select only those portions of handwriting favorable to her position, effectively permitting the proponent to rewrite the will. We further hold that a purported holographic will is invalid if the handwritten entries are interwoven with or joined to the typewritten material on the document, or continue from the typewritten material in physical form, by reference, or in sequence of thought.

Applying these principles, we conclude that the proffered holographic will fails as a matter of law because Louise's handwritten language considered as a whole is not self-contained such that it can be understood without reference to the typewritten text. Rather, that handwritten language is interwoven with the text, both physically and in sequence of thought, throughout the document.

Our conclusion is not altered by Esther's contention that the entries she did not proffer as part of the will may be disregarded as mere "surplusage." The "surplusage" **447 theory generally is limited to the striking of typewritten material, when the remaining portion of an instrument that is handwritten has meaning standing alone. See In re Estate of Teubert, 171 W.Va. 226, 298 S.E.2d 456, 459-60 (1982); see also 2 Page on the Law of Wills (rev.2003) § 20.5 at 279-80 ("the surplusage *302 test [requires that] the non-holographic material [be] stricken and the remainder of the instrument admitted to probate if the remaining provisions made sense standing alone"). Here, however, Esther mistakenly asks that we apply this theory to numerous handwritten, as well as typewritten, entries. Moreover, we are unable to apply the theory to disregard the typewritten entries that Esther seeks to exclude from consideration because, in the absence of the typewritten text, Louise's handwritten entries are either ambiguous or fragmented and unintelligible.

Accordingly, we consider the entire document that Louise returned to Mildred Slater and conclude that the document was not a valid will because it was neither wholly in Louise's handwriting nor duly attested by two competent witnesses. See Code § 64.1-49. We therefore hold that the circuit court erred in confirming the jury verdict that the selected portions of Louise's handwritten entries were a valid will. ...

For these reasons, we will... enter final judgment for Tamara admitting the 1993 will to probate.

In the 1950 *Bell v. Timmins* case to which the court referred in *Berry v. Trible*, the Supreme Court noted a couple of circumstances additional to the one it was addressing (minor clarifications inserted by a friend at testator's request) in which the presence of some writing on a will other than the handwriting of the testator should not prevent treatment of the will as a holograph. One example comes from an actual prior case, *Triplett's Ex'r v. Triplett*, 161 Va. 906, 172 S.E. 162 (1934), in which persons other than the testator signed their names as witnesses, though not in a manner that would allow the will to be probated as non-holographic (e.g., because they did not sign in the testator's presence). Another was hypothetical; the court opined in dictum that if a testator wrote a holographic will in a language other than English and then asked a friend to type in a translation above each line, the typed translation would not preclude treatment of the will as a holograph. 190 Va. 648, 656; 58 S.E.2d 55, 59.

Be clear about the effect of this conclusion, though; it is not to probate the entirety of a document containing writing other than the testator's handwriting but rather to probate only the portions of the document that were actually handwritten by the testator, while ignoring the rest (e.g., typed words on a pre-printed form, clarifying editing by someone else, translation, etc.).

Some circuit court applications of the handwriting requirement: In *Estate of Brown*, 85 Va. Cir. 235, 2012 WL 9737561, the Circuit Court for the City of Roanoke denied probate of an unwitnessed document that was entirely typed except for the decedent's signature, rejecting an argument that the typed content should be treated the same as handwriting because, according to witnesses, the decedent typed everything that she wanted to write. In *Klundt v. Klundt*, 77 Va. Cir. 162, 2009 WL 7326366, the Circuit Court for Fairfax County applied the holding of *Gooch v. Gooch*, 134 Va. 21, 29, 113 S.E. 873, 876 (1922), treating handwriting on a pre-printed will form as a holographic will, after finding that "nothing typewritten is included in the relevant paragraph" and "the typewritten portion is not referenced directly or indirectly by the handwritten paragraph."

§ 64.1–49.1, the informality forgiveness statute passed in 2007, reinforces these precedents allowing courts to simply ignore writing on a non-attested will that is typed or penned by someone other than the decedent. In *Schilling v. Schilling*, 280 Va. 146, 149-50, 695 S.E.2d 181 (2010), the Supreme Court held that § 64.1–49.1 applies to the estate of anyone dying after its enactment, even if the document proffered as a will was created before the statute was enacted, based on these principles:

> "A will is an ambulatory instrument, not intended or allowed to take effect until the death of the maker.... While he lives his written will has no life or force, and is not operative or effective for any purpose." Timberlake v. State–Planters Bank of Commerce & Trusts, 201 Va. 950, 957, 115 S.E.2d 39, 44 (1960). "The death of the maker for the first time establishes the character of the instrument." Spinks v. Rice, 187 Va. 730, 740, 47 S.E.2d 424, 429 (1948) (quotation marks omitted). Thus, a determination whether a writing offered for probate is a valid will applies the law in effect on the date of the maker's death. In this case, this is not a retroactive application of Code § 64.1–49.1.

The circuit court in *Schilling* had wrongly held that § 64.1–49.1 applies only to wills executed after its effective date, so the Supreme Court remanded for reconsideration of a purported holographic will in which a mother left her entire estate to her son, where the son had himself written in the address and the words "I bequeath to" in this brief writing "LAST WILL AND TESTAMENT OF ORA LEE SCHILLING, 40 PACIFIC HAMPTON VA. All this to be my last will and testament. Money in my Bank accoun[t]s and a Condo at 40 Pacific Dr., Hampton, VA and all of my Belongings, I bequeath to my son David Von Schilling." Unfortunately, no reported decision emanated from the remand proceedings.

3. Non-holographic wills

Wills not "wholly" in the testator's handwriting must be witnessed. § 64.2-403 prescribes a very particular way in which this should be done. Specifically:

- ✓ The testator must sign, or acknowledge his or her signature on, the will "in the presence of at least two competent witnesses"
- ✓ The witnesses must be "present at the same time"
- ✓ The witnesses must "subscribe the will in the presence of the testator."

All three of the particularities listed above has given rise to considerable litigation, because testators (and even some lawyers!) are not aware of them and because it is sometimes difficult to get a group of people all to stay put in one place for the length of time it takes to execute a will, especially in a busy professional office. They are all, however, also good candidates for application of recently-enacted § 64.2-404's rule of lenity. Long before the legislature adopted that rule, however, the Virginia Supreme Court interpreted the formalities generously to ensure form did not prevail over substance, as becomes evident from the cases below.

a. Testator signature

Section 1) presented cases concerning what constitutes a signature, for either a holographic or a non-holographic will. Also part of the signature requirement for non-holographic wills is that it have occurred in the presence of two competent witnesses.

At common law, beneficiaries of the proffered will were deemed not competent to act as witnesses to the will, because not disinterested, but the legislature abolished that requirement in the mid-nineteenth century. The Code today contains this provision:

Subtitle II, Chapter 4. Wills
SuperBrowse Article 1. Requisites and Execution

§ 64.2-405. Interested persons as competent witnesses.

No person is incompetent to testify for or against a will solely by reason of any interest he possesses in the will or the estate of the testator.

***

Also not required is that the witnesses be familiar with the contents of the will. Redford v. Booker, 185 S.E. 879, 166 Va. 561 (1936). What they attest is simply that they saw the testator sign the document or acknowledge having previously signed the document.

U.S. jurisdictions have divided in interpreting "presence," as between the view that a line of sight is a necessary and sufficient condition and the "conscious presence" view. On the latter, witnesses might be present even if there is a wall or other obstruction between them and the testator when the testator signs or acknowledges. On at least one occasion, the Virginia Supreme Court was presented with the unusual situation where the witnesses were physically present but the testator seemed not "conscious" of them. The court in Chappell v. Trent, 90 Va. 849, 19 S.E. 314, 344 (1893), reasoned:

> It is true that the two subscribing witnesses, with Dr. Nelson and Mr. Chappell, were present together at the deathbed scene, when the paper in question was executed; that the subscribing witnesses attested the paper right in front of him, and, as they say, Mr. Chappell was looking straight at them. But it is equally true that, when they were called in to attest the paper, Mr. Chappell did not even extend to them the ordinary greeting, when he had not seen one of them (Terrell) for some two days. Mr.

Chappell uttered not even a word to them, nor they to him. He did not request them to attest his will, nor did either of them ask him if he desired them to do so. They simply stood by and acquiesced in the pantomimic display being conducted by Dr. Nelson. This was not presence, in the true sense. The word "presence," so used in the statute, means "conscious presence." Baldwin v. Baldwin's Ex'r, 81 Va. 405; Tucker v. Sandidge, 85 Va. 546, 8 S. E. 650. They were present, and alive to what was going on, but how was it with Mr. Chappell? He was there, a dying man, and still breathing and living; but, in the light of all that transpired at the execution of this pretended will, he was no longer possessed of the essential elements of intelligent consciousness, without which there could be no valid will.

b. Witness signing

§ 64.2-403 explicitly disavows prescribing a particular form of attestation – that is, specific words the witnesses must write or affirm. Courts will treat a signature alone, with no other words, as a sufficient "subscription" if in context it appears intended as an attestation of witnessing the will execution. However, the Supreme Court has allowed for extrinsic evidence to prove that persons said to have witnessed a will did not in fact do so despite the presence of their signatures on the document offered for probate. A 1918 decision, Albert v. Stafford, 123 Va. 338 (1918) denied probate to a will with two signatures additional to that of the testator, with this brief explanation:

John R. Stafford wrote the paper as and for the will of Jennie A. Stafford, who was 84 years old, and … called in J. E. Stafford and J. T. Durham to witness it. The paper was folded up so as to conceal any writing which may have been on it, and the subscribing witnesses were asked to sign their names to the paper thus folded. J. E. Stafford, one of the subscribing witnesses, objected to signing it, because he did not know what he was signing; but John R. Stafford assured the subscribing witnesses that there was nothing in it that would hurt them, and because of their confidence in John R. Stafford, as they say, they signed their names to the paper while so folded. They did not see the name of Jennie A. Stafford on the paper, if it was on there; they did not know whether her signature was on it or not, and did not know whether Jennie A. Stafford knew what they were signing; that she was there, but said nothing, and did nothing; that she did not ask them to witness her signature, or to witness her will, and did not sign the paper in their presence, nor acknowledge that she had signed it, or that it was her will; and there is an entire lack of testimony from which it can be inferred that she ever signed it, or that she knew that these witnesses were attesting her signature. That the circuit court erred in admitting the paper to probate is manifest, because the proponents have failed to show that Jennie A. Stafford either signed or acknowledged its execution in the presence of the subscribing witnesses.

In the absence of such evidence raising a suspicion of foul play, the Supreme Court has been inclined to find the witness-signature requirement satisfied even in doubtful circumstances.

Supreme Court of Virginia.
Robinson v. Ward
239 Va. 36, 387 S.E.2d 735 (1990)

COMPTON, Justice.

… Prior to her death, Joane G. Tannehill, who was not married, resided in Staunton and on her 75–acre farm *39 near Deerfield, where she grew and sold Christmas trees. Appellee Katherine D. Ward, a close friend of Tannehill, moved to the farm several days before the events in question to assist her in the operation of the business. **737

During the morning of May 18, 1986, Tannehill, 52 years of age and apparently in good health, became ill with "a violent headache." Shortly, Tannehill directed Ward to obtain "a legal pad." Tannehill stated: "Write exactly what I say, and do not interrupt me." As Tannehill dictated, Ward wrote by hand with a pencil on a page of the pad. The writing follows, complete with spelling and other errors:

> To Katherine D. Ward I leave everything I own for her life time. She is to maintain the farm & provide employment for Penny Guin for as long as Penny cares to stay.

> I would hope that Katherine can maintain the farm & herself with the income from the farm & interest on my principal. At her death, the principal that is left is to be used as an endowment as maintaing this farm, which I wish to go to Covington Boys Home. The farm is to used by them as a teaching facility. If they do not wish to use it that way than the entire request is to go to VPI to be used in the same manner.

After Ward "finished writing the will," Tannehill "read it over, signed her name, dated it [May 18, 1986]," and "handed it back" to Ward. She placed the document on a table in Tannehill's bedroom, where the events in question occurred.

After trying unsuccessfully to reach several local physicians, Ward was directed by Tannehill to call a friend, Colonel George A. Knudson, a retired Marine and a member of the local rescue squad. Upon arrival, Knudson took Tannehill's blood pressure, which "was rather high." Tannehill then told Knudson that she had dictated her will to Ward and asked him to "please read it and witness it—which he did." Present in the room at the time were Tannehill, Ward, and Knudson. The following appears on the lower left portion of the document:

> Witness
>
> George A. Knudson
>
> May 18, 1986

*40 The will again was placed on the bedside table.

Tannehill took some medication and "a short time after that, she kind of cried out, her body jerked, she lost control, and she was unconscious." She was rushed to a Staunton hospital and, shortly after noon on May 18, was flown to a Charlottesville hospital where she remained in a coma.

Distraught by the grave condition of her friend, Ward "felt" that she needed "legal advice" to determine what she "should do step-wise for Joane or anything." With the aid of her sister, Ward contacted a Maryland attorney on May 19 who "said that he felt that in Virginia there should be two witnesses—two witness signatures on the will." The attorney suggested that Ward sign "on the bottom" and have Ward's "name witnessed."

On May 19, Ward returned to the farm and signed the document in the presence of Gwin, the farm employee. Ward signed below Knudson's signature and Gwin signed on the lower right portion. Both affixed the date "May 18, 1986" under their signatures. When asked why the date of May 18, instead of May 19, was written, Ward testified that she "was extremely upset" and that she "just picked up what was on the will." She stated, "I wasn't even thinking what day of the month or year it was." She said, "there was no evil intent or anything on my part."

The testatrix died later on May 19 without regaining consciousness. ... In a letter opinion sustaining the validity of the will, the trial court made the following findings.

> In this case there is no question, but that the writing expressed the testamentary intent of Joane G. Tannehill. That is conceded by all parties. The testatrix was a well educated and very intelligent person. At all times she was a strong willed individual and was in full control of her mental faculties. At age 52, she was enjoying good health, and had no reason to expect to die. Her only problem was anxiety caused by the unexpected **738 death of her fiance ten days before. She clearly had the capacity to make a will, and she expressed her testamentary intentions in the document which she dictated. When she completed her dictation, she took it, reviewed it, and then signed and dated it. She clearly recognized the accuracy of the transcription of her dictation and *41 accepted it as the authentic expression of her testamentary intentions. This was done in the presence and with the knowledge of Katherine Ward, a person in whom she placed great trust and confidence.

Accordingly, the court ruled that Ward's name appearing in the first sentence of the document "constitutes a sufficient compliance with prerequisites of the Statute of Wills to permit the document to be admitted to probate." The court said: "Even though the name appearing in the first sentence was not made as a signature, it does link the second witness with the writing and its execution, and it does identify her with it." The court concluded: "The words 'Katherine D. Ward' written by her while not a signature when made were sufficient subscription under the unique facts of this case to constitute satisfactory compliance" with the statute in question.

On appeal to this Court, the contestant argues… that there is "no compliance with the Will statute where the second witness does not subscribe the will as a witness." The contestant says: "When Katherine Ward wrote her name on the first line of the will at the direction of Joane Tannehill, she neither signed nor subscribed the will. When Katherine Ward placed her name on the first line, she merely wrote her name as a beneficiary of the estate." …

The purpose of the statute in requiring subscription of a will by competent witnesses in the presence of the testator is to prevent fraud, deception, mistake, and the substitution of a surreptitious document. These requirements, however, "are not intended to restrain or abridge the power of a testator to dispose of his property. They are intended to guard and protect him in the exercise of that power." *42 French v. Beville, 191 Va. 842, 848, 62 S.E.2d 883, 885 (1951). The safeguards of the statute "are not designed to make the execution of wills a mere trap and pitfall, and their probate a mere game." Bell v. Timmins, 190 Va. 648, 657, 58 S.E.2d 55, 59 (1950).

Accordingly, and while the statute must be strictly followed, it is vital that the provisions not be construed in a manner which would "increase the difficulty of the transaction to such an extent as to practically destroy" the right of the uninformed lay person to dispose of property by will. Savage v. Bowen, 103 Va. 540, 546, 49 S.E. 668, 669–70 (1905). The statute should be given "a sound and fair construction" with rigid insistence "upon substantial compliance with its requirements." Bell, 190 Va. at 657, 58 S.E.2d at 59–60.

The function of the witnesses' subscription "is to establish and prove the genuineness of testator's signature." Ferguson v. Ferguson, 187 Va. 581, 591, 47 S.E.2d 346, 352 (1948). "To attest a signature means to take note mentally that the signature exists as a fact." Id., 47 S.E.2d at 351. Formal attestation is unnecessary and the statute mandates no specific form nor particular place on the document for the witness' signature. Indeed, there is no statutory guidance for what constitutes a sufficient subscription of a will. **739

We agree with the trial court and hold that, under the facts of this case, there was sufficient subscription by Ward to constitute substantial compliance with the statute in question. Most importantly, there is no hint of fraud disclosed by the evidence. Furthermore, there is no dispute that the testatrix had the capacity to make a will and that the document accurately expresses her testamentary intentions. Nevertheless, the contestant seeks to invalidate the will, principally on the ground that Ward, when she wrote her name in the first line of the document, did not "do so with the intention of acting as a witness."

The case of Pollock v. Glassell, 43 Va. (2 Gratt.) 439 (1846), is particularly appropriate here. In that case, an ill testatrix expressed her wishes for disposition of her property to one S.S. Ashton, who recorded the information as the testatrix dictated it. At the foot of the paper, Ashton wrote, "Written by S.S. Ashton for," intending to add the testatrix' name if the latter should be unable to authenticate the paper by her own signature. The testatrix *43 did, in fact, sign her name to the document and Ashton struck the word "for." At the testatrix' request, another person signed the paper as a witness. When the testatrix asked Ashton to sign as a witness, she responded that it was unnecessary for her to sign the paper again because her name was already on it.

Rejecting the argument that the attestation by Ashton was insufficient under the statute (because she intended to act as a scribe when she wrote her name), this Court upheld the validity of the document as a codicil. The Court said that plainly the statutory requirement means "nothing more than that the instrument itself should be attested, in order to identify the witnesses, and designate who are to prove its due execution." Id. at 464. The Court stated: "The subscription of their names by the witnesses denotes that they were present at, and prepared to prove, the due execution of the instrument so attested, and nothing more." Id. Further, the Court noted that Ashton's "subscription alone was a sufficient attestation, and the memorandum ['Written by S.S. Ashton for'] does not disprove it was so intended. At most, it can only call for explanation, and that given by her testimony is completely satisfactory." Id. at 465.

The *Ferguson* decision is also instructive. There, a notary public, who had prepared a will at the testator's request, signed the document as "C.E. Trout, Notary Public," after the testator had affixed his mark to the document in the presence of Trout and at least one other witness. In ruling that Trout was an attesting witness to the will, even though he had signed solely in his capacity as a notary public, this Court said: "Where, as in Virginia, a formal attestation is unnecessary, any form of signing a will with the intention of acting as a witness is sufficient." 187 Va. at 591, 47 S.E.2d at 351. But the Court ruled: "Conceding the general rule to be that a witness must intend to attest the will as a witness, the language of the certificate, the actions and the testimony of Trout all declare that he acted as a witness, no matter how he regarded himself." Id. at 594, 47 S.E.2d at 353.

Likewise, in French v. Beville, supra, one Pitts signed his name to a will for the purpose of certifying as a notary public that another witness had observed the testator's execution of the document. The Court held that Pitts signed as a witness to the will, citing *Pollock* and *Ferguson*, and stated that the witness' attestation "may be contradicted or explained." 191 Va. at 850, 62 S.E.2d at 886. *44

As the proponents contend, the general rule "that a witness must intend to attest the will as a witness," is not applied mechanically. The important fact, as noted in *Ferguson*, is not how the witness regarded himself during execution of the will, but what he observed, because the witness' signature serves mainly to identify to whom the testator acknowledged the instrument. In other words, as the proponents argue, the witness need not realize his status during execution of the will.

Ashton in *Pollock*, Trout in *Ferguson*, and Pitts in *French* did not intend to attest the respective documents when they wrote **740 their names on the instruments upheld in each case. In those cases, as here, each person was declared to be a witness because the transaction was free of fraud, the document expressed the testamentary intent of a competent testator, the witness had written his or her name, and the will was acknowledged before at least two witnesses present together.

Similarly, Ward did not intend to act as a witness when she wrote her name in the first line of the document. Yet, she was a subscribing witness to the execution of the will, within the meaning of the statute. While the testatrix never formally asked Ward to be a witness to the will, the evidence establishes that Tannehill expected her to act as a witness and treated her as one, as the trial court noted. Moreover, Ward's testimony, and the other evidence, establishes that she, in fact, acted as a witness to the preparation and execution of the will and that she was present with Colonel Knudson when the testatrix acknowledged her signature to the document. Under these circumstances, the statute requires no more.

A statement from Sturdivant is apropos here: "Upon the whole, ... there has been a reasonable and substantial, if not a literal, compliance with the requirements of the statute shown in this case, sufficient for all practical purposes, and which in favor of the testamentary right ought to be sustained. To reject the will ... would be ... to sacrifice substance to form, and the ends of justice to the means by which they are to be accomplished." 51 Va. (10 Gratt.) at 89. ...

CARRICO, C.J., with STEPHENSON and WHITING, JJ., dissenting.

*45 Code § 64.1–49 provides that a witness to a will "shall subscribe the will in the presence of the testator, but no form of attestation shall be necessary." What the majority does in this case is to dispense not only with form, which the Code section permits, but also with substance, which, I submit, is impermissible. The substantive element of subscription requires "signing a will with the intention of acting as a witness." Ferguson v. Ferguson, 187 Va. 581, 591, 47 S.E.2d 346, 351 (1948) (emphasis added). Here, there is absolutely nothing in the record to support the proposition that when Katherine D. Ward placed her name on the first line of the will in question, she did so with the intention of acting as a witness. Indeed, the record is conclusive of the proposition that the only reason Ms. Ward wrote her name in the will was to identify herself as a beneficiary. ...

So we see that the Virginia Supreme Court applied the attestation requirement quite loosely for decades before passage of the informality forgiveness statute. The court recognized but treated as inconsequential the problem that the purpose of placing Katherine Ward's name in the first line of the will was clearly not to designate her as a witness. An additional problem the court did not recognize is that Ward likely did not write her name in signature form; she likely printed it, whereas people generally use a personalized cursive form when signing something. Further, what is arguably the greatest problem, which the court also did not recognize, is the temporal one; Ward wrote her name before the testator executed the will by signing herself. The very purpose of witness *sub*-scription (i.e., writing *below*) is to affirm that the person witnessing saw the testator (rather than an imposter) sign that document. Ward could not possibly have been doing that when she wrote her name, because Tannehill had not yet signed the document. The only basis we have for believing that Ward did in fact observe Tannehill sign the document is Ward's oral testimony after Tannehill's death, and if that suffices then the attestation requirement is out the window. The court no doubt gained confidence in the correctness of the outcome from the fact that there was one proper attestation, by Colonel George A. Knudson, but the court did not rest its decision on a holding that one is close enough to two when it comes to witnessing, but rather on the implausible contention that printing one's name in a dispositive provision in a will, before the testator has executed it, is equivalent to signing below the testator's signature after the testator signs and with the intention of confirming having witnessed the execution.

Robinson's holding might seem to be of limited applicability. It was essential to the holding that Ward was the "scrivener" of the will; she could not be treated as a signing witness if she had not herself written her name in the will. But apparently it is not uncommon for testator's to ask a principal beneficiary to transcribe the will and for both to fail to recognize that the scrivener should also sign his or her name at the end of the will if expected to serve as a witness. A subsequent similar decision of the Supreme Court reads *Robinson* as also resting on the facts that Ward was present when the second witness signed, after the testator acknowledged the document as her will, and that the will contestant offered no basis for thinking there had been any fraud.

Supreme Court of Virginia.
Draper v. Pauley
Jan. 10, 1997.

LACY, Justice.

… Irene Draper and her brother lived with their niece Patricia Pauley and her family for a number of years. In March 1995, Draper was a patient at Martha Jefferson Hospital in Charlottesville. On March 1, Pauley, Alice Butler, Darlene Butler, and two children visited Draper at the hospital. During this visit, Draper indicated she wanted to execute a will. Tracy Collier, a hospital employee who was a notary public, was called to Draper's room. When she arrived, Collier wrote **496 the following at the top of each of two blank pieces of paper:

> This is to verify that the signature below is the true signature of Irene Draper.

This statement was followed by Draper's signature and Collier's attestation as notary public. *80

Draper then began to dictate her testamentary disposition of a house she owned. Pauley took the first piece of paper and, below Draper's notarized signature, transcribed Draper's statement that, if anything should happen to her, she wanted Pauley to have the house. When Pauley finished writing, she read the document back to Draper, who stated that the document was exactly as she wanted it. Then Darlene Butler signed the document beside Collier's name.

Draper died on September 4, 1995. ... Draper's two sons, John W. and Charles E. Draper, ... alleg[ed] that the will was not valid. ... *81

Draper's signature on the will in question satisfies the requirements of the statute, notwithstanding the fact that Draper signed it before the document contained the disposition of her property. There is no dispute that the signature is Draper's and that, following the transcription of the statement and its recitation back to her, Draper stated that the document was exactly as she wanted it. Under these circumstances, the signature was "intended as a signature" and the "will acknowledged" by Draper in the presence of "at least two competent witnesses" ...

Likewise, at least two competent witnesses subscribed the will in the presence of the testator. All parties agreed that Darlene Butler's signature satisfied the statutory requirements. Pauley's signature was contained in the body of the document and was made when she was transcribing Draper's instruction that Pauley was to receive the house. The contestants' argument that subscription by a witness to the will in this manner is insufficient was addressed and answered in *Robinson*. ... Writing one's name in the body of the will was held to substantially comply with the statutory requirements for a subscribing witness because the scrivener/witness acted as a witness to the execution of the will by the testator, was present when a second witness subscribed to the will, and the transaction **497 was free of fraud. Id. at 44, 387 S.E.2d at 740.

The facts in *Robinson* and this case are virtually identical, and the holding in *Robinson* is applicable here. There are no suggestions of fraud or duress. Pauley wrote her name in the body of the will, witnessed the execution and preparation of the will by the testator and, in the presence of the testator, witnessed the subscription of the will by the other witness, Butler. Under these circumstances, Pauley, like the witness/scrivener in *Robinson*, was a subscribing witness to Draper's will within the meaning of § 64.1-49. Therefore, the trial court was correct in holding that the will was properly admitted to probate. ...

Supreme Court of Appeals of Virginia.
Savage v. Bowen
103 Va. 540, 49 S.E. 668 (1905)

HARRISON, J.

Ann C. Savage, of Mecklenburg county, departed this life in July, 1883, leaving a will, whereby she devised her tract of land in that county to her grandchildren, who are the appellants here. This will was dated the 7th day of June, 1883, and was in the following words:

In the name of God, Amen. After the Bowen debt becomes due and is settled, then I give to G. L. Savage's children my tract of land on which he, Bowen, has a deed; it contains sixty acres more or less. I want Geog's children to have my land and its benefits: this is my wish and will.

Then follows the signature of the testatrix and those of two attesting witnesses, namely, N. C. Bugg and T. A. Savage. ...

In March, 1902, E. T. Bowen and B. E. Cogbill, administrator of George L. Savage, deceased, who are the appellees here, filed their bill in the circuit court of Mecklenburg county, in which they allege that Ann C. Savage died intestate, leaving surviving her George L. Savage as her only child and heir at law, and that upon her death the tract of land mentioned in the alleged will descended to him as her sole heir at law and next of kin; that after the death of his mother George L. Savage and his wife had sold and conveyed the land to the complainant Bowen by deed with general warranty dated December 4, 1890, and that he is now the owner of the same... The grandchildren of Ann C. Savage, who are the children of George L. Savage, deceased, are made parties defendant... *669 ... George L. Savage, as heir of Ann C. Savage, would have had the right to impeach the will, and no reason is perceived why those claiming under and through him are not entitled to his rights in that respect. ...

T. A. Savage had united with her husband, George L. Savage, in this deed conveying the land in question to Bowen. ... T. A. Savage... was one of the attesting witnesses in the will...

The purpose of the statutory requirements with respect to the execution of wills was to throw every safeguard deemed necessary around a testator while in the performance of this important act, and to prevent the probate of a fraudulent and supposititious will instead of the real one. To effectually accomplish this, the statute must be strictly followed. It is, however, quite as important that these statutory requirements should not be supplemented by the courts with others that might tend to increase the difficulty *670 of the transaction to such an extent as to practically destroy the right of the uninformed layman to dispose of his property by will.

As said by Judge Moncure in the case of Parramore v. Taylor, 11 Grat. 220:

> The law of wills should be plainly written, and no room should be left for doubt or implication. It is a law of almost universal application, and must often be acted on by unlearned persons in a situation which precludes the possibility of obtaining professional aid. The most important family settlements, which are often postponed to the last day or hour of life, may depend upon an observance of its requisitions. How important, then, that it should impose no needless requisition; none that is not productive of some substantial good; and that it should plainly express what it means. ...

A casual glance at the statute shows that there is no peremptory requirement that the will shall be attested at the request of the testator; indeed, the word "request" does not appear in the statute. If ... such request is necessary to the validity of a will, then... how is the fact that the request was made to be evidenced? We are of opinion that it may appear from the facts and circumstances surrounding the transaction, as well as by an express and formal announcement of the invitation.

In the case at bar it appears that T. A. Savage was the daughter-in-law of the testatrix, and that they lived together in the same house; that the will was executed in a small room, 10 by 12 or 14 feet. It further appears that the will was written by T. A. Savage at the earnest request of the testatrix. This witness, who was not asked if she had been requested by the testatrix to witness the will, testifies that when N. C. Bugg, who had been sent for to witness the will, arrived, she handed the will to the testatrix, who raised up in her bed without assistance, and signed the will in the presence of N. C. Bugg and herself; that, after the testatrix had signed the will, Mr. Bugg signed his name as witness, at the bed; and that she then took the will, and went over to the bureau, and signed her name under Mr. Bugg's at the bureau; that the testatrix signed and acknowledged the will in the presence of N. C. Bugg and herself; that N. C. Bugg signed his name thereto in the presence of the testatrix and herself, and that she signed her name thereto in the presence of the testatrix and N. C. Bugg; that the testatrix, from the position occupied by her on the bed, could have seen the witness sign her name to the will at the bureau without changing her position, and simply by looking; that Mr. Bugg, from his position at the bed, could have seen her sign her name by simply turning his head; that the testatrix was in clear and strong mind at the time, mentally as sound as a dollar.

The witness N. C. Bugg says that he was sent for to witness the will; that when he arrived the testatrix said to him: "Napoleon, I want you to witness my will. I want to give what I have to George's children, because I do not think he will take care of it;" that he did not see the testatrix sign the will, but that she acknowledged it as her will to him, in the presence of Mrs. T. A. Savage; that the testatrix raised up in bed, and her mind was clear and all right; that he went around to the foot of the bed and signed the will; that he signed it in the presence of Mrs. T. A. Savage and of the testatrix; that after he had signed it Mrs. T. A. Savage took the paper, and went with it to the bureau; that he could have seen her if he had turned his head and looked, but that he did not see her sign the paper; that the testatrix, from her position on the bed, could have seen Mrs. T. A. Savage sign the paper without change of her position, as the bureau sat in front of the bed. This witness further states that he does not remember anything being said about Mrs. T. A. Savage witnessing the will; that, if anything was said about it, he did not recollect it; that he did not know T. A. Savage was to be a witness; thought that Mr. Gregory was to be the other witness.

It is clear from the evidence that the testatrix knew that two witnesses to the will were necessary, and she and the two whose names are signed to the will were the only persons present at the time of the transaction. From this testimony, if true, the implication is plain that the witness T. A. Savage signed the will at the request of the testatrix, and the jury should have been instructed that, if they believed the same, it constituted all the proof necessary to show that T. A. Savage had been requested by the testatrix to attest the will.

The fourth instruction goes a step further, and tells the jury that it is necessary for them to believe from the evidence that the testatrix had authorized or requested T. A. Savage to subscribe her name to the paper as an attesting witness before she attested the same.

The vice in this instruction, in addition to the inference that an express request was necessary, is the proposition that such request must have been made at some time prior to the act of attesting the will. This position is not tenable. The request might have been made at the time the will was being subscribed as well as before; or the *671 testatrix might have acquiesced in and ratified the act of attestation at the time it was done. In this case the witness T. A. Savage wrote the will at the urgent request of the testatrix, and signed it as a witness in the plain view and conscious presence of the testatrix, without objection on her part; and yet the jury are told that, though they believe these facts, they must find against the validity of the will.

In addition to the general objection pointed out, the sixth instruction is erroneous, because it, in effect, tells the jury that at some time prior to the signing each of the witnesses must have known that the other was to be an attesting witness, and each must also have known that the other had been requested to act in that capacity. This instruction imposes unnecessary requirements, not called for or suggested by the statute, which would be likely to defeat the probate of many otherwise valid wills. The witness T. A. Savage, who wrote the will, may have been asked to attest it before N. C. Bugg came to the house...

As said by Judge Moncure in Parramore v. Taylor, supra: "Nothing is more common or natural than for a scrivener to subscribe a will as a witness before his fellow witness is called in to join him in the attestation; or for a witness called on to attest a will, after doing so, to turn his back, and walk off, without noticing what is done by others afterwards."

In the matter of executing a will the statutory requirements must be complied with, but substance must not be sacrificed to form, and the end of the law to the means used for attaining it. For these reasons the ... the verdict of the jury [must be] set aside, and the cause remanded for a new trial of the issue... in accordance with the views herein expressed.

The process of probating a non-holographic will historically entailed obtaining the testimony or affidavit of the persons who signed as witnesses, affirming that the signatures on the document belong to them and, to the extent they can recall, their having witnessed the testator sign the will. Even today, however, despite tools on the internet for searching for people, it can be quite difficult to track down witnesses, especially if the testator chose employees of a bank or other business rather than family and friends, and even more so if those people had common names. Moreover, testators sometimes outlive their witnesses. What is to be done in such a case?

A circuit court decision in 1992 pulled together several authorities that speak to the question:

> The court starts with a presumption of the will's validity. "It has long been the rule in Virginia that courts lean strongly in favor of upholding the validity of wills fairly made, where there is no imputation of fraud." Martin v. Coleman, 234 Va. 509, 513, 362 S.E.2d 732, 735 (1987). Under normal circumstances, the burden of proof is on a will's proponent to show, by a preponderance of the evidence, that the writing offered was executed as required by statute. See Wilroy v. Halbleib, 214 Va. 442, 447, 201 S.E.2d 598, 602 (1974). However, wills offered for probate long after the death of the testator offer peculiar evidentiary problems. "If the witnesses to the will are dead, or if there is failure of recollection on their part, the court will often presume (the will being in other respects regular) that the requirements of the statute have been complied with in the formal execution of the instrument." Young v. Barner, 68 Va. 402, 405, 27 Gratt. 96, 106 (1876).
>
> In re Prob. of Will of Chadick, 28 Va. Cir. 403 (1992)

The legislature has also acted to address such situations, and more generally to facilitate probate of wills in the most efficient manner. Virginia Code today contains provisions allowing for an additional formality carried out at the time of will execution to substitute for, and obviate, later testimony or affidavit by the will's witnesses. Standard estate practice today entail including a "self-proving affidavit" in the initial will-execution ceremony.

§ 64.2-452. How will may be made self-proved; affidavits of witnesses.

A will, at the time of its execution or at any subsequent date, may be made self-proved by the acknowledgment thereof by the testator and the affidavits of the attesting witnesses, each made before an officer authorized to administer oaths under the laws of the Commonwealth or the laws of the state where acknowledgment occurred..., and evidenced by the officer's certificate, attached or annexed to the will. The officer's certificate shall be substantially as follows in form and content:

STATE OF VIRGINIA

COUNTY/CITY OF _____

Before me, the undersigned authority, on this day personally appeared _____, _____, and _____, known to me to be the testator and the witnesses, respectively, whose names are signed to the attached or foregoing instrument and, all of these persons being by me first duly sworn, _____, the testator, declared to me and to the witnesses in my presence that said instrument is his last will and testament and that he had willingly signed or directed another to sign the same for him, and executed it in the presence of said witnesses as his free and voluntary act for the purposes therein expressed; that said witnesses stated before me that the foregoing will was executed and acknowledged by the testator as his last will and testament in the presence of said witnesses who, in his presence and at his request, and in the presence of each other, did subscribe their names thereto as attesting witnesses on the day of the date of said will, and that the testator, at the time of the execution of said will, was over the age of eighteen years and of sound and disposing mind and memory.

_____
Testator

_____
Witness

_____
Witness

Subscribed, sworn and acknowledged before me by_____,
the testator, and subscribed and sworn before me by_____
and _____, witnesses, this _____ day of
_____, A.D., _____.

SIGNED _____

_____
(OFFICIAL CAPACITY OF OFFICER)

The affidavits of any such witnesses taken as provided by this section, whenever made, shall be accepted by the court as if it had been taken *ore tenus* before such court, notwithstanding that the officer did not attach or affix his official seal thereto. Any codicil that is self-proved under the provisions of this section that, by its terms, expressly confirms, ratifies, and republishes a will except as altered by the codicil shall have the effect of self-proving the will whether or not the will was so executed originally.

***

Another provision, § 64.2-453, is identical except for allowing an acknowledgement rather than affidavit by the witnesses. Self-proving affidavits, when executed properly, can spare executors, courts, and others significant time and expense. Unfortunately, adding another step also creates the possibility for more mix-ups.

Supreme Court of Virginia.
Hampton Roads Seventh-Day Adventist Church v. Stevens
275 Va. 205, 657 S.E.2d 80 (2008)

OPINION BY Chief Justice LEROY R. HASSELL, SR.

*207 ... Cora Lee Watson executed a will on March 12, 1996. After she died, the Hampton Roads Seventh–Day Adventist Church, a beneficiary identified in the will, requested that the clerk of the Circuit Court of the City of Hampton admit the will to probate pursuant to Code § 64.1–77. The clerk entered an order denying the request to probate the will because "[t]he purported will [was not] properly witnessed; to wit: where signatures of the witnesses should be, the names of the witnesses are printed."
...

Matthew Watson was the sole residuary beneficiary under the will, but the Church was the beneficiary of several specific bequests and legacies under the will including the testatrix' home and substantial bank accounts. ...

The testatrix signed a non-holographic document, entitled "Last Will and Testament of Cora Lee Watson," which consisted of five pages that were numbered one through five and included a self-proving affidavit on pages four and five of the will.

On page three of the will, the following paragraph appears that includes the testatrix' signature: *208

> IN WITNESS WHEREOF, I have hereunto set my hand and seal to this, my Last Will and Testament, consisting of five pages, this 12 day of March, 1996.
>
> Cora L. Watson (Seal)

The will contained designated spaces for witnesses to affix their signatures immediately below the above-referenced paragraph. A notary public, who was present when the testatrix signed the will, printed the names of the three witnesses in the designated spaces on page three of the will. The notary placed the address of each witness on page three of the will beside each witness' printed name, and each witness affixed his or her initials beside his or her address. The record does not reflect that the witnesses requested or directed the notary to print their names on the will.

The following paragraph appears on page 4 of the will:

> Before me, the undersigned authority, on this day, personally appeared Cora Lee Watson, Testator, Herbert N. Charles, Sr., Patricia A. Charles, and Thomas N. Boggess, known to me to be the Testator and the witnesses, whose names are signed to the attached or foregoing instrument and, all of these persons being by me first duly sworn, the Testator declared to me and to **82 the witnesses in my presence that said instrument is Testator's Last Will and Testament and that Testator had willingly signed and executed it in the presence of said witnesses as Testator's free and voluntary act for the purposes therein expressed; that said witnesses stated before me that the foregoing Will was executed and acknowledged by the Testator as Testator's Last Will and

Testament in the presence of said witnesses who, in Testator's presence and at Testator's request, and in the presence of each other, did subscribe their names thereto as attesting witnesses on the day of the date of said Will, and that the Testator, at the time of the execution of said Will, was over the age of 18 years and of sound and disposing mind and memory.

Cora L. Watson

Testator

Herbert N. Charles, Sr.

Witness *209

Patricia A. Charles

Witness

Thomas N. Boggess

Witness

The testatrix and each witness, Herbert Charles, Patricia Charles, and Thomas Boggess, signed their names immediately below this paragraph on page four of the will.

Herbert Charles testified that he recognized the will as the Last Will and Testament of Cora Watson and that he was present when she placed her signature on the will. When Mr. Charles placed his signature on page four of the will, which was also the self-proving affidavit, he did so in the testatrix' presence, and he intended to act as a witness when she affixed her signature on the will.

Patricia Charles also testified that she was present when the testatrix signed the will. When Ms. Charles signed her name on page four of the will, she did so in the presence of the testatrix and the other witnesses, and she intended to act as a witness when the testatrix affixed her signature to the will. No attorney was present when the will was executed. The record does not reflect any testimony was received from the third witness, Thomas Boggess. ... *210 ... **83 ...

Code § 64.1–49 requires that the testatrix, Cora Watson, sign and acknowledge the will in the presence of at least two competent witnesses. This requirement was satisfied and is not an issue in this appeal. The litigants disagree, however, whether the will was subscribed by two witnesses in the presence of the testator as also required by Code § 64.1–49. ... *211 ...

Even though the requirements in Code § 64.1–49 must be strictly followed, the statute must not be construed in a manner that would "increase the difficulty of the transaction to such an extent as to practically destroy" an uninformed layperson's right to dispose of property by will.

In French v. Beville, we applied former Code § 64–51, which is the precursor of, and identical to, Code § 64.1–49. We stated: "The literal meaning of the word 'subscribe,' as used in the statute, is 'to write underneath; sub, under; scribere, to write.'" 191 Va. at 850, 62 S.E.2d at 886. Applying these principles to the facts in the present case, we conclude that the testatrix' will was subscribed in a manner prescribed by Code § 64.1–49. As we have already stated, on page three of the will, she specified that her last will and testament consisted of five pages. The testatrix signed her name below the statement that described the number of pages contained in her will. On the next page of her will, page number four, the testatrix signed the self-proving affidavit, which, in this instance, is a part of her will. Herbert Charles and Patricia Charles placed their signatures below the testatrix' signature on that page. The placement of their signatures on page four of the will below the testatrix' signature satisfies the statutory requirement of subscription contained in Code § 64.1–49. Additionally, we note there is absolutely no evidence of fraud in the record before this Court, and the record is clear that the will consisted of five pages, including the self-proving affidavit on pages four and five. ... *212 ... *

> * We recognize Code § 64.1–49.1, which became effective July 1, 2007, states in part:
>
>> Although a document, or a writing added upon a document, was not executed in compliance with § 64.1–49 the document or writing shall be treated as if it had been executed in compliance with § 64.1–49 if the proponent of the document or writing establishes by clear and convincing evidence that the decedent intended the document or writing to constitute (i) the decedent's will....
>
> We do not, and we need not, consider the effect, if any, this statute has upon the legal issues presented in this appeal.

B. Will contests

In addition to alleging that a decedent lacked capacity to execute a will or that non-compliance with formalities calls into question whether the decedent intended to execute a will, persons who stand to gain by invalidating a will commonly argue that someone else wrongfully induced the testator to execute the will or to include certain things in the will by fraud or coercion. The latter form of wrongdoing goes by the name "undue influence" in the law of wills. The Virginia Code does not contain substantive rules for fraud or undue influence in the context of wills. Instead, this is a common law basis for challenging all or part of a will, developed by the courts over nearly two centuries. An undue influence claim is often coupled with an allegation of testator incapacity.

1.   Fraud

A court will invalidate all or part of a will if contestants show that all or part of it resulted from fraud. Ordinarily, the burden lies entirely on the contestants to present evidence of fraud, but in some circumstances a presumption of fraud arises, as the following illustrates.

Supreme Court of Virginia.
Carter v. Williams
246 Va. 53, 431 S.E.2d 297 (1993)

STEPHENSON, Justice.

… In 1974, Mary Alice Thompson executed her last will and testament devising and bequeathing her entire estate to her cousin, Mary Claudia Essig. Thompson had raised Essig as a daughter. Thompson named Essig and Bertha L. Claus, a friend, co-executors.

In 1979, Thompson initially contacted Gerald E. Williams in his capacity as an attorney at law. At that time, Williams rendered professional services to Thompson relating to a real estate settlement. In 1981, Thompson executed a general power of attorney, drafted by Williams and naming him as her attorney-in-fact. *56

Sometime in 1982, Thompson conversed with Williams about making a new will. At the time, Williams read Thompson's 1974 will and took extensive notes of their conversation. Thereafter, Williams drafted and personally typed the will in question. The will provided that Thompson's entire estate, except for a vase, a buffet, and an automobile, would go to Williams' wife, Peggy E. Williams. The will named Williams executor of the estate. A clause in the will stated that Thompson was making no provision for Essig because Thompson had "established a savings account or certificate of deposit" payable to Essig upon Thompson's death. Williams' notes, however, make no mention of any gift to his wife or of any reason why Essig was being excluded as a beneficiary in Thompson's new will. Williams did not send a copy of the draft of the new will to Thompson before its execution. **299

On October 8, 1982, Thompson returned to Williams' office to execute the will. At the time, she suffered from cataracts in both eyes. Williams did not read the will to Thompson, nor did he see Thompson read the will. Williams' brother and an associate in Williams' office witnessed the execution of the will. After the will had been executed, Williams retained the original will and a copy. He did not charge Thompson a fee for preparing the will.

Five of Thompson's intimate friends testified that, to their knowledge, Thompson had had no contact with Peggy Williams prior to the time the 1982 will was executed. During the nearly seven years between the execution of the 1982 will and her death, Thompson told various friends that she was leaving her house to Essig or to her friend, John Alan Cummings. The record does not reveal that Thompson ever told anyone that she was leaving the bulk of her estate to Peggy Williams. ... *57 ... *58 ... **300 ...

Barnes v. Bess, 171 Va. 1, 197 S.E. 403 (1938), is... similar to the present case in that the draftsman of a will was charged with fraud. In that case, the draftsman was a notary public and a substantial beneficiary in the will. The will contained devises and bequests different from those expressed by the testator in a prior will. Other suspicious circumstances were in evidence relating to the physical appearance of the contested document.

In *Barnes*, we stated that direct evidence is not necessary to impeach a will and that circumstantial evidence will suffice if it is strong enough to convince a jury that the writing is not the true last will of the decedent. 171 Va. at 7, 197 S.E. at 405. After noting that "suspicious circumstances place a burden upon the proponents of a will to make a satisfactory explanation," id. at 8, 197 S.E. at 405, we stated the following:

> We have repeatedly subscribed to the principle that where the draftsman
> holds a position of trust or confidence, and is himself made a major
> beneficiary in the will, his participation creates a presumption of fraud.
> The courts view such conduct with disfavor. It is necessary to overcome
> this presumption by evidence which satisfies the jury, and it is for the
> jury to determine whether the burden has been borne. Id.

In the present case, Williams, as Thompson's attorney and attorney-in-fact, held a position of great trust and confidence. Although Williams' wife was made a major beneficiary in Thompson's will, nothing in the record suggests that Thompson and Peggy Williams were related or were close friends at the time the will was executed. Indeed, the record supports the inference that Thompson barely knew Peggy Williams. This is a suspicious circumstance.

Moreover, other suspicious circumstances surround the execution of the will. Although Williams took copious notes of his conference *59 with Thompson, his notes made no mention of the gift to his wife. His notes also failed to address the reason why Essig, whom Thompson had raised as a daughter and who was the sole beneficiary in Thompson's 1974 will, was not a beneficiary in Thompson's new will. Williams did not send a draft copy of the will to Thompson before the will was executed. He did not read the will to her, nor did he see her read the will. After the will was executed, Williams retained the original will and a copy.

We think these circumstances, as well as others in evidence, gave rise to a presumption of fraud that operated to shift to Williams the burden of producing evidence to rebut the presumption. It was for the jury to determine whether this burden had been met. We reach this conclusion even though Williams was not the direct beneficiary in the will. By naming his wife as a beneficiary, Williams became an indirect beneficiary, and that, coupled with the other suspicious circumstances, was sufficient to raise the presumption. ... The ultimate burden of persuasion, however, remains upon the contestants. Martin v. Phillips, 235 Va. 523, 526, 369

S.E.2d 397, 399 (1988). ... **301 ...*60 ... Accordingly, we will ... remand the case for a new trial limited to the issue of fraud.

In the earlier case of Barnes v. Bess (1938), the court upheld a jury finding, approved by the trial court, that a document offered for probate was not the will of the decedent, but rather a product of fraud. In that case, the drafter of the will was a notary, and as in *Carter* had no substantial relationship with the decedent otherwise. Yet the proffered will devised to the notary himself "a valuable piece of real estate, with a two-story building thereon, containing five or six rooms," and the notary offered as explanation only the implausible suggested that the devise was in lieu of his being paid for his will-drafting services. In addition:

> A physical inspection of the typewritten will of 1932, offered for probate, consisting of three pages, shows on its face the following irregularities: (1) The first page is an original and the second and third pages are carbon copies; (2) different pens were apparently used in signing the names, different ink was used, and the fastening on the manuscript cover shows that more than one set of brads had been put therein; (3) between the lines of the paragraph near the bottom of the first page making the devise to Barnes and the short following paragraph there is a difference in spacing; and (4) all of the clauses containing the devises and bequests are numbered except the devise clause immediately following the devise to Barnes. The devise to Barnes is number three. The following devising *7 clause on the first page has no number and the first devising clause on page two is numbered four. Both of the attesting witnesses testified that they thought the will they signed contained only two sheets of paper, and that they signed on the second sheet. One said that each of the pages contained the same character of type, and that there was no mixture of original and carbon sheets. One of these attesting witnesses twice said in reply to questions from the trial judge that he couldn't say that he saw Bess sign the paper. The draftsman and executor was not sure whether he had made original and carbon copies at the time the will was drawn. The evidence points plainly to numerous suspicious circumstances. ... There is here more than vague suspicion and surmise. Direct proof is not necessary to overthrow a will. Any facts and circumstances are sufficient as evidence that will satisfy the jury as reasonable and fair-minded men that the paper writing is not a true last will and testament. *8 ...But suspicious circumstances place a burden upon the proponents of a will to make a satisfactory explanation. If they fail to carry that burden, they should not profit thereby.

171 Va. 1, 6-8, 197 S.E. 403, 405

Both *Carter* and *Barnes* involved "fraud in the execution" – that is, deceiving the testator as to what he was signing. Fraud in the execution almost always results in invalidation of the entire will. Another type of fraud is "fraud in the inducement," which means deceiving the testator as to facts regarding persons, things, or events with the intent to cause the testator to execute a will with content different from what it would be in the absence of the lies. Fraud in the inducement can result in invalidation of only a part of the will, but if the effect of the fraud was a substantial alteration of the testamentary plan, then the court might invalidate the entire will.

What happens if a court invalidates only one provision in a will – for example, a specific bequest to one person that resulted from fraud, such as a lie about the person's deservingness or about the value of the bequeathed property? The following statutory provision applies in that case, as well as in cases in which a court invalidates only part of a will because of undue influence, application of the slayer rule, in cases of lapsing (discussing below), and other situations.

Subtitle II. Wills and Decedents' Estates
Chapter 4. Wills
Article 3. Construction and Effect

§ 64.2-416. Devises and bequests that fail; how to pass

A. Unless a contrary intention appears in the will…:

1. If a devise or bequest other than a residuary devise or bequest fails for any reason, it shall become a part of the residue; and

2. If the residue is devised or bequeathed to two or more persons and the share of one fails for any reason, such share shall pass to the other residuary devisees or legatees in proportion to their interests in the residue.

***

The statute does not address the case of a residuary clause with only one beneficiary that is a result of fraud. It would be unusual for a court to invalidate only a residuary clause, rather than the entire will, because that clause usually governs a substantial portion of the estate. But were a court to do so, the result would be partial intestacy, and the residuary should pass in accordance with the intestacy rules of Chapter Two.

2.   Undue Influence

Supreme Court of Virginia.
Weedon v. Weedon
283 Va. 241, 720 S.E.2d 552 (2012)

OPINION BY Justice CLEO E. POWELL.

**554 *245 ... Dorothy Rose Weedon, the decedent, was the mother of five children: Larry S. Weedon, L. Perry Weedon ("Perry"), Billie Thomas Weedon, Gloria Weedon Sharp and Mary Ann Weedon. In 2000, Dorothy was diagnosed with multiple myeloma. At that time, Mary Ann decided that she would help take care of her mother.

In 2003, Dorothy contacted J. Richmond Low, Jr., an attorney, for assistance in drafting a will, a power of attorney, and an advanced medical directive. Low's assistant, Rosalind Garnett, met with Dorothy and characterized her as a woman who was "very adamant" and "once [Dorothy] told you this is what she wanted, you knew that's what she wanted." When Low met with Dorothy to draft *246 her will, he found her to be a woman of few words who knew what she wanted and got it.[1]

> [1] Low met Mary Ann for the first time when Mary Ann sought assistance to probate her mother's 2008 will.

In the 2003 will, Dorothy made a monetary gift to her church. In addition, she gifted a burial plot to Billie, Perry, Larry and Gloria. Mary Ann, Billie and Larry would receive a gift of real property upon Dorothy's death. In the event that Mary Ann predeceased Dorothy, Mary Ann's gift was to be split between Billie and Perry.

As Dorothy's illness progressed, Mary Ann took on additional responsibilities in caring for her mother and spent more time with her, including taking her mother to her dialysis treatments. By 2006, Mary Ann left her job to be able to devote more time to her mother's care.

On Christmas Eve of 2006, Dorothy had a quarrel with Billie about Dorothy's unwillingness to allow Gloria into her home for Christmas. Mary Ann witnessed this disagreement and Billie blamed her for it. After the incident, Dorothy informed Mary Ann, Larry and Perry that she was taking Billie out of her will.

In May of 2007, Dorothy contacted Garnett to have Low draft a new will for her. In it, she again gave a monetary gift to her church. She also devised real property to Mary Ann, Perry and Larry, but not Billie. This will provided that should Mary Ann predecease her mother, Billie was not to receive any portion of Mary Ann's share. Dorothy also removed Billie as the alternate agent in her advanced medical directive.

On May 20, 2008, Dorothy was admitted to the Medical Center at the University of Virginia ("UVA Hospital") for an unplanned orthopedic surgery. During the next week to ten days, a number of pain medications were prescribed for and administered to Dorothy, and she was confused at times as a result. During her hospitalization, doctors discovered that surgery was required to regulate Dorothy's blood pressure so that she could continue with dialysis. If Dorothy were required to stop dialysis treatments, doctors expected that she would lapse into a coma within 72 hours.

When the doctor told Dorothy the prognosis, she simply stated that she wanted to contact Low. Mary Ann described her mother's mental state at the time as being "fine." Mary Ann suggested that Dorothy wait until after her surgery to contact Low but Dorothy *247 insisted that she wanted to do it then. Paula Capobianco, a social worker in the palliative care unit, told Mary Ann that she should help Dorothy contact Low before her surgery so that she could have her affairs in order and have some measure of peace. **555

On June 19, 2008, Garnett received a telephone call from Mary Ann who told her that Dorothy was going to have surgery and wanted to change her will. Garnett remembered Dorothy as a previous client. Garnett told Mary Ann that Low was out of the office but that she would get back to Mary Ann and Dorothy as soon as she had spoken to Low. When Garnett spoke to Low, he told her to call back and speak directly with Dorothy. Garnett knew this to mean that she was to determine if Dorothy was mentally competent to execute a will.

When Garnett spoke with Dorothy, she recognized Dorothy's voice.[2]

> [2] When asked to describe how Dorothy's voice sounded, Garnett said that it sounded "very fine."

Garnett explained to Dorothy that they would need to go through each provision in her 2007 will even though Dorothy had already told Garnett that she desired to give everything to Mary Ann. In response to each bequest of real property in the 2007 will, Dorothy stated that she wanted Mary Ann to get each item. Garnett did not review the sections that were already making gifts to Mary Ann. Garnett made notes on a copy of the 2007 will as she spoke with Dorothy.

Dorothy asked that the new will be drawn up immediately because she was having surgery soon. Garnett testified that Dorothy's voice sounded "exactly the same" as it did when they spoke in 2007 regarding the modifications to the 2003 will. When asked whether she had any concerns that someone was pressuring Dorothy to make this change, Garnett responded "[a]bsolutely not." Although Garnett did not specifically inquire as to Dorothy's mental capacity, she was confident that Dorothy knew what she was doing and was doing what she wanted. Garnett denied that there was anything in Dorothy's voice that would indicate that she was being threatened to leave everything to Mary Ann.

After this initial phone call, Garnett realized that she had not reviewed the section about the burial plots with Dorothy, so she called her back. Mary Ann answered the phone and Garnett asked her to ask Dorothy what she wanted to do with the plots. Dorothy *248 said that she wanted to keep the plots as planned in the 2007 will but informed Garnett that there were three additional plots. She said that she would like to use one plot herself and would like to leave the remaining two to Mary Ann.

Upon his return to the office, Low drafted a new will using Garnett's notes. Low did not speak with Dorothy or Mary Ann nor did he meet with Dorothy. Based on what Garnett told him, he believed that Dorothy "was of herself, knew what she was doing, and that nobody was going to hold a gun to her head." Low trusted Garnett's judgment of Dorothy's mental state because Garnett had been his assistant since 1993 or 1994. After Low made the changes to the will, Garnett typed it and faxed it to a social worker in Charlottesville.

Mary Ann was present when her mother executed the will in the presence of Capobianco, Vicki Marsh, and Betsy Townsend. Marsh is a patient representative at UVA Hospital. Marsh served as a witness to the execution of the will, but she could not remember who asked her to do so. Marsh did not recall many specifics of this will execution but she knew that they "would not have witnessed ... the document if [Dorothy] was not alert."

Capobianco also witnessed Dorothy execute her 2008 will, but she later testified that she could not testify to Dorothy's mental capacity at that time. Like Marsh, Capobianco did not recall many details from that day. However, she explained that she would have declined to witness the execution of the will had she had any concerns about the proceeding. She testified that Dorothy signed without assistance. Capobianco described Dorothy as alert and stated that she was able to sit up by herself. At no time during the execution of the will did she think that Dorothy appeared confused or disinterested. In fact, Capobianco testified that during her hospital stay, Dorothy was only confused once or twice because of "some trouble I think related to infection." **556

Townsend, a patient representative, served as the notary during the execution of Dorothy's will. In her capacity as a patient representative and notary, Townsend has refused to serve as a notary when "it's either obvious that the patient is not even awake enough to, or capable enough to understand or to talk to or whatever, or if I go up and one of the staff says this person is not competent...." Townsend had no recollection of serving as the notary in this case. *249

The next day, during the surgery, the lower lobe of Dorothy's left lung collapsed. On the morning of Monday, June 23, 2008, Dorothy was "agitated and not doing well." Mary Ann called her siblings. Dorothy died later that day.

In addition to gifts made in her will, Dorothy left a certificate of deposit for Gloria, valued at $5,700, and another certificate of deposit for Mary Ann, valued at approximately $16,000.

Following Dorothy's death, Mary Ann probated the 2008 will and qualified as executor for the 2008 will. Larry, Perry, Billie, and Gloria sued Mary Ann, individually and as executor, to challenge the 2008 will. At the trial, the circuit court allowed Dr. Frederick A. Phillips, the medical examiner for the City of Fredericksburg and surrounding counties, to be qualified... as an expert to give "an opinion as to a person's mental state as it relates to the cause of death." Based solely on a review of Dorothy's medical records, Dr. Phillips opined that during the last week of her life, Dorothy would have been confused with intervals of lucidity. He further testified that "[c]ommunication skills would be I think—I know would be quite limited." He opined that she "would become less responsible for her words, her thoughts, her activities. She would be literally in a chemical fog, if you will." ...

Gloria and Billie believed that their mother was very protective of Mary Ann and Larry said that Dorothy often told him that she had to do things for Mary Ann because "she hasn't got anybody." They all claimed to have a good relationship with their mother. Despite this, Gloria admitted that she had not visited her mother during hospitalizations since 2006 or 2007 because she received an email from Perry or his wife telling her not to visit because it was too upsetting for Dorothy. The children also stated that they helped their mother financially and physically by taking her to appointments and doing work around her home.

With the exception of Gloria, the children described visiting their mother in the hospital. They opined that Dorothy's health was deteriorating during this time. Billie stated that Dorothy did not immediately recognize him when he came to visit. He described a telephone *250 conversation that he overheard her have with Mary Ann on June 16th as "disoriented." He said that on most visits, "you had to extract a response from [Dorothy]." Perry testified that around June 14 or 15, he brought Dorothy her favorite food but she had no interest in eating it. Larry said that on June 15, his mother stopped calling him by the nickname she gave him at birth, and he counts that as the day that she died. He also testified that Dorothy often called him by his brothers' names or referred to his children by the wrong names.

Larry and Perry claimed that Mary Ann attempted to deny them access to their mother and her doctors. Without going into specifics, Perry testified that Dorothy frequently told him things that she did not want Mary Ann to hear.

Nancy Cable testified ... that she knew Dorothy "very well" from 1992 until her death in 2008. ... Nancy also testified that she is "close, personal friends" with Mary Ann. ... **557 ... Nancy saw Dorothy on June 1, 2008 and then again on June 22, 2008. Nancy described Dorothy as being much weaker and thinner than the last time she had seen Dorothy. She also testified that Dorothy had difficulty getting comfortable.

Nancy testified that when she visited Dorothy on June 22, 2008, the day before Dorothy died, Dorothy immediately recognized her and that they began "talking about everything" including Nancy's recent travels. Nancy agreed to Dorothy's request that she spend the night with her. During this time, conversation would stop and then resume. At one point, Dorothy mentioned that she had decided to change her will. Dorothy also mentioned that she had not seen Perry since Nancy had left on June 1. Nancy said that Dorothy told her "very declaratively" that she wanted "Mary Ann [to] have what she had." The two then talked about Nancy's children and her doctors. Nancy brought her food from the cafeteria. During the night of June 22 and the early morning hours of June 23, the chaplain came in several times and the three prayed. Dorothy requested the Lord's Prayer but did not say it. Nancy did not know

whether Dorothy could not or chose not to say it. Dorothy died later that day. ...
*251 ... **558

II. ANALYSIS

A. Testamentary Capacity

... *253 The parties do not appear to question that the will was duly executed. Therefore, the presumption [of testamentary capacity] arises. ... The trial court in this case found that Mary Ann did not meet her burden of proving that Dorothy had testamentary capacity at the time that she executed the contested will. The court largely based this decision on its ruling that Low, the attorney who drafted the will, never met or spoke with Dorothy himself and impermissibly delegated the determination of Dorothy's capacity to his assistant. The basis for this ruling, however, is unsupported by the law. ...

[W]e recently found testamentary capacity based, in part, on testimony from a paralegal who drafted a will. Parish v. Parish, 281 Va. 191, 195, 704 S.E.2d 99, 102 (2011). ... We have never ruled, nor do we here, that the weight ascribed to the testimony of the professional speaking to the testatrix for the purpose of drafting the will is lessened if that person *254 does not actually draft the will. ...**559 ...

We also conclude that the court erred in placing undue weight on the fact that Dorothy did not place the call to Low's office herself. The fact that she did not place the call is clearly outweighed by the fact that she spoke with Garnett and clearly expressed her desires as to how she wanted her will changed.

Finally, we hold that the trial court erred in placing more weight on the testimony of Dr. Phillips and Dorothy's children who were not present when she executed the will than it did on the testimony of the witnesses, the notary, and Mary Ann who were present when the will was executed. "'[I]t is the time of execution of the will that is the critical time for determining testamentary capacity.' '[T]he testimony of those present at the factum—when the will is executed—is entitled to the greatest consideration.'" Parish, 281 Va. at 200, 704 S.E.2d at 104. "'Neither sickness nor impaired intellect is sufficient, standing alone, to render a will invalid.'" Pace v. Richmond, 231 Va. 216, 219, 343 S.E.2d 59, 61 (1986). None of the witnesses testified that Dorothy did anything that caused them concern. ... *255 ...

B. Undue Influence

We have previously held that

> in the will context "a presumption of undue influence arises when three elements are established: (1) the testator was old when his will was established; (2) he named a beneficiary who stood in a relationship of confidence or dependence; and (3) he previously had expressed an intention to make a contrary disposition of his property." Parish, 281 Va. at 202, 704 S.E.2d at 105–06.4

Undue influence must be established by clear and convincing evidence.

The evidence here proves that Mary Ann, who was the sole recipient of all of Dorothy's real property under the contested will, had a close relationship with her elderly mother and spent a great deal of time with her. Mary Ann also had power of attorney for her mother and had acted in that capacity. The evidence also proves that Dorothy had at least two prior wills that expressed contrary dispositions of her property. Thus, the evidence gives rise to the presumption of undue influence, but this does not end the inquiry.

"The undue influence which will vitiate a will must be of such a character as to control the mind and direct the action of the testator." "[I]t must be sufficient to destroy free agency on the part of the **560 ... testator; it must amount to coercion— practically *256 duress. It must be shown to the satisfaction of the court that the party had no free will." "Resistable persuasion, solicitation, advice, suggestions, and importunity do not constitute sufficient evidence of undue influence." "The burden of showing undue influence rests upon those who allege it, and it cannot be based upon bare suggestion, innuendo, or suspicion." Pace, 231 Va. at 224, 343 S.E.2d at 64.

> Not all influence is undue in the legal sense. "To be classed as 'undue,' influence must place the testator in the attitude of saying: 'It is not my will but I must do it.'" To support a jury verdict of undue influence, the evidence must be "sufficient to show that the person executing the will was deprived of his volition to dispose of his property as he wished. There must be manifest irresistible coercion which controls and directs the testator's actions." Wilroy v. Halbleib, 214 Va. 442, 446, 201 S.E.2d 598, 601 (1974).
>
> Gill v. Gill, 219 Va. 1101, 1105–06, 254 S.E.2d 122, 124 (1979).

In Gill, Dr. John Russell Gill married Patricia Wing Gill in 1957, four years after the death of his first wife. "In 1972, he executed a formal will granting [Patricia] a life estate in a trust and the marital residence, with remainder to his grandchildren. [He] died April 30, 1976 leaving a holographic will dated January 22, 1976 bequeathing five dollars to each of his two sons by his first marriage and the residue of his estate in fee to his widow." In that case, the evidence proved that

> gradually over the course of [the] marriage, Mrs. Gill became the dominant spouse, persuading her husband to change his fiscal policies, his religious affiliation, his work routine, his societal views, and his personal habits; that her influence increased as his health declined; that the holographic instrument was not witnessed the day it was dated as Dr. Brown and *257 Markham testified; that, indeed, it was not even written until later at a time when testator was confined to his home, alone with his wife; and that testator wrote and pre-dated the instrument, at his wife's direction, to give the appearance it had been executed in anticipation of surgery.
>
> Id. at 1105, 254 S.E.2d at 124.

Based on this evidence, a jury determined that the January 22, 1976 instrument was not the testator's true last will and testament. On appeal, this Court held "as a matter of law that the evidence was insufficient to support a finding of undue influence" and reversed the circuit court. Id. at 1107, 254 S.E.2d at 125.

"The ultimate burden of proof 'is always upon him who alleges fraud.'" Id. at 1106, 254 S.E.2d at 125. Here, the trial court focused on the circumstantial evidence that raised the presumption of undue influence5 while overlooking the ultimate inquiry: whether Dorothy's will was overridden. Although a presumption of undue influence was established, in the final analysis the evidence falls short of establishing undue influence by clear and convincing evidence. The evidence shows that Dorothy had strained relationships with some of her other children and spent more time with Mary Ann than her other children. Even the other children testified that Dorothy was protective of and concerned about Mary Ann. That Billie and Lewis claimed that Mary Ann blocked their access to Dorothy's doctors is of little consequence as it has nothing to do with whether Dorothy executed **561 the 2008 will against her own wishes. As to her previously executed wills, no one asserts that Mary Ann exerted undue influence over Dorothy when either of those wills *258 were drafted even though the first will specifically omitted Gloria and the second will omitted Gloria and Billie from gifts of real property. Garnett testified that in 2003 and 2007, Dorothy knew what she wanted done and demanded that it be done right away. Importantly, Garnett further testified that Dorothy was no different in 2008 when Dorothy decided to draft a new will in advance of impending surgery that could, if not successful, result in her lapsing into a coma and dying.

Indeed, as previously stated, Garnett testified that Dorothy "knew what she was doing and was doing what she wanted."[7]

> [7] Though relevant to the issue of testamentary capacity, this evidence also has bearing upon undue influence. ... Garnett's testimony similarly reveals that Dorothy, who was "doing what she wanted," was acting of her own volition and not as the result of external influence.

This testimony was in clear contrast to that of the siblings who testified in generalities that they believed that Mary Ann was the reason the will was changed. Perhaps one of the most telling pieces of evidence is the discussion that Dorothy had with Nancy when Mary Ann was not present. On the day before she died, Dorothy volunteered that she had changed her will because she wanted to leave everything to Mary Ann.

Similar to the evidence in *Gill*, testimony that the beneficiary of the contested will in this case asked the siblings not to visit, was the only sibling who was talking to the doctor, and isolated the testator is insufficient to prove undue influence by clear and convincing evidence. Although the evidence in this case certainly proves that Dorothy was very ill, in a great deal of pain, and dying, the contestants did not prove by clear and convincing evidence that Dorothy was in the position of saying "'[i]t is not my will but I must do it.'" Gill, 219 Va. at 1105–06, 254 S.E.2d at 124. Thus, we conclude that the evidence in this case rebuts the presumption of undue influence. ...

Justice MIMS, dissenting.

… Upon review of a trial court's finding of undue influence, this Court asks whether that finding was plainly wrong or without evidence to support it. See Parish v. Parish, 281 Va. 191, 201–02, 704 S.E.2d 99, 105 (2011)… In my view, there is such credible evidence to support the circuit court's finding that Dorothy was the victim of Mary Ann's undue influence. …*260 …

Mary Ann's evidence… predominantly focused upon rebutting the allegation of testamentary incapacity and only touched peripherally upon the question of undue influence. … [I]n both 2003 and 2007 there was a precipitating causal event that angered Dorothy that was not present in 2008. … *261 … The record is replete with additional testimony regarding Mary Ann's unusual and domineering relationship with Dorothy, especially in the final sad weeks of Dorothy's life. Lewis characterized that relationship as Dorothy being afraid of Mary Ann "get[ting] mad" and "throwing a fit on her." Most tellingly, Mary Ann spent approximately 12 hours per day alone with her in the hospital and limited her siblings' access to their mother. In the hospital, Dorothy was confused as to the identities of her children and grandchildren and was curled up in a fetal position much of the day, reluctant to contravene Mary Ann's wishes. **563

Billie testified that during one of his visits to the hospital, he asked Dorothy about an abrasion on her head. Dorothy told him that Mary Ann shoved her up the garage steps at Mary Ann's house, and that she fell into a wall. Billie also testified that Mary Ann used her power of attorney to block her siblings' access to Dorothy's doctors. Lewis testified that Mary Ann threatened to have him "locked up" for visiting his mother in the hospital. He testified that on another occasion, he spoke with his mother on the phone about visiting, but that she called back a few minutes later and, with Mary Ann in the background commanding her to cancel the visit, submitted to Mary Ann's demand.

In light of this evidence, the trial judge reasonably could give less credibility to the testimony of Mary Ann, who at trial was the sole witness regarding what transpired when Dorothy decided to draft a new will. …

In Parish v. Parish, cited in *Weedon* and presented earlier in this chapter in the context of testamentary capacity, in which a young man had been hit in the head with a metal bar and spent the rest of his life under a guardianship, the Supreme Court held that a presumption of undue influence should arise even though the testator was not old and had not previously expressed an intention to do something different from what the will contained. The court explained:

> The factors discussed in Martin [v. Phillips, 235 Va. 523, 369 S.E.2d 397 (1988)] regarding persons of advanced age are equally applicable to other testators who have weakness of mind, whether from injury as in this case or from any other cause. We hold that when a person with such weakness of mind has named a beneficiary with whom the testator stood

in a relationship of confidence or dependence, and when the testator either previously had expressed a contrary intention or previously had expressed no intention regarding the disposition of his property, a presumption of undue influence arises.

Our prior decisions contemplated undue influence in the context of elderly testators, not of young victims of brain injuries. [citations omitted] Such a requirement is too restrictive in this case, since Eugene was 22 years old at the time of his severe brain injury and 41 when he executed his first and only will. Likewise a "contrary expression" regarding disposition of property would be highly unusual at age 22. The record in this case does not demonstrate that Eugene even had significant property until after his brain injury. We therefore hold that the age and contrary disposition requirements discussed in *Martin* are inappropriate in determining whether Eugene was unduly influenced by David Wayne, his conservator, his translator during the drafting of the will, and his major beneficiary who would have taken nothing had the estate passed by intestacy.

281 Va. 191, 202-03; 704 S.E.2d 99, 106 (2011).

The court nevertheless upheld a circuit court decision rejecting the undue influence allegation, which was based on a conclusion that the presumption was overcome by evidence that "notwithstanding the impairments that he suffered, [Eugene] was a stubborn man.... if he did not want to do something, he damn well knew how to resist."

In its Carter v. Williams decision, presented above in the subsection on fraud, the case in which an attorney had drafted a will leaving nearly all a testator's estate to the attorney's wife, whom the testator might never have met, the Supreme Court rejected an undue influence claim. It stated: "There was no direct evidence of undue influence, and the circumstantial evidence was insufficient to raise a presumption of undue influence." Although there was a fiduciary relationship between the main beneficiary's spouse and the testator, and although the testator previously had expressed a contrary intention regarding disposition of her property, "there was no evidence to support the first [requirement for a presumption], i.e., that Thompson was enfeebled in mind." 246 Va. 53, 59 431 S.E.2d 297, 300-301 (1993).

Undue influence claims are typically decided by comparison with precedents, so reading several decisions applying the general rules is worthwhile to get a clearer sense of what sort of facts tend to sway the courts.

Supreme Court of Virginia.
Jarvis v. Tonkin
238 Va. 115, 380 S.E.2d 900 (1989)

RUSSELL, Justice.

*117 ... Ella Myers Wood died in Portsmouth in 1984 at the age of 89. She was the widow of the Reverend John W. Wood, who had died in 1978. No children were born of the marriage, but the Woods were survived by an adopted daughter, Mary Ella Wood Wickers Jarvis (Mary Ella), whom they adopted when she was about five years of age. In addition, the Woods had taken into their home two foster children, sisters who came from Brazil, Julie Pierce (Julie) and Nadir Tonkin (Nadir). Julie came to the Woods' home in 1961 and Nadir arrived in 1968. Julie and Nadir were never adopted. At the time of Mrs. Wood's death, Mary Ella had moved to Richmond. She later moved to Virginia Beach. Julie and Nadir lived in Portsmouth, not far from Mrs. Wood's home.

In 1971, the Woods executed similar reciprocal wills whereby each left all property to the survivor and the survivor left all property to Mary Ella. Soon after Mr. Wood's death in 1978, Mrs. Wood executed a second will which divided her property equally among Mary Ella, Julie, and Nadir. In 1981, Mrs. Wood executed a third will, the subject of this suit, which left $3,000 to each of the foster daughters and left the bulk of her estate to her adopted child, Mary Ella. The foster daughters contest the third will.

The evidence was in substantial conflict with respect to Mrs. Wood's relationships with her three beneficiaries, the frequency and nature of her contacts with them, and their treatment of her and attitudes toward her. In our view, however, the crucial evidence concerns the circumstances surrounding the execution of the 1981 will; accordingly, we focus upon that aspect of the case.

In 1981, Mrs. Wood was in poor physical health but was mentally competent. Indeed, the foster daughters concede her testamentary capacity, the commissioner in **902 chancery so reported to the court, and the chancellor confirmed the report in that respect. As stated above, the sole issue is that of undue influence. In January 1981, Mary Ella became concerned that Mrs. Wood, who was living alone in Portsmouth, was in precarious physical condition and was not receiving adequate medical care. She was suffering from swollen ankles, weakness, and impaired breathing. Mary Ella drove Mrs. Wood to her home in Richmond and placed her in the care of Dr. John M. Daniel, III, a physician whose practice consisted largely of caring for elderly patients. Mary Ella had no *118 prior acquaintance with Dr. Daniel. Dr. Daniel treated Mrs. Wood on five successive office visits and prescribed medication for her. He testified, as did other witnesses, that her condition improved substantially during the period of this treatment.

Dr. Daniel reported that Mrs. Wood was suffering from congestive heart failure, that she was incapacitated, and that she required continuing supervision. As a result, Mary

Ella, on application to the Circuit Court of Henrico County, was appointed guardian of Mrs. Wood's person and property in March 1981.

After revisiting her home in Portsmouth in April, Mrs. Wood returned to Mary Ella's Richmond home in May 1981. When Mrs. Wood expressed a desire to change her will, Mary Ella secured an appointment for her with Lee R. Gordon, a Richmond attorney with whom Mary Ella had no prior acquaintance. Mrs. Wood visited Mr. Gordon's office on two occasions—on the first visit to discuss with him her intended testamentary dispositions, and on the second visit to execute her new will. Mr. Gordon testified that he met Mary Ella when she brought Mrs. Wood to his office, but that he conferred with Mrs. Wood alone on both occasions. On both visits, Mary Ella remained in his waiting room, or left the office and returned later to pick up Mrs. Wood. He said, "She [Mary Ella] was out of the office. The door was shut." Mary Ella's testimony was to the same effect.

Mr. Gordon testified that Mrs. Wood brought the 1978 will with her, explained that she and her husband had intended to divide their estate equally among the three beneficiaries, but that she now "felt different from her husband and wanted to leave the majority of her estate to her daughter." He said that she was specific in stating her wishes, that she knew what she wanted, that her mind was clear, and that she did not appear to be "under the influence of any person." Nevertheless, because Mrs. Wood was changing an earlier disposition to favor one beneficiary over others, and because she was elderly, Mr. Gordon suggested that Mrs. Wood obtain a physician's statement. When she returned to execute the will on May 11, 1981, she brought with her a handwritten note from Dr. Daniel, dated the same day, which stated: "Ms. Ella Wood was seen in my office today & is aware of her circumstances. She understands she plans to change her will and give Mary Ella Wickers power of attorney." Mr. Gordon testified that when Mrs. Wood executed the will, it was "obvious that she was an adult of sound mind and knew what she was doing." *119

Mary Ella testified that her mother never told her what the new will provided, and that Mr. Gordon did not discuss it with her at the time. She said that when her mother emerged from Mr. Gordon's office after executing the new will, he handed it to her in a sealed envelope and Mrs. Wood asked her to keep it. Mary Ella also testified that when she was driving Mrs. Wood home, she asked Mrs. Wood what she wanted to do with the 1978 will. Mrs. Wood, who had the old will with her, said, "'[w]ell, I won't need this anymore,'" and "just tore it in a couple of pieces." Except for the testimony of Dr. Daniel concerning Mrs. Wood's physical and mental condition at the time, Mr. Gordon and Mary Ella were the only witnesses to the circumstances surrounding the execution of the 1981 will.

Mrs. Wood returned to Portsmouth in 1981 and remained there until her death in 1984. After her death, Mary Ella offered the 1981 will for probate in the Circuit Court of Henrico County, but that court ruled that probate was not proper in Henrico County. Julie and Nadir then instituted **903 this proceeding by bill of complaint filed in Portsmouth, seeking to establish a copy of the 1978 will as Mrs. Wood's true last will, the original of which "has been lost or destroyed by accident or design." Mary Ella filed a cross-bill seeking admission of the 1981 will to probate. ... *120 ...

"Undue influence ... is a species of fraud." Thornton v. Thornton's Ex'rs, 141 Va. 232, 240, 126 S.E. 69, 71 (1925). "[I]t cannot be based upon bare suggestion, innuendo, or suspicion." Core v. Core's Adm'rs, 139 Va. 1, 14, 124 S.E. 453, 457 (1924). Before a will may be set aside on the ground of undue influence, that influence "must be sufficient to destroy free agency on the part of the ... testator." Wood v. Wood, 109 Va. 470, 472, 63 S.E. 994, 995 (1909). It must be of such character as to control the testator's mind and actions. It must amount to coercion or duress. Mullins v. Coleman, 175 Va. 235, 239, 7 S.E.2d 877, 878 (1940). A party seeking to raise a presumption of undue influence is required to establish each prerequisite element by clear and convincing evidence. Martin v. Phillips, 235 Va. 523, 528–29, 369 S.E.2d 397, 400 (1988).

A presumption of undue influence may arise in the case of a will where the contestant proves by clear and convincing evidence that "(1) the testator was enfeebled in mind when the will was executed, (2) the requisite confidential or fiduciary relationship was accompanied by activity in procuring or preparing the favorable will, and (3) the testator previously had expressed a contrary intention to dispose of his property." Id. at 528, 369 S.E.2d at 400. ... In the present case, the record is devoid of evidence that Mrs. Wood was "enfeebled in mind" when she executed the 1981 will. The evidence was strongly to the contrary.

The second prerequisite element requires the existence of a "confidential or fiduciary relationship." Such a relationship might arise in the present case from the formal appointment of *121 Mary Ella as Mrs. Wood's guardian, see Waddy v. Grimes, 154 Va. 615, 647–49, 153 S.E. 807, 817 (1930), or from the less formal relationship of parent and child, see Hartman v. Strickler and Wife, 82 Va. 225, 237–38 (1886). Nevertheless, such a "confidential or fiduciary relationship" in the abstract is an **904 insufficient predicate for the creation of a presumption of undue influence. To constitute the second element of the presumption, "the relationship must be accompanied by activity on the part of the dominant person in procuring or preparing the will." Martin, 235 Va. at 528, 369 S.E.2d at 400. In the present case, the only evidence concerning the procuring or preparing of the will was that Mrs. Wood dealt independently with her attorney, that Mary Ella was absent when the will was discussed, formulated, and executed, and that, far from dictating its contents, she had no knowledge of her mother's testamentary intentions.

The chancellor, in evident disagreement with the conclusion drawn from the evidence by the commissioner in chancery, also made a finding that the 1978 will was "fraudulently destroyed by [Mary Ella] in the lifetime of the said testatrix." As noted above, the only evidence on this point was Mary Ella's own testimony which was directly to the contrary. Her testimony was unimpeached, uncontradicted, and not inherently incredible. The chancellor was not at liberty to disregard it. We have repeatedly held that although a trier of fact must determine the weight of the testimony and the credibility of witnesses, it may not arbitrarily disregard uncontradicted evidence of unimpeached witnesses which is not inherently incredible and not inconsistent with facts in the record, even though such witnesses are interested in the outcome of the case. ...

*122 .... Accordingly, we will reverse the decree and enter final judgment here, holding the 1981 will to be the true last will and testament of Ella Myers Wood and ordering it admitted to probate in the court below.

––––––––––––––––––––

In Rudwick v. Lloyd, 69 Va. Cir. 139 (2005), the Circuit Court declined to find undue influence by the testator's daughter, who received a much larger bequest than her brother, on these facts:

> The will was prepared by Theresa Mihalik, a divorce lawyer who had represented Regina Rudwick in her recent divorce proceedings... Ms. Mihalik had advised Regina Rudwick and Nancy Lloyd [daughter] that Ms. Rudwick should have a new will since her old one left everything to her husband... Ms. Mihalik had drafted the will on April 2, 2001, at the request of Ms. Lloyd, who told Ms. Mihalik that her mother wanted to draft a new will that left $50,000 to Lawrence Rudwick and the remainder of the estate to Ms. Lloyd. On April 3, 2001, Ms. Lloyd drove her mother to Ms. Mihalik's office, whereupon Ms. Mihalik showed them into a conference room and allowed Regina Rudwick to read the will on her own. When Ms. Mihalik returned, either Ms. Lloyd or Regina Rudwick told Ms. Mihalik that a change to the will was desired to increase the bequest to Lawrence from $50,000 to $100,000. Ms. Mihalik made the change to the document, gave it to Regina Rudwick to read once more, and then called three members of her staff into the conference room to witness and notarize Regina Rudwick's execution of the will. ...

> [T]here is some evidence that raises concerns regarding Regina Rudwick's mental condition prior to the date of execution... [A]t most, Regina Rudwick was suffering from the early stages of Alzheimer's or mild dementia in the spring of 2001. ... Ms. Mihalik testified that throughout March of 2001, she spoke to both Ms. Lloyd and Regina Rudwick regarding the Property Settlement Agreement with Bernard Rudwick. Ms. Mihalik stated that Regina Rudwick was involved in identifying the relevant assets for purposes of the Agreement, and that she signed the Agreement on March 23, 2001. ... Ms. Mihalik stated that she had no concern about a lack of mental capacity on her client's part when she came in to sign the will.... Ms. Lloyd testified that it was her mother who told her lawyer to increase the amount of the bequest.

... The amount of the bequest was also consistent with Lawrence's requests to his mother and father in January of 2001, when he asked his parents on separate occasions to lend him $100,000. ... [A] manager of the SunTrust bank where Regina Rudwick carried out many of her financial affairs... testified that on April 3, 2001, Regina Rudwick met with her to guarantee her signature on stock transfer documents relating to the Property Settlement Agreement with her husband. Ms. Rivera stated that there was nothing abnormal about Regina Rudwick's behavior on that date, which was the same day as the will execution... [T]he family therapist... testified that she had not noticed any signs of confusion or mental difficulties during their conversations. Much of the testimony indicated that any mental difficulties that Regina Rudwick may have had during this period were relatively mild and intermittent. ...

The court found a confidential relationship, because "[n]ot only did Ms. Lloyd live in the same house as her mother for a number of months during the relevant period in this case, but she was closely involved in Regina Rudwick's medical, legal and financial matters." It found that "Ms. Lloyd was active in the preparation of the will." And it found that an earlier will had a significantly different disposition, dividing the estate equally between son and daughter. However, the court concluded that the testatrix was not "enfeebled in mind" at the time of will execution, noting that a "number of witnesses... established that Regina Rudwick was aware of what was going on around her and that she was not suffering from any debilitating mental condition," and stating that "[e]ven if Regina Rudwick was suffering from a mild mental impairment or the beginning stages of Alzheimer's disease, that alone does not establish that she was 'enfeebled in mind' when she executed her will." Thus, no presumption of undue influence arose. The court further suggested that "[e]ven if such a presumption was established, it was sufficiently rebutted by the witnesses who testified" that they had observed the daughter's relationship with the mother over a long time and had never seen the daughter attempting to influence her mother's decisions or isolate her.

In Beek v. Speakman, 57 Va. Cir. 501 (2000), the Circuit Court also rejected allegations of incapacity and undue influence, on these facts:

Mrs. Speakman executed the challenged documents on May 22, 1997. At that time, Mrs. Speakman exhibited signs of dementia. Taken together, these documents substantially disinherited three of Mrs. Speakman's four daughters. This disposition did not comport with a Will Mrs. Speakman executed in 1986, which directed that Mrs. Speakman's four daughters share her estate equally. Mrs. Speakman died on August 30, 1998...

[T]here... was testimony regarding signs of Alzheimer's disease as early as 1996. This diagnosis was confirmed by the autopsy. ... Mr. Melnick, the attorney who prepared the documents... found Mrs.

Speakman to be "sharp as a tack…" On May 6, 1997 Dr. Peter Cook saw Mrs. Speakman and assessed her capacity to execute the documents. Dr. Cook wrote a letter on May 12, 1997 stating unequivocally that in his medical opinion, Mrs. Speakman was able to execute legal documents at that time. … As late as February 17, 1998, the medical records reveal that the health care provider found Mrs. Speakman "oriented to person and place." … Mr. Melnick stated that Mrs. Speakman was concerned that Bonnie would not have a place to live after Mrs. Speakman's death. Because Mrs. Speakman considered the sisters to be well provided for, she wished to change her earlier will. … Mrs. Speakman was also aware that the sisters would be unhappy with the disposition she was making. …

Mrs. Speakman was in Bonnie's care during the final years of her life. … Mrs. Speakman suffered from dementia and Alzheimer's disease. … Mrs. Speakman was easily persuaded, and Bonnie conceded this point. [H]owever, … Mrs. Speakman was acutely aware of the family dynamic among the four daughters. … Mrs. Speakman knew precisely what she was doing when she executed the documents and had a rational reason for doing so. Accordingly, the sisters cannot show that Mrs. Speakman was legally "enfeebled in mind" by clear and convincing evidence. …

Bonnie's role as caregiver, coupled with the familial relationship is sufficient to give rise to a fiduciary relationship. Nevertheless, … although Bonnie drove Mrs. Speakman to both the appointments with Mr. Melnick and the appointment with Dr. Cook, this evidence is not sufficient to support a finding that Bonnie acted to procure or prepare the documents. … Mr. Melnick testified that Bonnie waited in the reception area while he and Mrs. Speakman met. Bonnie did not participate in any of the meetings that led to the drafting and execution of the documents. … This simply is not a case where Bonnie had the documents prepared without Mrs. Speakman's knowledge or participation. Nor is this a case where Mrs. Speakman was presented with documents that purported to be something other than what they were to get her signature. … Bonnie brought Mrs. Speakman to family events, and therefore, it cannot properly be argued that Bonnie was isolating Mrs. Speakman from the sisters. [T]he sisters' hostility toward Bonnie was palpable to the Court. Given the level and intensity of the animosity, the Court does not find Bonnie's reluctance to allow the sisters unrestricted access to her home "suspicious." …

Bonnie would say on the telephone, apropos of nothing, "No, I'm not going to put Mom in a nursing home." … Clearly this was an effort to hold the possibility of going to a nursing home to influence Mrs. Speakman. Nevertheless, "earnest entreaty, importunity and persuasion may be employed, but if the influence is not irresistible it is not undue, and its existence is immaterial, even though it is yielded to." … Mrs.

Speakman was aware of another option. Carol testified that she had offered to have Mrs. Speakman live with her. Mrs. Speakman refused, preferring to live in her own home with Bonnie. ... Bonnie admitted hitting her mother and kicking her once in 1995; however, the evidence also shows that Bonnie voluntarily checked in to a mental health facility for treatment immediately following (and because of) this incident. Bonnie testified that there was never a repeat of the 1995 incident. Moreover, that single incident is too remote in time to form the basis of a finding of undue influence.

Because the sisters cannot prove any of the three required elements for a presumption of undue influence by clear and convincing evidence, the Court must find in favor of validity.

3.   No contest clauses

It is almost inevitable that a will that deviates substantially from intestacy rules in its disposition of wealth is going to be subject to challenge by would-be heirs, based on allegations of incapacity, fraud, or undue influence. Is there anything a client can do to discourage this? Writing an explanation in the will or in a contemporaneous writing is dangerous; it could end up being used as evidence to support the allegation, if there is anything in the explanation that is factually inaccurate, sounds eccentric, or suggests the testator was influenced by things a will beneficiary said to him or her. An alternative strategy is to include a "no contest clause" in the will. This is a provision stating that any will beneficiary who challenges the will is to be excluded from the will entirely. Such a clause, *along with* sufficient provision in the will for all would-be intestate heirs so that they have something to lose, can be an effective deterrent. A no-contest clause can do nothing to discourage a would-be heir for whom the will makes no provision at all, or so small a provision that a disgruntled beneficiary would not suffer significantly by losing it.

Virginia law has long supported enforcement of no-contest clauses. Litigation arises principally over whether particular actions triggered the clause and whether such a clause is overridden if a challenger successfully shows the will was invalid. The following is the seminal case.

Supreme Court of Appeals of Virginia
Womble v. Gunter
198 Va. 522, 95 S.E.2d 213 (1956)

HUDGINS, C.J., delivered the opinion of the court.

George F. Parramore, Sr., died testate on June 4, 1945. His somewhat complicated will, including five codicils, was duly probated and Benj. T. Gunter, Jr., and Quinton G. Nottingham qualified as executors. The testator devised and bequeathed all of his property in various amounts and proportions to his ten living children and numerous grandchildren.

On May 16, 1947, all the legatees and devisees of the testator, one being named as respondent for the purpose of pleading, filed a bill in chancery attacking the validity of the will on the ground of mental incompetency of the testator. ... A final decree dismissing the suit was entered on March 26, 1952, the effect of which makes the validity of the will unquestionable.

Benj. T. Gunter, Jr., and Quinton G. Nottingham, as executors of the estate of the testator, filed the bill in this cause alleging, among other things, that all of the thirty children and grandchildren of the testator named as beneficiaries in the will, except Lafayette H. Parramore, J. Morrison Parramore, Lafayette H. Parramore, Jr., Jacqueline P. Phister, Sophie Faison Mitchell and Dora W. Pike, had instituted legal proceedings to contest the validity of the will and thereby had breached the condition of paragraph XIII of the will, which provided that if any one or more of the legatees or devisees should contest the *524 will, then such contestants should forfeit any and all benefits made for him or her. ...

K. Addison Jarvis, Trustee of Christ Episcopal Church of Eastville, filed an answer to the bill in which it is alleged that all of the thirty children and grandchildren named as beneficiaries in the testator's will had joined in the former suit contesting the validity of the same and had thereby forfeited all their interest in the estate of the testator, which, under the conditions stated in paragraph XIV of the will, passed to the church. This paragraph provides: 'Should all my legatees and devisees contest my will, then my entire estate shall pass to Christ Episcopal Church in Eastville.' ... **216 ... *525 ...

Appellants and appellees agree that a condition against contesting a will or attempting to set it aside is generally held valid and enforceable. However, the twenty-four appellants contend that the general rule is subject to an exception, namely, that such provision is not effective as to the beneficiaries who unsuccessfully contest the will if it affirmatively appears that the contest was instituted by them in good faith and with probable cause to believe the will to be invalid.

The reason generally advanced by the authorities in support of the view that the 'no contest' condition should be held ineffective where the contest is based on good faith and probable cause is that a sound public policy demands that the truth of a disputable claim should be ascertained as the law provides, and that since courts are created to administer justice there should be no penalties inflicted upon those who seek their performance of that function. It is argued that if a will is actually invalid, a strict and literal application of such 'no contest' clause would tend to prevent the establishment of this fact, and thus thwart the course of justice. The persons, who may have been instrumental in the creation of the invalid document and who were to profit most by its admission to probate, would be provided a helpful cover for their wrongful acts. [citations omitted]

Some authorities maintain that in passing upon the defense of good faith and probable cause to a 'no contest' provision in a will, consideration *526 should be given to the grounds of the contest. A will is usually contested on one or more of six grounds; namely, lack of testamentary capacity, fraud, undue influence, improper execution, forgery, or subsequent revocation by a later will. These authorities declare that where the contest is based upon the claim of revocation by a later will, the public has an interest in having all the documents properly presented to the court; a person knowing of such instrument has the moral if not the legal duty of presenting the instrument for consideration; it would be against public policy to deter such person from presenting the same if he knew that he would risk the loss of all benefits under the will if he took any action on it. The conclusion of these authorities is that if such person's action in instituting the contest is based on good faith and probable cause he should **217 not be deprived of his benefits by the 'no contest' provision.

The same authorities argue that the public is interested in the discovery of the commission of the crime of forgery, and such forgery or subsequent revocation by a later will is usually based upon evidence more definite in character than that tending to establish the shadowy lines of demarcation involved in mental capacity, undue influence or fraud. They also argue that since this element is not involved in a contest based upon fraud, undue influence or lack of testamentary capacity, the balance of public policy favors sustaining the defense of good faith and probable cause where the contest is based upon forgery or the production of a later instrument believed to be the true will and should be rejected where the contest is based upon other grounds. Restatement, Property, § 428, p. 2499; 146 A.L.R. 1204 and cases therein cited, and Ann. 1211.

Other authorities of equal dignity hold that 'good faith and probable cause' do not protect the contesting legatees or devisees. The reasons advanced in support of this view are well expressed by Chief Justice Rugg in Rudd v. Searles, 262 Mass. 490, 160 N.E. 882, 58 A.L.R. 1548, 1555, as follows: 'The ease with which plausible contentions as to mental unsoundness may be supported by some evidence is also a factor which well may be in the mind of a testator in determining to insert such a clause in his will. Nothing in the law or in public policy, as we understand it, requires the denial of solace of that nature to one making a will. A will contest not infrequently engenders animosities and arouses hostilities among the kinsfolk of the testator, which may never be put to rest and which contribute to *527 general unhappiness. Moreover, suspicions or beliefs in personal insanity, mental weakness, eccentricities, pernicious habits, or other odd characteristics centering in or radiating from the testator, may bring his family into evil repute and adversely affect the standing in the community of its members. Thus a will contest may bring sorrow and suffering to many concerned. A clause of this nature may contribute to the fair reputation of the dead and to the peace and harmony of the living. Giving due weight to all these considerations, we are unable to bring our minds to the conviction that public policy requires that a testamentary clause such as here is involved be stamped as unlawful, even if the contestant had good grounds for opposing the allowance of the will. It seems to us that, both on principle and by weight of authority, this is the right result.' ...

The record in this case clearly reveals the adverse and disturbing effect upon family relations... Prior to the institution of the suit in 1947 to contest the will the children and grandchildren of the testator seemed to have been bound together with the usual and normal family ties, each having respect for and confidence in the other. As one of the sons, William P. **218 Parramore, said: 'There were eleven children in that family, and all our life we were in agreement, and I never knew them to disagree on any matter until this matter arose, and I thought it was a shame that we couldn't get together ....'

After the contest of the will had been settled adversely to the contentions of the contestants the family seemed to have been split *528 asunder, charging each other with misrepresentation, fraud and deceit. In the answer of the twenty-four respondents it is alleged that the other six beneficiaries were parties to the contest 'with full knowledge of their rights, obligations, duties and burdens with respect thereto, and the results to be had therefrom, and collaborated in all respects therein until the day of and during the hearing . . . (they) in order to gain advantage over other parties to said litigation wilfully, fraudulently, deceitfully and wickedly withdrew as parties complainant.' Five of the other six beneficiaries in their brief say: 'The other 24 appellants who are separately appealing this matter and who actively and consistently have attacked the Will can hardly hope to escape the forfeiture provision under any interpretation of the law; they have produced no evidence of any probable cause or good faith and a careful examination of the testimony in record tends to indicate the exact opposite. It would appear that the caveat suit was impetuously brought to satiate their dissatisfaction and impatience.'

It is unnecessary, however, for the court at this time and in this case to pass upon the question whether good faith, probable cause and reasonable justification afford a defense to a 'no contest' provision in a will. This is a question that must be affirmatively established by the parties making the allegation. It was not made an issue in the pleadings other than as heretofore stated. No testimony bearing on the question was introduced except the opinion of one witness, who did not state the facts upon which he based his conclusion, nor was the question raised in the lower court. It is well settled that this court will not determine questions not raised in the court below. ...

The evidence on the issue as to who were parties to the suit to contest the will is not in substantial conflict. The twenty-four beneficiaries (four of whom were minors) who filed a joint answer in this case admit that they were parties to the suit to contest the will and *529 alleged that the other six beneficiaries were likewise parties thereto. James H. Parramore filed no answer to the bill and took no part in the proceedings in the lower court or in this court. The decree as to him is final. Lafayette H. Parramore was a party complainant to the original bill in 1947 to contest the will, but after the jury were sworn to try the issue *devisavit vel non* [a document that sets forth the questions of fact pertinent to the validity of an alleged will and is sent from a court of probate or chancery to a court of law for a jury trial for judgment as to the validity of the will] and before it was submitted he, on his own motion, was made a party defendant instead of a party complainant. Some time after the jury had reported that they were unable to agree and had been discharged, the other four of the five appellants, three of whom were infants and had appeared as parties complainant by their respective parents as next friend, were on motion transferred from parties complainant to parties respondent. Later the case was dismissed without trial on its merits. None of these five named appellants filed an answer to the bill in this case or in the pleadings denied the averments made in the answer of the twenty-four beneficiaries **219 and in the answer filed by the Trustee of Christ Episcopal Church alleging that they were parties complainant in the bill to contest the will and charging that they were as much bound by the 'no contest' provision as the other beneficiaries.

The preponderance of the oral testimony tends to show that soon after the death of the testator on June 4, 1945, the executors sent each of the legatees and devisees a copy of the will, including the codicils; that between the date of the testator's death and the institution of the suit on May 16, 1947, to contest the will there were numerous family conferences of all the legatees and devisees in which their rights under, and the validity of, the will were fully discussed and all agreed to institute legal proceedings to contest its validity. One of the testator's sons said: 'We had been discussing at length the will at breakfast, dinner and supper.'

What activity or participation constitutes a contest or attempt to defeat a will depends upon the wording of the 'no contest' provision and the facts and circumstances of each particular case. The general rule is that 'a resort to the means provided by law for attacking the validity of a will amounts to a contest, although the contestant subsequently withdraws before the final hearing and even though the contestant subsequently treats the will as valid and seeks construction.' Page on Wills, Lifetime Ed., Chapter 1306, p. 823; Restatement, § 428, p. 2507; 26 A.L.R. 764; 57 Am. Jur., Wills, § 1513, p. 1026.

We find no error in the finding of the trial court that all the *530 beneficiaries named in the testator's will participated in the contest of the same.

The five appellants' next contention is that the infants who joined in the contest by their respective parents as next friend are not bound by the 'no contest' provision in the will.

Code § 8-87 authorizes an infant to sue by his next friend. The practice in Virginia is for such suits to be instituted in the name of the infant by one of the parents or other near relative without formal appointment. If the suit or action proceeds without objection, it is a recognition by the court that the infant is a party to the proceeding. In Kirby v. Gilliam, 182 Va. 111, 28 S.E.2d 40, it was held that the consent of the infant was not necessary for a suit to be maintained in her name by her next friend. In numerous cases we have held that in absence of fraud an infant is as much bound by a decree or judgment of a court as is an adult. The law recognizes no distinction between a decree against an infant and a decree against an adult, and, therefore, an infant can impeach it only upon grounds which would invalidate it in case of an adult party. Harrison v. Wallton, 95 Va. 721, 30 S.E. 372.

Whether an infant beneficiary is bound by the 'no contest' provision in a will has not been decided in express terms in Virginia, and the decisions of the courts on the question in other states are not in accord. Some authorities declare that the 'no contest' provision is invalid and unenforceable as against public policy when applied to gifts to infants. 57 Am. Jur. Wills, § 1512, p. 1026; Bryant v. Thompson, 14 N.Y.S. 28, 28 N.E. 522. Other authorities hold that the 'no contest' provision in a will is as binding upon an infant beneficiary as it is upon an adult. Persuasive reasons for this view are stated in Moorman v. Louisville Trust Company, 181 Ky. 30, 43, 203 S.W. 856:

> It is not so easy to comprehend the argument that to ascertain whether or not a conditional devise is against public policy it must first be learned who is affected thereby, and that a testator, because of good morals or a sound public **220 policy, may attach a condition to a gift to his adult child that he may not attach to a gift by the same instrument to his infant child. If such should be declared to be the law, no person, no matter how perfect his mind, could prevent a contest of his will by the objects of his bounty, some of whom were infants, no matter how sound his reasons for so desiring *531 might be considered, if some next friend regarded the provision made for the infant unfair or a provision for the infant's issue unwise; and the practical result of such a decision would be that a person without infant dependents could exercise a control over the disposition of his property that another with such dependents could not. The rule is universal that infants are bound, just as adults are bound, by judgments in actions prosecuted in their names and for their supposed benefit in the manner prescribed by law, even though the result might prove the action unwise and not for their good; and we cannot believe that public policy demands they shall not be responsible likewise for the legal consequences of such action. We are convinced that whatever the true doctrine with reference to such clause, it must apply alike to all.

In Alper v. Alper, 2 N.J. 105, 115, 65 A.2d 737, 741, it is said that 'the condition [no contest provision] is also enforceable against the infant grandchildren. The testator so willed; and there is no consideration of policy which forbids nonenforcement of the provision. It is in no sense a punitive measure, but a device or bequest upon condition subsequent with a gift over, and therefore an executory limitation. Upon the happening of the prescribed contingency, the gift over becomes effective.' Rudd v. Searles, supra; Old Colony Trust Co. v. Wolfman, 311 Mass. 614, 42 N.E.2d 574 (1942); Harrison v. Foote, 9 Tex.Civ.App. 576, 30 S.W. 838.

George F. Parramore, Sr., the testator, in his early life had been a practicing attorney. No one knew better than he that he had named in his will seven infant beneficiaries. In imposing the condition he made no distinction between his adult and his infant beneficiaries. He stated the condition in his will as follows: 'I have endeavored to distribute fairly and impartially all of my estate among my children and my deceased son George F. Parramore, Jr's., children, and as it seems best for their interests. I sincerely hope that each of them will receive as I have given unto them, but if any one or more of them should contest my will, I hereby expressly revoke any provisions herein made for the one or more so contesting my will, and the share the contestant would have received shall revert to my estate. Any charge of any kind brought against my estate by any beneficiary, the one so making such a claim shall forfeit any benefit herein made for him or her.' *532

If the testator had desired to except his infant beneficiaries from the 'no contest' provision he could have very easily used appropriate language to that end. He did not do so. On the contrary, in making the 'no contest' provision applicable to all his beneficiaries, he used the following all-inclusive language: 'Should all my legatees and devisees contest my will, then my entire estate shall pass to Christ Episcopal Church in Eastville.' (Italics supplied)

The court is not concerned with whether an heir or a devisee receives the property of a decedent. The normal freedom of the owner to dispose of his property as he sees fit should not be curtailed unless the disposition violates some rule of law or is against public policy. Where the language is clear and unambiguous, it is the duty of the court to give force and effect to the intention expressed by the testator and carry out the objects desired by him in disposing of his property. If the court held the 'no contest' paragraph valid as to **221 adults and invalid as to infants, it would be making a new and different will for the testator, and one contrary to his clearly expressed intention to restrain both the adult and infant beneficiaries from making a public exposure of essentially private and personal matters. ...

The Supreme Court has decided a few cases subsequently involving no-contest clauses in a trust, and those are discussed in Chapter Five. It appears to have issued only one decision subsequently in a case involving a will. In Virginia Found. of Indep. Colleges v. Goodrich, 246 Va. 435, 436 S.E.2d 418 (1993), the court held that a beneficiary's complaint seeking a declaratory judgment as to the meaning of "personal property" in a will, following the executor's interpretation of the clause to include only tangible personal property and to exclude intangible personal property, was not a will contest and so did not trigger the forfeiture provision in the will. The court explained: "As a general principle, one who seeks the guidance of a court in interpreting a provision in a will is not considered to have "contested" the will... While forfeiture clauses or 'no contest' clauses effectuate the testator's legitimate interest in preventing attempts to thwart his intent, a request for interpretation does not challenge the intent of the testator..." 246 Va. at 438, 436 S.E.2d at 420 The court implied, however, that if the no-contest clause explicitly included within its ambit any challenge to the judgment of the named executor in interpreting the will, then a complaint of this sort would result in forfeiture; all depends on the language the testator used in the will.

A recent circuit court decision also applied *Womble* to a will. In Estate of Rohrbaugh, 80 Va. Cir. 253 (2011), the court applied a no-contest clause in a will that stated:

> 14.3. Contests to Will. To the extent permitted by law, it is my intention, and I hereby direct, that any person who contests this Will or any provision hereof, claims against this Will or fails to dismiss any such contest or claim, shall ipso facto forfeit any rights, titles or interest such person has or may at any time have under this Will and/or in any property distributable hereunder, except for the sum of One Hundred Dollars ($100).

The decedent and his wife had, before marrying, executed a pre-nuptial agreement in which the wife waived all statutory rights of a surviving spouse and agreed instead to receive only certain listed property at the husband's death. The husband's will gave that property to her, and everything else to his children, some of whom had a mother other than the wife. After the husband's death, the wife initially filed a suit seeking to void the pre-nuptial agreement, find the husband breached that agreement, and claim her statutory rights as a surviving spouse. After a court held she was barred by the doctrine of laches from challenging the validity of the Antenuptial Agreement, she filed another suit accusing her husband's executors with conversion of personal property and re-alleging two breach of contract claims – namely, that the will did not comply with their pre-nuptial agreement and that it did not comply with a later oral agreement as to death-time transfer of certain real estate.

The court held that these legal actions triggered the no-contest clause, resulting in the wife receiving only $100 under the will from an estate worth over two million dollars, explaining:

> A court's determination of which "activity or participation constitutes a contest or attempt to defeat a will depends upon the wording of the 'no-contest' provision and the facts and circumstances of each particular case." In general, "a resort to the means provided by law for attacking the validity of a will amounts to a contest," even if the will contestant subsequently retreats from her position. Womble, 198 Va. at 530, 95 S.E.2d at 219. ... *6 In this case, by directing that the no-contest provision be applied "[t]o the extent permitted by law," Mr. Rohrbaugh clearly and unambiguously mandated an expansive construction of this clause to the furthest extent possible under the law. Such intent is further evidenced by his direction that the provision applies to "any person who contests this Will or any provision hereof, claims against this Will or fails to dismiss any such contest or claim." Thus, Mr. Rohrbaugh analogizes a "contest" to the Will and a "claim against" the Will, and further provides that the clause applies to anyone who contests not only the entire Will itself, but also any individual provision thereof.
>
> …

Mrs. Rohrbaugh's cumulative actions constitute an indirect contest or claim against Paragraph 3 of the Will. She intended to repudiate the Will because she disagreed with what she was given under what she described as the "will from hell." She explicitly acknowledged that she did not want to live "under the domination" of the Executors/Trustees, who were responsible under the Will for distributing net trust income to her and who could, in their "sole and absolute discretion," further distribu te portions of the principal to her as well. This is precisely the type of behavior that Mr. Rohrbaugh apparently sought to prevent by drafting the broad no-contest provision in his Will. Nonetheless, Mrs. Rohrbaugh sought to thwart his testamentary intent by filing her claims against the Estate. Indeed, she continued on this path knowing that she was actually contesting a provision of the Will, and with full knowledge of the consequences of her actions. Thus,… this Court finds that Mrs. Rohrbaugh's conscious and intentional acts invoked the no-contest provision of Mr. Rohrbaugh's Will.

The wife could still seek to recover on the contract claims, however; this decision concerned only interpretation of the will. And note that the court based its decision on the wife's "cumulative actions" and stated that it "need not address whether, standing alone, Mrs. Rohrbaugh invoked the no-contest clause of the Will by filing her lawsuits for breach of contract and claim to an elective share." It noted that "although the Supreme Court of Virginia has not touched upon the subject, non-binding authorities are supportive of the proposition that an independent action for breach of contract generally does not constitute a "contest" to the will" and "[c]ourts in foreign jurisdictions have generally held that a spouse's attempt to elect to take under the laws of succession does not result in a forfeiture of the spouse's interest under the will." [citations omitted]

III.   Establishing the Contents of Will

A court's probating (i.e., approving) a will is hardly the end of difficulties for effectuating a testator's estate plan. Many sorts of questions can arise concerning the precise contents of the will. Section A below addresses situations where a will refers to another document for guidance as to how particular items of property should be dispose. Section B addresses the problem of mistakes and ambiguities in will drafting. Section C concerns changes in relationships and property subsequent to will execution. Section D covers partial and complete bars to certain beneficiaries taking under a will.

A. Incorporation of extrinsic documents

In addition to the various ways Virginia courts have interpreted § 64.2-403 to allow for deviations from the formalities requirements, and in addition to the informality forgiveness rule, Virginia law authorizes incorporation into a will's testamentary disposition other documents that do not themselves comply with the requirements for a will. There are four possibilities:

1. The common law rule of "incorporation by reference"

2. A modern statutory provision authorizing incorporation of a "legal list"

3. A modern statutory provision authorizing incorporation of a document guiding the executor's discretion

4. Pour-over into a trust

1. Common law rule

A long-standing common-law rule has authorized probate of, in effect, documents that comport with none of the formalities, so long as a particular document

✓ was in existence when the will was executed
✓ is specifically referred to in the will

Supreme Court of Appeals of Virginia
Lawless v. Lawless
187 Va. 511, 47 S.E.2d 431 (1948)

SPRATLEY, J., delivered the opinion of the court.

Valentine Browne Lawless, a soldier, was killed in action October 16, 1944. On December 15, 1945, his last will and testament was admitted to probate in the Corporation *513 Court of the city of Norfolk. The will, wholly written in the handwriting of the testator, reads as follows:

Norfolk, Va.

November 13, 1941.

I, Valentine Browne Lawless (V. B. Lawless), do hereby make, declare and **432 publish this my last will and testament, drawn in my own hand.

1. My most valued possession, the Cloncurry gold seal ring, given me by my father, I give to Joseph Thomas Lawless, son of my brother, deceased, and who is my nephew; the seal ring to be given to him upon his reaching his twenty-first (21st) birthday, and to be held for him until that time in a safe deposit box at one of the local banks, the rental expense of which to be prepaid from any cash I may have in my name at the time of my death.

2. Any title I may have in any real estate and any title I may have in furniture (other than my Philco Radio Phonograph and records), I bequeath, share and share alike, to my surviving brothers and sister, with the same request being passed on to them that my father made in his will, i.e., that if practicable, to keep the furniture intact.

3. Any boats or boating equipment which I may own at my death, I request be sold and the cash be given my brother, Kirwan, whom I will later name Executor of this will and testament, this cash to be used as I shall later request.

4. Any automobile which I may have at the time of my death, I request be sold, and that the cash be also turned over to my brother, Kirwan for purposes herein written later on.

5. My insurance policy now listing my deceased father as beneficiary, I request be paid to my brother, Kirwan.

6. To a man whom I consider a friend and know to be kind and thoughtful, I bequeath my Philco Radio and Phonograph and records, the man is Geo. Manine Hughes.

7. All my other possessions, small or inconsequential as they are, I leave to my brother Kirwan to do with as he may see fit, with one exception. My black rosary, with *514 large oblong beads (given me for reverence and fidelity at the altar), somewhere in my possession, this I request be put in good repair at some jewelers, and to be sent to one of the finest women I've ever known, and one whom I shall always respect and admire, I refer to Sister Ariana, who taught me at Sacred Heart School some years ago.

I appoint my brother Edward Kirwan Lawless Executor of this will and request that no appraisement be made. I request that no surety be required of the appointed executor, and that no report be made of his disposition of my possessions, either cash possessions or other possessions. I believe neither to be necessary as I know my brother.

I request that the cash on hand at my death and resulting cash from sale of my possessions be applied to my funeral expenses and that the balance be given to Kirwan on a special purpose.

Published and declared as and for my last will.

(Signed) VALENTINE BROWNE LAWLESS

(V. B. Lawless).

The testator left no descendants and his parents were dead. His heirs-at-law were Margaret E. Lawless, a sister, Gregory B. Lawless and Edward Kirwan Lawless, brothers, and five nephews and one niece, the infant children of a deceased brother, Joseph T. Lawless, Jr.

Edward Kirwan Lawless, the executor named in the will, declining to qualify as such, Margaret Elward Lawless, was appointed and duly qualified as administratrix c.t.a. of the estate of her deceased brother.

In June, 1947, Margaret Elward Lawless, administratrix c.t.a., instituted this proceeding in chancery against all of the heirs-at-law of the testator, praying for a construction of the will of her decedent and advice as to the disposal of his assets.

The bill of complaint alleged that the testator had cash in hand amounting to $1,796.04 at his death and that since his death she had collected from the United States arrears in his army pay amounting to $1,814.46. It averred that the 'special purpose' mentioned in the will was indefinite *515 and unknown, but that a letter, in the handwriting of the testator, bearing the same date as the will and addressed to Edward Kirwan Lawless disclosed his intention; that this letter was merely in the **433 nature of an instruction to Kirwan Lawless as to the disposition of the money mentioned in the will or a request to so use the money, and was not intended to be a part of the will or a codicil thereto; that Kirwan Lawless had no intention of complying with the instructions of the letter, claiming that he was personally entitled to the money directed to be used for a 'special purpose;' and that Gregory Lawless contended that the attempted trust was null and void because of the failure of the 'special purpose' mentioned in the will, and the money set aside for such purpose should be paid to the heirs-at-law of the testator.

The infant defendants answered the bill by their guardian ad litem, duly appointed.

Edward Kirwan Lawless answered, admitting that the letter referred to in the will was written by his brother; but averred that despite its instructions it was illegally and improperly opened and read by the administratrix before it was turned over to him; and that he considered the contents thereof a private matter and subject to the dictates of his conscience. He denied that there had been a failure of the 'special purpose' mentioned in the will. He prayed that all funds in the hands of the administratrix, after payment of all debts due by the estate, be paid to him, and that all personal property, other than that specifically left to others, be turned over to him. ...

The letter of the testator was not probated nor offered *516 for probate as a will or codicil thereto. Wholly written in the handwriting of the testator, it reads as follows:

Nov. 13-'41.

Dear Kirwan:

Please be executor of my will and remember me as one who thought a lot of you and wishes you success which I believe of & hope for you.

I want you to take whatever cash no matter how much left over after my death & funeral & marker, and make a contract with a florist, to send one rose each Saturday morning before ten A.M. to the residence of a girl whom I have loved very dearly for over three years at this writing, and shall continue to love for the duration of my life. This is not a sentimental, love sick statement. I know the girl much better than any one realizes and she is one of the finest persons it has ever been my privilege to be associated with and I want the one perfect rose of any color (to vary) to be sent to her because I have wanted so much to give her some pleasure while I lived but not being the type of person who is able to give any one pleasure by company, & (company, dates, etc.,) would be necessary or she would not accept any other presents which I've wanted so much to give to her, because of these reasons, I have to request that the flower be sent to her and possibly she may sometimes wear it to church on Sunday, or, at least receive some enjoyment out of it. Please do this with the understanding that the bill & contract be paid for in advance and that no name ever be divulged as to the sender.

This is the most important part. Talk to only one person make only one contract and with that person, and make part of the agreement that no name be divulged ever, on request of the girl, or any one else.

I love her very much, Kirwan, and would like to be the type of person that could make her love me and marry me and be able to support & provide her with those things which it is such a pleasure to give to one you love. But, as I'm not a personality which is likable and as I do not *517 have mental qualifications requisite of one who is likely to be successful socially or financially, I must make this request.

Mention this letter to no one, not a single soul. My idea is to furnish the girl with the pleasure of receiving a rose, not have her think a lot of me because I sent it to her. **434

I've written a lot of letters to her in the last three years, some of them have been destroyed, most all of them, but there are some of them left in a brown envelope in my set of files on the closet shelf. Please see that those are sent her and that she be aware that they are personal and are to be read, if at all, in private. They are only my expressions of reactions to what has gone on in our association in business & love letters in general.

(She works for Southern Steve. Corp.) Her name is Mildred Fitz Patrick and she is one of the most beautiful girls in character & looks, I've ever known. Thanks and pray for me.

VAL

On the back of the letter appears, in the handwriting of the testator, the following legend:

To E. K. LAWLESS: - To be read by him only, and to be read by him in private. I ask that all details of the above request be carried out literally, that he be sure to read the letter while alone.

From: Val Lawless.'

... *518 ... In jurisdictions where a document extrinsic to a will is allowed to be incorporated therein, three things are essential to such incorporation. This is known as the doctrine of incorporation by reference. ... The limitations and conditions attendant upon the application of this doctrine are concisely stated in Harrison on Wills and Administration, Vol. 1, section 102(7), page 190, and approved in Triplett v. Triplett, 161 Va. 906, 921, 172 S.E. 162, as follows:

First, It (the extrinsic document) must be a paper in actual existence at the date of the execution of the will. Second, It must appear from the face of the will that it is a paper in actual existence; and Third, It must be identified and described with reasonable certainty in the will.

The reasons for the limitations are sound. Otherwise the wise provisions of the law relating to the making and execution of wills might be nullified. If the existing document sought to be incorporated was not in actual existence at the time of the execution of the will, then a decedent might write a will without complying with the statutory requirements relating to wills. If the extrinsic document is not referred to in the will as in existence, there can be no certainty that it is the paper referred to. If it is not sufficiently described in the will then parol evidence will be required to establish it as a part of the will. This is forbidden by statute. *519

While, under certain circumstances and conditions, extrinsic evidence may be admissible to explain ambiguous language in a will, or to describe a legatee not precisely named or described, such evidence cannot be admitted for the purpose of incorporating in a will either the nature of a purpose or the name of a beneficiary undisclosed in the will itself, in the absence of the three essential things required under **435 the doctrine of incorporation by reference.

In the present case not a single one of the required conditions has been complied with. There is not in the language of the will any clear and explicit reference to any specific document as existing at the time the testator executed his will. In fact, there is no reference to a letter of the testator. Whatever reference there is, is to 'a later request' or to purposes to be 'written later on.' Any letter or letters written by the testator any time after the will was executed, or any oral request made by him, would answer the reference. The reference is so vague and uncertain as to be capable of being applied to any document in particular existing at the time of the execution of the will.

The letter may have been written on the same day as the will but later in that day, or the date may have been subsequently inserted, or another letter submitted for it written at a different time and dated back. Nor was the letter of a testamentary nature as shown by the legend written on its face. It was intended only for the eyes of Kirwan Lawless. It was purely an attempt to make a personal agreement with his brother to be kept secret. It was manifestly never intended as a part of the will or as a codicil thereto. While the will, drawn by an intelligent testator, declares in both its first and last sentences that it shall be published, the letter imperatively commands that its contents be divulged to no one.

The proper decision of the case, therefore, depends upon the construction of the probated will alone. In this construction, we must, if possible, without violating well settled rules of law, give force to every word of the will. *520 The purpose of the law of wills is to allow the owner of property to dispose of it as he wishes. But the command of the testator must be expressed in writing and the words used must be sufficient for the purpose.

It will be noted that where the testator makes a bequest or devise in the will, he does so without any reservation whatever. In item 1, he gives his gold seal ring to his nephew; in item 2, he gives his realty and furniture to his brothers and sister; in item 5, he gives his insurance to his brother, Kirwan; in item 6, he gives his radio and records to George Hughes; and in item 7, he gives 'all my other possessions, small or inconsequential as they are, 'to Kirwan absolutely, except his black rosary. The bequest in this item clearly did not include the cash mentioned in paragraphs 3 and 4. The 'special purpose' therein mentioned was not intended for Kirwan's benefit. In item 3, the testator evidently had in mind 'a later request,' oral or written. In item 4, he manifestly intended the bequests therein mentioned be devoted to 'purposes' to be set out 'later on' in the will. Otherwise, there can be no reason why the specific property, - the boats and the automobile, or the proceeds therefrom, were not given directly to Kirwan, if the legacies were intended for his sole benefit.

Obviously the testator did not, at any time, have in mind the arrears in pay due him as a soldier of the United States. The balance mentioned in the last clause of the will refers specifically to the balance remaining from the cash on hand at the time of his death and the cash proceeds from the sale of his possessions, after payment of his funeral expenses. There was no intention to give such balance to Kirwan absolutely, because it was to be devoted to 'a special purpose.' The words of the will qualifying the use to which the cash of the testator was to be devoted cannot be struck out so as to make Kirwan the absolute beneficiary without violating the plain intendment of the testator. Here the testator had a special purpose in mind, a purpose which is not disclosed in the will. He simply did not set out in the will the nature of his purpose or disclose therein the beneficiary of that purpose.

In Sims v. Sims, 94 Va. 580, 27 S.E. 436, 64 Am.St.Rep. 772, this is said:

Where a trust is created by a will, if the beneficiary is not disclosed or cannot be discovered from the will itself, the trustee holds the devise or bequest for the benefit of the heirs or distributees of the **436 testator. The equitable interest goes to them by way of a resulting trust.

In Harrison on Wills and Administration, Vol. 1, in section 279, this is said:

No particular form of words are necessary to create a trust. * * *

It is necessary however, that the entire trust shall be disclosed by the will itself. The law imperatively requires that a will be in writing, and therefore no oral trusts outside of the will can be established, except in the cases of fraud to which we have referred in another place.

We conclude that the language of the will lacks sufficient words to create a trust, because we can ascertain from the will no definite subject nor any certain or ascertainable object. We cannot supply this by incorporating in the will a letter not referred to in the will.

Because of the reasons set forth, we are of opinion that the heirs-at-law of the decedent, Valentine Browne Lawless, are entitled absolutely to the monies, directed, under items 3 and 4 of the will, and in the last disposal paragraph, to be devoted to an undetermined 'special purpose,' the same to be distributed in accordance with the Virginia statute of descents and distributions...

In a recent circuit court application of the common law rule of incorporation by reference, Freeman v. Anderson, 55 Va. Cir. 353, 2001 WL 668350 (2001), the court analyzed a will provision stating: "I hereby request that the administrator of my estate shall give gifts to those persons whose names are listed on the volunteer list dated February 6, 1980." The court treated this, along with another provision directing the administrator to give gifts to people who had been of service to the testator, as a residuary clause, based on a presumption that "every testator intends to dispose of his entire estate." The court then held that this provision was a successful incorporation by reference:

The list is dated at the top February 6, 1980 and a handwritten addition is dated April 8, 1980. As the will is dated June 18, 1980, all portions of the list were in existence at the time of the will. The will identifies the paper as the 'volunteer list dated February 6, 1980.' The paper itself does not contain the words 'volunteer list' but states that those listed 'have consented and agreed to look after, care for the welfare and wellbeing of Lillian M. Taliaferro. Each shall assume responsibilities interchangeably.' That language coupled with the context of the Sixth and Seventh clauses satisfies the court that the will identified and described with reasonable certainty the volunteer list.

2.   Legal lists

Two statutory provisions enacted in this century allowance for incorporation of a document that comes into existence after will execution. The common law rule required testators to have figured out already at the time of will execution to whom all bequests would go, which is somewhat burdensome given that both relationships and property owned can change substantially over time, or else revise their will repeatedly. § 64.2-400 and § 64.2-104 reflect a legislative aim of giving testators more flexibility, with freedom to make such minor alterations in an estate plan right up until the time of death without having repeatedly to go through the steps of executing a will.

Note, though, that even under traditional common law rules, a holographic will was always effectively a work in progress, modifiable at any time, with edits in the testator's handwriting accepted as modifications even if demonstrably added long after the testator signed the will. (Though writing below the signature could raise questions about whether they were intended to be part of the will.) So someone content with a holographic will can simply write on the will ongoing decisions about who should get what. Note also that one can easily accomplish the purpose of incorporation by reference simply be creating a holographic codicil – that is, by creating a list on a separate paper in one's own handwriting, with an introductory line that says "The following is an amendment to my will" and a signature at the end. However, if one is determined to incorporate a separate non-testamentary document with a list, perhaps because one prefers to type it, one must comply with either the rule of incorporation by reference and create it prior to will execution, or comport with one of the modern statutes below.

§ 64.2-400. Separate writing identifying recipients of tangible personal property; liability for distribution; action to recover property.

A. If a will refers to a written statement or list to dispose of items of tangible personal property not otherwise specifically bequeathed, the statement or list shall be given effect to the extent that it describes items of tangible personal property and their intended recipients with reasonable certainty and is signed by the testator although it does not satisfy the requirements for a will. Bequests of a general or residuary nature, whether referring only to personal property or to the entire estate, are not specific bequests for the purpose of this section.

B. The written statement or list may be (i) referred to as one that is in existence at the time of the testator's death, (ii) prepared before or after the execution of the will, (iii) altered by the testator at any time, and (iv) a writing that has no significance apart from its effect on the dispositions made by the will. When distribution is made pursuant to such a written statement or list, a copy thereof shall be furnished to the commissioner of accounts along with the legatee's receipt.

...

***

There are several key aspects to this provision:

- ✓ The will must refer to the external document
- ✓ The incorporated document is effective only as to specific bequests of tangible personal property
- ✓ The testator must sign the incorporated list

The signature requirement is not found in the common law rule; it counter-balances the greater danger of fraud that arises from allowing for incorporation of documents that come into existence only after will execution.

3.   Guidance to executor

Subtitle I, Chapter 1. Definitions and General Provisions
SuperBrowse Article 2. General Provisions

§ 64.2-104. Incorporation by reference into a will, power of attorney, or trust instrument.

A. The following original documents may be incorporated by reference into a will…:

> 1. A letter or memorandum to the fiduciary or agent as to the interpretation of discretionary powers of distribution where the will… grants the fiduciary or agent the power to make distributions to beneficiaries in the discretion of the fiduciary or agent…

B. No provision in the original document sought to be incorporated by reference under this section is enforceable if it contradicts or is inconsistent with a provision of the incorporating will…

C. This section shall not prevent the incorporation by reference of any writing into any other writing that would otherwise be effective under § 64.2-400 or under any other law of incorporation by reference.

D. The maker shall sign and have notarized the documents referenced in subsection A and may prepare the documents before or after the execution of the will…

***

This provision further liberalizes the rule by allowing for incorporation of an external document that indirectly effects general bequests as well as disposition of tangible personal property. It does not explicitly say that the will must refer to the external document, but the legislature might have intended for "incorporated by reference" to mean precisely that. Like § 64.2-400, it allows for the external document coming into existence only after execution of the will and requires signing. The extra formality unique to this rule, again arguably counter-balancing the greater liberalization, is the requirement of notarization, something neither the common-law rule nor § 64.2-400 requires.

4.   Pour-over into a trust

A will can itself create a trust, by simply including a bequest or devise to a trust or to an individual or institution qua trustee, and providing direction in the will as to administration of the trust. In addition, though, testators can separately create a trust during their life, an *inter vivos* trusts, perhaps as a bucket to receive lifetime transfers, non-probate transfers at death, and also testamentary dispositions, thereby combining into one pool assets from several sources, all for the sake of the same beneficiaries and subject to the same set of directions, which could be quite elaborate and therefore seem to lengthy to include in the will. The law today takes an extremely liberal stance toward pouring over probate property into an *inter vivos* trust.

Subtitle II, Chapter 4. Wills
Article 3. Construction and Effect

§ 64.2-427. Testamentary additions to trusts after June 30, 1999.

A. A will may validly devise or bequeath property, including by the exercise of a power of appointment, to the trustee of a trust established or to be established (i) during the testator's lifetime by the testator, by the testator and some other person, or by some other person including a funded or unfunded life insurance trust, although the settlor has reserved any or all rights of ownership of the insurance contracts or (ii) at the testator's death by the testator's devise or bequest to the trustee, if the trust is identified in the testator's will and its terms are set forth in a written instrument, other than a will, executed before, concurrently with, or after the execution of the testator's will or in another individual's will if that other individual has predeceased the testator, regardless of the existence, size, or character of the corpus of the trust. The devise or bequest is not invalid because the trust is amendable or revocable, or because the trust was amended after the execution of the will or the testator's death.

...

C. Unless the testator's will provides otherwise, a revocation or termination of the trust before the testator's death causes the devise or bequest to lapse. [see discussing of lapsing below]

...

E. This section applies to a will of a testator who dies after June 30, 1999, and it shall be applied and construed to effectuate its general purpose to make uniform the law with respect to the subject of this section among states enacting it.

***

B. Mistakes and ambiguities

Even when a lawyer drafts a will, what gets written might not be exactly what the testator intended to say. In fact, "scrivener" error might be more common than testator error, because there is the extra step of communication between testator intent and inscription in the will, but testators have also been known to write carelessly. Sometimes mistakes are apparent on the face of the will – for example, an allocation of percentages of a particular asset or of an entire estate that add up to more than 100%. Other times people will allege based on facts in the outside world that the testator made a mistake – for example, that the testator misremembered which nephew had joined the priesthood; that the testator mistakenly made a large bequest to someone he never knew, someone bearing the same name as a boyhood friend, because the testator included an address he got out of the phone book and guessed wrong; that the testator mistakenly used the name his gardener "went by," a name that is actually the legal name of someone else in town, rather than the gardener's legal name; that the testator meant to leave a gift to his nursing home but mistakenly named a corporation that owns hundreds of nursing homes; or that there is no property with the address the will uses to describe real property that the testator devised.

Virginia has long followed the prevailing rule in the U.S. that where the words written in the will are clear and unambiguous, there is no room for rules of construction nor for extrinsic evidence offered to show that the testator actually wanted to do something else. In other words, courts will not rewrite wills based on claims of mistake. See, e.g., Gasque v. Sitterding, 208 Va. 206, 210, 156 S.E.2d 576, 579-80 (1967). Nationally, there is some movement away from this, with a small number of states authorizing courts to engage in reformation of wills (as those in Virginia can now do in limited circumstances with trust instruments), but Virginia has not yet joined that movement. If they can show they were "intended third-party beneficiaries" of the testator's contract with the attorney, persons harmed by the drafting attorney's mistakes can seek recovery in a malpractice suit.

Supreme Court of Virginia.
Thorsen v. Richmond Society for the Prevention of Cruelty to Aniimals
786 S.E.2d 453 (2016)

OPINION by Senior Justice Leroy F. Millette, Jr.

… In 2003, Alice Louise Cralle Dumville, then a resident of Chesterfield County, met with James B. Thorsen, an attorney, at his office in Richmond, Virginia, in order to prepare her last will and testament. At the end of the initial meeting, Thorsen understood that Dumville wanted him to prepare a will that would, upon her death, convey all of her property to her mother if her mother survived her, and, in the event her mother predeceased her, to the Richmond Society for the Prevention of Cruelty to

Animals ("RSPCA"). At the time, Dumville was forty-three and her mother was in her late seventies or early eighties. Dumville lived with three cats, which she desired to go to the RSPCA upon her death.

Thorsen prepared the will. At no time in the preparation of the will did Thorsen provide any tax advice, such as attempting to minimize tax burdens on the estate. On April 16, 2003, Thorsen wrote a letter to Dumville informing her of the completion of her will, and Dumville executed the will as drafted by Thorsen.

Dumville died on May 16, 2008, her mother having predeceased her. Thorsen, in his capacity as co-executor of the estate, notified the RSPCA that it was the sole beneficiary of Dumville's estate. Thorsen was subsequently informed that, in the opinion of the title insurance company, the will left only the tangible estate, not real estate, to the RSPCA.

Thorsen brought suit in a collateral proceeding to correct this "scrivener's error" based on Dumville's clear original intent. The Circuit Court of Chesterfield County, however, found the language unambiguously limited the bequest to the RSPCA to tangible personal property, while the intangible estate passed intestate to Dumville's heirs at law, Helen Boyle and Kathleen Davis. Thorsen v. Boyle, Rec. No. CL09-718 (April 9, 2010) (unpublished).

On April 14, 2011, the RSPCA brought suit against James B. Thorsen, Thorsen & Scher, LLP, and James B. Thorsen, P.C. (collectively, "Thorsen") for breach of contract-professional negligence, as a third-party beneficiary of the contract between Thorsen and Dumville. ... At trial, the parties stipulated that Thorsen, as Dumville's attorney, had a duty to incorporate her intent into her will accurately and that he did not accurately incorporate her intent as to the disposition of real property to the RSPCA. The RSPCA received $72,015.60 from the tangible estate, but the ultimate bequest, less expenses, would have totaled $675,425.50 absent the error. The circuit court... found damages for the RSPCA in the amount of $603,409.90. ...

II. DISCUSSION

A. Requirement of a Written Contract

... Code § 55-22 states:

> An immediate estate or interest in or the benefit of a condition respecting any estate may be taken by a person under an instrument, although he be not a party thereto; and if a covenant or promise be made for the benefit, in whole or in part, of a person with whom it is not made, or with whom it is made jointly with others, such person, whether named in the instrument or not, may maintain in his own name any action thereon which he might maintain in case it had been made with him only and the consideration had moved from him to the party making such covenant or promise.

Thorsen argues that the language of Code § 55-22 refers to the third-party beneficiary of an "instrument." An instrument is a "written legal document that defines rights, duties, entitlements, or liabilities, such as a statute, contract, will, promissory note, or share certificate." Black's Law Dictionary 918 (10th ed. 2014) (emphasis added). Thorsen therefore contends that, under the plain language of the statute, the oral nature of the contract in question is fatal to the RSPCA's cause of action, and the RSPCA has no recourse.

The parties do not dispute, nor can they in good faith, that the plain meaning of the term "instrument" as employed in this statute refers to a written document. Because the benefit to the third-party referred to in the first phrase of the statute derives from an "instrument," Code § 55-22 must refer to a benefit from a written document. This interpretation is bolstered by the second half of the statute: although the term "covenant or promise" is not preceded by a modifier specifying "written," it is nonetheless closely followed by reference to "the instrument" (emphasis added). The definite article makes clear that the source of the benefit referred to in this statute must be a written agreement or other benefit that is memorialized in a written document.

While we agree with Thorsen's construction of the statute, we cannot agree that this statute abrogates the common law so as to prohibit the ability of third-party beneficiaries to sue upon oral contracts. We have previously noted:

> At common law, the general rule was that, whether the contract was express or implied, by parol or under seal, or of record, the action must be brought in the name of the party in whom the legal interest was vested, and that this legal interest was vested in the person to whom the promise was made, and consequently that he or his privy was the only person who could sue in a court of law upon such contract. [citations omitted] However, "in contracts not under seal, it has been held, for two centuries or more, that any one for whose benefit the contract was made may sue upon it." Thacker, 122 Va. at 387, 94 S.E. at 931 (emphasis in original).

> Ward v. Ernst & Young, 246 Va. 317, 329, 435 S.E.2d 628, 634 (1993).

Oral contracts are not under seal, and the Court has never held, in the centuries prior to Thacker or the century since, that the oral nature of a contract limits a third-party beneficiary's ability to sue upon it.

Code § 55-22 is silent as to oral contracts. By its plain terms, it applies only to written contracts. Its enactment therefore does not affect the ability of a third-party beneficiary to bring a common law action based on an oral contract made for his or her benefit, which remains intact.

Additionally, "statutes are not to be considered as isolated fragments of law, but as a whole, or as parts of a great connected, homogenous system, or a single and complete statutory arrangement." Code § 11-2, entitled "When written evidence required to maintain action," more commonly known as the Statute of Frauds, sets forth limitations on oral contracts under some circumstances. A third-party beneficiary cannot sue upon an oral promise to answer for his or her debt, for example. Code § 11-2(4). However, there is no prohibition in Code § 11-2 on the ability of third-party beneficiaries to sue upon oral contracts generally. ...

Because the RSPCA had the authority to proceed under common law as a third-party beneficiary of an oral contract, and the circuit court had the authority to enter judgment accordingly...

B. Standing

Thorsen next assigns error to the circuit court's holding that the RSPCA has standing to sue for breach of contract while not party to the attorney-client relationship. ... This assignment of error requires us to consider... whether Virginia recognizes a cause of action for breach of contract against attorneys by third-party testamentary beneficiaries...

1. The Cause of Action

While, as a general rule, strangers to a contract acquire no rights under such contract, third-party beneficiary contracts represent a well-recognized exception in our law under which a nonparty can nevertheless enforce the contract under certain circumstances. A primary rationale for supporting third-party beneficiary claims was that donee contracts, of which testamentary instruments are one example, otherwise could rarely be enforced, as the promisee could recover only nominal damages upon nonperformance: "The party to the contract would have no action for its breach except nominal damages since he was not the one who suffered by the promisor's default. If the beneficiary could not sue there could be no adequate recovery even though the breach was established." ...

While this rule remains throughout many aspects of the attorney-client relationship, courts in the majority of our sister states have recognized some form of cause of action against negligent drafters of estate instruments by frustrated beneficiaries, through contract or tort principles, or both. In Virginia, "an action for the negligence of an attorney in the performance of professional duties, while sounding in tort, is an action for breach of contract." Oleyar v. Kerr, 217 Va. 88, 90, 225 S.E.2d 398, 400 (1976). In the Commonwealth, the cause of action alleged today therefore lies in contract, and the exception to the privity rule lies there as well. Indeed, this Court is among those which have previously addressed the privity requirement in terms of the attorney-client relationship in Copenhaver v. Rogers, 238 Va. 361, 384 S.E.2d 593 (1989), in which grandchildren who were remaindermen under their grandparents' testamentary trust were precluded from bringing a legal malpractice action. The fatal aspect of the claim, however, was that they had asserted they were intended beneficiaries of the estate rather than intended beneficiaries of the contract. Id. at 369, 371, 384 S.E.2d at 597-98. ...

While a party may reap a benefit from an estate, such party may not proceed in Virginia against one who negligently drafted testamentary documents without showing that the party was a "clearly and definitely intended" beneficiary of the contract to draft the testamentary documents. By way of illustration, the Court in Copenhaver offered these polar hypotheticals:

> There is a critical difference between being the intended beneficiary of an estate and being the intended beneficiary of a contract between a lawyer and his client. A set of examples will illustrate the point: A client might direct his lawyer to put his estate in order and advise his lawyer that he really does not care what happens to his money except that he wants the government to get as little of it as possible. Given those instructions, a lawyer might devise an estate plan with various features, including inter vivos trusts to certain relatives, specific bequests. . . [and] many people and institutions might be beneficiaries of the estate, but none could fairly be described as beneficiaries of the contract between the client and his attorney because the intent of that arrangement was to avoid taxes as much as possible. By contrast, a client might direct his lawyer to put his estate in order and advise his lawyer that his one overriding intent is to ensure that each of his grandchildren receive one million dollars at his death and that unless the lawyer agrees to take all steps necessary to ensure that each grandchild receives the specified amount, the client will take his legal business elsewhere. In this second example, if the lawyer agrees to comply with these specific directives, one might fairly argue each grandchild is an intended beneficiary of the contract between the client and the lawyer. Id.

Because the Copenhavers "never alleged that their grandparents and Rogers entered a contract of which they were intended beneficiaries," they had no claim. ...

> In short, there is an agreement out of which arises an obligation to benefit a third party, the breach of which causes damages to that third party. Accordingly, "where the intent to benefit the plaintiff is clear and the promisee (testator) is unable to enforce the contract," our precedent recognizes a cause of action among the narrow class of third-party beneficiaries to enforce claims which would otherwise have no recourse for failed legacies resulting from attorney malpractice. Fabian v. Lindsay, 765 S.E.2d 132, 140 (S.C. 2014).

... Thorsen argues that Johnson v. Hart, 279 Va. 617, 692 S.E.2d 239 (2010), overrules Copenhaver. Yet *Johnson* applies specifically to an attempt to bring suit under Code § 8.01-13, pertaining to assigns and beneficial owners. The appeal concerned whether a sole testamentary beneficiary could bring a legal malpractice action in her own name against the attorney for the estate for negligent services rendered. Because the attorney-client relationship existed between the attorney and the estate, Johnson never argued that she was an intended third-party beneficiary. Johnson sought to bring suit as a beneficial owner under Code § 8.01-13, but the Court found that such action was barred by the rule prohibiting assignment of legal malpractice actions in the Commonwealth. Id. at 626, 692 S.E.2d at 244. We thus find the holding in *Johnson* inapplicable to the question before this Court today. ...

Because this cause of action requires that one of the primary purposes for the establishment of the attorney-client relationship is to benefit the nonclient, the scope of such claims is necessarily limited; as this Court has previously stated, "it will no doubt be difficult for a litigant, in a case of this kind, to meet the requirements of third-party beneficiary claims." *Copenhaver*, 238 Va. at 371, 384 S.E.2d at 598. Indeed, it has proved so difficult that this Court has not seen another such case in the nearly three decades from *Copenhaver* until this day.

2. Allegations of Third-Party Beneficiary Status

... A nonparty must allege facts sufficient to conclude it was a "clearly and definitely intended beneficiary" of the contract; "[a]n incidental beneficiary has no standing to sue." Kelly Health Care, Inc., v. Prudential Ins. Co., 226 Va. 376, 380, 309 S.E.2d 305, 307 (1983). ... An incidental beneficiary is so far removed from the obligations assumed by the contracting parties that a court will not allow him to sue on that contract, whereas an intended beneficiary is such an integral part of the obligations assumed by the contracting parties that a court will permit him to sue on that contract. Radosevic v. Virginia Intermont College, 651 F.Supp. 1037, 1038 (W.D. Va. 1987). ... Here, the facts sufficiently allege that the contract was entered into for the benefit of Dumville's mother and the RSPCA. The RSPCA sufficiently alleges that Dumville... sought Thorsen's professional expertise to accomplish this task; that Dumville and Thorsen contracted so that Dumville would confer a benefit, and that Thorsen accepted that obligation, thus creating the clear and definite intent to create a benefit to the RSPCA. ... The RSPCA has standing to proceed.

C. Contingent, Residuary Beneficiaries as Third Party Beneficiaries

Thorsen next argues that a contingent, residuary beneficiary to a will cannot be a "clearly and definitely intended" third-party beneficiary as a matter of law. We disagree. Thorsen seeks... a per se rule against certain classes of testamentary beneficiaries. The class of beneficiary in a will is one of many factors to be considered in weighing whether the nonparty was a "clearly and definitely intended beneficiary" to the contract.

1. Residuary Beneficiaries

First, we consider the residuary beneficiary, the beneficiary who takes after specific bequests. It is patently obvious that this beneficiary can be a "clearly and definitely intended beneficiary" under the law.

Consider the following example: a widowed and remarried woman living in a nursing home with her husband retains an attorney to create a will for the benefit of her own biological son. She leaves a specific bequest to her husband of her wedding ring and bequeaths the entire residue of her estate to her son. Although the residuary taker, the son receives nearly the entirety of the estate, and, although there may have been multiple purposes to the will, the son was a "clearly and definitely intended beneficiary" of the contract and not an incidental beneficiary.

Depending on circumstances, a residuary beneficiary may take all of the estate, none of the estate, or anything in between. Evidence may support a finding that the residuary beneficiary was clearly and definitely intended by the testator, or may support the conclusion that the residuary was an incidental beneficiary, such as if the testator instructed the attorney to select a charity for the residuary estate. Whether the residuary beneficiary is a third-party beneficiary is a fact-intensive inquiry; the residuary beneficiary is not precluded from third-party beneficiary status as a matter of law. ...

2. Contingent Beneficiaries

At the time a will is drafted, the testator cannot know or at least could not be certain whether any particular contingency will be removed such that a contingent beneficiary will in fact take. Thorsen argues, therefore, that a contingent beneficiary by definition cannot be a "definitely intended beneficiary."

Yet one of the most common scenarios in which parents enter into their first set of testamentary instruments shows this to be contrary to reason. Consider the couple who retains an attorney to draft reciprocal wills at the birth of their child. They will likely name each other as the primary beneficiaries, desiring that if something were to happen to only one of them, the other would benefit from the will. The child is a contingent beneficiary, sometimes through a trust if a minor and in his or her own name as an adult. An overriding purpose in entering into the contract with the attorney to draft such a will at this time is generally to account for the possibility that both parents might perish, perhaps in a common accident, and to provide for the child's long-term care. Although the surviving spouse remains the primary beneficiary of the will, and the child takes only as a contingent beneficiary, this does not alter the fact that the child is a "clearly and definitely intended beneficiary" of the contract to draft the will.

Contrary to Thorsen's claims, the viability of a third-party contract claim in this context does not depend on identifying, or being able to identify, the specific party being benefitted when the contract is made. Contingent beneficiaries exist to accommodate changing circumstance, particularly age, and to direct the progression of beneficiaries without the constant need to revisit the instrument as time and eventuality goes by. Thus, the fact that beneficiaries do not take first does not mean that they are not "clearly and definitely intended beneficiar[ies]" under the contract, but rather that they were not intended as the first takers given the circumstances at the time the will was drafted; yet, the will might still have been drafted, perhaps even primarily as in the example above, for their benefit. Whether a contingent beneficiary in a will is a third-party beneficiary of the contract to draft the will is a fact-intensive inquiry. ...

D. Plea in Bar

In Virginia, actions for legal malpractice are actions for breach of contract and are thus governed by the limitations periods prescribed for contract claims. Code § 8.01-246 states that "actions founded upon a contract ... shall be brought within the following number of years next after the cause of action shall have accrued: ... 4. In actions upon any unwritten contract, express or implied, within three years."

Code § 8.01-230 states that:

> In every action for which a limitation period is prescribed, the right of action shall be deemed to accrue and the prescribed limitation period shall begin to run from the date the injury is sustained in the case of injury to the person or damage to property, when the breach of contract occurs in actions *ex contractu* and not when the resulting damage is discovered, except where the relief sought is solely equitable or where otherwise provided under ... other statute.

Thorsen maintains that, if he breached the contract, it was when he drafted the will, thus completing his legal services, on April 16, 2003 (citing MacLellan v. Throckmorton, 235 Va. 341, 345, 367 S.E.2d 720, 722 (1988) ("[T]he breach of contract or duty occurs and the statute of limitations begins to run when the attorney's services rendered in connection with that particular undertaking or transaction have terminated.")). In his view, the statute of limitations then expired three years later, on April 16, 2006. We disagree.

... A cause of action is the operative set of facts giving rise to a right of action. "A right of action cannot arise until a cause of action exists because a right of action is a remedial right to presently enforce an existing cause of action." "Some injury or damage, however slight, is essential to a cause of action." In the case of a testamentary beneficiary, no injury, however slight, can be sustained prior to the testator's death, because "[a] testator may, during his lifetime, alter his will or other testamentary papers as he pleases and whenever he chooses." Van Dam, 280 Va. at 462, 699 S.E.2d at 482. "While [the testator] lives, no beneficiary has anything more than a bare expectancy and no person has suffered any injury or damage as a result of his tentative dispositions." Id. Because of this mutability and bare expectancy, no testamentary beneficiary has a cause of action prior to the death of the testator.

In accordance with Code § 8.01-246, the three-year statute of limitations cannot begin to run as to the testamentary beneficiary until a cause of action accrues, after the death of the testator. Thus Code § 8.01-246 can, under the proper circumstances in which no injury is sustained, provide one of the referenced statutory exceptions to the rule set forth in Code § 8.01-230 that contractual rights of action accrue at breach. ...

The RSPCA... was unable to bring suit in the years following the execution of the will: lacking a vested interest and possessing only a bare expectancy, it had no standing to sue. Not even slight harm or damage accrued to the RSPCA until the testator's death. ... Because the RSPCA's cause of action could not have accrued until the testator's death, we [reject the defense] premised on the statute of limitations.

E. Sufficiency of the Evidence

… To review the circuit court's finding that the RSPCA was a third-party beneficiary of the contract, we review both the evidence as to Dumville's intent and Thorsen's intent at the time of the contract to consider whether the RSPCA was a "clearly and definitely intended" beneficiary.

1. Dumville's Intent

… Thorsen's answer to an interrogatory from the prior collateral proceeding stated: "The decedent was clear in her instructions to Thorsen … that she wanted her entire estate to go to her mother and if her mother predeceased her, then her entire estate be to the Richmond SPCA. These were her instructions and intentions at the time of the initial interview and the creation of her last will and testament and throughout the drafting period." The RSPCA introduced a letter from Thorsen to the title insurance company stating:

> [I]t was the clear intent of Alice and the intent in my drafting, to make a full and complete conveyance of Alice's estate to her mother if she survived Alice, and if not, a full and complete bequeath/conveyance of all of Alice's entire estate to the RSPCA. Moreover, I had no idea Alice had any relative other than her mother, and did not become aware of Ms. Boyles [sic] until sometime after [Dumville's mother] died.

The parties stipulated that Dumville was forty-three and her mother was in her late seventies or early eighties when the will was drafted. Thorsen testified that he was aware that Dumville had a relationship with the RSPCA, had an affinity for the organization, and wanted her cats to go to the RSPCA after her death. Thorsen testified in the previous matter that these three cats "were her babies" and she "probably cared for her cats more than she did herself." Finally, although there is error in the drafting, the RSPCA is named specifically in the will instrument. …

Here, a single woman with an uncomplicated estate created a simple will devising her entire estate to the only relative with whom evidence suggests she had a close relationship, her elderly mother, or, if her mother predeceased her, a charity with which she had a preexisting relationship, upon her death. It is a fair inference that the client entered into a contract to draft a will for the purpose of benefiting one of those parties upon her death. Given the deference afforded to the factfinder, we find no error in the circuit court's conclusion that the primary or overriding purpose of the contract was for the benefit of the will beneficiaries.

The evidence was also sufficient to support Dumville's intent for the RSPCA specifically to benefit. There was testimony as to her relationship with the RSPCA, supporting the RSPCA as a purposeful choice. The ages of Dumville and her mother at the time the will was drafted make it not unlikely and, in fact, foreseeable that

Dumville's mother would predecease her and the RSPCA would take the entirety of Dumville's estate. Finally, in the case of a residuary charitable beneficiary, affirmatively being named in the instrument lends additional support to the testator's clear and definite intention to benefit the charity in her contract with her attorney and his understanding of that obligation. Taking these facts together, we find no error in the trial court's finding of sufficient evidence to conclude that Dumville clearly and definitely intended the RSPCA to be a third-party beneficiary of the contract.

2. Thorsen's Intent

Thorsen alleges that there was no evidence that Thorsen agreed to benefit the RSPCA in entering into the retention agreement to draft the will, and so the RSPCA cannot be a third-party beneficiary of the contract. A third-party beneficiary rule "has no application unless the party sought to be held liable has assumed an obligation for the benefit of the third party." Thorsen argues that, in the *Copenhaver* hypothetical, this Court explicitly included a requirement that a lawyer comply with the testator's specific directives at the outset of their retention. 238 Va. at 369, 384 S.E.2d at 597. Thorsen desires the Court to distinguish between the obligation undertaken to make a will in a retention agreement and the obligation to benefit the parties in the will.

We disagree that *Copenhaver* requires some specific language in the contract between a testator and her attorney that the lawyer must comply with her directives or there will be no contract, and we do not find this cause of action necessarily so limited. The Copenhaver hypothetical indeed emphasizes that mutual understanding of the benefit to the third party is essential to the contract. Id. at 369, 384 S.E.2d at 597 (e.g., "unless the lawyer agrees ... the client will take his legal business elsewhere"; "if the lawyer agrees to comply with these specific directives"). Yet, the agreement to comply with specific directives is implied when the client contracts with the attorney to perform a specific service which the attorney then undertakes to perform. We cannot separate the obligations of the client's intent from the agreement because, without the intent and the assent to take on those specific directives, there would be no retention agreement.

For this reason, when a client can terminate a contract at any time, a client's request six months into an attorney-client relationship to make a third party his or her beneficiary has the same weight as a request on the first day of the relationship: refusal of the attorney to draft the will according to his or her wishes would likewise result in the termination of the attorney-client relationship. Thus, we do not find it necessary to prove that this mutual assent was expressed prior to retention, but rather that, prior to the completion of the attorney's services, the attorney became aware of the directives of the client and agreed to undertake the obligation.

There may be many reasons for drafting a testamentary instrument which would not result in the creation of third-party beneficiaries to the attorney-client contract. But the evidence in this case supports the trial court's finding that Dumville went to Thorsen to draft a will for the purpose of benefiting her mother and the RSPCA. The parties stipulated that, at the end of their initial meeting regarding preparation of the will, "Thorsen understood that Ms. Dumville wanted him to prepare a Will which would accurately incorporate and effectuate Ms. Dumville's decisions as to the distribution of her estate upon her death, i.e. that upon her death all of her property would be left to her mother if her mother survived her, and in the event her mother predeceased her, all of her property would be left to the RSPCA." Thorsen stated under oath that "There was no doubt in my mind what she wanted in terms of the will, no doubt what she expressed." In that meeting, which Thorsen testified was their only meeting regarding the will prior to his drafting, Thorsen agreed to draft a will according to those specifications. ...

Thus, taking these findings together as a whole, we find no error in the trial court's holding that the RSPCA was a clearly and definitely identified third-party beneficiary of the contract.

———————————

There is no recourse, though, when it was the testator who made a mistake, if there is no uncertainty of interpretation to justify extrinsic evidence.

Many wills do, however, contain ambiguities, and then courts can look to rules of construction or to extrinsic evidence to clarify the testator's intent. A "patent ambiguity" is apparent on the face of the will. An example is a term with no legal meaning, such as "dearest friends," or more than one meaning, such as "partner," and lacking any further explanation of who was meant. There can be uncertainty whether an expression of preference was meant to be binding, creating a conditional gift, or merely precatory. Or whether a gift of real property to a surviving spouse "so she may have it for her life" conveys a life estate or fee simple. Other examples:

> "I give my house to one of my brothers."

> "I give one of my houses to my sister Janet."

> Para. 4: "I give my golden sword to my friend John." Para. 11: "I give my golden sword to my brother Joe."

With such patent ambiguities, one can tell just by looking at the language of the will that there will be a problem in effectuating it.

A "latent ambiguity" is a will provision that becomes difficult to apply once the executor looks at the outside world. A residuary clause leaves the remainder to "my cousin Beth Rose," but it turns out the executor had two cousins by that name. A will provision with a beneficiary designation that fits more than one person, or with a description of property that fits more than one thing the testator owned (e.g., "my Fender guitar"), is also sometimes called an "equivocation."

The Virginia Code provides a little, but only a little, guidance to aid construction of ambiguous language in wills. First, if uncertainty arises because the testator referred to an asset that he or she later replaced with a like item, as people commonly do with houses and cars, the Code says to interpret the will as if it were written immediately before the testator's death.

Subtitle II, Chapter 4. Wills, Article 3. Construction and Effect

§ 64.2-414. When wills deemed to speak.

A. A will shall be construed, with reference to the real and personal estate comprised in it, to speak and take effect as if it had been executed immediately before the death of the testator, unless a contrary intention shall appear by the will.

B. Every will reexecuted or republished, or revived by any codicil, shall be deemed to have been made at the time it was reexecuted, republished, or revived.

***

Thus, if the will refers to "my Lamborghini," the executor should construe it as applying to the 2014 Lamborghini the testator owned at death rather than the 1990 Lamborghini the testator owned at the time of will execution and later sold. This provision will be relevant in the next subsection, relating to changes in persons or property since will execution.

Another code provision targets class gifts – that is, gifts to a group whose description might be ambiguous or whose composition might change.

Subtitle I, Chapter 1, Article 1. Definitions

§ 64.2-101. Construction of generic terms.

In the interpretation of wills and trusts, adopted persons and persons born out of wedlock are included in class gift terminology or terms of relationship in accordance with rules for determining relationships for purposes of intestate succession unless a contrary intent appears on the face of the will or trust. In determining the intent of a testator or settlor, adopted persons are presumptively included in such terms as "children," "issue," "kindred," "heirs," "relatives," "descendents" or similar words of classification and are presumptively excluded by such terms as "natural children," "issue of the body," "blood kindred," "heirs of the body," "blood relatives," "descendents of the body" or similar words of classification. ...

***

Otherwise the legislature has left it to the courts to sort out what to do about apparent or alleged mistakes and ambiguities. There are also some common law rules of presumptive interpretation of ambiguous language, as reflected in the *Lane* case below. The will in this case reflects the not uncommon situation in which a testator wants to leave specific properties to beneficiaries, but the properties are of such great value that the devise or bequest could create an unbalanced estate plan unless the testator requires the beneficiaries to pay into the estate some portion of the value.

Supreme Court of Virginia.
Lane v. Starke
279 Va. 686, 692 S.E.2d 217 (2010)

OPINION BY Senior Justice CHARLES S. RUSSELL.

*688 ... Willard W. Lane, Sr. (the testator), a resident of Surry County, died on December 5, 1991. He was survived by his wife, Bernice J. Lane (the life tenant). His will, dated in 1982, was admitted to probate. The will appointed the testator's son, W.W. Lane, Jr., (Lane, Jr.) executor but he did not qualify as executor until 2006.

*689 The testator's will contained the following provisions: Article II bequeathed all tangible personal property to the testator's wife; Article III devised the testator's home place, with 18 acres of land, to the testator's wife in fee simple absolute. Article IV provides: "All the rest and residue of my estate I give, devise and bequeath to my wife, BERNICE J. LANE, for and during her natural life or until she remarries." Article V provides:

> Upon the death of my wife, she having survived me, or upon her remarriage, I give, devise and bequeath the property herein devised to her for her life or until her remarriage as follows:
>
> 1. I give, devise and bequeath that portion of the ROWELL PLACE [metes and bounds description] to my son, W.W. LANE, JR., upon the EXPRESS condition that he pay into my estate ONE–HALF (1/2) of the ASSESSED VALUE of such property.
>
> 2. I give, devise and bequeath the TWO HOUSES AND LOTS at SCOTLAND to my two daughters, JANICE L. STARKE and MOLLY L. RICKMOND, upon the EXPRESS condition that they pay into my estate ONE–HALF (1/2) of the ASSESSED VALUE of such property.

The life tenant died on March 27, 2002, having never remarried. ... In 2006 Lane, Jr., individually and as executor of his father's will, filed this suit in the circuit court requesting aid and direction as to the appropriate date upon which to determine the assessed valuations of the real property in which he and his sisters had been devised remainder interests by their father. He asked the court to determine whether the date upon which the assessed valuations were to be determined should be (A) the date of the will, (B) the date of the testator's death, or (C) the date of the life tenant's death. *690 ... **219 ...

[T]he circuit court... held that Article V of the testator's will created contingent remainders, not vested remainders; that the conditions had to be met before the death of the life tenant, which was not done; that the failure of the contingencies caused the properties to revert to the testator's estate to be distributed through the residuary clause of his will; that the residuary clause devised the residue of the testator's estate to the life tenant only for her life and that the residuary clause failed because the life tenant was deceased; and that the testator was therefore intestate as to the property devised under Article V, which would pass to the testator's heirs at law under the statute of descent and distribution. ...

The testator's will is ambiguous in that it may be construed in different ways. It does not explicitly provide for the time the assessed valuation of the devised parcels is to be ascertained. That uncertainty creates doubt as to the amounts to be paid. Those issues raise the fundamental legal questions whether the remainders are *691 contingent on payment of the amounts due the estate, or whether the remainder interests vested at the testator's death, leaving the requirements of payment as conditions subsequent. In the latter case, the required payments would constitute liens upon the land, enforceable in equity, but would not defeat the remainder interests. Gilley v. Nidermaier, 176 Va. 32, 41, 10 S.E.2d 484, 487–88 (1940).

When testamentary language is clear and unambiguous, it will be applied as written unless it contravenes the law or public policy, because the testator's intent is the "guiding star" in testamentary construction. When the language of a will is ambiguous, however, leaving the testator's intent unclear, the courts are guided by certain well-settled rules of construction. Perhaps the most time-honored of these canons of construction in Virginia is the "early-vesting" rule. This Court, in Catlett v. Marshall, 37 Va. (10 Leigh) 83, 96 (1839), construing the will of Thomas, Lord Fairfax dated in 1777, established the rule that "where no special intent to the contrary is manifested, the vesting of legacies shall be referred to the death of the testator."

More recently, we said:

> Our purpose of course is to find the testamentary intent. If a will reflects a clear intent that the determination of beneficiaries be postponed until a life tenant's death, rather than the testator's death, we honor that intent. See Griffin v. Central Nat'l Bank, 194 Va. 485, 74 S.E.2d 188 (1953). But if a will is ambiguous in this regard, we invoke the aid of the canon of construction known as the early vesting rule. Under that rule, "devises and bequests are to be construed as vesting at the testator's death, unless the intention to postpone the vesting is clearly indicated in the will". Chapman v. Chapman, 90 Va. 409, 411, 18 S.E. 913 (1894).

> Clark, 213 Va. at 8–9, 189 S.E.2d at 47 (footnote omitted).

Although the will in the present case postpones their enjoyment of the devises made to the remaindermen, there is no language in the testator's will evidencing an intent to postpone the vesting of their remainder interests. **220 Accordingly, the early vesting rule applies. *692 We hold that the remainder interests vested at the time of the testator's death.

Similarly, when testamentary language requires that a monetary payment be made prior to the vesting of a future interest in a remainderman, the requirement will be treated as a condition precedent, but if the language does not necessarily provide that the payment must precede vesting, the condition is treated as a condition subsequent. Wenner v. George, 129 Va. 615, 618, 106 S.E. 365, 366 (1921). As we have previously observed:

> The courts have, wherever possible, construed a provision for the payment of a legacy, or a sum of money, as a charge rather than a condition precedent, in order that the estate may vest in the devisee. Thus, where it appears from the language of the will that the testator intended to couple the payment of the legacy by the devisee with the devise of the land, so that the payment is to be made, because, or as a condition on which, the devise has been made, then the real estate is, in equity, chargeable with the payment of the legacy. Gilley, 176 Va. at 41, 10 S.E.2d at 487.

We therefore hold that the monetary payments required by the will are conditions subsequent, constituting liens on the land devised, enforceable in equity.

The circuit court's construction of the will leads to a partial intestacy.

> No principle of testamentary construction is more firmly settled in Virginia than that there is a strong presumption that every testator intends to dispose of his entire estate ... and the courts are inclined very decidedly against adopting any construction of wills which leaves the testator intestate as to any portion of his estate, unless that result is inescapable.
>
> First Nat'l Exchange Bank v. Seaboard Citizens Nat'l Bank, 200 Va. 681, 685, 107 S.E.2d 408, 411 (1959).

Even though the remainder interests vested at the time of the testator's death, the testator postponed their enjoyment by the remaindermen until the death of the life tenant. Therefore, their duty to make payment of one-half the assessed valuations of the lands *693 devised to them did not arise until the death of the life tenant. The amounts they are required to pay are therefore to be ascertained by the real estate assessments existing on that date.

Supreme Court of Virginia.
Gaymon v. Gaymon
258 Va. 225, 519 S.E.2d 142 (1999)

LACY, Justice.

... The testator was survived by Violeta N. Gaymon, his widow, and two adult children from his former marriage, William Victor Gaymon and Nicole G. Gaymon (the Gaymon children). The Fifth Article (Article 5) of testator's will provides:

FIFTH. I give and bequeath to my children, WILLIAM V. GAYMON and NICOLE G. GAYMON, share and share alike, the following described property, subject to any encumbrances upon the same upon the date of transfer *and the mortgage remaining shall be paid by the remainder persons*:

> a. My residence, together with improvements thereon, located at 2619 Fox Mill Road, Reston, Virginia. ... **144

> It is understood that in the case that Mrs. VIOLETA N. GAYMON and I have residence at the Fox Mill address at the time of my demise, she would have a life estate in the same for the remainder of her life.

The language in Article 5 that is italicized above was a handwritten addition initialed by the testator. ... *229 ...

Acting as the Executor, William V. Gaymon... asked the chancellor to determine... whether Article 5 created a "mandatory or precatory life estate" in favor of Violeta in the property. The Executor also asked the chancellor to declare that, under the terms of the will, Violeta is obligated to pay expenses on the property, including interest on the deed of trust notes, taxes, and insurance. ... *230 ...

The legal principles applicable to the construction of a will are well established. The objective in construing a will is to determine the testator's intent by initially looking to the four corners of the document. Extrinsic evidence may be considered only if the language of the will is ambiguous, that is, susceptible to more than one interpretation. **145 Gillespie v. Davis, 242 Va. 300, 303-04, 410 S.E.2d 613, 615 (1991).

I. Life Estate

... The Executor argues that the phrase "It is understood" contained in Article 5 reflects the testator's request or desire that Violeta be allowed to remain on the property but does not give her the right to do so. In support of this position, the Executor relies on Carson v. Simmons, 198 Va. 854, 856, 96 S.E.2d 800, 802 (1957), in which the phrase "with the understanding" was determined to be precatory rather than mandatory, thereby defeating a claim that a spendthrift trust was created. However, although the phrases in Carson and in this case are similar, the context in which they appear is quite different. Thus, applying the principles discussed in *Carson* to this case does not lead to the same result.

The will in Carson gave the testator's daughters an apartment building "with the understanding that" the daughters would rent out one of the apartments and use the rental income for the upkeep of the property until the youngest grandchild reached 16 years of age. The Court concluded that this phrase was precatory because it directed the legatees to perform some act, rather than directing actions of the executor. The Court reached this conclusion even though the use of *231 the same phrase in a subsequent paragraph of the will was mandatory. Id. at 858-59, 96 S.E.2d at 804.

In this case, however, reading the phrase "it is understood," within the context of Article 5 leads to only one interpretation, that the testator intended to create a life estate. As noted by the chancellor, Article 5 refers to the Gaymon children as "remainder persons." That reference is consistent only with the conclusion that a life estate was created in the property because, without such an estate, the Gaymon children would have a fee simple interest, not a remainder interest. And, unlike the direction in Carson, Article 5 gives no direction to the Gaymon children, but only declares the interest created. The only contingency attached to the interest given Violeta was that she and the testator be living at the property at the time of the testator's death. There is nothing in the will which supports a conclusion that the Gaymon children, the remainder persons, had the discretion to determine whether Violeta Gaymon could remain on the property during her lifetime.

The Executor also relies on the rule of construction recited in Smith v. Baptist Orphanage, 194 Va. 901, 75 S.E.2d 491 (1953), and McKinsey v. Cullingsworth, 175 Va. 411, 9 S.E.2d 315 (1940), that when an estate is conveyed in one part of an instrument by clear and unambiguous words, only words of equal clarity and decisiveness can diminish or destroy that estate. According to the Executor, the phrase "it is understood" is too imprecise to effectively diminish the fee simple estate granted the Gaymon children in the property by Article 5 of the will. We disagree.

No specific words are required to create a life estate. Robinson v. Caldwell, 200 Va. 353, 356-57, 105 S.E.2d 852, 854 (1958). Nevertheless, the language of Article 5-"a life estate in the [property] for the remainder of her life"-is not a vague or general description of the interest conveyed. Rather, this is the formal, technical language associated with the creation of a life estate. Furthermore, in both the cases upon which the Executor relies, the Court was required to consider whether certain phrases allegedly describing the interests at issue were mandatory or precatory and, in both cases, we concluded that the phrases only indicated a desire of the testator and thus were not mandatory. Obviously, if a phrase in a will is precatory and creates no interest, it cannot be of equal dignity with words creating an interest. In this case, as we have already said, the language of Article 5 is not precatory. Therefore, the rule of construction *232 cited by the Executor does not defeat the intent of the testator as expressed in Article 5 under the circumstances of this case.

For these reasons, we conclude that there is no error in the chancellor's conclusion that the language of Article 5 unambiguously creates **146 a life estate in the property in favor of Violeta Gaymon.

II. Liability of Remainder Persons

… Although we agree with the chancellor that extrinsic evidence was not necessary to determine the testator's intent in adding the language directing the remainder persons to pay the mortgages, we disagree with the chancellor's ultimate interpretation of the added language. Apparently, the chancellor concluded that the testator used the word "mortgage" to mean both the principal and interest due on the deeds of trust. By using that word, the chancellor concluded, the testator intended the remainder persons to pay both principal and interest, thus altering the common law principle that a life tenant must pay the interest on any encumbrance on the devised life estate property. Livesay v. Boyd, 164 Va. 528, 532-33, 180 S.E. 158, 159-60 (1935).

However, there is nothing in the word "mortgage" itself that indicates inclusion or exclusion of interest due on the encumbrance, and there is no other language in the added phrase or elsewhere in the will that addresses the treatment of interest. Therefore, in the *233 absence of more precise direction, we cannot conclude that by using the word "mortgage," the testator intended to deviate from the well-established common law principle regarding the obligation of a life tenant. ...

[W]e conclude nevertheless that the added language had a meaning independent of other instructions in the will. That language shows the testator's intent to make the remainder persons personally liable for payment of the mortgage principal. The general rule in this Commonwealth is that if property encumbered with a lien is devised in a will, and the lien secures a personal debt of the testator, the decedent's personal estate, not the encumbered property, is the primary fund for discharge of that debt. Brown, Adm'r v. Hargraves, 198 Va. 748, 750, 96 S.E.2d 788, 790 (1957). Operation of this rule can be altered by the testator if he directs in his will that the encumbered property be the primary source of his estate for satisfaction of the lien. Id.

To determine the priority of the property in the testator's estate for satisfaction of such liens, the language of the will is reviewed to ascertain the intent of the testator, as in all cases of will construction. In this case, by devising the property "subject to any encumbrances," the testator indicated his intent that the encumbered property, not his personal estate, be the primary source of his estate for payment of the deeds of trust.[*]

> [*] Of course, if the property were sold to satisfy the liens but proceeds were insufficient, the unpaid balance could be satisfied out of the personal estate.

However, while devising the property subject to the deeds of trust changed the order in which the component parts of the decedent's estate were to be looked to for satisfaction **147 of his debts, it did not go so far as to make the remainder persons personally liable for the debts secured by the deeds of trust. Personal liability was imposed when the testator added the language directing that the mortgages "shall be paid by the remainder persons." This added language imposed a condition on the disposition of the testator's estate, that the remainder persons would assume personal liability for the debt secured by the deeds of trust. This condition has meaning and effect independent of the direction devising the property "subject to *234 any encumbrances" and unrelated to the common law apportionment of the obligations of life tenants and remainder persons to make mortgage payments.

Thus, we conclude that the testator's intent in adding the interlined phrase was to make the remainder persons personally liable for the debts secured by the deeds of trust, but not to negate the common law principle that the life tenant has the obligation to preserve the property, including among other things the duty to pay the interest on any liens on the property. ...

Where no rule of construction governs and suffices to resolve an ambiguity, courts frequently must decide whether "extrinsic evidence" can be admitted, and if so what kind – specifically, can it include "declarations of intent" that the testator made before dying, or only "facts and circumstances" evidence. Our first such case provides a scenario where only the latter type of extrinsic evidence is admissible.

Supreme Court of Virginia.
Gillespie v. Davis
242 Va. 300, 410 S.E.2d 613 (1991)

COMPTON, Justice.

... William J. Gillespie, the testator, was a resident of Wallops Island in Accomack County. He was a civil engineer and a successful contractor engaged for many years in the manufacture of ready-mix concrete and concrete abutments. The business was conducted on the property in question, one of eight parcels of realty owned by the testator; it was "a fenced-in compound of approximately *302 four-and-a-half acres" located at a highway intersection near Chincoteague.

Appellee C. Lee Davis, a friend of the testator's for "approximately thirty years," became the testator's business associate in 1980. Several years later, the testator decided to retire from the business, which Davis continued to operate at the site. Davis leased the property from the testator who maintained an office on the premises. During the next few years, the testator gave Davis "invaluable" assistance in the operation of the business, refusing "many times" Davis's offer of compensation. According to Davis, "it was almost like he was a father to me."

In May 1988, the testator executed the will in question, a three-page typewritten document. He died on February 3, 1989, and the will was duly probated. The appellants, Anne L. Davis Gillespie, Martha Louise Storer, and Caroline Denmon Wyly are the devisees under the will. Gillespie, also known as Anne L. Davis, is the testator's widow and qualified as executrix of the estate. Storer and Wyly are the testator's stepdaughters.

This controversy was generated by the third and sixth clauses of the will. They **615 provide as follows, complete with spelling errors:

> Third, I give and devise all of my realestate to Mrs. H.E. Storer, Mrs. C.J. Wyly, Jr., and Mrs. Anne L. Davis. They are to share equally and the disposal will be in their hands.
>
> ....
>
> Sixth —It is my desire that Lee Davis, the present renter of the shop area, (fenced-in compound) be allowed to purchase that area and the equipment I own in that area for the fair market value. The equipment includes one D–7 Catepillar bulldozer, John Deere backhoe, Lorain 25–

ton crane with 100′ of boom, Mack tractor and 33–ton capacity LaCrosse trailer, acetelyne cutting touch with bottles and Cart, Dewalt radial saw (in carpenter shop) and a 4″ electric threading machine. The fixed equipment includes a cement silo, aggregate bins, shop building, quonset huts, carpentry shop and sheds. In the event Lee Davis does not desire to buy the moving equipment it shall be sold at auction and the proceeds divided equally among the before-mentioned heirs.

In August 1990, Mr. Davis instituted the present proceeding by a bill for declaratory judgment in equity, naming the devisees defendants. *303 ... Davis asserted that he desired to purchase the realty in question from the devisees for what he alleged was the fair market value of $189,500, but that the devisees had "failed and refused to convey same to him pursuant to the provisions of the will." ... [T]he devisees asserted that the proper interpretation of the will is that the testator gave all his real property, including the parcel in question, to them "to do with as they saw fit." They asserted that the language in the sixth clause "is merely precatory in nature and expresses a wish or request of the testator, not a positive command or directive necessary to establish rights of [Davis] in or to the subject real property..." Additionally, the devisees alleged that the property's fair market value was $300,000. ...

"The cardinal principle of will construction is that the intention of the testator controls; the problem is to ascertain it." Clark v. Strother, 238 Va. 533, 539, 385 S.E.2d 578, 581 (1989). A court construing a will must determine the testator's intent from the language of the document, if possible. Baker v. Linsly, 237 Va. 581, 585, 379 S.E.2d 327, 329 (1989).

Extrinsic evidence may never be used in aid of the interpretation of a will if the language is clear and unambiguous. Coffman's Adm'r v. Coffman, 131 Va. 456, 461, 109 S.E. 454, 456 (1921). But there are various ways of expressing the same thought and there are many different shades of meaning which a group of words may convey; individuals differ in their knowledge of grammar and in their manner of expression. These factors often *304 give rise to cases where the language of a will is ambiguous, susceptible to more than one interpretation. In such cases, two classes of extrinsic evidence may be admitted: (1) so-called "facts and circumstances" evidence and (2) so-called "declarations of intention" evidence. Id. at 461–64, 109 S.E. at 456–57. **616

The first class involves evidence about the testator, the testator's family and property; the claimants under the will and their relationship to the testator; the testator's hopes and fears; the testator's habits of thought and language; and similar matters. The second class is confined to cases of "equivocation," that is, where the words in the will describe equally well two or more persons or two or more things. Under this narrow category, extrinsic statements by the testator of his actual testamentary intentions, that is, what he has done or designs to do by the will, are admissible. Id., 109 S.E. at 456–58. Accord Baker, 237 Va. at 586, 379 S.E.2d at 330; Baliles v. Miller, 231 Va. 48, 57–58, 340 S.E.2d 805, 810–11 (1986).

Contrary to the devisees' contention, we conclude, as did the trial court, that the third and sixth clauses create an ambiguity in the will and that this was a proper case for the use of extrinsic evidence. In the first sentence of the third clause, the testator gives "all of" his real estate to the devisees, but states in the second sentence that the "disposal" of it "will be in their hands." The only other will reference to his real property is contained in the sixth clause in which he expresses the "desire" that Davis be permitted to purchase the parcel in question. This, of course, deals with the disposition of realty and could reasonably be construed to refer back to the "disposal" reference in the third clause, giving Davis a right to purchase from the devisees. But the provisions could also reasonably be construed to mean that the realty in the hands of the devisees was to be unaffected and unencumbered by the "desire" expressed in the sixth clause. If this was the testator's intention, however, the second sentence of the third clause was unnecessary; the gift to the devisees would have been unrestricted by use of the first sentence alone.

While this is a case where the use of extrinsic evidence was warranted, this is not a case of equivocation; the parties and the property are clearly designated. This is a case, however, where evidence of facts and circumstances concerning the testator properly were admitted. And this evidence is overwhelming that the *305 testator intended for Davis to have the right to purchase the shop area for its fair market value.

The widow testified that the testator made a draft of the will in his own handwriting and that she typed it as he stood beside her. During this process, there was no discussion about the disposition of the "concrete plant property" except that the handwritten draft provided that the property could be purchased for $400,000; the testator directed her to type that it could be bought for "the fair market value."

The evidence was undisputed, indeed corroborated by the widow, that Davis and the testator had a close business and personal relationship for at least nine years prior to his death. According to the testimony, the testator unselfishly assisted Davis in operating the business, giving advice and financial assistance when necessary. Davis was operating on a monthly lease and attempted to obtain a long-term lease but the testator always refused. The testator told Davis that if he decided to sell the property, Davis could purchase it or, at his death, could buy it from the estate.

Significantly, the widow testified that the testator, in discussing the continuation of the concrete business, said that he "wanted Lee [Davis] to have it, but he's going to have to pay for it." The widow testified there was "no question" in her mind about Davis's right to purchase the property but "he was going to have to pay [me] and the daughters the fair market value."

Confronted with this abundant evidence of the testator's intention that Davis have the right to purchase the subject property from the devisees, they nevertheless contend that the "desire" and "be allowed" language in the sixth clause are mere precatory words of entreaty, request, wish, or recommendation as distinguished from direct or imperative terms. They point out that throughout other clauses of the will, the testator expressed "in clear and concise terms the disposition of his estate" by using the words "I direct" or "I give and devise," or "I give." They say that the language in the sixth clause "is a wish, a **617 personal charge to his heirs, and does not establish a right in Davis to the shop area." We do not agree.

Precatory words are generally defined as terms expressing direction, recommendation, desire, wish, or request. Such words are usually deemed mandatory when addressed to an executor, but when directed to devisees generally are not considered imperative unless it appears that they were meant to create a legal obligation. *306 Carson v. Simmons, 198 Va. 854, 859, 96 S.E.2d 800, 804 (1957). We have held that "words of request or expectation are presumably indicative of nothing more, unless the context, or the circumstances surrounding the testator when he made the will, show that he really meant to leave the devisee no option in the matter." Smith v. Trustees of the Baptist Orphanage, 194 Va. 901, 905, 75 S.E.2d 491, 494 (1953). As we have said already, the circumstances surrounding this testator when he made the will show that he really meant to leave these devisees no option but to sell the shop area to Davis for its fair market value. It follows, therefore, that the sixth clause establishes a right in Davis to purchase the property in question. ...

Next we have two Supreme Court decisions allowing declarations of intent. The first involved an equivocation as to property, the second an equivocation as to persons.

Supreme Court of Virginia.
Baker v. Baker
237 Va. 581, 379 S.E.2d 327 (1989)

RUSSELL, Justice.

... Alberta Virginia Baker, a resident of Virginia Beach, died on November 27, 1985. She was unmarried and childless. Aware that she was terminally ill, she had a will prepared by her attorney shortly before her death, which was thereafter admitted to probate. Its pertinent provisions are as follows: *583

Article I

[A direction to the executor to pay all just unsecured debts and expenses of administration as soon as possible after death.]

Article II

I hereby direct my Executor to sell my home at 1347 Little Neck Road, Virginia Beach, Virginia, and the net proceeds of such sale to be applied to the payment of my just debts, including the costs of administration and to the extent net proceeds remain, to be used to satisfy the specific cash bequests set forth below and the remainder, if any, to be passed under the residue of my estate.

Article III

[A series of bequests of specific items of personal property and cash legacies to 22 named individuals and organizations. Some beneficiaries were to receive cash only; some, tangibles only; and others, a combination of cash and tangible items. The cash legacies came to a total of $315,000.00. One of these clauses, containing the largest single legacy, gives to Barnabus William Baker "my daddy's handmade silver with CPB initials engraved and Twenty Five Thousand ($25,000) dollars." The article ends with the following paragraphs:]

It is my desire and intent that the specific bequests made above be carried out by my Executor, whose decision and identification of the individual named articles to the named beneficiary shall be conclusive and final, and if there isn't sufficient monies to make all the above **329 bequests, then all the money bequests shall be proportionately reduced.

All the rest and residue of my property, both real and personal, wherever situate and however held, including lapses, legacies and devises, I devise and bequeath to BARNABUS WILLIAM BAKER.

... *584 The executor took the position that the entire estate should be devoted to the satisfaction of the cash legacies in Article III, but represented to the court that Barnabus Baker, as residuary legatee, was contending that the cash legacies in Article III were to be funded solely from the proceeds of the sale of Miss Baker's home, pursuant to Article II. The executor further alleged that the sale of the home would yield proceeds between $120,000 and $150,000, but that the personal estate contained money market funds totalling approximately $210,000. Thus, if the executor's interpretation were correct, there would be nearly enough in the estate after payment of debts and expenses to pay the Article III legacies in full, but there would be little, if any, money to pass under the residuary clause. If Mr. Baker's view prevailed, the Article III legacies would abate pro-rata to less than half the sums mentioned in the will, and the $210,000 in money market funds would pass to Mr. Baker under the residuary clause. ...

Mr. Baker argues ... that Article II designates a fund, the proceeds of sale of the house, which is expressly devoted "to satisfy the specific cash bequests set forth below," and that ..."Monies" ... is merely the plural of "money," and the only source of ready money provided by the will is the proceeds of sale of the home under Article II. Thus, he contends, it is apparent from the face of the will that the testatrix intended that the legacies abate if the proceeds of sale of the home were insufficient to pay them in full.

The will is indeed subject to the foregoing interpretation, but that is not the only tenable view. The term "monies" is not *585 necessarily limited to cash. In Dillard v. Dillard, 97 Va. 434, 438, 34 S.E. 60, 62 (1899), we said:

It seems to be well settled that a gift in a will of "money," with nothing in the context to explain or define the sense in which it is used, includes cash, bank notes, and money in bank, but does not include choses in action or securities. The word, however, is often popularly used as synonymous with personal estate, and has been construed to include, besides money literally so called, not only debts and securities, but the whole personal estate, and even the proceeds of realty. What is meant by the word "money" must in each case depend upon the will and its context.

It is equally well settled that a court construing a will must, if it can, determine the testator's intent from the language of the will itself. If in doubt, the court must place itself in the position of the testator at the time the will was drafted, and must consider the surrounding facts and circumstances as they then appeared to the testator. See Collins v. Hartford Acci., Etc., Co., 178 Va. 501, 511-512, 17 S.E.2d 413, 417 (1941); 2 Harrison on Wills and Administration § 258 (G. Smith 3rd ed. 1986). Such a consideration is aided by the presumption that a testator, when drafting his **330 will, knows what he owns and what he owes. ...

[T]he executor points out that Miss Baker's dominant intent was clearly expressed in Article III: "It is my desire and intent that the specific bequests made above be carried out...." Presuming that she knew that the proceeds of sale of her home would serve to pay less than 50% of the stated amounts of the legacies, the only way of effectuating her intent would be to devote her money market funds also to their payment. That course, the executor suggests, would result in paying the legacies in full, or nearly so, as she clearly intended. Therefore, the executor argues, Miss Baker must have used the word "monies" in the broader sense, including her money market funds as well as the proceeds of sale of her home as a combined source for the payment of the legacies. Only if that combined source were insufficient would the legacies abate. *586

We agree with the executor. It is true that his analysis depends upon circumstances outside the words of the will, but the will is ambiguous and the ambiguity, although latent, amounts to an "equivocation." Depending upon the definition assigned to the word "monies," either construction of the will is tenable. We have defined "ambiguity" as "the condition of admitting of two or more meanings, of being understood in more than one way...." Berry v. Klinger, 225 Va. 201, 207, 300 S.E.2d 792, 796 (1983). It follows that the chancellor correctly admitted evidence extrinsic to the will to aid in determining Miss Baker's intent.

In Baliles v. Miller, 231 Va. 48, 57-58, 340 S.E.2d 805, 810-11 (1986), we expressly adopted the rules set forth by Professor Graves in 1893:

(1) If the language of a will is plain and unambiguous, extrinsic evidence is never admissible to contradict or alter its meaning.

(2) Extrinsic evidence of facts and circumstances, such as "the state of [the testator's] family and property; his relations to persons and things; his opinions and beliefs; his

hopes and fears; his habits of thought and of language" are "always admissible in aid of the interpretation of the will-i.e., as explanatory of the meaning of the words as used by the testator"; and "the same doctrines should apply to all ambiguities, whether patent or latent, admitting evidence of the facts and circumstances in all cases, and of declarations of intention in the one case of equivocation."

(3) An "equivocation" exists "where the words in the will describe well, but equally well, two or more persons, or two or more things" and "all extrinsic statements by a testator as to his actual testamentary intentions-i.e., as to what he has done, or designs to do, by his will, or as to the meaning of its words as used by him" are admissible to show which person or thing he intended and, thus, to resolve the equivocation.

The extrinsic evidence heard by the chancellor gave overwhelming support to his finding. Several of the witnesses who testified to Miss Baker's statements were also legatees, and could have been affected by bias. Her attorney, who drafted the will, *587 however, had no personal interest in the outcome. He testified that her last will revoked and replaced an earlier will and substantially increased the legacies contained in the earlier will. He further testified that Miss Baker was well aware that the proceeds of sale of the home would be far too small to pay the increased legacies, and that he discussed with her "where was this money coming from." She responded that the increased gifts were made possible by "an appreciable increase in the values of her mutual funds and other securities." He stated that she had no intention to restrict the legacies to the proceeds of sale of the real estate.

For the foregoing reasons, the decree will be Affirmed.

Supreme Court of Virginia.
Baliles v. Miller
231 Va. 48, 340 S.E.2d 805 (1986)

POFF, Justice.

We granted and consolidated these appeals, each challenging the chancellor's holding that one of the two bequests in a residuary clause was void for indefiniteness. ... The appellants are Gerald L. Baliles, Attorney General of Virginia, Commonwealth of Virginia; The Medical College of Virginia, Health Sciences Division of Virginia Commonwealth University, and The Rector and Visitors of the University of Virginia (collectively, the Universities); and American Heart Association, Virginia Affiliate, Incorporated (Virginia Affiliate).

Virginia Fletcher Wood (testatrix) and her husband, Robert Eugene Wood, died on the evening of August 28, 1979. Their car stalled on a bridge over the Thornton River during a flash flood, and both were drowned. Mr. Wood left a holographic will dated February 20, 1948, which read in pertinent part:

I ... leave my entire estate ... to my (wife) Virginia Fletcher Wood....

In the event my (wife) Virginia Fletcher Wood and myself die at the same time I leave my estate as follows:

> 2nd The balance of my estate is to be divided between the canser [sic] and heart funds of Virginia.

Mrs. Wood also left a holographic will dated December 4, 1948. Only four paragraphs are relevant to this appeal: *53

> Second; I give all my property, both real and personal, with the exception of five thousand dollars, in fee simple, to **808 my husband, Robert Eugene Wood, if he be living at my death.

> Third; I give to Giles H. Miller, Jr. the sum of five thousand dollars, if he be living at the time of my death....

> Sixth; If Robert Eugene Wood, my husband be not living at the time of my death, or if our deaths should occur at the same time, I wish my estate divided as follows:

> I leave twenty five thousand dollars to my friend and a good friend of my father, Giles H. Miller, Jr., if he then be living....

> All the rest and residue of my estate I wish be divided equally into two parts. One part I wish and direct go to the Virginia Division of the American Cancer Society; the other part I wish and direct to go to the State of Virginia Organization or Foundation engaged in research concerning ailments of the Heart and Heart Trouble.

Appellee Miller offered both wills for probate, qualified as executor of each, and filed separate suits seeking the advice and guidance of the court in the administration of the estates. ... The parties agreed that the decedents had died simultaneously (see Code § 64.1–97), and the issue focused primarily upon the residuary clauses of the two wills.

Reserving a ruling on objections, the chancellor permitted Ralph Deacon to testify concerning certain conversations he had held with the Woods during the year preceding their deaths. Deacon testified that he had urged Mr. Wood to consider making a gift or a bequest to Bridgewater College or to Culpeper Memorial Hospital "to build a Fletcher-Wood memorial wing". Mr. Wood told Deacon that "they had a will", that they "had left half of [their money] to the Cancer Fund, half of it to the Heart Fund", and that they were concerned that their money not "go to New York, to the National Association, and be squandered there". "He also made the comment," Deacon said, "that he didn't have any close relatives, and he didn't want any of his relatives to have any." Mrs. Wood was present during some of these conversations. *54 "Her concerns," Deacon stated, "were the same as Gene's, yes. She expressed that they had left it half to the Heart Fund, half to the Cancer Fund, and, again, they were concerned about the organization."

Evidence was adduced to show that, at the time the Woods drafted their wills, the Virginia Division of the American Cancer Society was popularly known as "the Cancer Society" or "the Cancer Fund." An officer of the American Heart Association testified that "[t]he Heart Fund ... is a name that was given to us by the public and the media," that this name was later registered as a trademark, and that the Virginia Affiliate, formally incorporated in 1949, was authorized to use the name. The evidence showed that the Universities were engaged in cardiovascular research at the time the wills were written, and the chancellor found that the Virginia Afilliate "funds such research and in a broader sense itself engages in such research".

In a letter opinion, the chancellor ruled that ... Mr. Wood's residuary estate "must pass to the American Cancer Society, Virginia Division, Incorporated and the American Heart **809 Association, Virginia Affiliate Incorporated to be divided equally."

Concerning Mrs. Wood's bequest to "the Virginia Division of the American Cancer Society", the chancellor held that "one-half of the net residuary estate ... shall be paid over and delivered to the American Cancer Society, Virginia Division, Inc...." However, construing her bequest to "the State of Virginia Organization or Foundation engaged in research concerning ailments of the Heart and Heart Trouble", he concluded that he could not "seek the aid of Mr. Deacon's testimony to resolve the uncertainty", that "this provision must fail for indefiniteness", and that *55 "the remaining one-half net residuary estate ... shall vest in the heirs-at-law of Virginia Fletcher Wood, deceased." ...**810 *56 ...

We begin our analysis by reviewing certain established principles.

> The only reason anyone can have for making a will is to change the devolution of his property from that prescribed by the statutes of descent and distributions. Hence there is a strong presumption that the testator intended to dispose of *57 his entire estate, and courts are decidedly averse to adopting any construction of a will which leaves a testator intestate as to any portion of his estate, unless compelled to do so. The judicial expositor, therefore, starts out with this presumption.

> McCabe v. Cary's Ex'r., 135 Va. 428, 433–34, 116 S.E. 485, 487 (1923).

> All of the refinements of the law must yield to the power of the testator to dispose of his property as he desires. When this intention, which is the guiding star, is ascertained and can be made effective, the quest is ended and all other rules become immaterial.

> Wornom v. Hampton N. & A. Inst., 144 Va. 533, 541, 132 S.E. 344, 347 (1926).

...

As we distill the views of Professor Graves [C. Graves, "Extrinsic Evidence in Respect to Written Instruments," 14 Va.L.Reg. 913 (1909)], we perceive three rules pertinent to our inquiry [see quoted passage in Baker, supra]: ... **811 ... *58

Nothing in the decisions of this Court contradicts these rules, and we endorse them as the law of this Commonwealth. ... [T]he chancellor gave special emphasis to the passage which stated that, in order for an equivocation to exist, "[t]he words of the will must be descriptive of concrete objects; that is, of some person or thing whose identification is the purpose of the declarations of intention. Such declarations are not now allowed ... to explain the meaning of ambiguous expressions in a will ... [or] to explain generic terms...." Graves at 934. The chancellor found that the language employed by Mrs. Wood is "generic", concluded that no equivocation existed, and ruled that he could not consider Mrs. Wood's declarations of intention "to resolve the uncertainty".

We do not agree that the language of the will is "generic" in the sense of that word as "relating or applied to or descriptive of all members of a genus, species, class, or group". Webster's Third New International Dictionary (1971). The term "State of Virginia Organization or Foundation engaged in research concerning ailments of the Heart and Heart Trouble" is descriptive of a geographical segment of a larger class. It is particular rather than general.

The heirs argue that the term is patently ambiguous and that the only extrinsic evidence competent to resolve a patent ambiguity is evidence of facts and circumstances surrounding the making of the will. ... Mrs. Wood's "description is not on its face applicable to two or more organizations or foundations". The words of her will describe a particular, concrete object, viz., the organization or foundation engaged in cardiovascular research. The ambiguity is latent; the "uncertainty" to which the chancellor referred did not appear until the evidence disclosed that more than one organization or foundation was engaged in heart research.

> As defined by Lord Bacon, 'a latent ambiguity is that which seemeth certain and without ambiguity for anything that appeareth on the deed or instrument; but there is some *59 collateral matter out of the deed that breedeth the ambiguity.'
>
> A latent ambiguity therefore exists in a sentence or expression only when the real meaning or intention of the writer is hidden or concealed. It does not appear on the face of the word[s] used nor is its existence known until those words are brought into contact with collateral facts. It is only when you come to apply the words, bringing them alongside the facts which existed when used, and to read them in the exact light in which they were written that you make up the latent ambiguity, if one exists.
>
> Hawkins v. Garland's Adm'r Et Als., 76 Va. 149, 152 (1882).

An equivocation which becomes apparent only when evidence discloses that the language of a will applies equally well to two or more persons or things fits this definition of a latent ambiguity.

"[T]he American courts have generally admitted declarations to resolve latent ambiguities as to the beneficiaries or the property devised, without regard to whether or not there was technically 'an equivocation.'" 94 A.L.R. 280 (1935). In Grimes v. Crouch, 175 Va. 126, 7 S.E.2d 115 (1940), the testator left a holographic will which read: "Ever thing left to sister for life times." The testator was survived by two sisters. The **812 trial court admitted the evidence of a witness who testified that the testator told him that he "was accustomed to speak of his sister, Eva J. Crouch, as 'sister,' a term which he did not apply to his other sister, Mrs. Ridgeway." Although this Court made no reference to "equivocation", we held that "[t]he gift is to 'sister.' ... Any latent ambiguity which might be caused by this incomplete designation has been wiped away by competent evidence." Id. at 136, 7 S.E.2d at 119.

Even if, as the heirs insist, the ambiguity is patent rather than latent, Mrs. Wood's declarations of intention were admissible. Under the second rule we have excerpted from Professor Graves' paper, "the same doctrines should apply to all ambiguities, whether patent or latent, admitting evidence of the facts and circumstances in all cases, and of declarations of intention in the one case of equivocation." Graves at 942. Accord J. Thayer, "The 'Parole Evidence' Rule (II)," 6 Harv.L.Rev. 417, 424 (1893). *60

Applying the third rule we have approved, we hold that "the words in [Mrs. Wood's] will describe well, but equally well, two or more persons, or two or more things", Graves at 926; that an equivocation exists; and that the chancellor erred in excluding Deacon's testimony concerning Mrs. Wood's declarations of intention.

We must now construe the language of Mrs. Wood's residuary clause in light of those declarations and other facts and circumstances in evidence. Preliminarily, we reject the suggestion that the term "State of Virginia Organization or Foundation" was intended to apply solely to governmental bodies. The language is in the disjunctive, and while each of the Universities is a state "Organization", neither is a "Foundation". We interpret the term to mean an organization or foundation operating within the State of Virginia. Deacon's testimony that the Woods did not want their money squandered in another state reinforces our interpretation.

From the evidence adduced by the Universities and the Virginia Affiliate, the chancellor found that these organizations and "likely ... others not before the court" were engaged in heart research. In effect, this was a factual finding that the words in the will described equally well more than one Virginia organization. It is clear, however, that Mrs. Wood had in mind a specific organization or foundation engaged in heart research, for she made her bequest to "the ... Organization or Foundation", and, significantly, she capitalized the nouns. Neither University introduced any evidence to show that it was the entity she had in mind. On the other hand, it appears that the Virginia Affiliate is the one Virginia organization engaged exclusively in heart research and the funding of heart research by other Virginia institutions.[8]

[8] These include the University of Virginia, the Medical College of Virginia, Eastern Virginia Medical School, Old Dominion University, George Mason University, Fairfax Hospital, and the Veterans Administration Hospital in Richmond.

Citing Tracy v. Herring, 48 N.C.App. 372, 268 S.E.2d 875 (1980), and other cases, the Attorney General states on brief that "this is a proper case for construing the will of Virginia Fletcher Wood in light of her husband's will which was drawn some nine months earlier." We agree. A comparison of the two wills reveals parallels in structure and substance which support the conclusion that Mrs. Wood was familiar with the content and effect of her husband's will and shared his testamentary purposes. *61 We believe this is a "fact or circumstance" within the meaning of the second rule we have borrowed from Professor Graves' paper.

Mr. Wood left his "entire estate" to his wife; Mrs. Wood left "all [her] property to [her] husband". Each made alternative bequests in the event one predeceased the other or both died simultaneously. Mr. Wood divided his residuary bequest between "the canser [sic] and heart funds of Virginia"; Mrs. Wood divided her residuary **813 bequest between "the Virginia Division of the American Cancer Society" and "the State of Virginia Organization or Foundation engaged in research concerning ailments of the Heart and Heart Trouble".

The pattern of the two wills is similar. True, the language is different.[9]

> [9] The evidence suggests the reason for the difference. At the time the wills were written, the Virginia Affiliate had not been given the proper name under which it was incorporated. Mr. Wood defined the two charitable organizations in the vernacular. Mrs. Wood was simply groping for more definitive language.

In our view, however, its import reflects an identity of testamentary intent on the part of husband and wife to make the same bequests to the same legatees for the same charitable purposes. And the declarations of intention reported by Deacon strengthen our view.

The chancellor held that Mr. Wood intended half of his residuary estate to pass to the Virginia Affiliate. Reading Mrs. Wood's will in context with that of her husband and considering Mrs. Wood's declarations of intention, we hold that Mrs. Wood intended the same and that the chancellor erred in declaring her bequest void for indefiniteness.

This does not end our inquiry. The chancellor ruled that the $5,000.00 and $25,000.00 legacies to Giles H. Miller, Jr., contained in Mrs. Wood's will "are cumulative, and not substitutional" and ordered that both be paid to the legatee. The Attorney General assigns error to that ruling.

We resolve this issue from the face of the will. Mrs. Wood obviously intended to divide her whole estate in one manner if her husband survived her and in a different manner if he did not. She wanted her husband, if alive, to have all her property except the $5,000.00 she wanted Miller to have. If her husband was dead, she wanted Miller to receive a larger legacy, $25,000.00, before the residue was paid to the charities she named. Thus, the two bequests, expressly separated by a common contingency, were mutually *62 exclusive alternatives, and we hold that the chancellor erred in ruling that the legacies were cumulative. Because "there is no sufficient evidence that the persons have died otherwise than simultaneously, the property of each person shall be disposed of as if he had survived", Code § 64.1–97, and the $5,000.00 legacy must fail.

… [W]e will enter final judgment here awarding the $25,000.00 legacy to Giles H. Miller, Jr., and one-half the net residuary estate of Virginia Fletcher Wood to the American Heart Association, Virginia Affiliate, Incorporated.

Note that the court misinterpreted Grimes v. Crouch. The evidence allowed in that case, that the testator "was accustomed to speak of his sister, Eva J. Crouch, as 'sister,'" was not a declaration of intent; it was 'facts and circumstances' evidence. Yet declarations of intent – for example, if a witness testified the testator had told him "I'm leaving everything to Eva, who is the one I really think of as my sister" – would have been allowable in that case, because "to sister" is an equivocation. Because *Grimes* actually did not involve a declaration of intent, and because both *Grimes* and this *Baliles* did present an equivocation, anything the court said in *Baliles* suggesting that declarations of intent are admissible to resolve even non-equivocation ambiguities is only dictum. The rule the court squarely embraces in *Baliles*, and reaffirms in *Baker supra*, that which Professor Graves' paper articulated, clearly limits admission of declarations of intent to equivocations.

In Roller v. Shaver, 178 Va. 467, 475-76; 17 S.E.2d 419 (1941), alternative takes argued that the court should rule void for uncertainty a will provision directing the executor to "sell all real estate and personal property, if any, and the proceeds from same be given to the Trustees of some Methodist Institution or Institutions for the poor or what in his judgment is worthy of the same, and any other moneys or bonds." The court rejected the argument, stating:

> A number of cases which have been decided by this court… hold that such general expressions as 'to the poor', 'for the benefit of the poor', or 'for the relief of the poor', and other like general expressions, are too indefinite and uncertain to be enforceable. But this case is not of that sort. The gift is not to the poor but to some Methodist institution or institutions for the poor or what in the judgment of the executor is worthy of the same. The taker of the gift and the application of its benefits is perfectly plain. But if there is any doubt about any particular Methodist institution satisfying the intention of the testator, in the opinion of his executor, then he is authorized to employ his own judgment as to what prospective recipient is worthy.

Some Circuit Court decisions on construing ambiguities:

In re Estate of Martin, 68 Va. Cir. 58 (2005), addressed a residuary clause in a will stating "to my children surviving at my death per stirpes," where one adult child had predeceased the testatrix, leaving two offspring. The Circuit Court for the City of

Roanoke stipulated that this provision "clearly constitutes an 'equivocation,'" and then allowed both evidence of the two grandchildren's close relationship with the testatrix (facts-and-circumstances evidence) and declarations of intent – namely, testimony by one grandchild "that his grandmother had explicitly expressed to him that he and his brother would 'split' their father's share and that she had a will to take care of that," and testimony by the other grandson "that his grandmother had been quite upset about another family situation where the children had not inherited the share of the parent and she had spoken to him about that at length after his father's death, stating that result would not happen in her situation due to the way she had prepared her will."

In Kasabian v. Littleton, 52 Va. Cir. 39 (2000), the Circuit Court for Warren County analyzed a will provision stating:

> I hereby request that all currency and monetary accounts of which I may have ownership at the time my Last Will and Testament takes effect to be liquidated and placed in one fund. This will include my Paine Webber Investment Accounts, … the contents of my safe deposit box and bank account, located at …, and my account number 3029 at the Congressional Credit Union…. This fund is to be divided equally, share and share alike, between the following surviving persons: [certain relatives and a friend].

The residuary beneficiary wanted to exclude from the meaning of "monetary accounts" (so they would go into the residue) two items – first, the anticipated refund of an entrance fee the decedent had paid to a continuing care facility, which the facility had placed in escrow at a bank; and second, a class action settlement payment that resulted from a civil suit on behalf of investors in "Payne Webber Income Properties 8." The court based its decision on both a rule of construction and extrinsic evidence:

> The term "monetary account" is not a technical legal term, and its meaning is ambiguous when applied to the facts of this case. Therefore, the Court may consider the nature and extent of the decedent's estate at the time when she wrote her will and her intention as expressed in her will in construing Item Fourth. The testatrix did not own any real estate when she wrote her will, and it appears that when she wrote her will, her estate's major assets were her "monetary accounts."

> When words used in a will do not have a technical legal meaning, … the words are given their ordinary meaning in the context in which the word is used in the will. Accordingly, the word "money" has been held to include both cash and securities and even the whole personal estate of the decedent. "The word 'money' or 'cash' as it is used in testamentary instruments is a term of flexible meaning, having either a restricted or a wide signification, according to the context of the will in which it occurs and those surrounding circumstances which the court is bound to take into consideration." …

"[I]n the construction of legal instruments, when the listing of an item with a specific meaning is followed by a word of general import, the general word will not be construed to include things in its widest scope but only those things of the same import as that of the specific item[s] listed," Turner v. Reed, 258 Va. 406, 518 S.E.2d 832 (1999)(applying ejusdem generis construction principles). The decedent used the word monetary account by which she clearly intended to include a term that was broad enough to embrace bank accounts, security accounts, and similar accounts. The term account has been defined as "a claim or demand by one person against another creating a debtor-creditor relationship." 1A M.J., Accounts and Accounting, § 2. Applying this definition, a monetary account would be any claim of the decedent against another for a sum which was either liquidated or specifically quantified, as opposed to an unquantified chose in action. Addendum A to the contract with the Southerlands specified a formula for the determination of the refund of the Entrance Fee, so it was a monetary account within the contemplation of the term used by the testatrix.

In Item Fourth of her will, the decedent used the term "monetary account" and she listed those items which she then owned which comprised her monetary accounts, and she listed her bank account and her stock account by way of both inclusion and illustration. The Payne Webber Account mentioned in the 1992 will was converted into the Merrill Lynch Account which the decedent owned when she died in 1998. The Merrill Lynch Account is clearly a monetary account as contemplated by the decedent. The class action settlement payment of $1,339.29 was not a monetary account even if it derived from a security investment in the Payne Webber Fund formerly held by the Decedent, so it would pass under the residuary clause. See Baker v. Linsly, 237 Va. 581, 585, 379 S.E.2d 327 (1989) (the term "money" does not include choses in action).

In Witt v. Dooley, 50 Va. Cir. 7 (1999), the testatrix had left the bulk of her estate "unto those of my issue who may survive me, share and share alike." She was survived by some offspring and by some grandchildren who were children of the testatrix's predeceased offspring. The Circuit Court for Bedford County first noted that the Supreme Court had long held that "issue" has a specific legal meaning – namely, "heirs of the body" or, in other words, "natural descendants of a common ancestor," distinguishing it "from seemingly similar words such as 'children.'" Citing Hyman v. Glover, 232 Va. 140, 142, 143, 348 S.E.2d 269 (1986) and Vicars v. Mullins, 227 Va. 432, 437, 318 S.E.2d 377 (1984). So it should include grandchildren as well as children. And indeed, "the Supreme Court of Virginia has specifically ruled: 'The word "issue" includes grandchildren....' Mullins v. Simmons, 235 Va. 194, 197, 365 S.E.2d 771 (1988)." However, the circuit court noted, the Supreme Court has also stated that when the language of a will clearly manifests an intention on the part of the testator that a term is to have a meaning different from its technical legal meaning, then the testator's manifest intention trumps the legal meaning, citing Driskill v. Carwile, 145 Va. 116, 120, 133 S.E. 773 (1926).

The circuit court in Witt was equivocal about whether there was an ambiguity. It noted that the will was extremely brief and included no other language that would give any guidance, but rather than conclude from that, consistent with Driskill, that the legal meaning must therefore be used, it decided to allow consideration of extrinsic evidence without clearly deciding the matter, because extrinsic evidence had been presented without objection. The only suggestion of why it might be justifiable to treat "issue" as ambiguous was that giving the term its legal meaning would lead to an odd result, because the "share and share alike" phrase would require that every descendant of the testatrix receive an equal share, unlike the normal per stirpes distribution under intestacy law and the language of most wills. Then the "legal meaning of 'issue' becomes strained and therefore unclear and ambiguous."

Assuming the term "issue" is ambiguous, then all types of extrinsic evidence would be allowed, because it would constitute an equivocation. The court ultimately decided to interpret "issue" to mean only children, in part because two of the children testified that at will execution the testatrix had declared "that she wanted her estate distributed equally among her children who were living at the time of her death," had "specifically asked the attorney about the word 'issue' and … the attorney told her in response that 'issue' meant 'children.'" That was declaration-of-intent evidence. In addition, there was facts-and-circumstances evidence: Family members testified "that Mrs. Dooley had very little contact with her grandchildren during her lifetime, and that her estate was not very large." Further:

> [T]hrough her six children, Mrs. Dooley had a multitude of natural descendants, some of whom it may not be possible to identify or locate. If surviving 'issue' is to be defined in the context of this will as all of Mrs. Dooley's surviving natural descendants, and that each of these natural descendants is to receive an equal share of her estate, as would be required, in my opinion, by the phrase "share and share alike," such per capita distribution of this apparently modest estate would be a nightmare. I readily acknowledge that the difficulty of distributing an estate under a will is not ordinarily a proper consideration for the court when construing a will. Nevertheless, when there is evidence admitted to this effect, the court can consider whether Mrs. Dooley actually intended such wide-spread, equal distribution of her estate as application of the legal definition of "issue" would require.

Lastly, the will in Stoller v. Andrews, 42 Va. Cir. 310 (1997), gave one-third of Mrs. Andrews' estate each to her son and two of her grandsons, but it also specifically devised her home and its land and furnishings to one of the grandsons with an indication that the home was to make up part of his one-third share. Upon looking outside the will to real world circumstances, and finding that the home was worth roughly half the value of the entire estate, the executor realized that it would be impossible to fulfill both provisions of the will. When Mrs. Andrews wrote the will, her total estate was much larger, but her husband's long-term stay in a nursing home depleted much of their other wealth. The Circuit Court for the City of Roanoke treated this as a latent ambiguity, which it defined as "an uncertainty that arises entirely from the state of facts extrinsic to the will," citing 2 Harrison on Wills and Administration, 58 (3d ed. 1986). This would allow for admission of extrinsic facts and circumstances evidence, but the parties all agreed there was none that would help determine what the testator would have wanted in this circumstances. Instead the court applied rules of construction to try to reconcile the two clauses, and held that the home should be sold so that all three beneficiaries could receive shares of equal value, explaining:

> Virginia has long followed the "doctrine which enjoins upon the expositor to look for the intention of the testator in the general tenor and context of the instrument and to qualify or even reject any clause or phrase that may be found incompatible with it; and though first expressed, this general intent shall overrule the particular intent afterwards disclosed." Hooe & als. v. Hooe, 54 Va. (13 Gratt.) 245, 251 (1856), as quoted in Picot v. Picot, 237 Va. 686 , 689-90, 379 S.E.2d 364 (1989). In this case, the expositor (the chancellor) has no need to qualify the potentially incompatible clause or phrase; Mrs. Andrews has done so by making the specific gift to Michael "a part of his share." Applying the rules of construction, it is obvious that the testatrix's general intent is clear and definite, and that the specific gift to Michael-- as qualified by the words of the will and its placement within the dispositive sentence--is not repugnant to the general provisions for distribution.

The court noted a contrary rule of construction, that "[t]he specific provisions of a will control over a provision that is general in nature," citing 2 Harrison at 29, but did not explain why it chose one rule of construction over another. As a sort of consolation prize, the court gave the grandson the option of taking all the furnishings in the house as part of his one-third share of the estate.

C. Changes in property and persons

If substantial time elapses between will execution and death, much can change in the particular property the testator owns and in the composition of the testator's family and social circle.

1. Changes in property

A basic rule of will interpretation is that, at least with respect to the property it distributes, it "speaks at the time of death." In other words, an executor or court presumptively should apply the terms of the will to the testator's property and family as they were when the testator died, as if the testator had just executed it.

Subtitle II, Chapter 4. Wills, Article 3. Construction and Effect

§ 64.2-414. When wills deemed to speak

A. A will shall be construed, with reference to the real and personal estate comprised in it, to speak and take effect as if it had been executed immediately before the death of the testator, unless a contrary intention shall appear by the will.

B. Every will reexecuted or republished, or revived by any codicil, shall be deemed to have been made at the time it was reexecuted, republished, or revived.

***

This rule reflects in part an assumption that people who leave their wills as is over time are constantly reaffirming that they want the will to be as it is, for they are free until they die to change it. There are important exceptions to this general principle, mostly reflecting the reality that in some circumstances the testator was actually incapable of changing the will for some time before dying in order to reflect circumstances unanticipated at the time of initial execution.

Property identified in a will can increase in value before the testator's death, though more commonly it decreases in value or disappears altogether.

a.   Increased value

Supreme Court of Appeals of Virginia.
Carper v. Reynolds
211 Va. 567, 179 S.E.2d 482 (1971)

PER CURIAM.

When Walter Edgar Reynolds made his will, he owned an undivided one-half interest in a 245-acre farm in Craig County, and when he died he owned the entire interest in that farm. Reynolds' will provided:

> 'FIRST: I hereby give and devise all my right, title and interest (being a one-half undivided interest) in and to that certain farm or tract of land, situate in Craig County, Virginia, containing approximately 245 acres, * * * unto June Lugar, wife of the said Russell Lugar, in fee simple and absolutely.'

... Since a will speaks as of a testator's death, Va.Code Ann. s 64.1-62 (1968), the words of Article FIRST 'all my right, title and interest' operated to devise the testator's entire interest at his death. The succeeding parenthetical words 'being a one-half undivided interest' merely identified the testator's interest when he made the will.

In these will construction cases, there is almost always going to be a loser as well as a winner. In Carper, it would have been the residuary beneficiaries; if the court had focused on "one-half undivided interest" instead of "all my right, title and interest," then half the decedent's interest in the Craig County property would have fallen into the residue. But it avoids treating this as a situation of latent ambiguity, and therefore one in which extrinsic evidence could be admitted to demonstrate actual intent, by treating the parenthetical phrase as merely an inaccurate description rather than an independently effective devise.

b. Ademption

The general rule as to property specifically bequeathed or devised in a will that the testator no long owns at the time of death is that the devise or bequest is ineffective; the gift fails. If my will leaves "my Taylor guitar" to my friend Glen, and at my death I own no guitar, then that provision in my will is utterly ineffective and Glen will receive nothing thereby. If I sold the guitar before dying, Glen will not receive the proceeds; the law presumes I sold the guitar knowing this would revoke that gift to Glen. In the common law, this was termed "ademption by extinction." The legislature has created certain exceptions to this general rule, however, in code provisions that appear below.

It seems most ademption litigation concerns proceeds from sale of real estate, which might be so because a) a high percentage of people expect to live in their home till death but then to have the house sold, so they bequeath 'the proceeds from sale of my home' or something like that, and b) a large portion of those people actually end up selling their home before they die, because old age forces them to move to a care facility, to a relative's home, or to some other new situation. With items of personal property, in contrast, testators expecting to retain them till death simply bequeath the items without directing sale or leave it to the executor to distribute all personal property in his or her discretion. Note that if a will devises the testator's home *simpliciter*, and the testator has sold the home before dying, it is a clear case of ademption; there is no authority to support a claim that the named beneficiary should receive the proceeds from the sale. So, too, with any bequest of personal property.

The Supreme Court's most recent ademption case presented the unusual situation of a contingent sale of the home, contracted by the testator before dying but not yet completed by the time of death, because the contingency had not yet materialized.

Supreme Court of Virginia.
Bauserman v. Digiulian
224 Va. 414, 297 S.E.2d 671 (1982)

POFF, Justice.

... *416 ... By will executed March 10, 1966, Inez devised a fractional fee simple interest in two parcels of land to the devisees and bequeathed her personal property to the residuary legatees. On July 8, 1977, Inez entered into two conditional contracts to convey the land to strangers for a total price of $590,820. ... The contract recites that the purchasers had paid $1,000 as a deposit which was to be credited against the purchase price if the sale was consummated. Paragraph (4) provides that "[t]his contract is subject and contingent upon the subject property being rezoned" but that "[t]he forfeiture provisions of paragraph (11) hereof shall apply regardless of the **673 status of the rezoning." Paragraph (11) provides that, if the purchasers fail to make settlement on or before a fixed date, "the deposit ... and prepaid real estate taxes shall be forfeited as liquidated damages to the Seller, and all parties released from further liability hereunder."

Inez died on November 16, 1977, and her will was admitted to probate. The property was rezoned on June 19, 1978. On December 15, 1978, the executors delivered deeds to the purchasers, and the purchasers paid the contract purchase price. A question arose whether the proceeds of sale should be distributed to the devisees or to the residuary legatees, and the executors sought the guidance of the court. ...

To begin our analysis, we construe the provisions of the contract. The rights and duties of the seller and the purchasers were geared to the happening of an uncertain event. If rezoning occurred, Inez was obligated to sell upon demand. While, arguably, *417 the purchasers had an implicit right to waive the rezoning condition and buy the property as zoned, they were not obligated to do so and they did not do so. Even if the rezoning condition was satisfied, the purchasers had the right to choose whether to buy or to refuse to buy, subject to forfeiture as liquidated damages a sum less than one-half of one percent of the purchase price. Thus, the duty to sell and the duty to buy were not reciprocal obligations, and we construe the contract as a contract of sale upon the purchasers' option.

If the purchasers had exercised their option before Inez's death, the prior devise would have been adeemed by extinction. Collup v. Smith, 89 Va. 258, 15 S.E. 584 (1892) (delivery of deed of gift during testator's lifetime revoked prior devise). In fact, the purchasers did not exercise their option until after her death. Nevertheless, the chancellor ruled that the devise "was adeemed by the sale of the property which was the subject thereto prior to [Inez's] death and that the proceeds of such sale passed to the [residuary legatees]." Necessarily inherent in that ruling was a holding that the sale by the executors converted the realty into personalty; that the conversion was retroactive to the moment the contract was executed; and, hence, that the conversion "adeemed" the earlier devise. In effect, the chancellor applied what may be loosely termed the doctrine of retroactive equitable conversion. ... *418

Durepo v. May, 73 R.I. 71, 54 A.2d 15 (1947), concluded: **674

> ... The decided trend of the decisions in this country is that the exercise of an option to purchase real property after the death of the owner does not relate back to the time of the option agreement so as to affect, under the doctrine of equitable conversion, the rights of the owner's heirs or devisees.

... When the testamentary intent of the donor is clear, the doctrine of equitable conversion will not be applied to defeat a testamentary gift of land. *419 Robinson v. Lee, 205 Va. 363, 136 S.E.2d 860 (1964) (land granted by specific devise not equitably converted by conditional installment-sales contract).

One of the first American opinions repudiating the rule [was] Rockland-Rockport Lime Co. v. Leary, 203 N.Y. 469, 480-92, 97 N.E. 43, 46-47 (1911). ... [T]he court reasoned:

> The doctrine of equitable conversion rests on the presumed intention of the owner of the property and on the maxim that equity regards as done what ought to be done.... As [the lessor] intended no conversion unless the contingent event happened, he is presumed to have intended none until that event happened, for that would be the natural date to have it take effect in order to avoid confusion if not disaster.... The maxim underlying the doctrine of equitable conversion rests on a duty to do something, but in this case until the option was exercised there was no duty and it could not be known whether there ever would be a duty.... If the lessor had made the duty absolute instead of contingent, he could fairly be said to have intended that conversion must take place at some time, but as he made it contingent he could not have intended that result.... We hold that conversion was effected only from the date when conveyance became a duty and that it did not relate back to the date of the lease.

Invoking a similar rationale, the Supreme Court of Wisconsin has held that equitable conversion does not occur on the date of an option contract because such a contract is not subject to specific performance on that date.

> [N]o conversion will be deemed to take place until there is a certainty that there will be a change of title. Equity regards that as done which is clearly intended to be done, or which is contracted to be done, but not that which only may be done. .... To relate the conversion back to the date of the option is to relate it back to a time when there was and could be no conversion .... Granted that conversion **675 takes place at the *420 moment there is in existence a mutual right to enforce conveyance and compel acceptance of title, such moment, in the case of an option, does not occur until the option is exercised.

Estate of Bisbee, 177 Wis. 77, 80-81, 187 N.W. 653, 655 (1922).

We are persuaded that logic supports the majority American view, and we adopt that view as the rule in this Commonwealth. Applying the rule in this case, we hold that the devise was not adeemed, and, hence, that the right to the proceeds of the sale devolved upon the devisees.

––––––––––––

In the following, earlier case, in which the testator sold the real estate in question before executing the will and bequeathed a share of ongoing purchase payments, we see the Supreme Court willing to rely on extrinsic evidence to determine the testator's intentions as to ademption.

Supreme Court of Appeals of Virginia
Home Mission Board of the Southern Baptist Convention
181 Va. 395, 25 S.E.2d 281 (1943)

CAMPBELL, C.J., delivered the opinion of the court.

This appeal involves the construction of the will of Emily C. Pryor. The pertinent provisions of the will are as follows:

> Papers have been legally prepared to transfer the payments due each month from the property known as 1342 Monroe St. N.W., Washington, D.C., to my two nieces, Mary S. Diuguid and Anna D. Turner, after my death. **282

> I want the payments of forty-five dollars due each month from the property on Wilson Boulevard in Arlington, Va., now: (but formerly known as Ballston, Va.) paid to my sister, Nora A. Diuguid, after my death.

> If my sister does not survive me, these monthly payments from the property on Wilson Boulevard, now owned by Mr. U. M. Gaile must be made to my two nieces after my death, each niece having an equal share. *397

> I request each niece to bequeath at her death a sum of money equal to that she has received from properties here mentioned, to a hospital, or some institution for the benefit of the sick or poor.

> * * *

> All the remainder of my possessions which consist of real estate or property I bequeath to the Home Mission Board of the Southern Baptist Convention, located at Atlanta, Ga.

> * * *

> If my two nieces prefer the property, 230 Warwick Lane to the property, 1342 Monroe Street, N.W., Washington, D.C., and the Home Mission Board will agree to an exchange, I would like it.

…*398 … Some years prior to the execution of her will, the testatrix and her sister, Clara C. Baird, owned jointly the real estate situated in Washington. On November 12, 1929, Clara C. Baird died testate and by her will her one-half interest in the property was devised to Emily C. Pryor for life, with remainder to Mary S. Diuguid and Anna D. Turner.

On March 2, 1936, Emily C. Pryor, Mary S. Diuguid and Anna D. Turner united in a conveyance of this property to Leroy F. Dodson, for the sum of $10,000, payable $500 in cash and the balance in monthly installments. Subsequently, Dodson conveyed the property to one Harry A. Lane, the consideration being the assumption of the unpaid purchase money then due. Sometime after the conveyance to Lane, Emily C. Pryor, Mary S. Diuguid and Anna D. Turner agreed with Lane to accept a cash payment of $8,000. This sum was paid in November, 1939, and $4,000 of said sum was deposited on savings account in Emily C. Pryor's name, for life, with remainder to Mary S. Diuguid and Anna D. Turner, and the other $4,000 was deposited in the bank on the personal savings account of Mrs. Pryor.

The evidence shows, without cavil, that this deposit was kept intact by Mrs. Pryor in the savings account until her death. The evidence also discloses that though urged by her nieces to use this money to pay her hospital bill, she stated that she considered the money belonged to them because it had been put in the bank for them after her death; that she wanted them to have it and declined to spend any part thereof. ...

The rule for construction of wills has been so repeatedly stated by this court that it is needless to cite all of the authorities dealing with the question. The accepted criterion, that intention of the testator is the polar star in the construction of wills, is found in *399 Conrad v. Conrad's Ex'or, 123 Va. 711, 97 S.E. 336. There it is said:

> In ascertaining this intention, the language used, and the sense in which it is **283 used by the testator, is the primary source of information, as it is the expressed intention of the testator which is sought.
>
> Isolated clauses or sentences are not to be considered by themselves, but the will is to be considered as a whole, and its different clauses and provisions examined and compared so as to ascertain the general plan and purpose of the testator, if there be one. Nothing is to be added to or taken from the language used, and every clause and every word must be given effect, if possible.

It is the contention of appellant that the legacy in the will of Mrs. Pryor was adeemed by reason of the fact that the legacy was of the purchase money note, and not of the proceeds of the sale of the interest of testatrix in the Washington property.

This contention is untenable. The fact that the proceeds of the Washington property were left intact and preserved, admittedly for appellees, demonstrates that no ademption was intended. All that occurred by reason of the deposit of the $4,000 was merely a change in form of the proceeds of sale. This conclusion is further fortified by the intention of the testatrix, as shown by the language of the will. ... In the first sentence of the will, testatrix declares her intention that appellees should have the 'payments' from the Washington property after her death. The second and third sentences in the will clearly show that testatrix intended her nieces to receive a 'sum of money' and, necessarily, it was to be derived from her estate. In the last sentence of the will, 'proceeds' must have been intended, for, at the time of the execution of the will, the Washington property had then been *400 sold and the 'proceeds' deposited in the bank at the direction of the testatrix.

This conclusion is not only fortified by the frequently expressed intention of testatrix to make her nieces her legatees, but also by a letter written by her to Washington Loan and Trust Company on March 2, 1936. While it is true the request contained in the letter – that the Trust Company collect the Dodson note – was not carried out, the language employed in the letter has a significant bearing on the question of intention:

> Gentlemen:
>
> I hereby deposit with you for collection a first deed of trust note of $9,500.00, signed by LeRoy F. Dodson, dated - March 2, 1936, - payable in monthly instalments of $75.00 per month including interest at 6% per annum, until paid, and secured on Lot 39 in Square 2837, known as premises 1342 Monroe Street, N.W., which note is payable to my order and is endorsed by me.
>
> You are hereby authorized to apply the collections to be made by you on said note as follows:
>
> 1. Such portion of said collections as is in payment of interest on the principal of the debt represented by said note you are to remit to me for my lifetime.
>
> 2. One-half of such portion of said collections as is in amortization payment of said principal you are also to remit to me for my lifetime.
>
> 3. The other one-half of said principal-amortization collections you are to remit in equal proportions to Mary S. Diuguid and Anna D. Turner, 616 Court Street, Lynchburg, Virginia.
>
> 4. After my death, all the principal of said debt, uncollected or unremitted to me, as well as all interest thereafter collected on said debt, shall be paid to said Mary S. Diuguid and Anna D. Turner, equally as aforesaid.

That the testatrix at no time intended appellant to receive the money deposited in bank is, we think, conclusively shown by the residuary clause of the will: *401

> All the remainder of my possessions which consist of real estate or property I bequeath to the Home Mission Board of the Southern Baptist Convention, located at Atlanta, Ga.

There is not even an implication in this residuary clause that testatrix intended to dispose of any property except real estate. The word 'bequeath,' used in the clause, is a misnomer, as real estate is devised, not bequeathed. In our opinion appellant is entitled to receive only what testatrix clearly intended it to receive, viz: valuable real estate situated in Virginia and Georgia.

The seminal case on ademption presented the classic scenario of sale anticipated after death but actually occurring before death.

Supreme Court of Appeals of Virginia.
May v. Sherrard's Lgatees
115 Va. 617, 79 S.E. 1026 (1913)

BUCHANAN, J.

... [In] the last will and testament of Mrs. Maria L. Sherrard, ... the second clause is as follows:

> Second-I give, bequeath and devise my dwelling house and the lot on which the same stands, situated on North New street, in the city of Staunton, Virginia, and now known by the street number of 307 North New street, to be sold and equally divided between Tate Boys Sterrett, of Hot Springs, Virginia, and John Bishop of Charlestown, West Virginia, great nephews of mine, and sons of Maria B. Sterrett of Hot Springs, Virginia, and Margaret Bishop of Charlestown, West Virginia.

The only other portions of the will which, it is claimed, throw any light upon the meaning to be given the clause quoted are contained in the fifth clause, which, after making certain bequests to Margaret Bishop, a greatniece of the testatrix, provides that, "in the event of the death of her brother, John Bishop, I will one-half of the 307 North New street house, when sold, to pass in fee simple absolute to Margaret Bishop of Charlestown, West Virginia;" and the codicil, which states, among other things, *1027 that the testatrix had sold the house No. 307 North New street for $3,500, and invested $2,650 thereof in two houses and lots in the city of Roanoke, which were worth $3,000 at the time the codicil was written. The trial court held that the devise or bequest made in the second clause was specific and not demonstrative, and that by the sale of house No. 307, mentioned therein, in the lifetime of the testatrix the gift made by that clause was adeemed or revoked, and that the devisees or legatees named therein took nothing under it.

The distinction made between specific and demonstrative gifts is well understood; but it is sometimes difficult to determine whether a particular gift belongs to the one class or the other. ...

Mr. Pomeroy, in his work on Equity Jurisprudence, ... defines a specific legacy as "a bequest of a specific article of the testator's estate, distinguished from all others of the same kind, as, for example, a particular horse, or piece of plate, or money in a certain purse, or chart, a particular stock in the public funds, a particular bond or other instrument for the payment of money." Volume 3 (3d Ed.) § 1130. He defines "demonstrative legacies" as "bequests of sums of money, or of quantity or amounts having a pecuniary value and measure, not in themselves specific, but made payable primarily out of a particular designated fund or piece of property belonging or assumed to belong to the testator." Same volume, § 1133.

The general rule is that a legacy will not be construed as specific unless it appears clearly to have been so intended (Corbin v. Mills, 19 Grat. [60 Va.] 27 438, 468), and that whether or not it is specific depends wholly upon the language of the will (3 Pom. Eq. Jur. § 1130). ...

Whether this be gift of the house and lot itself, and the sale directed was merely for the purposes of partition between the devisees, as the appellee insists, or a gift of the proceeds or fund arising from the sale of the house and lot, there can be no question that the thing given is so described, pointed out, and identified as to distinguish it from all the other property of the testatrix. It is not a gift of a certain sum of money or other thing "payable primarily out of a particular designated fund or piece of property." There is nothing in the language of the clause or of the will which manifests any intent to give the persons named in that clause any particular sum, or amount, or quantity, to be paid primarily out of the proceeds of the sale of the house and lot, and, if for any reason that fund should fail, then to be paid out of the general estate; but, on the contrary, the gift is either of the house and lot, or it is a gift of the fund arising from the sale. If it be a gift of the house and lot, it is manifestly a specific devise; if it is a gift of the fund arising from the sale directed, it is equally specific as it seems to us. That the testatrix intended the gift made by that clause as specific, either of the house and lot, or of the fund produced by its sale, is emphasized and made clearer, if possible, by the fifth clause of her will, which provides: "That in the event of the death of her brother John Bishop" (one of the beneficiaries under the second clause) "I will one-half of 307 North New street house, when sold, to pass in fee simple to Margaret Bishop. ***"

The conclusion that we have reached, that the gift in question is specific, and not demonstrative, is fully sustained by the case of King v. Sheffey, 8 Leigh (35 Va.) 614, in which the provision of the will construed was substantially the same as that now under consideration. ... The question in that case was whether or not the devise or bequest of the Fincastle estate or its proceeds was revoked or adeemed by the alienation of the testator in his lifetime. President [St. George] Tucker, in delivering the opinion of the court, said, among other things: "... For here it is clear the testator had no design that his general estate should ever be charged with those legacies. *** Moreover, it was not a bequest of a certain sum (as of $500) chargeable upon the land, which, according to the case of Fowler v. Willoughby, 2 Sim. & Stuart, 354, might be charged on the general assets, if the land failed; but it was a devise of an uncertain interest, which would be more or less, according to the price for which the land might sell, the amount of which did not admit of being ascertained except by sale."

After holding that, if the gifts in that case were treated as legacies, they were specific, and were adeemed by the alienation of the Fincastle estate by the testator, he continues: "To come to a just understanding of this case, however, we must consider it more closely. This is a case of a devise, and a devise of real estate." After giving the reasons why the claim in question was a will of real estate, and citing authorities to sustain that view, he says: "So completely, indeed, is it a devise of the land to the three beneficiaries that, if it had not been sold, Finley, Mitchell, and Allen might now by their concurrent act demand a conveyance of the land itself, and arrest the sale, for a right to the whole proceeds of the estate is a right to the estate itself." After citing authorities to sustain that view, he says: "The devise, then, being of real estate-that is, of an equitable interest in land-was revoked by alienation. This principle is too plain to require support." ...*1028 ...

If the gift in this case be treated as a devise of real estate, the whole current of authority is that it was revoked by the alienation of the house and lot by the testatrix. If it be regarded as a bequest or legacy, then the weight of authority is, it seems, in favor of the conclusion reached by this court in King v. Sheffey. The text-books generally, as we understand them, so state the rule, and the decided cases sustain that statement.

In discussing the subject of specific legacies, Mr. Roper, in his work (4 Am. Ed. p. 200), says that: "If a testator direct his freehold or his leasehold estates to be sold, and dispose of the proceeds in such a form as to evince an intention to bequeath them specifically, the testamentary disposition will be specific, the money is sufficiently identified and severed from his other property, and, since he has sufficiently marked his intent to distribute the identical proceeds, the bequests are accompanied with all the requisites of specific legacies."

In a note to 3 Pom. Eq. Jur. § 1130, at p. 2210, it is said that: "Where the testator deals with specific property belonging to himself, not by giving legacies or sums of money out of it, but by dividing and apportioning out the very property itself, or the proceeds of it, if it is directed to be sold and converted into money, then the bequests of the parts thus apportioned among the legatees will be specific." ...

In 18 Am. & Eng. Enc. Law (2d Ed.) p. 716, it is said: "A gift on a specific thing to be sold and divided in certain shares among several persons is a specific bequest." ...

King v. Sheffey ... was rendered by President Tucker, one of the most distinguished jurists that ever sat on this bench, and concurred in by all the other members of the court-Cabell, Carr, Brockenbrough, and Brooke. ... There is nothing in our other cases referred to, as we understand them, which is not in harmony with the principles announced in King v. Sheffey.

Having reached the conclusion that the gift in question was specific, it follows that the appellants can take nothing under the second clause of the will, whether the gift be treated as a devise or a bequest; for the alienation of the property by the testatrix worked a revocation if it was a devise, and an ademption if it was a bequest. Liability to ademption is said to be the most distinctive feature of a specific legacy.

In Hood v. Haden, 82 Va. 588, 599, it was held that if the identical thing bequeathed was not in existence, or had been disposed of by the testator, so that it does not form a part of the testator's estate at the time of his death, the legacy is extinguished and the legatee's rights are gone.

In Skipwith v. Cabell's Ex'r, 19 Grat. (60 Va.) 758, in which one of the questions was whether or not certain stock given had been adeemed, it was held that a mere nominal or formal change in the thing given did not work an ademption. In that case the gift was of "my guaranteed bonds of the James River & Kanawha Company to be equally divided between" the beneficiaries. After the date of the will an act was passed which authorized the holders of the bonds of that company, for which the state was bound, to surrender them and receive in lieu thereof bonds of the state for the same amount, and under this act the testatrix exchanged her guaranteed bonds for state bonds, which she held at her death. While it was held in that case that there was no ademption, it was upon the ground that the thing given had been changed in name and form only and was substantially the same; but Judge Joynes recognizes fully the general rule that where the thing given is not in existence or has been alienated the bequest is adeemed. He says: "Where stock specifically bequeathed has been sold by the testator, *** the subject of the bequest is extinguished or annihilated; nothing exists upon which the will can operate, and the legacy is adeemed and gone. But 'where the thing specifically given has been changed in name and form only, and is in existence, substantially the same, though in a different shape, *** it will not be *** adeemed by such nominal change.'" Page 795. ...

This case is a stronger one [than King v. Sheffey] for the ademption of the bequest than that, since in this case not only was the house and lot, given and directed to be sold and its proceeds divided, sold during the lifetime of the testatrix, but the proceeds in part were invested in other real estate, and the residue of the proceeds otherwise used or disposed of.

The fact that the testatrix states in the codicil to her will what she had done with the Staunton property, and the disposition she had made of a portion of the proceeds, does not affect the question of ademption. Ademption with us, and generally, depends upon a rule of law, and not upon the intention of the testator. King v. Sheffey, 8 Leigh (35 Va.) 617; Skipwith v. Cabell, 18 Grat. (60 Va.) 794, 795; 1 Roper on Legacies, 329.

The final sentence is a bit jarring; modern doctrine and statutes regarding will construction, such as the one immediately below, emphasize the overriding aim of discerning the testator's intent. And the codicil would not even be extrinsic evidence; a codicil becomes part of the will itself. Courts today presumably would consider seriously whether the words of the codicil manifest a particular intent by the testator regarding the alienated property.

Lower courts still cite May as the seminal case on ademption. In Estate of Dorsey, 80 Va. Cir. 253 (2011), the Circuit Court for Fairfax County cited May in rejecting a surviving wife's claim to proceeds from the sale of a vacation home in Florida that had been specifically devised to her in the husband's will. The will said nothing about proceeds from the property, but rather simply devised the property. The wife claimed she was entitled to another property that the husband had purchased with the money he received for the Florida property, because he had promised her that she would own the new property upon his death. But oral wills are not recognized, and so the wife was essentially asking the court to interpret the provision in the will regarding the Florida property in a manner irreconcilable with the "clear and unambiguous language" of the will.

The Code section that specifically addresses ademption deals only with situations where the testator no longer possessed devised or bequeathed property but the reason for that was actions by other persons or by God without the testator's consent.

Subtitle II, Chapter 4. Wills, Article 3. Construction and Effect

§ 64.2-415. How certain bequests and devises to be construed; nonademption in certain cases.

... B. Unless a contrary intention appears in the will:

1. A bequest of specific securities, whether or not expressed in number of shares, shall include as much of the bequeathed securities as is part of the estate at the time of the testator's death, any additional or other securities of the same entity owned by the testator by reason of action initiated by the entity, excluding any securities acquired by the exercise of purchase options, and any securities of another entity acquired with respect to the specific securities mentioned in the bequest as a result of a merger, consolidation, reorganization, or other similar action initiated by the entity;

2. A bequest or devise of specific property shall include the amount of any condemnation award for the taking of the property which remains unpaid at death and any proceeds unpaid at death on fire and casualty insurance on the property; and

3. A bequest or devise of specific property shall, in addition to such property that remains part of the estate of the testator, be deemed to be a bequest of a pecuniary amount if such specific property, during the life of the testator and while he is under a disability, was sold by a conservator, guardian, or committee for the testator, or if proceeds of fire or casualty insurance as to such property are paid to the conservator, guardian, or committee for the testator. For purposes of this subdivision, the pecuniary amount shall be the net sale price or insurance proceeds, reduced by the sums received under subdivision 2. ...

C. [Language identical to B.3 except substitute "agent acting within the authority of a durable power of attorney for the testator" for conservator, etc..] ... This subsection shall not apply (a) if the agent's sale of the specific property or receipt of the insurance proceeds is thereafter ratified by the testator or (b) to a power of attorney limited to one or more specific purposes.

...

***

There have been no court decisions interpreting this statutory provision. It codifies a presumption as to what the testator would have intended in certain circumstances. That presumption is subject to rebuttal, by showing "a contrary intention appears in the will." Case law predating the statute construing intent from will language therefore provides some guidance as to what wording might suggest a contrary intention.

For example, in Warner v. Baylor, 204 Va. 867, 134 S.E.2d 263 (1964), the Supreme Court held that legatees of bequests of specific numbers of securities should receive additional shares resulting from stock splits, where the splits occurred while the testator had become paralyzed and confined to a hospital. The will gifted some of the securities to two trusts, and with respect to each trust the will said that trustee commissions should be paid from the residue of the estate rather than from the trust property, which suggested to the court an intention to preserve the entire value of the securities for the beneficiaries. This confirmed the common law presumption that a bequest of a certain number of securities should be interpreted to include additional share resulting from stock splits. 204 Va. at 877, 134 S.E.2d at 270. The court seemed also to infer from the testator's having made bequests of specific amounts of money to other beneficiaries that the testator intended the stock bequests to have a certain value, independently of how many shares represented that value at the time of her death. 204 Va. at 877, 134 S.E.2d at 270.

2.   Changes in persons

Both loss of persons and addition of persons are quite common when a long time passes between will execution and the testator's death. Either can result in effectively rewriting the will to reflect a presumption about what the testator would have wanted if he or she anticipated the event.

a.   Lapsing

As with property that is gone when the testator dies, the presumptive effect when a person is gone (predeceased) is that the will provision is rendered entirely ineffective. With a predeceased person, this is called lapsing; the gift to that person fails, or "lapses," and the property intended for that person goes to someone else. I might still own a Taylor guitar at my death, but if Glen is already gone, that gift fails and my guitar becomes part of my residuary estate, going to whoever the residuary beneficiaries are. A Code provision directs the fate of the property intended for the predeceased beneficiary:

§ 64.2-416. Devises and bequests that fail; how to pass.

A. Unless a contrary intention appears in the will, and except as provided in § 64.2-418 :

1. If a devise or bequest other than a residuary devise or bequest fails for any reason, it shall become a part of the residue; and

2. If the residue is devised or bequeathed to two or more persons and the share of one fails for any reason, such share shall pass to the other residuary devisees or legatees in proportion to their interests in the residue. ...

***

This statutory provision leaves intact the common law rule that when a residuary clause fails because no named beneficiary survives the testator, then partial intestacy results and the residue passes by means of intestacy rules. But it embodies the modern treatment of residuary bequests to two or more persons as a class gift, so that if one member drops out the others presumptively take more, thus avoiding intestacy. This rule is subject, however, to the "anti-lapse rule" presented below, applicable to bequests to close family members, which applies to class gifts as well as to bequests and devises to individuals.

The Supreme Court has had little occasion to apply the lapse rule in the past century, because it is fairly straightforward. In addition, Virginia has long had an anti-lapse rule that prevents lapsing with close relatives, and most predeceased will beneficiaries are close family members. Circuit courts in the state have, though, issued several decisions in recent years resolving novel issues that might someday receive Supreme Court attention.

Circuit Court of Virginia, City of Salem
Ayers v. Aid and Guidance of City of Salem Circuit Court
84 Va. Cir. 276 (2012)

ROBERT P. DOHERTY, JR., Judge.

Dear Counsel and Beneficiaries:

… [T]estator made his will twenty-three years before his death, and in the interim, seven of the named beneficiaries of the estate predeceased him. His will did not contain a residuary clause. An inquiry has to be made… whether a class gift was made, and whether a lapse of a devise and a bequest as at common law occurred. …

The testator's intent is clear. After payment of his bills and the costs of administration of his estate, he gave his entire estate to his wife, if she survived him. She did not. He then directed that if his wife should predecease him, the estate was to be divided into moieties, or half shares, one-half of the assets from each moiety to go to testator's mother if she survived him, and if not, to his stepfather if he survived testator. The other moiety or one half of the estate was to go to testator's wife's father, if he survived testator. Testator's mother, stepfather and father-in-law predeceased him.

Upon the failure of the above beneficiaries of each moiety to survive him, testator's will directed that from each moiety of his estate, one-fourth of his entire estate should go to a named beneficiary, Finese Wilbourne, who in fact survived him. From each moiety, one-eighth of the entire estate was to be given to Saint Jude's Children's Hospital, Memphis, Tennessee. The remaining one-eighth of the entire estate from each moiety was to go to testator's wife's five nieces and nephews, all of whom testator named. Three of those named nieces predeceased testator. There was no residuary clause in the will, ostensibly because the above fractional shares combine to total one hundred percent of the entire estate.

Each beneficiary of each moiety of the estate was given the same fractional share of the estate, twice, once from each moiety. That has the effect of doubling each beneficiary's share of the estate. Accordingly, Finese Wilbourne will receive a gift of one-quarter of the estate two times, for a total of one-half of the estate. The same applies to Saint Jude's Children's Hospital. It will receive one-eighth of the estate from each moiety, for a total share of one-quarter. The shares of the remaining five named nieces and nephews also double, as they were to receive their one-eighth share twice, once from each moiety, for a total share of one-quarter of the estate. That one-quarter share of the estate was to be divided equally among the five nieces and nephews so that each was to receive one-twentieth of testator's estate, if they survived him.

CLASS GIFTS

*2 Richard N. Moore and Kenneth W. Moore are the two surviving named members of the testator's wife's nieces and nephews, that being the group that was to inherit a one-quarter share of testator's estate. Had the testator simply said that one quarter of his estate was to go to his wife's nieces and nephews, then it would have been a class gift and that one-quarter of decedent's estate would have been divided equally between the two surviving members of the class. "[A] gift to a class is an aggregate sum to a body of persons uncertain in number at the time of the gift, to be ascertained at a future time, who are to take in equal or some other definite proportions, the share of each being dependent for its amount upon the ultimate number." Saunders v. Saunders, 109 Va. 191, 194, 63 S.E. 410 (1909). However, "... when all are named, each by his or her name in full, and an equal share is given to each, the presumption is that they are to take in their individual capacity and not in their collective capacity...." Kent v. Kent, 106 Va. 199, 205, 55 S.E. 564 (1906). In other words, the beneficiaries are treated as individuals and not as members of a class. In this case, because they were all named, they were not members of a class. At common law the shares of the three potential beneficiaries who predeceased testator would simply have lapsed. The inquiry at this stage then, is whether Virginia's anti-lapse statute prevents that result.

VIRGINIA'S ANTI–LAPSE STATUTE

The Virginia General Assembly enacted legislation to prevent lapses of devises and bequests under certain circumstances. That legislation, the Virginia anti-lapse statute,... does not help save these potential bequests and devises in this case because, although all three of testator's wife's nieces were dead at the time the testator's death, they were not a grandparent or descendant of a grandparent of the testator. They were not related to decedent by blood in any manner. The fact that two of them had children who survived them does not alter the result.

RESIDUARY CLAUSE

Had a residuary clause existed in the will, and no contrary intention having been shown by the language of the will, § 64.1–65.1, Code of Virginia (1950) [now § 64.2-416] would have come into play. It reads in pertinent part "... if a devise or bequest other than a residuary devise or bequest fails for any reason, it shall become part of the residue." As part of the residuary, the potential one-twentieth share of the estate that was to have been given respectively to Cary Lynn Roop, Marilyn V. Francisco and Sue V. Johnson, would have been divided equally, or as directed in the residuary clause, among the residuary legatees and devisees. However, no residuary clause was contained in testator's will. Accordingly, those three potential one-twentieth shares of the entire estate that would have gone to wife's deceased nieces, lapsed.

TESTATE DISTRIBUTION, LAPSE AND INTESTACY

*3 The decedent is deemed to have died intestate as to any lapsed devise or bequest. Therefore, three-twentieths of decedent's estate descends as if he died without a will. ... Insofar as the testate estate is concerned, Finese Wilbourne will inherit one-half of the estate, one-quarter goes to Saint Jude's Children's Hospital, Memphis, Tennessee, one-twentieth goes to Richard N. Moore, one twentieth goes to Kenneth W. Moore, and three-twentieths should be delivered to the administrator or the administratrix of decedent's intestate estate. Once a qualification occurs on the intestate estate, the administrator or administratrix would be able to file a petition for aid and guidance of the court to determine who are the heirs at law of the intestate decedent. ...

The following case addressed language in a will bequest to a spouse that heirs of the spouse argued expressed the testator's intent to avoid application of the lapse rule and to effect application of something like the modern statutory anti-lapse rule to the predeceased spouse (whom the anti-lapse statute would not cover).

Circuit Court of Virginia, County of Accomack
In re Estate of Peterson
64 Va. Cir. 428 (2004)

TYLER, J.

... Grace Hickman Peterson, deceased, who departed this life in 2002..., by Will executed in 1958, devised her Estate to her husband, Harold E. Peterson, "his heirs and assigns forever." However, he predeceased her in 1992. The question is whether the heirs of Grace or the heirs of Harold inherit her estate. ...

Harold and Grace, husband and wife, executed essentially identical Wills in 1958, each giving his or her entire estate to the other. ... At the time of his death, Harold's sole heir was his wife, Grace. They had no descendants; their grandparents had no descendants. ...

The heirs of Grace were served with process... The heirs of Harold were unknown to the Administrator at the time of the filing of his petition for aid and direction and were served by order of publication. ... Responding to the publication, the heirs of Harold sent letters to the Clerk... In her Will, Grace provides in pertinent part as follows:

> I give, devise and bequeath to my husband, Harold E. Peterson, his heirs
> and assigns forever, all of my property, real, personal and mixed ...

She neither named a substitute beneficiary if her husband should predecease her nor provided a residuary clause. ...

To paraphrase the Rule in Shelley's case, 1 Co. Rep. 93b (1581), it says whenever a person takes an estate and in the same writing the estate is limited by remainder to the person's heirs, the word "heirs" ... does not create a remainder in the person's heirs. The statute [Va. Code § 55-14] simply reverses the Rule and provides that a remainder is created. But Harold has not taken any estate by any writing. ... Harold does not take an estate of freehold as required by § 55-14.

This case involves simply a lapsed devise and legacy. A lapse is not affected by the fact that words of limitation are used in the gift. George P. Smith, Jr., Harrison on Wills and Administration, § 422 (3rd ed.1985). ... "[T]he doctrine ... that the words 'and his heirs'... are regarded merely as words of limitation and not as words of substitution ... and hence must be regarded as not preventing a lapse ... is well established in modern jurisprudence." 80 Am Jur 2d Wills, § 1429 (2002). This Court concludes that the heirs of Grace Hickman Peterson, deceased, have inherited her entire Estate. ...

Virginia, like all other states, long ago concluded that lapsing in every case of a predeceased beneficiary is not consistent with what most people would want to happen with their estates in that circumstances. When the beneficiaries are close biological family members, such as offspring or siblings, testators generally would prefer that the share of any predeceased beneficiary go to his or her descendants (but not so with a predeceased spouse who had children from another relationship). So, Virginia has codified an "anti-lapse rule" for such cases:

§ 64.2-418. When children or descendants of devisee or legatee to take estate.

Unless a contrary intention appears in the will, if a devisee or legatee, including a devisee or legatee under a class gift, is (i) a grandparent or a descendant of a grandparent of the testator and (ii) dead at the time of execution of the will or dead at the time of testator's death, the children and the descendants of deceased children of the deceased devisee or legatee who survive the testator take in the place of the deceased devisee or legatee. The portion of the testator's estate that the deceased devisee or legatee was to take shall be divided into as many equal shares as there are (a) surviving descendants in the closest degree of kinship to the deceased devisee or legatee and (b) deceased descendants, if any, in the same degree of kinship to the deceased devisee or legatee who left descendants surviving at the time of the testator's death. One share shall pass to each such surviving descendant and one share shall pass per stirpes to such descendants of deceased descendants.

***

This anti-lapse rule is consistent with intestacy rules, under which descendants of a deceased offspring or sibling take and divide amongst themselves the share of the predeceased offspring or sibling. Prior to the mid-1980s, the anti-lapse rule covered all beneficiaries. See, e.g., Thomas v. Copenhaver, 235 Va. 124, 127, 365 S.E.2d 760, 762 (1988) (stating that daughters of the decedent's former and predeceased neighbor, "by virtue of the anti-lapse statute then in effect (former Code § 64.1-64), take the interest their mother would have taken"). Now it is limited to close family members, reflecting an assumption that affection for non-family members is less likely to extend to descendants than is affection for siblings and other immediate family members. Note that it applies to class gifts, not just gifts to individuals, so the members of the class "my children" could ultimately include children and grandchildren, and members of the class "my siblings" could ultimately include siblings and nieces and nephews.

As with the basic lapse rule, the Supreme Court has rendered few decisions regarding application of the anti-lapse rule. In Hester v. Sammons, 171 Va. 142, 198 S.E. 466 (1938), the court ruled that a will provision creating a trust for the decedent's sister should be treated like a legacy and so be governed by the anti-lapse rule, given that the sister had predeceased the testator, with the result that the money designated for the trust would pass to the sister's children. In other words, the trust form of the bequest does not change the outcome. In Wildberger v. Cheek's Ex'rs, 94 Va. 517, 27 S.E. 441 (1897), the court held that the anti-lapse rule would apply even in a case where a specifically-named beneficiary was already deceased at the time of will execution.

One relatively recent circuit court decision addresses the question what sort of language in a will expresses an intent to override the anti-lapse rule.

Circuit Court of Virginia, Greene County.
Deane v. Tennyson
34 Va. Cir. 538 (1994)

PAUL M. PEATROSS, JR., Judge.

… Clara V. Deane died in 1953… Clara devised a tract of land containing approximately eighteen acres in fee simple to her son, Russell K. Deane… Clara explained her reasons for making the gift to Russell: (1) Russell had been of great assistance to her in the years preceding her writing the will and (2) he bore a financial liability which Clara's other children did not have, caring for an invalid daughter, Marjorie. …

After Clara's death, Russell and his wife, Blanche M. Deane, resided on the property in question. ... In 1979, their daughter, Marjorie, died. In 1986, Russell died intestate, survived by Blanche, who continued to reside on the property until her death in 1992.

Blanche's will… purports to devise and divide the property among Barbara Ann Grover, Hazeltine Deane, Dorothy Tennyson, Buddy Deane, Wayne Deane, and Charles D. Deane. Tennyson, however, claims sole ownership of the eighteen acre tract under Clara's will, which Tennyson asserts vested no more than a life estate in Blanche. The language upon which Tennyson bases her claim appears in paragraph four of Clara's will:

> In the event of the death of my son, Russell K. Deane, if prior to that of his wife, Blanche Deane, I hereby desire and instruct that tract of land mentioned in item no. 2 be conveyed to his widow as long as she remains his widow, otherwise or at her death, I further desire and

instruct that this tract of land be conveyed equally to all of my remaining children.

... *2 ... Clara Deane's will clearly reveals Clara's intention to make a special provision for her son, Russell. ... Paragraph three reveals Clara's intention to treat her children equally in all other respects regarding the disposition of her estate. ...

[T]he very existence of paragraph four, as well as the language contained therein, discloses Clara's intention to create a defeasible fee in Russell. If Clara had intended to grant Russell a fee simple absolute, paragraph four as it is written would not exist. ... Clara, however, intended to provide for a special circumstance: the death of Russell "if prior to that of his wife Blanche." Thus, Clara created the defeasible fee which appears in paragraph four. If Russell predeceased Blanche, Blanche maintained the right to remain on the property until her death or remarriage; after her death or remarriage, the property would revert to Clara's children. ...*3 ... [B]y granting Russell a defeasible fee, Clara did provide Russell with a crucial component of caring for his daughter: a home. Moreover, Clara's creating a defeasible fee is consistent with Clara's desire to treat all of her children equally, as revealed in paragraphs three and four. By granting a defeasible fee contingent upon Russell's predeceasing Blanche, Clara ascertained before her death that while Blanche would have a home until her death or remarriage, Clara's property would eventually pass to her own children, not to those to whom Blanche might devise the property. ... Russell's predeceasing his wife granted Blanche a life estate. Upon Blanche's death, the property passed to the remaindermen, Clara's remaining children.

For the interpretation of the phrase "remaining children," Complainants point the Court's attention to the "early vesting rule," which provides that "devises and bequests are to be construed as vesting at the testator's death, unless the intention to postpone the vesting is clearly indicated in the will." Clark v. Whaley, 213 Va. 7, 8-9, 189 S.E.2d 46 (1972). They argue that "remaining children" in the context of this case refers to those children living at Clara's death (all seven) rather than those living at the time of Blanche's death (only one, Ms. Tennyson).

However, as the rule itself states, the early vesting rule does not apply when the intention of the testatrix is clear from the will and the Court finds that Clara made her intentions clear. The text of paragraph four, supra, contains several indications that, in Clara's mind, the "remaining children" who would receive the land if Russell predeceased Blanche would be those who were living at Blanche's death. For example, the phrase which introduces the provision for the remainder to pass to the "remaining children" is "otherwise or at her [Blanche's] death"; this phrase seems quite time specific, as there could be only one point in time when Blanche either remarried or died. *4

Moreover, a contextual examination of paragraph four also indicates that Clara's intention was to grant the remainder to her children "remaining" at Blanche's death. In paragraph three, after granting the land in question to Russell, Clara specified that after all her expenses were paid, she granted all her other property "to all of my living children equally." In that context, in which she was clearly referring to the time of her own death and the settlement of her estate, she used the word "living" to classify the children who were to take. In paragraph four, however, she replaced the word "living" with "remaining"; otherwise, the two phrases would be identical (save the placement of the adverb "equally"). Thus, it seems that Clara had in mind a time other than her own death regarding the remainder vesting in her children and that the children who gained possession of the remainder would be those who were living at that later time, Blanche's death.

The Complainants argue, however, that "[i]t is strained to say that Clara would leave it to chance whether any child would survive Russell's wife, and then intend to leave all of the real estate in question to that child." Instead,... Clara intended each child receive an equal share, whether personally or, if deceased, through his or her heirs via the anti-lapse statute, Va.Code Ann. § 64.1-64.1, and, furthermore, that the presumption of the law supports this contention:

> Where an ambiguity exists in a will, unless there is a manifest intention to the contrary, the presumption is that the testator intended that his property should go in accordance with the laws of descents and distributions. See, Blankenbaker v. Early, 132 Va. 408, 412, 112 S.E. 599 (1922).

However, the *Blankenbaker* court went on to state the familiar rule that the intention of the testator is determined from the language which he used and that "[i]f the meaning of that language is plain, the will must be given effect accordingly." Id. On its face, the term "remaining" children in context seems plain. The Complainants may propose other theories about what Clara Deane would or would not leave to chance, but the language itself which Clara used in writing her will seems to indicate that she intended her children, not her grandchildren or some other more distant relatives whom she might not know, to inherit her estate after Blanche died.

With respect to predeceasing, bear in mind that the Simultaneous Death Act applies to will construction as well as to intestacy (and trusts).

Subtitle V. Provisions Applicable to Probate and Nonprobate Transfers
Chapter 22. Uniform Simultaneous Death Act

§ 64.2-2202. Requirement of survival by 120 hours under donative dispositions in governing instruments.

Except [when the will says otherwise], an individual who is not established by clear and convincing evidence to have survived an event, including the death of another individual, by 120 hours is deemed to have predeceased the event.

Sometimes a testator will stipulate a longer survival period for a spouse, if concerned that the entire estate would go to heirs of the spouse who are not also heirs of the testator (e.g., if the spouse has children from another relationship), rather than actually benefiting the spouse. Common language is something like "to my wife if she survives until the time of estate distribution." The state legislature created a special statutory provision for such cases, to deal with the possibility that estate administration could drag on for years, during which time the spouse survives and perhaps borrows money in anticipation of repaying with the bequest when it is disbursed, a scenario the testator likely did not contemplate.

§ 64.2-421. Construction of certain conditions of spouse's survivorship.

A. If property passes from the decedent or is acquired from the decedent by reason of the decedent's death under a will or trust that provides that the spouse of the decedent shall survive until the distribution of the gift, the will or trust shall be construed as requiring that the spouse survive until the earlier of the date on which the distribution occurs or the date six months after the date of the death of the testator or decedent, unless the court shall find that the decedent intended a contrary result. ...

b.   New persons

Testators might marry after executing a will and fail to revise it to provide for the new spouse. In addition, new births might add to the number of children the testator leaves behind or might increase the size of some class to which the testator made a testamentary gift. In addition, some wills leave gifts to a class of unrelated persons, such as members of an organization, whose membership can change over time.

i.   New spouse

Chapter Four presents the several protections in the law for surviving spouses, one of which is the "elective share" entitlement to a fraction of the estate. The elective share is aimed at situations in which a decedent tried intentionally to disinherit a spouse without the spouse's consent and without adequate alternative provision, and it reflects a "partnership view" of marriage by which the spouse in a sense has an equitable entitlement to a share of marital wealth, as well as a state interest in avoiding welfare dependency.

There is also, however, a statutory rule aimed at situations of presumed inadvertence in omission of a spouse from a testator's estate plan – specifically, ones in which the testator was not yet married at the time of will execution to the person who ultimately becomes his or her surviving spouse. This provision is potentially more generous to a surviving spouse than the elective share rule, ensuring the spouse "an intestate share" – that is, what he or she would receive under the intestacy rules if there were no will.

§ 64.2-422. When omitted spouse to take intestate portion.

If a testator fails to provide by will for a surviving spouse who married the testator after the execution of the will, the omitted spouse shall receive the same share of the estate such spouse would have received if the decedent left no will, unless it appears from the will or from the provisions of a valid premarital or marital agreement that the omission was intentional.

***

Supreme Court of Virginia.
Caine v. Freier
264 Va. 251, 564 S.E.2d 122 (2002)

Opinion by Senior Justice A. CHRISTIAN COMPTON.

… Dr. Andrew A. Freier, resident of Fairfax County, died testate on January 27, 1998 at age 74. … The widow made an election against the will pursuant to the omitted spouse statute. *254 …

The testator conducted an active medical practice for many years prior to his retirement in 1996. In November and December of 1997, he was hospitalized due to medical problems associated with congestive heart failure. Following the hospitalization, discussions took place among the testator, his wife, and their separate attorneys. These discussions were designed to effectuate a change to the testator's estate plan. Under the provisions of the 1990 will, the testator's entire estate was left to his two children. A portion of the estate consisted of three Individual Retirement Accounts (IRAs), two of which named the children as beneficiaries; the third named the testator's estate as beneficiary.

The first change to his existing estate plan was accomplished on January 21, 1998, when the testator executed the proper documentation to make his wife the sole beneficiary of the three IRAs. On January 22, 1998, a draft marital agreement was prepared by the testator's attorney to implement additional changes to the estate plan. The wife's attorney added an additional provision to the draft and a final copy of the agreement was prepared by the testator's attorney.

**124 On January 24, 1998, the agreement was brought to the Freier home and the wife executed it. On that day, the testator's attorney planned to present the agreement and a newly prepared will to Dr. Freier for his signature. However, the testator was unable to communicate with his attorney due to his failing health. When he died on January 27, 1998, he had not signed the marital agreement or the new will.

In September 1998, the Freier children filed a suit in the court below seeking to void the designation of the widow as beneficiary of the IRAs. They alleged forgery of the signatures of the IRA beneficiary forms, lack of capacity of the decedent to execute the forms, and fraud and undue influence by the widow.

Prior to the June 1999 trial in the IRA litigation, presided over by the same judge who presided in the present suit, the children learned that the widow had executed the marital agreement prior to the decedent's death. … However, the children did not pursue the *255 issue of the agreement's enforceability during trial, even though the court raised it sua sponte.

The circuit court ruled against the children and in favor of the widow in the IRA suit. The children's petition for appeal from that judgment was refused by this Court.

The August 2000 bill of complaint in the present suit... identified a number of issues.... The first issue was whether the proposed marital agreement executed by the widow is fully or partially enforceable against the widow by the decedent's estate. ... The proposed agreement provided, inter alia, that the widow accepted the jointly owned family home. The document stated she would not seek payment of any portion of the mortgage debt from the husband's estate and would be solely responsible for payment of that sum. After providing for disposition of certain personalty and for transfer of the IRAs, the document provided that the widow "waive[d] the right to take an elective share of [decedent's] estate as otherwise accorded her by the Virginia Code." The draft will referred to the proposed agreement, made certain bequests to the widow, and gave the residue of the estate to the children in equal shares. ...

**125 ...*257 ... The analysis begins with the observation that the children have not assigned error to the trial court's rulings... sustaining the demurrer regarding the unenforceability of the proposed marital agreement. .. Because the unenforceability of the proposed marital agreement has been finally decided in this case, the... **126 ... only issues that have any possible viability are (1) whether the trial court erred in refusing to find there was an "enforceable oral *258 agreement" (as distinguished from the proposed formal written agreement) for the testator's general estate plan between Dr. and Mrs. Freier that was binding upon Mrs. Freier...

For purposes of this discussion, we will assume but not decide that Virginia law permits an oral, unwritten, enforceable estate distribution plan. But see Code § 64.1-49 (will not valid unless in writing and signed by testator); Code §§ 20-155 and-149 (marital agreements shall be in writing). We do not need to address that question of law, because here there is no credible testimony that Dr. and Mrs. Freier had a definite oral agreement for the distribution of his estate.

Indeed, there was evidence... that the Freiers contemplated a formal written agreement regarding the distribution. For example, Dr. Freier's attorney confirmed in testimony that, from the first meeting about estate planning held in December 1997, the parties "were working towards a written formal agreement ... that would provide for her in accordance with his estate distribution." The evidence established that the terms of the proposed written agreement were being modified up until the date of the testator's death.

This issue is not controlled by cases... in which the Court has approved enforcement of oral agreements. For example, in Snyder-Falkinham v. Stockburger, 249 Va. 376, 457 S.E.2d 36 (1995), we gave effect to an oral agreement to settle a lawsuit even though the parties had contemplated a formal written settlement agreement. In that case, however, unlike the present case, there was no dispute that all parties and counsel had agreed to all aspects of the settlement, when one party rejected the deal before a *259 formal agreement was drafted but after the case had been dismissed with prejudice. ...

Questions can also arise as to whether the testator did in fact modify a will after marrying. In Estate of Pan Tai Liu, 49 Va. Cir. 431 (1999), a circuit court rejected an argument by the decedent's son, who was the sole named beneficiary in the decedent's will, that by making his new bride the beneficiary of annuities under his retirement plan, the decedent had effectively modified – to include the wife -- a provision in his will bequeathing his beneficial interest in various types of bank deposits and securities to the beneficiaries or co-owners of such deposits and securities. In other words, the son argued that the wife was provided for in the will, because that provision describing a class of people to receive bequests now included her. The court ruled that the son had not met his burden of showing "by a preponderance of the evidence that the decedent, in amending his retirement annuity contracts and naming Mrs. Chen as the beneficiary, also created a Codicil to his Will."

ii. New children

The law presumes that a parent would want to provide for any children he or she might have, and to an equal degree. As with intestacy law, though, when the other parent was married to the decedent and survives the decedent, the law presumes the decedent would want the survivor to take in the short-term and then pass on what remains at the survivor's death to their offspring. So the following statutory rules more or less apply intestacy rules to "pretermitted" children.

§ 64.2-419. Provision for omitted children when no child living when will made.

A. If a testator executes a will when the testator has no children, a child born or adopted after the execution of the testator's will, or any descendant of his, who is neither provided for nor mentioned in the will is entitled to such portion of the testator's estate as he would have been entitled to if the testator had died intestate.

B. The devisees and legatees shall contribute ratably to the portion of the testator's estate to which the afterborn or after-adopted child is entitled, either in kind or in money, out of what is devised and bequeathed to them, as the court deems proper. However, if such afterborn or after-adopted child, or any descendant of his, dies unmarried, without issue, and before reaching 18 years of age, his portion of the estate, or so much of his portion as may remain unexpended, shall revert to the person to whom it was given by the will.

§ 64.2-420. Provision for omitted children when child living when will made.

A. If a testator executes a will that makes provision for a living child of the testator, a child born or adopted after execution of a testator's will who is neither provided for nor expressly excluded by the will is entitled to the lesser of (i) such portion of the testator's estate as the afterborn or after-adopted child would have been entitled to if the testator had died intestate or (ii) the equivalent in amount to any bequests and devises to any child named in the will, and if there are bequests or devises to more than one child, then to the largest aggregate bequest or devise to any child.

B. [identical to paragraph B in § 64.2-419]

***

There appear to be no Virginia court decisions applying or interpreting these statutory rules in their modern form.

iii.   Class gifts

The subsection above covering lapsing and the anti-lapse statute addressed loss of class members who predecease a testator. It is also possible, though, that new members will enter a class between will execution as the testator's death. In that situation, the basic principle that a will speaks at the time of death governs, § 64.2-414 (above), so whoever is a member of the class described at the time of the testator's death gets included, even if the testator never met them and even if they had not yet been born at time of will execution.

D.   Obstacles to Enforcement of Will Provisions

Even after a will has been probated, the meaning of all its provisions determined, and corrections made for inadvertent omission of immediate family members, some will provisions – indeed an entire testamentary plan – might fail for several reasons. First, there are a few reasons why particular individuals might not take what a will provision gifts to them – disclaimer, satisfaction, and the slayer rule. Second, there might be obligations of the decedent or the estate that trump the will and require reducing the share of one or more beneficiaries, including commercial debts, taxes, and contractual undertakings relating specifically to execution of a will. These obstacles to enforcing will provisions we address here. An additional and very important one – the rights of a surviving spouse – merits its own chapter, and that is the subject of Chapter Four.

1.   Failure of individual bequests and devises

Sometimes beneficiaries do not wish to accept a testamentary gift, perhaps preferring to have the property pass to the next in line in the estate plan or wanting to keep property out of the hands of creditors or tax agencies. Other times, beneficiaries are disqualified from receiving, either because they already got what was coming to them or because they committed serious wrongdoing against the testator.

a. Disclaimer

As with non-probate transfers and inheritance under intestacy laws, no one is forced to accept a decedent's property through probate of a will. Refer to the discussion of disclaimer in Chapters One and Two for the pertinent statutory provisions, Chapter 26 (§ 64.2-2600 et seq.) of Title 64.2, Subtitle V. Va. Code Ann. § 64.2-2603 states that a disclaimer of a will bequest or devise becomes irrevocable when it is delivered to the executor or (if none has yet been appointed) filed with the probate court. § 64.2-2604 provides that disclaimer of a benefit under a will is treated as effective from the time of the testator's death, and that the effect of the disclaimer is to treat the disclaimant as having predeceased the testator (i.e., the lapse and anti-lapse rules would apply). A will beneficiary can forfeit the ability to disclaim, however, by certain actions:

Supreme Court of Virginia.
Niklason v. Ramsey
233 Va. 161, 353 S.E.2d 783 (1987)

THOMAS, Justice.

… In January 1971, Marshall Ramsey and William Boardman obtained separate judgments against Hugh [Niklason]. … Ramsey and Boardman tried unsuccessfully for several years to collect these judgments. …

On August 13, 1979, Hugh's mother, Ellowene D. Niklason executed a will. At the time the will was executed, Ellowene's family consisted of her two sons, Hugh and Don D. Niklason, and seven grandchildren, four by Hugh and three by Don. The evidence established that she had expressed **784 the desire that her seven grandchildren share equally in her estate. Ellowene died July 4, 1981. Her will was probated on July 6, 1981. The will did not divide her estate equally among her grandchildren. Instead, it gave virtually all of her estate to one of her grandchildren, Scott F. Niklason, Hugh's son.

On July 10, 1981, Ellowene's other son, Don… challenged the paper writing on two grounds. First, he contended that at the time the August 1979 paper was executed his mother lacked testamentary capacity. Second, he contended that the paper writing was the result of undue influence exerted upon his mother. Don's suit was placed on the docket as a fiduciary proceeding.

*163 The fiduciary proceeding-of which Ramsey and Boardman were unaware and in which they played no part-never came to trial. The parties settled that dispute. The commissioner found as a fact, and the trial court confirmed the finding, that all the parties to the fiduciary suit, including Hugh, entered into a contract as to the method of dividing Ellowene's estate. This contract provided that the will of Ellowene D. Niklason was invalid. This contract was entered into prior to any disclaimer being made by Hugh.

On January 28, 1982, two things occurred in the fiduciary suit. Hugh signed a disclaimer and then the trial court entered the consent decree which embodied the agreement previously reached by all the parties. The consent decree read in part as follows: "ADJUDGED, ORDERED and DECREED that the paper writing dated August 13, 1979 is not the Last Will and Testament of Ellowene D. Niklason...." The consent decree went on to provide the method by which the estate was to be divided among the seven grandchildren of Ellowene Niklason. ...

[T]he instant suit was initiated in March 1982. Ramsey and Boardman contend that because Hugh, prior to disclaiming, entered into a contract to divide his mother's estate he exercised dominion over her estate and thus was not permitted to disclaim.

Code § 64.1-194 [now § 64.2-2611} is controlling. It reads in pertinent part as follows:

> Any ... assignment, conveyance, encumbrance, pledge or transfer of property or interest therein or contract therefor ... bars the right to disclaim as to the property or interest.

Here, the commissioner found and the trial court confirmed the following matters:

> [T]he facts clearly show that a contract was entered into prior to the execution by F. Hugh [Niklason] of his disclaimer. The contract provided that the will of Ellowene D. [Niklason] was invalid and her estate was to be divided in accordance with the agreement. The children of F. Hugh Niklason would receive his notes of $10,000.00 and $24,000.00 the payment of which were certainly doubtful, and other assets and the children of Don D. [Niklason] would receive certain assets all in accordance with the agreement. *164 F. Hugh Niklason certainly contracted as to the assets which he later attempted to disclaim.
> .... F. Hugh Niklason entered into a contract for the transfer of his interest in the estate prior to execution of the disclaimer and his right to disclaim was [barred] under Section 64.1-194 of the code.

We are persuaded that by contracting away whatever interest he may have had in his mother's estate, Hugh exercised dominion over her estate contrary to the language of Code § 64.1-194. ...

A bankruptcy court in Virginia has held that a disclaimer while under a bankruptcy trusteeship is ineffective under federal bankruptcy law, which trumps state estate law.

In re Farrior
344 B.R. 483 (U.S. Bankruptcy Ct., W.D. Virginia, 2006)

ROSS W. KRUMM, Bankruptcy Judge.

... On February 17, 2004, Charles R. Farrior and Katherine L. Farrior, the debtors, filed a joint voluntary petition for Chapter 7 relief, and an Order for Relief was entered. Roy V. Wolfe III, Esq., qualified as Chapter 7 Trustee.

On March 25, 2004 the trustee filed a § 341 meeting report that declared *485 that no assets were available for distribution. On May 25, 2004 the debtors received their discharge.

On or about May 5, 2004, Ruth M. Farrior died testate. Under the provisions of her Last Will and Testament, the debtor, Charles R. Farrior and his sister, the Defendant, Janet Farrior von Gal, each inherited a one-half (1/2) undivided interest in [certain real estate], and in certain items of personal property owned by Mrs. Farrior on the date of her death. On or about March 11, 2005, Charles Farrior filed a Partial Disclaimer in the Frederick County Circuit Court disclaiming all but $5,902.00 of his interest in the Property. On March 16, 2005 the debtor filed Amended Schedules A and C with this court, together with copies of the Amended Homestead Deed and Partial Disclaimer. The Trustee was properly noticed with those filings on that date. ...

The filing of a joint case under the Code creates a bankruptcy estate comprised of all legal or equitable interests in property held by each debtor on the date of filing. 11 U.S.C. § 541(a). In general, property acquired by the debtor post petition is not considered property of the estate and may be retained by the debtor. See United States v. Gold (In re Avis), 178 F.3d 718, 720 (4th Cir.1999). However, an exception to the general rule is provided by the Code whereby property acquired by inheritance, bequest or devise within 180 days of the filing of the petition becomes property of the estate. 11 U.S.C. § 541(a)(5)(A).[2]

> [2] Interests acquired or arising after petition. If... the debtor acquires or becomes entitled to acquire any interest in property, the debtor shall within 10 days after the information comes to the debtor's knowledge... file a supplemental schedule in the chapter 7 liquidation case, chapter 11 reorganization case, chapter 12 family farmer's debt adjustment case, or chapter 13 individual debt adjustment case. If any of the property required to be reported under this subdivision is claimed by the debtor as exempt, the debtor shall claim the exemptions in the supplemental schedule. The duty to file a supplemental schedule in accordance with this subdivision continues notwithstanding the closing of the case, except that the schedule need not be filed in a chapter 11, chapter 12, or chapter 13 case with respect to property acquired after entry of the order confirming a chapter 11 plan or discharging the debtor in a chapter 12 or chapter 13 case. Fed. R. Bankr.P. 1007(h)

The debtors filed their Chapter 7 bankruptcy petition on February 17, 2004, and the male debtor inherited the property on May 5, 2004, within the 180–day time extension for inclusion of the property within the bankruptcy estate. Hence, his inheritance became property of the estate.

Under 11 U.S.C. § 363, the trustee may sell an interest in property of the estate and the interest of any co-owner in property in which the debtor had, at the time of the commencement of the case, an undivided interest as a tenant in common or joint tenant. *486 The debtors argue that the provisions of § 363(h) do not apply to the proposed sale because the male debtor made a partial disclaimer of his inheritance, and he amended his homestead deed to exempt $5,902, the full value of inherited property which he did not disclaim. In summary, the debtors assert that the right given Mr. Farrior under Virginia law to disclaim his inheritance permits exclusion of the disclaimed interest as property of the estate even when the disclaimer occurs after the filing of the bankruptcy petition.

Federal law, not state law, determines what constitutes the property of the estate. The term "property of the estate" encompasses "all legal or equitable interests of the debtor in property as of the commencement of the case." 11 U.S.C. § 541(a)(5)(A) includes as property of the estate property inherited within 180 days of the filing. ... Once he filed Mr. Farrior lost any right to exercise disclaimer under Virginia law because 11 U.S.C. § 704(a)(1) gives the Chapter 7 trustee the duty to "collect and reduce to money the property of the estate...." ... To hold otherwise would permit state law to preempt the Federal Bankruptcy Code.[6]

> [6] Cf. United States v. Irvine, 511 U.S. 224, 240 (1994) (holding federal tax law is not "struck blind" by state law right to inheritance disclaimer where Congress has shown no intent to support state law legal fictions as touchstones of taxability).

For the reasons state this court holds that the post-petition disclaimer by Charles R. Farrior in the property inherited from Ruth Farrior was ineffective. Accordingly, it is

ORDERED:

That the post petition partial disclaimer of Charles R. Farrior filed in the Clerk's Office of the Circuit Court of Frederick County, Virginia, be and hereby is declared VOID and the undivided one half interest of Charles R. Farrior in Tax Parcel *487 no. 86–A–265 is property of the estate pursuant to 11 U.S.C. § 541(a)(5)(A) to be administered by the Chapter 7 Trustee, and it is

FURTHER ORDERED:

That further hearing shall be conducted on the Trustee's complaint to sell the real estate interest of the debtor, Charles R. Farrior...

Sometimes prospective will beneficiaries execute an advance disclaimer of rights under any will of a certain other person, and this can be binding on them. It is called a "release" rather than a disclaimer, and it is somewhat different from a waiver of rights under intestacy law or spousal statutory rights. Its purpose is generally not to protect the person as to whose estate the release pertains; that person could simply choose not to execute a will leaving anything to the releasing party. Its purpose is rather to benefit other potential takers of an estate and to prevent the person to whose estate it applies from leaving property to the releaser despite the release. For example, siblings might enter into an agreement that one of them will execute a release as to their parent's estate, in exchange for receiving some other benefit at the time of the agreement. Contrast that with a prospective spouse's waiver of intestacy or elective share rights as to the other's estate in a pre-nuptial agreement; the other spouse would nevertheless be free to execute an effective will bequeathing some or all of his or her estate to the one who waived entitlements, choosing not to enforce the waiver.

Supreme Court of Virginia.
Ware v. Crowell, 251 Va. 116465 S.E.2d 809 (1996)

KEENAN, Justice.

*118 ... Edna Jensen Buric and her two adult children, Shirley M. Crowell and Robert W. Jensen, owned real property in Illinois as tenants in common. In 1985, Buric wanted to sell the property, but Crowell refused. Buric then brought an action in an Illinois circuit court, seeking a ruling that a quitclaim deed to the property conveyed a fee simple interest to her alone.

In December 1985, Crowell entered into a written agreement with her mother and brother settling the Illinois action. Under the settlement agreement, Crowell received $16,000, which represented one-third of the proceeds of sale of the property. The agreement further provided that Jensen would receive no proceeds from the sale.

The settlement agreement included the following release.

> [Crowell] does hereby disclaim any and every right, benefit, title and interest which she might or could receive from Buric now or at the time of her death, including, but not without limiting the generality of the foregoing, each and every bequest and devise that may be contained in the last will and testament of Buric, any and all rights which she might or could have as an heir at law of Buric, ... and any and all other rights which might or could be conferred upon her as a result of any act done by Buric. She further agrees not to file any petition to contest the validity of Buric's will or any inter vivos transfers at the time of her death or in any manner interfere in the orderly process of the administration of the estate of Buric.

In August 1989, Buric executed a will which provided a specific bequest of $16,000 to Jensen. The will also contained a residuary clause devising the balance of Buric's estate to Crowell and Jensen in equal shares. **811 At the time of her death on March 13, 1990, Buric owned the real property in Virginia that is the subject of this appeal.

Following Buric's death, Jensen borrowed the sum of $100,000 from Southside Bank. The notes were secured by two deeds of trust on the Virginia property. Crowell later filed a bill of complaint seeking a declaratory judgment that she owned a one-half *119 interest in the property free from the deeds of trust executed by Jensen. ...

[T]he issue presented is one of first impression regarding the effect of a release on the right to take property under a will. At least twenty-two of the twenty-five jurisdictions that have addressed the issue recognize the enforceability of a release of an expectancy interest in an ancestor's estate. *120 [citations omitted] Under the majority rule, which we adopt for purposes of testate succession, a release of an expectancy interest in an estate, freely and fairly made, is binding on the releasing beneficiary and excludes that beneficiary from participation in the ancestor's estate.

The release must be based on a valuable consideration and must be made in good faith and free from circumstances of fraud or oppression. As a contract, the release effectively conveys the expectancy interest to the other beneficiaries when the interest becomes vested at the time of the ancestor's death.

In the present case, the parties' 1985 agreement was a contract among three adults that eliminated Crowell's right to share in Buric's estate. The record contains no evidence that the agreement was made in bad faith or under circumstances of fraud or oppression. In consideration of the provision eliminating Crowell's right to take property under Buric's will, Crowell acquired the right to receive a share of the proceeds from the **812 Illinois property. Buric could not alter by will the rights Jensen acquired in this agreement. Foremost among these rights was the exclusion of Crowell from taking property under Buric's will. When Buric died, Crowell's expectancy interest in Buric's estate vested in Buric's other beneficiaries. Thus, we conclude that Crowell's release of her expectancy interest in Buric's estate is binding. ... [2] ...

> [2] We also note that Code §§ 64.1-188 to -196 are not relevant to our decision. Those sections apply only to instruments disclaiming succession to property passing under a will or by descent or distribution, which may be filed after the death of the decedent.

---

b.   Satisfaction

In the context of intestate succession, a claim that some heir "already got his" was called "advancement." In the will context, it is called "satisfaction."

Subtitle II, Chapter 4. Wills, Article 3. Construction and Effect

§ 64.2-417. When advancement deemed satisfaction of devise or bequest.

Property that a testator gave during his lifetime to a person shall not be treated as a satisfaction of a devise or bequest to that person, in whole or in part, unless (i) the will provides for deduction of the lifetime gift, (ii) the testator declares in a writing made contemporaneously with the gift that the gift is to be deducted from the devise or bequest or is in satisfaction thereof, or (iii) the devisee or legatee acknowledges in writing that the gift is in satisfaction of the devise or bequest.

***

The Supreme Court has not rendered a decision applying or interpreting this provision, which is more restrictive than the rule for advancement in the intestacy context. There is just one, unreported circuit court decision involving a situation of satisfaction. In Feld v. Priebe (2004), the Circuit Court for the City of Richmond probated a will with a provision clearly expressing an intention for some lifetime transfers to be treated as satisfaction, and the only dispute concerned which transfers the testator would have meant to include. The will stated:

> A. Remaining Estate. It is my intent to treat my children as equally as possible ...

> I hereby direct that all such transfers and all other gifts which I have made after January 1, 1996 shall be treated as advancements, shall be brought back into hotchpot, without interest, and shall be deducted from the shares to be formed for my children or their descendants. Moreover, all such transfers and all other gifts made after January 11, 1996 that are made to my child shall be treated as advancements to that child's descendants should my child predecease me. For the purposes of this paragraph, the value of such gifts shall be the fair market value of the gift on the date of the gift... The value of any life insurance policies shall be valued not less than the value of the proceeds paid at the time of my death.

c.   Slayers

As in the contexts of non-probate transfers and intestacy, the law does not permit people to profit through a will by killing.

Subtitle V. Provisions Applicable to Probate and Nonprobate Transfers
Chapter 25. Acts Barring Property Rights

§ 64.2-2502. Property passing by will or intestate succession
... B. The slayer shall be deemed to have predeceased the decedent as to property that would have passed to the slayer by the will of the decedent; however, the antilapse provisions of § 64.2-418 are applicable ...

§ 64.2-2507. Powers of appointment

A. The slayer shall be deemed to have predeceased the decedent as to any exercise in the decedent's will of a power of appointment in favor of the slayer and the appointment shall be deemed to have lapsed.

d. Ex-spouses

The law presumes testators would not still wish to leave much or any of their estate to someone who is an ex-spouse, and it recognizes that it many people do not think about their wills when going through the often-traumatic experience of a divorce. So it effects a partial or complete revocation of any will that was executed prior to divorce and makes provision for the spouse.

Subtitle II, Chapter 4. Wills, Article 2. Revocation and Effect

§ 64.2-412. Revocation by divorce or annulment; revival upon remarriage

A. If, after making a will, the testator is divorced from the bond of matrimony or his marriage is annulled, the divorce or annulment revokes any disposition or appointment of property made by the will to the former spouse. Unless the will expressly provides otherwise, any provision conferring a general or special power of appointment on the former spouse or nominating the former spouse as executor, trustee, conservator, or guardian is also revoked.

B. Property prevented from passing to a former spouse because of revocation pursuant to this section shall pass as if the former spouse failed to survive the testator. Provisions of a will conferring a power or office on the former spouse shall be interpreted as if the former spouse failed to survive the testator.

C. If the provisions of the will are revoked solely pursuant to this section, and there is no subsequent will or inconsistent codicil, the provisions shall be revived upon the testator's remarriage to the former spouse. ...

***

Significantly, this current version of the rule regarding ex-spouses, at least with respect to the effect of divorce on property distribution, includes no exception for instances in which the will expresses a contrary intention. The omission appears deliberate, because paragraph B essentially codifies a 1978 decision of the Supreme Court – Jones v. Brown, 219 Va. 599, 602; 248 S.E.2d 812, 814– holding that "property devised to a former spouse, which is prevented from passing because of statutory revocation, shall pass as if the former spouse failed to survive the decedent *unless a contrary intention is apparent from the provisions of the will*." (emphasis added) The question presented in that case was whether a will provision stating "In the event my said Wife shall not survive me…" should be read literally to require the actual death of the wife or should instead apply also where a bequest to the wife is revoked by operation of statute; the court adopted the latter view. If Virginia courts now interpret this statutory provision literally, it seems a testator would need to execute a new testamentary document after the divorce in order to include an ex-spouse in his or her disposition of property (unless, perhaps, a contractual obligation to the former spouse is effective, as discussed in the next section); no language in the pre-divorce will could override the operation of the statute. But the courts have yet to address such a situation in a published decision.

2.   Obligations to others

With the rules discussed in the previous subsection, reducing or voiding a bequest or devise to a particular beneficiary, the result is to take from that beneficiary and give to other beneficiaries or heirs. The only loser is the person whose own actions (disclaiming, accepting a lifetime gift, murdering) are the basis for denying effect to some portion of the will. The present subsection addresses situations in which some beneficiaries must lose out, through no fault of their own, because the decedent had or the estate has a legal obligation to some persons, institutions, or agencies that trumps the testamentary disposition of the estate. After discussing of such obligations, the subsection includes analysis of the rule for apportioning among will beneficiaries responsibility for fulfilling those obligations.

a.   Contracts to make a will

People sometimes promise recompense, in the form of a will bequest, to others who have helped and supported them. If the will does not actually make any provision for the promisee, the promisee might claim a contractual right to take from the decedent's estate. Another common situation in which contract law potentially intrudes into estate administration is when someone alleges that a decedent and his or her surviving spouse had at some point, before or during marriage, entered into an agreement with respect to the distribution of their wealth at the point when both are deceased. Virginia courts have taken a fairly restrictive approach to recognizing and giving effect to such contracts.

i.   Promise to repay for services

Supreme Court of Virginia.
Virginia Home for Boys and Girls v. Phillips
279 Va. 279, 688 S.E.2d 284 (2010)

OPINION BY Senior Justice CHARLES S. RUSSELL.

*282 …William Ray Phillips (Phillips) grew up in Sussex County. He lived with his parents about a mile away from the farm of Wayland and Margaret Council. Wayland Council (Wayland) was Phillips' uncle. At the age of ten, Phillips moved to the Council home and lived with them, helping with the farm work, until he graduated from high school. The Councils had no children and Phillips was described by another relative as "the closest thing they had to a son." Phillips went to college after high school. In 1970, shortly after finishing college, he was employed by a tobacco company in Petersburg. Thereafter, he married and lived with his wife in a home they acquired about five minutes away from his place of employment.

In 1977, Phillips' uncle Wayland asked him to come to the Councils' farm in Sussex County to discuss a proposal. During a conference at the Councils' kitchen table, both Councils were present but Wayland "did ... most of the talking." He proposed that Phillips move to the farm where the Councils would sell him a parcel of land on which to build a home for his family. Phillips would then work on the farm, assisting his uncle until 1980, when Wayland planned to retire. Thereafter, Phillips would take over the farming operation, paying rent to the Councils for the land, machinery and farm equipment, and a wage to Wayland for any farm work he might do. Phillips was also to be **286 available for any business or personal help the Councils might need in their later years. In return, Phillips testified, the Councils promised to leave him whatever assets they had, real or personal, when the last survivor of them died. Phillips testified that he agreed to this proposal, understanding that the Councils might consume all their assets while living and that he could ultimately *283 receive "everything or nothing, whatever was left in their estate was to go to me." The agreement was entirely oral and no written memoranda of it existed. Only Phillips and the Councils were present at the conference.

In reliance on the agreement, Phillips sold his home, purchased 1.618 acres of the farm from the Councils, took out a construction loan, built a new home on the lot and moved there with his family, which now included a three-year-old son. Phillips continued to commute to his job at the tobacco company in Petersburg from 1977 until his uncle retired in 1980, adding about 40 miles per day to his travel to and from work. He also helped his uncle with farm work.

In 1980, when Wayland retired, Phillips took over the farming operation. He paid rent to the Councils for the farm land and equipment, paid wages to Wayland and assisted the Councils with their affairs. In 1980, Phillips' first year of farming operations, the area experienced a severe drought. In order to pay expenses for that year and to have "start-up money" for the next, Phillips borrowed $30,640 from a federal agency to be repaid over 20 years, secured by a second deed of trust on his home. The Councils were not liable for this debt. Phillips repaid the loan in 2001.

Wayland died in 1982. His will left all his property to his wife but provided that if she predeceased him, his entire estate would go to his nephew, Phillips. Phillips testified that Margaret Council (Margaret) showed the will to him when they went to the clerk's office to offer it for probate and told him "mine is just like it."

In 1987, the plant in Petersburg was closed. The tobacco company, however, offered Phillips an opportunity to transfer to another plant in Georgia. Phillips declined the offer because he would be unable to fulfill his agreement with the Councils if he moved. He was compelled to accept a position in Hampton with a considerably lower salary and benefits that required him to travel 100 miles per day to and from work.

After Wayland died, other witnesses testified that Margaret became "angry ... that he died," "very eccentric," "very reclusive," and "would change her mind from one day to the next on what she was going to do." Phillips testified that her attitude toward him changed. "She had become a little more reclusive. Wanted to be by herself more. Wanted to make decisions on her own." She gave Phillips a durable power of attorney in 1992, but in October 1996 Phillips received a letter from her attorney advising him that she had *284 "made some changes in her estate plan." The letter enclosed a revocation of Phillips' power of attorney.

Margaret died on April 6, 2005. Her will was admitted to probate. Except for a few household furnishings, it leaves all her real and personal property to the "Virginia Home for Boys in Richmond, Inc." The name of that entity was changed in 2004 to Virginia Home for Boys and Girls (the Home)...

Phillips... seeks imposition of a trust on Margaret's assets and specific performance of the parol agreement he had made with the Councils in 1977. Phillips contested neither the validity of the will nor Margaret's testamentary capacity. ... **287

ANALYSIS

Code § 8.01-397 ["Dead man's statute] provides, in pertinent part:

> In an action by or against a person who, from any cause, is incapable of testifying, or by or against the committee, trustee, executor, administrator, heir, or other representative of the person so incapable of testifying, no judgment or decree shall be rendered in favor of an adverse or interested party founded on his uncorroborated testimony.

... Phillips agrees that no written memorandum of *285 the agreement was made and that no other witnesses testified to its existence, but contends that the circumstantial evidence strongly corroborates his testimony. ... Code § 11-2 provides, in pertinent part:

> When written evidence required to maintain action.-Unless a promise, contract, agreement, representation, assurance, or ratification, or some memorandum or note thereof, is in writing and signed by the party to be charged or his agent, no action shall be brought in any of the following cases: ....

> > 6. Upon any contract for the sale of real estate, or for the lease thereof for more than a year; ...

This section has repeatedly been held applicable to oral contracts to devise real estate. See, e.g., Hill v. Luck, 201 Va. 586, 589, 112 S.E.2d 858, 860 (1960) [other citations omitted].

A parol contract to devise land may, however, be taken out of the Statute of Frauds by evidence of part performance on the promisee's part. To prevail, the promisee must establish: (1) that the parol agreement relied on is "certain and definite in its terms," (2) that his acts of part performance were done "in pursuance of the agreement proved," and (3) that the agreement has been "so far executed that a refusal of full execution would operate a fraud" upon him. Clark v. Atkins, 188 Va. 668, 674-75, 51 S.E.2d 222, 225 (1949). ... *286

At common law, when one who would have been a party litigant had been rendered incapable, by death or incapacity, from testifying in his own behalf, an adverse party litigant was disqualified as a witness in his own behalf on the ground of interest. The Dead Man's Statute substituted the more flexible requirement that the testimony of the surviving witness be corroborated in place of the harsh common-law rule.

We have, in many cases, considered the nature and degree of the corroboration required under this statute. Because the statute's purpose is remedial, the kind and quantity of corroboration required depend largely upon the facts of each case and no general rule of universal application exists. It is well established that corroboration may be shown by circumstantial evidence, that not **288 every material point upon which the surviving party testifies must be corroborated, and that corroboration need not rise to the level of confirmation, but need only serve to strengthen the surviving witness' account. Nevertheless, one essential requirement is implicit in all our cases: evidence, to be corroborative, must be independent of the surviving witness. It must not depend upon his credibility or upon circumstances under his control. It may come from any other competent witness or legal source, but it must not emanate from him. Leckie v. Lynchburg Trust and Savings Bank, 191 Va. 360, 370, 60 S.E.2d 923, 928 (1950).

Our review of the record, in light of that requirement, discloses no evidence that is independent of Phillips' testimony corroborating the existence or the terms of the parol agreement on which he relies. Phillips' personal credibility is not in question, and the circuit court was entitled to weigh it and find it persuasive. The requirement of corroboration, however, imposed a separate burden upon Phillips that is independent of the weight and sufficiency of his own testimony. The General Assembly chose to impose that burden to replace the heavier burden formerly imposed by the common law *287 on a litigant claiming against an opponent incapable of testifying. Although the requirement of corroboration might sometimes lead to results not intended by parties to an oral agreement, it is evident that the legislative judgment was that such occasional unfortunate results were preferable to a state of the law in which every will would be subject to challenge after the testator's death by a claimant asserting an oral agreement contrary to the will's provisions, based only on the claimant's self-serving testimony.

Because Phillips failed to carry the burden of proving corroboration imposed upon him by the Dead Man's Statute, his claim also fails to satisfy the Statute of Frauds. As noted above, Code § 11-2(6) applies to parol contracts to devise land. Part performance may only be relied on to take the case out of the Statute of Frauds when the claimant establishes that the parol agreement is "certain and definite in its terms" and that his part performance was done "in pursuance of the agreement proved." Clark, 188 Va. at 674-75, 51 S.E.2d at 225. Because of the effect of the Dead Man's Statute, Phillips failed to meet the legal standard for proving either the terms of the parol agreement or its existence. We... enter final judgment in favor of the Home.

Supreme Court of Virginia.
Runion v. Helvestine

256 Va. 1, 501 S.E.2d 411 (1998)

CARRICO, Chief Justice.

... Dorothy Marie Runion and her husband, David L. Runion, sought to enjoin the alienation of Lots A and B, as shown on a certain plat, in which the plaintiffs claimed an interest under an oral contract whereby Dorothy W. Helvestine agreed to make a will devising the plaintiffs Lot A and an option to purchase Lot B.[1] ...

> [1] Dorothy W. Helvestine was still living at the time of the proceedings below, so a bill seeking specific performance of the alleged agreement to make a will would have been inappropriate.

Upon the death of her husband, Frank Helvestine, Jr., in 1986, Dorothy Helvestine became the owner of a tract of land containing *4 approximately 25 acres which includes Lots A and B. Lot A contains 1.86 acres and Dorothy Helvestine's residence, located at 5931 Cotton Hill Road, S.W., in Roanoke **413 County. Lot B contains 2.446 acres and a frame house adjoining Lot A.

The amended bill alleged that Dorothy Helvestine "is currently not competent" and requested that a guardian ad litem be appointed to represent her. Jeffrey L. Dorsey, Esquire, was appointed to perform this function.

The amended bill also alleged as follows: After the death of Frank Helvestine, Jr., but before the incompetency of Dorothy W. Helvestine, [she] came to the Plaintiffs and requested them to move in with her at the above stated address in order to take care of her. In March, 1986, the Plaintiffs moved in with Dorothy W. Helvestine. At that time, they entered into an oral contract to make a will whereby if the Plaintiffs provided the day-to-day care for Dorothy W. Helvestine as long as possible, she would will to them the house and lot at the address above-stated. The Plaintiffs specifically relied upon these representations. Further, Defendant, Dorothy W. Helvestine, also stated that in addition to devising them the house and lot aforesaid, she would further devise to them an option to purchase a second tract of land. In furtherance of this oral contract to make a will, Dorothy W. Helvestine directed a survey to be made in April, 1991... Lot A represents the property that Dorothy W. Helvestine contracted to be devised by will to the Plaintiffs. Lot B is the property that was agreed the Plaintiffs could purchase upon the death of Dorothy W. Helvestine from her estate for the sum of $35,000.00. This $35,000.00 purchase price was agreed to in 1991 and the Plaintiffs were given first refusal as to this property upon which representations the Plaintiffs relied.

The amended bill alleged further that the plaintiffs "performed under the contract from March, 1986, to October, 1993, when Dorothy W. Helvestine became so frail and infirm because of advanced age that her care required her to be transferred to the South Roanoke Nursing Home." In addition, the amended bill alleged that "[d]espite the performance on behalf of the Plaintiffs done in reliance on the oral contract to make a will with Dorothy W. Helvestine, the Defendants, *5 Frank Helvestine, III and Eric Helvestine, are denying that any such arrangement ever existed and ... are taking any and all steps necessary to defeat the oral contract and work a fraud upon the Plaintiffs." Finally, the amended bill alleged that Frank Helvestine, III, had entered into a contract for the sale of Lot B... to Strauss Construction Corporation (hereinafter, Strauss).[2]

> [2] The copy of the contract attached to the amended bill is signed only by Eric F. Helvestine as attorney-in-fact for Dorothy W. Helvestine.

The amended bill prayed that the plaintiffs "be granted a permanent injunction preventing the Defendants, Frank Helvestine, III, and Eric Helvestine, from alienating Lots A and B... The bill also prayed that the contract for the sale of Lot B to Strauss "be rescinded as inequitable." ... **414 ...*6 [4]

> [4] Since the plaintiffs do not assign error relating to their claim that they were entitled to a right of first refusal with respect to Lot B, we will not consider that claim.

The Statute of Frauds provides that "[u]nless a ... contract ... is in writing and signed by the party to be charged or his agent, no action shall be brought ... [u]pon any contract for the sale of real estate...." Code § 11–2(6). The defendants agree, however, that an oral contract relating to land, including an oral contract to make a will and an oral option to purchase, is enforceable when there has been partial performance and certain legal requirements are met. Those requirements are well-established. In Wright v. Pucket, 63 Va. (22 Gratt.) 370 (1872), this Court stated:

> ... From the numerous decisions on the subject the following principles may be extracted and briefly stated as follows: 1st. The parol agreement relied on must be certain and definite in its terms. 2d. The acts proved in part performance must refer to, result from, or be made in pursuance of the agreement proved. 3d. The agreement must have been so far executed that a refusal of full execution would operate a fraud upon the party, and place him in a situation which does not lie in compensation. Id. at 374; see also Story v. Hargrave, 235 Va. 563, 570, 369 S.E.2d 669, 673 (1988).

*7 Here, the arguments of the defendants focus upon the first two of the Wright v. Pucket requirements, viz., that the oral agreement relied on must be definite in its terms and that the acts proved in part performance must refer to, result from, or be made in pursuance of the agreement proved. The defendants maintain that the plaintiffs' oral agreement relating to the devise of an option to purchase fails to satisfy either requirement.

Strauss argues that "[t]o be enforceable, the terms of an oral contract involving the conveyance of land must be clear, definite, and certain at the time the alleged agreement [is] entered into." Here, Strauss says, when the agreement to devise an option was purportedly made in 1986 it was not definite in its terms because the land to be optioned had not yet been clearly defined and the purchase price had not been determined. Strauss points out that the purchase price and the description of the property were not ascertained until 1991, five years after the agreement was entered into, and it argues that what occurred in 1991 "does not make a legally unenforceable 'agreement' entered into in 1986 an enforceable contract in 1991."

Frank and Eric Helvestine... also argue... the plaintiffs... had already moved in with Dorothy Helvestine and were caring for her **415 in reliance upon her 1986 promise to devise Lot A. Therefore, their moving in could not have been in reliance upon a promise made in 1991 with respect to Lot B. Hence, ... "[p]art performance and reliance were already in place ... because of the 1986 'agreement' as to Lot A" and "the 1991 option was without any consideration."

We are of opinion that when the allegations of the amended bill are fairly read they state a case for an agreement requiring Dorothy Helvestine to do two things in consideration of the plaintiffs' moving in with her and providing her day-to-day care as long as possible, (1) make an outright devise to them of the house and lot *8 located at 5931 Cotton Hill Road, S.W., and (2) devise them an option to purchase a second tract of land. While the terms of the option were not then certain and definite because the land and the price to be paid therefor were not specified, the terms were made certain and definite in 1991 when Lot B was created at Dorothy Helvestine's direction and the parties agreed upon a purchase price of $35,000.

Strauss has not cited, nor have we found, any authority for its contention that, for an oral contract to be enforceable, its terms "must be clear, definite, and certain at the time the alleged agreement [is] entered into" and that nothing occurring later can "make a legally unenforceable 'agreement' ... an enforceable contract." We think subsequent occurrences can make enforceable an otherwise unenforceable contract, provided the rights of innocent parties without notice have not intervened. ...

With respect to the argument of Frank and Eric Helvestine that there was no consideration for what they call "the 1991 option," we hold that no additional consideration was necessary. What was done in 1991 merely filled in the details of the 1986 agreement and became part and parcel of the bundle of rights the plaintiffs acquired at the outset in consideration of their moving in with Dorothy Helvestine and providing her day-to-day care as long as possible. That bundle consisted of a promise to devise what became Lot A and a promise to devise an option to purchase what became Lot B, and the plaintiffs' acts of part performance resulted from or were made in pursuance of both those promises.

Even so, the defendants submit, there are no allegations in the amended bill as to time of performance, conditions of exercise, or payment arrangements. However, because the alleged agreement involved the making of a will, the time of performance is implied from the event that would make the will effective, i.e., the death of Dorothy Helvestine. The defendants do not suggest what conditions of exercise are lacking from the allegations or whether such conditions would relate to the formation of the contract or merely to matters of performance, *9 the latter being non-essential allegations. Townsend v. Stick, 158 F.2d 142, 145 (4th Cir.1946). And the defendants are correct in saying that the alleged agreement provides for a purchase price of $35,000 without specifying the terms of payment. But, in such circumstances, the law implies that the purchase price will be paid in cash. See Lacey v. Cardwell, 216 Va. 212, 221, 217 S.E.2d 835, 842 (1975) **416 ...

[T]he chancellor held that the plaintiffs were not entitled to rescission of the contract for the sale of Lot B to Strauss because the plaintiffs have an adequate remedy at law for any damages they may sustain. The plaintiffs argue that when a right to acquire an interest in land is involved, money damages are inadequate because there is no substitute for the land itself, and equity will enforce the right in an appropriate proceeding. ... We agree with the plaintiffs that if they establish an interest in Lot B, an award of damages would not provide an adequate remedy.

In Story v. Hargrave, supra, we reversed an award of $1,000 per month as compensation to a couple who cared for an elderly woman in return for her promise to leave her property to them in her will. We held that the couple's claim was not compensable in damages and that they were entitled to the benefit of their contract in the form of the transfer of the property to them at the promisor's death. 235 Va. at 569, 369 S.E.2d at 672–73. In Everton v. Askew, 199 Va. 778, 102 S.E.2d 156 (1958), this Court affirmed the enforcement of an oral agreement made by a husband *10 and wife whereby she was to devise to him all real estate he had conveyed to her; instead, she left the property to her sister. We said, "[t]here is no way [the husband] can be put in statu quo except by enforcing the agreement." 199 Va. at 784, 102 S.E.2d at 160. And in Wright v. Dudley, 189 Va. 448, 53 S.E.2d 29 (1949). we held that an oral agreement by an elderly woman to make a will devising her real estate to a caretaker in return for the latter's maintenance and support should be specifically enforced. We stated: "Contracts of this kind are taken out of the operation of the statute of frauds and enforced in equity because the remedy at law is not adequate...." Id. at 455, 53 S.E.2d at 32.

It does not follow, however, that the plaintiffs are entitled to rescission of the contract for the sale of Lot B to Strauss. They are not parties to that contract; they allege no misconduct on Strauss's part in inducing the contract... This does not mean that the plaintiffs are without a remedy. The amended bill contains an explicit prayer for a permanent injunction preventing Frank Helvestine, III, and Eric Helvestine, Dorothy Helvestine's attorneys-in-fact, from alienating Lot B. If the plaintiffs prove the allegations of the amended bill and it is determined that Strauss had notice of the plaintiffs' claim to Lot B, the chancellor will have injunctive relief at his disposal to protect the plaintiffs' rights in that lot. ...

Supreme Court of Virginia.
Vaughn v. Shank
248 Va. 224, 445 S.E.2d 127 (1994)

KEENAN, Justice.

… [P]ursuant to a foster care agreement of the Shenandoah County Board of Public Welfare, Helen Vaughn began *226 living in the [Ruth B.] Conner household in 1970 at age 12 and remained there until her marriage in 1976. … Vaughn maintained a close, filial relationship with Conner until Conner's death on September 23, 1990.

Conner was survived by her two daughters, Linda Himelright and Nancy L. Plaugher, and her son, William Conner, who were her sole heirs at law. Her last will, executed on October 18, 1988, … bequeathed $1,000 to her daughter, Linda, and devised and bequeathed the residue of her estate to the Brethren's Home of Indiana, Incorporated.

In March 1991, Vaughn filed a notice of claim against Conner's estate… Vaughn stated:

> I herewith make claim on the estate of Ruth M. Conner for services rendered and pursuant to the attached affidavit of indebtedness for the house and lot located at 301 North Water Street in Woodstock, Virginia or its value based on the purchase price of $31,000.

… The evidence at the hearing showed that, at some time before 1986, Conner converted her residence into a nursing home that she operated as the Dutch Haven Home for Adults (Dutch Haven), and that Vaughn was employed at Dutch Haven from the time of its opening until Conner's death in 1990. In 1987, Conner purchased the house on Water Street referred to in Vaughn's notice of claim. Vaughn testified that Conner asked her to live in the Water Street house because it was closer to Dutch Haven than Vaughn's previous residence. Vaughn also stated that Conner told her that the house was purchased for Vaughn and Vaughn's daughter, and that if they liked the house, "it would be [theirs]." **129

Vaughn testified that, after she and her daughter had lived in the Water Street house for a month and a half, Conner asked Vaughn to leave the house and move into Dutch Haven. According *227 to Vaughn, Conner "needed someone there with CPR" training and wanted Vaughn to be available to work "on call." Vaughn stated that, at that time, Conner "made me a promise, that if I moved in to Dutch Haven[,] she would see that we got the Water Street house. Me and my daughter." According to Vaughn, Conner agreed to fulfill this promise on her expected date of retirement, which was Christmas, 1991.

Vaughn testified that, in 1987, she moved into Dutch Haven, as Conner had requested, and assumed additional duties. Although her previous employment at Dutch Haven had involved a 40-hour week, she now began working 80 to 90 hours per week. She stated that, since she was the only employee qualified to administer cardiopulmonary resuscitation (CPR), she had to remain "on call" at Dutch Haven 24 hours per day, with the exception of a few hours each Friday and Sunday. Vaughn asserted that, although she performed these additional duties, she continued to be paid for only 40 hours of work per week. She also stated that, once in residence at Dutch Haven, she continued to work the above-described schedule of hours until Conner's death.

Eilene McClelland, who rented the Water Street house from Conner after Vaughn moved to Dutch Haven, testified that Conner told her on two occasions that "the house was purchased for [Conner's] step daughter" and that "the house was bought for Helen and her daughter." Vaughn's daughter, Shannon, age 12, testified that Conner told her "that when she retires that we would be taken care of." According to Shannon, Conner also stated that she would give them the Water Street house, and "that we would have a roof over our head when she died or when she retired."

Finally, William Glenn Sweeney, a resident of Dutch Haven, testified that Vaughn worked in excess of 40 hours per week. Sweeney stated that no other employee worked as many hours as Vaughn, and that, because she lived on the premises, she was available at all times. ... *228 *

> *   Vaughn... seeks specific performance of the alleged contract for the conveyance of the Water Street house, rather than compensation for the value of her services. We note, however, that specific performance is purely an equitable remedy, and Vaughn did not file a bill of complaint in equity; instead, she filed a notice of claim pursuant to Code § 64.1-171. In light of our holding, we need not further address this issue.

**130 ... Since Vaughn seeks to enforce an oral contract allegedly made with a party who is now deceased, we must consider her evidence in accordance with the requirements of corroboration set *229 forth in Code § 8.01-397. ... The purpose of the statute is to prevent the survivor from prevailing against the decedent's estate solely because the executor has been deprived of the decedent's version of the transaction. ...

In the present case, Code § 8.01-397 requires corroboration of Vaughn's testimony that she entered into the alleged contract with Conner, because that is the sole essential allegation on which her claim is based. However, ... only Vaughn's testimony relates to the issue whether a contract was formed. Although Shannon Vaughn testified that Conner said she would "give us [the] house," and Eilene McClelland stated that Conner told her the Water Street house was purchased for Vaughn and her daughter, this testimony does not show that Vaughn and Conner entered into an agreement that the house *230 would be transferred in consideration for services, or that Conner recognized an obligation to convey the house to Vaughn pursuant to the terms of their agreement. The testimony of these witnesses is equally consistent with an unenforceable promise on the part of Conner to make Vaughn a gift of the house.

Moreover, the surrounding circumstances do not corroborate the existence of a contract between Vaughn and Conner. While Vaughn asserts that Conner promised in 1987 to convey the house to her, there was no evidence that Conner planned or attempted to have a deed drawn. In addition, Conner's will, executed in 1988, shows that Conner contemplated another disposition of her property in the event of her death. **131 William Sweeney's testimony dealt only with the number of hours that Vaughn worked at Dutch Haven. This testimony provides no corroboration of

Vaughn's assertion that she performed the work at Dutch Haven in consideration for Conner's promise to give her the Water Street house.

In previous cases… where a plaintiff was held entitled to relief, the testimony and evidence of surrounding circumstances provided the kind of clear corroboration that Vaughn's evidence lacks. For example, in Timberlake v. Pugh, 158 Va. 397, 163 S.E. 402 (1932), two witnesses testified that the decedent had asked them to prepare his will conveying certain property to the plaintiff, thus strengthening the plaintiff's testimony that the decedent had promised to will her the same property in return for her housekeeping services. In Clark v. Atkins, 188 Va. 668, 51 S.E.2d 222 (1949), Atkins's contention that Clark had promised to leave him all his property if Atkins would help run Clark's business was corroborated by "nine witnesses, most of whom [were] not interested or related to the parties, who testified that Clark had stated to them on various occasions that he expected to leave the meat market business" to Atkins.

Similarly, in Everton v. Askew, 199 Va. 778, 782, 102 S.E.2d 156, 158 (1958), the decedent was shown to have told numerous persons that the plaintiff, her husband, had titled his real estate in the *231 decedent's name in return for her promise to make a will leaving the property to the plaintiff. In Purcell v. Purcell, 188 Va. 91, 49 S.E.2d 335 (1948), the plaintiff alleged that the decedent, his brother, had agreed to make monthly payments if the plaintiff would provide a home for their sister. This assertion was corroborated by evidence that the decedent sent payments to the plaintiff for several years, and by the decedent's statements and letters showing that the amounts were paid in return for the plaintiff's assistance.

In the present case, Vaughn failed to provide such corroborative evidence of the alleged oral contract; thus, the trial court properly denied her claim against Conner's estate. …

In Browder-Martin v. Meneses, 81 Va. Cir. 199 (2010), the Circuit Court for the City of Norfolk rejected a claim to enforce a contract to make a will, asserted by a neighbor of a decedent, who presented evidence that she and her late husband were good friends of the decedent, and that when the decedent was 77 years old and in good health she asked them to care for her for the duration of her life in exchange for receiving in her will real property she owned in Norfolk. The decedent had in fact executed a will devising the property, subject to a condition that her granddaughter have the option of purchasing the property from the neighbors, and explaining in the will the contractual basis for this devise. After the husband in the neighboring couple died, the wife continued to care for the decedent, but nine years later she moved to Chesapeake and could only manage to visit the decedent a few times per week to help with cooking, driving, and paying bills. The decedent's son and daughter-in-law then took over most of the duties the neighbor had previously performed, and eventually the decedent moved into their house and remained there for a year and a half until her death. During a brief stint in a nursing home, the decedent executed a new will leaving the real property to her granddaughter. The court found that a valid contract existed. Further, citing Story v. Hargrave, 235 Va. 563, 369 S.E.2d 669 (1988), the court determined that damages for the value of services provided was an inadequate remedy in such cases, that "the promisee is entitled to the benefit of his bargain, i.e., the land," but that the promise may instead seek damages in the form of the value of the land if she so chooses. However, the court ultimately concluded that the neighbor had not fulfilled her obligation under the contract and so could recover nothing. The efforts of the son and daughter-in-law could not substite for those of the neighbor as fulfillment of the obligation. The former neighbor would have had to show "(1) the decedent agreed to release her from her obligation to provide personal services and to accept the substituted services of the Browders, (2) that the Browders fully performed the services, and (3) that the decedent still agreed to convey the property—not to the Browders—but to the plaintiff." In fact, the evidence suggested the decedent viewed the contract as a nullity after the neighbor moved.

ii.   Agreements between spouses

The most recent Supreme Court decision on this issue addresses a claim that a contract was implicit in execution of reciprocal wills.

Supreme Court of Virginia.
Keith v. Lulofs
283 Va. 768, 724 S.E.2d 695 (2012)

OPINION BY Justice CLEO E. POWELL.

... Arvid and Lucy were married in 1972. At the time of their marriage, each had a *771 child from a previous marriage: Arvid had a son, Keith, and Lucy had a daughter, Venocia W. Lulofs ("Lulofs"). Arvid and Lucy executed wills on December 9, 1987, that were "mirror images" of each other. Each will left the estate first to the surviving spouse and then to Keith and Lulofs equally.

Arvid died on March 21, 1996, and his estate passed to Lucy pursuant to the 1987 will. Following Arvid's death, Lucy executed a new will on May 17, 1996, in which she left the entirety of her estate to Lulofs and made no provision for Keith. Lucy died in 2006. After Lucy's death, Lulofs attempted to probate Lucy's will, which Keith challenged.

The evidence also demonstrated that in 1994, Arvid and Lucy took out an insurance policy naming both Keith and Lulofs as the primary beneficiaries, each with a 50% share of the proceeds. Lucy changed the beneficiary percentages on the insurance policy on April 1, 1996, such that Keith would receive 22% and Lulofs would receive 78%. Lucy **697 changed the insurance policy again on May 30, 1996, so that Lulofs received 100%.

Keith testified ... that in 1991, his father told him that he and Lucy made "reciprocal wills" leaving everything to Lulofs and him in equal shares. He testified that in 1994 Lucy mentioned the life insurance policy, saying that they did this so there "won't be any money to fight over once we die." He also testified that shortly before Arvid died, Arvid told him to "watch out for [Lucy]." Arvid told him that he was going to ensure that everything was divided evenly. Keith testified that Lulofs told him in 2006 that their parents had reciprocal wills. ...

Keith argued that Arvid and Lucy executed reciprocal wills in 1987 that became an irrevocable contract upon the death of either party. He also alleged that the estate was to be funded with the proceeds of the life insurance policy and that the policy was evidence of the testators' intent to make the 1987 wills irrevocable. ... *772 ...

II. ANALYSIS

... Where a party asserts that the wills are reciprocal and irrevocable, it is important to distinguish the law of wills and the law of contracts. A significant distinction between the two areas of law is that wills, unlike contracts, generally are unilaterally revocable and modifiable. A *773 will does not become irrevocable or unalterable simply because it is drafted to "mirror" another testator's will. See Williams v. Williams, 123 Va. 643, 646, 96 S.E. 749, 750 (1918).

> [T]he fundamental reason for this rule is that every purely testamentary disposition of property is in the nature of a gift, and a different rule applies where a contract "is disguised under the name and appearance of a will." In the latter event the contractual **698 nature of the instrument does not necessarily defeat its character as a will, but enables the party for whose benefit the contract was made to prevent, by resorting to a court of equity, a revocation which would destroy the compact or the trust created thereby.

> Id. at 646–47, 96 S.E. at 750.

Thus, "when reciprocal testamentary provisions are made for the benefit of a third party, there is sufficient consideration for the contractual element of the will to entitle the beneficiary to enforce the agreement in equity, provided the contract itself is established." Salley v. Burns, 220 Va. 123, 131, 255 S.E.2d 512, 516 (1979). Proof of the contractual nature of this agreement between the testators must be "clear and satisfactory." Id. Such proof "may expressly appear in the language of the instrument, or it may be supplied by competent witnesses who testify to admissions of the testators, or it may result as an implication from the circumstances and relations of the parties and what they have actually provided for by the instrument." Id. at 131–32, 255 S.E.2d at 516–17.

In Black v. Edwards, 248 Va. 90, 93, 445 S.E.2d 107, 109 (1994), this Court held that the mutual and reciprocal wills at issue were irrevocable contracts. We based that decision upon the unimpeached testimony of the drafting attorney who testified that the parties intended to draft reciprocal, irrevocable wills. Id. Here, the attorney who drafted the wills for Arvid and Lucy in 1987 had no recollection of the wills or the circumstances under which they were prepared, nor did he remember the 1996 will that he drafted for Lucy after Arvid's death.

By contrast, in *Salley*, we determined that the evidence was insufficient to establish an irrevocable contract where a joint will stated that if either spouse survived the other, the property at issue *774 vested in the survivor. The third paragraph of the will also contained a clause providing that

> [b]oth parties ... jointly and severally agree not to sell, encumber or otherwise hypothecate or dispose of any property ... without the written consent of the other party, it being the mutual desire and will of both parties to this indenbture [sic] to hold all property now owned of [sic] hereafter acquired by either for the use and benefit of their natural offsprings....

The will further specified that if neither testator survived, the property vested in the daughters "share and share alike." Salley argued that the language of the third paragraph created a binding contract. This Court held that no binding contract was created by the joint will because so holding would have required the surviving testator to hold the entire estate for the benefit of the daughters. 220 Va. at 134, 255 S.E.2d at 518. Such a strained interpretation would have left the surviving testator destitute. Id.

> Such an unreasonable result is completely foreign to the testamentary scheme established by the other provisions of the will. If achievement of that goal had been the testators' purpose, language more explicit could have been used. When an estate in fee simple is devised in one part of a will, by clear and unambiguous words, such estate is not diminished nor destroyed by terms contained in another part of the instrument, unless such terms which reduce the estate be as clear and decisive as the words by which it was created.

> Id. (citing Smith v. Trustees of the Baptist Orphanage, 194 Va. 901, 908, 75 S.E.2d 491, 495–96 (1953)).

The language at issue in *Salley* is very similar to the language in the 1987 wills:

> I give, devise and bequeath unto my beloved [spouse] if [spouse] survives me by thirty days, all of my property and estate, real, personal and mixed, wherever situate, whether now acquired or acquired hereafter, to be [spouse's] in fee simple and [spouse's] absolute property.

> *775

> In the event that my [spouse] predeceases me or fails to survive me by thirty days, I give, devise and bequeath all of my property of every sort, kind and description, real, personal, and mixed, unto [Keith] and [Lulofs] in equal shares, share and share alike.

**699 In both wills, the testators' clear intent was to transfer the estate to the surviving spouse.

Moreover, language in *Salley* was even more conducive to an argument that it created a contract because it expressly precluded either spouse from divesting himself or herself of any property without the consent of the other—an action that could only occur during the life of both. Despite this language, when focusing on the will as a whole, this Court found no clear and convincing evidence of an intent to form a binding contract.

The interpretation urged by Keith would create the very real risk that any testator who executes a will that "mirrors" another will and contains language similar to that contained in the wills at issue here, would be unintentionally hamstrung by the death of the purportedly reciprocal testator. In fact, the testator would be unable to provide for any future spouse or any child born or adopted during a later marriage. Such an interpretation is unreasonable.

The language of these "mirror image" wills is insufficient alone to form a contract and, therefore, Keith failed to meet his burden to show that the 1987 wills were irrevocable. ...

Keith argued that even if the express language of the wills was not sufficient to establish a contract, he presented sufficient circumstantial evidence to establish that Arvid and Lucy intended for the wills to be contracts. We disagree.

In pertinent part the Dead Man's Statute, Code § 8.01–397, provides:

> In an action by or against a person who, from any cause, is incapable of testifying, or by or against the committee, trustee, executor, administrator, heir, or other representative of the person so incapable of testifying, no judgment or decree shall be *776 rendered in favor of an adverse or interested party founded on his uncorroborated testimony.

This statute was enacted largely to provide relief from the harsh common law rule that would have prohibited testimony from the surviving witness and, therefore, the nature and quantity of the corroboration will vary depending on the facts of the case. Virginia Home for Boys & Girls v. Phillips, 279 Va. 279, 286, 688 S.E.2d 284, 287 (2010). Corroboration may, and often must, be shown through circumstantial evidence, but each point need not be corroborated nor must the corroboration rise to the level of confirmation as long as the corroboration strengthens the testimony provided by the surviving witness. Id. at 286, 688 S.E.2d at 287–88.

Here, Keith provided no independent evidence or testimony to corroborate his testimony regarding the contractual nature of the wills. Keith's argument that Lulofs' testimony corroborates his is without merit. Lulofs merely testified that she recalled a discussion about the insurance policy between herself, Keith, Arvid and Lucy, but Lulofs could not recall the specifics of that conversation. Further, the existence of the insurance policy itself does not provide corroboration. An insurance policy taken out seven years after the wills were executed cannot provide evidence as to the intent of the testators at the time the wills were drafted. Thus, no evidence in this record corroborates Keith's testimony as required by the Dead Man's statute. ...

In an earlier case, there clearly was an agreement, but its terms were somewhat unclear.

Supreme Court of Virginia.
Plunkett v. Plunkett
271 Va. 162, 624 S.E.2d 39 (2006)

LEMONS, Justice.

*165 ... The marital agreement at issue was executed by Linda and Carroll H. ("Pete") Plunkett about five years into their marriage. The Agreement provided in paragraphs 1 and 2:

> 1. Testamentary Disposition of Separate Estates. The parties each agree that in light of the fact that this was a second marriage for each of them, and that Pete has children from his previous marriage, that their separate property be devised and bequeathed to his children. Accordingly, the parties agree that they will execute the wills, copies of which are attached to this Agreement, and make no subsequent changes in testamentary disposition of their separate property to Pete's children.

> 2. Testamentary Disposition of Marital Estate. The parties agree that they will execute the wills, copies of which are attached to this Agreement, and make no subsequent changes ... in contravention [of] their intent to leave their marital property as set forth and described in this **41 Agreement first to the survivor and then equally to all of Pete's children.

Attached to the Agreement are two wills, one signed by Pete and one signed by Linda. All three documents were executed simultaneously.

Upon Pete's death, Linda submitted his will to probate. Article IV of the will states in pertinent part: "I give and bequeath my jewelry, personal effects, automobiles and other tangible personal property, to my spouse, if said spouse survives me; and if not, to my children." The residuary clause, contained in Article V states: "My Residuary Estate, I give, devise, and bequeath to my spouse, if [she] survives me. If said spouse shall not survive me, I give, devise, and bequeath said property to my children and their descendants." The will further provided that "[i]f ...any share of my [r]esiduary [e]state becomes distributable to my son, Peter" such share would be held in a separate trust until Peter reached a certain age or completed college. There is no other provision in the will regarding disposition of Pete's property. ...

Pete's three children, appellees herein, alleged that Pete had, "upon information and belief, *166 significant separate property, including ... real estate, stocks, and ... items of personal property" with a value "greater than the federal and state estate tax exemption amount." They also asserted that the language of the will was inconsistent with his intent, the Agreement, and Pete's "prior relationship with and devotion to his children." They filed a bill of complaint seeking imposition of a constructive trust on Pete's separate property. Linda argued to the trial court that the terms of the Agreement are not ambiguous, the will conforms to the Agreement, and conforms to the intent she shared with Pete in executing the Agreement. ...

II. Analysis

The construction of a marital agreement is subject to the rules of contract construction generally. Southerland v. Estate of Southerland, 249 Va. 584, 588, 457 S.E.2d 375, 378 (1995) (applying general contract rules of construction to property settlement agreements). Marital agreements written "for the purpose of settling the rights and obligations of either or both [spouses]" have the same effect and are subject to the same conditions as premarital agreements. Code § 20-155. The parties may contract with respect to "the making of a will." Code § 20-150(3)-(5). ...

*167 ... **42 ... Black v. Edwards, 248 Va. 90, 445 S.E.2d 107 (1994) [and] Williams v. Williams, 123 Va. 643, 96 S.E. 749 (1918)... stand for the general proposition that an agreement to make mutual and reciprocal wills, where properly proven, will be enforced against a breach of the agreement by a subsequent non-conforming will. We do not find it necessary or proper to consider these decisions because, as a matter of law, this will cannot "breach" this Agreement. It is axiomatic that a party cannot breach a contract in the formation of the contract itself. ... This particular Agreement incorporates the wills by reference, and we must consider all of the terms of this Agreement, including the terms contained in the incorporated wills together. ...

Contracts are construed as written, without adding terms that were not included by the parties. Where the terms in a contract are clear and unambiguous, the contract is construed according to its plain meaning. A contract is not ambiguous merely because the parties disagree as to the meaning of the terms used. Furthermore, contracts must be considered as a whole "without giving emphasis to isolated terms." *168

Paragraphs 1 and 2 of the Agreement set forth seemingly distinct treatment of the "separate" and "marital" property. "When two provisions of a contract seemingly conflict, if, without discarding either, they can be harmonized so as to effectuate the intention of the parties as expressed in the contract considered as a whole, this should be done." ... [T]he provisions may be harmonized "without discarding any of its provisions or doing violence to any of its language." First, we note that the Agreement incorporates Linda's will, which contains provisions reciprocal to those found in Pete's will. Articles IV and V of Linda's will, read together, leave her entire estate to Pete, and then to his children if he does not survive her. The practical effect is that all assets in Linda's estate will pass to Pete's children upon her death. She is not free to make changes to this will, as paragraphs 1 and 2 of the Agreement require that there be "no subsequent changes" to the testamentary disposition. As a result, any children who survive Linda will receive an equal share of the entire estate upon Linda's death.

We also note that paragraph 1, which appears to be the real center of this controversy, refers to "their separate property" rather than "his" or "her" separate property. Such language is not frequently used when referring to separate property, and we think it is significant that the separate property is referred to in plural rather than singular form. The use of the plural form demonstrates the intent of both parties that the separate property of each spouse will be joined together and then devised to the children. This can only occur upon the deaths of both spouses, rather than each spouse. Clearly, paragraph 1 does not mean that the separate property of both Linda and Pete will be devised to the children upon his death. Alternatively, if the **43 language is supposed to mean "each" set of separate property owned by each spouse, and Linda had predeceased Pete, it would be most unusual for Linda to devise only her separate property to Pete's children while devising all other property to Pete first, which would be the result reached if we were to adhere to the trial court's interpretation of this language. *169

A far more reasonable interpretation is that the spouses intended this language to reflect what was actually provided in the wills. On this point, we reject the contention that paragraph 1 must necessarily mean that Pete's separate property would be devised to the children upon Pete's death. The language of paragraph 1 does not refer specifically to "his" separate property, nor to "his" death, and we are not permitted to add language to that which already exists on the face of the Agreement. The language used, "their separate property," therefore leads to the conclusion that it must have referred to some combination of the separate property owned by Linda and Pete.

Most significantly, we cannot ignore the language requiring the simultaneous execution of the wills and the circumstances under which this was accomplished. The Agreement states specifically "that they will execute the wills, copies of which are attached to this Agreement." This language required the spouses to read and execute these particular wills in conjunction with the Agreement. The wills employed specific language regarding the identification of Pete's three children, appointment of the named Executor, disposition of property, appointment of a guardian for Peter during his minority, and the trust to be established for Peter. Surely if the spouses intended an estate plan that split the marital and separate property apart, then the failure to include this language in these particular wills would have been readily apparent. The simultaneous execution of all these documents demonstrates that the Agreement and the incorporated wills accomplish precisely what the spouses intended.

Upon these considerations, we conclude that Linda and Pete intended to leave their property first to the surviving spouse, and then to Pete's children. The terms of this Agreement and the wills incorporated therein are not ambiguous and can be harmonized in a reasonable manner. There is no need to resort to extrinsic evidence to resolve the questions raised here.

We hold that the trial court erred in considering extrinsic evidence pertaining to the Agreement, and erred in imposing a constructive *170 trust in favor of Pete's children. We will reverse the judgment of the trial court and enter final judgment in favor of Linda.

———————

b.   Contracts retricting disposition of particular assets

Sometimes it turns out that the decedent entered into an agreement during life concerning what shoul happen to particular assets at his or her death, an agreement that does not effect a non-probate transfer but that is enforceable and operates on the estate's personal representative to compel the PR to dispose of those assets in the agreed-upon way.

Supreme Court of Virginia
Jimenez v. Corr
288 Va. 395, 764 S.E.2d 115 (2014)

Opinion by Justice LEROY F. MILLETTE, JR.

*402 … This appeal arises from a dispute over the disposition of shares of stock in a family held business after the death of that business's founding generation. ... Lewis S. Corr, Sr. ("Mr. Corr") and Norma F. Corr were married prior to their deaths. Mr. Corr and Norma had three children: Lewis S. Corr, Jr. ("Lewis"), Patricia Corr Williams, and Nancy Corr Jimenez. Patricia is married to Thomas M. Williams.

Mr. Corr established Capitol Foundry of Virginia in 1970 as a broker and reseller of castings of heavy infrastructure. Capitol Foundry was incorporated in 1976 with Mr. Corr initially as the sole shareholder. Lewis joined the business when it incorporated and later, in 1981, Mr. Corr allowed Lewis to purchase 5 newly issued shares of Capitol Foundry stock. That same year, Nancy joined the business.

In 1999, Mr. Corr passed away, and all of his outstanding shares in Capitol Foundry were transferred outright to his wife Norma. In 2002, Norma conveyed 5 of her shares to Nancy. At the time of Norma's death in 2012, Norma owned 95 shares of Capitol Foundry stock, Lewis owned 5 shares of Capitol Foundry stock, and Nancy owned the remaining 5 shares of Capitol Foundry stock. *403

After Norma's death, Nancy filed suit in the Circuit Court of the City of Virginia Beach against Lewis, the executors of Norma's estate, and Capitol Foundry. Nancy alleged that Norma, Lewis, and Nancy entered into an agreement (the "Shareholders' Agreement") which required Norma's executors to make Norma's 95 shares of Capitol Foundry stock available for purchase by Capitol Foundry, and required Capitol Foundry to purchase those shares.

The defendants countered that Norma's estate planning documents, and not the Shareholders' Agreement, controlled disposition of Norma's 95 shares of Capitol Foundry stock. Therefore, in accordance with the estate planning documents, those shares were to go into an inter vivos trust rather than being subject to purchase under the Shareholders' Agreement. ...

While this litigation was ongoing, the parties entered into an agreement that permitted Capitol Foundry to purchase 64.4 shares of Norma's Capitol Foundry stock so that **118 Norma's estate would obtain tax benefits under Internal Revenue Code § 303 (the "Stock Redemption Agreement"). The disposition of Norma's remaining 30.6 shares of Capitol Foundry stock remained at issue subsequent to this purchase. ... *404 ...

II. Discussion

... When construing a particular legal instrument, if other documents were "executed at the same time or contemporaneously between the same parties, in reference to the same subject matter" as the legal instrument, then all such documents "must be regarded as parts of one transaction, and receive the same construction as if their several provisions were in one and the same instrument." Bailey v. Town of Saltville, 279 Va. 627, 633, 691 S.E.2d 491, 493 (2010) (internal quotation marks and citation omitted). Norma's Last Will and Testament ("Norma's Will") and the Norma F. Corr Revocable Trust document (the "Trust Document") were both executed on July 17, 1992, were both executed by Norma, and reference one another. We therefore consider these two documents together "as parts of one transaction."

Norma's Will nominated and appointed Lewis and Joseph L. Lyle, Jr. as co-executors of the will, and named Thomas as co-executor in the event that Joseph became unwilling or unable to serve as executor. The parties agree that, at the time of Norma's death, Lewis and Thomas were co-executors. *405 Norma's Will contains numerous specific bequests and devises. Article VII of the Will governs disposition of the residue of Norma's estate:

> All the rest, residue, and remainder of my property of every kind and description, and wherever located, including any lapsed or void legacy or devise, after satisfying all the bequests and devises hereinabove set out and after the payment or provision for payment of all administrative expenses and all death taxes as hereinabove directed, I give, devise, and bequeath to the Trustee of a trust agreement between me as Grantor and as Trustee dated July 17, 1992, which is now in existence, to be held, administered, and distributed in accordance with its terms.

**119 In the event any such property given, devised or bequeathed to the Trustee of such trust agreement is, under the terms of such trust agreement, to be distributed immediately to any beneficiary thereof, outright and free of trust, then such property may be transferred directly to such beneficiary by my Executor, without the necessity of passing through such trust.

Article VII is a pour-over provision. ... Article VII operates to gather up the entirety of what remained of Norma's estate after all debts, bequests, and devises had been settled, and "pours over" that residuary estate into a trust which was already existing and created by Norma. ...

The Trust Document *406 named Lewis and Joseph L. Lyle, Jr. as successor co-trustees in the event that Norma became unable to serve as trustee, and named Thomas as a successor co-trustee in the event that Joseph became unwilling or unable to serve as trustee. The parties agree that, at the time of Norma's death, Lewis and Thomas were co-trustees. ...

Article IV, Section (B)(3) of the Trust Document provides:

> 288.   To the extent not appointed by [Norma's] husband, upon the death of [Norma's] husband, the then remaining trust assets, if any, shall be divided, per stirpes, into equal shares, one share for each child of [Norma] then living and one share for each child of [Norma] then deceased with surviving issue. Each living child of [Norma] shall then be entitled to request and receive, outright and free of trust, his or her entire share. ...

Norma had three children, all living, when Norma's residuary estate poured over into Trust A and became subject to the per stirpes division: Lewis, Nancy, and Patricia. Thus, any such property would be divided equally into three shares.

Article IV, Section (B)(6) of the Trust Document provides in relevant part: **120 *407

> Notwithstanding anything herein to the contrary, upon the second to die of [Norma] and her husband, [Norma's] son, Lewis S. Corr, Jr., is hereby granted and given the exclusive right and option to purchase[:]

> 289.   any or all shares of stock in Capitol Foundry of Virginia, Inc., or any successor entity thereto, which Trust A herein may own, and

> (ii) any or all interests Trust A may own in [certain real property]. ....

To the extent shares of Capitol Foundry stock are owned by Trust A, this would allow Lewis to purchase and acquire those shares so that his siblings Nancy and Patricia, fellow beneficiaries of Trust A, would not be able to acquire those shares through the per stirpes distribution scheme set forth in Section (B)(3). However, because Lewis's purchase of these shares would put money back into Trust A, that money would be subject to the per stirpes distribution. Thus, Nancy and Patricia would ultimately receive the cash value of *408 their shares of Capitol Foundry stock held by Trust A, just not the shares themselves. ...

Reading these two documents together, they operate so that pursuant to Article VII of her Will, Norma's shares of Capitol Foundry stock would pour over into Trust A upon Norma's death, and then, pursuant to Article IV, Section (B)(6) of the Trust Document, Lewis would be able to exercise his exclusive option to purchase those shares.

However, the analysis does not end here because these are not the only two documents relevant to this appeal. Norma also entered into the Shareholders'

Agreement in December of 2002, subsequent to executing her estate planning documents in July of 1992. This Shareholders' Agreement is a contract separate and distinct from Norma's Will. Nonetheless, the Shareholders' Agreement could affect the operation of Norma's **121 Will because, even though these two documents were not executed contemporaneously, a will and a contract are instruments that both can relate to the same subject matter—the disposition of property upon death of the owner—and simultaneously embody the testator's intent on that subject. *409

Further, it is clear from the substance of Norma's Will and the Shareholders' Agreement that these two documents operate in harmony. That is, Norma's Will created a general provision—Article VII-governing the disposition of the general residue of Norma's estate upon her death. The Shareholders' Agreement, in turn, created a specific provision—Section 3-governing the particular disposition of Norma's shares of Capitol Foundry stock upon her death. Norma's shares are property that would fall into Norma's residuary estate because they were not otherwise specifically devised or bequeathed in Norma's Will. Although the general provision set forth in Norma's Will still has effect, the scope of its operation is necessarily limited to the extent it would govern disposition of Norma's shares of Capitol Foundry stock, which is instead governed by the more specific provision set forth in the Shareholders' Agreement. Cf. Condominium Servs., Inc. v. First Owners' Ass'n of Forty Six Hundred Condominium, Inc., 281 Va. 561, 573, 709 S.E.2d 163, 170 (2011) (" [A] specific provision of a contract governs over one that is more general in nature."). ...

The Shareholders' Agreement was executed by Norma, Lewis, and Nancy as shareholders of Capitol Foundry. Section 3, titled "Mandatory Sale and Purchase of Stock," provides in relevant part:

> 290. Death of an Agreeing Shareholder. Subject to subparagraph (d) hereof, on the death of an Agreeing Shareholder, all of the Shares of Stock owned by such Agreeing Shareholder shall be sold by his personal representative and shall be purchased by the Company or the remaining Shareholders for the purchase price and under the terms set forth in Section 4. ....
>
> > (d) An Agreeing Shareholder shall have the right to convey or bequeath his/her shares to a member of such Agreeing Shareholder's immediate family. Such right shall apply during such Agreeing Shareholder's lifetime and shall also apply subsequent *410 to the demise of such Agreeing Shareholder, and then be applicable to such Agreeing Shareholder's executor or administrator. The term "immediate family" shall be defined as children, spouses, parents and siblings of such Agreeing Shareholder.

... The parties agree that Paragraph (d) allowed Norma to bypass the mandatory purchase scheme of Paragraph (a) by bequeathing her Capitol Foundry stock to her children. The parties disagree whether Paragraph (d) permitted Norma to do so by way of the pour-over provision in Norma's Will, which, as discussed, would convey Norma's shares of Capitol Foundry stock to Trust A for the benefit of Norma's children. **122

Resolving this dispute requires ascertaining the nature of an inter vivos trust. An inter vivos trust is not like a corporation, which is "a legal entity entirely separate and distinct from the shareholders or members who compose it." Cheatle v. Rudd's Swimming Pool Supply Co., 234 Va. 207, 212, 360 S.E.2d 828, 831 (1987). ... [A]n inter vivos trust is inseparable from the parties related to it, and the trust does not have separate legal status. Indeed, the term "trust" refers not to a separate legal entity but to "a fiduciary relationship with respect to property, subjecting the person by whom the title to the property is held to equitable duties to deal with the property for the benefit of another person, which arises as a result of a manifestation *411 of an intention to create it." Restatement (Second) of Trusts § 2 (1959). When such a trust exists, it is not a separate legal entity being referred to, but a fiduciary relationship between already existing parties, be they real persons or other legal entities.3

Those parties have specific titles to denote their various roles within the trust relationship. There is the "settlor," or the "person who creates a trust," the "trustee," or the "person holding property in trust," and the "beneficiary," or the "person for whose benefit property is held in trust." Restatement (Second) of Trusts § 3 (1959); see also Code § 64.2–701. Because there is no trust entity which retains title over property held in trust, a settlor who will not also be a trustee must convey title of trust property to another party in order for a trust to be created. Code § 64.2–719(1). In most trusts, the trustee acquires legal title to the trust property, while "[t]he beneficiary is the equitable owner of trust property, in whole or in part." Fletcher v. Fletcher, 253 Va. 30, 35, 480 S.E.2d 488, 491 (1997). Thus, legal and equitable ownership of property entered into Trust A in this case is split between the trustees and beneficiaries.

It would be incorrect, then, to adopt Nancy's argument that because a trust is not defined in Paragraph (d) as a type of "immediate family," Paragraph (d) prevented Norma from bequeathing her shares of Capitol Foundry stock by way of Trust A. Trust A, like all inter vivos trusts, is simply a method to transfer property to another party including, potentially, members of Norma's "immediate family." The question is thus whether Trust A constitutes a mechanism by which Norma bequeathed her Capitol Foundry stock to persons who qualify as members of Norma's "immediate family." If so, disposition of Norma's shares of Capitol Foundry stock by way of Trust A was permitted by Paragraph (d) as an alternative to the mandatory purchase scheme of Paragraph (a). *412

In undertaking this inquiry, we must determine whether both the trustees and the beneficiaries of Trust A qualified as members of Norma's " immediate family." This is because both a trustee and a beneficiary have a substantial ownership interest in trust property. On the one hand, a beneficiary's equitable title permits the beneficiary to enforce the terms of the trust and to seek judicial remedy in the event of a breach.

See **123 Code § 64.2–792(B) (setting forth methods for a court to "remedy a breach of trust that has occurred or may occur"). On the other hand, a trustee's legal interest is more than nominal. A trustee, though "a mere representative," must "attend to the safety of the trust property and ... obtain its avails for the beneficiary in the manner provided by the trust instrument." Fletcher, 253 Va. at 35, 480 S.E.2d at 491. A trustee's legal title in trust property allows him to utilize and, if appropriate, dispose of trust property so as to effectuate his duty to administer the trust. See Code § 64.2–763. In fact, unless limited by the terms of the trust, a trustee may exercise "[a]ll powers over the trust property that an unmarried competent owner has over individually owned property." Code § 64.2–777(A)(2)(a). And, specifically, "[w]ith respect to stocks" such as Norma's shares, a trustee has the power to "exercise the rights of an absolute owner." Code § 64.2–778(A)(7).

In light of the substantial nature of both a beneficiary's and trustee's ownership interest in trust property, disposing of property by trust is a method of conveying such property to both the trustee and beneficiary. As such, although the Shareholders' Agreement did not outright prevent Norma from bequeathing her Capitol Foundry stock by way of Trust A, the Shareholders' Agreement prevented Norma from bequeathing her Capitol Foundry stock by way of Trust A if both the trustees and beneficiaries do not qualify as Norma's "immediate family."

In this case, at the time Norma's shares of Capitol Foundry stock were to pour over into Trust A, all the beneficiaries of Trust A qualified as members of Norma's "immediate family" because each beneficiary—Lewis, Nancy, and Patricia—is either Norma's son or daughter, and therefore qualify as Norma's "children." However, at the time Norma's shares of Capitol Foundry stock were to pour over into Trust A, all the trustees of Trust A did not qualify as members of Norma's "immediate family." Lewis and Thomas were co-trustees of Trust A at the time of Norma's death. Thomas, being Patricia's husband, is Norma's son-in-law. Because a son-in-law is not *413 one of Norma's "children, spouses, parents [or] siblings," Thomas is not a member of Norma's "immediate family" as that term is defined in Paragraph (d). We therefore hold that, because Norma's method of bequeathing her shares by way of Trust A did not satisfy the terms of Paragraph (d), Paragraph (d) did not exempt those shares from the mandatory purchase scheme of Paragraph (a).

It is now necessary to construe the exemption in Section VII of Norma's Will. As previously stated, that exemption permits property that would otherwise pass into Trust A to instead pass directly to the trust beneficiaries if such property would be "distributed immediately to any beneficiary" under the terms of the Trust Document. Appellees argue that this exemption applies to Norma's shares of Capitol Foundry stock because the beneficiaries of Trust A will "immediately" receive all of Norma's shares. Consequently, the argument goes, because Section VII of Norma's Will permits Norma's shares to bypass Trust A and be distributed directly to the beneficiaries, and because all the beneficiaries are members of Norma's "immediate family," the disposition of Norma's shares in accordance with the terms of Norma's Will actually falls within the scope of Paragraph (d).

We find this argument unconvincing because it stretches the term "immediate" beyond its ordinary meaning. "The language of the will itself must be relied on as the chief guide [to understanding how the will operates]. If that language be ordinary and popular, its meaning is to be construed according to its usual acceptation." Senger v. Senger's Ex'r, 81 Va. 687, 696 (1886). Immediate means "[o]ccuring without delay" and "instant." Black's Law Dictionary 866 (10th ed.2014). We thus disagree with the appellees because Norma's shares of Capitol **124 Foundry stock could not be instantly distributed to any beneficiary under the terms of the Trust Document.

Unlike most other property poured over into Trust A, which automatically underwent a per stirpes division under Article IV, Section (B)(3) of the Trust Document, Norma's shares were first subject to Lewis's exclusive purchase option under Article IV, Section (B)(6) of the Trust Document. Lewis's exclusive purchase option thus prevented every beneficiary from "immediately" having their per stirpes division of Norma's shares "distributed" to them. And Lewis himself could not "immediately" have Norma's shares "distributed" to him pursuant to that exclusive option because he was required to first determine how many of the shares he wanted to acquire, purchase such shares, arrange or make *414 payment under a specified payment plan, and act within a set schedule as established by the terms of Section (B)(6). This is not the type of automatic and instant distribution contemplated by the term "immediate" as that term would apply to most property poured over into Trust A.

In sum, Lewis's exclusive purchase option prevented Norma's shares of Capitol Foundry stock from simply passing through Trust A and being "distributed immediately" to any beneficiary. The exemption provision of Section VII of Norma's Will does not apply to Norma's shares, and those shares were required to pass through Trust A by the terms of Norma's Will and the Trust Document. This argument therefore does not alter our conclusion that Norma's estate documents failed to bequeath Norma's shares in a manner consistent with Section 3, Paragraph (d) of the Shareholders' Agreement. As the exemption of Section 3, Paragraph (d) of the Shareholders' Agreement does not apply, … Paragraph (a) requires Norma's personal representatives to sell all of her Capitol Foundry shares to either the Company or the remaining shareholders upon Norma's death. *415 …

"It is well settled that a contract must be complete and certain[,] and that the essential elements … must have been agreed upon[,] before a court … will specifically enforce the contract." Rolfs v. Mason, 202 Va. 690, 692, 119 S.E.2d 238, 240 (1961). Appellees argue that Paragraph (a) is uncertain when, as in this case, disagreement exists about which parties will purchase Norma's **125 stock, as well as the quantities of stock each party would purchase. We reject this argument. "The law does not favor declaring contracts void for indefiniteness and uncertainty, and leans against a construction which has that tendency." Reid v. Boyle, 259 Va. 356, 367, 527 S.E.2d 137, 143 (2000) (internal quotation marks omitted). We do not "permit parties to be released from the obligations which they have assumed if this can be ascertained with reasonable certainty from language used, in light of all the surrounding circumstances." Id. Such surrounding circumstances include other provisions of the contract, as we "construe [a] contract as a whole." Schuiling v.

Harris, 286 Va. 187, 193, 747 S.E.2d 833, 836 (2013). Thus, we review the entire Shareholders' Agreement to determine whether the contracting parties established a mechanism to provide certainty to this potentially indefinite term.

Section 14 of the Shareholders' Agreement, titled "Survival of Benefits," establishes such a mechanism. Section 14 provides, in pertinent part:

> Any covenant or agreement made by the Company herein shall also constitute a covenant and agreement by the Agreeing Shareholders to vote the Shares of the Company held by them to cause the Company to perform any such covenant or agreement.

The Company, through its shareholders, agreed to purchase Norma's shares of Capitol Foundry stock upon her death in Section 3, Paragraph (a) of the Shareholder's Agreement. By way of Section 14 of that agreement, Lewis, Nancy, and Norma, as "Agreeing Shareholders," have an overriding obligation to ensure that the Company performs that agreement. Thus, in the event that the Company, Lewis, Nancy, and *416 Norma's executors cannot agree as to who will purchase Norma's stock, and in what quantities, Section 14 obligates Lewis, Nancy, and Norma's executors to vote their respective shares of the Company so that the Company will perform its agreement by purchasing all of Norma's stock.

In this manner, Section 3, Paragraph (a) of the Shareholders' Agreement is not uncertain as to who will ultimately purchase Norma's shares, and in what quantity. Paragraph (a) certainly allows for an array of options as to what might happen: either the Company, Lewis, or Nancy, or any combination thereof, may make such a purchase, and in whatever quantity they determine. But Section 14 provides definiteness to this term in the event of disagreement by requiring the Agreeing Shareholders to vote their shares to have the Company purchase all of Norma's stock.

… Paragraph (a) allows for the parties to first attempt to come to an agreement how such a disposition shall occur. We will remand this case to the circuit court so that the parties may, in the first instance, attempt to resolve who will purchase Norma's 30.6 shares, and in what quantities. If the parties cannot reach such an agreement, Section 3, Paragraph (a) and Section 14 of the Shareholders' Agreement require the shareholders, including Norma's executors on Norma's behalf, to ensure that Norma sells all 30.6 of her shares to Capitol Foundry. …

We hold that the Shareholders' Agreement governs disposition of Norma's shares of Capitol Foundry stock, and will **126 remand this case for further proceedings consistent with this opinion.

*417 Justice McCLANAHAN, dissenting.

The majority opinion elevates form over substance... "The presumption in commercial contracts is that the parties were trying to accomplish something rational. Common sense is as much a part of contract interpretation as is the dictionary or the arsenal of canons." … The "apparent object of the parties" to the Shareholders'

Agreement... was to limit ownership of Capitol Foundry stock to family members... The Agreement, however, placed no restrictions on the method used for effecting such transfer of ownership. Through her inter vivos trust, Norma provided for the transfer of actual ownership of her Capitol Foundry stock to her three children, subject to Lewis' option to purchase. Indeed, such a trust is "a device for making dispositions of property" to such beneficiaries, not trustees. Collins v. Lyon, Inc., 181 Va. 230, 246, 24 S.E.2d 572, 579 (1943). Accordingly, at the time of the momentary interim transfer of the stock from Norma's estate (where it is being held) to the trust, the trustees would hold no more than "bare" legal title to the stock. See Restatement (Third) of Trusts § 42 cmt c (2003) ("[A] trustee ... ordinarily takes only what is generally described as the 'bare' legal title to the trust property."). That is, at no time would the trustees, solely in that capacity, possess any beneficial ownership interest in the stock. See id. (a trustee is a "mere representative whose function is to attend to the safety of the trust property and to obtain its avails for the beneficiary in the manner provided by the trust instrument") (quoting Bogert, The Law of Trusts and Trustees § 961, at 2 (rev.2d ed.1983)). *418 No part of this transaction, based on a reasonable reading of the Shareholders' Agreement, should be deemed a violation of the Agreement. ...

---

c.   Debts

As explained in Chapter One, before distributing to will beneficiaries or intestate heirs, the PA must pay the estate's debts and expenses. There are some special rules relating to debts in cases where a will disposes of the probate estate, mostly allowing for direction in a will to override default rules for what the source of money for paying debts should be.

Subtitle II, Chapter 5. ... Administration of Estates
Article 6. Liability of Real Estate to Debts

§ 64.2-526. What personal estate to be sold; use of proceeds

A. Subject to [statutory provisions regarding rights of surviving spouse to personal property] and excluding personal estate that the will directs not to be sold, the personal representative shall sell such assets of the personal estate where the retention of such assets is likely to result in an impairment of value. ...

B. If, after the sale pursuant to subsection A, the personal estate is not sufficient to pay the funeral expenses, charges of administration, debts, and legacies, the personal representative shall sell so much of the remaining personal estate as is necessary to pay such obligations. In conducting such a sale, the personal representative shall give as much consideration as practicable to preserving specific bequests in the will and to the provisions of Article 2 (§ 64.2-309 et seq.) of Chapter 3.

C. Unless necessary for the payment of funeral expenses, charges of administration, or debts, the personal representative shall not sell personal estate that the will directs not to be sold.

§ 64.2-532. Real estate of decedent as assets for payment of debts

If a decedent's personal estate is insufficient to satisfy the decedent's debts and lawful demands against his estate, all real estate of the decedent, including such real estate that remains after satisfying the debts with which the real estate was charged or was subject to under the decedent's will, are assets for the payment of the decedent's debts and all lawful demands against his estate.
...

To understand the next statutory provision, you need to know what "exoneration" means. Virginia formerly had a common law rule known as "exoneration of liens." In *Owen v. Lee*, 185 Va. 160, 164, 37 S.E.2d 848, 850 (1946), the Supreme Court stated: "In this State it is well settled that, in the absence of a contrary testamentary direction, the personal estate of a decedent is the primary fund for the payment of his debts, even though they may be secured by a lien given by the decedent in his lifetime on real estate." In other words, if a will left the family home to the testator's children, and the house was serving as security on a loan (e.g., mortgage or home equity loan), the children would take the house free of the debt. The PA should first use the testator's personal property to pay off the loan, and only after that is exhausted impose the remaining liability on the takers of the real property. However, in 2007 the General Assembly reversed this rule by statute:

§ 64.2-531. Nonexoneration; payment of lien if granted by agent

A. Unless a contrary intent is clearly set out in the will or in a transfer on death deed, (i) real or personal property that is the subject of a specific devise or bequest in the will or (ii) real property subject to a transfer on death deed passes, subject to any mortgage, pledge, security interest, or other lien existing at the date of death of the testator, without the right of exoneration. A general directive in the will to pay debts shall not be evidence of a contrary intent that the mortgage, pledge, security interest, or other lien be exonerated prior to passing to the legatee.

B. Subsection A shall not apply to any mortgage, pledge, security interest, or other lien existing at the date of death of the testator against any specifically devised or bequeathed real or personal property, or any real property subject to a transfer on death deed, that was granted by an agent acting within the authority of a durable power of attorney for the testator while the testator was incapacitated. ... This subsection shall not apply (a) if the mortgage, pledge, security interest, or other lien granted by the agent on the specific property is thereafter ratified by the testator while he is not incapacitated, or (b) if the durable power of attorney was limited to one or more specific purposes and was not general in nature.

C. [similar to B, but for instances where a "conservator, guardian, or committee of the testator" created a lien on the testator's real estate]

***

As to a mortgage or other debts of the estate, disputes arise as to whether certain bequests in a will are general or specific, because the rule of "abatement" states that general bequests should be used first before any reduction of specific bequests.

Supreme Court of Appeals of Virginia
Chavis v. Myrick
190 Va. 875, 58 S.E.2d 881 (1950)

BUCHANAN, J., delivered the opinion of the court.

Edward Hatcher, of Norfolk, died September 17, 1948, leaving a will dated March 12, 1948, the first clause of which directed his debts to be paid, and the second clause, which is the point of controversy here, was as follows: *877

> 2. I give, devise and bequeath to my daughter, Bernice Hatcher Myrick, Norfolk, Virginia, my one (1/2) half interest in our business, and real and personal property, 'Morning Glory Funeral Home', Norfolk, Virginia, in fee simple.

By clause 3 he gave to his sister, Sue Hatcher Coleman, his home for life, remainder to his niece, Anna Haynes. 'I also give my said sister Sue Hatcher Coleman, Five Thousand (5,000.00) Dollars cash.'

By clause 4 he gave to Martha D. Harris 'Three Thousand ($3,000.00) Dollars cash.'

By clause 5 he gave to his executrix, Blanche Chavis, his personal and real property located at 1439 East Princess Anne road, in fee simple.

By clause 6 he gave 'all the rest and residue of my estate not herein disposed of,' to his said daughter, Bernice Hatcher Myrick.

By clause 7 he appointed said Blanche Chavis as his executrix.

The executrix brought this suit claiming that the daughter, Bernice Hatcher Myrick, did not take, under clause 2 of the will, the testator's one-half interest, amounting to $4,947.01, in the money in bank to the credit of the funeral home; and asking the court to construe the will. ...

The only evidence introduced was in regard to the condition of the testator's estate when he died. That showed that he then had an individual bank account of $6,862.66. His total cash assets, exclusive of his interest in the bank account of **883 the funeral home, which was a partnership in which he was one of two partners, were $7,902.66. His debts were $3,380.98. Thus, without the funeral home money there was not enough left after paying debts to pay in full the $8,000 of bequests in clauses 3 and 4 of the will.

Appellant's brief states that she has since discovered that *878 the funeral home had bills receivable amounting to $9,958.34, of which $4,629.57 had been collected. Nothing is said about what the partnership may owe. The partnership assets are first liable for the partnership debts. We cannot, of course, consider matters not in the record. Nor is this material, in view of the way the will must be construed.

The judicial function in construing a will is to determine what the testator meant by what he said, not what it might be supposed he intended to say or should have said. If the meaning of the words is plain there is no room for construction. The property being the testator's, his will is the law of the court unless it be against the law of the land.

Clause 2 of the will, quoted above, gave to the testator's daughter his one-half interest in the business and real and personal property of the funeral home, in fee simple. Words could hardly be broader or more inclusive. Plainly they embraced his interest in all that belonged to the funeral home, all that pertained to it as a going business. This money in bank was an asset of the business, part of its working capital for the purchase of goods and payment of debts. Testator's interest in the money came from his interest in the business, of which it was a part. The gift of his whole interest necessarily included the money which was a part of the whole.

Appellant argues that the testator's intention not to give the daughter his interest in the partnership money is shown by the fact that there was not enough money, aside from the partnership funds, to pay in full the bequests in clauses 3 and 4. As well might it be conjectured that he had sufficient money in his individual account when he made his will, or expected to provide money for other sources to meet these bequests. Speculations as to his intention are not *879 admissible when the words of the will are plain. The will gave the testator's interest in the funeral home business and its real and personal property to the daughter, and it must be taken that he meant to do what he did.

The gift of the funeral home interest to the daughter in clause 2, being a gift of a particular entity or thing, was a specific legacy, while the $5,000 legacy to Sue Hatcher Coleman in clause 3 and the $3,000 legacy to Martha D. Harris in clause 4, were general legacies.

A specific legacy is a bequest of a particular, individualized article or portion of the testator's personal estate, set apart from the balance of his property. A general legacy is one which is designated by quantity or amount and which may be satisfied out of the general assets of the estate. In the settlement of a testator's estate, when there are not sufficient assets to satisfy both debts and legacies, debts come first, and legacies abate, that is, they are reduced by the amount needed to pay debts. But as between general legacies and specific legacies, the general legacies abate first, and pro rata among themselves. See Harrison, Wills and Administration, vol. 1, secs 295-6. The general legacies in clauses 3 and 4 are, therefore, first subject to any deficiency in assets to pay debts and abate ratably between themselves for that purpose. ...

When a will leaves shares of stock or money in an institutional account, disputes often arise about whether this constitutes a general or specific bequest for abatement purposes.

Supreme Court of Appeals of Virginia
Friedman v. Sabot
205 Va. 318, 136 S.E.2d 845 (1964)

I'ANSON, J., delivered the opinion of the court.

**847 ... *320 ... The testator, who died on July 15, 1961, executed his will on June 11, 1959, and a codicil revoking two cash legacies was dated September 6, 1960. ... [T]he testator made eleven cash bequests in varying amounts to certain individuals and charitable associations. Three of these individuals were nephews of the testator and one was a great niece. He bequeathed shares of stock in various corporations to nine nephews and nieces. Three parcels of real estate were devised to two of his nephews and a niece.

Following the residuary clause of the will the testator provided in a separate paragraph:

> I hereby direct my executor, in the event any of the shares of stock
> heretofore bequeathed shall be disposed of during my lifetime, he shall
> pay to the beneficiary of such shares an equivalent amount in cash,
> based upon the market value of such stock as of the day of my death.

The codicil to the will merely revoked two cash bequests and directed that these amounts become a part of the residuary estate.

The appellants contend that the bequests of stock are general and not specific. If these legacies are general, they, together with the cash bequests, abate ratably to pay the debts, taxes and administrative costs of the testator's estate. On the other hand, if the legacies are specific, the beneficiaries are entitled to receive the exact shares of stock enumerated in the will without abatement. Chavis v. Myrick, 190 Va. 875, 879, 58 S.E.2d 881..

A general legacy was recently defined by this Court to be 'one which is not limited to any particular fund or thing, does not direct the delivery of any particular property, and may be satisfied out of the general assets of the testator's estate;' **848 while a specific legacy is a bequest 'of a specific thing, or some particular portion of the testator's estate, which is so described by the testator as to distinguish it from other articles of the same nature.' Warner v. Baylor, Ex'r, 204 Va. 867, 874, 134 S.E.2d 263, 269. It is a firmly established principle that the intention of the testator, as

gathered from his entire will, determines whether a legacy is general or specific. Id.
...

[T]he language used in testator's will shows it was his intention to make the bequests of stock specific rather than general. The clause containing the alternate provision indicates that he owned the exact stocks bequeathed when he executed the will, and that he meant to give to the beneficiaries named the interests in the various corporations which his stock certificates represented. If the testator had intended the gifts of stock to be only claims against his general estate, and thus constitute general legacies, then the clause creating an alternate claim against his general estate would be meaningless. *322 The testator, anticipating the danger of ademption, although probably not known to him by that name, made the alternate provision so that in the event he disposed of any of the stocks during his lifetime the beneficiaries would not be barred from receiving an equivalent of the interests in the corporations which he bequeathed to them. ...

Appellants say that since most of the individuals named in the will in question were nieces and nephews of the testator, **849 thus being the same degree of blood relationship to him, it must be presumed that testator intended to treat them all equally by making general bequests to each of them in the form of stock or money.

This argument is not supported by the provisions of the will. The testator bequeathed varying sums of money to some of his nieces and nephews and to others he gave stock in several corporations in different total shares. Still others were devised parcels of real estate. Such provisions do not give even the slightest indication that the testator intended to provide for his relatives on a uniform basis. On the contrary, these provisions show that the testator intended to give these individuals interests in his estate differing in character and amount.

Appellants also argue that the failure of the testator to use the possessive word 'my' in referring to the stock bequeathed is a clear indication that he intended the stock legacies to be general and not specific. There is no merit in this argument. It is true that the authorities generally agree that the use of the word 'my' indicates an intention to make legacies of stocks specific, but the law is not so technical as to insist upon the use of the word 'my' when other language in the will clearly indicates the intention of the testator to bequeath the shares of stock he owned at the time the will was executed. Warner v. Baylor, Ex'r, 204 Va. at p. 876, 134 S.E.2d at p. 270.

For the reasons stated, we hold that the shares of stock given to the nine beneficiaries named in testator's will constitute specific legacies, and thus they are entitled to receive the exact shares of *323 stock specified in the will. Thus the cash bequests, which are clearly general legacies, must be reduced pro rata to pay the debts, taxes and administrative costs of the decedent's estate. ...

A more recent case, decided by a circuit court, Walters v. Walters, 69 Va. Cir. 334 (2005), analyzed a situation where the cause for abatement was a surviving spouse's claim of statutory allowances – specifically, $15,000 in exempt property and an $18,000 family allowance. The court noted that the executor must pay these allowances before distributing anything to will beneficiaries, and that ordinarily this would be accomplished by abatement of legacies. In this instance, however, the surviving spouse had signed a pre-marital agreement waiving her statutory rights to the decedent's separate property, so the assets in the estate that represented what a divorce court would treat as separate property (wealth acquired before marriage or by gift or inheritance at any time) were off limits and would pass to beneficiaries as indicated in the will. The surviving spouse did retain the right to pursue the spousal allowances out of the couple's marital property, so will bequests tied to marital assets were subject to abatement. The court also held that a bequest of "all the rest of my tangible personal property" was a specific bequest, not a general one, so abatement should first come from intangible personal property that was the subject of general bequests. The court first reaffirmed the rule of priorities:

> Under Virginia law, there is a well-established hierarchy for the abatement of gifts under a will. Bequests of personal property abate first, in the following order: first the residuary legacy, then general legacies, followed by specific legacies. The legacies in each category abate ratably. See Frasier v. Littleton's Ex'rs, 100 Va. 9, 13, 40 S.E. 108 (1901). The bequests of real estate abate only if the personal property in the estate is insufficient.

The court then held that the bequest of "all the rest of my tangible personal property" was not a residuary clause, because "the Will contains a clearly designated residuary clause leaving all the residue of the testator's property of any kind to his wife and two children in equal shares." It then concluded that it is a specific bequest because this provision

> is subject to ademption by extinction. If the decedent had used a list to bequeath all his non-business, tangible personal property to other people, Ms. Walters would take nothing under Article Four of the Will. Alternatively, the decedent could have sold all of his non-business personal property before his death, again leaving Ms. Walters with a void gift. Unlike a general bequest, "all the rest of my tangible personal property" cannot be satisfied out of other assets of the estate. Thus, the gift fits more appropriately in the category of specific bequests.

By way of supporting authority, the court cited only a like decision by another circuit court, in Estate of Brockenbrough, Jr., 68 Va. Cir. 95 (Nelson County 2005), holding that a bequest of "all my tangible personal property" was a specific bequest "subject to ademption by sale, destruction, or conveyance prior to death." Finally, the court ruled that the executor should first liquidate "valuable personal property, including a boat, fishing equipment, and shares of stock, before using the wife's "unclaimed portion of the proceeds from the sale of the home to pay estate debts," consistent with the law's greater protection of real property devises over bequests of personal property.

The *Brockenbrough* court also held that a bequest of "all of my money on hand and on deposit in my checking accounts, savings accounts, and money market accounts" was a specific legacy, because the testator used the word "my," and "[i]n the context of stock certificates, it has been held that use of the "my" to describe a stock certificate indicates the intention to make the legacy of the stock specific," (citing Friedman v. Sabot, Va. 205 Va. 318, 322 (1964)), and because "any of the monetary accounts described in Article Three (A) could have been sold or liquidated prior to debt and subject to ademption." 68 Va. Cir. 95. In contrast, a bequest of $25,000 each to the testator's children was a general bequest, and so those must be sacrificed first to pay debts. In addition, it held that the testator had written around the nonexoneration rule of § 64.2-531 by directing "that all mortgage indebtedness be paid by his executor" and that "the executor '… not sell any of my real estate to raise money to fund the legacies…'"

d. Taxes

An estate might be liable for several categories of tax. The most common is income taxes – federal and state -- for the decedent, on income earned prior to death in the year of death and possibly also the preceding year (if tax returns for that year were not yet filed at the time of death). Also common are income taxes – federal and state – for the estate, if the estate generates income – for example, by earning interest, dividends, or capital gains during the probate period. Quite uncommon are federal estate taxes, which apply only to estates with a value over roughly five and a half million dollars ($5.45 million in 2016, and increasing each year by the rate of inflation). Virginia does not have an estate or inheritance tax anymore. 2006 General Assembly House Bill 5018.

The rule for payment of income taxes, personal or estate, is the same as for debts – namely, take first from the residue, then from general bequests, then from specific bequests of personal property, and last from real property. The rules for estate taxes are different and complex. First, the estate tax is based not on income but on total wealth, and (as with the elective share rule presented in Chapter Four) the law aims to prevent attempts to evade the legal obligation in the form of inter vivos and non-probate transfers, so the taxable "gross estate" for federal estate tax purposes includes some inter vivos gifts and non-probate transfers. In addition, the General Assembly has created a different rule of apportionment for estate taxes. The core of it is this:

Article 7. Apportionment of Estate Taxes.

§ 64.2-540. Apportionment required.

A. … [W]henever… an executor… has paid an estate tax levied… upon or with respect to any property required to be included in the gross estate of a decedent…, the amount of the tax so paid… shall be prorated among the persons interested in the estate to whom such property is or may be transferred or to whom any benefit accrues. Such apportionment shall be made in the proportion that the value of the property, interest, or benefit of each such person bears to the total value of the property, interests, and benefits received by all such persons interested in the estate. However, in making such proration each person shall have the benefit of any exemptions, deductions, and exclusions allowed by law in respect of the person or the property passing to him…

§ 64.2-541. Recovery by executor when part of estate not in his possession.

If any property required to be included in the gross estate is not in the possession of the executor, administrator, or other fiduciary, he shall recover from the person who is in possession of such property, or from the persons interested in the estate, the amount of tax payable by the persons interested in the estate that is chargeable to such persons under the provisions of this article.

§ 64.2-542. Transfers not required until tax ascertained or security given.

An executor, administrator, or other fiduciary is not required to transfer, pay over, or distribute any fund or property subject to an estate tax imposed by the Commonwealth, any other state, or the United States until the devisee, legatee, distributee, or other person to whom such property is transferred pays such fiduciary the amount of such tax due, or, if the apportionment of tax has not been determined, furnishes adequate security for such payment.

§ 64.2-543. Contrary provisions of will or other instrument to govern.

A. For purposes of this section:

"Includable beneficial interest" means any property, interest, or benefit included in a person's estate for estate tax purposes that passes pursuant to an instrument other than such person's will.

B. The provisions of this article shall not impair the right or power of any person by will or by written instrument executed *inter vivos* to make direction for the payment of estate taxes and to designate the fund or property out of which such payment shall be made. Such designated funds or property may, in addition to any property passing by testate or intestate succession, include any includable beneficial interest. …

***

Supreme Court of Virginia.
Stickley v. Stickley
255 Va. 405, 497 S.E.2d 862 (1998)

KINSER, Justice.

... Daniel C. Stickley (the Testator)... died on May 4, 1995. Article One of his will addresses the payment of death taxes and administration expenses: **863

> All estate, inheritance, and other death taxes including interest and penalties together with the expenses of my last illness and all administration expenses including an appropriate marker for my grave, payable in any jurisdiction by reason of my death, (including those taxes and expenses payable with respect to assets which do not pass under this will) shall be paid out of and charged generally against the principal of my residuary estate. I waive any right of reimbursement for or recovery of those death taxes and administration expenses.

... Daniel C. Stickley, Jr., and William S. Stickley, the Testator's two sons, qualified as co-executors of the estate... They are also the beneficiaries of the residuary estate. The Testator's estate is solvent, but the residuary estate is insufficient to pay all the administration costs, debts, funeral expenses, and estate taxes as directed in Article One. A dispute arose... *408 whether the estate taxes should be apportioned upon depletion of the residuary estate. ...

When an estate owes estate taxes, Code § 64.1–161 requires that such taxes be apportioned. This statute is "based on the principle that estate taxes should be equitably apportioned among the taxable legatees." Lynchburg College v. Central Fidelity Bank, 242 Va. 292, 296, 410 S.E.2d 617, 619 (1991). However, an individual may avoid apportionment by making directions in a will "for the payment of such estate taxes and ... designat [ing] the fund or funds or property out of which such payment shall be made." Code § 64.1–165.

In this case, the parties agree that the Testator, in Article One of his will, exercised his right under Code § 64.1–165 to avoid apportionment of the estate taxes as otherwise would have been required by Code § 64.1–161(A). However, the... co-executors... disagree as to which fund or *409 property should bear the burden of paying the estate taxes after the residuary estate is exhausted. ...

[O]ur decision in Lynchburg College is dispositive. In that case, the decedent's will directed **864 that all debts and expenses of administration, including any taxes levied against the estate, be paid as soon as practicable. The decedent did not, however, specify any particular fund out of which the expenses and taxes were to be paid. The sole question on appeal was whether that provision in the will was "sufficient direction to prevent the application of Virginia's apportionment statute, Code § 64.1–161, or, stated differently, contains sufficient direction to meet the requirements of Virginia's anti-apportionment statute..." Lynchburg College, 242 Va. at 295, 410 S.E.2d at 619. We answered the question in the affirmative and concluded that, although the decedent did not designate the fund out of which the taxes were to be paid, the decedent, nevertheless, intended that the taxes be paid from the same fund which bore the burden of the other debts and administration expenses. In short, the decedent intended that the estate taxes, debts, and administration expenses be treated as a charge against the estate, thus avoiding apportionment of the estate taxes.

We find the same intent in this case. The Testator, in Article One of his will, directed that the estate taxes, debts, funeral expenses, and administration costs be treated in the same manner by specifying that they all be paid from the residuary estate. An insufficient residuary estate does not change that intent. When the Testator initially directed identical treatment of all these expenses, he successfully invoked the anti-apportionment statute, and having done so, apportionment does not apply, absent some direction to that effect by the Testator. See Baylor v. Nat'l Bank of Commerce, 194 Va. 1, 5, 72 S.E.2d 282, 284 (1952) (finding that since decedent made no distinction between debts, funeral expenses, and estate taxes, decedent intended that these obligations "be treated alike and be paid in the same manner and from the same fund"). *410

Nor is it relevant that the Testator in this case designated a particular fund out of which to pay the estate taxes and administration costs while the decedents in *Lynchburg College* and *Baylor* did not. The pertinent inquiry is not whether a particular fund was identified but whether the Testator intended that the debts, administration costs, and estate taxes be treated alike. ... In the present case, the Testator's intent to avoid apportionment of his estate taxes, even if the residuary estate is depleted, is further evidenced by his waiver in Article One of any right of recovery of the estate's taxes. ... [A]ny estate taxes outstanding after exhaustion of the residuary estate should not be apportioned but should be charged generally against the probate estate. ...

Supreme Court of Virginia.
Lynchburg College, The College of William and Mary, and the American Cancer Society v. Central Fidelity Bank
242 Va. 292, 410 S.E.2d 617 (1991)

COMPTON, Justice.

Louis G. Pittard, a resident of Clarksville, Mecklenburg County, died in February 1989, leaving a will drawn by an attorney dated in September 1987. Item I of the will provides:

> I desire my just debts and all expenses of the administration of my estate, including such taxes as may be levied against my estate, paid as soon after my death as practicable. *295

In the will, the testator made 38 cash bequests, a gift of mineral rights, two devises of real estate (one with a bequest of tangible personal property), and two equal residuary bequests-one to a group of nine tax-exempt organizations and the other to a group of relatives (a nephew, a niece-in-law, and two greatnephews). ... **619 ... *296 ...

In Virginia, all the debts and liabilities of a testator must be paid before any bequests can be effectual... Edmunds v. Scott, 78 Va. 720, 726 (1884). ... Without an apportionment statute, the burden of estate taxes, unless otherwise directed by the testator, would fall upon the residuary estate, which ordinarily benefits the natural objects of the testator's generosity. To correct this apparent inequity, Virginia, along with a number of other states, has enacted an apportionment statute. The statute, Code § 64.1-161 [now § 64.2-540], is based on the principle that estate taxes should be equitably apportioned among the taxable legatees.

The statute provides that estate taxes assessed upon an estate shall be charged against the share of each beneficiary of the estate in the proportion that the value of the beneficiary's interest bears to the total value of the estate, "except that in making such proration each such person shall have the benefit of any exemptions, deductions and exclusions allowed by ... law in respect of such person or the property passing to him." § 64.1-161.

The statutes dealing with apportionment, found in Article 7, Chapter 6 of Title 64.1 of the Code, expressly preserve, however, "the right of a testator to designate such parts of his assets as he desires to bear the burden of all taxes." Baylor v. National Bank of Commerce, 194 Va. 1, 7, 72 S.E.2d 282, 285 (1952). ... Code § 64.1-165 [now § 64.2-543], ...**620 ... So the pertinent inquiry, as we have indicated, is whether Pittard's will discloses an intention by the testator that the burden of estate taxes should fall entirely upon the probate estate, contrary to the statutory rule of apportionment. In responding to this *297 query, we apply ordinary rules of construction relating to wills. In construing a will, a court must ascertain the intent of the testator from the language of the document, if possible. If it is made "clear" that the testator intended there should not be an apportionment of taxes, such intent must be given effect. Simeone v. Smith, 204 Va. 860, 863, 134 S.E.2d 281, 283-84 (1964).

The appellants argue that the testator "merely expressed a general desire to have taxes on his estate paid in a timely fashion," and that Item I is "no more than simple 'boilerplate' language," insufficient to invoke the anti-apportionment statute. They say that the emphasis of the words in Item I is not "on speculative tax allocation instructions, but rather on the time for paying all obligations-'as soon after my death as practicable.'" According to the appellants, "Pittard wanted his legatees to receive their distributions promptly, and the sooner the debts and taxes were paid, the sooner the legatees could enjoy their gifts. To read any more into his request for prompt payment would require speculation and conjecture." We do not agree.

In Baylor, this Court considered similar language. In that case, the testator in Item 1 directed his executors to pay "all my just debts, funeral expenses and any inheritance, estate, and transfer taxes which may be assessed against my estate, or any beneficiary under this Will, including any share of Federal Estate or other taxes which may be chargeable against any person or persons who may receive any proceeds of life insurance upon my life ... as soon as practicable after my death." 194 Va. at 3, 72

S.E.2d at 283. The question presented was whether the testator's widow, who was given "one-third of my personal estate," was entitled to receive one-third of the gross personal estate or one-third of the personal estate diminished by the payment of costs of administration, funeral expenses, debts, and estate and inheritance taxes.

The Court said: "The testator made no distinction between debts, funeral expenses and State inheritance and Federal transfer taxes. It is clear from the language used that he intended all of the items to be treated alike and to be paid in the same manner and from the same fund." Id. at 5, 72 S.E.2d at 284. Quoting the *Baylor* trial judge, the Court stated: "'As the debts must be deducted from the personal estate before the widow's one-third thereof may be determined, it follows ... that the funeral expenses *298 and taxes mentioned must likewise be deducted therefrom prior to such determination. Any other conclusion would fail to give effect to the provisions of the will.'" Id. at 5-6, 72 S.E.2d at 285. ... This Court, after quoting the anti-apportionment statute, stated that the testator, in making the provision for the payment of debts and taxes, "simply exercised the right expressly reserved to him in the Apportionment statutes," noting that the point "was not seriously argued before the trial judge." Id. at 7-8, 72 S.E.2d at 286. Again quoting the trial judge, this Court noted that the language of the will "'constituted an effective direction relieving the executors from the necessity of complying with the requirements of the Apportionment statute,'" and that "'this appears to be in accordance with the great weight of authority.'" Id. at 8, 72 S.E.2d at 286.

Baylor, 39 years later, is still in accord with the great weight of authority. An annotator has summarized the majority rule, referring to so-called "tax clauses" like Item I of Pittard's will: "Where there **621 is no express designation of the fund which is to be burdened with taxes but there is a general direction to the executor to pay all debts, expenses, and taxes, there is an implied direction that the taxes are to be paid from the fund which also bears the burden of debts and expenses." Annotation, Construction and Effect of Will Provisions Expressly Relating to the Burden of Estate or Inheritance Taxes, 69 A.L.R.3d 122, 130, 445 (1976 and Supp.1991).

This is precisely the situation with Pittard's will. In clear language, there is a general direction to pay all debts, expenses of administration, and taxes; that command, "I desire," implicitly is addressed to the executors.* There is no express designation of the fund to be burdened with taxes but there is an implied direction that the taxes are to be paid from the fund which bears the burden of debts and administration expenses. Indeed, the testator specifically stated that he considered debts and expenses of administration as "including" estate taxes. *299

> * Precatory words expressing desire, recommendation, or request are uniformly considered imperative when addressed to an executor. Smith v. Trustees of the Baptist Orphanage, 194 Va. 901, 75 S.E.2d 491 (1953).

Paraphrasing *Baylor*, we find that the testator made no distinction between debts, administration expenses, and estate taxes. ... Accordingly, we hold the trial court correctly ruled that the language of Pittard's will, particularly that contained in Item

I, demonstrates the testator's intention to relieve the executors from the necessity of complying with the requirements of the apportionment statute, Code § 64.1-161. ...

In re King, 63 Va. Cir. 362 (Fairfax County 2003), found no intent to deviate from the statutory apportionment rule for estate taxes wasw manifest in the opening will statement: "I direct that *after payment of all my just debts*, my property be bequeathed in the manner following...".

IV.   Revocation and Revival

The prior Part addressed situations in which some act other than a testamentary decision by the testator works a partial or complete revocation, including predeceased beneficiaries and persons treated as predeceased beneficiaries (e.g., ex-spouses, slayers). In addition, a testator is free at any time, absent contractual obligation (as discussed in the prior Part), deliberately to revoke all or part of a will. There are many ways of doing it, and disputes often arise after the testator's death about whether and to what extent a revocation was intended, what the testator wished to happen subsequent to a revocation, and whether the testator wished to revive a revoked will.

Subtitle II, Chapter 4, Article 2. Revocation and Effect

§ 64.2-410. Revocation of wills generally.

A. If a testator with the intent to revoke a will or codicil, or some person at his direction and in his presence, cuts, tears, burns, obliterates, cancels, or destroys a will or codicil, or the signature thereto, or some provision thereof, such will, codicil, or provision thereof is void and of no effect.

B. If a testator executes a will in the manner required by law or other writing in the manner in which a will is required to be executed that expressly revokes a former will, such former will, including any codicil thereto, is void and of no effect.

C. If a testator executes a will or codicil in the manner required by law that (i) expressly revokes a part, but not all, of a former will or codicil or (ii) contains provisions inconsistent with a former will or codicil, such former will or codicil is revoked and superseded to the extent of such express revocation or inconsistency if the later will or codicil is effective upon the death of the testator.

***

From this statutory provision, we see that there are both physical acts and expressions of intent that can effect a revocation, that one can revoke only one provision of a will or the entire thing, and that revocation is sometimes implicit – namely, when the testator executes a later will that does not expressly revoke a prior will but is inconsistent with the prior will. Physical acts including tearing up a will, putting it through a shredder, throwing it in the fire, crumpling it and throwing it in the trash, and crossing out particular lines or putting a big X across entire pages. In addition, we saws in the context of ademption that a testator can effectively partially revoke a will be destroying or alienating specifically bequeathed property. A statutory provision clarifies that this does not otherwise affect the operation of the will.

§ 64.2-413. Effect of subsequent conveyance on will.

Except for an act that results in the revocation of a will pursuant to this article, any conveyance or other act done subsequent to the execution of a will shall not prevent the operation of the will with respect to such interest in the estate as the testator may have power to dispose of by will at the time of his death.

Supplementing the statutory rules are court decisions engrafting certain presumptions in particular situations, such as when the original copy of a will cannot be found.

Supreme Court of Virginia.
Edmonds v. Edmonds
290 Va. 10, 772 S.E.2d 898 (2015)

Opinion by Chief Justice DONALD W. LEMONS.

*13 ... **900 James A. Edmonds, Jr. ("Edmonds") died on April 30, 2013. Edmonds was survived by his wife, Elizabeth Cashman Edmonds ("Elizabeth"), his daughter from that marriage, Kelly Elizabeth Edmonds ("Kelly"), and a son from a previous marriage, James Christopher Edmonds ("Christopher"). ...

November 8, 2002, Edmonds executed a will ("2002 Will") which left all of his personal property to his wife, Elizabeth, and the remainder of his property to a revocable living trust ("Trust"). The 2002 Will stated that in the event Elizabeth predeceased Edmonds all of Edmonds' personal property would go to his daughter Kelly. The 2002 Will intentionally omitted Christopher as a beneficiary. The documents creating the Trust were also executed on November 8, 2002. Elizabeth and Kelly are the beneficiaries of the Trust. The Trust documents state that Christopher was intentionally omitted as a beneficiary. *14

At the same time Edmonds executed his 2002 Will and Trust documents, Elizabeth also executed her will and trust documents. Her estate planning documents were a mirror image of Edmonds' documents, leaving all of her estate to Edmonds, and if Edmonds predeceased her, leaving everything to Kelly.

After Edmonds died, his original 2002 Will could not be located. However, photocopies of the 2002 Will and Trust documents were found in a green binder in Edmonds' filing cabinet in his office. Thereafter, Elizabeth filed a "Complaint to Establish Copies of the Will and Trust Where Originals Cannot Be Located," in the Circuit Court of Arlington County ("trial court") and named Kelly and Christopher as defendants. ... Kelly and Christopher would both be heirs at law if Edmonds was deemed to have died intestate...

Elizabeth presented numerous witnesses who described conversations they had with Edmonds regarding his testamentary intentions. Patrick J. Vaughn, an attorney who prepared wills and trust documents for Edmonds and Elizabeth in 1973, and again in 1989, testified that in the 1973 will, Edmonds left his estate to Elizabeth, and expressly excluded any child of his born from a previous marriage. In the 1989 will, Edmonds again left everything to Elizabeth. In the event Elizabeth predeceased him, he left everything to his daughter, Kelly.

Marc E. Bettius ("Bettius") testified that he had been friends with Edmonds and Elizabeth for more than 30 years. Bettius stated *15 that in the fall of 2012, he had gone by Edmonds' auto business to have his car serviced, and he and Edmonds had a conversation. During that conversation, Bettius asked Edmonds what plans he had made for the future of his business, and Edmonds indicated that everything was taken care of in his estate and it would all go to Elizabeth. Edmonds also stated that he made the appropriate decisions to maximize estate tax benefits. Bettius knew Edmonds had a son from a previous marriage and asked Edmonds if he'd ever thought about having a relationship with his son. Edmonds responded in the negative and said that, "the boy had never been a part of his life and never would be a part of his life."

Paul C. Kincheloe ("Kincheloe"), an attorney who had been friends with Edmonds since the 1970s, testified that he was not professionally engaged to do any estate planning for Edmonds, but they did discuss the subject on several occasions. At one point, **901 Edmonds asked Kincheloe to serve as substitute trustee, and Kincheloe agreed. Edmonds told Kincheloe he was leaving everything to his wife and daughter, and nothing to his son.

John A. Bell, Jr. ("Bell") testified that he had been friends with Edmonds and Elizabeth since the 1980s. The last time he was with Edmonds was during the first week of March 2013, when Edmonds invited him to Florida for a four-day golf tournament. Bell testified that he brought up the subject of estate planning because he was deciding what do with his own estate. During that conversation, Edmonds said, "As soon as I go, everything goes to Liz. And as soon as she goes, everything goes to Kelly." When asked if Edmonds ever said anything negative about Christopher, Bell responded that Edmonds had never mentioned his son. Bell testified that about three or four years before this March 2013 conversation, he and Edmonds had another discussion about their estates. During that discussion, Edmonds said he was trying to set up his estate so that Kelly would receive her inheritance in increments. Bell testified that Edmonds was concerned that Kelly would spend the money all at once.

Edmonds was also concerned that he had paid for Kelly to have a great education, and he was not sure she was using it wisely.

Raymond Knight, one of Edmonds' employees in his auto business, testified that approximately six years before Edmonds *16 died, they had a conversation about the future of the business if anything happened to Edmonds. Edmonds told him that "Liz would carry on the business."

Donald Manning ("Manning") was the attorney who prepared the 2002 Will. Manning testified that when he met with Edmonds and Elizabeth to prepare their wills in 2002, Edmonds made it clear that he did not want Christopher to be a beneficiary. Manning testified that after Edmonds and Elizabeth executed their wills and trust documents, he made photocopies of the originals. Several weeks later, Edmonds picked up both the originals and the photocopies. Manning testified that the photocopies were placed in a green binder before Edmonds picked them up. Manning also testified that Edmonds never completed several of the items related to the estate plan, such as funding a family trust or retitling stock, but Manning agreed that those items did not affect the 2002 Will.

Meta Jane Mortensen ("Mortensen"), who prepared Edmonds' taxes each year, testified that she had a discussion with Edmonds wherein she told him she was concerned about the tax implications of his estate plan and wanted to see the documents governing it. Edmonds finally brought her his estate documents in 2011. The documents Edmonds showed her in 2011 were the 2002 Will and Trust.

Dina Knight, the bookkeeper for Edmonds' auto business, testified that although Edmonds did not discuss his estate plan in specific terms with her, he told her that one day the business would belong to his wife and daughter. Knight also testified that Edmonds kept all of his important papers in the filing cabinet in his office. After Edmonds died, Knight looked through the cabinet for important papers Elizabeth would need, and that is where she found life insurance papers, lease agreements, and the green binder with the copies of the 2002 Will and Trust documents. Knight did not know the documents in the green binder were photocopies when she found them. Upon learning that those documents were not originals, Knight assisted Elizabeth in looking through all the cabinets and drawers in the auto business, but they never found the original 2002 Will.

Elizabeth testified that she and Edmonds were married in 1972. She explained that Edmonds had three serious surgeries during their marriage, one in 1992, another in 1998, and the last one in *17 2003. Prior to each of these surgeries, he always told her that all the important papers she would need, including his will, were in the top drawer of his filing cabinet in his office. Elizabeth testified that when they prepared their wills in 2002, Edmonds was clear that he wanted to exclude Christopher as a beneficiary. Elizabeth also testified that in late March or early April of 2013, while they were still in Florida, Edmonds stated that when they got back to Virginia they should make an appointment with their estate attorney to starting putting **902 into place several of the estate planning items, including funding the family trust and retitling some of their stock.

Christopher testified that he had never met or spoken to Edmonds, although he did make two attempts to contact him. ...*18 ...

II. Analysis

... Over the past century, this Court has decided numerous cases involving missing wills, and the law controlling this case is well-established. The most recent case this Court decided involving this issue was Brown v. Hardin, 225 Va. 624, 304 S.E.2d 291 (1983), where we stated:

> Where an executed will in the testator's custody cannot be found after his death there is a presumption that it was destroyed by the testator animo revocandi. *19 This presumption, however, is only prima facie and may be rebutted, but the burden is upon those who seek to establish such an instrument to assign and prove some other cause for its disappearance, by clear and convincing evidence, leading to the conclusion that the will was not revoked. **903

> Id. at 626, 304 S.E.2d at 292.

Neither party in this appeal disagrees that, where an executed will in the testator's custody cannot be found after his death, there is a presumption that it was destroyed by the testator with the intent of revoking it. In this case, the 2002 Will was traced to Edmonds' custody, but could not be found at his death. Accordingly, the trial court properly applied the presumption in this case that the 2002 Will was destroyed by Edmonds.

The parties also do not appear to disagree that the presumption of revocation can be overcome by the proponent of the will upon presentation of clear and convincing evidence, leading to the conclusion that the will was not revoked by the testator. ... Christopher argues that to meet her burden of proof, Elizabeth was required to prove "some other cause" for the disappearance of the will, and that evidence of general intent and affection alone is not clear and convincing evidence, sufficient to overcome the presumption of revocation. ...

In 1913, we provided a synthesis of the operation of the lost will presumption and the evidence sufficient to rebut it, in deciding the case of Jackson v. Hewlett, 114 Va. 573, 77 S.E. 518 (1913). In *Jackson*, the evidence proved that the decedent had made a will in which he devised the bulk of his estate to his illegitimate daughter, and left only a few minor devises to others, including his legitimate daughter. The will was kept in an unlocked drawer, but after decedent's death the will could not be located. The *20 proponent of the will introduced numerous declarations by the testator regarding his intentions to leave the bulk of his estate to her, and not to his other relatives. We explained that these declarations were not introduced for the purpose of proving the will, its due execution, or its contents. Rather,

> [t]hey were introduced as evidence showing a strong and unvarying adherence by the testator to his purposes with respect to the disposition of his estate, which had obtained for years prior to his death, both as to

the beneficiaries thereunder and as to those omitted therefrom; and for the purpose of rebutting the presumption that this testator deliberately destroyed, with intent to revoke, a will he had so carefully prepared, and to which he had so firmly adhered. Id. at 578, 77 S.E. at 520.

We held that, in a case like *Jackson*, the presumption could only be overcome by this type of evidence, since "[i]t is impossible for the beneficiaries under the will to say what became of it; they can only assert that, whatever may have happened to it, the testator did not revoke it." Id. at 580, 77 S.E. at 521. We concluded that:

> It must be generally the case, in such a status, that the best evidence, if not the only evidence, that can be adduced to rebut the presumption of revocation is that the testator's mind for many years contemplated a certain disposition of his property; that when he disposed of that property by will his mental attitude was precisely the same that it had been during the previous years, and that after he made such disposition his mind remained in the same state practically until his death, supplemented by the consistency of his mental attitude towards his various relatives. Id. at 581, 77 S.E. at 521.

Our decision in Jackson recognizes that it may very well be impossible for the proponent of a missing will to explain what happened to the will, and therefore the statements of the testator regarding his testamentary intentions may be the best evidence to rebut the presumption of revocation. *21

The next case we decided involving a missing will was Bowery v. Webber, 181 Va. 34, 23 S.E.2d 766 (1943)...— **904 the decision that appellant contends is an "outlier," but which in fact gave another concrete illustration of the nature of the evidence required to rebut the presumption of revocation for a lost will. In *Bowery*, the decedent had prepared a will which left her estate to her step-granddaughter, whom she had raised as her daughter, but excluded other relatives. At the time of the testator's death, the will could not be found... The proponent of the will put on evidence that the decedent repeatedly stated to her intimate associates that she desired and intended to leave all of her property to her adopted daughter. In contrast, there was no evidence of any such affection or intention toward her other relatives. There was also no evidence of any incidents occurring which would have induced the decedent to revoke or change her will. We held that this evidence was sufficient to support the conclusion that the testator did not destroy her will with the intent to revoke it. Id. at 39, 23 S.E.2d at 768.

Three years after *Bowery*, we decided Tate v. Wren, 185 Va. 773, 40 S.E.2d 188 (1946), holding that the evidence presented in that case was not sufficient to overcome the presumption of revocation. We explained that, unlike the record before the trial court in *Bowery*, there was no evidence in *Tate* of declarations by the testator that his 1933 will was still in effect. Id. at 785–86, 40 S.E.2d at 194. To the contrary, there was evidence that the testator had made numerous statements that he intended to change his 1933 will, and that he had actually prepared a new holographic will. Id. at 786, 40 S.E.2d at 194. It is important to note, however, that in distinguishing the facts in *Tate* from the facts in *Bowery*, we never indicated that *Bowery* was an "outlier" or no longer correct.

Later cases have confirmed the continued application of *Jackson* and *Bowery* in lost will cases. For example, in Sutherland v. Sutherland, 192 Va. 764, 66 S.E.2d 537 (1951), we referenced our decisions in Bowery and Jackson, and stated that, in our opinion, the facts in those two cases "were clear and convincing." Id. at 774, 66 S.E.2d at 543. We determined that the facts in *Sutherland* did not "measure up" to the facts present in *Bowery* and *Jackson*, *22 and therefore we held that the proponent of the missing will had failed to meet his burden of proof to overcome the presumption of revocation. Id. at 774–75, 66 S.E.2d at 543–44. Our opinion in *Sutherland* makes clear that we viewed *Jackson* and *Bowery* to be correct, and to be examples of factual scenarios where the proponent of the missing will had met the necessary burden of proof to overcome the presumption of revocation.

Where the will-proponent's proof fails to clearly and convincingly rebut the presumption of revocation, the burden is not met and the will cannot be probated. In Harris v. Harris, 216 Va. 716, 222 S.E.2d 543 (1976), for example, the proponents of the missing will argued that the will was not actually in the decedent's possession at the time of his death, and for that reason the presumption of revocation should not apply. However, we disagreed and held that the evidence proved that the will remained in the decedent's house, and therefore the presumption of revocation applied. Id. at 719–20, 222 S.E.2d at 545. Further, we determined that the proponents had not met their burden of overcoming the presumption, because the only evidence presented was that other relatives were frequently in the house and could have had access to the will. We held that this evidence left the competing inferences "equally probable," and was not enough to constitute clear and convincing evidence that the will was not revoked by the testator. Id. at 720, 222 S.E.2d at 546.

The most recent decision by this Court on the issue of a missing will was the *Brown* case. In *Brown*, there was no dispute that the decedent had made a will in which he left the majority of his estate to a family friend instead of his sister. There was evidence presented that the decedent had told numerous witnesses that he intended to leave everything to the friend, and that he was not leaving anything to his sister because she **905 was already well off and did not need the money. 225 Va. at 636–37, 304 S.E.2d at 298. We emphasized that:

> The declarations of a testator, after he has made his will, as to its continued existence, its contents, or its revocation, where the will cannot be found after his death, [are] recognized under certain circumstances as entitled to great weight. *23 Id. at 636, 304 S.E.2d at 298

Evidence was also presented that the sister had access to the decedent's personal papers within 36 hours of his death, which might have explained the disappearance of the will. Id. The Court stated that to overcome the presumption that the will was destroyed by the testator with the intention of revoking it, the burden was on [the proponent of the will] to prove by clear and convincing evidence that the will was not destroyed by [the testator] but was destroyed or secreted by some other person with intent to prevent its probate or recordation, or was lost or misplaced; that it was not incumbent upon [the proponent] to prove that the [will] was destroyed or suppressed by any certain person nor specifically what became of said will; and that [the proponent] only had to prove by clear and convincing evidence that [the testator] did not destroy the will with the intention of revoking it. Id. at 637, 304 S.E.2d at 299.

It is clear from a review of our extensive caselaw on this topic that a proponent of a missing will is not required to specifically prove what became of the missing will. ... The evidence presented by a proponent of a missing instrument will take different forms depending on the facts and context of each individual case. In some cases, the proponent may present evidence regarding what could have happened to the will; and in other cases, there may be no evidence to explain why the will is lost or missing. ... What remains the same is that each proponent of a missing will must prove, by clear and convincing evidence, that the testator did not destroy the will with the intention of revoking it. That is the standard that we *24 have articulated in all our cases over the past century, and it remains the law of the Commonwealth today. ...

We have defined clear and convincing evidence as:

[t]hat measure or degree of proof which will produce in the mind of the trier of fact a firm belief or conviction as to the allegations sought to be established. It is intermediate, being more than a mere preponderance, but not to the extent of such certainty as is required beyond a reasonable doubt as in criminal cases. It does not mean clear and unequivocal.

Brown, 225 Va. at 637, 304 S.E.2d at 299

**906 ... The trial court found that Elizabeth had proven that fact by clear and convincing evidence. Elizabeth is entitled to have this Court review the evidence and all reasonable inferences therefrom in the light most favorable to her, the prevailing party at trial. Viewing the evidence in the light most favorable to Elizabeth, the *25 evidence is sufficient to support the trial court's finding that she had rebutted the presumption...

Edmonds and Elizabeth had been married for more than 40 years and had complementary estate plans in place to provide for each other and then to pass their estate to their daughter Kelly after they both died. On numerous occasions, Edmonds stated his intent that his estate be handled in such a manner, declarations that are both admissible and entitled to great weight. See Brown, 225 Va. at 636, 304 S.E.2d at 298; Shacklett, 97 Va. at 644, 34 S.E. at 494.

Christopher testified that he had never spoken with or met Edmonds. Edmonds stated to his friend Bettius that he had no interest in having a relationship with Christopher. Edmonds had at least three wills, and each time he changed his will, he had a new one prepared. Christopher was never listed as a beneficiary in any of Edmonds' wills.

During the preparation of his 2002 Will, Edmonds was clear that he did not want Christopher to be a beneficiary. Because Edmonds did not want Christopher to be a beneficiary, he would know that he needed to have a will to exclude Christopher from inheriting part of his estate. Therefore, even if he lost confidence in his daughter, there is no indication that he would want his property to pass through intestate succession under any circumstances.

It is important to note in this instance that a neatly bound photocopy of Edmonds' 2002 Will and Trust was found in a drawer in the filing cabinet in Edmonds' office, exactly where Edmonds had stated he kept his important papers. The photocopy was fully executed. However, the original of the document could not be found. The fully executed photocopy was found where Edmonds stated he would keep his important papers. If he had intended to revoke the 2002 Will by destroying the original, it would have been logical that he would have removed the photocopy from his file of important papers.

Edmonds never indicated to his wife, or anyone else, that he had destroyed the couple's 2002 estate planning documents. He also made a number of statements in the last two years of his life that reflected his intention that, when he died, his estate would be *26 governed by the 2002 Will and Trust. In the fall of 2011, he gave a copy of the 2002 Will and Trust to his long-term tax advisor for her review. In the fall of 2012, he told his close friend, Bettius, that he had no interest in developing a relationship with Christopher, that he had made appropriate decisions to maximize his estate tax benefits, and that after he died all the decisions regarding the management of his business would be in Elizabeth's hands. This is inconsistent with Edmonds having revoked the will, leaving no estate plan in place.

In March 2013, Edmonds told his close friend Bell that, "as soon as I go, everything goes to Liz. As soon as she goes, everything goes to Kelly." In late March or early April, just weeks before his death, Edmonds told Elizabeth that they should meet with their attorney when they returned to Arlington from Florida to begin funding their trust and taking the other steps their attorney had recommended as part of the 2002 estate plan.

As in *Jackson* and *Bowery*, ... in all of his statements Edmonds confirmed the intention that his wife and daughter were to be the objects of his bounty, and that he specifically did not intend to leave anything to his son. There is also no evidence in the record of anything that might have happened to **907 change Edmonds' mind in the period prior to his death. Accordingly, we hold that these facts are sufficient to support the trial court's finding of clear and convincing evidence that Edmonds did not destroy the original 2002 Will with the intention of revoking it. ...

An earlier decision of the Supreme Court addresses a claim that the testator's lawyer is to blame for the fact that the original of the will cannot be located.

Supreme Court of Virginia.
Johnson v. Cauley
262 Va. 40, 546 S.E.2d 681 (2001)

LACY, Justice.

**683 ... Josephine S. Howell executed a will in 1985 and three codicils in 1987, 1990, and 1992. Upon her death in 1999, the original of the 1990 codicil was discovered in a safe in Howell's former home, but only copies of the will and the other two codicils were found. Three of her daughters, Amelia H. Spivey, Lynda H. Bond, and Geneva H. Cauley, and their children (collectively "Spivey") brought suit to establish the missing original documents as lost and to probate a copy of the missing will and codicils along with the original 1990 codicil. A fourth daughter, Peggy H. Johnson, and her children (collectively "Johnson") filed a counterclaim, charging that the missing documents had been destroyed by Howell and were therefore revoked, not lost. ...

Howell executed each of her testamentary documents in the offices of her attorney, J. Louis Rawls, Jr., pursuant to a comprehensive estate plan. Furthermore, the trial court held that the evidence clearly established that the missing documents "were last specifically known to be in the possession of Mr. Rawls at his law office." Rawls predeceased Howell, and the current members *43 of Rawls' law practice did not know what happened to the original documents. ... [T]he trial court ... found, as a matter of fact, that Howell had no "reasonable possibility" of access to the will and codicils while they were kept at the law offices. ...

I.

We begin by reviewing familiar principles applicable in instances when original testamentary documents are missing. Under such circumstances, two different presumptions are available, depending on the last known location of the missing documents. First, if an executed will was known to be in the testator's custody but cannot be found after death, there is a presumption that it was destroyed by the testator *animo revocandi*, that is with the intention to revoke. Under these circumstances, the proponents of a copy of the will must show by clear and convincing evidence that the will was simply lost and not revoked by the testator. Second, if the evidence shows that after execution the will was not in the possession of the testator and not accessible to her, then a presumption of loss arises. The presumption of loss must then be rebutted by clear and convincing evidence that the will was revoked by the testator. Harris v. Harris, 216 Va. 716, 719, 222 S.E.2d 543, 545 (1976); Ballard v. Cox, 191 Va. 654, 659–60, 62 S.E.2d 1, 3 (1950). Which presumption is applied in a specific case depends on the threshold factual determination of whether the will was in the possession of the testator at *44 death and, if not, whether the testator nevertheless had access to it prior to death.

II.

... **684 ... Johnson asserts that the conclusion that the testamentary documents were in the possession of Howell's attorney "flies in the face" of the evidence that the only remaining original document was found in Howell's former home, that no original documents were found in Rawls' law offices, that originals of prior wills and codicils were kept by Howell personally, that members of Rawls' firm testified that they had never lost an original testamentary document in their possession, and that, although the records of the firm showed the firm's possession of testamentary documents, the records did not show that these documents were in the firm's possession.

As a trier of fact, a chancellor evaluates the testimony and credibility of witnesses. Thus, a finding of fact, made by a chancellor who has heard the evidence ore tenus, carries the weight of a jury verdict, and will not be disturbed unless plainly wrong or without evidence to support it. Here, in addition to the evidence cited by Johnson, there was testimony that Howell stated to others that her testamentary documents were at Rawls' offices and notations on copies of these documents indicated that the originals were at Rawls' offices. In light of this evidence, we cannot say that the trial court's finding that the documents were in Rawls' possession was plainly wrong or without evidence to support it.

III.

... Johnson argues that in considering Howell's "accessibility" to the testamentary documents, the trial court required a "reasonable possibility of access" rather than simply a "possibility of access" as *45 set out in our prior cases. *Harris*, 216 Va. at 719, 222 S.E.2d at 545. Johnson claims that, by requiring proof that Howell had a "reasonable possibility" of access, the trial court transformed the standard from one of possibility to one of probability.

Johnson's argument is one of semantics. The trial court's addition of the word "reasonable" was superfluous and did not impose a higher standard than that required by *Harris*. To the extent "reasonable" modifies "possibility," it restricts the circumstances of access to those that are "reasonable" rather than "unreasonable." A "reasonable possibility" does not require probability.

Finally, Johnson argues that testamentary documents left with an attorney as custodian "obviously are accessible to clients," and, therefore, unless the custodial attorney testifies that the testator did not claim the documents or that the attorney lost or destroyed them, a testator must be considered to have access to the documents. Such a definition of access, however, reflects the legal right of the testator to retrieve her documents but does not address the practical acts necessary to access testamentary documents for purposes of revoking them or reasserting physical control over them.

For example, in *Ballard*, the testatrix directed her attorney to mail the original will to her sister, Miss Ballard, who in turn put the will in her safe deposit box where it remained until the testatrix's death. Miss Ballard delivered the original will to the deceased testatrix's husband, who denied having received the will. Miss Ballard sought to have a copy of the will admitted to probate. In admitting the copy to probate, the Court found that the evidence clearly showed that after executing the will, it was never again in the possession of the testatrix and the presumption of loss arose. Id. at 659–60, 62 S.E.2d at 3. Clearly, the testatrix had "access" to her will in the sense that she had the legal right to recover possession of it from her sister. Nevertheless, the facts indicated that the testatrix was in the hospital when she made her will and that she died **685 approximately four months later. The lack of access necessary for the imposition of the presumption of loss was based on the factual record developed. It was not dependent on the testimony of any single witness or a generalized right of access to one's documents.

Thus, for purposes of determining whether the presumption of loss applies, a testator's access to testamentary documents entrusted to a custodian is a matter to be resolved by the fact finder based on the evidence produced. *46 ... This principle is also consistent with our decision in *Harris*, in which we stated, "[i]f the possibility of access is shown that is controlling." 216 Va. at 719, 222 S.E.2d at 545. In *Harris*, the testator did not entrust his will to a custodian. The daughter who sought to have a copy of the will probated testified that, unknown to her father, she took his will to the second floor of his home, put it in her bureau drawer, and subsequently discovered it was missing. Sometime later the testator was transferred to a nursing home where he died. We concluded that the testator had access to the will because the will was in his home and he was physically active before he entered the nursing home "long after [his daughter] discovered that the will was missing." Id. at 720, 222 S.E.2d at 545. The determination of accessibility in *Harris*, as in *Ballard*, was based on a consideration of the facts, not the legal entitlement of the testator to possession of his will.

Having rejected Johnson's contention that access was established in this case because the testator had a legal right to repossess her documents or because there was no affirmative testimony by the custodial attorney that the documents were either retrieved by the testator or lost or destroyed by the attorney, we now turn to Johnson's argument that the record was insufficient to show lack of access. Johnson relies primarily on the fact that Howell enjoyed good health, was able to go to Rawls' law offices by herself, and was not generally known by sight to Rawls' staff as evidence that supports a finding of access. In addition, Johnson cites testimony that the testator expressed concern about the fairness of her estate plan. However, the evidence in this case also shows that Howell entrusted the documents to Rawls, knew her documents were with Rawls, intended that they remain there, and commented that she had "everything on paper with my lawyers." *47 ...

[T]he trial court, as the finder of fact, was entitled to weigh the evidence and credibility of the witnesses. We cannot set aside a finding of fact unless it is clearly erroneous or without evidentiary support. We agree with the trial court that, on this record, only pure speculation would support a finding that Howell exercised her ability to access the missing will and codicils and retrieved them from Rawls' law offices after leaving them there in 1992. Accordingly, we conclude that the record supports the trial court's determination that the missing testamentary documents were not in the possession of the testator and that she did not have access to them.

Thus, the documents were properly presumed lost and the burden shifted to Johnson to prove that Howell revoked the missing will and codicils by clear and convincing evidence. Johnson has not assigned error to the trial court's conclusion that Johnson did not produce clear and convincing evidence of revocation to rebut the presumption of loss. **686 Accordingly, we will affirm the judgment of the trial court.

<hr>

The next case addresses a situation where the original will is found but there appears to have been a physical act of partial revocation. It also discusses the somewhat-perplexing doctrine of dependent relative revocation.

Supreme Court of Virginia.
Goriczynski v. Poston
248 Va. 271, 448 S.E.2d 423 (1994)

COMPTON, Justice.

… Charles Roach McCowen, the testator and a resident of Norfolk, died September 4, 1989. The testator's will, dated October 27, 1983, was probated by the clerk of the court below on September 6, 1989. … In September 1990, the executor filed the present suit seeking aid and direction in ascertaining the estate's distributees. The executor, a beneficiary under the will, joined as defendants the 15 other beneficiaries originally named in the will. Also joined as *273 defendants were the testator's seven heirs at law, none of whom were beneficiaries under the will. …

Labelled "Last Will And Testament Of Charles Roach McCowen," the typewritten document contains two pages of substantive provisions and is attested by two witnesses. Following a preamble, the writing contains four Articles. Article I directs payment of debts, funeral expenses, and taxes. Article II appoints an executor and a substitute.

Article III contains paragraphs A, B, C, D, E, F, G, H, I, J, K, and L. Paragraph A gives the testator's Norfolk business, "Mac's Cycle Shop," to Newton [the executor]. Paragraphs B through K contain a devise of the testator's Norfolk residence, the gift of an airplane, and gifts of specific sums of money to named individuals. Paragraph L is the residuary clause naming "the Salvation Army, Heart Fund, and American Cancer Society" as residuary beneficiaries. Article IV grants to the personal representative the powers specified in the applicable statute.

The following additional facts are not disputed on appeal: The will was drawn by an attorney; no handwritten marks, except signatures and dates, were on the will at the time of its execution; the testator had testamentary capacity when the will was executed; the testator had continuous possession of the document from its execution until his death; and, the will was found at the testator's residence "at or near the time of his death."

As found, the will contains certain handwritten markings. There is no dispute on appeal that the handwriting and marks on the will were made by the testator and that he had testamentary capacity on the date or dates these changes were made. ...

Subsequent to the execution of the will, the testator drew with a pen some red lines and some black lines through a number of the provisions. The lines mostly **425 are wavy and run horizontally over the typewritten words. *274 The words in paragraphs A, B, C, D, G, and I of Article III are marked through virtually in their entirety. The testator also drew a horizontal line through the words "Salvation Army" in paragraph L, the residuary clause.

In addition, along the left margin of the first and second pages of the document, the testator wrote the word "Delete" in seven places adjacent to paragraphs A, B, C, D, G, I, and L of Article III. Also, where the words "Delete" were written in the margin, the testator signed his name and placed the date "1–20–89" at each signature. The writings in the left margin do not touch any typewritten portions of the document.

In paragraphs J and K of Article III, the testator had given to Henry Driver and Virginia Driver the sum of "Twenty Thousand ($20,000.00) Dollars" and to Gary (Red) Chandler the sum of "Five Thousand ($5,000.00) Dollars," respectively. After execution of the will, the testator drew mostly straight, horizontal lines through the words and figures representing the dollar amounts in each paragraph. In the Driver paragraph, he inserted "10,000" and in the Chandler paragraph he inserted "$10,000." Both insertions were made at the end of each paragraph on the blank parts of the page. ...

[T]he chancellor ruled the testator had accomplished a partial revocation of the will. The chancellor decided that the deletions without substitutions in paragraphs A, B, C, D, G, I, and L of Article III caused those devises and bequests to fail. The chancellor also ruled that the gifts of cash in the unchanged paragraphs, that is, paragraphs E, F, and H, are valid bequests, and that the residuary legatees under paragraph L are the Heart Fund and the American Cancer Society by virtue of the deletion without substitution of the Salvation Army.

The chancellor also ruled that the deletions with substitutions of the numerical amounts in the Driver and Chandler paragraphs are ineffective, and that those provisions, under the doctrine of dependent relative revocation, will be read as if no changes were attempted. According to the doctrine, if a testator performs any act to vitiate a will with the present intention of making a new will immediately, and the new one is not made, or if made fails for any reason, then the old will, having been conditionally revoked, still stands. Bell v. Timmins, 190 Va. 648, 659, 58 S.E.2d 55, 61 (1950). The basis for the rule is that if a testator's *275 whole testamentary intent cannot be carried out in making the new will, or in making changes to the old one, then the law presumes that the testator prefers the old will to intestacy and that the revocation was conditioned upon the new testamentary disposition being effective. Id. at 659–60, 58 S.E.2d at 61. ...

The principal issue is whether the testator effected a partial revocation of his will by the physical acts of drawing lines through the typed words of the will. That query must be answered in the affirmative. Code § 64.1–58.1 [now § 64.2-410]... refers to acts directed to a "provision" of the testamentary document, [so] it permits partial revocation of a duly attested will without further formalities. See Etgen v. Corboy, 230 Va. 413, 416–18, 337 S.E.2d 286, 288–89 (1985). And, whenever any of the foregoing statutory methods are employed by the testator with an intent to revoke, the changes are effective, even though made after execution of a duly attested **426 will, provided "they sufficiently support an inference of cancellation." Triplett's Ex'r v. Triplett, 161 Va. 906, 917, 172 S.E. 162, 166 (1934).

 In the present case, the physical act of drawing lines through the typed provisions of Article III unambiguously supports an inference of cancellation. Furthermore, there is the unrebutted presumption that the testator made these changes with the intent to revoke. When, as here, the will presented for probate had been in the testator's custody after execution and was found among his effects at death with provisions marked through that constitute a sufficient act of cancellation within the meaning of the applicable statute, a rebuttable presumption arises that such marks were made with the intention of revoking the affected provisions. See Franklin v. McLean, 192 Va. 684, 689, 66 S.E.2d 504, 506 (1951). In addition, even though the marginal notes are of no legal effect, they do support the conclusion drawn from an examination of the document left by the testator that he meant a partial, not complete, revocation of the will.

Also, despite the cancellations made in Article III, the will that remains is complete and has "the finality of testamentary intent." Jessup v. Jessup, 221 Va. 61, 73, 267 S.E.2d 115, 122 (1980). The will, still carrying the label of "Last Will And Testament," provides for payment of debts, expenses, and taxes; names a personal representative with specified powers; provides for specific gifts to named individuals; and leaves the residue of the estate to named charitable organizations. Indeed, the will carries out the testator's manifest intention, that is, he did not want his estate to pass to his heirs.

The heirs' second contention is that the chancellor erred in applying the doctrine of dependent relative revocation to the Driver and Chandler bequests. We do not reach the merits of that assignment of error because the heirs lack standing to raise the issue. The heirs will inherit the testator's estate only if the will is declared entirely revoked and of no effect. The doctrine of dependent relative revocation was applied to only two specific bequests in which the testator retained the named legatees, but attempted to change the amount given to each. The chancellor's ruling impacts only the size of the residuary estate under the will. The heirs receive nothing under the will and thus have no cognizable interest in this issue. ...

———————

The next case addresses revocation by subsequent execution of another testamentary instrument and also "revival" of an earlier will when a later one is revoked. The latter is now governed by this statutory provision:

§ 64.2-411. Revival of wills after revocation.

Any will or codicil, or any part thereof that has been revoked pursuant to § 64.2-410 shall not be revived unless such will or codicil is reexecuted in the manner required by law. Such revival operates only to the extent that the testator's intent to revive the will or codicil is shown.

***

The version of the statute effective in 1960 is slightly different and presented in this opinion:

Supreme Court of Appeals of Virginia
Timberlake v. State-Planters Bank of Commerce and Trusts
201 Va. 950, 115 S.E.2d 39 (1960)

BUCHANAN, J., delivered the opinion of the court.

*951 The question for decision in this case [turns on] the proper interpretation **40 of [the revocation provision in the Code] considered in connection with § 64-60.[2]

> [2] § 64-60. Revival of wills after revocation. — No will or codicil, or any part thereof, which shall be in any manner revoked, shall, after being revoked, be revived otherwise than by the re-execution thereof, or by a codicil executed in the manner hereinbefore required, and then only to the extent to which an intention to revive the same is shown.

The testatrix, Kate Miller Levering, made two wills, both executed and attested in accordance with [required formalities], and left them both in the custody of the Trust Department of a Richmond bank, which was named as executor in both. The first will was dated October 29, 1954. The second was dated January 31, 1955, and in the first clause thereof stated that the testatrix makes 'this my last Will and Testament, hereby expressly revoking any and all wills and/or codicils by me at any time heretofore made.'

Afterwards, on November 20 or 21, 1956, the testatrix went to the bank and made request to withdraw the 1955 will, giving as her reason that she wanted to make some changes in it and expected to do so by a new will rather than by a codicil. This 1955 will was accordingly delivered to her and was never later found. It is consequently presumed that it was destroyed by her with intent to revoke it. An unsigned carbon copy of it was preserved by the bank...

After the death of the testatrix, which occurred on November 1, 1958, the 1954 will was presented to the chancery court and offered for probate by the beneficiaries and the executor named therein... *952 [T]he appellants, heirs at law of the deceased, ...

contend that the 1954 will was revoked by the 1955 will and that the deceased died intestate. The holding of the chancery court was based on the proposition that a will is ambulatory, speaks only at the death of the maker, and the 1955 will having been destroyed in the lifetime of the testatrix, it never had the effect of revoking the 1954 will. The appellants contend that the revocation clause in the 1955 will became effective immediately upon the execution of that will, was not affected by the destruction of it, and hence the 1954 will was without force or effect.

It will be observed that the statute... provides that a will may be revoked only (1) by a subsequent will or codicil, or (2) by some writing declaring an intention to revoke the same executed as a will is required to be executed, or (3) by mutilating or destroying it with the intent to revoke it.

This statute first appeared in the Code of 1849 ... in the identical words of the present statute, but its prototype has been in the statute laws almost since the birth of the nation. ... Bates v. Holman, 13 Va. (3 Hen. & Munf.) 502, was decided first in 1808 and on a rehearing in 1809. ... **41 ... [T]he testator had made a will in 1799 and then in 1803 made another which he signed and under his signature made and signed a postscript stating 'I revoke all other wills heretofore made by me.' He later cut off his signature to the 1803 will but left the postscript as written and signed. The question was whether the 1799 will was thereby revoked. By a court divided 3 to 2 it was held, opinion by Judge Tucker, that the postscript was separately signed by the testator 'as an express statutory revocation of all former wills made by him, utterly independent of, and unconnected with, his second will; and by the maker left in full force, at the time of cancelling that second will, and remaining in full force at the time of his death.' *953 ... There seems to have been no disagreement among the five judges that if the postscript was part of the canceled 1803 will, it fell with that will and would not have been effective to revoke the 1799 will.

In Barksdale v. Barksdale, 39 Va. (12 Leigh) 535, decided in 1842, the question was whether a will of real and personal property duly executed in 1838 was revoked by a writing dated in 1839, intended to be a will but having only one witness and hence invalid. In its opening sentence declaring the instrument to be the maker's will were the words 'revoking all other wills' previously made. It was held that the revoking clause could not be abstracted from the will and made to serve as a declaration of revocation under the statute, but that 'the invalidity of the instrument, which defeats the new disposition of his property, must also defeat the revocation of the former instrument.' ... Judge Baldwin, for a unanimous court, said:

> There are two modes of written revocation contemplated by the law just quoted, one by a will or codicil in writing, the other by a *954 declaration in writing. For the sake of distinction, the first may be called a testamentary revocation, and the last a declaratory revocation. . . . The distinction between the two modes of revocation is not formal, but essential. In the testamentary revocation, the testator contemplates a new disposition of his property, and the revocation may be implied from inconsistency . . . or it may be express, in order that the testator may do

his new testamentary **42 work without being in any wise fettered by the contents of his former will. The declaratory revocation, on the other hand, is always express, . . . and is in contemplation by the testator of that disposition of his property made by the law governing in cases of intestacy.

In every testamentary revocation, the testator always acts upon the supposition that his whole purpose will be accomplished, that his entire testamentary act will be effectual, as well in regard to the new disposition of the subject, as the revocation of that which he had made by the former instrument; and his revocation is in fact part and parcel of his new testamentary action. . . . nor can I conceive, when he makes a new disposition of his property, and *eodem flatu* a revocation of a former disposition of it, how he can do so with any other expectation than that both will share the same fate. . . .

He further said: 'Besides, no man, I should think, ever made provision by last will and testament for dying intestate. If such had been the testator's design, he would have torn up the will of 1838 or thrown it into the fire, or if out of his possession and control, would have simply executed a naked instrument of revocation.'

Rudisill v. Rodes, 70 Va. (29 Gratt.) 147,... did not cite Barksdale or discuss the question of revocation, but dealt with the question of revival. There Rudisill made three wills, one each in 1868, 1871 and 1872. The second and third contained clauses revoking all former wills. He destroyed the third will with intent to revoke it, leaving the other two uncancelled. The court said the question was whether by the destruction of the third will the second was revived, and that the solution depended on § 9, Ch. 118 of the Code of 1873, which was in the identical language of present § 64-60, supra. Revocation seems to have been assumed or conceded. That the court did not have that question in mind appears from the statement in the opinion that it was not aware that § 9, the revival section with which it was dealing, had ever been construed by this court, and that there was no reported case about it. It was held, however, that there was no *955 error in the judgment of the circuit court that the 1871 will had been revoked by the 1872 will, was not revived by the destruction of the latter, and therefore was not entitled to probate.

In Bell v. Timmins, 190 Va. 648, 58 S.E.2d 55, the chancery court probated the holographic will of the testatrix, dated in 1935, after deleting interlineations made by a Miss O'Brien. ... Miss O'Brien testified that there was in existence a subsequent will, holographic and signed, which started out with a revocation clause, followed by a disposition of identical purport and effect as the will which was probated. The court was asked by the contestant 'to rip this introductory clause of the supposed subsequent will out of its setting, and use it to cancel this 1935 will; but without going further and undertaking to set up, here or elsewhere, the whole of the subsequent will.' In rejecting this request the court applied the doctrine of dependent relative revocation, which it explained, and then stated:

... The law takes the view that if the testator is not able to carry out his whole testamentary intent in making the new will, or in making changes in the old one, then it is to be presumed that he prefers his old will to intestacy; that the revocation was conditioned upon the new testamentary disposition being effective. **43

The court added that the doctrine is nowhere more clearly recognized than in Barksdale v. Barksdale, supra, which is quoted from at length in the opinion.

In Poindexter v. Jones, 200 Va. 372, 106 S.E.2d 144, the testatrix had made two holographic wills, one dated in 1938 and the other in 1939. Later she made two other holographic wills, one dated in 1947 and the other in 1950, which impliedly revoked the 1938 and 1939 wills but which she subsequently canceled with intent to revoke by tearing off her signature. The question was whether the 1938 and 1939 wills were revoked by the 1947 and 1950 wills when either or both of the latter were executed. Neither of the latter wills contained a revoking clause or declared an intent to revoke the earlier wills, but they were wholly inconsistent with the earlier wills and if unrevoked would have supplanted them.

There, as here, the heirs of the testatrix relied upon the *Rudisill* case, supra, to support their contention that the 1938 and 1939 wills were immediately revoked on the execution of the subsequent wills and that the testatrix died intestate. But we referred to the fact *956 that in the *Rudisill* case the court dealt with the revival statute (§ 64-60), did not refer to the *Barksdale* case, and did not comment on what is now ... the revocation statute, which was equally pertinent 'because unless the subsequent will revoked the former when executed, the issue of whether or not there is a revival is never reached.'

We then proceeded, after discussing the *Barksdale* case, to hold that where there are two inconsistent wills and one has been destroyed by the maker, 'no conflict arises or can arise between the two instruments, for wills are ambulatory and operate only upon and by reason of death.' Consequently, we said, the 1938 and 1939 wills must be probated because they were not revoked by the 1947 and 1950 wills 'as there can, in fact, be no conflict between these ambulatory instruments — these wills — until death, and as the latter were destroyed animus revocandi, they thus never constituted wills... and never revoked the 1938 and 1939 wills.' ...

The testamentary revocation is made to clear the way for a new disposition of testator's property; the declaratory revocation does not dispose of property but renders the maker intestate. The testamentary revocation would not occur unless the testator intended to change his previous will. The testamentary revocation is thus part and parcel of his new testamentary action. When he destroys the revoking will, how can he do so with any other expectation or belief than that he is destroying it all, the revoking provision along with the disposing provisions, both imbedded in the same document? Barksdale v. Barksdale, supra.

Here we know that Mrs. Levering did not intend to die intestate. The evidence shows it and the chancellor found it to be true. At the bank she asked only for the 1955 will and left the 1954 will intact in the bank where she had placed it. She intended to make some changes in the 1955 will. Instead of doing so she destroyed that will. Then how could we know that she then meant or thought that the revocation would remain effective although she knew the *957 dispositions of her property in the instrument of which it was a part would not be?

In *Poindexter* we spoke of the paradoxical situation of a testator's dying intestate with an intact will in his hand. As **44 the chancellor said in his opinion in the present case, this testatrix left her will in a better and safer place than if she had died with it in her hand. She died 'with a valid, unblemished will in the custody of the executor named therein, upon whose integrity and good faith to propound that will for probate and to carry out its testamentary provisions she had a right to rely.'

A will is an ambulatory instrument, not intended or allowed to take effect until the death of the maker. It may be changed during life as often as the mind and purpose of the testator change. While he lives his written will has no life or force, and is not operative or effective for any purpose. 95 C.J.S., Wills, § 310, p. 110. If a testator elects to use the first method provided by the statute and puts a revocation provision in a will which he knows he may change at pleasure and which he knows will not be effective until he dies, it would seem to be wholly illogical to say that if he afterwards destroyed the will with intent to revoke it, he did not thereby destroy all of it, but that, regardless of his intention, the revocation caluse, although without physical form or existence, remained alive and vital with power to destroy all the wills he had ever written. Under such a rule the most solemn and deliberate will of a testator may be refused probate on the testimony of a witness, as in Bell v. Timmins, supra, that he saw the testator write and sign a later will which revoked the will not proffered.

We specifically held in *Barksdale* that a revoking clause in a will is a part and parcel of the will itself, without independent and immediate life or power, and that it survives or perishes with the will. We specifically held in Poindexter that a will which revokes a prior will by being wholly inconsistent with it, does not effect such revocation when executed but may do so only if it subsists when the testator dies. We are unwilling now to turn from the reasoning or the result of those two cases.

Our conclusion is that *Barksdale* and *Poindexter* announced the safer and better rule, a rule that keeps in step with the historic character and function of wills and is consonant with the language of the statute; that is, when a revocation of a prior will is made under the statute... by a subsequent will, the revocation clause *958 speaks when the will speaks, not at the time of the execution of the will, but at the death of the testator; and if in the testator's lifetime he destroys or cancels the revoking will with the intent to revoke it, the revocation provision falls with the will and is not effective to revoke the prior will. So far as Rudisill v. Rodes, supra, 70 Va. (29 Gratt.) 147, is in conflict with this conclusion, it is overruled.

SPRATLEY, J., dissenting:

... **45 ... Here we have a second will dated January 31, 1955, duly executed, wherein testatrix expressly declaring her intention to revoke all former wills by her made. It is clear that she did not intend her former will dated October 29, 1954, to stand, both by that declared intention and by her different property disposals in the two instruments. The execution of the second will was the last testamentary act of the testatrix. Thereafter, she told a friend that she intended to execute a new will, and on some unnamed date she presumptively destroyed the second instrument. She did not later make a new will, undertake to revise, or to re-execute either of the two wills she had made, in any of the methods provided by statute. ... *959 ... **46 ...

In Barksdale v. Barksdale, ... there was no second will and consequently no question of the effect of revoking a subsequent instrument. ... In Bell v. Timmins, the court held that a second instrument had not been established as a last will and that the evidence was insufficient to establish such a will, and relying upon *961 the *Barksdale* case, supra, permitted the first will to stand. ... In Poindexter v. Jones, it is sufficient to say that neither of the last two of four wills made by the testatrix contained a revoking clause, 'nor did either declare an intention to revoke any previous wills.' In distinguishing the *Rudisill* case, supra, Mr. Justice Miller pointed out that the will in the Rudisill case 'contained a revoking clause; it was a writing "declaring an intention to revoke * * *."' 200 Va., supra, page 380. In... Clark v. Hugo, (1921) 130 Va. 99, 107 S.E. 730, the court in extending the rule in the *Rudisill* case, supra, said: 'The legal rules and purposes which must control are decisive and clear. A will is revoked by a **47 subsequent inconsistent will; and after such revocation the destruction of the latter will does not have the effect of reviving the former, even though the testator so intends. ...

As Mr. Justice Eggleston... said in In Re Will of Bentley, (1940) 175 Va. 456, 462, 463, 9 S.E.2d 308, 311, where there were two inconsistent wills executed on different dates.

> It is true that both instruments cannot stand. But the first will is revoked by the act of the testator in executing a subsequent will, and not by the judgment of the court in admitting the later will to *962 probate. The result flows not from any proceeding attacking the probate of the first will, but from the law which gives vitality and force to the last testamentary act of the testator.' 175 Va., pages 462 and 463

If the foregoing statement of Justice Eggleston be said to be dictum, 'it was the dictum of a distinguished judge, concurred in by the entire court, and is entitled to much respect.' ...

[I]n the *Bates* case, supra, there was a subsequent inconsistent will which was cancelled by the testator, and that there was a duly signed postscript to that will which revoked all former wills, but there was no revocation of the postscript. ... Moreover, since in the *Bates* case there was no revocation of the revoking instrument, it cannot be said to support the view that the revocation of a revoking instrument restores a revoked instrument.

In the case before us the trial court gave no consideration to § 64-60, which section was expressly held in the *Rudisill* case, supra, to have changed the rules of law in effect prior to the revisal of the general laws in force before 1849. ... Section 64-60 provides how and when a will 'in any manner revoked' may be revived. The latter section eliminates any distinction between *963 the effect of a testamentary act of revocation and a separate and independent act. **48 In § 64-59 [predecessor to § 64.2-410] no difference is made between a will, or a codicil, or a writing, containing a revocation clause, as to the time when such a clause and either type of instrument becomes effective; and there is no indication that the legislature intended to make a difference. There is no provision that the revocation of a prior will is conditioned upon the existence of a subsequent will containing a revocation clause at the death of the testator, or that the second will be admitted to probate in order that its revocation clause can be made effective. If that condition had been provided, a revival statute such as § 64-60 would be useless because the potential survivor, himself, would be past reviving. The act declaring the intention to revoke is the essence and heart of the revocation process, an act which has immediate effect at the time of commission. In Re Will of Bentley, supra, 175 Va. Moreover, § 64-60, in the employment of the language 'in any manner revoked' encompasses all types of revocation in writing, whether by testamentary act or by a separate and independent instrument, duly executed.

A will being ambulatory in its provisions from its very nature constitutes a recognition that a testator may revoke any of its provisions, make a new instrument with new dispositions, or re-execute or republish a former will, in accordance with statutory requirements. ...

It is all very nice to say that the testatrix here could have destroyed her first will, and that since she did not do so that will remained alive and vital. That she desired the first will to remain alive is contrary to the evidence as declared by her in the execution of the second will, and by her statement that she intended to make a third will. She changed her mind when she made the second will, she changed her mind when she destroyed the second will, and we have no means of knowing whether she subsequently changed her mind again, preferring that her property be disposed of according to the laws of intestacy. May it not be as well presumed that in destroying the subsequent will and in failing to make a new will she elected to die intestate? The intentions of the testatrix with respect to disposal of her property are as ambulatory as are the provisions *964 of a will. I am not inclined to believe that she had any knowledge of the doctrine of dependent relative revocation. ....

I'ANSON, J., concurs in this dissent.

A final source of uncertainty regarding revocation the Supreme Court has addressed is a subsequent testamentary document that does not expressly revoke an earlier one.

Supreme Court of Appeals of Virginia
Bradshaw v. Bangley
194 Va. 794, 75 S.E.2d 609 (1953)

SPRATLEY, J., delivered the opinion of the court.

*795 ... **610 ... J. N. Alexander, a resident of the City of Suffolk, Virginia, died April 18, 1943, leaving surviving him his wife, Virgie E. Alexander. Mrs. Alexander died May 5, 1950. No children were born of their marriage. Appellants are the brothers and sisters of Mrs. Alexander and her sole heirs at law. Appellees are the nieces and nephews of J. N. Alexander and his sole heirs at law. ...

[O]n April 7, 1936, the date of the first paper writing, J. N. Alexander was individually seized of three parcels of land, Lots 14 and 15 in Block H and Lot 7 in Block K. He and his wife then jointly owned the parcel consisting of *796 parts of Lots 11, 12 and 13 in Block H. On May 7, 1942, the date of the second paper writing, and on April 18, 1943, the date of his death, J. N. Alexander individually owned Lots 7 and 15, and he and his wife owned jointly two parcels, Lot 14 and the Grace Street lot.

J. N. Alexander made and executed at separate dates two wills. Both wills were wholly in the handwriting of the testator. That of April 7, 1936, hereinafter referred to as his first will, reads as follows:

> <(This is my Will)>
>
> To Whom it May Concern:
>
> In case of my death I want my wife, Virgie E. Alexander, to have all money lots of land and every thing that I have in my name as her own. That she shall have full possession of every thing at my death.
>
> This April 7th, 1936.
>
> Sign J. N. ALEXANDER.

The second, dated May 7, 1942, hereinafter referred to as his second will, reads as follows:

> May 7th, 1942
>
> In case of my death I want my wife, Virgie Alexander to have full right to everything her lifetime to do as she thinks best for herself, so long as she lives At her death every lot that Deeded to J. N. & Virgie Alexander be sold and 1/2 go to her brothers and sisters, the other half to my nieces nephews.
>
> J. N. ALEXANDER.

On April 26, 1943, eight days after the death of Alexander, the second will was admitted to probate in the Clerk's Office of the Circuit Court of the City of Suffolk. No appeal was taken from the probate. On December 14, 1950, seven months after the death of Virgie E. Alexander, the first will was offered for probate in the Clerk's Office of the said Court, as a part of the last will and testament of the testator. Probate was refused by the clerk on the ground that the will dated May 7, 1942, had already beey duly proved and probated. An appeal was taken to the Circuit Court of the City **611 of Suffolk by appellants, the brothers and sisters of Mrs. Alexander. ... *797 ...

... [In the second will,] testator made no disposition *798 of the remainder in his individually owned property. ... [T]he court... correctly construed the second will, standing alone, as bringing about a partial intestacy of the estate of J. N. Alexander. ... [H]owever, ... under such a construction the second will is not wholly inconsistent with the first will....

In In Re Will of Bentley, 175 Va. 456, 461, 9 S.E.2d 308, Mr. Justice Eggleston, **612 citing considerable authority, pointed out that 'a man's last will may consist of different testamentary papers of different dates and that it is not indispensable that they should be probated at the same time.' In accord therewith is Gordon v. Whitlock, 92 Va. 723, 727, 24 S.E. 342, where the following statement is quoted from Schultz v. Schultz, 10 Gratt. 358, 373: 'A man's last will must not of necessity be confined to one testamentary paper. It may consist of several different testamentary papers, of different dates, and executed and attested at different times.'

The general rule is summed up in 57 Am. Jur., Wills, § 466, page 326, where this is said:

> Ordinarily, a will does not revoke a former will unless it purports to do so, or makes a disposition of the testator's property so inconsistent with that made in the former will that the two instruments cannot stand together. *799

Further, we find in § 474, page 332:

> The general rule is that two or more instruments, each purporting to be a will, may be admitted to probate if they are not so inconsistent or repugnant that they cannot stand together as constituting the will of the testator, and the date of execution of the respective instruments is ascertainable. While a revocation by implication may be either complete or partial, the rule is to give effect to both the earlier and later wills so far as possible, and to hold that the earlier will was entirely revoked by a later inconsistent will only where it appears that the testator so intended or the wills are so plainly inconsistent as to be incapable of standing together.

Also, in § 476, page 333, the subject is continued:

Generally speaking, the courts do not favor revocation by implication, and incline to such a construction as will give effect as far as possible to both instruments, rather than sacrifice the earlier will by declaring a total revocation by implication. Unless the two instruments are so inconsistent as to be incapable of standing together in any of their parts, the earlier one is deemed to be revoked only to the extent necessary to give the later one effect, and both instruments are to be admitted to probate as constituting together the last will and testament of the decedent.

Where two instruments are probated jointly as constituting one will, they are construed so as to give effect as far as possible to both, sacrificing the earlier so far only as it is clearly irreconcilable with the later instrument. In general, a will does not entirely revoke a prior one if it bequeaths different property or fails to dispose of substantial interests of the testator which are covered by the prior instrument.

The subject is summed up with the following statement, 57 Am. Jur., Wills, § 543, page 375:

The execution of the later will does not necessarily import the revocation of the earlier one, and it is incumbent upon the contestant asserting the revocation to prove the contents of the later will, and to show either that it contained express words of revocation or that there was an implied revocation because its provisions were so inconsistent with those of the former will that they could not exist together.

In 68 C.J., Wills, § 491, page 803, we find:

The weight of authority supports the rule that a later will *800 is not necessarily a revocation of a prior will unless by it the prior will is in terms revoked and canceled, or by the later will a disposition is made of all the testator's property, or it is so inconsistent with the former will that the two cannot stand together.

'When a later testamentary instrument does not revoke a former testamentary instrument they are to be **613 construed together as one.' 69 C.J., Wills, § 1163, page 120.

The will of May 7, 1942, contains no clause revoking the former will of April 7, 1936, expressly or by implication. Nor is there anything on the face of it to indicate that it was intended to stand alone, and be in complete substitution for the first. On the other hand, it shows that the welfare of his wife was the paramount desire of the testator. In the first sentence he gave to her the 'full right to everything her lifetime to do as she thinks best for herself, * * *.' This language clearly shows that he intended to give her the absolute power of disposal of all the property he possessed, if she thought 'best for herself.' Then, in the second sentence, he made a limitation over only as to the property he jointly owned, omitting any such limitation as to his individually owned property in which his wife failed to exercise the power of disposal during her life. The two paper writings read together show that the testator was desirous of making a complete testamentary disposition of his entire property. The effect of the writing of May 7, 1942, read alone is to leave the testator intestate as to the remainder over in his individually owned estate, - a result not favored by the law. If he had not desired that the first will operate together with the later testamentary paper to dispose of his entire estate, he could have destroyed it.

In Virginia, we have consistently followed the rule that where a will has been executed, the reasonable and natural presumption is that the testator intended to dispose of his entire estate. Gallagher, et al. v. Rowan's Adm'r., et al., 86 Va. 823, 827, 11 S.E. 121. '... Accordingly, where two modes of interpretation are possible, that is preferred which will prevent *801 either total or partial intestacy.' Honaker v. Starks, 114 Va. 37, 39, 75 S.E. 741. '... There is a strong presumption against partial intestacy, * * * and the courts have for a long time inclined very decidedly against adopting any construction of wills which leaves the testator intestate as to a part of his estate, unless that result is absolutely unescapable.' Coffman's Adm'r. v. Coffman, 131 Va. 456, 466, 109 S.E. 454.

'The only reason anyone can have for making a will is to change the devolution of his property from that prescribed by the statutes of descent and distributions. Hence there is a strong presumption that the testator intended to dispose of his entire estate, and the courts are decidedly adverse to adopting any construction of a will which leaves a testator intestate as to any portion of his estate, unless compelled to do so.' McCabe v. Cary's Ex'r., 135 Va. 428, 433, 116 S.E. 485. 'Partial intestacy is looked upon with disfavor. Wills are written for the purpose of disposing of property.' Neblett v. Smith, supra, at page 847. 'An intestacy is a dernier result in the construction of wills, and the abhorrence of the courts to intestacy under a will has been likened to the abhorrence of nature to a vacuum.' 57 Am. Jur., § 1158, page 755. '...[W]here a will is fairly open to more than one construction, a construction resulting in an intestacy as to any part of the estate will not be adopted if by any reasonable construction it can be avoided.' 69 C.J., Wills, § 1147, page 91.

The construction of the first will gives us no trouble. By it testator devises and bequeaths to Mrs. Alexander a fee simple estate in all of his real property and an absolute estate in all his personalty. In ordinary and common acceptation, the word 'everything' means: 'All; all that pertains to the subject under consideration.' Webster's New International Dictionary, Second Edition. **614

In the second will testator again uses the word 'everything.' *802 First, he gives his wife an estate for her life in all of his property, with full power of disposal without limitation in remainder over. In the next sentence, he provides that the remainder over in the property conveyed to him and his wife shall go at her death to their respectively named kindred. Nowhere does he mention the remainder over in his individually owned property. Obviously, he wanted his kindred to have only the remainder over in his share of his jointly owned property, and his wife's kindred to have the remainder in her share of such property.

The two wills deal with the same quantity of property, that is, all of the property of the testator. They are inconsistent only in the quality of the estate bequeathed and devised. The testator obviously knew that unless he disposed of his property by will, his heirs at law would succeed to a portion of it. That he originally desired to exclude them from any portion is manifest in the express provisions of the first will. The second instrument expressed his desire that they share therein only so far as his jointly owned property was concerned. The intention of the testator, we think, in view of the circumstances, is fairly plain and necessarily implies that he meant only to give his heirs at law an interest in his share of the jointly owned property. We find nothing inconsistent in law or fact with that intention, and it should be effectuated by construing the two wills as a whole. ...

For the reasons stated, we conclude that the trial court erred *803 in refusing to admit the first will to probate as a part of testator's true last will and testament. We find that the first will gave Mrs. Alexander a fee simple estate in all that the testator owned, and that the second will reduced that estate to one for life, but failed to dispose of the remainder over in his individually owned property, hence that remainder passed to her by virtue of the first will. Giving effect to the provisions of both instruments, Virgie E. Alexander took all of the individually owned estate of her husband, absolutely and in fee simple, together with an estate for her life in his share of the real property jointly owned, with the remainder in his share of the jointly owned property to his nieces and nephews. Under the facts of this case, the one-half share of Mrs. Alexander in the jointly owned real estate descended according to our statute of descent and distribution to her heirs at law. Her husband could not, of course, dispose of her estate by his will. ...

One circuit court decision regarding revocation is worth noting:

In Estate of Doughtie, 70 Va. Cir. 329 (2006), the testator had died in a car accident at age 91. She had a will, but it was "clear from the evidence that, but for the accident, Ms. Doughtie would have revised her will." She had told at least three trusted persons what changes she planned to make, and she had made an appointment to discuss her will with her lawyer. Her brother, to whom her will left a third of the estate, had died ten months earlier. When her will was produced after her death, "Wilford's name had been obliterated by the use of an opaque correction fluid... [and] [a]nother name had been handwritten above Wilford's name; that name had been obliterated in the same fashion." The court cited Timberlake v. State Planters Bank for the proposition that a will "may be changed during life as often as the mind and purpose of the testator change" and Goriczynski v. Poston for the proposition that the revocation statute "permits partial revocation of a duly attested will without further formalities." After concluding that the provision for Wilford was legally revoked, and after noting that uncontradicted testimony of several witnesses revealed a clear and firm conviction on Mrs. Doughtie's part as to what she wanted to do with her estate instead, the court said: "Can a court order such a division, if satisfied by the evidence that it knows what Ms. Doughtie said and meant? The answer, of course, is no." The court then noted that Ms. Doughtie herself did not believe she had executed a new will simply by telling people what she wanted, so there was no mistake on her part as to the effect of the revocation. The last step was deciding what to do with Willard's one-third share of the estate. The court referred to the well-established principle that courts should "'a strong presumption that the testator intended to dispose of his entire estate, and courts are decidedly averse to adopting any construction of a will which leaves a testator intestate as to any portion of his estate'" (quoting) Baliles v. Miller, 231 Va. 48, 57, 340 S.E.2d 805 (1986); to the rule embodied in Code § 64.1–65.1 [now § 64.2-416] that "if the residue is devised or bequeathed to two or more persons and the share of one fails for any reason, such share shall pass to the other residuary devisees or legatees in proportion to their interests in the residue"; and to precedent establishing that revocation is "any reason" why a bequest fails, citing Saunders v. Saunders, 109 Va. 191, 195, 63 S.E. 410 (1909). Thus, "the residue of the estate must be divided proportionally (which in this case means equally) between the two remaining residuary beneficiaries."

Chapter Four
Special Protections for Surviving Spouses

We saw in Chapter One that a surviving spouse has priority in distribution of an intestate estate – specifically, the entire estate if the decedent had no children or only children in common with the surviving spouse, and one third of the estate if the decedent had separate children. But that is not the only way estate law today favors and protects surviving spouses. The inheritance priority is based on an assumption of decedent intent, but protection of surviving spouses is one realm in which fairness and public policy now play a significant role.

The fairness consideration is primarily embodied in the "elective share" rule, first enacted in 1991 and substantially revised in 2016, which gives surviving spouses a right against being directly disinherited by a will or effectively disinehertied by lifetime gifts and non-probate transfers to others (e.g., decedent just before or at the time of death transfers all his wealth to children from a prior marriage). The fairness notion here is tied to a fundamental principle of domestic relations law -- namely, that both spouses contribute to generation of wealth during a marriage, regardless of who the nominal income earner is. This principle is the basis of equitable distribution in divorce, and it would be highly anomalous if the law required transfer of wealth from a primary breadwinner to a homemaker spouse in a divorce, when the breadwinner probably would prefer not to make that transfer, but did not ensure it at the time of the breadwinner's death, when it is more likely (though certainly not always true) that a less-than-normal outcome for the surviving spouse was unintentional.

Thus, the law today ensures a surviving spouse a share of a decedent's estate whether the less-than-normal intestate or testate award to the survivor was intentional or unintentional. Although ordinarily heirs are not deemed to have any "right" to inherit, there is an exception in the case of spouses, because of this marital property/equitable distribution idea. The elective share rule in Virginia does not perfectly track the equitable distribution rules, as explained below, but it comes close.

The elective share rule also derives normative support from the public policy of privatizing dependency – that is, keeping non-self-sufficient people off of public assistance. That rationale also clearly underlies the other (typically less significant) protections surviving spouses enjoy regardless of whether there is a will, which primarily serve to avoid short-term hardship of a surviving spouse while the probate process goes on. We study these incidental protections first.

I. Incidental Protections

The less significant protections entitle a surviving spouse to remain in the marital home for a period of time and to take ownership of some wealth immediately in order to subsist.

Subtitle II. Wills and Decedents' Estates
Chapter 3. Rights of Married Persons
Article 1.1. Elective Share of Surviving Spouse of Decedent Dying on or After January 1, 2017

§ 64.2–308.16. Rights in family residence

Until the surviving spouse's rights in the principal family residence have been determined and satisfied by an agreement between the parties or a final court decree, in cases (i) where the principal family residence passes under the provisions of § 64.2–200 [intestacy rule] and the decedent is survived by children or their descendants, one or more of whom are not children or their descendants of the surviving spouse, or (ii) where the surviving spouse claims an elective share in the decedent's augmented estate under this article, the surviving spouse may hold, occupy, and enjoy the principal family residence and curtilage [land attached to the residence] without charge for rent, repairs, taxes, or insurance. ...

*   *   *

This provision addresses two situations in which a surviving spouse is likely to receive half or less of the decedent's estate – namely, when the he or she will take just one third under the intestacy laws and when he or she will take half or less of the "marital-property portion" of the decedent's "augmented estate" under the elective share rule (see Part II, below). In most other cases, the surviving spouse will be receiving more than half of the decedent's estate, and therefore likely title to the family residence. But there could be instances where the residence constitutes less than two-thirds of the decedent's estate and the decedent arranged for it to pass by non-probate transfer or will to persons other than the surviving spouse (e.g., children from a former marriage), thereby resulting in the ouster of the surviving spouse. It seems odd, then, that the General Assembly chose not to extend this temporary protection to surviving spouses in all cases, for who else would have urgent cause to possess the couple's residence immediately?

The final clause of § 64.2-307 suggests that, regardless of what financial resources the survivor has, the PA must pay any mortgage, rent, repair, tax, and insurance bills for the survivor during the probate period. Cf. Colbert v. Priester, 214 Va. 606, 608, 203 S.E.2d 134, 135 (1974) (holding that the estate must reimburse a widower for his payments during probate toward a loan secured by the property, repairs, and property taxes; Boyle v. Boyle, 30 Va. Cir. 438 (Albemarle County, 1993) (holding that an executor should make ongoing mortgage payments during probate, "since their duty to preserve the estate for ultimate distribution means they must make reasonable efforts to prevent the property from going into foreclosure," but should not use estate funds to pay the widow's utility bills, which "are necessary for the widow's personal enjoyment of the residence, not for preservation of the estate for future distribution"). It is not clear, though, against whom § 64.2-307 operates. The initial phrase suggests that the protection only applies when the surviving spouse might have some right to the property. A circuite court decision, In re Estate of Shoemaker-Liebel, 70 Va. Cir. 361 (2006), implicitly supposed that to be true, in holding that a widower must vacate a family house the decedent had placed into a trust prior to their marriage, because the house would not be part of the augmented estate. This reading would rule out applicadtion to situations in which the couple was renting a property from a third party, so the statutory provision would not operate against a landlord.

Subtitle II, Chapter 3, Article 2. Exempt Property and Allowances.

§ 64.2-309. Family allowance.

A. In addition to any other right or allowance under this article, upon the death of a decedent who was domiciled in the Commonwealth, the surviving spouse and minor children whom the decedent was obligated to support are entitled to a reasonable allowance in money out of the estate for their maintenance during the period of administration, which allowance shall not continue for longer than one year if the estate is inadequate to discharge all allowed claims. The family allowance may be paid as a lump sum not to exceed $24,000, or in periodic installments not to exceed $2,000 per month for one year. It is payable to the surviving spouse for the use of the surviving spouse and minor children or, if there is no surviving spouse, to the person having the care and custody of the minor children. If any minor child is not living with the surviving spouse, the family allowance may be made partially to the spouse and partially to the person having the care and custody of the child, as their needs may appear. If there are no minor children, the allowance is payable to the surviving spouse.

B. The family allowance has priority over all claims against the estate.

C. The family allowance is in addition to any benefit or share passing to the surviving spouse or minor children by the will of the decedent, by intestate succession, or by way of elective share. ...

***

This provision creates a near-absolute right of a surviving spouse to the first $24,000 of a decedent's estate, which for a substantial percentage of estates would constitute all or most of the assets. The family allowance is in addition to any other claim a surviving spouse has and takes priority over the claims of any other persons, organizations, or agencies. The final sentence of paragraph A makes clear that a surviving spouse is entitled to the allowance even if the decedent was not survived by any minor children, overruling a strange 1986 decision of the Circuit Court for City of Roanoke denying the family allowance to a widower, based on reasoning that the family allowance applied only if there were a "family" surviving the decedent and that a single person living alone could not constitute a family. In re Estate of Hess, 8 Va. Cir. 256 (1986).

§ 64.2-310. Exempt property.

A. In addition to any other right or allowance under this article, the surviving spouse of a decedent who was domiciled in the Commonwealth is entitled from the estate to value not exceeding $20,000 in excess of any security interests therein in household furniture, automobiles, furnishings, appliances, and personal effects. If there is no surviving spouse, the minor children of the decedent are entitled in equal shares to such property of the same value. If the value of the exempt property selected in excess of any security interests therein is less than $20,000, or if there is not $20,000 worth of exempt property in the estate, the spouse or minor children are entitled to other assets of the estate, if any, to the extent necessary to make up the $20,000 value.

B. The right to exempt property and other assets of the estate needed to make up a deficiency of exempt property has priority over all claims against the estate, except the family allowance.

C. The right to exempt property is in addition to any benefit or share passing to the surviving spouse or minor children by the will of the decedent, by intestate succession, or by way of elective share.

***

In addition to the family allowance, then, a surviving spouse is entitled to take another $20,000 in personal property out of the estate, before any intestate right or will provision operates. This effectively raises to $44,000 the threshold value an estate must have before any of the rules for distribution we studied in Chapters Two and Three even come into play.

Disputes can arise when a surviving spouse claims a portion of assets other than tangible personal property, on the grounds that the value of exempt property is less than the statutory amount (now $20,000). Thus, in Landram v. Sullivan, 29 Va. Cir. 190 (1992), the Circuit Court for Spotsylvania County had to address objections by a decedent's daughter and executrix that the decedent's wife had already received several "transfers in satisfaction of the allowances." The court found this to be true with respect to a social security check intended to help pay for burial expenses, the rental value of the home the wife occupied after the husband's death, and the tangible personal property in the couple's house. But it rejected the characterization of other things the wife received as satisfaction of her statutory rights, and so ordered the daughter to make up the difference from a bank account whose money the daughter was designated to receive by non-probate transfer, because there were not enough assets in the probate estate to fulfill the spousal rights. The follow Code provision authorizes this remedy.

Title 6.2. Financial Institutions and Services
Subtitle II. Depository Institutions and Trust Organizations
Chapter 6. Deposits and Accounts
Article 2. Multiple-Party Accounts

§ 6.2-611. Liability of surviving party for debts of decedent's estate

A. If the assets of a deceased party's estate, other than the assets in a multiple-party account, are not sufficient to pay the debts, taxes, and expenses of estate administration, including statutory allowances to the surviving spouse, minor children, and dependent children, no transfer of account funds, to which the deceased party was beneficially entitled immediately before his death, shall be effective, by virtue of a party's survivorship of the decedent, against the estate of such deceased party to the extent such funds are needed to pay such liabilities of the estate.

B. A surviving party, P.O.D. payee, or beneficiary who receives payment from a multiple-party account after the death of a deceased party shall be liable to account to his personal representative for amounts the decedent owned beneficially immediately before his death to the extent necessary to discharge the claims and charges described in subsection A that remain unpaid after application of the decedent's estate. ...

C. This section shall not affect the right of a financial institution to make payment on multiple-party accounts according to the terms thereof, or make it liable to the estate of a deceased party unless, before payment, the institution has been served with process in a proceeding by the personal representative.

***

This statutory rule prevents a married person from depriving his or her surviving spouse of statutory rights by arranging for non-probate transfer of the bulk of his or her assets. See also Bray v. Ireland, 69 Va. Cir. 270 (2005) (applying § 6.2-611 to decide that "the funds beneficially owned by Mr. Bray [the decedent] in the joint Wachovia Bank account should be used to satisfy [widow] Ms. Bray's statutory allowances because the assets of the estate are otherwise insufficient").

A final incidental statutory right is called a "homestead allowance," but really is just another entitlement to money "off the top" where the estate is fairly small, albeit one less commonly available to a surviving spouse than those discussed above.

Subtitle II, Chapter 3, Article 2. Exempt Property and Allowances

§ 64.2-311. Homestead allowance.

A. In addition to any other right or allowance under this article, a surviving spouse of a decedent who was domiciled in the Commonwealth is entitled to a homestead allowance of $20,000. If there is no surviving spouse, each minor child of the decedent is entitled to a homestead allowance amounting to $20,000, divided by the number of minor children.

B. The homestead allowance has priority over all claims against the estate, except the family allowance and the right to exempt property.

C. The homestead allowance is in lieu of any share passing to the surviving spouse or minor children by the decedent's will or by intestate succession; provided, however, if the amount passing to the surviving spouse and minor children by the decedent's will or by intestate succession is less than $20,000, then the surviving spouse or minor children are entitled to a homestead allowance in an amount that when added to the property passing to the surviving spouse and minor children by the decedent's will or by intestate succession, equals the sum of $20,000.

D. If the surviving spouse claims and receives an elective share of the decedent's estate ..., the surviving spouse shall not have the benefit of any homestead allowance.

***

A surviving spouse would claim under this statutory provision only if he or she a) would not be receiving $20,000 or more from the probate estate (after deduction of the family allowance and exempt property allowance) and b) is not claiming the elective share. So, in other words, a surviving spouse seeking to maximize his or her take from the estate would claim the homestead allowance only if the decedent made little or no provision for him or her in a will and the surviving spouse's claim under intestacy rules or the elective share rule would be less than $20,000.

In Johnston v. Rosenthal, 31 Va. Cir. 368 (1993), the Circuit Court for Warren County held that the words "any share passing to surviving spouse... by the decedent's will" in § 64.2-311 "are clear and unambiguous and require no interpretation" and must include a "right to receive one third of the income from a [testamentary] trust." Thus, if the decedent's husband "persists in claiming the... Homestead Allowance..., this will be in lieu of any interest passing to him under the will of his wife, and he will thereby forfeit his [much more valuable] joint survivorship life estate in the residuary trust."

With any of the above spousal rights, the question arises as to who, among heirs or beneficiaries of will provisions or non-probate transfers, should sacrifice to pay them. The Code provides a little guidance:

§ 64.2-312. Source, determination, and documentation of family allowance, exempt property, and homestead allowance; petition for relief.

A. Property specifically bequeathed or devised shall not be used to satisfy the right to exempt property and the homestead allowance if there are sufficient assets in the estate otherwise to satisfy such rights. Subject to this restriction, the surviving spouse or the guardian of the minor children may select property of the estate as exempt property and the homestead allowance. The personal representative may make these selections if the surviving spouse or the guardian of the minor children is unable or fails to do so within a reasonable time, or if there is no guardian of the minor children. ...

***

There has been some litigation concerning whether the spousal rights have been properly claimed. A Code provision specifies what is required:

§ 64.2-313. When and how exempt property and allowances may be claimed.

Any election to take a family allowance, exempt property, or a homestead allowance shall be made within one year from the decedent's death. The election shall be made either in person before the court having jurisdiction over probate or administration of the decedent's estate, or by a writing recorded in the court, or the clerk's office thereof, upon such acknowledgment or proof as would authorize a writing to be admitted to record under Chapter 6 (§ 55-106 et seq.) of Title 55.

***

The Supreme Court appears not to have addressed any disputes about proper claiming of the incidental protections, but a decision relating to claiming of the elective share likely would extend to these other spousal rights. Code § 64.2-302, governing how the elective share may be claimed, contains language virtually identical to the second sentence of § 64.2-313. The following case addresses the not uncommon situation where the offspring of a surviving spouse, who are not also offspring of the decedent, want the surviving spouse to get as much from the estate as possible, in expectation some of the wealth will ultimately devolve to them (rather than to heirs or beneficiaries of the decedent).

Supreme Court of Virginia.
Jones v. Peacock
267 Va. 16, 591 S.E.2d 83 (2004)

OPINION BY Justice ELIZABETH B. LACY.

… Geraldine M. and B. Franklin Jones (the Joneses) were married for 15 years. During the marriage the Joneses lived at Westminster Canterbury, a retirement home and nursing facility. For the last five years of the marriage, Mrs. Jones resided in the health care section of the facility. Although they lived apart, the Joneses saw each other on a daily basis and generally dined together.

Mrs. Jones died on May 15, 2000. Her will, dated April 11, 1995, was admitted to probate. According to the terms of the will, the majority of Mrs. Jones' estate was to be held in trust for the lifetime benefit of Franklin Jones. Upon his death, any remaining assets were to be distributed to certain named beneficiaries. Mrs. Jones had no children, but Franklin had two sons by a prior marriage.

At the time of his wife's death, Franklin resided in the assisted living section of Westminster Canterbury. On August 22, 2000, he was moved to a nursing home level of care because he refused to take food, fluids, or medication, had expressed a desire to die, and was found wrapping a call bell cord around his neck.

On August 24, 2000, Richard Jones visited his father. During this visit Richard gave his father a completed but unsigned Notice of Claim for Elective Share of Augmented Estate (Notice of Claim). Franklin signed the Notice of Claim and his signature was notarized by Harriet Smith, an employee of Westminster Canterbury. Richard Jones filed the Notice of Claim with the clerk of the Circuit Court *19 for the City of Virginia Beach later that day. Franklin died two days later on August 26, 2000 at the age of 90.

David W.K. Peacock, Executor and Trustee of Mrs. Jones' estate (Executor), filed an amended bill of complaint for advice and guidance asserting that the Notice of Claim was not valid because Franklin Jones was not competent to execute it on August 24, 2000. The executor argued that Code § 64.1-13 [now § 64.2-302] requires a notice of claim to be recorded under the same conditions as other recorded instruments such as deeds and contracts, and thus, a notice of claim is analogous **86 to a contract. Therefore, according to the Executor, the mental capacity required to validly execute a deed or contract should also be required in order to validly execute a notice of claim under Code § 64.1-13.[1]

> [1] A party is competent to execute a deed or contract if at the time of execution, the party has sufficient mental capacity to understand the nature of the transaction and agree to its provisions. Hill v. Brooks, 253 Va. 168, 175, 482 S.E.2d 816, 821 (1997).

Based on the deposition testimony and medical records in this case, the Executor argued that Franklin Jones did not have the requisite mental capacity to validly execute the Notice of Claim on August 24, 2000.

The respondents, Charles and Richard Jones, asserted that the Notice of Claim was analogous to a testamentary document and, therefore, the requisite mental capacity should be that applicable to the execution of wills.[2]

> [2] A party is competent to execute a will if the party has sufficient mental capacity at the time of execution to "recollect[] his property, the natural objects of his bounty, and their claims upon him, and kn[o]w the business about which he was engaged and how he wished to dispose of his property." Fields v. Fields, 255 Va. 546, 550, 499 S.E.2d 826, 828 (1998).

Continuing, the sons maintained that regardless of which standard was applied, Franklin Jones was competent to validly execute the Notice of Claim on August 24, 2000. …

[W]e have not previously considered the appropriate competency standard for executing *20 a notice of claim under the augmented estate statutes. …

Subsection A of [§ 64.1-13] prescribes that a written notice of claim filed with the clerk of court be "upon such acknowledgment or proof as would authorize a writing to be admitted to record under Chapter 6 (§ 55-106 et seq.) of Title 55." The trial court concluded… that Code § 64.1-13 implicitly suggests a similarity between contracts, deeds, and notices of claim because the referenced sections in Chapter 6 of Title 55 govern other recorded instruments such as deeds and contracts. We do not find this argument persuasive. The referenced sections in Title 55 address only the form that a document must meet to be admitted to record. There is nothing in these statutory provisions, or any other, that establishes the level of competence required to execute a notice of claim. ... **87 ... A contract involves a bilateral exchange, a meeting of the minds, and an understanding of obligations undertaken-factors not present in taking an elective share. A will requires action by only the testator and does not affect *21 the testator's present or future interests. Choosing an elective share over provisions made in a will, although a unilateral act, does affect future interests of the surviving spouse. ... [T]he distinct nature of an election warrants a level of competency uniquely connected to that act.

We hold that at the time an election is made under Code § 64.1-13, the surviving spouse must have the capacity to understand his right to elect against the will and receive a share of the estate established by law and to know that he is making such an election. Competency to execute the notice of claim does not require a surviving spouse to know the specific amount that will be received as a result of such an election. Indeed, that amount may not be determined without litigation. Whether a surviving spouse exercises good judgment when making an election is not relevant to the issue of mental capacity to make such a choice. See, e.g., Thomason v. Carlton, 221 Va. 845, 855, 276 S.E.2d 171, 177 (1981) (an unwise decision or mistake in judgment in making a will is not evidence of incompetency); Smyth Bros.-McCleary-McClellan Co. v. Beresford, 128 Va. 137, 169-70, 104 S.E. 371, 382 (1920) (capacity to make a contract controls, not the propriety or impropriety of any dispositions of the maker's property that may be made therein). ... *22 ....

In determining whether a party was competent to make an election under Code § 64.1-13, we begin with the presumption that all persons are competent, and the party challenging this presumption has the burden of establishing incompetency. Brown v. Resort Developments, 238 Va. 527, 529, 385 S.E.2d 575, 576 (1989).

Franklin Jones' two treating physicians testified by deposition. Dr. Jerry H. Morewitz, a psychiatrist, began treating Franklin Jones for mild to moderate depression in February 2000. Throughout his treatment, Dr. Morewitz found Jones alert and with appropriate mental skills. The last time Dr. Morewitz saw Jones was August 22, 2000, the day Jones had been transferred to the health care facility because he would not take food, water, or medications. On that occasion, Jones would not communicate with Dr. Morewitz. Dr. Otarod Bahrani, Jones' primary care physician, also saw Jones on August 22, 2000. Jones did communicate with Dr. Bahrani. **88 According to Dr. Bahrani, Jones was alert and oriented on that date. Both doctors testified that Franklin's weakening condition could cause his mental state to fluctuate, but neither doctor could form an opinion as to whether Franklin Jones was competent to sign the Notice of Claim form on August 24, 2000.[3]

[3] Dr. Bahrani testified that he did not think Franklin Jones was competent to execute a contract, to buy a car, or purchase a house. However, on cross-examination he explained that the complexity of matters associated with buying a house such as finances and insurance would be difficult for someone "just in the hospital" to undertake, although many people at the end of life can make decisions "in the last minute" and he did not know "about Mr. Jones in this case."

Nothing in the testimony of either physician indicates that Franklin Jones lacked the capacity to understand his right to claim an elective share under Code § 64.1-13 or to know that he was executing such a claim on August 24, 2000. In fact, the evidence of record suggests the contrary.

Ms. Harriet Smith testified that she knew Franklin Jones "fairly well" and visited him throughout his residency at Westminster Canterbury. She recalled that when she was called to his room to notarize the Notice of Claim on August 24, 2000, he recognized her and called her by name. Ms. Smith testified that when he signed the Notice of Claim he "was alert." *23

Richard Jones testified that he brought the Notice of Claim to his father on August 24, 2000 pursuant to his father's request. Franklin recognized Richard and "appeared glad" to see him. Richard told his father about the Notice of Claim and told him that his signature would have to be notarized if he chose to sign the document. Richard testified that his father read the Notice of Claim before signing it. Richard also testified that his father raised the subject of the elective share some years before and that Richard had assisted his father in getting the answers to some questions regarding the elective share.

Based on the record before us, we conclude that the Executor failed to satisfy his burden of establishing that on August 24, 2000, Franklin Jones did not have the mental capacity to understand his right to elect against the will and take a share of the estate as prescribed by statute or to understand that he was executing such an election when he signed the Notice of Claim ...

In Walters v. Walters, 69 Va. Cir. 334 (2005), a surviving spouse claimed the exempt property and family allowance rights (she had waived the elective share in a marital agreement). She had filed a written request, but it was not notarized, and other potential takers from the estate argued that the request was therefore not in compliance with the statutory requirement that the "writing recorded in the court" have "such acknowledgment or proof as would authorize a writing to be admitted to record under Chapter 6 (§ 55–106 et seq.) of Title 55." The court viewed the statutory language as ambiguous and therefore concluded that it could consider equitable arguments. Because all parties were on notice of the intent to claim and no one was prejudiced by the omission of notarization, the court held that the wife could pursue the claims.

II. The Elective Share

Until 2017, Virginia law entitled a surviving spouse, regardless of the length of the marriage, to half of a decedent's entire "augmented" estate if the decedent was not survived by any children from another relationship, and one third if the decedent was survived by one or more children from another relationship. New legislation in 2016 changed the calculation of the elective share dramatically. First, it made the existence of children from another relationship irrelevant, making the elective share fraction one-half in all instances. Secondly, however, the elective share fraction is now applied to "the marital-property portion of the augmented estate," rather than to the entire augmented estate, and those two things become identical only after fifteen years of marriage. For marriages of less than fifteen years, the marital portion of the augmented is some percentage less than one hundred and increases over time, starting at merely 3% for marriages of less than a year. Thus surviving spouses of decedents who had no children or only children with the survivor are worse off now under the elective share rule if they were married less than fifteen years when one died, and after fifteen years their lot is the same as under prior law. However, surviving spouses of decedents survived by children from another relationship are better off than under prior law once the marriage has lasted eleven years; they are entitled to half the augmented estate rather than one third. An additional complication, though, making comparison of outcomes under the old and new rules quite complex, is some change in what property composes the augmented estate – most importantly, the surviving spouse's own earnings.

Chapter 3. Rights of Married Persons.
Article 1.1. Elective Share of Surviving Spouse of Decedent Dying on or after January 1, 2017.

§ 64.2–308.1. Applicability; definitions

A. The provisions of this article shall apply to determining the elective share of a surviving spouse for decedents dying on or after January 1, 2017.

B. As used in this article, unless the context requires a different meaning:

"Presently exercisable general power of appointment" means a power of appointment under which, at the time in question, the decedent, whether or not he then had the capacity to exercise the power, held a power to create a present or future interest in himself, his creditors, his estate, or creditors of his estate, and includes a power to revoke or invade the principal of a trust or other property arrangement.

"Property" includes values subject to a beneficiary designation.

"Right to income" includes a right to payments under a commercial or private annuity, an annuity trust, a unitrust, or a similar arrangement.

"Transfer," as it relates to a transfer by or of the decedent, includes (i) an exercise or release of a presently exercisable general power of appointment held by the decedent, (ii) a lapse at death of a presently exercisable general power of appointment held by the decedent, and (iii) an exercise, release, or lapse of a general power of appointment that the decedent created in himself and of a power described in subdivision 2 b of § 64.2–308.6 that the decedent conferred on a non-adverse party.

§ 64.2–308.3. Elective share amount; effect of election on statutory benefits

A. The surviving spouse of a decedent... has a right of election... to take an elective-share amount equal to 50 percent of the value of the marital-property portion of the augmented estate.

B. If the right of election is exercised..., the surviving spouse's homestead allowance, exempt property, and family allowance, if any, are not charged against but are in addition to the elective-share amount. ...

§ 64.2–308.4. Composition of the augmented estate; marital property portion

A. Subject to § 64.2–308.9, the value of the augmented estate, to the extent provided in §§ 64.2–308.5, 64.2–308.6, 64.2–308.7, and 64.2–308.8, consists of the sum of the values of all property, whether real or personal, movable or immovable, tangible or intangible, wherever situated, that constitute:

1. The decedent's net probate estate;

2. The decedent's non-probate transfers to others;

3. The decedent's non-probate transfers to the surviving spouse; and

4. The surviving spouse's property and non-probate transfers to others.

B. The value of the marital-property portion of the augmented estate consists of the sum of the values of the four components of the augmented estate as determined under subsection A multiplied by the following percentage:

If the decedent and the spouse were married to each other:	The percentage is:
Less than 1 year	3%
1 year but less than 2 years	6%
2 years but less than 3 years	12%
3 years but less than 4 years	18%
4 years but less than 5 years	24%
5 years but less than 6 years	30%
6 years but less than 7 years	36%
7 years but less than 8 years	42%
8 years but less than 9 years	48%
9 years but less than 10 years	54%
10 years but less than 11 years	60%
11 years but less than 12 years	68%
12 years but less than 13 years	76%
13 years but less than 14 years	84%
14 years but less than 15 years	92%
15 years or more	100%

***

So, § 64.2–308.3 sets a surviving spouse's share of the augmented estate at one half, and then § 64.2–308.4 first spreads a very wide net to draw into that pool everything either spouse owned, more or less, when one spouse died, but then says a survivor's claim on the estate should increase over time and be rather slight in the early years of a marriage.

The two major innovations here are 1) including the surviving spouse's assets in the augmented estate, and 2) having the elective share value depend on the length of the marriage. It might seem odd to include in the decedent's augmented estate non-probate transfers from the decedent to the survivor and also the survivor's own property, as if already having or receiving a lot of property should entitle the survivor to more, but another provision below says that such property should be treated as partial or complete satisfaction of the survivor's elective share. So the law includes such property in order to create a complete picture of the couple's "marital property," and then aims to ensure the survivor receives a fair share of that (consistent with the partnership view of marriage) but no more.

The increasing percentage approach is potentially inconsistent with the law's approach to equitable distribution in divorce. In practice, courts generally apply a presumption of 50-50 split of marital property in divorce. The equitable distrubtion law, Va. Code § 20-107.3, does make "duration of the marriage" a factor to consider in determining what division of marital property would be equitable, but courts can and do divide marital property more or less equally even in short-term marriages. This is more justifiable in the divorce context because divorce law includes in the marital pie to be divided only wealth acquired by effort during marriage and not pre-marital wealth. Thus, if the couple has been married only a couple of years, there might be very little marital wealth compared to the pre-marital wealth one or both brought into the marriage. As we see below, the elective share rule includes pre-marital wealth in the "marital property" subject to division, and that makes the increasing-percentage approach more defensible, even requisite. One might think divorce law should incorporate an explicit increasing-percentage approach, even though it excludes pre-marital wealth from the pie, on the theory that early in a marriage each spouse's earning potential mostly reflects all his or her pre-marital efforts in education, training, and job performance, and does not reflect support or assistance received from the other spouse, whereas later in the marriage a spouse's support for one's ongoing efforts play a larger role. But at present it only authorizes judges subjectively to take into account the length of the marriage.

Now we look to several other Code provisions for specification of the content of "the four components of the augmented estate" in Paragraph A of § 64.2–308.4:

    1. The decedent's net probate estate;

    2. The decedent's non-probate transfers to others;

    3. The decedent's non-probate transfers to the surviving spouse; and

    4. The surviving spouse's property and non-probate transfers to others.

§ 64.2–308.5. Decedent's net probate estate

The value of the augmented estate includes the value of the decedent's probate estate, reduced by funeral and administration expenses (excluding federal or state transfer taxes), homestead allowance, family allowances, exempt property, and enforceable claims.

***

By excluding the surviving spouse's other statutory rights, the Code avoids diminishing the value of those rights, ensuring that they are "in addition to" the elective share rather than partially "in lieu of" the elective share. Excluding debts and death-related expenses effectively entitles a decedent to pay off his or her debts and have a decent burial without running up against the demands of a surviving spouse. Excluding debts also means acting on the basis of the estate's "net value" rather than gross value. And unlike the rules for incidental protections, this elective-share rule, which is more about 'getting one's fair share' rather than bare subsistence, gives creditors priority over the surviving spouse.

The next provision, capturing non-probate transfers from the decedent, prevents married persons from depriving their spouses from a fair share of marital property by arranging for it all to go to third parties by non-probate transfer, keeping it out of the probate estate. A recurring term in the next few code provisions is "general power of appointment." This is a right to dictate to whom property will go at the end of a life estate, and it is "general" if it could be directed into the power holder's own estate. This device for passing property exists so that an original owner of property can let someone else choose in the future to whom the property should go following a gifted life estate. Thus, for example, suppose my mother gave me in her will a life estate and general power of appointment with respect to a beachfront vacation property. That is pretty close to fee simple; I own the property "in substance." If I exercise the power of appointment in favor of my estate, then the property would be in the probate estate and captured by § 64.2–308.5. Because I could do that, if I choose not to – that is, if I choose to exercise the power in favor of my children from a prior marriage, my siblings, or a friend, that is effectively a gratuitous transfer of property rights by me to someone other than my spouse, so essentially the same as giving them in my will property that I held in fee simple. The law therefore treats that property as part of my augmented estate.

The rule also captures decedents' interests in joint tenancies with rights of survivorship, even if the decedent never had more than a joint tenancy interest (i.e., did not own solely and then gratuitously add someone else as joint tenant) and even though people generally do not control which joint tenant dies first, given that the decedent could have sought severance of the joint tenancy before death and thus secured his or her fractional interest for the probate estate. Bank accounts and life insurance proceeds are forms of wealth the decedent more obviously could have allowed to pour into his or her probate estate but chose to pass to others outside of probate.

Lastly, Part 3 of the next Code provision captures inter vivos transfers to persons other than the surviving spouse, but with only a less-than-three-year look-back and only to the extent the property transferred was worth more than the federal Gift Tax Annual

Exclusion, which is currently $14,000. This means that a married person could deliberately deprive his or her spouse of a fair share of marital property by either a) giving away unlimited amounts of wealth more than three years before dying or b) giving gifts worth less than $14,000 per person to many individuals immediately before dying. So the law aims to capture any non-probate transfer, regardless of value, so could include a $1,000 certificate of deposit with a POD designation naming a grandchild or nephew, but the law excludes the first $14,000 of any gift given to any person a week before dying. The value threshold for gifts might reflect the greater difficulty in identifying and valuing gifts of tangible personal property, relative to non-probate transfers (which are generally of money in accounts, with an easily-ascertainable value, or of large assets such as real estate).

§ 64.2–308.6. Decedent's non-probate transfers to others

The value of the augmented estate includes the value of the decedent's non-probate transfers to others... of any of the following types, in the amount provided respectively for each type of transfer:

1. Property owned or owned in substance by the decedent immediately before death that passed outside probate at the decedent's death. Property included under this category consists of:

   a. Property over which the decedent, alone, immediately before death, held a presently exercisable general power of appointment. The amount included is the value of the property subject to the power, to the extent the property passed at the decedent's death ... to or for the benefit of any person other than the decedent's estate or surviving spouse.

   b. The decedent's fractional interest in property held by the decedent in joint tenancy with the right of survivorship... to the extent the fractional interest passed by right of survivorship at the decedent's death to a surviving joint tenant other than the decedent's surviving spouse.

   c. The decedent's ownership interest in property or accounts held in Payable on Death or Transfer on Death designations or co-ownership registration with the right of survivorship... to the extent the decedent's ownership interest passed at the decedent's death to or for the benefit of any person other than the decedent's estate or surviving spouse.

   d. Proceeds of insurance, including accidental death benefits, on the life of the decedent, if the decedent owned the insurance policy immediately before death or if and to the extent the decedent alone and immediately before death held a presently exercisable general power of appointment over the policy or its proceeds. The amount included is the value of the proceeds, to the extent they were payable at the decedent's death to or for the benefit of any person other than the decedent's estate or surviving spouse.

2. Property transferred in any of the following forms by the decedent during marriage:

a. Any irrevocable transfer in which the decedent retained the right to the possession or enjoyment of, or to the income from, the property if and to the extent the decedent's right terminated at or continued beyond the decedent's death. The amount included is the value of the fraction of the property to which the decedent's right related, to the extent the fraction of the property passed outside probate to or for the benefit of any person other than the decedent's estate or surviving spouse.

b. Any transfer in which the decedent created a power over income or property, exercisable by the decedent alone or in conjunction with any other person, or exercisable by a non-adverse party, to or for the benefit of the decedent, creditors of the decedent, the decedent's estate, or creditors of the decedent's estate. The amount included with respect to a power over property is the value of the property subject to the power, and the amount included with respect to a power over income is the value of the property that produces or produced the income, to the extent the power in either case was exercisable at the decedent's death to or for the benefit of any person other than the decedent's surviving spouse or to the extent the property passed at the decedent's death, by exercise, release, lapse, in default, or otherwise, to or for the benefit of any person other than the decedent's estate or surviving spouse. If the power is a power over both income and property and the preceding sentence produces different amounts, the amount included is the greater amount.

3. Property that passed during marriage and during the two-year period next preceding the decedent's death as a result of a transfer by the decedent if the transfer was of any of the following types:

a. Any property that passed as a result of the termination of a right or interest in, or power over, property that would have been included in the augmented estate under subdivision 1 a, b, or c, or under subdivision 2, if the right, interest, or power had not terminated until the decedent's death. The amount included is the value of the property that would have been included under those subdivisions if the property were valued at the time the right, interest, or power terminated...

b. Any transfer of or relating to an insurance policy on the life of the decedent if the proceeds would have been included in the augmented estate under subdivision 1 d had the transfer not occurred. ...

c. Any transfer of property, to the extent not otherwise included in the augmented estate, made to or for the benefit of a person other than the decedent's surviving spouse... to the extent the transfers to any one donee in either of the two years next preceding the date of the decedent's death exceeded the amount excludable from taxable gifts under 26 U.S.C. § 2503(b), or its successor, on the date of the gift.

***

The next component of the augmented estate reflects recognition that a married person might choose to bestow a fair share of his or her estate, or indeed the vast bulk of the estate, on a surviving spouse outside of probate. In fact, the law today aims to facilitate that approach to passing on one's wealth at death, for reasons discussed in Chapter One. When a decedent has done that, fairness would not support enabling the survivor also to grab a large share of the rest of the decedent's wealth. So the elective share rule adds in non-probate to the surviving spouse, before calculating the total value of the augmented estate, and then – as shown below -- counts those non-probate and inter vivos transfers as partial or complete satisfaction of the spouse's elective share.

§ 64.2–308.7. Decedent's non-probate transfers to the surviving spouse

Excluding property passing to the surviving spouse under the federal social security system, the value of the augmented estate includes the value of the decedent's non-probate transfers to the decedent's surviving spouse, which consist of all property that passed outside probate at the decedent's death from the decedent to the surviving spouse by reason of the decedent's death, including:

   1. The decedent's fractional interest in property held as a joint tenant with the right of survivorship…;

   2. The decedent's ownership interest in property or accounts held in co-ownership registration with the right of survivorship, or with Payable on Death or Transfer on Death designations…; and

   3. All other property that would have been included in the augmented estate under subdivision 1 or 2 of § 64.2–308.6 had it passed to or for the benefit of a person other than the decedent's spouse, surviving spouse, the decedent, or the decedent's creditors, estate, or estate creditors.

***

Finally, the elective share calculation takes into account that the surviving spouse might already have owned some of the couple's marital property. This is a new feature of the elective share rule, added in 2016. In a divorce, a court would look to all assets the couple owned, regardless of who held title, and include all such property that *either* spouse acquired a) by labor and b) during marriage as part of the marital pie subject to division. The elective share rule is consistent with that practice to the extent it includes in the marital pie wealth that had been held by the survivor in her or her name. That would include, significantly, inter vivos gifts to the survivor from the decedent, so account for the possibility that the decedent already provided for the surviving spouse by lifetime transfers. It would also include, though, the surviving spouse's own earnings, because under the partnership view of marriage the decedent had an equitable claim to part of those earnings, so the survivor's retention of them means he or she got from that source as well some wealth from the decedent.

A significant difference between "marital property" for divorce purposes and "marital property" for elective share purposes remains in the Code even after the 2016 revisions. As suggested above, in a divorce, a court would treat as a spouse's separate property, excluded from the marital estate, both property a spouse received by gift or inheritance and any property the spouse owned prior to the marriage and "brought into the marriage." Divorce law assumes that a spouse made no contribution to the earnings the other spouse acquired before the two were married. But § 64.2–308.9 below excludes from the marital estate for elective share purposes only the first type of separate property – that is, wealth acquired by gift or inheritance, while including pre-marital wealth. The effect of this is that over time (the first 15 years of marriage), each spouse's pre-marital wealth increasingly gets treated as part of the marital estate. This might be justifiable on the grounds that the line between pre-marital and marital wealth blurs as a marriage goes on, with spouses inter-mingling assets and continually making decisions about which pool of resources to use for various expenses (e.g., repairs to a pre-marital property) without assiduous attention to the separate-marital distinction.

The following Section includes not only property already in the surviving spouse's possession but also (in Subsection A.2) property the survivor gave away to third parties in the last few years of the decedent's life. This prevents the surviving spouse from extracting more from the decedent's estate by depleting his or her own estate, perhaps by transfers to his or her own family members, friends, or favorite charities.

§ 64.2–308.8. Surviving spouse's property and non-probate transfers to others

A. Except to the extent included in the augmented estate under § 64.2–308.5 or 64.2–308.7, the value of the augmented estate includes the value of:

1. Property that was owned by the decedent's surviving spouse at the decedent's death, including:

a. The surviving spouse's fractional interest in property held in joint tenancy with the right of survivorship;

b. The surviving spouse's ownership interest in property or accounts held in co-ownership registration with the right of survivorship; and

c. Property that passed to the surviving spouse by reason of the decedent's death, but not including the spouse's right to homestead allowance, family allowance, exempt property, or payments under the federal social security system.

2. Property that would have been included in the surviving spouse's non-probate transfers to others, other than the spouse's fractional and ownership interests included under subdivision 1 a or b, had the spouse been the decedent. [5]

---

[5] The section continues with rules for valuation:

§ 64.2–308.9. Exclusions, valuation, and overlapping application

A. The value of any property is excluded from the decedent's non-probate transfers to others:

1. To the extent the decedent received adequate and full consideration in money or money's worth for a transfer of the property; or

2. If the property was transferred with the written joinder of, or if the transfer was consented to in writing before or after the transfer by, the surviving spouse.

B. 1. The value of any property otherwise included under § 64.2–308.5 or 64.2–308.6, and its income or proceeds, is excluded from the decedent's net probate estate and non-probate transfers to others to the extent such property was transferred to or for the benefit of the decedent, before or during the marriage to the surviving spouse, by gift, will, transfer in trust, intestate succession, or any other method or form of transfer to the extent it was (i) transferred without full consideration in money or money's worth from a person other than the surviving spouse and (ii) maintained by the decedent as separate property.

2. The value of any property otherwise included under § 64.2–308.8, and its income or proceeds, is excluded from the surviving spouse's property and non-probate transfers to others to the extent such property was transferred to or for the benefit of the surviving spouse, before or during the marriage to the decedent, by gift, will, transfer in trust, intestate succession, or any other method or form of transfer to the extent it was (i) transferred without full consideration in money or money's worth from a person other than the decedent and (ii) maintained by the surviving spouse as separate property.[6]

B. Property included under this section is valued at the decedent's death, taking the fact that the decedent predeceased the spouse into account, but, for purposes of subdivision A 1 a or b, the values of the spouse's fractional and ownership interests are determined immediately before the decedent's death if the decedent was then a joint tenant or a co-owner of the property or accounts. For purposes of subdivision A 2, proceeds of insurance that would have been included in the spouse's non-probate transfers to others under subdivision 1 d of § 64.2–308.6 are not valued as if the spouse were deceased.

C. The value of property included under this section is reduced by enforceable claims against the surviving spouse.

[6] The section continues with rules for valuation:
C. 1. The value of property:
1. Included in the augmented estate under § 64.2–308.5, 64.2–308.6, 64.2–308.7, or 64.2–308.8 is reduced in each category by enforceable claims against the included property; and
2. Includes the commuted value of any present or future interest and the commuted value of amounts payable under any trust, life insurance settlement option, annuity contract, public or private pension, disability compensation, death benefit or retirement plan, or any similar arrangement, exclusive of the federal social security system. Except as provided herein for interests passing to a surviving spouse, life estates and remainder interests are valued in the manner prescribed in Article 2 (§ 55–269.1 et seq.) of Chapter 15 of Title 55 and deferred payments and estates for years are discounted to present value using the interest rate specified in

Though the above provisions represent a substantial change in the elective share rule as a result of legislation in 2016, some precedents applying and interpreting the pre-2016 elective share rules remain pertinent, because they concerned aspects of the law that carried over from old to new. The first case below addresses a dispute over whether the surviving spouse had consent to the decedent's gift to a third party.

Supreme Court of Virginia.
Tuttle v. Webb
284 Va. 319, 731 S.E.2d 909 (2012)

OPINION BY Chief Justice CYNTHIA D. KINSER.

*322 ... In 2010, Grace died and was survived by her husband, Lloyd, their two adopted children, and Henry B. Webb (Henry), her son from a previous marriage. In her will,... Grace named Henry as the executor of her estate, and devised and bequeathed her entire estate to him. Lloyd timely filed a claim for an elective share in Grace's augmented estate...

In 2005, Lloyd and Grace sold their jointly owned real property located in Chesterfield County and deposited the sale proceeds of $118,000 into their joint checking account. After *323 using a portion of the proceeds to pay jointly owed debts, Lloyd executed two checks drawn on the joint checking account, each in the amount of $41,750. One check was payable to Lloyd, and the other check was payable to Grace. Lloyd never cashed his

---

§ 55–269.1. In valuing partial and contingent interests passing to the surviving spouse, and beneficial interests in trust, the following special rules apply:

    a. The value of the beneficial interest of a spouse shall be the entire fair market value of any property held in trust if the decedent was the settlor of the trust, if the trust is held for the exclusive benefit of the surviving spouse during the surviving spouse's lifetime, and if the terms of the trust meet the following requirements:

        (1) During the lifetime of the surviving spouse, the trust is controlled by the surviving spouse or one or more trustees who are non-adverse parties;

        (2) The trustee shall distribute to or for the benefit of the surviving spouse the entire net income of the trust at least annually;

        (3) The trustee is permitted to distribute to or for the benefit of the surviving spouse out of the principal of the trust such amounts and at such times as the trustee, in its discretion, determines for the health, maintenance, and support of the surviving spouse; and

        (4) In exercising discretion, the trustee may be authorized or required to take into consideration all other income assets and other means of support available to the surviving spouse.

    b. To the extent that the partial or contingent interest is dependent upon the occurrence of any contingency that is not subject to the control of the surviving spouse and that is not subject to valuation by reference to the mortality and annuity tables set forth in §§ 55–271 through 55–277, the contingency will be conclusively presumed to result in the lowest possible value passing to the surviving spouse.

    c. To the extent that the valuation of a partial or contingent interest is dependent upon the life expectancy of the surviving spouse, that life expectancy shall be conclusively presumed to be no less than 10 years, regardless of the actual attained age of the surviving spouse at the decedent's death.

D. In case of overlapping application to the same property of the subsections or subdivisions of § 64.2–308.6, 64.2–308.7, or 64.2–308.8, the property is included in the augmented estate under the provision yielding the greatest value, and under only one overlapping provision if they all yield the same value.

check, and his $41,750 remained in the joint checking account. Grace, however, used the proceeds from her check to obtain two cashier's checks, each issued in the amount of $20,875 and payable to Henry. Henry testified that the cashier's checks were a gift from Grace and that Lloyd knew of the gift. Lloyd, however, testified that Grace told him that she gave Henry the money to invest for her. **911 ...*324 ...

As relevant to this appeal, the term

> augmented estate means the estate passing by testate or intestate succession, real and personal, after payment of allowances and exemptions ... to which is added the sum of the following amounts: *325

> > 3. The value of property transferred to anyone other than a bona fide purchaser by the decedent at any time during the marriage to the surviving spouse, to or for the benefit of any person other than the surviving spouse, to the extent that the decedent did not receive adequate and full consideration in money or money's worth for the transfer, if the transfer is of any of the following types: **912 ....

> > > d. Any transfer made to or for the benefit of a donee within the calendar year of the decedent's death or any of the five preceding calendar years to the extent that the aggregate value of the transfers to the donee exceeds $10,000 in that calendar year. Code § 64.1–16.1(A)(3)(d).

To prevent one spouse from disinheriting the other by transferring property before the transferor dies, this statutory provision imputes to the decedent's augmented estate the value of property transferred by the decedent during the marriage. If, however, property was "transferred by the decedent during marriage with the written consent or joinder of the surviving spouse," the value of the transferred property is not included in the transferring spouse's augmented estate. Code § 64.1–16.1(B)(i). ... The party seeking such an exclusion of property from a decedent's augmented estate carries the burden of establishing it. Chappell v. Perkins, 266 Va. 413, 418, 587 S.E.2d 584, 587 (2003). ...

Lloyd's execution and gift of the check to Grace did not remove those funds from, or decrease the value of, Grace's estate. In other words, the check represented Lloyd's consent to the transfer of joint property to Grace alone but it did not **913 signify his consent to remove the property from or diminish the value of Grace's estate. ... Lloyd's gift to Grace did not exclude those funds from her augmented estate. Consequently, *327 Lloyd's written consent to or joinder in Grace's subsequent gift to Henry was still required. Thus, the circuit court erred by excluding the sum of $41,750 from Grace's augmented estate.

Supreme Court of Virginia.
Chappell v. Perkins
266 Va. 413, 587 S.E.2d 584 (2003)

OPINION BY Justice ELIZABETH B. LACY.

... Walter and Carole were married from 1988 until Carole's death in 1997. Both had children from prior marriages, but they had none together. Walter was not a beneficiary under Carole's will. Walter timely filed a claim for his elective share of Carole's augmented estate...**586 ...

The property at issue included two investment accounts and a parcel of real property known as the Elliotts Creek property, all held *417 in Carole's name. The Estate asserted that the funds in the investment accounts were proceeds Carole received from her first husband's retirement program following his death, from her first husband's life insurance policy, and from the sale of their home.

Walter and Carole purchased the Elliotts Creek property in 1989 as tenants by the entirety. In 1991, they jointly executed a deed of gift conveying the property solely to Carole in fee simple. In 1992, they built a residence on the property with funds from the sale of other jointly owned property, a construction loan secured by securities owned by Carole, and funds contributed by both Carole and Walter. Carole transferred the property to the Carole K. Chappell Revocable Living Trust in 1997. ... *418 ...

The legislation defining the augmented estate begins with the value of the property in the decedent's probate estate. That value is increased by the value of certain property previously transferred by the decedent. The value of the augmented estate is then decreased by excluding the value of certain property....[4]

> [4] The provisions of the augmented estate apply whether the decedent dies testate or intestate.

[T]he party seeking inclusion of property under Subsection A of Code § 64.1–16.1 [now § 64.2–308.5 – 308.8] has the burden of proof under that subsection and the party seeking exclusion of property under Subsection B of that section [now, inter alia, § 64.2–308.9] carries the burden of establishing such exclusion. Accordingly, the circuit court did not err in placing on the Estate the burden to establish that the investment accounts and the Elliotts Creek property should be excluded from the augmented estate ...

B. The Investment Accounts

... Subsection B of Code § 64.1–16.1... *419 ... provides in pertinent part:

> B. Nothing herein shall cause to be included in the augmented estate ... (ii) the value of any property, its income or proceeds, received by the decedent by gift, will, intestate succession, *or any other method or form of transfer to the extent it is received without full consideration in money or money's worth*, before or during the marriage to the surviving spouse, from a person other than the surviving spouse to the extent such property, income, or

proceeds were maintained by the decedent as separate property[.] (Emphasis added.)

... *420 ... **588 ... Rules of statutory construction... assume that words in a statute are read according to their common meaning; however, if a term has a known legal definition, that definition will apply unless it is apparent that the legislature intended otherwise. "Gift" is a commonly used legal term and there is nothing to indicate that the General Assembly intended that the term have some other or additional meaning in this statute. A "gift" requires donative capacity and intent, delivery, and acceptance. The term does not include the mere receipt of property "without full consideration in money or money's worth." Indeed, at oral argument, counsel for the Estate could not identify any instance in which the receipt of funds from an insurance policy, from a retirement plan, from the sale of a house, or by operation of law qualified as receipt of property by gift. ... [B]ecause there is no evidence in this record showing that the funds in the investment accounts came from a gift, a will, or intestate succession,... the Estate failed to carry its burden to establish that investment accounts should be excluded from the augmented estate... *421

C. The Elliotts Creek Property

...The Estate argues that the transfer of the property by Carole and Walter to Carole in 1991 was a transfer of property by Carole made with the written consent or joinder of Walter and therefore, that the value of the property should be excluded from Carole's augmented estate... The Estate's position is based on the literal application of subparagraph (B)(i)...: "Nothing herein shall cause to be included in the augmented estate (i) the value of the property transferred by the decedent during marriage with the written consent or joinder of the surviving spouse."

The Estate argues that a plain reading of this subparagraph is that, once consent to the transfer of the property is made, the value of that property can never be included in the transferring spouse's estate. Such an application of the statutory provision leads to absurd results. For example, if the transferring spouse subsequently repurchases the transferred property, under the Estate's construction of Subsection (B)(i), that property could never be part of the transferring spouse's augmented estate, even though the property was part of the transferring spouse's probate estate because of the subsequent reacquisition. Accordingly, the provision eliminates value attached to a specific conveyance of property, not to specific property.

The Estate's construction is also inconsistent with the purpose of the augmented estate legislation, which is to prevent one spouse from disinheriting the other by transferring property prior to the transferor's death and thereby diminishing the transferor's estate. To achieve this purpose, the value of certain property transferred by the decedent during marriage is imputed to the decedent's augmented estate. If, however, a spouse had agreed to the transfer, the value of the transferred property is not included in the transferring spouse's augmented estate. This exception is based on principles of fairness. When a spouse agrees to a transfer of property that diminishes the transferor's estate, that spouse should not be allowed to reclaim the value of the transferred *422 property in the transferring spouse's **589 augmented estate.

If a transfer does not remove the property from the transferring spouse's estate, the consent of the non-transferring spouse, while a consent to the transfer, is not a consent to any diminution in the estate by virtue of that transfer. Accordingly, we conclude that that subparagraph (B)(i) of Code § 64.1–16.1 applies when a spouse consents to a specific conveyance that removes the property from, or decreases the value of, the transferring spouse's estate. In this case, the transfer of the Elliotts Creek property to Carole in fee simple did not remove the property from, or decrease the value of, Carole's estate. Although consenting to that transfer, Walter did not consent to a decrease in the value of Carole's estate. ... [T]herefore, the circuit court did not err in including the Elliotts Creek property in Carole's augmented estate.

In Kibler v. Kibler, 60 Va. Cir. 266 (2002), the Circuit Court of Shenandoah County looked to domestic relations law doctrine for interpretation of the phrase "to the extent such property, income, or proceeds were maintained by the decedent as separate property" in the statutory provision excluding from the augmented estate property received by gratuitous transfer. The court concluded that keeping the property (a farm in that case) titled solely in the name of the initial recipient "is part of maintaining the property as separate property," but not conclusive, and the court asked the parties to return with evidence as to whether some part of the value of the property might be marital for augmented estate purposes because of the couple's investing of marital wealth or effort into "improvements or additions which clearly increased the value of the real estate."

As with debts and other spousal rights, the question naturally arises how a surviving spouse's elective share is to be satisfied – that is, which beneficiaries of will provisions, non-probate transfers, or inter vivos gifts are going to have to give up some of their windfall for the sake of ensuring the spouse his or her fair share. The following Section first looks to property the surviving spouse would possess even if not claiming the elective share, including a) transfers the survivor received already directly from the decedent, by inter vivos or non-probate death-time transfer, b) property the surviving spouse acquired independently of the decedent that is marital property (i.e., property as to which the decedent would have had a claim in divorce or by elective share if the order of death were reversed), and c) what the surviving spouse stands to take by intestacy or will from the probate estate. If all that does not add up to the elective share value (i.e., augmented estate x % based on years of marriage x 50%), then all who would be beneficiaries of probate and non-probate transfers must contribute pro rata. Thus, in contrast to the rule for satisfying debts and other statutory spousal rights, there is no prioritization of special bequests and devises over general and residuary ones. Finally, if there is not enough in the probate estate and non-probate transfers combined to meet the elective share amount (because the decedent "gave away the farm" before dying), then the probate court and PA should go after people who received inter vivos gifts, who must contribute pro rata to the remaining balance.

§ 64.2–308.10. Sources from which elective share payable

A. In a proceeding for an elective share, the following are applied first to satisfy the elective-share amount and to reduce or eliminate any contributions due from the decedent's probate estate and recipients of the decedent's non-probate transfers to others:

1. The value of property excluded from the augmented estate under subsection A of § 64.2–308.9, which passes or has passed to the surviving spouse;

2. Amounts included in the augmented estate under § 64.2–308.5 that pass or have passed to the surviving spouse by testate or intestate succession and amounts included in the augmented estate under § 64.2–308.7; and

3. The marital property portion of amounts included in the augmented estate under § 64.2–308.8.

B. The marital property portion under subdivision A 3 is computed by multiplying the value of the amounts included in the augmented estate under § 64.2–308.8 by the percentage of the augmented estate set forth in the schedule in subsection B of § 64.2–308.4 appropriate to the length of time the spouse and the decedent were married to each other.

C. If, after the application of subsection A, the elective share amount is not fully satisfied, amounts included in the decedent's net probate estate, other than assets passing to the surviving spouse by testate or intestate succession, and in the decedent's non-probate transfers to others under subdivisions 1, 2, and 3 b of § 64.2–308.6 are applied first to satisfy the unsatisfied balance of the elective share amount. The decedent's net probate estate and that portion of the decedent's non-probate transfers to others are so applied that liability for the unsatisfied balance of the elective share amount is apportioned among the recipients of the decedent's net probate estate and of that portion of the decedent's non-probate transfers to others in proportion to the value of their interests therein.

D. If, after the application of subsections A and C, the elective share amount is not fully satisfied, the remaining portion of the decedent's non-probate transfers to others is so applied that liability for the unsatisfied balance of the elective share amount is apportioned among the recipients of the remaining portion of the decedent's non-probate transfers to others in proportion to the value of their interests therein.

E. The unsatisfied balance of the elective share amount as determined under subsection C or D is treated as a general pecuniary bequest.

***

As with the other spousal protections, there is a time limit and prescribed procedure for claiming the elective share.

§ 64.2–308.12. Proceeding for elective share; time limit

A. The election by the surviving spouse... must be made no later than six months after the later of (i) the time of the admission of the decedent's will to probate or (ii) the qualification of an administrator on the decedent's intestate estate, by a writing recorded in the court or the clerk's office thereof, upon such acknowledgment or proof as would authorize a writing to be admitted to record under Chapter 6 (§ 55–106 et seq.) of Title 55. ...

B. The surviving spouse must file the complaint to determine the elective share no later than six months after the filing of the election as set forth in subsection A. No later than 30 days after the filing of the complaint, the surviving spouse must provide a copy of the complaint to all known persons interested in the estate and to the distributees and recipients of portions of the augmented estate whose interests will be adversely affected by the taking of the elective share. The decedent's non-probate transfers to others are not included within the augmented estate for the purpose of computing the elective share if the complaint is filed more than 12 months after the decedent's death.

C. ... [T]he election for an elective share may be withdrawn by the surviving spouse at any time before entry of a final determination by the court and such election shall be extinguished.

D. ... The proceeding may be maintained against fewer than all persons against whom relief could be sought, but no person is subject to contribution in any greater amount than such person would have been... had relief been secured against all persons subject to contribution. ...

§ 64.2–308.13. Right of election personal to surviving spouse; incapacitated surviving spouse

A. The right of election may be exercised only by or on behalf of a surviving spouse who is living when the election for the elective share is filed... [I]it may be made on the surviving spouse's behalf by his or her conservator or agent under the authority of a durable power of attorney.

B. If the election is made on behalf of a surviving spouse who is an incapacitated person, ... the court must... appoint a trustee to administer that property for the support of the surviving spouse. [rules governing the trust follow]

***

Supreme Court of Virginia.
Haley v. Haley
272 Va. 703, 636 S.E.2d 400 (2006)

OPINION BY Justice G. STEVEN AGEE.

**401 *705 ... Hoover Clifton Haley ("H.C.") died intestate on October 22, 2003. Surviving H.C. were his widow, Betty Kersey Haley ("Haley"), and his son from a previous marriage, James Clifton Haley ("James"). Haley qualified as the administrator of H.C.'s estate on December 22, 2003. On February 12, 2004, a document was filed in the clerk's office of the trial court claiming an elective share for Haley in H.C.'s estate. The February 12th document showed the following typed words in a signature block at the end of the document: "Betty Kersey Haley / By Counsel / _____ / Lonnie L. Kern" and was signed by Mr. Kern as Haley's attorney. The February 12th document did not contain Haley's personal signature and was not acknowledged.

Haley filed a petition for contribution and bill of complaint to enforce her claim to the elective share. James filed a demurrer, asserting that Haley's claim to an elective share was ineffective because the February 12th document failed to meet the requirements of Code § 64.1–13 in that it was not personally executed by the claimant and failed to contain the acknowledgment required by the statute. By order dated December 30, 2004, the trial court sustained James' demurrer, but granted Haley leave to file an amended bill of complaint.

Haley filed a new claim for elective share, personally executed by her and properly acknowledged by a notary public, on January 28, 2005. That same day, she filed an amended bill of complaint and petition for contribution to enforce her right to an elective share. James again demurred because "the amended claim to [an] elective *706 share was, and can be of no legal effect, not having been filed within six (6) months of plaintiff's qualification as administrator of the H.C. Haley intestate estate as required by Code § 64.1–13." ...

II. ANALYSIS

Haley alleges... the requirements of Code § 64.1–13 were "substantially met" when Haley's attorney "signed as her agent the election for her share" in H.C.'s estate and James "received actual notice of Mrs. Haley's Election." ... **402 ... *707 ...

The text of Code § 64.1–13 is unambiguous: "The claim to an elective share shall be made ... by writing recorded in [the court having jurisdiction], or the clerk's office thereof, upon such acknowledgment or proof as would authorize a writing to be admitted to record under Chapter 6 (§ 55–106 et seq.) of Title 55." Code § 55–106 unequivocally requires that in order for a writing to be admitted to record, the original signature of the person executing the document "shall have been acknowledged by him." This requirement also applies to a writing when executed on behalf of another: "When such writing is signed by a person acting on behalf of another, or in any representative capacity, the signature of such representative may be acknowledged or proved in the same manner." Code § 55–106. To claim an elective share, the claimant must strictly comply with the requirements set forth in the statute.

The February 12th document does not bear the requisite acknowledgment or proof to be admitted to record under Code § 55–106. As a matter of law, the February 12th document was thus ineffective to make a claim of an elective share because it failed to comply with the Code § 64.1–13 acknowledgement requirement. The later filing on January 28, 2005 was also ineffective because it was not filed within the six-month time period required by Code § 64.1–13 and therefore also fails as a matter of law.

Contrary to Haley's argument, "actual notice" and substantial compliance are not sufficient to satisfy the requirements for claiming an elective share under Code § 64.1–13. The clear and unambiguous requirements of Code § 64.1–13 are mandatory. ...*708 Code § 64.1–13 sets forth the means for claiming an elective share, and requires the election to be acknowledged. To permit "actual notice" to suffice would create an exception that has no basis in the text of the statute. Accordingly, actual notice does not satisfy the requirements for claiming an elective share under Code § 64.1–13. ...*

* Because we find... the February 12, 2004 document fails to satisfy the requirements of Code § 64.1–13 because it does not contain an acknowledgment or proof, we need not address Haley's argument that an attorney can make a claim of an election under Code § 64.1–13 for his or her client and express no opinion in that regard.

Because the elective share and other spousal rights operate against written instruments upon which others might justifiably rely, the Code also addresses their liability and predicament. § 64.2–308.15 protects persons and institutions that pay out probate or non-probate assets to designated beneficiaries if they act "in good faith reliance on the validity of a governing instrument,... before the payor or other third party received written notice from the surviving spouse or spouse's representative... that a complaint for the elective share has been filed." Once banks, life insurance companies, executors etc. have "received written notice that a complaint for the elective share has been filed," then they are liable for payments made in contravention of the spouse's rights. This Section also authorize such holders of property to transfer the property to the probate court, rather than requiring them to hold on to the property while the court determines the spouse's entitlement.

III.   Waiver of Spousal Rights

A married person can waive the elective share and other statutory rights at the time of the spouse's death by simply not claiming them; the new elective share rules (unlike the pre-2016 rules) do not authorize the court or PA to assert the right on the survivor's behalf. In addition, many people waive spousal claims to decedents' estates in a pre-nuptial agreement when they get married, especially when either has children from another relationship. Less commonly, spouses execute such an agreement during marriage, which is most likely when they both have children from another relationship. The new elective share rule adopts the enforceability rule from the Code provision in the Domestic Relations title for enforcement of pre-nups, Va. Code § 20-151. In addition, a married person can incidentally waive statutory rights against a spouse's estate by abandoning the spouse. Whether an intentional or unintentional waiver has occurred is one of the most frequently litigated issues relating to rights of surviving spouses.

§ 64.2–308.14. Waiver of right to elect and of other rights; defenses

A. The right of election of a surviving spouse and the rights of the surviving spouse to homestead allowance, exempt property, and family allowance, or any of them, may be waived, wholly or partially, before or after marriage, by a written contract, agreement, or waiver signed by the surviving spouse.

B. A surviving spouse's waiver is not enforceable if the surviving spouse proves that:

1. The waiver was not executed voluntarily; or

2. The waiver was unconscionable when it was executed and before execution of the waiver because:

a. A fair and reasonable disclosure of the property or financial obligations of the decedent was not provided;

b. Any right to disclosure of the property or financial obligations of the decedent beyond the disclosure provided was not voluntarily and expressly waived, in writing; and

c. The surviving spouse did not have, or reasonably could not have had, an adequate knowledge of the property or financial obligations of the decedent.

C. An issue of unconscionability of a waiver is for decision by the court as a matter of law.

D. Unless it provides to the contrary, a waiver of all rights, or equivalent language, in the property or estate of a present or prospective spouse or a complete property settlement entered into after or in anticipation of separation or divorce is a waiver of all rights of elective share, homestead allowance, exempt property, and family allowance by each spouse in the property of the other and a renunciation by each of all benefits that would otherwise pass to one spouse from the other by intestate succession or by virtue of any will executed before the waiver or property settlement.

E. If a spouse willfully deserts or abandons the other spouse and such desertion or abandonment continues until the death of the other spouse, the party who deserted or abandoned the deceased spouse shall be barred of all interest in the decedent's estate by intestate succession, elective share, exempt property, family allowance, and homestead allowance.

***

Supreme Court of Virginia.
Dowling v. Rowan
270 Va. 510, 621 S.E.2d 397 (2005)

DONALD W. LEMONS, Justice.

*514 ... On July 10, 1993, Daniel Dowling ("Dowling") and his future wife, Wilma, entered a premarital agreement. The Agreement stated in prefatory language that "[t]he purpose of this Agreement is to settle the rights and obligations of each of them, during their marriage, upon the death of either or both of them, or in case of dissolution of the marriage." In paragraph nine of the Agreement, they agreed "[t]he property currently belonging to each party *515 and titled in his or her name shall remain his (her) separate property." Both of them came into the marriage with significant assets that were listed in appendices to the Agreement.

During their marriage, Wilma established the Wilma P. Dowling Revocable Trust ("Revocable Trust"), the Wilma P. Dowling Irrevocable Life Insurance Trust ("Insurance Trust"), and executed a Last Will and Testament ("will") that devised her tangible personal property to her husband, Dowling, except for "that tangible personal property identified in our Prenuptial Agreement" which was devised to Wilma's daughter by a former marriage, Vivianne Rowan.

After Wilma's death, her will was submitted to probate and Dowling qualified as Executor of her estate in accordance with the will. Thereafter Dowling timely filed claims for an elective share of Wilma's augmented estate, family allowance..., and exempt property... Dowling also claimed reimbursement of expenses related **399 to administering the estate, funeral expenses, his Executor's commission, and attorney's fees, which brought the total sum of his claims to $371,678. Rowan opposed all of Dowling's claims.[1] Dowling is an attorney licensed in Virginia and he represented himself in the elective share litigation.

> [1]   Rowan answered in her personal capacity, as Trustee of the Insurance Trust, and as Co–Trustee of the Revocable Trust.

... In calculating Dowling's elective share, the trial court... [i]ncluded... bank accounts, jointly owned property, and tangible personal property not listed in the Agreement. The court excluded all real and personal property listed in the Agreement, certain real property located in Peru, the proceeds of Wilma's life insurance policies, and the value of benefits conferred upon Dowling under the Revocable Trust. The value of the property included in the augmented estate was $63,893. This amount was reduced by *516 $44,606, the total amount of funeral expenses, various fees, and costs for administration of the estate.[2] The remaining amount, $19,287, was the value of the augmented estate as determined by the trial court.

> [2]   The trial court granted Dowling's claims for reimbursement for expenses including $8,604 for costs of administration of the estate, $15,439 for funeral expenses, and $13,922 for legal fees related to administration of the estate, and $6,641 for accountant fees.

Pursuant to the trial court's conclusions, Dowling's elective share, one-third of the augmented estate [under the old rule], was $6,429. Since Dowling had already received assets from the estate totaling $52,806, and those assets must be deducted from the elective share, the trial court held that the estate would owe nothing to Dowling. ...

II. ANALYSIS

A. Property excluded from the augmented estate

Parties to a premarital agreement can contract with respect to disposition of property upon separation, marital dissolution, death, or any other event. Code § 20–150. Premarital agreements "are contracts subject to the rules of construction applicable to contracts generally." Pysell v. Keck, 263 Va. 457, 460, 559 S.E.2d 677, 678 (2002). ... Where contracts are "plain upon their face, they are to be construed as written, and the language used is to be taken in its ordinary significance unless it appears from the context it was not so intended. They are to be construed as a whole." *517 **400 ...

In *Pysell*, we held that no such waiver existed in the premarital agreement because "nowhere ... do we find a reference to either party's rights in the property of the estate of the other." 263 Va. at 460, 559 S.E.2d at 679 (construing a premarital agreement to apply only while the parties were living). This case is different. The plain language of the Agreement in this case contains an express waiver of rights to specific property of the decedent upon death. The Agreement sets forth in prefatory language that "[t]he purpose of this Agreement is to settle the rights and obligations of each of them, during their marriage, upon the death of either or both of them, or in case of dissolution of marriage." The explicit reference to rights "upon the death" is precisely the language that was lacking in *Pysell*.

Furthermore, there is an implicit reference to survivor's rights in paragraph five, which states:

> Each party fully understands that, in the absence of this Agreement, the law would confer upon him or her certain property rights and interests in the assets and property owned by the other, and it is the intent of each party, by this Agreement, to relinquish certain of such property rights and interests in such assets as specified herein.

Many property rights may arise by operation of law upon marriage. Lacking any language to the contrary, and considering the stated purpose of the Agreement, we hold that the foregoing language refers to all property rights accrued during the marriage, including a surviving spouse's rights to an elective share, family allowance, and exempt property. ... *518

However, Dowling did not completely waive his survivorship rights by executing the Agreement. Rather, paragraph five limits the waiver to "*certain of* such property rights and interests in such assets as specified herein." (Emphasis added.) Under paragraph seven, each item of individually owned property is listed in the two appendices of the Agreement. Consequently, the waiver pertains only to a specific list of property. This interpretation is supported by paragraph nine wherein the parties agreed that "[t]he property currently belonging to each party and titled in his or her name shall remain his (her) separate property." This language does not conflict with any other portion of the Agreement. In fact, it appears to accord perfectly with the stated intent in paragraph five to "relinquish" certain rights in the property of the other.

This court is duty bound to construe a contract as a whole, considering every word and every paragraph, if there is a sensible construction that can be given. Read together, the quoted portions of the Agreement establish that (i) the Agreement applies upon death, (ii) it pertains to certain rights in certain assets specified therein, and (iii) separate property is to remain separate. There is no conflicting language within the four corners of the Agreement. ... Accordingly, Dowling's claims to elective share, family allowance, and exempt property cannot be satisfied **401 using any property listed in the appendix to the Agreement. *519

At the time of her death, Wilma held a remainder interest in various real properties located in Peru that she acquired by intestate succession. This property is not listed in the Agreement. Wilma acquired this interest after she was married to Dowling. The trial court excluded the value of these properties from the augmented estate pursuant to Code § 64.1–16.1(B)(ii) [former elective share rule] which directs exclusion of property from the augmented estate which is "received by the decedent by gift, will, intestate succession ... to the extent such property, income or proceeds were maintained by the decedent as separate property." The question before us is whether Wilma "maintained" this property as separate property. ...

We are bound by the plain meaning of the words used "unless a literal interpretation would result in a manifest absurdity." Dowling urges this Court to require physical repair or maintenance upon the property to consider it "maintained as separate" under the statute. We disagree. The properties at issue were located in Peru and Wilma's relatives who held a similar interest occupied several of the properties. It would be manifestly absurd to require that Wilma travel to another country, enter upon land occupied by another person, and perform physical improvements as an act of "maintenance" in order to retain the "separate" nature of the property.

Looking to the context of the word "maintain" in the statute, the language does not refer to physical maintenance of "property," "income" or "proceeds." Rather, the language of the statute refers to keeping a legal interest in the property separate.

At times we consider statutes relating to the same subject matter to help provide meaning to the statute before us. There is ample authority on the matter of separate property within *520 domestic relations law. The equitable distribution statute defines separate property to include "all property acquired during the marriage by bequest, devise, descent, survivorship or gift from a source other than the other [spouse]." Code § 20–107.3(A)(1) (ii). Such property will retain its "separate" status for purposes of equitable distribution unless one of several circumstances transmutes the nature of the property, such as commingling separate assets with marital assets or retitling the property in the joint names of the spouses. Code § 20–107.3(A)(3)(d), (e), and (f). Since the primary purpose of the equitable distribution statute is to provide a fair manner for classifying assets accumulated during a marriage, we find that this body of law is sufficiently analogous to the issue at hand to inform our decision.

Dowling did not argue that Wilma took any action, such as commingling or retitling, which would defeat the separate status of her remainder interest in the Peruvian properties. In fact, Dowling emphatically argued that Wilma did nothing with regard to these properties. On this basis we conclude that Wilma's interest in the Peruvian properties was maintained as separate and ... **402 properly excluded... from the augmented estate.

Wilma owned two life insurance policies that were not listed in the Agreement. Three years before her death, Wilma established an irrevocable life insurance trust, transferred the policies to the trust, and named her daughter as beneficiary of the trust. The policies had no investment or "cash" value on the date of transfer.[5]

> [5] The Midland National Life Insurance policy was a "graded" whole life policy with no cash value until Wilma reached 80 years of age. The Garden State Life Insurance policy was a term life policy with no cash value.

A life insurance policy subject to the decedent's control on the date of an irrevocable transfer is treated as "property" within the augmented estate statute. Property transferred to a third party donee within five years prior to death [now two years] will be included in the augmented estate to the extent that the transferred value exceeds $10,000 in the calendar year of transfer [now $14,000]. The party seeking inclusion of property in the augmented estate... has the burden of proof. Chappell v. Perkins, 266 Va. 413, 418, 587 S.E.2d 584, 587 (2003). Accordingly, Dowling has the burden to show that the value of the *521 life insurance policies exceeded $10,000 in the calendar year they were transferred. Valuation of a life insurance policy is governed by Code § 64.1–16.1(C)(2), which states that

> [t]he value of an insurance policy that is irrevocably transferred during the lifetime of a decedent is the cost of a comparable policy on the date of transfer or, if such a policy is not readily available, the policy's interpolated terminal reserve.

... Dowling maintains that evidence of a "comparable policy" is not available for the date of transfer, and there was no interpolated terminal reserve. Dowling urges the Court to recognize the "full proceeds of the existing policies" as the appropriate measure of value. Were we to adopt Dowling's position, it would effectively rewrite the plain language of Code § 64.1–16.1(C). "... [I]t is not the province of the judiciary to add words to the statute or alter its plain meaning." Jackson v. Fidelity & Deposit Co., 269 Va. 303, 313, 608 S.E.2d 901, 906 (2005). Moreover, we think it is self evident that the value of a term life insurance policy upon transfer before death of the named insured is not the full death benefit.

Having rejected Dowling's position that the value of the policies is the face value of the death benefit, the only remaining evidence in the record is that offered by Rowan which is the annual premiums in the year of transfer, a sum far less than $10,000. Consequently, Dowling has failed to prove the $10,000 threshold to trigger the "pull back rule" in the statute. We hold that upon this record the life insurance policies were properly excluded from the augmented estate.

B. Attorney's fees

... Dowling argues that the trial court erred in denying his claim for attorney's fees related to the elective share litigation. We adhere to the "American rule" which embodies the principle that each litigant must pay his own attorney's fees in the absence of a statute or contractual provision that would shift the burden *522 of payment to the unsuccessful party. In Virginia, there is no statutory basis for an award of attorney's fees to the surviving spouse in elective share litigation. ... Code § 26–30... states that the commissioner **403 "shall allow the fiduciary any reasonable expenses incurred by him as such." In construing this statute, we have held that reasonable expenses can be paid out of the estate when the fiduciary, in execution of his duties, proceeds in good faith and the aid of counsel is reasonably necessary for performance of the fiduciary's duties. Clare v. Grasty, 213 Va. 165, 170, 191 S.E.2d 184, 188 (1972) (partially denying appellant's claims to attorney's fees for those portions of his litigation that were detrimental to the estate). ... In Clare, we specified that attorney's fees will not be awarded to an executor whose litigation seeks to frustrate the testator's expressed wishes. 213 Va. at 171, 191 S.E.2d at 188–89. In this case, Dowling's personal interests are adverse to those of the estate, to which, as a fiduciary, he owes a duty of utmost fidelity. See Pritchett v. First Nat'l Bank of Danville, 195 Va. 406, 412, 78 S.E.2d 650, 653 (1953) (fiduciaries have the duty to exercise "the highest fidelity" and "utmost good faith" in how they deal with an estate).

Our opinion in O'Brien v. O'Brien, 259 Va. 552, 526 S.E.2d 1 (2000) is particularly instructive on this point. There, two brothers who were co-executors of their deceased mother's estate sued the third brother, in his individual capacity and as co-executor, to collect a debt to the estate. O'Brien, 259 Va. at 554, 526 S.E.2d at 2. We approved the trial court's ruling which granted attorney's fees to the co-executors who sued on behalf of the estate to recover the debt and denied attorney's fees for the defendant brother. Id. at 557–58, 526 S.E.2d at 4. We reasoned that the defendant's attorney's fees "were incurred for his personal benefit and not to benefit the estate or to aid him in his duties as executor." Id. The critical distinction in O'Brien among the brothers was based upon function, not form, with regard to the interests of the estate. *523 Such is the case here. Dowling's attempt to characterize his elective share litigation as "necessary" to settle the estate confuses his function as Executor with his personal interests. The only issues that need settling are those created by Dowling. Certainly he has a right to pursue his elective share litigation but he is not entitled to be compensated from the estate for doing so. ...

Supreme Court of Virginia.
Flanary v. Milton
263 Va. 20, 556 S.E.2d 767 (2002)

Opinion by Justice ELIZABETH B. LACY.

768 ... Linda and Ross E. Flanary married on February 5, 1982 and separated on July 7, 1995. Mrs. Flanary filed for divorce on the grounds of desertion and/or cruelty and Mr. Flanary filed a cross-bill seeking a divorce based upon desertion. On April 17, 1997, during Mrs. Flanary's deposition taken in conjunction with the divorce proceedings, an oral agreement between the parties was recited into the record by ***22 the parties' attorneys. The agreement provided that Mrs. Flanary, in exchange for a lump sum payment of $45,000, would release "any interest in any assets [ ] in [Mr. Flanary's] possession and/or name and in further release of any interest or any rights she has to any additional or future spousal support." Mrs. Flanary agreed to this arrangement and agreed that it would serve as "a full and final settlement of all rights accrued by virtue of this marriage." Mr. Flanary died the day after the deposition. The divorce proceeding was subsequently dismissed.

Mrs. Flanary filed a petition of surviving spouse... for determination of the appropriate family allowance, exempt property, and an elective share of the augmented estate. Mr. Doss Jackson Milton, Jr., as executor of Mr. Flanary's estate (the Executor), filed a responsive pleading asserting that Mrs. Flanary was estopped from pursuing these claims because she contracted away all her marital interests in Mr. Flanary's estate in the oral agreement made during her deposition. ...

The General Assembly has identified agreements between spouses involving rights and obligations arising from the marital relationship as a unique category of agreements subject to specific requirements. Code § 20–155 provides that:

> Married persons may enter into agreements with each other for the purpose of settling the rights and obligations of either or both of them, to the same extent, with the same effect, and subject to the same conditions, as provided in §§ 20–147 through 20–154 for agreements between prospective spouses, except that such marital agreements shall become effective immediately upon their execution. However, a reconciliation of the parties after the signing of a separation or property settlement agreement shall abrogate such agreement unless otherwise expressly set forth in the agreement.*23

Code § 20–150 identifies the various subjects that such agreements may properly address, including the parties' rights regarding spousal support and disposition of property upon separation or divorce. The agreement at issue purported to settle, among other things, spousal support and property rights. However, the agreement was not in writing, nor was it signed by the parties as required by Code § 20–149. ...

Richardson v. Richardson, 10 Va.App. 391, 398; 392 S.E.2d 688, 691 (1990)... held that "compromises and settlement agreements to pending litigation which incidentally include issues of property and spousal support" are not within the purview of Code § 20–155 and, thus, do not need to comply with the requirement that such agreements be in writing. ...

Code § 20–155 by its terms applies to agreements between spouses **769 affecting the "rights and obligations" arising from the marital relationship. While agreements made in contemplation of settling litigation can be enforced even though not reduced to writing, see, e.g., Snyder–Falkinham v. Stockburger, 249 Va. 376, 457 S.E.2d 36 (1995), nothing in the language of Code § 20–155 exempts from its application a property or spousal support agreement made in contemplation of resolving a pending divorce action. Nor can such an exemption be read into the statute. ...

Additionally, collateral statutes within the Premarital Agreement Act clearly contemplate marital agreements entered into for the purpose of resolving a pending divorce action. The language of Code § 20–150(3) specifically includes agreements made regarding the disposition of property upon "marital dissolution" within its provisions. Furthermore, the 1998 amendment to Code § 20–155 anticipates agreements made during proceedings for dissolution of a marriage, by providing that a signed separation or property settlement agreement is abrogated if the parties reconcile unless otherwise specifically provided in the agreement. ... *24

We hold that Mrs. Flanary's oral agreement made in conjunction with the divorce proceedings was subject to the provisions of Code § 20–155. The agreement was not in writing and not signed by the parties, as required by statute. Therefore,... we will... remand the case for further proceedings.

In Higham v. Williams, 2008 WL 2076188 (2008), the Circuit Court for Fairfax County rejected the argument of a decedent's children that their surviving step-father had waived his right to an elective share, an argument based on evidence of how the mother and step-father had lived their lives and these confirming statements in their mother's will: "Prior to our marriage, my husband and I each owned separate property and, following the marriage, we have continued to have separate property. Each of us have controlled our separate property during the marriage except when we have placed certain property in joint tenancy. We have maintained our separate property for the reason that in the event of our death that each of us reserved the right to direct the distribution of our property free and clear of any claim of the surviving spouse except for the property held in joint tenancy." The court simply pointed to the statutory requirement that an agreement waiving spousal rights must be in writing.

What happens to any claim a surviving spouse has under intestacy law or as a will beneficiary, if he or she claims the elective share and then is found to have waived it? Is the other benefit then lost? In Perez v. Draskins, 89 Va. Cir. 298 (2014), the Circuit Court for Roanoke County answered that question in the negative when a decedent's offspring presented it, following a ruling that the decedent's surviving spouse had waived the elective share in a pre-marital agreement. The court reasoned that the surviving spouse's election of the forced share was not binding on her if she lacked "full knowledge of ... her rights," and that this surviving spouse did lack such full knowledge, because she "claimed her elective share under the mistaken belief that the Agreement with Testator was void and unconscionable." As an alternative theory, the court mused: "In effect, Ms.

Draskinis did not make an election as her claim was a nullity." In First Nat. Exch. Bank of Roanoke v. Hughson, 194 Va. 736, 746, 74 S.E.2d 797, 804 (1953), the Supreme Court had stated that "election to take under the statute forfeits all rights enjoyed and provisions made for him or her in the will." The Circuit Court paraphrased this to say that "a surviving spouse may not take both under the elective share statute and under the will," which is probably in fact what the Supreme Court meant in *Hughson*; there is little reason to discourage surviving spouses from invoking the elective share rule by making it perilous for them to do so.

The last form of waiver the statute contemplates is the implicit one of "abandonment," a vague concept that has produced disputes in many family law contexts.

Supreme Court of Virginia.
Purse v. Patterson
275 Va. 190, 654 S.E.2d 885 (2008)

OPINION BY Senior Justice ELIZABETH B. LACY.

**886 ... *193 ... Dorothy and Marrill were married in July 1988. Dorothy had many health problems throughout the marriage and, while the couple lived together, friends and neighbors often took Dorothy to doctors' appointments, cleaned the home, and cooked meals. Dorothy's daughter, Vanessa C. Patterson, testified that Marrill did not visit Dorothy in the hospital during her illnesses and did not take care of her when she returned home.

Marrill and Dorothy had a tumultuous marriage. Dorothy complained to her daughter and friends of Marrill's treatment of her. In April 1997, Dorothy obtained a protective order against Marrill based on his physical abuse of her, and she renewed the order a few months later. The protective order expired in June 1998, and the parties resumed cohabitation. In October of 1998, Dorothy sought another protective order, claiming she was under severe stress because Marrill's girlfriend was harassing her, Marrill was drinking and staying out late every night, and she was afraid that she might have a stroke. The court denied the protective order.

In June 2000, Dorothy and Marrill agreed that Dorothy would leave the marital residence. After the separation, in August 2000, Dorothy sought a third protective order, claiming Marrill had threatened to kill her; the petition was denied. Dorothy filed a fourth petition for a protective order in June 2002, claiming among other things that Marrill hurt her arm and threatened her; however, she withdrew this petition.

Dorothy filed for a divorce in January 2003, identifying the grounds for the divorce as living separate and apart for more than one year. The divorce decree was never issued, and the parties remained legally married at the time of Dorothy's death.

Dorothy brought into the marriage rental properties she owned. Marrill, on the other hand, was retired during most of the marriage. Marrill did not participate in the management of the rental properties, and he did not provide any financial support to Dorothy after the separation. During her last illness, Dorothy lived with her daughter in

New Jersey. Marrill did not know Dorothy was in New Jersey, nor did he visit, call, or otherwise communicate with her. *194 ...

Marrill first asserts that... post-separation conduct is not relevant to whether one spouse abandoned the other. We disagree. ... The clear language of this Code section requires a court to determine whether the willful desertion or abandonment continued "until the death of the spouse" and that determination is not limited to consideration of actions occurring prior to a separation, should one have occurred. "In construing a statute, we must apply its plain meaning, and 'we are not free to add [to] language, nor to ignore language, contained in statutes.'" **887 ...

Whether Marrill abandoned Dorothy is a mixed question of law and fact. ...The term "abandonment" is not defined in the statutes governing elective share claims. We agree with the parties that principles *195 developed in domestic relations law relating to abandonment are helpful in determining the issue of abandonment under Code § 64.1–16.3 [now § 64.2–308.14].

In the domestic relations context, "abandonment" is generally used synonymously with "desertion." This Court has defined desertion as "a breach of matrimonial duty—an actual breaking off of the matrimonial cohabitation coupled with an intent to desert in the mind of the deserting party." Petachenko v. Petachenko, 232 Va. 296, 298–99, 350 S.E.2d 600, 602 (1986). Domestic relations cases have considered "matrimonial duty" to include cooking, cleaning, support, and contributing to the well-being of the family. See Goodwyn v. Goodwyn, 222 Va. 53, 54–55, 278 S.E.2d 813–14 (1981); Fussell v. Fussell, 182 Va. 720, 722, 30 S.E.2d 555, 556 (1944). Mindful of these domestic relations cases, in resolving the issue in this case we will use the word "abandonment" to mean a termination of the normal indicia of a marital relationship combined with an intent to abandon the marital relationship.

While the term "abandonment" is similarly defined for purposes of domestic relations and elective share matters, there are significant differences in the analysis of the evidence when resolving the issue in the domestic relations and elective share contexts. For example, as we have noted, the relevant time period for determining abandonment for purposes of Code § 64.1–16.3 extends to the time of the deceased spouse's death and is not limited to the moment of separation, or the filing of a petition for divorce, as it is when abandonment is the ground upon which a divorce is sought. Compare Sprott v. Sprott, 233 Va. 238, 242, 355 S.E.2d 881, 883 (1987) (finding desertion by wife based on her actions leading to her departure from the marital home), Breschel v. Breschel, 221 Va. 208, 212, 269 S.E.2d 363, 366 (1980) (finding no desertion because wife was legally justified in leaving based on facts leading up to her departure), and Hudgins v. Hudgins, 181 Va. 81, 87, 23 S.E.2d 774, 777 (1943) ("[T]he absenting of one spouse from the other after the institution and during the pendency of a suit for divorce ... is not desertion in law."), with Code § 64.1–16.3. A second distinction is the effect of the parties' agreement to separate or to seek a divorce. In an elective share analysis, an agreed separation or petition for divorce is relevant evidence of the termination of cohabitation, but is not evidence which defeats a finding of willful abandonment. In contrast, such an agreed separation or divorce petition may preclude a claim *196 of abandonment in a divorce action because a finding of abandonment in that context is based on fault which is inconsistent with parties agreeing to terminate cohabitation or to seek a divorce. With these distinctions in mind, we now turn to the evidence in this case. ...

The relevant evidence is Marrill's conduct and his intent. Here, the record shows that both before and after Dorothy and Marrill agreed to separate, Marrill's conduct showed a lack of support for Dorothy and the marital relationship. While living together or apart, **888 Marrill provided Dorothy with little or no support or care during her illnesses and recoveries. Financially, Dorothy brought her rental properties into the marriage and managed the properties alone while living with Marrill. Marrill did not contribute to Dorothy's support in this regard.

After the separation, Marrill apparently did not communicate with Dorothy in any meaningful way because he did not even know she was living in New Jersey and did not acknowledge her final illness in any way. He did not support Dorothy financially, emotionally, or physically. Although he testified that he did not want the marriage to end, the trier of fact was not required to believe this testimony; indeed, the trial court found Marrill's testimony incredible. Nothing in the record showed Marrill tried or intended to reconcile with Dorothy. At the time of Dorothy's death, Marrill had ceased to perform any marital duties. Therefore, we conclude that the evidence is sufficient to support the trial court's holding that Marrill abandoned Dorothy prior to and continuing until the time of her death under Code § 64.1–16.3.

Accordingly, we will affirm the judgment of the trial court that Marrill was not eligible for an elective share of Dorothy's augmented estate.

In an earlier circuit court decision, Royer v. Royer, 65 Va. Cir. 476 (2004), the Circuit Court for the City of Richmond reached the obvious conclusion that a wife had not abandoned her husband, for purposes of waiving the elective share, by moving out of the marital home to an apartment after the husband had several times ordered her to leave.

Chapter Five
Trusts

A trust is a legal device whereby an individual or entity, a trustee, holds legal title to certain property and manages it for the benefit of other persons, called beneficiaries, or to serve the charitable or other aims of the person or organization that created the trust. A trustee as such has no equitable or "beneficial interest" in the trust property (though someone can be both the trustee and a beneficiary of a trust). Beneficiaries as such do not have legal title to or control over trust property, but they possess a beneficial or equitable interest in the property. This division of legal title and beneficial interest enables a trust creator – called a "settlor" or "grantor" -- to use property to benefit persons without handing over control or legal ownership of the entire property to them. The settlor might belive the persons benefited incapable of managing the property, or the settlor might want the property used for the benefit of particular persons only to the extent those persons actually need it (e.g., a surviving spouse whose future needs might be uncertain), and otherwise to go to others (e.g., the settlors' descendants). A settlor could use a trust instead for long-term support of a public-welfare cause, setting aside a large amount of wealth for that purpose now but only gradually doling out smaller amounts to persons and organization who serve that cause, while preserving a corpus so the fund endures.

The trustee possesses extensive power in relation to trust property; except to the extent curtailed by the settlor, the power approaches that of an outright owner of property. Yet a trustee is also subject to several duties, which include managing the property prudently, making distributions to beneficiaries in accordance with the settlor's instructions, and periodically giving an accounting of actions taken and status of the trust assets.

The most common forms of trust, called "settlor trusts," are created by an individual property owner (the settlor) during the owner's life (an "inter vivos trust") or by Last Will and Testament (a "testamentary trust"). These break down further into private trusts, charitable trusts, and honorary trusts. But there are also trusts -- constructive trusts and resulting trusts – that arise by court order or by automatic operation of law.

In addition to allowing for division of control and beneficial ownership, inter vivos trusts are an effective means of transferring property at death outside of probate. A settlor can put property into a trust for his or her own benefit during life, with the remainder going immediately at death to "remainder persons." As we learned in Chapter One, transfers outside of probate deliver wealth to surviving family members or others more quickly, more privately, and with fewer deductions for courts costs and fiduciary commissions. Testamentary trusts do not serve this purpose; any property directed by will into a trust passes through probate.

The main categories of legal rules pertaining to trusts are:

    I.   Requirements for creating a trust

    II.   Trust contests

    III.   Modification and termination of trusts

    IV.   Trusts and creditors

    V.   Trustee duties

Virginia adopted the Uniform Trust Code in 2005, with an effective date of July 2006, thereby effecting a wholesale reformation of the law of trusts in this state. Pre-2006 court precedents remain relevant to a limited degree – namely, as to any common law rules that survive or any precedents applying prior statutes with terms sufficiently similar to the UTC. A decade is not a very long time for courts to address any uncertainties or ambiguities in the law. So this chapter will present a lot of Code and less judicial analysis than one might wish. That is the predicament of an estate planning attorney in Virginia today. Fortunately, the UTC is a relatively well-drafted piece of legislation.

The UTC's scope of application in Virginia is fairly extensive, encompassing express inter vivos trusts, most testamentary trusts, charitable trusts, honorary trusts, and "trusts created pursuant to a statute, judgment, or decree that requires the trust to be administered in the manner of an express trust." Principal among the trusts not within the scope of the UTC Article of the Virginia Code are trusts used for business operations, such as pension funds and trusts used for paying salaries and other employment benefits. Va. Code § 64.2-700.

Note, however, that the state where a trust instrument is executed or where the settlor lives is not necessarily the state whose laws govern the trust. The UTC authorized settlors, to a substantial degree though not completely, to choose the state whose laws will govern the trust and also to waive or replace many of its own provisions.

Title 64.2. Wills, Trusts, and Fiduciaries
Subtitle III. Trusts
Chapter 7. Uniform Trust Code
Article 1. General Provisions and Definitions

§ 64.2-705. Governing law

The meaning and effect of the terms of a trust are determined by:

1. The law of the jurisdiction designated in the terms unless the designation of that jurisdiction's law is contrary to a strong public policy of the jurisdiction having the most significant relationship to the matter at issue; or

2. In the absence of a controlling designation in the terms of the trust, the law of the jurisdiction having the most significant relationship to the matter at issue.

§ 64.2-703. Default and mandatory rules

A. Except as otherwise provided in the terms of the trust, this chapter governs the duties and powers of a trustee, relations among trustees, and the rights and interests of a beneficiary.

B. The terms of a trust prevail over any provision of this chapter except:

1. The requirements for creating a trust;
2. The duty of a trustee to act in good faith and in accordance with the terms and purposes of the trust and the interests of the beneficiaries;
3. The requirement that a trust and its terms be for the benefit of its beneficiaries, and that the trust have a purpose that is lawful, not contrary to public policy, and possible to achieve;
4. The power of the court to modify or terminate a trust under §§ 64.2-728 through 64.2-734;
5. The effect of a spendthrift provision and the rights of certain creditors and assignees to reach a trust as provided in Article 5 (§ 64.2-742 et seq.);
6. The power of the court under § 64.2-755 to require, dispense with, or modify or terminate a bond;
7. The power of the court under subsection B of § 64.2-761 to adjust a trustee's compensation specified in the terms of the trust that is unreasonably low or high;
8. The effect of an exculpatory term under § 64.2-799;
9. The rights under §§ 64.2-801 through 64.2-804 of a person other than a trustee or beneficiary;
10. Periods of limitation for commencing a judicial proceeding; and
11. The power of the court to take such action and exercise such jurisdiction as may be necessary in the interests of justice.

I.   Requirements for Creating a Trust

The basic rule for a valid settlor trust to arise requires that a settlor deliver property to a trustee for the benefit of ascertainable beneficiaries or for a charitable cause or legally-recognized personal aim, with the intent to create a trust for a lawful purpose not contrary to public policy.

Article 4. Creation, Validity, Modification, and Termination of Trust

§ 64.2–719. Methods of creating trust

A. A trust may be created by:

1. Transfer of property to another person as trustee during the settlor's lifetime by the settlor or by the settlor's agent... under a power of attorney that expressly authorizes the agent to create a trust on the settlor's behalf; or by will or other disposition taking effect upon the settlor's death;

2. Declaration by the owner of property that the owner holds identifiable property as trustee;

3. Exercise of a power of appointment in favor of a trustee; or

4. A conservator acting in accordance with § 64.2–2023.

B. A circuit court, upon petition from an interested party, may create and establish a trust with such trustee and such terms as the court determines. ...

§ 64.2-720. Requirements for creation

A. A trust is created only if:

1. The settlor has capacity to create a trust; or when the trust is created by the settlor's agent under a power of attorney, which expressly authorizes the agent to create a trust on the settlor's behalf;

2. The settlor or his agent indicates an intention to create the trust;

3. The trust has a definite beneficiary or is:

   a. A charitable trust;

   b. A trust for the care of an animal, as provided in § 64.2-726; or

   c. A trust for a noncharitable purpose, as provided in § 64.2-727;

4. The trustee has duties to perform; and

5. The same person is not the sole trustee and sole beneficiary.

B. A beneficiary is definite if the beneficiary can be ascertained now or in the future, subject to any applicable rule against perpetuities.

C. A power in a trustee to select a beneficiary from an indefinite class is valid. If the power is not exercised within a reasonable time, the power fails and the property subject to the power passes to the persons who would have taken the property had the power not been conferred.

***

In stark contrast to wills, trusts can be created orally.

§ 64.2-725. Evidence of oral trust

Except as required by a statute other than this chapter, a trust need not be evidenced by a trust instrument, but the creation of an oral trust and its terms may be established only by clear and convincing evidence.

***

Our principal focus will be on private trusts, the type of trusts estate planning attorneys routinely create for clients. Let us first, then, glance at the few UTC provisions addressed specifically to the other types of settlor trusts authorized by § 64.2-720(A)(3) above.

§ 64.2-723. Charitable purposes; enforcement

A. A charitable trust may be created for the relief of poverty, the advancement of education or religion, the promotion of health, governmental or municipal purposes, or other purposes the achievement of which is beneficial to the community.

B. If the terms of a charitable trust do not indicate a particular charitable purpose or beneficiary, the court may select one or more charitable purposes or beneficiaries. The selection shall be consistent with the settlor's intention to the extent it can be ascertained.

C. The settlor of a charitable trust, among others, may maintain a proceeding to enforce the trust.

***

Paragraph B suggests that a property owner can create a charitable trust by conveying property during life or by will and stating simply "use this for charity" or language to that effect, without identifying any particular sort of charitable purpose. If the settlor cannot be consulted when someone seeks to effectuate the trust, because deceased or incapacitated, a court can choose a purpose after taking evidence about the sorts of public-minded values the settlor held – for example, what charitable works the settlor had performed or to which charitable organizations the settlor had contributed or belonged.

Paragraph C states that a trust settlor has standing to seek enforcement of trust terms, but what if the settlor is deceased or incapacitated The Virginia Code also empowers the state's Attorney General to oversee administration of charitable trusts, because of the interest the state has in use of wealth for public purposes. See, e.g., § 64.2-736 and § 64.2-1104 (conferring on the Attorney General a role in modification of trust terms) and § 64.2-757 (conferring on the Attorney General a role in replacement of a trustee).

Trusts that are neither for the benefit of ascertainable beneficiaries nor charitable may a personal aim of the settlor, such as care of a pet after the settlor death or incapacitation.

The problem with such trusts is not a policy aversion to letting people use their wealth after death to serve such purposes but rather the difficulty of enforcing the settlor's intentions once the settlor is deceased or incapacitiated. With a private trust, the beneficiaries can be expected to oversee trustee conduct and ensure compliance with terms benefiting them. If a trust has no ascertainable human beneficiaries, there might be no human with motivation to watch over the trustee's shoulder and standing to complain about non-compliance. The statutory provisions below aim to address this difficulty, but limit the potential duration of such trusts in recognition of the enforcement cost they entail.

§ 64.2-726. Trust for care of animal

A. A trust may be created to provide for the care of an animal alive during the settlor's lifetime. The trust terminates upon the death of the animal or, if the trust was created to provide for the care of more than one animal alive during the settlor's lifetime, upon the death of the last surviving animal. Funds from the trust may be applied to any outstanding expenses of the trust and for burial or other postdeath expenditures for animal beneficiaries as provided for in the instrument creating the trust. ...

B. ... Extrinsic evidence is admissible in determining the transferor's intent.

C. A trust authorized by this section may be enforced by a person appointed in the terms of the trust or, if no person is so appointed, by a person appointed by the court. A person having an interest in the welfare of the animal may request the court to appoint a person to enforce the trust or to remove a person appointed. The appointed person shall have the rights of a trust beneficiary for the purpose of enforcing the trust, including receiving accountings, notices, and other information from the trustee and providing consents. Reasonable compensation for a person appointed by the court may be paid from the assets of the trust.

D. Except as ordered by a court or required by the trust instrument, no filing, report, registration, periodic accounting, separate maintenance of funds, appointment, or surety bond shall be required by reason of the existence of the fiduciary relationship of the trustee.

E. Property of a trust authorized by this section may be applied only to its intended use, except to the extent the court determines that the value of the trust property exceeds the amount required for the intended use. Except as otherwise provided in the terms of the trust, property not required for the intended use shall be distributed to the settlor, if then living. If the settlor is deceased, such property shall be distributed pursuant to the residuary clause of the settlor's will if the trust for the animal was created in a preresiduary clause in the will or pursuant to the residuary provisions of the inter vivos trust if the trust for the animal was created in a preresiduary clause in the trust instrument; otherwise, such property shall be distributed to the settlor's successors in interest.

§ 64.2-727. Noncharitable trust without ascertainable beneficiary

Except as otherwise provided in § 64.2-726 or by another statute…:

1. A trust may be created for a noncharitable purpose without a definite or definitely ascertainable beneficiary or for a noncharitable but otherwise valid purpose to be selected by the trustee. The trust may not be enforced for more than 21 years.

2. A trust authorized by this section may be enforced by a person appointed in the terms of the trust or, if no person is so appointed, by a person appointed by the court.

3. Property of a trust authorized by this section may be applied only to its intended use, except to the extent the court determines that the value of the trust property exceeds the amount required for the intended use. Except as otherwise provided in the terms of the trust, property not required for the intended use shall be distributed to the settlor, if then living, otherwise to the settlor's successors in interest.

***

Now we concentrate our focus on the details of private trust creation. From § 64.2–725 above, we see that a written instrument is not necessary to create any trust; a trust can arise if there is clear and convincing evidence of an oral declaration of trust. Contrast this with the law of wills, in which a written instrument is essential, and which allows evidence of a testator's declarations of intent only in limited circumstances to facilitate interpretation of ambiguous terms or to infer the testator's intentions underlying certain actions (e.g., physical revocation of a will).

From §§ 64.2–719 and 64.2–720, we can extract these six elements of a private settlor trust:

(A)   Competent settlor

(B)   Property transferred

(C)   One or more trustees

(D)   Ascertainable beneficiaries

(E)   Intent to create a trust/Duties owed to beneficiaries

(F)   Legitimate trust purpose.

A.   Competent settlor

§ 64.2-701 defines "Settlor" as "a person, including a testator, who creates, or contributes property to, a trust," and goes on to state that a trust can have more than one settlor, in which case "each person is a settlor of the portion of the trust property attributable to that person's contribution except to the extent another person has the power to revoke or withdraw that portion."

A private trust can arise by testamentary disposition – that is, a will provision constituting a specific, general, or residuary bequest or devise to someone as trustee for the benefit of others. In that case, the statutory provision and case law presented in Chapter Three concerning the capacity required to execute a will apply to creation of the trust.

With respect to revocable inter vivos trusts (trusts a settlor creates during life while retaining the power to revoke it), the Virginia Code simply incorporates wills law on the issue.

Article 6. Revocable Trusts

§ 64.2-750. Capacity of settlor of revocable trust

The capacity required to create, amend, revoke, or add property to a revocable trust, or to direct the actions of the trustee of a revocable trust, is the same as that required to make a will.

***

Oddly, the Virginia Code contains no provision stating a capacity requirement for creating an irrevocable trust. There is reason to be more cautious in enforcing an irrevocable inter vivos trust against a settlor than there is in giving effect to a revocable trust or Last Will and Testament that might not reflect a decedent's genuine intentions. The settlor of an inter vivos trust might still be alive and in need of the wealth that is in the trust, whereas a deceased testator cannot suffer from thwarting his or her wishes-while-alive for disposition of property, and an irrevocability clause naturally makes it more difficult to undo execution of an inter vivos trust instrument and regain control of the property.

B. Property transferred

Historically a trust could come into existence legally only when the settlor transferred some standard form of property (money, stocks, real estate, etc.) to a trustee. Eventually this was expanded to include legal rights with potential value, such as contract or intellectual property rights. The Virginia Code in § 64.2-701 now provides a capacious definition of property as "anything that may be the subject of ownership, whether real or personal, legal or equitable, or any interest therein." But still there had to be something in the trust as to which the trustee could exercise duties, even if only a duty to enforce rights if and when they come to have value. This cut off for some people certain possible ways of transferring property into a trust whose terms are private – for example, money in a bank account that the owner wants to go into trust only after he or she becomes incompetent or dies. Once incompetent, it might be impossible to create a trust, and creating a trust by will makes it public.

So today Virginia law authorizes "unfunded trusts," which really means a trust that possesses only one or more contractual rights to transfer of wealth at the time of the settlor's death. We saw in Chapter Three that the Uniform Testamentary Addtions to Trusts Act, Va. Code § 64.2-427, allows for a will to pour probate property into an "unfunded life insurance trust." Such a trust can serve as a bucket for collection of assets from various sources, so that all serve the same purpose, under single management, subject to the same directions by the settlor. Of course, one could simply put $100 into a trust at its inception, thus satisfying any requirement of a trust having definite property, but then trustee duties of management, including earmarking of trust property, would kick in, and this is inefficient with a trust fund of trivial value. Thus, today an inter vivos trust can exixt even though there is no property for the trustee to manage and even though the trustee's only duty, practically speaking, is to accept receipt of material assets when transfer ultimately occurs.

C.   One or more trustees

Typically a settlor names a trustee. But occasionally a settlor expresses a simple desire that property be held in trust for the benefit of another, without specifying who is to hold the property in trust, and more commonly persons whom the settlor named as trustee decline the officr or later drop out of the role for one reason or another. It is not essential there be a willing trustee named at the outset, and a trust does not terminate simply because a trustee resigns or dies. A court can always appoint a trustee when needed.

§ 64.2-758. Resignation of trustee

A. A trustee may resign:

    1. Upon at least 30 days' notice to the settlor, if living, to all cotrustees, and to the qualified beneficiaries except those qualified beneficiaries under a revocable trust that the settlor has the capacity to revoke; or

    2. With the approval of the court.

B. In approving a resignation, the court may issue orders and impose conditions reasonably necessary for the protection of the trust property.

C. Any liability of a resigning trustee or of any sureties on the trustee's bond for acts or omissions of the trustee is not discharged or affected by the trustee's resignation.

§ 64.2-757. Vacancy in trusteeship; appointment of successor

A. A vacancy in a trusteeship occurs if:

    1. A person designated as trustee rejects the trusteeship;

    2. A person designated as trustee cannot be identified or does not exist;

    3. A trustee resigns;

    4. A trustee is disqualified or removed;

5. A trustee dies; or

6. An individual serving as trustee is adjudicated an incapacitated person.

B. If one or more cotrustees remain in office, a vacancy in a trusteeship need not be filled. A vacancy in a trusteeship shall be filled if the trust has no remaining trustee.

C. A vacancy in a trusteeship of a noncharitable trust that is required to be filled shall be filled in the following order of priority:

1. By a person designated pursuant to the terms of the trust to act as successor trustee;

2. By a person appointed by unanimous agreement of the qualified beneficiaries; or

3. By a person appointed by the court pursuant to §§ 64.2-1405 and 64.2-1406, or pursuant to § 64.2-712.

D. A vacancy in a trusteeship of a charitable trust that is required to be filled shall be filled in the following order of priority:

1. By a person designated pursuant to the terms of the trust to act as successor trustee;

2. By a person selected by the charitable organizations expressly designated to receive distributions under the terms of the trust, subject, however, to the concurrence of the Attorney General in any case in which he has previously requested of an organization so designated that he be consulted regarding the selection of successor; or

3. By a person appointed by the court pursuant to §§ 64.2-1405 and 64.2-1406, or pursuant to § 64.2-712.

E. Whether or not a vacancy in a trusteeship exists or is required to be filled, the court may appoint an additional trustee or special fiduciary whenever the court considers the appointment necessary for the administration of the trust.

F. A successor or surviving trustee shall succeed to all the rights, powers, and privileges, and shall be subject to all the duties, liabilities, and responsibilities imposed upon the original trustee without regard to the nature of discretionary powers conferred by the instrument, unless the trust instrument expressly provides to the contrary, or unless an order appointing the successor trustee provides otherwise.

***

Any competent adult individual can serve as trustee; one need not have special financial expertise. Often settlors name an institutional trustee, such as a bank that regularly engages in trust business. In a recent unpublished opinion, the Supreme Court ruled that a charitable corporation can be a trustee governed by the Uniform Trust Code just as much as can a for-profit corporation or an individual. Com. ex rel. Bowyer v. Sweet Briar Institute (2015).

Neither an individual nor an institution can be required to accept the trustee role. But once they do accept, many duties, discussed in Part V below, kick in. Sometimes it is unclear whether a named trustee did in fact accept the role.

Article 7. Office of Trustee

§ 64.2-754. Accepting or declining trusteeship

A. Except as otherwise provided in subsection C, a person designated as trustee accepts the trusteeship:

1. By substantially complying with a method of acceptance provided in the terms of the trust; or

2. If the terms of the trust do not provide a method or the method provided in the terms is not expressly made exclusive, by accepting delivery of the trust property, exercising powers or performing duties as trustee, or otherwise indicating acceptance of the trusteeship.

B. A person designated as trustee who has not yet accepted the trusteeship may reject the trusteeship. A designated trustee who does not accept the trusteeship within a reasonable time after knowing of the designation is deemed to have rejected the trusteeship.

C. A person designated as trustee, without accepting the trusteeship, may:

1. Act to preserve the trust property if, within a reasonable time after acting, the person sends a rejection of the trusteeship to the settlor or, if the settlor is dead or lacks capacity, to a qualified beneficiary; and

2. Inspect or investigate trust property to determine potential liability under environmental or other law or for any other purpose.

***

Circuit Court of Virginia, City of Norfolk.
Burton v. Dolph
89 Va. Cir. 101 (2014)

On May 17, 2002, the Plaintiff's father—Lester Hudgins—created three irrevocable trusts, the first of which was never funded. The second trust was funded by a Lincoln Financial term life insurance policy with a face value of $500,000. The third trust was also funded by a Lincoln Financial term life insurance policy with a face value of $650,000.1 Ann Archer was named the original trustee of the Irrevocable Trusts, with Defendant Old Point Trust named as the successor trustee. The Irrevocable Trusts each had multiple named beneficiaries. Lester Hudgins named Marsha Hudgins (his wife), Burton, and Branch Hudgins beneficiaries of Trust # 2.2 He named Burton and Branch Hudgins beneficiaries of Trust # 3.

Original trustee Ann Archer passed away on November 28, 2009. The Complaint alleges that Old Point Trust accepted trusteeship of the Irrevocable Trusts no later than December 21, 2009. In support of this allegation, Burton relies upon two Notices of

Crummey Withdrawal Rights... Specifically, Burton claims that Defendant Cyrus Dolph, in his capacity as a director of Old Point Trust, drafted these notices and sent them to the beneficiaries of the Irrevocable Trusts on behalf of Old Point Trust.

In 2010, the Lincoln Financial life insurance policies lapsed due to non-payment of premiums. Burton contends that when these policies lapsed, Old Point Trust was the trustee of, and Dolph was the attorney for, the Irrevocable Trusts. In support of her claims, Burton further asserts the following in her Complaint:

> • As trustee, Old Point Trust was empowered to borrow against the face value of the life insurance policies to pay the policy premiums, but failed to do so.

> • Old Point Trust, Dolph, and Lester Hudgins failed to provide notice to Burton, as a beneficiary of the Irrevocable Trusts, that the life insurance policies were on the brink of lapsing and that no further payments would be made. As a result, she was unable to take action to protect her interest as a beneficiary.

> • The Defendants took no action under either the terms of the trust or applicable law to protect Burton's interests as beneficiary of the Irrevocable Trusts.

> • In 2010, Defendant Hudgins Contracting Corporation—a company owned and controlled by Lester Hudgins—purchased a $2 million life insurance policy from The Hartford and a $1 million life insurance policy from ING, both on Lester Hudgins' life.

> • The applications for the Replacement Policies indicated that these policies were intended to replace the Lincoln Financial policies that comprised the Irrevocable Trusts. In this regard, Hudgins Contracting exercised dominion and control over the Lincoln Financial policies and represented that the Replacement Policies would supplant the Lincoln Financial policies in the Irrevocable Trusts.

> • After purchasing the Replacement Policies, Hudgins Contracting transferred ownership of the policies to Lester Hudgins. He in turn named a separate revocable trust as the sole beneficiary of the Replacement Policies.[4] Burton contends that the amendments to the revocable trust affected significant changes concerning the property to be left to its beneficiaries.[5]

> • Neither Old Point Trust nor Dolph adequately disclosed the existence of certain claims for breach of trust.

Based on these factual allegations, Burton asserts ... [a] direct action against Old Point Trust, alleging that it breached its duties as a trustee [and a] direct action against Dolph, alleging that he breached his duties as a de facto trustee... Old Point Trust filed demurrers ... alleging... that the Complaint fails to establish that Old Point Trust ever accepted trusteeship of the Irrevocable Trusts...; and Dolph filed demurrers... argu[ing] that there is no such thing as a "de facto" trustee under Virginia law. ...

II. Analysis.

... Virginia Code § 64.2–754... provides that a prospective trustee may accept trusteeship either by (i) substantially complying with a method of acceptance provided in the terms of the trust; or (ii) if the terms of the trust do not provide a method, or that method is not deemed exclusive, "by accepting delivery of the trust property, exercising powers or performing duties as trustee, or otherwise indicating acceptance of the trusteeship." Va.Code § 64.2–754(A). Part (B) of the statute explains that a designated trustee who has yet to accept trusteeship may reject trusteeship; it further states that if a reasonable time elapses during which a designated trustee has not yet accepted trusteeship, he is deemed to have rejected trusteeship. Va.Code § 64.2–754(B). ...

Old Point Trust... contends that it did not engage in conduct that would implicate Virginia Code § 64.2–754, nor did it even have notice that the previous trustee, Ann Archer, had passed away. ... But because the Court must accept the Complaint in the light most favorable to the Plaintiff at this stage, Old Point Trust's arguments fall short. Paragraph 18 of the Complaint clearly alleges that Old Point Trust had accepted trusteeship of the Irrevocable Trusts. Moreover, it cites to the Crummey Notices as evidence that Old Point Trust had, by the time the notices were dispatched, already assumed trusteeship. In addition to references to Old Point Trust as the successor trustee, both Crummey Notices (one for each of the Irrevocable Trusts) allude to Old Point Trust as the actual trustee of the Irrevocable Trusts. ("These rights can be exercised by you to require Old Point, as Trustee, to distribute to you a share of each gift to the Trust ..."). The Crummey Notices also reference Ann Archer's death, which thwarts Old Point Trust's assertion that it was unaware of her passing.

Moreover, although the Irrevocable Trusts do not contain a specific acceptance provision, the allegations contained in paragraph 18 of the Complaint can reasonably be read to satisfy the requirements of Virginia Code § 64.2–754(A)(2) (stating that acceptance of a trusteeship can be evidenced by "exercising powers or performing duties as trustee, or otherwise indicating acceptance of the trusteeship."). Certainly, notifying a beneficiary of her right to withdraw money from a trust falls within this statutory language. This reading is also consistent with the Official Comment to the analog provision in the Uniform Trust Code. See Comment to Uniform Trust Code § 701 ("... this section validates any other method demonstrating the necessary intent" to accept trusteeship.). ...

Dolph asserts that no Virginia statute or case law has recognized the status of de facto trustee under a written trust agreement, and that to do so would be inconsistent with the entirety of the Uniform Trust Code, specifically Virginia Code § 64.2–754, which governs the acceptance of trusteeship. ... Although a relatively under-developed concept in Virginia—and not discussed in the Comments to the Uniform Trust Code—Burton is correct that Virginia law recognizes de facto trustees. The Supreme Court's most recent discussion of the de facto trustee came in First National Bank v. Johnson, 183 Va. 227, 31 S.E.2d 581 (1944). In Johnson, a merchant's landlord re-entered the leased premises after the merchant had absconded. In the merchant's absence, the landlord continued to conduct the merchant's business, and shortly thereafter took full possession of all of his merchandise and personal property. Upon doing so, the landlord sold a portion of the lessee's property and used some of the property to satisfy debts owed to creditors. Noting that the landlord had unlawfully assumed management of the merchant's property and that it had dissipated the value of the merchant's assets, the Court held the landlord to be a trustee *de son tort*—in other words, a de facto trustee—and held it liable as if it were the trustee of the merchant's property.[7]

> [7] "A 'trustee de son tort' is one who of his own authority enters into the possession, or assumes the management, of property which belongs beneficially to another; a person subject to the same rules and remedies as other constructive trustees." 19 M.J. Trusts and Trustees § 2 (2013). See also Brown v. Lambert, 74 Va. 256 (1880).

227 Va. at 237, 31 S.E.2d at 585. The Court reads *Johnson* as the Supreme Court's approval of a cause of action brought against a de facto trustee. ... That the trust agreement in this case was written has no bearing on the Court's conclusion. ...

Why would anyone want to accept the role of trustee, with all the responsibilities and duties dicussed in Part V below? Settlors commonly do it themselves with a revocable inter vivos trust, if the principal purpose of the trust was to effect a non-probate transfer rather than to relieve themselves of the burden of managing property. Some people who agree to serve as trustee for a trust they themselves do not create do so without compensation, as a favor for the settlor. But trustees are presumptively entitled to a commission, as well as to reimbursement for any expenses incurred, and most who are not the trust settlor accept the commission.

§ 64.2-761. Compensation of trustee

A. If the terms of a trust do not specify the trustee's compensation, a trustee is entitled to compensation that is reasonable under the circumstances.

B. If the terms of a trust specify the trustee's compensation, the trustee is entitled to be compensated as specified, but the court may allow more or less compensation if:

1. The duties of the trustee are substantially different from those contemplated when the trust was created; or

2. The compensation specified by the terms of the trust would be unreasonably low or high.

§ 64.2-762. Reimbursement of expenses

A. A trustee is entitled to be reimbursed out of the trust property, with interest as appropriate, for:

1. Expenses that were properly incurred in the administration of the trust; and

2. To the extent necessary to prevent unjust enrichment of the trust, expenses that were not properly incurred in the administration of the trust.

B. An advance by the trustee of money for the protection of the trust gives rise to a lien against trust property to secure reimbursement with reasonable interest.

***

D. Ascertainable beneficiaries

A private trust must identify one or more persons to whom the trustee owes duties with respect to trust property. § 64.2-701 defines "Beneficiary" as "a person that (i) has a present or future beneficial interest in a trust, vested or contingent; or (ii) in a capacity other than that of trustee, holds a power of appointment over trust property." To be ascertainable, the trust instrument or declaration must describe persons sufficiently that the trustee can determine who is intended with some certainty. Problematic designations of beneficiaries would be descriptions like "those who have cared about me" or "my friends," and an apparent attempt at creating a trust that is no more definite than this about any beneficiaries will fail.

Under the common law, it was also problematic if a trust instrument created merely a contingent interest for some beneficiary and if it were possible that a very long time might pass before it became certain whether the interest would ever vest. For example, a trust instrument might create a life estate for a surviving spouse and direct the remainder to "such of my nieces and nephews who reach age 35" or "to the first of my descendants to swim the English Channel." The settlor's siblings might keep producing offspring long after the settlor's spouse is deceased, and the settlor's descendants might never include a long-distance swimmer. This uncertainty about the fate of property was economically inefficient, so the law would treat some such provisions as invalid, under the Rule Against Perpetuities, the details of which law students no longer need to learn. Today Title 55 of the Virginia Code essentially provides that if a contingent interest in a trust instrument or other property conveyance has not vested ninety years after creation, then a court may reform the instrument to make it a vested interest.

Title 55. Property and Conveyances
Chapter 1. Creation and Limitation of Estates; Their Qualities

§ 55-12.1. Uniform Statutory Rule Against Perpetuities

A. A nonvested property interest is invalid unless:

1. When the interest is created, it is certain to vest or terminate no later than twenty-one years after the death of an individual then alive; or

2. The interest either vests or terminates within ninety years after its creation.

§ 55-12.3. Reformation

Upon the petition of an interested person, a court... shall reform a disposition in the manner that most closely approximates the transferor's manifested plan of distribution and is within the ninety years allowed by subdivision A 2... if:

1. A nonvested property interest... becomes invalid under § 55-12.1;

2. A class gift is not but might become invalid under § 55-12.1 and the time has arrived when the share of any class member is to take effect in possession or enjoyment; or

3. A nonvested property interest that is not validated by subdivision A 1 of §
55-12.1 can vest but not within 90 years after its creation.

***

E. Intent to create a trust

The main issue that arises with respect to this requirement is that sometimes people
express wishes without making clear whether they actually intend to impose a duty on the
recipient of property to use the property for fulfillment or those wishes or instead are
simply letting the recipient know the transferor would be happy to know the property
would be used in that way, if the recipient so chooses.

Supreme Court of Virginia.
Spicer v. Wright
215 Va. 520, 211 S.E.2d 79, (1975)

POFF, Justice.

Leila Wilson Spicer died March 22, 1968, survived by her husband, Meade T. Spicer, Jr.,
her sole heir at law. In her holographic will dated May 20, 1966, ...*521 [t]he third
paragraph... provided:

> 'My estate of every kind and description, personal, real estate, etc., I give to
> my sister, Anne Beecher Wilson to be disposed of as already agreed
> between us.'

... Mr. and Mrs. Spicer were married in June, 1953, when both were over 50 years of age.
Prior thereto, Mrs. Spicer and her sister, Miss Wilson, had lived together in an apartment,
caring for an aunt who was suffering a terminal illness. After the aunt's death, Miss
Wilson joined the Spicers in their apartment. She lived there in two separate rooms and
took her meals with her sister and brother-in-law. For three days in April, 1966,
approximately one month before the will was written, Mr. Spicer was hospitalized for a
cardiovascular condition, generalized arteriosclerosis, and mild diabetes. Hospital records
show that he sat staring into space or walked about aimlessly in a state of confusion.
Shortly thereafter, Mr. Spicer executed a power of attorney authorizing his wife to
conduct his affairs. The Spicers' joint federal income tax return, prepared from data
assembled by Mrs. Spicer, reflects an adjusted gross income of less than $1200.00 in
1966.

A doctor at Tucker Hospital, where Miss Wilson was employed for 50 years,
remembered granting Miss Wilson's request for free time to accompany her sister to
make a will relating to 'property of Miss Wilson's, Mrs. Spicer, and Mr. Spicer.' Nothing
in the record shows that Mrs. Spicer executed **81 a formal will or that she intended, by
executing her holographic will, to change an earlier will.

Pearl Latta, the sisters' maid for more than 40 years, could not remember any discussion between her employers concerning the agreement mentioned in the will, but she did recall hearing them say that they did not want any distant relatives to have *522 their property. When Mrs. Spicer died, Miss Wilson directed that no relatives should be notified of the death or funeral.

Appellant contends that the language of the will, 'to be disposed of as already agreed between us', is imperative and connotes an intent to create an express trust; that such testimony intent is corroborated by the extrinsic evidence; and that since the terms of the agreement are unknown and the express trust cannot be enforced, '(t)he property must be held as a resulting trust for Mrs. Spicer's heir and next of kin-her husband.'

In Burton v. Irwin, 212 Va. 104, 181 S.E.2d 624 (1971), the testatrix devised her estate by holographic will to her brother whom she named 'executor and trustee'. The last sentence of the will provided: 'My Brother knows my wishes and will carry them out, to the best of his ability.' The chancellor held that an express trust was intended, that the trust failed for indefiniteness, and that a 'naked trust was created or implied in favor of the heirs at law and distributees' of the testatrix. We said that '(t)he question is whether the testatrix intended to create a trust for undesignated beneficiaries and unspecified purposes which must fail for indefiniteness or whether she intended to leave her entire estate in fee simple to her brother. If she created a void trust then her net estate will be held by Burton as trustee under a resulting trust for the benefit of her heirs at law and distributees.' 212 Va. at 105-106, 181 S.E.2d at 626. Reversing the chancellor's decree, we held that 'the language found in Mrs. Mallory's will falls short of establishing an intent to create a trust and that it constitutes a devise and bequest of her property in fee simple and absolute estate to her brother William L. Burton.' 212 Va. at 110, 181 S.E.2d at 629.

Here, we are faced with essentially the same question. We must decide whether the language of Mrs. Spicer's will, read in context with the extrinsic evidence, is sufficient to establish an intent to create an express trust; if so, that trust fails for indefiniteness and a resulting trust arises in favor of Meade T. Spicer, now deceased; if not, Miss Wilson takes the entire estate in fee simple.

As we said in *Burton* '(p)recatory words are prima facie construed to create a trust when they are directed to an executor . . . (but) no trust is created by precatory language directed to a legatee unless there is testamentary intent to impose a legal *523 obligation upon him to make a particular disposition of property.' 212 Va. at 109, 181 S.E.2d at 628.

> '. . . (T)he question in all cases is whether a trust was or was not intended to be created; i.e., looking at the entire context of the will and the facts and circumstances properly admitted into evidence, did the testator intend to impose a binding obligation on the devisee to carry out his wishes, or did he mean to leave it to the devisee to act or not at his own discretion. (Citations omitted).' Smith v. Baptist Orphanage, 194 Va. 901, 905, 75 S.E.2d 491, 494 (1953).

The extrinsic evidence showing the close relationship between Mrs. Spicer and Miss Wilson reinforces the import of the language of the will that, at the time the will was written, the two sisters had 'already agreed' how the property of the testatrix was 'to be disposed of'. But such evidence fails to establish a 'testamentary intent to impose a legal obligation . . . to make a particular disposition of property' or to show that the agreement was one designed 'to impose duties which are enforceable in the courts.' Restatement of Trusts s 25, Comment a at 69 (2d ed. 1959). If the extrinsic evidence had sufficiently **82 identified the beneficiary agreed upon and the terms of the benefits agreed upon, that evidence and the precatory language considered together would be sufficient to established a testamentary intent to impose a legally enforceable duty, and to create a trust.[1]

> [1]   See, e.g., Lawless v. Lawless, 187 Va. 511, 47 S.E.2d 431 (1948), where a letter identifying the intended beneficiary and the terms of the benefits, although incompetent to be incorporated by reference in the will so as to create an express testamentary trust, was sufficient when read in context with precatory language in the will to show an intent to create a trust.

Since the evidence did not, the precatory language standing alone imposes nothing more than an undefined moral obligation.

As to the nature of that obligation, the evidence suggests several possible interpretations. Mr. Spicer was infirm and impecunious, and it is reasonable to surmise that the sisters agreed that upon Mrs. Spicer's death, Miss Wilson would receive her property and use part or all of the corpus or income for Mr. Spicer's maintenance and support.2 It is possible that they *524 agreed that Miss Wilson would make some provision out of what she received for Pearl Latta who had served them for more than 40 years. It is possible, too, that the only plan agreed upon was that Miss Wilson would take Mrs. Spicer's entire property and manage and dispose of it so that it would never pass to their distant relatives, or, upon Mr. Spicer's death, to his heirs or distributees. With no evidence of oral declarations of intent to create a particular trust for a particular beneficiary, nothing in the record aids us in choosing among these several interpretations. All that the extrinsic evidence fairly supports is an interpretation that the agreement mentioned in the will was a sisterly 'understanding' that upon Mrs. Spicer's death, Miss Wilson would receive her entire estate and that in the use and disposition of it, Miss Wilson would exercise her own discretion as to how their understanding should best be implemented. Such an 'understanding' imposes no legal obligation and engrafts no trust upon a testamentary grant. See Carson v. Simmons, 198 Va. 854, 96 S.E.2d 800 (1957).

We hold that the language Mrs. Spicer employed is precatory, that the extrinsic evidence is insufficient to render that language imperative or to establish a testamentary intent to impose a legal obligation to make a particular disposition of property, that no express trust was intended or created, and that the language constitutes an absolute testamentary grant to Miss Wilson. ...

It is worth reading some portion of the *Burton* case as well, as it provides additional guidance on how to construe particular language and what extrinsic evidence can inform as to intent.

Supreme Court of Appeals of Virginia.
Burton v. Irwin
212 Va. 104, 181 S.E.2d 624 (1971)

COCHRAN, Justice.

On this appeal we are concerned with the construction of the holographic will of the late Blanche Burton Mallory. Mrs. Mallory, a widow 86 years old, died without issue on November 10, 1967, leaving as her heirs at law and distributees two sisters, a brother, various nieces and nephews and great-nieces and great-nephews. Her will... reads as follows:

> Richmond Virginia
>
> June 26, 1962
>
> This is my last will & testerment.
>
> I appoint my Brother William L Burton as executor and Trustee of my estate. **626
>
> To my Brother William L Burton I present herewith & Without recourse the accompaning Bonds, Stocks, Mortage Notes, real estate, and Bank Accounts and valuables of all descriptions in my safty box, at First & Merchants Bank Richmond Va. or at home or any other place in Richmond Va.
>
> My Brother knows my wishes and will carry them out, to the best of his ability.
>
> Blanche Burton Mallory

... *106 Thereafter, a sister, the personal representative of a sister who died after Mrs. Mallory's death, five nieces and nephews, two great-nieces and a great-nephew... alleged that Mrs. Mallory's estate was devised and bequeathed to Burton to hold 'for the benefit of her heirs and next of kin.' ...

The will must be considered as a whole in order to determine the testamentary intent. It is apparent from her phraseology and errors in spelling and punctuation that Mrs. Mallory had little faculty for expressing herself in writing. Nevertheless, the chancellor concluded that the language of the will was clear and therefore, over objection, he excluded evidence adduced by Burton to show facts and circumstances surrounding the testatrix at the time the will was executed. Such extrinsic evidence is admissible for the purpose of determining testamentary intent where there is legitimate dispute as to the meaning of words used in the will. ...*107 We cannot agree that the language of the testatrix was so clear unambiguous as to make extrinsic evidence inadmissible.

Use in a will of the word 'trustee' by a lawyer may clearly indicate that a trust is intended, but the same word written by one not learned in the law, may have an entirely different meaning. A will may be construed to create a trust without use of the words 'trust' or 'trustee'. Conversely, it may be found that a testator did not intend to create a trust although he used such words. Scott, Law of Trusts s 24, p. 192 (3rd ed. 1967). **627 Likewise, a testator may bequeath and devise fee simple title to property without using the precise legal terminology normally employed to do so. See McKinsey V. Cullingsworth, 175 Va. 411, 9 S.E.2d 315 (1940).

Moreover, precatory words in a will may be construed to create a trust depending upon the language used in the light of all the circumstances. Various circumstances to be considered in determining the testator's intent include the imperative character of the words used, the relations between the parties, their financial situation and the motives which may have influenced the testator. Restatement, Trusts s 25, Comment b (2d ed. 1959). ...

The record... reveals that there was an unusually close relationship between Mrs. Mallory and her brother William. She was about 24 years older than he. After their father died when William was nine months old, he and his mother lived with the Mallorys and, after his mother's death, he continued to make his home with them until his marriage at the age of 24. The Mallorys gave him a lot about two blocks away upon which he and his wife built their house. He was in daily contact with Mr. Mallory, called on Mrs. Mallory several times a week and acted as general utility man around their house. *108

Mr. Mallory died in 1940 a few months after the death of Mr. McCulloh, the husband of a sister of Mrs. Mallory's and Burton's. Thereafter, Mrs. Mallory and Mrs. McCulloh lived together, each year spending six months in Florida in a home owned by Mrs. McCulloh and six months in Richmond in Mrs. Mallory's home. Burton would drive the two sisters to Florida each fall and fly home, returning to Florida each spring to drive them back to Richmond. Commencing about ten years before the hearing, Burton and his wife went to Florida with the sisters each fall and lived with them during the six months they were there. When Mrs. Mallory and Mrs. McCulloh were in Richmond, Burton went by every day to attend to Mrs. Mallory's needs. He saw to the upkeep of her property, shopped for her, and took her to the bank, the stockbroker's office and wherever she wanted to go.

Mrs. Mallory's property came from her husband. After his death she converted much of his real estate into stocks and bonds and had only three pieces of rental real estate at the time of her death. Burton had access to Mrs. Mallory's safety deposit box. He had no income of his own but receive some compensation from Mrs. Mallory, who had persuaded him to give up his own business as a manufacturer's representative 'in order to look after her problems.'

The evidence thus shows a relationship approaching that of mother-son between the testatrix and her brother, financial dependence of William upon his sister and a motive for her to leave her estate to him. In light of these circumstances we consider the language of the Mallory will.

Her brother is the only person mentioned by the testatrix, and he is referred to three times in the brief writing. The word 'trustee' is found only once and then in conjunction with 'executor'. No trust beneficiaries are named nor are any **628 trust purposes specified. The conclusion is inescapable that in naming her brother 'executor and Trustee' Mrs. Mallory, acting without knowledge of the legal terminology employed, merely intended that her brother administer her estate.

In the third sentence of the will Mrs. Mallory used the words 'I present herewith & without recourse' in disposing of her enumerated assets to her brother. While this is unusual usage of these words for testamentary purposes, there can be no misunderstanding of the verb 'present'. It is defined in Webster's Third New International Dictionary, p. 1793 (1969) as follows: '* * * to make a present or *109 donation to: furnish or provide (as a person) with something by way of a present or gift * * * deliver formally for acceptance.'

The meaning of the words 'without recourse', usually associated with negotiable instruments, is more obscure. But whether they were intended to mean without recourse to the testatrix or without recourse to Burton, the testamentary intent of the entire phrase was to make an unconditional gift, unless the precatory language of the concluding sentence imposed a trust.

Precatory words are prima facie construed to create a trust when they are directed to an executor. Smith v. Baptist Orphanage, 194 Va. 901, 905, 75 S.E.2d 491, 493-494 (1953); 1 Bogert, Trusts and Trustees s 48, p. 385 (2d ed. 1965). But here, while the brother is personal representative as well as sole devisee and legatee, the precatory words are addressed to him as 'Brother' and not as fiduciary. ...

Under the modern view, approved by us and by a majority of other courts, no trust is created by precatory language directed to a legatee unless there is testamentary intent to impose a legal obligation upon him to make a particular disposition of property. ... In following the majority rule we have stated that more than mere precatory words are required to create a trust. See McClure v. Carter, Ex'r, 202 Va. 191, 195, 116 S.E.2d 260, 264 (1961). The *110 precatory language will not be made imperative if it comprises merely words of suggestion and advice. See Carson v. Simmons, 198 Va. 854, 96 S.E.2d 800 (1957). In McKinsey v. Cullingsworth, Supra, 175 Va. at 412, 9 S.E.2d 316, we held that the words 'Vennor I want you to have my home and every thing and you take care of Lula the best you can' did not create a trust but gave to Vennor (Vernon S. Cullingsworth) the entire property of the testatrix in fee simple and absolute estate. **629

It has been said that if a supposed trust would be invalid for any reason 'the argument against a trust intent is apt to be conclusive'. Bogert, Supra, s 48, p. 391. Here, the argument for a trust intent is advanced by those who know that the trust, if established, would then be declared invalid and that the testatrix would be held to have died intestate except for the appointment of her personal representative.

The cases relied upon by the lower court, Sims v. Sims, 97 Va. 580, 27 S.E. 436 (1897) and Lawless v. Lawless, 187 Va. 511, 47 S.E.2d 431 (1948), are distinguishable. In Sims the trust language was clear and unequivocal, the property being given to a nephew 'to be disposed of by him as a private trust, about which I shall give him specific verbal directions * * *.' 94 Va. at 582, 27 S.E. at 436-437. The verbal directions were void and parol evidence was inadmissible to prove them. So the trust was vaid and the committee of the trust beneficiary was entitled to the property.

In *Lawless* the testator made various devises and bequests to designated beneficiaries. He also in three clauses left property to his brother 'as I shall later request', 'on a special purpose' and 'for purposes herein written later on', respectively. By letter of even date with the will the testator requested his brother to purchase and send a rose each week to a girl whom he admired. We held that, as the letter was not incorporated by reference into the will, no valid trust was created and the testator's heirs at law were entitled to the money and other property in controversy.

We conclude that the language found in Mrs. Mallory's will falls short of establishing an intent to create a trust and that it constitutes a devise and bequest of her property in fee simple and absolute estate to her brother William L Burton.

F.   Legitimate trust purpose

§ 64.2-722. Trust purposes

A trust may be created only to the extent its purposes are lawful, not contrary to public policy, and possible to achieve. A trust and its terms shall be for the benefit of its beneficiaries.

***

An obvious example of an unacceptable purpose would be direction that trust property be used to commit crimes. More common are trust provisions that make receipt of wealth turn on decisions relating to marriage. One possibility is that settlors believe a loved one will need more financial assistance if single than if married, so they provide that a beneficiary (e.g., a surviving spouse) will receive periodic payments from the trust for so long as they remain unmarried, or only after they get divorced. If the settlor's aim appears in this benign light, it will be valid, but if it looks like the purpose is to encourage the person to get divorced, that is contrary to public policy and a court will reform the trust to eliminate the condition for receipt. Another possibility is that the settlor wanted to constrain the potential benificiary's choices, or in other words reward decisions of which the settlor approves. Validity of such conditions will depend on just how constraining they are, whether they amount to coercision and are too narrow. So a condition on a multi-million dollar bequest that the potential beneficiary must marry a specific individual named by the settlor would be too restrictive and so violate the public policy favoring freedom of choice in marriage, but a condition that the potential beneficiary marry someone who is Catholic likely would not be. Likewise, a temporal condition can be too restrictive (e.g., "within one year").

II.   Trust Contests

§ 64.2-724. Creation of trust induced by fraud, duress, or undue influence

A trust is void to the extent its creation was induced by fraud, duress, or undue influence.

***

The following case addressing a fraud allegation is a rare instance of a federal court resolving a dispute in the field of trusts & estates, the reason for it doing so in this case being diversity jurisdiction.

Oliver v. Hines
965 F. Supp. 2d 708 (E.D. Va. 2013)

T.S. ELLIS, III, District Judge.

*709 In this removed diversity action, plaintiff seeks a declaratory judgment that the July 23, 2008 amended inter vivos trust of her father, Colonel William P. Oliver, is invalid. ... [A] concern arose that subject matter jurisdiction might be lacking by virtue of the judicially-created probate exception to federal diversity jurisdiction. ... Memorandum Opinion dated May 1, 2013... concluded that the probate exception did not apply to this case. ... Thereafter, the matter proceeded to a two-day bench trial...

• Plaintiff Jane Williams Oliver... is the sole surviving child of Colonel William P. Oliver, a decorated Marine Corps officer whose 2008 Amended Trust is at issue here.

• Defendant Charleyrene Danforth Hines, a resident of New Mexico, is a widow who lived in the same retirement community as Colonel Oliver and there developed a long-term, romantic relationship with him. The 2008 Amended Trust names Mrs. Hines the trustee of Colonel Oliver's trust upon his death and also names Mrs. Hines as the primary beneficiary *710 of the trust during her lifetime. She is sued both in her capacity as a trustee and in her individual capacity.

• Defendant Patricia D'Rene Danforth Lethgo is Mrs. Hines's daughter and a resident of New Mexico. Mrs. Lethgo regularly visited her mother and Colonel Oliver at the retirement community where Mrs. Hines and Colonel Oliver lived. Mrs. Lethgo is the primary residual beneficiary of the 2008 Amended Trust.

• Defendants Mary Kate Williams Johnson and Frederick Williams are Colonel Oliver's cousins. Defendant Daniel F. Johnson is married to Mary Kate Williams Johnson. All three are residents of Florida, and all three were named as beneficiaries of the 2008 Amended Trust. Although named as defendants, Mr. and Mrs. Johnson and Mr. Williams have not noticed an appearance. ...

• Colonel William P. Oliver, a decorated retired Marine Corps officer and an attorney, died on January 22, 2012 at age 91. Although Colonel Oliver had been married previously, he was not married at the time of his death and was then living alone at the

401

Fairfax, a retirement community for retired military officers in Fort Belvoir, Virginia. Colonel Oliver had lived at the Fairfax since 2000. … *722

Both parties agree that Virginia Code § 64.2–720(A) provides the relevant requirements for the creation of a trust. Those requirements are:

> (1) the settlor must have the capacity to form a trust;
>
> (2) the settlor must indicate his intention to create a trust;
>
> (3) the trust must have a definite beneficiary; *723
>
> (4) the trustee must have duties to perform; and
>
> (5) the same person must not be the sole trustee and the sole beneficiary.

Four of these elements are undisputed. Neither party disputes that (i) Colonel Oliver had the capacity to form a trust, (ii) that the trust has definite beneficiaries, (iii) that the trustee has duties to perform, and (iv) that the same person was not the sole trustee and the sole beneficiary. The remaining element requiring that Colonel Oliver have the intention to create a trust is disputed. More specifically, the parties do not dispute that Colonel Oliver intended to form and execute a trust on July 23, 2008. In fact, the parties do not dispute that Colonel Oliver executed the signature pages attached to the original duplicates of the 2008 Amended Trust on that date. Rather, plaintiff argues that Colonel Oliver did not intend to execute *these particular* trusts.

Plaintiff apparently advances two theories in support of her claim that the 2008 Amended Trust has been altered and does not reflect Colonel Oliver's intent with respect to his trust at the time he executed the 2008 Amended Trust. First, plaintiff all but accuses Mrs. Hines and Mrs. Lethgo of fraud by suggesting that they substituted pages of Colonel Oliver's executed trust for pages that made Mrs. Lethgo the primary residual beneficiary of the trust. Then, plaintiff vaguely argues that emails from the summer of 2009 indicate that another trust was executed after the 2008 Amended Trust and that that trust has since been destroyed or lost but should be given deference anyway, despite the fact that such a trust is nowhere to be found. There is no evidence that Colonel Oliver ever modified the 2008 Amended Trust, and in fact, emails from Colonel Oliver to plaintiff in November of 2011 indicate that at that time, the 2008 Amended Trust was still in effect and had not been changed by Colonel Oliver.

The facts recited above indicate that Colonel Oliver did, in fact, intend to create and execute a trust on July 23, 2008, and that the trust he intended to create and execute is the 2008 Amended Trust presented by defendants in this case. It is clear that Colonel Oliver had a strong and very close relationship with Mrs. Hines and Mrs. Lethgo, that he relied on them for assistance with his daily tasks and for the administration of his estate, and that he intended to thank them and to express his affection by naming them as beneficiaries in his trust. It is also clear that although Colonel Oliver loved and admired his daughter, his relationship with her was tumultuous and lacking in warmth. Colonel Oliver repeatedly requested that his daughter come to visit him and made pellucidly clear that plaintiff would not inherit substantial sums of money from him unless she visited him regularly. Yet, she chose not to visit Colonel Oliver regularly; indeed, she visited him only four times in the eleven years before his death. *724

As evidence that the 2008 Amended Trust documents did not reflect Colonel Oliver's intent, plaintiff argues that the original duplicates were printed on different printers and different types of paper and that the documents do not display consistent margins or fonts or staple marks throughout. Although these observations are accurate, they do not point persuasively to a conclusion that the duplicate originals of the 2008 Amended Trust were altered either by Mrs. Hines, Mrs. Lethgo, or someone else. Rather, the evidence persuasively points to the conclusion that Colonel Oliver was responsible for these differences and that the 2008 Amended Trust clearly reflects his intent at the time that he executed the original duplicates and that he never changed the document from that time until his death.

Plaintiff argues that the inconsistencies in the printers, paper, margins, fonts, and staple marks used within the 2008 Amended Trust duplicate originals show that they are altered documents. In this regard, plaintiff cites several cases holding that "if, on production of the [trust], it appears to have been altered, it is incumbent on *the party offering it* in evidence to explain this appearance." *Priest v. Whitacre,* 78 Va. 151, 155 (1883) (emphasis original). These cases are unpersuasive as they are easily distinguished. It was clear in all of the cases cited that the documents were, in fact, altered following their creation. *See Hodnett's Adm'x v. Pace's Adm'r,* 84 Va. 873, 6 S.E. 217, 219 (1888) (at trial it was shown based on the face of the bond and expert testimony that the date on a bond had been changed from 1852 to 1853); *Bashaw's Adm'r v. Wallace's Adm'r,* 101 Va. 733, 45 S.E. 290 (1903) (due dates on a bond had been altered); *Tull v. Benton State Bank,* 257 Ark. 386, 387, 516 S.W.2d 583 (1974) (a will had been altered by the testatrix after execution without complying with the formal execution requirements for wills in Arkansas).

But the only hint of evidence that the 2008 Amended Trust duplicate originals were altered after Colonel Oliver executed them is plaintiff's self-serving testimony that these documents are unlike anything else she had ever known her father to produce, even though on cross examination she admitted that she had never seen any wills or trust documents produced by her father and she had only seen her father four times in 11 years. No persuasive evidence shows that the duplicate originals were not in this condition at the time that Colonel Oliver executed them. Indeed, even if, under the burden-shifting scheme for altered documents, defendants were required to prove that the 2008 Amended Trust duplicate originals accurately reflected Colonel Oliver's intent, they have done so by demonstrating the facts laid out above. The record evidence, as a whole, points convincingly to the conclusion that the 2008 Amended Trust accurately reflects Colonel Oliver's intent at the time he signed the 2008 Amended Trust and at the time of his death, as he never changed the 2008 Amended Trust. The duplicate originals will not be treated as altered documents because there is no credible evidence *725 that they were altered after they were executed.

Defendants are also correct that if plaintiff is arguing that Mrs. Hines and Mrs. Lethgo substituted the pages naming Mrs. Lethgo as the primary residual beneficiary, plaintiff would need to make such a showing by clear and convincing evidence because she would be accusing defendants of fraud. There is not even a scintilla of evidence to show that Mrs. Lethgo and Mrs. Hines altered Colonel Oliver's 2008 Amended Trust or that they acted improperly in any way, much less fraudulently. Therefore, any fraud claims must fail.

Nor is there any doubt that Colonel Oliver created a valid trust on July 23, 2008 when he executed the duplicate originals of the 2008 Amended Trust. Plaintiff's contention that the 2008 Amended Trust does not accurately reflect Colonel Oliver's intent is wholly unpersuasive inasmuch as the record makes clear that the 2008 Amended Trust reflects Colonel Oliver's intent at the time that he executed the duplicate originals. There is also no evidence that he ever took any steps to alter the 2008 Amended Trust. Accordingly, the 2008 Amended Trust is not an altered document and will not be invalidated.

As with wills, a trust instrument can include an enforceable no-contest clause

Supreme Court of Virginia.
Rafalko v. Georgiadis
290 Va. 384, 777 S.E.2d 870 (2015)

Opinion by Justice S. BERNARD GOODWYN.

*388 ... Dimitri B. Georgiadis (Dimitri) established a revocable trust on December 21, 1989 that designated his new wife, Margaret Georgiadis (Margaret), and his only children, two sons from a previous marriage, Paul Georgiadis (Paul) and Basil Georgiadis (Basil) (collectively, the sons), as beneficiaries. The sons were named co-trustees of that trust. *389

On August 27, 2012, Dimitri amended and restated the trust (August trust). The August trust removed the sons as co-trustees and appointed Dimitri as the trustee with Celia Rafalko (Rafalko or trustee) [Dimitri's financial advisor] as the successor trustee after his death. Further, the August trust eliminated the previously required distribution to the sons upon Dimitri's death. Instead, Margaret was made the income beneficiary of those funds, thus deferring any distribution to the sons or other descendants until after Margaret's death.[1]

> [1] According to Rafalko, under the terms of the 1989 Trust, prior to the August 27, 2012 amendment, the sons would have received a distribution of approximately five million dollars upon the death of their father.

The sons complained to Dimitri about the changes to the trust and they exchanged several emails. The sons expressed their displeasure with their father not providing for them or their families during Margaret's lifetime. They also questioned the appointment of Celia Rafalko, whom they believed to be a close friend of their stepmother, as the contingent trustee of the trust.

Dimitri died on December 3, 2012. Paul wrote a letter dated January 3, 2013 to Timothy H. Guare (Guare), the attorney who drafted the August trust, asking him to preserve documents relating to Dimitri's estate plan, and stating that "the testamentary documents purportedly executed in your office on or about August 27, 2012 by my father shortly before his death will be the subject of a contest." On January 4, 2013, Paul wrote a letter to Margaret asking her to agree with the sons to terminate the August trust and distribute its assets with one-third going to her and one-third to each of the sons, claiming it would be in their mutual best interests to do so. The letter also warned that "[s]hould we be forced to contest the August 27, 2012 will and trust and file suit to set them aside," Basil and Paul would assert that there was undue influence upon Dimitri and challenge Dimitri's testamentary capacity when the changes were made.

Soon after Paul had sent the letters to Guare and Margaret, Paul and Basil received separate letters from Rafalko, ... which provided a copy of Dimitri's will and trust. Unbeknownst to the sons, the testamentary documents executed by Dimitri on August 27, 2012 had been superseded; Dimitri amended, ratified and reconfirmed the August trust on September 21, 2012 *390 (September trust). The September amendments added a provision allowing the trustee to distribute the trust assets to a charity of his or her choosing if Margaret and Dimitri died and no beneficiaries remained. Further, the September amendments added Article VII(L), which provided as follows in relevant part:

> L. No Contest Clause and Release of Claims. I intend to eliminate the possibility that any beneficiary of mine will challenge the decisions that I have made concerning the disposition of my assets during my lifetime or at my death, and my Trustee shall take all appropriate steps to carry out this intent. Accordingly, I direct the following: **873
>
> > 1. Absent proof of fraud, dishonesty, or bad faith on the part of my Trustee, if any beneficiary or potential beneficiary under this trust agreement shall directly or indirectly, by legal proceedings or otherwise, challenge or contest this trust agreement or any of its provisions, or shall attempt in any way to interfere with the administration of this trust according to its express terms, any provision I have made in this trust agreement for the benefit of such beneficiary shall be revoked and the property that is the subject of such provision shall be disposed of as if that contesting beneficiary and all of his or her descendants had predeceased me. Absent proof of fraud, dishonesty, or bad faith on the part of my Trustee, the decision of my Trustee that a beneficiary or potential beneficiary is not qualified to take a share of the trust assets under this provision shall be final.
> >
> > 2. My Trustee shall obtain from each then living adult child and adult grandchild of mine a written release of any and all legal claims that such child or grandchild might make against the personal representative of my estate, my Trustee, any person who acted as my attorney-in-fact under a power of attorney executed by me, or any beneficiary under this trust agreement, relating to the conduct of any financial affairs prior to my

death *391 and the disposition of assets passing pursuant to my will, this trust agreement, any beneficiary designation that I may have executed during my lifetime, or my decision to cause assets to be titled in joint names with rights of survivorship with myself and another individual as joint owners.

On January 7, 2013, Basil sent a letter to Margaret disavowing himself from the January 4 letter written by his brother. Neither Basil nor Paul were aware of the September amendments to the trust until after Paul had sent the letters.[2]

> [2] The circuit court attributed the letters to both Paul and Basil despite the fact that Paul authored both letters. Paul and Basil do not assign error to this finding.

In a letter dated January 31, 2013, Rafalko informed the sons that she was considering whether the letters sent by Paul violated the no contest clause and asked them for any information "you believe might bear on my decision," in writing on or before February 15, 2013. As required by the September trust, she also sent releases to be signed by the sons. She gave them thirty days to execute and return the releases. Rafalko acknowledges receiving the releases, which were signed on February 19, 2013 by both sons, and by which they released all claims concerning any challenge to the will or the trust or to their administration.

In providing information solicited by Rafalko, Paul's counsel informed her counsel that Paul was unaware of the no contest clause when he wrote the letters, would not be challenging or interfering with the administration of the trust in any way and that the "clear import" of the January 4 letter was "to introduce the concept of a non-judicial settlement agreement," expressly authorized by statute. He also claimed that the specter raised concerning challenging the August trust was at most a threat which did not constitute a challenge, contest or interference with the administration of the September trust. However, her counsel noted in his memorandum that he had been told that if Rafalko decided that Paul had violated the no contest clause, Rafalko would "be in for a dog fight." Basil's explanation admitted that he "was aware of Paul's January 4 letter when he wrote it, but thereafter immediately disavowed it." *392

In a letter dated May 28, 2013, Rafalko notified the sons that she had decided that the letters sent by Paul violated the no contest provision. Rafalko stated: "I have concluded that both of you have violated the No Contest Provision of the Trust. Therefore, neither of you is qualified to take a share of the Trust assets, and the descendants of each of you are also barred from taking a share of the Trust assets." Rafalko attached a memorandum drafted by her attorney. The memorandum concluded that the letters written by Paul were "an attempt" to "interfere" with the administration of the trust "according to its express terms," which justified disqualifying Dimitri's descendants as beneficiaries **874 to the trust and that ignorance of the "no contest" clause was irrelevant.

On June 24, 2013, the sons filed suit in the Henrico County Circuit Court seeking a declaratory judgment that the sons' conduct did not trigger the no contest clause and that they and their descendants are rightful beneficiaries of the trust. ... *393 ... **875 ... *395

ANALYSIS

... No contest clauses in trusts that are part of a testamentary estate plan are given full effect, as they are in wills. Keener v. Keener, 278 Va. 435, 442, 682 S.E.2d 545, 548 (2009). ... When determining whether a beneficiary's actions have triggered a no contest clause, we strictly construe the language of the clause because the drafter chose the language and forfeiture is disfavored in the law. Id. at 442–43, 682 S.E.2d at 548–49. ...

Rafalko notes that the trust states that a trustee's decision is final unless there is a showing of "fraud, dishonesty, or bad faith" on the part of the trustee [and that] the sons' complaint did not allege that she acted fraudulently, dishonestly or in bad faith when she decided that the sons violated the no contest clause and were disqualified as beneficiaries. ... In the complaint, they alleged that Rafalko's decision that they had violated the no contest clause "'relied upon an interpretation of the *396 terms of the No Contest Clause that is arbitrary and capricious, contrary to law, contrary to the clearly expressed intent of the Grantor,' and 'in violation of the public policy of the Commonwealth of Virginia.'" **876 ...

Code § 64.2–703(B)(2) states that a trust's language cannot remove "[t]he duty of a trustee to act in good faith and in accordance with the terms and purposes of the trust and the interests of the beneficiaries."[3]

> [3] Notably, Code § 64.2–703(B)(11) states, "[t]he power of the court to take such action and exercise such jurisdiction as may be necessary in the interests of justice" cannot be abrogated by the terms of a trust. Thus, it appears that a court can always review a trustee's decision if the court believes it is in the best interest of justice. ...

See also NationsBank of Virginia, N.A. v. Estate of Grandy, 248 Va. 557, 561–62, 450 S.E.2d 140, 143 (1994) ("Generally, a trustee's discretion is broadly construed, but his actions must be an exercise of good faith and reasonable judgment to promote the trust's purpose."). A trustee's exercise of discretion can be overruled by a court if the trustee has clearly abused the discretion granted him under the trust instrument or acted arbitrarily. ... *397 Thus, Virginia statutes and jurisprudence provide that, notwithstanding a broad grant of discretion or one specifically limited only by bad faith, fraud or dishonesty, a court is vested with the authority to evaluate whether the trustee's actions were consistent with the terms and purposes of the trust and in the best interests of the beneficiaries, and if they were not, to overrule the decision of the trustee as arbitrary and an abuse of discretion. ...

The sons' complaint stated that Rafalko's decision that the no contest clause could be triggered with actions short of "prosecuting a legal action" was "arbitrary and capricious, contrary to law, and contrary to the clearly expressed intent of the Grantor." Further, they alleged that Rafalko's interpretation of the no contest clause such that she deemed the letters to be an "attempt to interfere with the administration of [the Trust] according to its express terms" was "arbitrary and capricious, contrary to the Grantor's intent, contrary to law, and in violation of the public policy of the Commonwealth of Virginia." The complaint alleged that Rafalko's decision to disinherit the sons and their descendants was contrary to Dimitri's "clearly expressed intent" as articulated by the trust language. In other words, it alleged that her decision was without authority because it was contrary to the purposes of the trust and an abuse of the discretion she was afforded under the terms of the trust.

Thus, judicial review of the trustee's exercise of discretion is allowed pursuant to Virginia jurisprudence and Code § 64.2–703(B)(2) to discern whether the trustee has abused the discretion vested in her by the trust or acted arbitrarily. ... **877 ... *398 ...

A person acts in good faith when he or she acts with honest motives. ... *399 ... The stated purpose of Article L, which included the no contest clause and a provision for releases to be sent to the beneficiaries, was to "eliminate the possibility that a beneficiary would challenge the Trust." Upon notification of the existence of Article L and upon being presented with the releases required to be sent to them, the sons expressed their desire not to challenge the trust in any way and executed the releases. After the releases were signed, the intent of the no contest and release clauses was accomplished. The possibility that the beneficiaries would challenge the trust had been eliminated without litigation.

However, the trustee thereafter used the trust proceeds to spend three months collecting information and consulting attorneys and others concerning whether the actions taken by the sons, before they knew of the no contest clause, could possibly be considered a challenge to the trust or an attempt to interfere with the administration of the trust.

At trial, Rafalko offered into evidence several emails showing exchanges between the sons and their father after the sons found out that they would no longer be receiving a distribution from the trust upon their father's death. The emails say unflattering things about Dimitri, Margaret and Rafalko, including an accusation that Dimitri believed impugned Rafalko's honesty. Rafalko argued that the sons were "horrible people" **878 even though neither the emails nor the sons' behavior toward their father was relevant to whether the no contest clause had been violated.

Rafalko admitted that the named beneficiaries stood to gain nothing by her pursuing whether the letters violated the no contest clause, after the sons had signed releases of all claims and the stated purpose of Article L had been accomplished. Also, Rafalko had been told that declaring the sons in violation of the no contest clause based upon the January letters would result in a legal "dogfight" that would no doubt cost the estate some expense. Additionally, it was revealed through evidence at trial that if the *400 sons were eliminated as beneficiaries, the remainder of the trust would be left for distribution at Rafalko's discretion pursuant to the terms of the trust. There is sufficient evidence upon which a court could determine that Rafalko's decision to find the sons in violation of the no contest provision was not motivated by a desire to carry out the testator's intent or to protect the beneficiaries and was therefore done in bad faith.

Even if there was no evidence to support the circuit court's finding of bad faith, ... the circuit court's decision was grounded on its determination that the letters sent by the sons to Margaret and Dimitri's attorney concerned the trust as it existed on August 27, 2012. In its letter opinion, the circuit court, construing the no contest provision narrowly, clearly stated that the no contest provision which prohibited interference with "this trust agreement and any provisions made in 'this trust agreement,'" meant that the applicability of the no contest clause was restricted to challenges directed to the September trust documents. Accordingly, the circuit court concluded that "[t]here was no prohibition against challenging any prior agreement or the trust agreement as written in 1989 or August 27, 2012." This was the reason for the circuit court's determination that the sons' actions did not violate the no contest provision. ... At best, the finding of bad faith by the circuit court was an alternative or additional ground for the circuit court entering judgment in favor of the sons, in addition to the trustee acting arbitrarily or abusing her discretion by misapplying the terms of the trust. ... *401 ... **879 ...

"The question whether a no-contest clause in a [trust] has been triggered presents, on appellate review, a mixed question of law and fact." Keener, 278 Va. at 441, 682 S.E.2d at 548. Whether particular conduct "constitutes a contest or attempt to defeat a will depends on the wording of the 'no contest' provision and the facts and circumstances of each particular case." Womble v. Gunter, 198 Va. 522, 529, 95 S.E.2d 213, 219 (1956). "Accordingly, [this Court] accord[s] deference to the circuit court's findings of historical fact, but review[s] questions of law de novo." Keener, 278 Va. at 441, 682 S.E.2d at 548. ... *402 ...

The terms of the no contest clause that Rafalko claims the letters violated prohibit "an attempt in any way to interfere with the administration of this trust according to its express terms." ...We have stated that no contest clauses are strictly construed for two reasons. First, the testator or skilled draftsman acting at his direction has the opportunity to select the language that will most precisely express the testator's intent. See Womble, 198 Va. at 531–32, 95 S.E.2d at 220–21. Second, provisions that require forfeiture are not favored in the law generally and will not be enforced except according to their clear terms. See Trailsend Land Co. v. Virginia Holding Corp., 228 Va. 319, 323–24, 321 S.E.2d 667, 669 (1984). The no contest clause in this case does not prohibit discourse related to proposed conduct, even if actually undertaking that conduct would be prohibited. Construing this clause narrowly, as we must, it only prohibits actual attempts to interfere with the administration of the trust. Proposing actions whose goal, if accomplished, may interfere with the administration of the trust is not prohibited. Evidence that the sons "cherished a desire" to terminate the trust is not "sufficient to bring them under the ban of this clause." See Puller v. Ramsey, 198 Mo.App. 261, 200 S.W. 83, 87 (1918).

The trustee is charged with the administration of the trust and her responsibilities of administration are set forth in the trust. They include: dividing Dimitri's assets into the marital and family trusts; distributing income; paying debts; making productive use of Dimitri's property; allocating assets in the best interests of the beneficiaries; and dividing property into equal shares for distribution to Dimitri's descendants. Dimitri also incorporated by reference the numerous powers set forth in Code § 64.2–105. These are the "express terms" of the trust regarding its administration that Dimitri wanted free from interference.

The sons took no action that can be characterized as an attempt to interfere with the administration of the trust. Neither *403 letter sent by the sons implicate any of the trustee's powers of administration or affect her ability to exercise those powers. First, as the sons alleged in their complaint, neither letter was sent to the trustee herself. One was sent to a fellow beneficiary, Margaret, and the other was sent to Dimitri's former attorney who prepared the trust documents. The trustee fails to explain how words stated to third parties about a previous version of the trust could interfere with her administration of the trust.

Moreover, neither letter necessitated any action by the trustee, affected the trust's administration, or even attempted to do so. In their letter to their stepmother, the sons expressed their discontent with the terms of the trust and indicated their interest in a **880 non-judicial settlement pursuant to Code § 64.2–709. Regardless of whether the ultimate realization of their proposal could ever interfere with the administration of the trust, the sons did not pursue this matter further.[5]

> [5] Moreover, because the September amendment added a charitable contingent beneficiary, the stated goal of the letter was an impossibility, as the trustee noted in her decision memorandum. See Code § 64.2–709.

In the letter to Guare, the sons merely instructed him to retain relevant documents because a legal contest was likely. Again, this action had no effect whatsoever on the trustee's administration of the trust "according to its express terms." Telling Dimitri's former lawyer to retain documents did not interfere, or attempt to interfere, with any of the trustee's powers of administration as set forth in the trust and Code § 64.2–105. The letter accomplished nothing more than the preservation of evidence at a time when the sons were evaluating their rights and remedies respecting their father's estate. When the sons learned of the no contest clause, the provision had its intended prophylactic effect and the sons committed no further action in preparation for a contest. See Lavine v. Shapiro, 257 F.2d 14, 19 (7th Cir.1958) ("Plaintiff ... had a right to express her feeling of hostility as well as her opinion of defendant in any way, at any place, at any time she saw fit, without being vulnerable to the charge that she directly or indirectly aided in the contest of the will."); Estate of Wojtalewicz v. Woitel, 93 Ill.App.3d 1061, 49 Ill.Dec. 564, 418 N.E.2d 418, 421 (1981) (allowing a legatee a "right to express a feeling of hostility toward and an opinion of the executor [as] he sees fit" without forfeiting his interests).

*404 A trustee has discretion to determine if the terms of a trust have been violated but not the discretion to define those terms as he or she sees fit. Rinker, 159 Va. at 621–22, 166 S.E. at 549. A court must ensure that the trustee remains true to the intent of the testator as those intentions are expressed in the text of the trust. Accordingly, the record supports a conclusion that the letters at issue did not interfere with the trustee's administration of the trust, and should not have resulted in the disqualification of the sons as beneficiaries. ...

Paul D. Georgiadis and Basil D. Georgiadis and their respective descendants are rightful beneficiaries of the trust, subject to all provisions of the trust... [W]e also affirm the circuit court's judgment awarding the sons' attorneys' fees and costs in the amount of $45,977.58. ...

Justice MIMS, dissenting.

... *405 ... **881 ...The grantor of a trust in Virginia may not exempt a trustee from the fiduciary duties imposed by statute. Code § 64.2–777(B) expressly states that a trustee's exercise of power under a trust is subject to the statutory fiduciary duties. Those duties include administering the trust and investing its assets in good faith, Code § 64.2–763, so administration of the trust in bad faith is necessarily a breach of fiduciary duty. However, the statutory fiduciary duties are broader than mere bad faith or the two other grounds set forth in the trust agreement for challenging the trustee's decision to disqualify a beneficiary. As an illustrative, non-exclusive example of these statutory fiduciary duties, Code § 64.2–765 imposes a duty of impartiality. Partiality cannot be simply a form of bad faith because that would *406 make Code § 64.2–765 duplicative of Code § 64.2–763. Such an interpretation violates our canons of construction. Owens v. DRS Auto. FantomWorks, Inc., 288 Va. 489, 497, 764 S.E.2d 256, 260 (2014) ("We adhere to rules of statutory construction that discourage any interpretation of a statute that would render any part of it useless, redundant or absurd.")

The same reasoning applies to the other statutory fiduciary duties. Yet the trust agreement does not appear to permit a beneficiary to challenge a trustee's decision that he or she is disqualified on the ground that such a decision was not impartial, or breached any other statutory fiduciary duty. To the extent that the trust agreement purports to restrict a beneficiary's ability to do so, the agreement is superseded by law. Code § 64.2–703(B)(11). Accordingly, the trust agreement may not limit the sons' ability to challenge the trustee's decision solely on the bases of fraud, dishonesty, or bad faith. ... The sons' complaint recites the statutory "fiduciary duties of good faith and fair dealing, loyalty, impartiality, [and] prudent administration" and asserts that the trustee's interpretation of the no-contest clause was "contrary to law, and in violation of the public policy of the Commonwealth of Virginia." ...Thus, ... the complaint **882 was sufficient... *407 ...

Nevertheless, ... the sons failed to prove a breach of fiduciary duty at trial. ... The evidence indicated that the trustee had been a friend of the sons' father (the grantor) and step-mother and included letters and emails in which the sons disparaged their father, their step-mother, and the trustee. The trustee testified that these communications—or so many of them as the sons' father received while he lived—upset him. However, ... the trustee testified that she sent the sons copies of the trust documents as quickly after their father's death as she could gather the documents, identify who was entitled to them, and make and send copies. She sent them on January 3, 2013, sooner than required by law. Coincidentally, that day, scarcely a month after his father's death, was the same day Paul mounted his assault on the trust by informing their father's attorney that it would be contested. The next day, Paul wrote his step-mother that the trust would be challenged if she did not agree to divide its assets equally between her and the sons.

As soon as the trustee learned of Paul's letters, she met with counsel. She did not discuss the letters with the step-mother or ask *408 her opinion of whether the letters violated the no-contest clause. The trustee testified that her decision to disqualify the sons was based solely on Paul's letters and the legal advice of counsel. She expressly denied that her decision was tainted by her knowledge that the sons' communications had upset their father before he died. She testified that the decision was a difficult one for her because of its "far reaching implications." Nevertheless, she believed it was not her place as trustee to determine whether the outcome was fair, but whether the trust agreement compelled it. Neither the trustee nor the step-mother benefited from the trustee's decision. While the trustee's counsel referred to the sons as "horrible" in closing argument, there is no indication that was the trustee's personal view of them, or even if it was, that she had formed that view before reaching her decision.

In considering whether the sons violated the no-contest clause, the trustee was required by law to make a neutral assessment of whether Paul's letters and the sons' actions constituted a "direct[ ] or indirect[ ]" "challenge or contest" to the trust agreement, "by legal proceedings or otherwise." She bore a statutory burden of impartiality with regard to the sons and the contingent beneficiaries (who would share in the trust assets in their place if the sons violated the clause). Code § 64.2–765; see also Sturgis v. Stinson, 241 Va. 531, 534–35, 404 S.E.2d 56, 58 (1991) ("Under general trust law principles, where, as here, a trust is created for successive beneficiaries, the trustee has a duty to deal impartially with them."). The record reflects that she discharged this burden responsibly after deliberation and consultation **883 with counsel, and dutifully compared what the sons did to what the clause forbade. There is simply no evidence that she bore antipathy toward the sons or that it clouded her judgment. Likewise, no trace of bad faith, partiality, or any other breach of her statutory fiduciary duties in the record. ... *409 ...

The circuit court ruled that the words "this trust agreement" as used in the September amendment applied only to that amendment itself rather than to the entire trust agreement as amended and restated on August 27, 2012. However, the September amendment is not a trust agreement. Standing alone, it contains none of the elements required to create a trust. Massanetta Springs Summer Bible Conference Encampment v. Keezell, 161 Va. 532, 541, 171 S.E. 511, 514 (1933) (noting that an enforceable trust agreement "must be certain and definite in respect to the objects or persons who are to take, and also in respect to the subject matter thereof." Consequently, the words "this trust agreement" as used in the September amendment must refer not to that amendment alone but to that amendment together and collectively with the August 27, 2012 trust agreement it amends. ... *410 ...

[W]e have upheld no-contest clauses to "effectuate the [grantor's] legitimate interest in preventing attempts to thwart his intent." Virginia Found. of Indep. Colleges v. Goodrich, 246 Va. 435, 438, 436 S.E.2d 418, 420 (1993). ... [W]e enforce no-contest clauses "according to their clear terms." Keener v. Keener, 278 Va. 435, 443, 682 S.E.2d 545, 548–49 (2009). The no-contest provision in this case clearly prohibits a beneficiary from "directly or indirectly" "challeng[ing] or contest[ing]" the trust agreement, "by legal proceedings or otherwise." The sons' **884 argument would render the words "or otherwise" meaningless, contravening the clear terms of the no-contest clause. Further, Paul's January 3 letter to his father's attorney stated that the trust "will be the subject of a contest." Similarly, his January 4 letter to his step-mother threatened that if she did not accept the sons' proposal to disregard the trust and divide its assets equally between them, they "would be moving to have the [c]ourt recognize [their father's] long-established will and trust in place for over 23 years as against the current will and trust in place only in the last three months of his life." No clearer evidence of their intent to thwart their father's wishes as expressed in the trust agreement is required. ...

Justice KELSEY, with whom Justice McCLANAHAN joins, dissenting.

... The settlor specifically intended his trustee's determination—in *411 the limited context of the no-contest provision—to be "final" in the absence of a showing of "fraud, dishonesty, or bad faith on the part of [the] Trustee." No such showing has been made in this case. The underlying question in this case is not whether the no-contest provision was violated. It is who gets to make that call. Absent egregious circumstances, the settlor of this trust intended his trustee—not the litigation machinery of the court system—to umpire this dispute. ...

After the August 2012 restatement, the sons began a campaign to undo the changes to the trust. They wrote letters and emails and left messages on their father's voicemail. Basil wrote his father complaining that their stepmother, the income beneficiary of the trust, "will have won the lottery" when he dies. The closing lines of a letter from Paul to his father reads: "So much for loyalty to your own blood and fair play from Step–Mum. Dad, I have NOTHING more to say about this and won't debate it with your [sic] or discuss it with [your wife]. Your actions speak *412 volumes."[1]

> [1] Paul wrote the email on behalf of himself and his brother and forwarded it to Basil. "You have accurately and eloquently summarized the situation without emotion," Basil told his brother in response. "Your words are clear and true. Well-said Brother." The trial court, following a bench trial, made a factual finding that "Basil Georgiadis is bound by the letters because he agreed with the contents and authorized them to be sent by his brother." On appeal, the sons have waived any challenge to this finding.

In another email he warned, "[Y]ou cannot insist that we happily accept this and get along. I do not and will not." Another email from Basil lamented, "To pretend that we are happy **885 with your actions or that we are one big happy family would be a falsehood.... I will forever be disturbed by your actions."

The father was greatly upset by the reaction of his sons. One of his emails reminded them that he "always treated [them] with consideration, generosity and courtesy" and had "never lied" to them. He pointed out that their stepmother had been his "lifetime partner, over several decades and has consistently and faithfully shown complete loyalty and support to [him] and [his] family." Their views of her, the father declared, "are unfounded and totally unwarranted." If they continued to ignore his wishes, he flatly said: "I will be very angry as you impugn my character. Remember also that no one has any entitlements of any kind and if I so desire I can bequeath whatever I wish to whomever I wish." The father ended the email by telling his sons that they created "this nasty and regrettable situation." Whether the family remained "intact," he said, "is now up to you two."

Shortly thereafter, on September 21, 2012, the father amended the trust (as restated on August 27, 2012) to include a no-contest provision, which states:

> Absent proof of fraud, dishonesty, or bad faith on the part of my Trustee, if any beneficiary or potential beneficiary under this trust agreement shall directly or indirectly, by legal proceedings or otherwise, challenge or contest this trust agreement or any of its provisions, or shall attempt in any way to interfere with the administration of this trust according to its express terms, any provision I have made in this trust agreement for the benefit of such beneficiary shall be revoked and the property that is the subject of such *413 provision shall be disposed of as if that contesting beneficiary and all of his or her descendants had predeceased me. Absent proof of fraud, dishonesty, or bad faith on the part of my Trustee, the decision of my Trustee that a beneficiary or potential beneficiary is not qualified to take a share of the trust assets under this provision shall be final.

Another provision of the September 2012 amendment provided that, after the father died, his sons could not receive anything from the trust unless they executed a release of liability warranting that they would not sue the trustee, the personal representative of the father's estate, the father's attorneys in fact, or any other beneficiary under the trust. If either brother failed to execute the required release, that son's share "shall be revoked" by the trustee. The September 2012 amendment to the trust also created a new class of contingent remainder beneficiaries, charitable organizations recognized under the Internal Revenue Code, to replace the sons as remainder beneficiaries in the event that the trustee determined that they violated the no-contest or release provisions.[2]

> [2] According to the language of the September 21, 2012 trust amendment, ... it did nothing other than "amend" the August 27, 2012 restatement of the trust agreement. The September amendment otherwise affirmed all unaffected portions of the August restatement, explicitly stating, "In all respects not hereinabove altered, the [August 27, 2012] Trust Agreement is hereby ratified and confirmed." Settlors of revocable trusts may revoke (and restate entirely) or amend the trust agreement "[b]y substantial compliance with a method provided in the terms of the trust." Code § 64.2–751(C)(1).

The father died on December 3, 2012. At the time of his death, he had been married to his wife for 23 years. On January 3, 2013, Paul wrote to the attorney who had drafted the August 2012 restatement and who had served as the trustee's initial legal counsel, declaring that "the testamentary documents purportedly executed in your office on or about August 27, 2012 by my late father"—which replaced the sons as co-trustees with their father's financial advisor as successor trustee and increased their stepmother's ability to use the corpus of the trust during times of need—"will be the subject of a contest." He made this threat with the agreement of his brother, Basil.

A day after announcing that the trust "will be the subject of a contest," Paul wrote a letter to his stepmother, at Basil's urging, attempting to persuade her to terminate the trust outright and to agree to the immediate conveyance of two thirds of the trust assets to him and his brother. The letter asked for her agreement to the sons' desire "that the trust be set aside and dissolved." If she failed to capitulate, leaving the sons *414 "forced to contest" their father's trust and will, Paul warned his stepmother that she "would lose a substantial share of [her] income," that Basil and he **886 "would take the $5.1 million distribution," and that, upon her death, Basil and he "would still take the remainder." Paul added that he would "not belabor the legal issues of undue influence and lack of testamentary capacity," given that he and his brother would "save [their] arguments for the Court and jury if needed." Paul gave his widowed stepmother ten days to respond in writing to his threats, "[s]o that no one has to incur needless legal expenses." ...

Faced with an apparent violation of the no-contest provision of the trust, the trustee asked legal counsel to advise her on the proper course of action. The trustee's counsel investigated the matter and issued a lengthy legal memorandum opining that the sons had violated the no-contest provision of the trust. After seeking legal counsel from the amendment's drafting attorney, reviewing her independent counsel's legal opinion, and considering the arguments made by the sons and their counsel, the trustee informed the sons that she had made her own independent determination that, in fact, both of them had violated the no-contest provision of the trust. ... *415 ...**887 ...

[T]he sons conceded that they did not plead fraud, dishonesty, or bad faith by the trustee. They said a "specter of bad faith" may be present, but they were not attempting to plead or prove bad faith because, to obtain a court order nullifying the trustee's determination, it was "enough" for them "to simply establish that the Trustee 'got it wrong.'" They "were not required to establish bad faith," the sons reasoned, because the issue was merely "whether the Trustee had properly *416 interpreted the Trust's terms." With respect to the disjunctive clauses of the no-contest provisions, the sons argued that the court should find them overly broad and thus unenforceable. ... The trustee testified that she was a professional investment and wealth manager. She had no self-interest in any aspect of the trust distribution. ... *417 ... The no-contest provision, she explained, expressly placed on her shoulders the duty to apply its terms and to make a final determination. She consulted with the attorney who had drafted the amendment, she hired independent legal counsel to advise her on the subject, and she requested input from the sons and considered all information they provided to her. The trustee said that her deliberations "took a couple of months," but in the end, "the decision itself seemed very straightforward." ...

The trustee said that she never discussed the situation with the stepmother or "ever ask[ed] her" for input. The stepmother, as income beneficiary, stood to gain nothing from the trustee's determination. The consequences of the trustee's determination implicated only the primary remainder beneficiaries (the sons) and the contingent remainder beneficiaries (the charitable organizations that would later be named). ... **888 ...*418 ... *419 ...**889

II.

... The ultimate question in this case—whether the trial court correctly set aside the trustee's determination—requires us first to decide what, if any, judicial deference the trial court owed the trustee. ... *420 ... Consideration of this threshold issue should begin with a review of the history of no-contest provisions and the settled principles governing them. There appears to be something basic and natural about a giver wanting his gifts, particularly those given after his death, to be received without rancor and disputation. Examples of testamentary no-contest provisions date back to the ancient times. English common law and chancery courts enforced no-contest provisions, subject to various limiting principles, throughout the 17th and 18th centuries. Early American courts did as well. ..

We have made clear that no-contest provisions are prima facie valid in Virginia. See Womble v. Gunter, 198 Va. 522, 525, 95 S.E.2d 213, 216 (1956) (approving such a provision in a will); Keener v. Keener, 278 Va. 435, 442, 682 S.E.2d 545, 548 (2009) (extending approval of no-contest clauses to trusts). Equally clear is that we have adopted no hard-and-fast rules governing their scope. It is the settlor's intent that controls: "What activity or participation constitutes a contest or attempt to defeat a will depends upon the wording of the 'no contest' provision and the facts and circumstances of each particular case." Keener, 278 Va. at 441, 682 S.E.2d at 548 (quoting *421 Womble, 198 Va. at 529, 95 S.E.2d at 219). ... **890 ... "[C]ompelling reasons" justify the "strict enforcement" of such provisions, we held, because they protect the right of a testator or settlor "to dispose of his property as he sees fit" and safeguard "the societal benefit of deterring the bitter family disputes that will [and trust] contests frequently engender." Id. Somewhat paradoxically, however, *Keener* also said that no-contest provisions should be "strictly construed" because the testator or settlor "has the opportunity to select the language that will most precisely express [his] intent." Id. at 442–43, 682 S.E.2d at 548.

The synthesis of strict enforcement and strict construction makes sense only by separating the related, but conceptually distinct, issues of legal validity and textual construction. Virginia courts do not begrudgingly enforce no-contest provisions. To the contrary, the "clear terms" of such provisions must be "strictly enforced," id. at 442–43, 682 S.E.2d at 548–49, without regard to the severity of the result. On the other hand, the inflexibility of strict enforcement cannot be predicated on supposed inferences of settlor intent that are not reflected in the actual text of a no-contest provision. In this sense, we strictly construe the text to the extent necessary to ensure that the plain meaning of the provision clearly calls for forfeiture, which, admittedly, is a result typically disfavored in law. *422

Keener is a good example of both ideas working together. We reaffirmed that... such a provision should be strictly enforced. Even so, we held that the provision in that case, by its plain terms, applied only to contests of "any provision of this Trust " and did not purport to apply to contests of a related will. Id. at 443, 682 S.E.2d at 549; accord Virginia Found. of Indep. Colls. v. Goodrich, 246 Va. 435, 439, 436 S.E.2d 418, 420 (1993) (holding that seeking guidance from the court in interpreting a will was not a challenge "questioning" the testator's intent under the no-contest clause in that case). The principle of strict construction precluded us from judicially extending the no-contest provision beyond its plain terms.

In this case, the trustee...determination of whether a beneficiary has violated the no-contest provision "shall be final." I agree that the plain meaning of this provision has no textual ambiguity requiring judicial strict construction. Text that has a plain **891 meaning needs no judicial construction. See Conner v. Hendrix, 194 Va. 17, 25, 72 S.E.2d 259, 265 (1952) ("'The province of construction lies wholly within the domain of ambiguity.' If it is too plain to misunderstand, there is nothing to construe."); see also Virginia Broad. Corp. v. Commonwealth, 286 Va. 239, 249, 749 S.E.2d 313, 318 (2013); *423 ...

Contrary to the sons' view, nothing in the Virginia Uniform Trust Code precludes strict enforcement of their father's no-contest provision to the facts of this case. Code § 64.2–703(B)(2) requires trustees to "act in good faith and in accordance with the terms and purposes of the trust and the interest of the beneficiaries." The no-contest provision does not offend this statutory duty. The provision itself requires the trustee's determination to be disregarded if it is a product of "bad faith." It also removes finality from any trustee's determination infected by "fraud" or "dishonesty." ... *424 ...

I see no need to address whether the equitable duty of impartiality is merely a conceptual species within the genus of fiduciary good faith or, instead, whether the two involve wholly dissimilar concepts. The sons do not assert any violation of Code § 64.2–765, nor did the trial court find any evidence of impermissible partiality. This is understandable given that the stepmother did not gain any financial benefit from the trustee's determination on the no-contest provision. The only real monetary contest was between the sons, as named remainder beneficiaries, and the charitable organizations, as contingent remainder beneficiaries. ...

The no-contest provision is one of the "terms" of the trust that effectuates the "purposes" of the trust. If either brother violated the provision, it declares that his share "shall be revoked." The trustee complied with the terms and purposes of the trust when she shouldered the responsibility of determining whether the sons had violated their father's emphatically worded prohibition on conduct that "directly or indirectly, by legal proceedings or otherwise" constituted a "challenge or contest" of "this trust agreement or any of its provisions" or constituted an "attempt in any way to interfere with the administration of this trust according to its express terms." The trustee's exercise of **892 her duties under the no-contest provision did not violate "the terms and purposes of the trust." Code § 64.2–703(B)(2). ...

[A] trustee cannot protect the beneficiaries' interests more sedulously than the settlor intended. A no-contest provision represents strong medicine for the fractious intra-family contests that sometimes follow the death of a settlor. But it is the settlor's assets being distributed to his beneficiaries. Thus, it is the settlor, not the beneficiaries, who determines the legally recognizable "interests of the beneficiaries." The trustee cannot expand or contract those interests in violation of the settlor's expressed intent. *425 ...

Virginia has more than a century of jurisprudence addressing specific settlor grants of broad discretionary authority to trustees. A long line of authorities limits judicial review to allegations of trustee fraud, bad faith, or other misconduct of similar magnitude. [citations omitted] *426 **893 ... The sons... propose that we adopt an "arbitrary and capricious" standard of judicial review to cover situations when a trustee makes an outrageously wrong determination under a no-contest provision of this kind—but does so innocently, with honest motives, and in good faith. I find the argument purely academic in this case. Even if such a standard judicially supplemented the language of the no-contest provision in this case,[11] nothing in this record comes *427 close to showing that the trustee's determination was arbitrary and capricious. ...

> [11] I acknowledge our cases stating that a trustee may not abuse her discretion by exercising it "in such an arbitrary manner, as, in effect, to make it a means of destroying the trust." Rinker v. Simpson, 159 Va. 612, 621–22, 166 S.E. 546, 549 (1932); see also NationsBank of Va., N.A. v. Estate of Grandy, 248 Va. 557, 561–62, 450 S.E.2d 140, 143 (1994); Trout, 106 Va. at 443, 56 S.E. at 169. In both *Rinker* and *Trout*, however, the trust instrument vested absolute discretion in the trustee, making no express exception for the presence of fraud, dishonesty, or bad faith, as the father did here. In *Grandy*, we restated the equitable principle raised by *Rinker*, but we held that the trial court had "impermissibly substituted its judgment for that of the trustees." Grandy, 248 Va. at 562, 450 S.E.2d at 144. In these cases, we merely recognized, as the Virginia Uniform Trust Code does now, that broad trustee discretion cannot be employed to destroy the trust, which would be the ultimate defiance of the settlor's intent. See Code § 64.2–703(B)(2). Enforcing the no-contest clause in this case, which expressly nullifies the trustee's discretion in cases of "fraud, dishonestly, or bad faith," cannot reasonably be said to have this effect.

The father intended the forfeiture to be mandatory ("shall be revoked") if either son directly or indirectly asserted a challenge or contest via litigation ("by legal proceedings") or by any other means ("or otherwise"). He also intended the forfeiture to be similarly mandatory if his sons "attempt[ed] in any way to interfere with the administration" of the trust. No legitimate exercise in textual interpretation would justify the conclusion that this provision applies only to contests and challenges asserted in court. ... We have never held that Virginia law invalidates no-contest provisions worded in such a way as to apply to contests short of litigation, and I see no reason to do so now. ...

The law does not give parties an inviolate right to cure a fully consummated breach. Nor has any precedent ever suggested that the legal **894 efficacy of a conditional gift necessarily depends on the donee's knowledge of the condition. And for good *428 reason: If there were such a rule, a donor's condition could be avoided unilaterally simply by a donee willfully ignoring it, falsely claiming ignorance, or conceding knowledge of the condition but protesting his misunderstanding of it. I thus cannot conclude that the trustee acted arbitrarily or capriciously by not giving dispositive weight to the sons' expression of regret for their actions upon discovering their father's no-contest provision. Even in cases in which the no-contest provision applies only to litigation contests, the "general rule is that 'a resort to the means provided by law for attacking the validity of a will amounts to a contest, although the contestant subsequently withdraws before the final hearing and even though the contestant subsequently treats the will as valid and seeks construction.'" Womble, 198 Va. at 529, 95 S.E.2d at 219 (citation omitted). ...

The no-contest provision applies to challenges or contests of "this trust agreement or any of its provisions"—which would necessarily include provisions in earlier versions that the amendment explicitly "ratified and confirmed." The provision also applied to attempts to interfere with the administration of "this trust." There was, and still is, only one trust. *429 The trust agreement includes the August 2012 restatement and the September 2012 amendment. The September 2012 amendment was as much a part of the "trust agreement" as the August 2012 restatement. ... **895 ...

Few axioms of Virginia law are better settled than our view that a litigant's "[p]leadings are as essential as proof, and no relief should be granted that does not substantially accord with the case as made in the pleading." Therefore, "[n]o court can base its decree upon facts not alleged, nor render its judgment upon a right, however meritorious, which has not been pleaded and claimed." ... I need not hypothesize whether an allegation of bad faith connotes something different in a trust case than it does in any other civil case. Nor do I see the need to address whether any evidence in this record would be sufficient to prove an allegation of bad faith—because there never was any allegation of bad faith in this case. [15]

> [15] See also Trout, 106 Va. at 441, 56 S.E. at 168 (noting that "he who invokes the aid of the court to regulate and control the [broad] discretion with which the [trustee] was clothed must set forth facts and circumstances which will call into activity the power of the court to regulate the broad discretion conferred upon the trustee—must show that the trustee has acted in bad faith"); Virginia–Carolina Chem. Co. v. Carpenter & Co., 99 Va. 292, 293, 38 S.E. 143, 144 (1901) (stating that "a charge of fraud or bad faith must be clearly and distinctly proven").

From the beginning of this litigation until now, the sons have consistently maintained that they did not need to plead bad faith. Based on that view, they never did. *431 ... **896 ...

An additional obstacle to contesting a trust, in the case of an inter vivos trust that was revocable prior to the settlor's death, is a statutory limitations period.

§ 64.2-753. Limitation on action contesting validity of revocable trust

A. A person may commence a judicial proceeding to contest the validity of a trust that was revocable at the settlor's death within the earlier of:

1. Two years after the settlor's death; or

2. Six months after the trustee sent the person a copy of the trust instrument and a notice informing the person of the trust's existence, of the trustee's name and address, and of the time allowed for commencing a proceeding.

B. Upon the death of the settlor of a trust that was revocable at the settlor's death, the trustee may proceed to distribute the trust property in accordance with the terms of the trust. The trustee is not subject to liability for doing so unless:

1. The trustee knows of a pending judicial proceeding contesting the validity of the trust; or

2. A potential contestant has notified the trustee of a possible judicial proceeding to contest the trust and a judicial proceeding is commenced within 60 days after the contestant sent the notification.

C. A beneficiary of a trust that is determined to have been invalid is liable to return any distribution received.

***

A settlor might rest in the peace of knowing a trust contest cannot occur after his or her death by, immediately after creating the trust, sending to anyone who might be inclined to launch a contest the documents and information specified in Paragraph A.2. While still alive, a competent settlor should be able to defeat any trust contest.

III.   Modification and Termination of Trusts

Alteration or elimination of a trust is straightforward while it is revocable; the settlor has complete freedom. But even irrevocable trusts are quite susceptible to change, as the law aims to strike a balance between effectuating the intent of settlors and maximizing utility in light of changing circumstances.

A. Revocable Trusts

Setttlors of inter vivos revocable trusts retain absolute freedom at any time to modify the terms of the trust or to terminate or revoke the trust. Importantly, as reflected in the first paragraph of the first Code provision below, in Virginia today there is a presumption of revocability, so that if an inter vivos trust says nothing about revocability, by default it is revocable. In other words, a settlor wishing to create an irrevocable trust must state this intention explicitly. This reverses the historically-prevalent rule that trusts are presumptively irrevocable, consistent with the modern trend of giving property owners maximum flexibility.

Article 6. Revocable Trusts

§ 64.2-751. Revocation or amendment of revocable trust

A. Unless the terms of a trust expressly provide that the trust is irrevocable, the settlor may revoke or amend the trust. This subsection does not apply to a trust created under an instrument executed before July 1, 2006.

B. If a revocable trust is created or funded by more than one settlor:

1. To the extent the trust consists of community property, the trust may be revoked by either spouse acting alone but may be amended only by joint action of both spouses;

2. To the extent the trust consists of property other than community property, each settlor may revoke or amend the trust with regard to the portion of the trust property attributable to that settlor's contribution; and

3. Upon the revocation or amendment of the trust by fewer than all of the settlors, the trustee shall promptly notify the other settlors of the revocation or amendment.

C. The settlor may revoke or amend a revocable trust:

1. By substantial compliance with a method provided in the terms of the trust; or

2. If the terms of the trust do not provide a method, by any method manifesting clear and convincing evidence of the settlor's intent.

D. Upon revocation of a revocable trust, the trustee shall deliver the trust property as the settlor directs.

E. A settlor's powers with respect to revocation, amendment, or distribution of trust property may be exercised by an agent, acting in accordance with § 64.2-1612, under a power of attorney that expressly authorizes such action except to the extent expressly prohibited by the terms of the trust.

F. A conservator of the settlor or, if no conservator has been appointed, a guardian of the settlor may exercise a settlor's powers with respect to revocation, amendment, or distribution of trust property only (i) to the extent expressly authorized by the terms of the trust or (ii) if authorized by the court supervising the conservatorship or guardianship for good cause shown.

G. A trustee who does not know that a trust has been revoked or amended is not liable to the settlor or settlor's successors in interest for distributions made and other actions taken on the assumption that the trust had not been amended or revoked.

***

In addition, settlors can structure a trust so that some beneficiaries will be in a position like a settlor of a revocably trust, with the power to withdraw their interest at any time.

§ 64.2-752. Settlor's powers; powers of withdrawal

…

B. During the period the power may be exercised, the holder of a power of withdrawal has the rights of a settlor of a revocable trust under this section to the extent of the property subject to the power.

§ 64.2-701. Definitions

"Power of withdrawal" means a presently exercisable general power of appointment other than a power exercisable by a trustee that is limited by an ascertainable standard, or that is exercisable by another person only upon consent of the trustee or a person holding an adverse interest.

***

Moreover, so long as the trust is revocable, the settlor can effectively modify the terms by giving direction to the trustee.

Subtitle III, Chapter 7, Article 8. Duties and Powers of Trustee

§ 64.2-770. Powers to direct

A. While a trust is revocable, the trustee may follow a direction of the settlor that is contrary to the terms of the trust.

B. Irrevocable Trusts

Testamentary trusts are inherently irrevocable, as they come into being only when the settlor/testator's will becomes effective, at that person's death. In addition, many settlors of inter vivos trusts choose to make them irrevocable. To what extent is the settlor's intent at the time the trust became effective forever binding?

First note that a settlor can effectively continue to make modification decisions by proxy even after dying or becoming incapacitated, by naming a "trust director."

§ 64.2-770. Powers to direct

... B. If (i) the terms of a trust confer upon a person other than the settlor... power to direct certain actions of the trustee and (ii) subsection E does not apply, the trustee shall act in accordance with an exercise of the power unless the attempted exercise is manifestly contrary to the terms of the trust or the trustee knows the attempted exercise would constitute a serious breach of a fiduciary duty that the person holding the power owes to the beneficiaries of the trust.

C. The terms of a trust may confer upon a trustee or other person a power to direct the modification or termination of the trust. ...

E. The provisions of this subsection shall apply if the settlor incorporates this subsection into the trust instrument by specific reference. ...

> 1. For the purpose of this subsection, a "trust director" means any person who is not a trustee and who has, pursuant to the governing instrument, a power to direct the trustee on any matter. ...

> Notwithstanding anything in the trust instrument to the contrary, the trust director shall be deemed a fiduciary who, as such, is required to act in good faith with regard to the purposes of the trust and the interests of the beneficiaries. ... [A] term of a trust relieving a trust director of liability for breach of trust is unenforceable to the extent that it (i) relieves the trust director of liability for breach of trust committed in bad faith or with reckless indifference to the purposes of the trust or the interests of the beneficiaries or (ii) was inserted as the result of an abuse by the trust director of a fiduciary or

confidential relationship to the settlor. An exculpatory term drafted or caused to be drafted by the trust director is invalid as an abuse of a fiduciary or confidential relationship unless the trust director proves that the existence and contents of the exculpatory term were adequately communicated to the settlor.

2. A trustee who acts in accordance with a direction in the governing instrument that the trustee is to follow the trust director's direction or act only with the trust director's consent or direction shall not, other than in cases of willful misconduct or gross negligence on the part of the directed trustee, be liable for any loss resulting directly or indirectly from any act taken or not taken by the trustee (i) pursuant to the trust director's direction or (ii) as a result of the trust director's failure to direct, consent, or act, after receiving a request by the trustee for such direction, consent, or action.

3. A trustee shall not, except as otherwise expressly provided in the trust instrument, have any duty to (i) monitor the trust director's conduct;... (v) do anything to prevent the trust director from giving any direction or taking any action...

***

In addition, the UTC authorizes judicial modification or termination of a trust in some circumstances at the request of trustees and/or beneficiaries.

Article 4. Creation, Validity, Modification, and Termination of Trust

§ 64.2-728. Modification or termination of trust

A. In addition to the methods of termination prescribed by §§ 64.2-729 through 64.2-732, a trust terminates to the extent the trust is revoked or expires pursuant to its terms, no purpose of the trust remains to be achieved, or the purposes of the trust have become unlawful, contrary to public policy, or impossible to achieve. ...

§ 64.2-729. Modification or termination of noncharitable irrevocable trust by consent

A. If upon petition the court finds that the settlor and all beneficiaries consent to the modification or termination of a noncharitable irrevocable trust, the court shall enter an order approving the modification or termination even if the modification or termination is inconsistent with a material purpose of the trust. A settlor's power to consent to a trust's modification or termination may be exercised by an agent under a power of attorney only to the extent expressly authorized by the power of attorney or the terms of the trust; by the settlor's conservator with the approval of the court supervising the conservatorship if an agent is not so authorized; or by the settlor's guardian with the approval of the court supervising the guardianship if an agent is not so authorized and a conservator has not been appointed.

B. A noncharitable irrevocable trust may be terminated upon consent of all of the beneficiaries if the court concludes that continuance of the trust is not necessary to achieve any material purpose of the trust. A noncharitable irrevocable trust may be modified upon consent of all of the beneficiaries if the court concludes that modification is not inconsistent with a material purpose of the trust.

C. Upon termination of a trust under subsection A or B, the trustee shall distribute the trust property as agreed by the beneficiaries.

D. If not all of the beneficiaries consent to a proposed modification or termination of the trust under subsection A or B, the modification or termination may be approved by the court if the court is satisfied that:

    1. If all of the beneficiaries had consented, the trust could have been modified or terminated under this section; and

    2. The interests of a beneficiary who does not consent will be adequately protected.

***

This statutory provision establishes a rule for three scenarios: 1) Settlor and all beneficiaries agree (Para. A), 2) Settlor is unable (because deceased or incapacitated) or unwilling to consent but all the beneficiaies agree (Para. B), and 3) Settlor is unable or unwilling to consent and at least one beneficiary is unable or unwilling to consent (Para D). None of these scenarios make trustees' views relevant. Surprisingly, the Supreme Court has yet to decide a case that turns on this provision. There are just a couple of circuit court decisions applying it.

Circuit Court of Virginia, City of Norfolk.
Saunders v. AMG Nat. Trust Bank
88 Va. Cir. 389 (2014)

MARY JANE HALL, J.

... Mr. Braden Vandeventer executed his last will and testament on April 27, 1942, when his daughter Mary (now known as Mrs. Saunders) was 19 years old. He died on September 28,1943 and his will was probated thereafter. The will established a noncharitable irrevocable trust for Mary's benefit, with his son Braden serving as the trustee for his sister. Originally, the Trust assets consisted largely of real estate and stock in a privately-held corporation. Currently, the assets consist only of cash, marketable securities, and fixed-income bonds. The terms of the Trust provide that Braden manage its assets in trust for his sister's lifetime, with the remainder to her heirs and distributees on her death.

Petitioners Robert M. Saunders, Jr. and Eliza R. Saunders are Mrs. Saunders' only heirs and distributees and are the remainder beneficiaries of the Trust. Respondent is the successor to the Old Dominion Trust Company, which in turn succeeded Braden Vandeventer, Jr. as the trustee when he resigned.

Petitioners recite in much detail their acute dissatisfaction with Respondent's administration of the Trust, highlighting its poor performance and excessive fees, expenses and taxes. They seek to terminate the Trust in order for the assets to be paid into an account for Mrs. Saunders free of trust, with minimal fees and maintenance expenses, to be paid on death to her two children. Respondent defends its performance and disagrees with Petitioners' characterization of its handling of Trust assets. Whether Respondent has done a good or a bad job, however, is not the controlling issue. The only issue is whether a material purpose exists in continuing this Trust seventy-one years after a father established it to provide income for his 19–year old daughter. ... Identification of an original material purpose of the Trust and whether continuance is unnecessary to achieve any ongoing material purpose must be determined from the language of the Will that established the Trust. ...

The beneficiaries of the Trust are the three Petitioners, who consent to termination. The Court may thus terminate if it appears that continuance is not necessary to achieve any material purpose of the trust. Petitioners argue that the material purpose of the Trust is to provide lifetime income to Mrs. Saunders. They suggest that such purpose could be accomplished by termination of the Trust and establishment of an account with lower fees and maintenance charges, reducing costs and income taxes and thus providing more income for Mrs. Saunders. Respondent argues that the spendthrift provision in the Will, specifying that "the said property and said income shall not be assignable by the said Mary Dunn Vandeventer nor subject to her debts" states the material purpose of the Trust that would be defeated by termination.

Mr. Vandeventer did not spell out the material purpose that motivated him to create the Trust. The Court must divine the existence of such purpose from the words that he used and the uncontested evidence regarding the circumstances surrounding the creation of the Trust:

> Occasionally, a settlor expressly states in the will, trust agreement, or declaration of trust that a specific purpose is the primary purpose or a material purpose of the trust. Otherwise, the identification and weighing of purposes under this Section frequently involve a relatively subjective process of interpretation and application of judgment to a particular situation, much as purposes or underlying objectives of settlors in other respects are often left to be inferred from specific terms of a trust, the nature of the various interests created, and the circumstances surrounding the creation of the trust. Restatement (Third) of Trusts, § 65, comment (d).

The authors caution that "material purposes are not readily to be inferred." Id.

With no statement by the settlor about his material purpose, and no known circumstance cited by either party that would elevate the inclusion of a spendthrift provision to the material purpose of the Trust (such as, for example, a swarm of creditors surrounding Mrs. Saunders about whom her father was aware), the Court rules that the mere inclusion of a spendthrift restriction is not sufficient on its own to establish or create a presumption of a material purpose that prevents termination by consent of the beneficiaries. The Court is persuaded by the following discussion in the Restatement (Third) of Trusts, § 65, Comment (e):

> A spendthrift clause may be included as a routine or incidental provision of a trust (unimportant or even unknown to the settlor), as a part of a trust established for tax purposes, merely to provide successive enjoyment, or for other reasons not inconsistent with allowing premature termination upon application of all the beneficiaries. Thus, for example, the fact that a lawyer had explained the effect and advised the inclusion of a spendthrift provision is not alone sufficient to establish that it represents more than an advantage that the beneficiaries are free to relinquish by consenting to termination of the trust.

The Court also notes the language of Uniform Trust Code § 410(c):

> A spendthrift provision in the terms of the trust is not presumed to constitute a material purpose of the trust.

… The language of the actual Restatement section… is almost identical to Virginia Code § 64.2–729, suggesting that Virginia law does not diverge from Restatement principles in this area. Further, Virginia courts have cited with approval numerous sections of the Restatement of Trusts: [citations omitted] The Court has not located a Virginia decision relying upon the comments to Section 65, but those comments include citations to decisions that have referenced the section; and no decisions rejecting the section or the comments are listed. The Court thus concludes that this section, like most Restatement provision, states the broadly accepted common law rather than one side of a controversial issue. Application of the Restatement analysis leads to the conclusion that the spendthrift provision is not the material purpose of the Trust. Virginia Code § 64.2–743(c), cited by Respondent, does not shed any light on the materiality of a spendthrift provision and does not mandate continuation of trusts that have them when the beneficiaries consent to terminate.

The material purpose of the Trust is to provide income for Mrs. Saunders' life. The Court agrees that such purpose is not defeated by termination of the Trust, inasmuch as she can enjoy that income at a reduced cost to her if the Trust is terminated. … The Court finds… that Petitioners are entitled to termination of the Trust. Mr. Hatchett is directed to prepare an Order that accomplishes the termination of the Trust and directs Respondent to distribute all Trust assets into an account owned free of trust by Mrs. Saunders and designated as transferable on death to her two children.

In addition to formal modification or termination, the UTC authorizes beneficiaries and trustees effectively to modify the terms of a trust by agreement.

Article 1. General Provisions and Definitions

§ 64.2-709. Nonjudicial settlement agreements

A. For purposes of this section, "interested persons" means persons whose consent would be required in order to achieve a binding settlement were the settlement to be approved by the court.

B. Except as otherwise provided in subsection C, interested persons may enter into a binding nonjudicial settlement agreement with respect to any matter involving a trust.

C. A nonjudicial settlement agreement is valid only to the extent it does not violate a material purpose of the trust and includes terms and conditions that could be properly approved by the court...

D. Matters that may be resolved by a nonjudicial settlement agreement include:

1. The interpretation or construction of the terms of the trust; ...

3. Direction to a trustee to refrain from performing a particular act or the grant to a trustee of any necessary or desirable power; ...

5. Transfer of a trust's principal place of administration; and

6. Liability of a trustee for an action relating to the trust. ...

***

Further, two Code provisions empower trustees to terminate a trust themselves in limited circumstances. The first also authorizes a court to modify to terminate in those same circumstances.

Article 4. Creation, Validity, Modification, and Termination of Trust

§ 64.2-732. Modification or termination of uneconomic trust

A. After notice to the qualified beneficiaries, the trustee of a trust consisting of trust property having a total value less than $100,000 may terminate the trust if the trustee concludes that the value of the trust property is insufficient to justify the cost of administration.

B. The court may modify or terminate a trust or remove the trustee and appoint a different trustee if it determines that the value of the trust property is insufficient to justify the cost of administration.

C. Upon termination of a trust under this section, the trustee shall distribute the trust property in a manner consistent with the purposes of the trust.

D. This section does not apply to an easement for conservation or preservation.

§ 64.2-735. Combination and division of trusts

After notice to the qualified beneficiaries, a trustee may combine two or more trusts into a single trust or divide a trust into two or more separate trusts, if the result does not materially impair the rights of any beneficiary or adversely affect achievement of the purposes of the trust.

***

Several additional Code provisions authorize a court to terminate or modify in other circumstances, without specifying who may petition the court to do so. The first presents a clear contrast to the law of wills, which does not in Virginia permit reformation to correct alleged mistakes.

§ 64.2-733. Reformation to correct mistakes

The court may reform the terms of a trust, even if unambiguous, to conform the terms to the settlor's intention if it is proved by clear and convincing evidence that both the settlor's intent and the terms of the trust were affected by a mistake of fact or law, whether in expression or inducement.

§ 64.2-730. Modification or termination because of unanticipated circumstances or inability to administer trust effectively

A. The court may modify the administrative or dispositive terms of a trust or terminate the trust if, because of circumstances not anticipated by the settlor, modification or termination will further the purposes of the trust. To the extent practicable, the modification shall be made in accordance with the settlor's probable intention.

B. The court may modify the administrative terms of a trust if continuation of the trust on its existing terms would be impracticable or wasteful or impair the trust's administration.

C. Upon termination of a trust under this section, the trustee shall distribute the trust property in a manner consistent with the purposes of the trust.

§ 64.2-731. Cy pres

A. Except as otherwise provided in subsection B, if a particular charitable purpose becomes unlawful, impracticable, impossible to achieve, or wasteful:

1. The trust does not fail, in whole or in part;

2. The trust property does not revert to the settlor or the settlor's successors in interest; and

3. The court may apply cy pres to modify or terminate the trust by directing that the trust property be applied or distributed, in whole or in part, in a manner consistent with the settlor's charitable purposes.

B. A provision in the terms of a charitable trust that would result in distribution of the trust property to a noncharitable beneficiary prevails over the power of the court under subsection A to apply cy pres to modify or terminate the trust only if, when the provision takes effect:

1. The trust property is to revert to the settlor and the settlor is still living; or

2. Fewer than 21 years have elapsed since the date of the trust's creation.

§ 64.2-734. Modification to achieve settlor's tax objectives

To achieve the settlor's tax objectives, the court may modify the terms of a trust in a manner that is not contrary to the settlor's probable intention. The court may provide that the modification has retroactive effect.

Supreme Court of Virginia.
Ladysmith Rescue Squad, Inc. v. Newlin
280 Va. 195, 694 S.E.2d 604 (2010)

OPINION BY Senior Justice CHARLES S. RUSSELL.

**606 *198 ... Miller Hart Cosby (the testator) died a resident of Caroline County on March 17, 2004, unmarried and with no descendants. His will dated March 2, 1998, together with a codicil dated September 25, 2002, were admitted to probate. The third article of the will gave all of the testator's stocks, bonds and other securities to trustees, to hold in a charitable remainder unitrust as recognized by certain provisions of the Internal Revenue Code.[1]

---

[1] A charitable remainder unitrust "is a trust in which no more than a specified percentage of the fair market value of the trust's assets (as determined each year), for a specified period, can go to the noncharitable beneficiaries; the rest belongs to a charity or charities designated in the trust." 26 U.S.C. § 664(d)(2).

The terms of the trust required the trustees to invest and manage those assets for the benefit of four named individuals (the income beneficiaries) who were to receive the net income earned by the trust, or 6% of the value of the trust assets, whichever is less. The income was to be distributed annually, divided equally among them and payable in quarterly installments. At the death of the last surviving income beneficiary, the trustees were to distribute the residue of the trust assets to two named charitable beneficiaries: The Upper Caroline Volunteer Fire Department (Upper Caroline) and the Ladysmith Volunteer Rescue Squad (Ladysmith), in equal shares for their general purposes, provided those entities were charitable organizations within the contemplation of the Internal Revenue Code at the time of distribution.

The fifth article of the will contained a typical spendthrift clause, insulating the beneficiaries' interests from the claims of their creditors and denying the beneficiaries any right to encumber or otherwise control their shares until actually paid to them by the trustees.

The will appointed Donald H. Newlin and William J. Howell (the trustees) as executors and trustees. After they qualified, the trustees instituted this proceeding in the circuit court as a complaint for advice and guidance, asking the court to determine the assets of the *199 estate that were the residue subject to payment of debts, taxes and costs of administration. The trustees pointed out that the will had designated its fourth article as the residuary clause but that the assets passing under that fourth article would be insufficient to pay the estate expenses. They asked the court to ascertain what other bequests should abate in order to pay those expenses.

Several years of litigation ensued on the issues raised by the trustees' complaint. In April 2009, only two of the income beneficiaries, Gloria G. Essaye and William Welford Orrock, remained alive and the value of the trust corpus was between five and six million dollars. At that point, the trustees, the two surviving income beneficiaries and Upper Caroline (the moving parties) moved the court to authorize the trustees to divide the trust into two equal trusts, to be called the "Upper Caroline Trust" and the "Ladysmith Trust." Ladysmith objected to the division of the trust. The moving parties also moved the court to authorize the trustees to commute and terminate the Upper Caroline Trust by paying the income beneficiaries in cash the commuted value of their interests in that trust based upon their life expectancies and distributing the remainder of that trust to Upper Caroline without awaiting the death of the last surviving income beneficiary. The motions asked that the proposed Ladysmith Trust continue in effect, to be administered in accordance with the testator's will. Because **607 all other issues in the suit were resolved by settlement among the parties, this appeal concerns only those two motions. ...

[C]ounsel for the trustees argued: "Now, the only unanticipated circumstance[,] I submit, is that the beneficiaries ... have said: 'We would rather have our money today than wait.'.... I believe the Court has the authority to do that; particularly, where the beneficiaries have said: 'This is our property and we want it today so we can eliminate investment risk; we can eliminate mortality risk, and we can handle our own funds.'" ... *200 ...

ANALYSIS

In support of their motion to divide the testamentary trust, the moving parties relied on Code § 55–544.17 [now § 64.2-735, above]... In support of their motion to commute and terminate the Upper Caroline trust, the moving parties relied on Code § 55–544.12(A) [now § 64.2-730(A), above]...

With respect to division of the trust, the sole question before us is, therefore, whether division of the trust established by the testator's will would "materially impair rights of any beneficiary or adversely affect achievement of the purposes of the trust" .... The testator expressly provided in his will that the trustees had authority to amend the trust "for the sole purpose of ensuring *201 that this trust qualifies and continues to qualify as a charitable remainder unitrust." No contention is made by any party that the trust failed, or would have failed if undivided, to so qualify. Therefore, authority to divide the trust can be found, if at all, only within the language of Code § 55–544.17, not from any expressed intention of the testator.

Our analysis does not end with the decision of that question alone, however, because the two motions were inextricably intertwined parts of a common design. If either were denied, the other would be futile. The common design was simply to enable Upper Caroline and the income beneficiaries to "have [their] money today [rather] than wait." Ladysmith consistently objected to this common design on the ground that it would violate the testator's intent. Division of the trust would be necessary to isolate Ladysmith, depriving it of standing to object to the motion to commute and terminate the Upper Caroline **608 trust, because Ladysmith would have no pecuniary interest in that trust. Thus, after a division was made, all parties to the Upper Caroline trust would be in a position to present a draft of an agreed order to the court for its commutation and termination.

The trustees argue that the adoption of the Uniform Trust Code (UTC) in 2005 (2005 Acts ch. 935), of which both Code sections quoted above were a part, effected a "dramatic change" in the trust law of Virginia. We agree that the UTC materially changed the law, but not as dramatically as the moving parties contend. The framers of the UTC were careful to preserve the guiding principles that have historically been the foundations of trust law. The following provisions of the UTC, as adopted in Virginia, are illustrative: Code § 55–541.06 provides that the common law of trusts and the principles of equity supplement the UTC except when modified by statute.[5]

> [5] To the extent any provisions of the UTC are in derogation of the common law or the principles of equity, they must be strictly construed. Britt Construction, Inc. v. Magazzine Clean, LLC, 271 Va. 58, 63, 623 S.E.2d 886, 888 (2006).

Code § 55–541.05(B) provides that the express terms of a trust prevail over many provisions of the UTC, including the power to divide a trust under Code § 55–544.17. For the protection of charitable trusts, the Attorney General is given the rights of a "qualified beneficiary" by Code § 55–541.10(D).

We conclude that the UTC has not altered the fundamental principles that in construing, enforcing and administrating wills and trusts, the testator's or settlor's intent prevails over the desires of the *202 beneficiaries, and that intent is to be ascertained by the language the testator or settlor used in creating the will or trust. Walton v. Melton, 184 Va. 111, 115, 34 S.E.2d 129, 130 (1945). The UTC has not so altered the law as to permit beneficiaries, after the death of a testator, to defeat the terms of his will that postpone their enjoyment of his bounty, merely because they "would rather have [their] money today than wait."

There is no evidence in the record, and no contention is made, that the trust assets have been mismanaged, that the trust has become uneconomic, that its objects have become unattainable, or that any other factor, aside from the desires of the beneficiaries, justifies amending it in any way.

Under the express terms of Code § 55–544.12(A), the circuit court had authority to modify or terminate the trust only in "circumstances not anticipated by the settlor" and when such "modification or termination will further the purposes of the trust." The moving parties argue that the settlor could not have foreseen that the beneficiaries would "rather have [their] money today than wait" and that they would resort to expensive litigation among themselves. We do not agree. Unfortunately, an examination of the records of this Court and others having similar jurisdiction demonstrates that beneficiaries of wills and trusts have, for centuries, engaged in such litigation with depressing frequency. It may fairly be said that the likelihood of such litigation increases in direct proportion to the amount in controversy. Suits of this kind are most often based upon the beneficiaries' desires to enhance their shares or accelerate their payment.

There is no reason to suppose, and no evidence in the record to show, that the testator did not anticipate those risks. The moving parties' argument is based upon pure speculation. The burden was upon them to prove that the circumstances upon which they rely to justify modification of the trust were "not anticipated by the settlor." Code § 55–544.12(A). The moving parties failed to carry that burden.

Further, it cannot be said the modifications made by the circuit court would "further the purposes of the trust." Id. The settlor expressed a purpose to obtain for his assets the most favorable treatment possible for estate tax purposes, but that was not his only purpose. He also expressed a purpose **609 to provide a stream of income to named friends who were made income beneficiaries, but their distributions *203 were not to invade the trust corpus and were to be paid out of trust income for their lifetimes. The income beneficiaries' benefits were shielded from their creditors and from their own interference by spendthrift provisions. In no event was payment of their benefits to be accelerated. The trustees were to manage the corpus, preserving it until the death of the last income beneficiary, and only then were they to disburse the residue to the charitable beneficiaries. The modification made by the court did not further those purposes, but completely frustrated them.

The division of the trust was merely a device to accomplish the moving parties' desires without having to seek the approval of Ladysmith, the only party expressing a desire to defend the settlor's intent. Even that preliminary step "adversely affect[ed] achievement of the purposes of the trust" for the reasons stated above, and therefore contravened the provisions of Code § 55–544.17.

The moving parties contend that Ladysmith has no standing to dispute the commutation and termination of the Upper Caroline trust because Ladysmith has no pecuniary interest in that trust. The moving parties' argument is circular. Ladysmith's lack of standing is premised solely upon the validity of the circuit court's order dividing the testamentary trust into two parts, which we hold to be erroneous for the reasons stated. Ladysmith retains standing to object to the common design presented by both motions. … [We] remand the case to the circuit court with direction to enter orders denying both motions...

The only other Virginia decision addressing a request for modification following UTC enactment was a circuit court decision. It picks up on the *Ladysmith* court's inclination to apply narrowly the Code provisions authorizing a court to modify trust terms.

Circuit Court of Virginia, Fairfax County.
In re Estate of Brown
87 Va. Cir. 353 (2013)

ROBERT J. SMITH, J.

... Elbert Brown ("Brown"), a resident of Fairfax County, died June 2, 2012. ... The document purporting to be Brown's Will created a separate, pour-over trust entitled "The Elbert Brown Revocable Trust" ("Trust"). .... First American Bank of Virginia originally administered the trust; now the successor to First American Bank—Wells Fargo Bank— administers the trust. ... Brown's Will... left all of his estate to the Trust. According to probate, the only asset outside of the trust and, therefore, subject to probate, is Brown's real estate worth $400,000. ... [W]hen the estimated remaining Trust balance is $200,000, the Trust would become available to the descendants of Brown's parents to provide for their educational expenses. ...

The issues now before the Court... [include] whether the institutional trustees should be permitted to modify the trust to eliminate the requirement that an institutional trustee administer the estate. ... Petitioner cites two reasons for modification of the Trust. First,...that the value of the trust property is insufficient to justify the cost of administration. Secondly, petitioner cites Va.Code § 64.2–730(A), which states:

> The court may modify the administrative or dispositive terms of a trust or terminate the trust if, because of circumstances not anticipated by the settlor, modification or termination will further the purposes of the trust. To the extent practicable, the modification shall be made in accordance with the settlor's probable intention.

The burden is upon the party moving for modification of the trust to "prove that the circumstances upon which they rely to justify modification of the trust were 'not anticipated by the settlor.'" Ladysmiih Rescue Squad, Inc. v. Newlin, 280 Va. 195, 202 (2010)...

There are no cases on point in the Commonwealth that specify when a trust becomes uneconomical to administer. However, the National Conference of Commissioners on Uniform State Laws Comments state that:

> When considering whether to terminate a trust under either subsection (a) or (b), the trustee or court should consider the purposes of the trust. Termination under this section is not always wise. Even if administrative costs may seem excessive in relation to the size of the trust, protection of the assets from beneficiary mismanagement may indicate that the trust be continued. The court may be able to reduce the costs of administering the trust by appointing a new trustee.

In our present case, Brown specifically calls for an institutional trustee in Article XI(B)(1), along with three individual trustees, to manage the trust. Brown further indicates that if "after the grantor's death there is no institutional trustee, the individual co-trustees shall appoint as institutional trustee a corporation authorized to provide trust services." It seems clear to the Court that Brown intended for the trust to always have a non-individual trustee overseeing the administration of the trust. Brown anticipated the day where an institutional trustee may no longer exist to administer the estate, and even in that instance, Brown indicated that he' desired that a non-individual entity have a role in the administration of his estate.

Accordingly, the Court finds that the party moving for modification of the trust did not bear its burden. The motion to modify the trust to eliminate the requirement that the Trust be administered by an institutional trustee is denied.

---

§ 64.2-779. Distribution upon termination

A. Upon termination or partial termination of a trust, the trustee may send to the beneficiaries a proposal for distribution. The right of any beneficiary to object to the proposed distribution terminates if the beneficiary does not notify the trustee of an objection within 30 days after the proposal was sent but only if the proposal informed the beneficiary of the right to object and of the time allowed for objection.

B. Upon the occurrence of an event terminating or partially terminating a trust, the trustee shall proceed expeditiously to distribute the trust property to the persons entitled to it, subject to the right of the trustee to retain a reasonable reserve for the payment of debts, expenses, and taxes. ...

***

IV. Trusts and Creditors

Trusts can to some degree insulate wealth from the claims of the settlor's or the beneficiaries' creditors. In fact, one reason why people create trusts is to improve quality of life for a loved one who is, or threatens to become, deep in debt, because giving them wealth outright would simply mean the wealth goes to the creditors. When property is in a debtor's outright ownership, creditors can petition a court for an attachment to secure payment of debts. This is true even of property placed in trust once it is distributed to beneficiaries. A trust, however, allows for smaller periodic or occasional payments to beneficiaries, which they can use for immediate expenses and not hold to long enough for a creditor to attach them. Generally, for satisfaction of large financial obligations, creditors would need to be able to invade the trust corpus or get a court order attaching all future payments from the trust to a debtor/beneficiary. The UTC, however, enables settlors to set up a trust in such a way that most creditors can do neither. The first few provisions deal with debtors qua beneficiaries. This could include a trust settlor. Further below, though, are provisions dealing specifically with settlors as such who are debtors.

§ 64.2-701. Definitions

"Spendthrift provision" means a term of a trust that restrains both voluntary and involuntary transfer of a beneficiary's interest.

Article 5. Creditor's Claims; Spendthrift and Discretionary Trusts

§ 64.2-743. Spendthrift provision

A. A spendthrift provision is valid only if it restrains both voluntary and involuntary transfer of a beneficiary's interest.

B. A term of a trust providing that the interest of a beneficiary is held subject to a "spendthrift trust," or words of similar import, is sufficient to restrain both voluntary and involuntary transfer of the beneficiary's interest.

C. A beneficiary may not transfer an interest in a trust in violation of a valid spendthrift provision and, except as otherwise provided in this article, a creditor or assignee of the beneficiary may not reach the interest or a distribution by the trustee before its receipt by the beneficiary.

§ 64.2-742. Rights of beneficiary's creditor or assignee

To the extent a beneficiary's interest is not subject to a spendthrift provision, the court may authorize a creditor or assignee of the beneficiary to reach the beneficiary's interest by attachment of present or future distributions to or for the benefit of the beneficiary or other means. The court may limit the award to such relief as is appropriate under the circumstances.

The law gives special protection to several special "creditors" – namely, children to whom a beneficiary owes a support duty, government tax or welfare authorities, and, of course, lawyers.

§ 64.2-744. Exceptions to spendthrift provision

A. In this section, "child" includes any person for whom an order or judgment for child support has been entered in this or another state.

B. Even if a trust contains a spendthrift provision, a beneficiary's child who has a judgment or court order against the beneficiary for support or maintenance, or a judgment creditor who has provided services for the protection of a beneficiary's interest in the trust, may obtain from a court an order attaching present or future distributions to or for the benefit of the beneficiary.

C. Subject to the limitations of § 64.2-745, no spendthrift provision shall operate to the prejudice of the United States, the Commonwealth, or any county, city, or town.

D. A claimant against which a spendthrift provision cannot be enforced may obtain from a court an order attaching present or future distributions to or for the benefit of a beneficiary. The court may limit the award of such relief as is appropriate under the circumstances.

§ 64.2-745. Certain claims for reimbursement for public assistance

A. Notwithstanding any contrary provision in the trust instrument, if a statute or regulation of the United States or Commonwealth requires a beneficiary to reimburse the Commonwealth or any agency or instrumentality thereof, for public assistance, including medical assistance, furnished or to be furnished to the beneficiary, the Attorney General or an attorney acting on behalf of the state agency responsible for the program may file a petition in the circuit court having jurisdiction over the trustee requesting reimbursement. The petition may be filed prior to obtaining a judgment. The beneficiary, the guardian of his estate, his conservator, or his committee shall be made a party.

B. Following its review of the circumstances of the case, the court may:

1. Order the trustee to satisfy all or part of the liability out of all or part of the amounts to which the beneficiary is entitled, whether presently or in the future, to the extent the beneficiary has the right under the trust to compel the trustee to pay income or principal to or for the benefit of the beneficiary; or

2. Regardless of whether the beneficiary has the right to compel the trustee to pay income or principal to or for the benefit of the beneficiary, order the trustee to satisfy all or part of the liability out of all or part of any future payments that the trustee chooses to make to or for the benefit of the beneficiary in the exercise of discretion under the trust.

C. A duty in the trustee under the instrument to make disbursements in a manner designed to avoid rendering the beneficiary ineligible for public assistance to which he might otherwise be entitled, however, shall not be construed as a right possessed by the beneficiary to compel such payments.

D. The court shall not issue an order pursuant to this section if the beneficiary is a person who has a medically determined physical or mental disability that substantially impairs his ability to provide for his care or custody, and constitutes a substantial handicap.

***

With non-settlor beneficiaries, the law affords substantial protection against creditors for their interest in a trust because the trust settlors owed no obligation to the creditors to pay off the beneficiary's debts, and because it is utility-maximizing to enable property owners to use their wealth as they desire, and desires to benefit loved-ones (rather than impersonal entities or less close persons) are generally quite strong. The law is less indulgent of property owners' desires to avoid paying their debts by placing assets behind a trust wall. The provisions below allow for some protection of trust assets against the settlor's debts, but only in very limited circumstances, with complex rules for qualification. Basically, they require that transfers to the trust not have been the cause of default on loans and that the settlor has given up control over the assets placed in trust – in other words, approximating an outright gift to others that was not for the purpose of evading debts, though allowing for the settlor's having retained some beneficial interest.

§ 64.2-745.1. Self-settled spendthrift trusts

A. A settlor may transfer assets to a qualified self-settled spendthrift trust and retain in that trust a qualified interest, and, except as otherwise provided in this article, § 64.2-747 shall not apply to such qualified interest.

B. Section 64.2-747 shall continue to apply with respect to any interest held by a settlor in a qualified self-settled spendthrift trust, other than a qualified interest.

C. A settlor's transfer to a qualified self-settled spendthrift trust shall not, to the extent of the settlor's qualified interest, be deemed to have been made with intent to delay, hinder, or defraud creditors, for purposes of § 55-80, merely because it is made to a trust with respect to which the settlor retains a qualified interest and merely because it is made without consideration. A settlor's transfer to a qualified self-settled spendthrift trust may, however, be set aside under § 55-80 or § 55-81 on other bases, such as if the transfer renders the settlor insolvent.

D. A settlor's creditor may bring an action under § 55-82 to avoid a transfer to a qualified self-settled spendthrift trust or otherwise to enforce a claim that existed on the date of the settlor's transfer to such trust within five years after the date of the settlor's transfer to such trust to which such claim relates.

E. A creditor shall have only such rights with respect to a settlor's transfer to a qualified self-settled spendthrift trust as are provided in this section. No creditor and no other person shall have any claim or cause of action against any trustee, trust adviser, trust director, or any person involved in the counseling, drafting, preparation, or execution of, or transfers to a qualified self-settled spendthrift trust.

F. If a settlor makes more than one transfer to the same qualified self-settled spendthrift trust, the following rules shall apply:

    1. The settlor's making of a subsequent transfer shall be disregarded in determining whether a creditor's claim with respect to a prior transfer is valid under this section;

    2. With respect to each subsequent transfer by the settlor, the five-year limitations period provided in subsection D, with respect to actions brought under Chapter 5 of Title 55 with respect to the subsequent transfer, commences on the date of such subsequent transfer; and

3. Any distribution to a beneficiary is deemed to have been made from the latest such transfer.

...

§ 64.2-745.2. Definitions; vacancies; right to withdraw

A. As used in this article, unless the context requires a different meaning:

"Independent qualified trustee" means a qualified trustee who is not, and whose actions are not, subject to direction by:

1. The settlor;

2. Any natural person who is not a resident of the Commonwealth;

3. Any entity that is not authorized under Title 6.2 to engage in trust business within the Commonwealth;

4. The settlor's spouse;

5. A parent of the settlor;

6. Any issue of the settlor;

7. A sibling of the settlor;

8. An employee of the settlor;

9. A business entity in which the settlor's holdings represent at least 30 percent of the total voting power of all interests entitled to vote;

10. A subordinate employee of the settlor; or

11. A subordinate employee of a business entity in which the settlor is an executive.

"Qualified interest" means a settlor's interest in a qualified self-settled spendthrift trust, to the extent that such interest entitles the settlor to receive distributions of income, principal, or both, in the sole discretion of an independent qualified trustee. A settlor may have a qualified interest in a qualified self-settled spendthrift trust and also have an interest in the same trust that is not a qualified interest, and the rules of § 64.2-747 shall apply to each interest of the settlor in the same trust other than the settlor's qualified interest.

"Qualified self-settled spendthrift trust" means a trust if:

1. The trust is irrevocable;

2. The trust is created during the settlor's lifetime;

3. There is, at all times when distributions could be made to the settlor pursuant to the settlor's qualified interest, at least one beneficiary other than the settlor (i) to whom income may be distributed, if the settlor's qualified interest relates to trust income, (ii) to whom principal may be distributed, if the settlor's qualified interest relates to trust principal, or (iii) to whom both income and principal may be distributed, if the settlor's qualified interest relates to both trust income and principal;

4. The trust has at all times at least one qualified trustee, who may be, but need not be, an independent qualified trustee;

5. The trust instrument expressly incorporates the laws of the Commonwealth to govern the validity, construction, and administration of the trust;

6. The trust instrument includes a spendthrift provision, as defined in § 64.2-743, that restrains both voluntary and involuntary transfer of the settlor's qualified interest; and

7. The settlor does not have the right to disapprove distributions from the trust.

"Qualified trustee" means any person who is a natural person residing within the Commonwealth or a legal entity authorized to engage in trust business within the Commonwealth and who maintains or arranges for custody within the Commonwealth of some or all of the property that has been transferred to the trust by the settlor... [and] materially participates within the Commonwealth in the administration of the trust. A trustee is not a qualified trustee if such trustee's authority to make distributions of income or principal or both are subject to the direction of someone who, were that person a trustee of the trust, would not meet the requirements to be a qualified trustee.

B. [provision for filling a vacancy in the position of qualified trustee]

C. [provision for filling a vacancy in the position of independent qualified trustee]

D. A trust instrument shall not be deemed revocable on account of the inclusion of any one or more of the following rights, powers, and interests:

1. A power of appointment, exercisable by the settlor by will or other written instrument effective only upon the settlor's death, other than a power to appoint to the settlor's estate or the creditors of the settlor's estate;

2. The settlor's qualified interest in the trust;

3. The settlor's right to receive income or principal pursuant to an ascertainable standard;

4. The settlor's potential or actual receipt of income or principal from a charitable remainder unitrust or charitable remainder annuity trust... and the settlor's right, at any time, and from time to time, to release, in writing delivered to the qualified trustee, all or any part of the settlor's retained interest in such trust;

5. The settlor's receipt each year of a percentage, not to exceed five percent, specified in the trust instrument of the initial value of the trust assets or their value determined from time to time pursuant to the trust instrument;

6. The settlor's right to remove a trustee and to appoint a new trustee;

7. The settlor's potential or actual use of real property held under a personal residence trust ...;

8. The settlor's potential or actual receipt or use of a qualified annuity interest…;

9. The ability of a qualified trustee, whether pursuant to discretion or direction, to pay, after the settlor's death, all or any part of the settlor's debts outstanding at the time of the settlor's death, the expenses of administering the settlor's estate, or any estate inheritance tax imposed on or with respect to the settlor's estate; and

10. A settlor's potential or actual receipt of income or principal to pay, in whole or in part, income taxes due on trust income, or the direct payment of such taxes to the applicable tax authorities, pursuant to a provision in the trust instrument that expressly provides for the direct payment of such taxes or the reimbursement of the settlor for such tax payments.

E. A beneficiary who has the right to withdraw his entire beneficial interest in a trust shall be treated as its settlor to the extent of such withdrawal right, when such right to withdraw has lapsed, been released, or otherwise expired, without regard to the limitations otherwise imposed by subsection B of § 64.2-747.

§ 64.2-746. Discretionary trusts; effect of standard

A. In this section, "child" includes any person for whom an order or judgment for child support has been entered in this or another state.

B. Except as otherwise provided in subsection C and § 64.2-745, whether or not a trust contains a spendthrift provision, a creditor of a beneficiary may not compel a distribution that is subject to the trustee's discretion, even if:

1. The discretion is expressed in the form of a standard of distribution; or

2. The trustee has abused the discretion.

C. To the extent a trustee has not complied with a standard of distribution or has abused a discretion:

1. A distribution may be ordered by the court to satisfy a judgment or court order against the beneficiary for support or maintenance of the beneficiary's child; and

2. The court shall direct the trustee to pay to the child such amount as is equitable under the circumstances but not more than the amount the trustee would have been required to distribute to or for the benefit of the beneficiary had the trustee complied with the standard or not abused the discretion.

D. This section does not limit the right of a beneficiary to maintain a judicial proceeding against a trustee for an abuse of discretion or failure to comply with a standard for distribution.

E. A creditor may not reach the interest of a beneficiary who is also a trustee or cotrustee, or otherwise compel a distribution, if the trustee's discretion to make distributions for the trustee's own benefit is limited by an ascertainable standard.

§ 64.2-701. Definitions

"Ascertainable standard" means a standard relating to an individual's health, education, support, or maintenance within the meaning of § 2041(b)(1)(A) or 2514(c)(1) of the Internal Revenue Code of 1986.

§ 64.2-747. Creditor's claim against settlor

A. Whether or not the terms of a trust contain a spendthrift provision...:

1. During the lifetime of the settlor, the property of a revocable trust is subject to claims of the settlor's creditors.

2. With respect to an irrevocable trust, except to the extent otherwise provided in §§ 64.2-745.1 and 64.2-745.2, a creditor or assignee of the settlor may reach the maximum amount that can be distributed to or for the settlor's benefit. If a trust has more than one settlor, the amount the creditor or assignee of a particular settlor may reach may not exceed the settlor's interest in the portion of the trust attributable to that settlor's contribution. ...

3. After the death of a settlor, and subject to the settlor's right to direct the source from which liabilities will be paid, the property of a trust that was revocable at the settlor's death is subject to claims of the settlor's creditors, costs of administration of the settlor's estate, the expenses of the settlor's funeral and disposal of remains, and statutory allowances to a surviving spouse and children including the family allowance, the right to exempt property, and the homestead allowance to the extent the settlor's probate estate is inadequate to satisfy those claims, costs, expenses, and allowances. ...

B. For purposes of this section:

1. During the period the power may be exercised, the holder of a power of withdrawal is treated in the same manner as the settlor of a revocable trust ...

§ 64.2-748. Overdue distribution

A. In this section "mandatory distribution" means a distribution of income or principal that the trustee is required to make to a beneficiary under the terms of the trust, including a distribution upon termination of the trust. The term does not include a distribution subject to the exercise of the trustee's discretion even if (i) the discretion is expressed in the form of a standard of distribution or (ii) the terms of the trust authorizing a distribution use language of discretion with language of direction.

B. Whether or not a trust contains a spendthrift provision, a creditor or assignee of a beneficiary may reach a mandatory distribution of income or principal, including a distribution upon termination of the trust, if the trustee has not made the distribution to the beneficiary within a reasonable time after the designated distribution date.

§ 64.2-749. Personal obligations of trustee

Trust property is not subject to personal obligations of the trustee, even if the trustee becomes insolvent or bankrupt.

V.   Trustee Duties

Most disputes regarding trusts arise from challenges to the trustees' execution of that role. Trustees presumptively owe a great number of duties, to the settlor in the case of a revocable trust (see § 64.2-752) and to the beneficiaries of an irrevocable trust. For everyone concerned – settlor, beneficiaries, and trustee – the content of trustee duties is of great importance. This Part first considers what recourse there is against a trustee who breaches a duty, then sets out the different types of duties to which trustees are subject, then concludes with rules as to settlor's freedom to waive duties or beneficiaries' power to authorize or excuse a breach of duty.

A.   Recourse for trustee breach of duty

The Virginia Code once required trustees to post bond, in order to guard against breach of duty, but today it creates a presumption against so requiring.

§ 64.2-755. Trustee's bond

A. Except as otherwise provided in Part A (§ 64.2-1200 et seq.) of Subtitle IV, a trustee shall give bond, or bond with surety or other security, to secure performance of the trustee's duties only if the court finds that a bond is needed to protect the interests of the beneficiaries or is required by the terms of the trust and the court has not dispensed with the requirement. ...

C. A regulated financial service institution qualified to do trust business in the Commonwealth need not give bond, even if required by the terms of the trust.

***

There is still recourse against a trustee for breach of duty, even in the absence of a bond; the settlor or beneficiary may bring suit and seek an injunction or a finding of personal liability the supports an order against the trustee to compensate the trust for any loss the breach caused.

Article 10. Liability of Trustees and Rights of Persons Dealing with Trustee

§ 64.2-792. Remedies for breach of trust

A. A violation by a trustee of a duty the trustee owes to a beneficiary is a breach of trust.

B. To remedy a breach of trust that has occurred or may occur, the court may:

1. Compel the trustee to perform the trustee's duties;

2. Enjoin the trustee from committing a breach of trust;

3. Compel the trustee to redress a breach of trust by paying money, restoring property, or other means;

4. Order a trustee to account;

5. Appoint a special fiduciary to take possession of the trust property and administer the trust;

6. Suspend the trustee;

7. Remove the trustee as provided in § 64.2-759;

8. Reduce or deny compensation to the trustee;

9. Subject to § 64.2-803, void an act of the trustee, impose a lien or a constructive trust on trust property, or trace trust property wrongfully disposed of and recover the property or its proceeds; or

10. Order any other appropriate relief.

§ 64.2-793. Damages for breach of trust

A. A trustee who commits a breach of trust is liable to the beneficiaries affected for the greater of:

1. The amount required to restore the value of the trust property and trust distributions to what they would have been had the breach not occurred; or

2. The profit the trustee made by reason of the breach.

B. Except as otherwise provided in this subsection, if more than one trustee is liable to the beneficiaries for a breach of trust, a trustee is entitled to contribution from the other trustee or trustees. A trustee is not entitled to contribution if the trustee was substantially more at fault than another trustee or if the trustee committed the breach of trust in bad faith or with reckless indifference to the purposes of the trust or the interests of the beneficiaries. A trustee who received a benefit from the breach of trust is not entitled to contribution from another trustee to the extent of the benefit received.

§ 64.2-794. Damages in absence of breach

A. A trustee is accountable to an affected beneficiary for any profit made by the trustee arising from the administration of the trust, even absent a breach of trust.

B. Absent a breach of trust, a trustee is not liable to a beneficiary for a loss or depreciation in the value of trust property or for not having made a profit.

§ 64.2-795. Attorney fees and costs

In a judicial proceeding involving the administration of a trust, the court, as justice and equity may require, may award costs and expenses, including reasonable attorney fees, to any party, to be paid by another party or from the trust that is the subject of the controversy.

§ 64.2-796. Limitation of action against trustee

A. A beneficiary may not commence a proceeding against a trustee for breach of trust more than one year after the date the beneficiary or a representative of the beneficiary was sent a report that adequately disclosed the existence of a potential claim for breach of trust and informed the beneficiary of the time allowed for commencing a proceeding.

B. A report adequately discloses the existence of a potential claim for breach of trust if it provides sufficient information so that the beneficiary or representative knows of the potential claim or should have inquired into its existence.

C. If subsection A does not apply, a judicial proceeding by a beneficiary against a trustee for breach of trust shall be commenced within five years after the first to occur of:

1. The removal, resignation, or death of the trustee;
2. The termination of the beneficiary's interest in the trust; or
3. The termination of the trust.

D. Whenever fraud has been perpetrated in connection with any proceeding or in any statement filed under this chapter, or if fraud is used to avoid or circumvent the provisions or purposes of this chapter, any person injured thereby may obtain appropriate relief against the perpetrator of the fraud or restitution from any person benefiting from the fraud, whether innocent or not, except for a bona fide purchaser. Any proceeding shall be commenced within two years after the fraud is discovered, but no proceeding may be brought against one not a perpetrator of the fraud later than five years after the time the fraud is committed. This section does not apply to remedies for fraud practiced on a decedent during his lifetime that affects the succession of his estate.

E. The provisions of this section shall not operate to reduce the period of limitations applicable to actions and suits governed by § 8.01-245 [which provides: "No action shall be brought upon the bond of any fiduciary except within ten years next after the right to bring such action shall have first accrued."].

§ 64.2-797. Reliance on trust instrument

A trustee who acts in reasonable reliance on the terms of the trust as expressed in the trust instrument is not liable to a beneficiary for a breach of trust to the extent the breach resulted from the reliance.

§ 64.2-798. Event affecting administration or distribution

If the happening of an event, including marriage, divorce, performance of educational requirements, or death, affects the administration or distribution of a trust, a trustee who has exercised reasonable care to ascertain the happening of the event is not liable for a loss resulting from the trustee's lack of knowledge.

§ 64.2-801. Limitation on personal liability of trustee

A. Except as otherwise provided in the contract, a trustee is not personally liable on a contract properly entered into in the trustee's fiduciary capacity in the course of administering the trust if the trustee in the contract disclosed the fiduciary capacity.

B. A trustee is personally liable for torts committed in the course of administering a trust, or for obligations arising from ownership or control of trust property, including liability for violation of environmental law, only if the trustee is personally at fault.

C. A claim based on a contract entered into by a trustee in the trustee's fiduciary capacity, on an obligation arising from ownership or control of trust property, or on a tort committed in the course of administering a trust, may be asserted in a judicial proceeding against the trustee in the trustee's fiduciary capacity, whether or not the trustee is personally liable for the claim.

§ 64.2-803. Protection of person dealing with trustee

A. A person other than a beneficiary who in good faith assists a trustee, or who in good faith and for value deals with a trustee, without knowledge that the trustee is exceeding or improperly exercising the trustee's powers, is protected from liability as if the trustee properly exercised the power.

B. A person other than a beneficiary who in good faith deals with a trustee is not required to inquire into the extent of the trustee's powers or the propriety of their exercise.

C. A person who in good faith delivers assets to a trustee need not ensure their proper application.

D. A person other than a beneficiary who in good faith assists a former trustee, or who in good faith and for value deals with a former trustee, without knowledge that the trusteeship has terminated is protected from liability as if the former trustee were still a trustee.

E. Comparable protective provisions of other laws relating to commercial transactions or transfer of securities by fiduciaries prevail over the protection provided by this section.

§ 64.2-804. Certification of trust

A. Instead of furnishing a copy of the trust instrument to a person other than a beneficiary, the trustee may furnish to the person a certification of trust containing the following information:

    1. That the trust exists and the date the trust instrument was executed;

    2. The identity of the settlor;

    3. The identity and address of the currently acting trustee;

    4. The powers of the trustee;

    5. The revocability or irrevocability of the trust and the identity of any person holding a power to revoke the trust;

    6. The authority of cotrustees to sign or otherwise authenticate and whether all or less than all are required in order to exercise powers of the trustee;

    7. The trust's taxpayer identification number; and

    8. The manner of taking title to trust property.

B. A certification of trust may be signed or otherwise authenticated by any trustee.

C. A certification of trust shall state that the trust has not been revoked, modified, or amended in any manner that would cause the representations contained in the certification of trust to be incorrect.

D. A certification of trust need not contain the dispositive terms of a trust.

E. A recipient of a certification of trust may require the trustee to furnish copies of those excerpts from the original trust instrument and later amendments that designate the trustee and confer upon the trustee the power to act in the pending transaction.

F. A person who acts in reliance upon a certification of trust without knowledge that the representations contained therein are incorrect is not liable to any person for so acting and may assume without inquiry the existence of the facts contained in the certification. Knowledge of the terms of the trust may not be inferred solely from the fact that a copy of all or part of the trust instrument is held by the person relying upon the certification.

G. A person who in good faith enters into a transaction in reliance upon a certification of trust may enforce the transaction against the trust property as if the representations contained in the certification were correct. ...

***

Some trusts have more than one trustee, so questions can arise regarding the responsibility and liability of a trustee who believes a course of action the other trustees have proposed would constitute a breach of duty.

§ 64.2-756. Cotrustees

A. Cotrustees who are unable to reach a unanimous decision may act by majority decision.

B. If a vacancy occurs in a cotrusteeship, the remaining cotrustees may act for the trust.

C. A cotrustee shall participate in the performance of a trustee's function unless the cotrustee is unavailable to perform the function because of absence, illness, disqualification under other law, or other temporary incapacity, or the cotrustee has properly delegated the performance of the function to another trustee.

D. If a cotrustee is unavailable to perform duties because of absence, illness, disqualification under other law, or other temporary incapacity, and prompt action is necessary to achieve the purposes of the trust or to avoid injury to the trust property, the remaining cotrustee or a majority of the remaining cotrustees may act for the trust.

E. A trustee may delegate to a cotrustee the performance of any function other than a function that the terms of the trust expressly require to be performed by the trustees jointly. Unless a delegation was irrevocable, a trustee may revoke a delegation previously made.

F. Except as otherwise provided in subsection G, a trustee who does not join in an action of another trustee is not liable for the action.

G. Each trustee shall exercise reasonable care to:

    1. Prevent a cotrustee from committing a serious breach of trust; and

    2. Compel a cotrustee to redress a serious breach of trust.

H. A dissenting trustee who joins in an action at the direction of the majority of the trustees and who notified any cotrustee of the dissent at or before the time of the action is not liable for the action unless the action is a serious breach of trust.

***

Paragraphs G and H appear to draw a distinction between a serious breach of trust and a non-serious breach of trust. As to the former, a trustee has an affirmative obligation to try to prevent co-trustees from doing it, and to seek redress from co-trustees if they go ahead and do it anyway. As to the latter, a trustee's duty is simply to express dissent to the other trustees.

In extreme cases, a court may remove a trustee from the position.

§ 64.2-759. Removal of trustee

A. The settlor, a cotrustee, or a beneficiary, or, in the case of a charitable trust, the Attorney General may petition the court to remove a trustee, or a trustee may be removed by the court on its own initiative.

B. The court may remove a trustee if:

1. The trustee has committed a serious breach of trust;

2. Lack of cooperation among cotrustees substantially impairs the administration of the trust;

3. Because of unfitness, unwillingness, or persistent failure of the trustee to administer the trust effectively, the court determines that removal of the trustee best serves the interests of the beneficiaries; or

4. There has been a substantial change of circumstances or removal is requested by all of the qualified beneficiaries, the court finds that removal of the trustee best serves the interests of all of the beneficiaries and is not inconsistent with a material purpose of the trust, and a suitable cotrustee or successor trustee is available.

C. Pending a final decision on a request to remove a trustee, or in lieu of or in addition to removing a trustee, the court may order such appropriate relief under subsection B of § 64.2-792 as may be necessary to protect the trust property or the interests of the beneficiaries.

§ 64.2-760. Delivery of property by former trustee

A. Unless a cotrustee remains in office or the court otherwise orders, and until the trust property is delivered to a successor trustee or other person entitled to it, a trustee who has resigned or been removed has the duties of a trustee and the powers necessary to protect the trust property.

B. A trustee who has resigned or been removed shall proceed expeditiously to deliver the trust property within the trustee's possession to the cotrustee, successor trustee, or other person entitled to it.

C. Title to all trust property shall be owned and vested in any successor trustee, upon acceptance of the trusteeship, without any conveyance, transfer, or assignment by the prior trustee.

B.   Content of trustee duties

The Virginia Code contains dozens of provisions spelling out the content of trustees' presumptive duties. To make the matieral more digestible, this Part divides the topic into each category of presumptive duty and then concludes with a Subpart on settlor's freedom to waive trustee duties. The basic categories of presumptive duty are:

1. Loyalty

2. Impartiality

3. Communication

4. Management

1. Duty of Loyalty

In a nutshell, trustees should avoid any transactions that amount to self-dealing or that create a conflict of interests for them.

§ 64.2-764. Duty of loyalty

A. A trustee shall administer the trust solely in the interests of the beneficiaries.

B. ...[A] sale, encumbrance, or other transaction involving the investment or management of trust property entered into by the trustee for the trustee's own personal account or that is otherwise affected by a conflict between the trustee's fiduciary and personal interests is voidable by a beneficiary affected by the transaction unless:

1. The transaction was authorized by the terms of the trust;

2. The transaction was approved by the court;

3. The beneficiary did not commence a judicial proceeding within the time allowed by § 64.2-796;

4. The beneficiary consented to the trustee's conduct, ratified the transaction, or released the trustee in compliance with § 64.2-800; or

5. The transaction involves a contract entered into or claim acquired by the trustee before the person became or contemplated becoming trustee.

C. A sale, encumbrance, or other transaction involving the investment or management of trust property is presumed to be affected by a conflict between personal and fiduciary interests if it is entered into by the trustee with:

1. The trustee's spouse;

2. The trustee's descendants, siblings, parents, or their spouses;

3. An agent or attorney of the trustee; or

4. A corporation or other person or enterprise in which the trustee, or a person that owns a significant interest in the trustee, has an interest that might affect the trustee's best judgment.

D. A transaction between a trustee and a beneficiary that does not concern trust property but that occurs during the existence of the trust or while the trustee retains significant influence over the beneficiary and from which the trustee obtains an advantage beyond the normal commercial advantage from such transaction is voidable by the beneficiary unless the trustee establishes that the transaction was fair to the beneficiary.

E. A transaction not concerning trust property in which the trustee engages in the trustee's individual capacity involves a conflict between personal and fiduciary interests if the transaction concerns an opportunity properly belonging to the trust.

F. An investment by a trustee in securities of an investment company, investment trust, mutual fund, or other investment or financial product to which the trustee, or an affiliate of the trustee, sponsors, sells, or provides services in a capacity other than as trustee is not presumed to be affected by a conflict between personal and fiduciary interests if the investment otherwise complies with the Uniform Prudent Investor Act and § 64.2-1506. The trustee may be compensated by the [entity]..., and such compensation may be in addition to the compensation the trustee is receiving as a trustee if the trustee notifies the persons entitled to receive a copy of the trustee's annual report under § 64.2-775 of the rate and method by which that compensation was determined...

G. In voting shares of stock or in exercising powers of control over similar interests in other forms of enterprise, the trustee shall act in the best interests of the beneficiaries. If the trust is the sole owner of a corporation or other form of enterprise, the trustee shall elect or appoint directors or other managers who will manage the corporation or enterprise in the best interests of the beneficiaries.

H. This section does not preclude the following transactions, if fair to the beneficiaries:

   1. An agreement between a trustee and a beneficiary relating to the appointment or compensation of the trustee;

   2. Payment of reasonable compensation to the trustee;

   3. A transaction between a trust and another trust, decedent's estate, or conservatorship of which the trustee is a fiduciary or in which a beneficiary has an interest;

   4. A deposit of trust money in a regulated financial service institution operated by the trustee; or

   5. An advance by the trustee of money for the protection of the trust.

I. The court may appoint a special fiduciary to make a decision with respect to any proposed transaction that might violate this section if entered into by the trustee.

***

Supreme Court of Appeals of Virginia
Parsons v. Wysor
180 Va. 84, 21 S.E.2d 753 (1942)

HUDGINS, J., delivered the opinion of the court.

... E. Lee Trinkle was named as trustee of certain property in the will of J. P. M. Simmerman, which was probated on *87 March 26, 1914. This property was sold in a suit instituted for the purpose, and on December 19, 1921, the proceeds of this sale, totaling $24,798.40, were by decree placed in the hands of the trustee to invest 'in accordance with the laws of Virginia for the investment and handling of trust funds.' E. Lee Trinkle, a former Governor of Virginia, died in 1939. There was found in his ledger a typewritten statement, dated March 30, 1938, containing a list of the securities held by the trustee of the Simmerman estate as of February 2, 1937. The securities listed on the statement were found in a separate envelope marked 'E. Lee Trinkle, Trustee, J. P. M. Simmerman Estate.' These notes and bonds, and the securities for their payment were as follows:

1. Four notes dated December 23, 1934, totaling
    $2,000.00
    Signed Tico Factories, payable to and endorsed by Roy W. Sexton and Helen S. Trinkle.

2. One note dated November 1, 1935, totaling
    500.00
    Payable to the order of E. Lee Trinkle, Secured by a vendor's lien on property in Arkansas.

3. Balance due on one bond of $1,000, dated October 27, 1926, signed by Howerton-Henry Realty Co., Inc., F. M. Hughson and May C. Hughson, payable to bearer one year after date.
    500.00

4. Two bonds of $500 each, dated Oct.22, 1927, Signed by F. M. and May C. Hughson, Due one year after date.
    1,000.00

5. One bond dated February 25, 1921, Signed F. M. and May C. Hughson, Due three years after date.
    3,500.00

6. Seven bonds, dated Dec. 12, 1930, totaling
    8,000.00
    Signed Ethel K. Spence, in her own right and as executrix of Will S. Trinkle, payable to bearer one year after date, payment secured by deed of trust on Dublin farm.

7. One bond, dated July 16, 1934. Signed by Ethel Trinkle Spence, Ethel Lee Trinkle and E. Norred Trinkle.
    $750.00

8. One bond, dated December 12, 1930, Signed by Ethel K. Spence, in her own right and as administratrix of Will S. Trinkle, Payable to bearer one day after date, Payment secured by undivided one-half interest in Sand Mountain farm.
    8,500.00

**755 The obligations stated in items 1, 2, 6 and 7 were collected in full by the substituted trustee. The obligations in items 3, 4 and 5 show on their face that recovery from the makers was barred by the statute of limitations prior to the death of the trustee. Neither the general creditors nor the personal representative of the Trinkle estate offered any evidence tending to exonerate the trustee for his failure to collect the notes before they were barred. The trial court very properly held that the fact that the notes showed on their face that they were out of date created a prima facie presumption that the trustee had not used due diligence in making the loans, or in preserving the securities and collecting the amounts due. These obligations were declared to be preferred claims owing by the Trinkle estate.

The only assignment of error is to the action of the trial court in refusing to allow the substituted trustee to recover from the estate of E. Lee Trinkle the amount of loss on the $8,500 bond mentioned in item 8 above. Mrs. Ethel K. Spence executed a deed of trust on December 12, 1930, conveying to a trustee her one-half undivided interest in the Sand Mountain farm, located in Wythe County near Wytheville, containing 600 acres, to secure the payment of the $8,500 bond in question. The entire farm was sold at auction in this suit on February 24, 1941, for $14,455. One-half of the net proceeds of this sale was approximately $3,000 less than sufficient to pay the full obligation due the Simmerman estate. *89 ...

The standard of care, by which the management of trust funds by a fiduciary is measured, is that he must act in good faith and must exercise the same degree of discretion in the management of the trust that a prudent man of discretion and intelligence would exercise in his own like affairs. What constitutes this care, diligence and discretion depends on the facts and circumstances disclosed. ... Specific references were made to Harrison on Wills and Administration, volume 1, page 705, wherein this noted author said: 'The inquiry in every case in which it is sought to fix a liability upon a fiduciary is: 1. Did he act within the scope of his powers and duties? 2. Did he act in good faith? 3. Did he act with ordinary prudence? If he did so act, he is not responsible for the consequences of the act, though it result in the loss of the trust fund, or some part of it.' Mr. Justice Holt, in Harris v. Citizens Bank, etc., Co., 172 Va. 111, 200 S.E. 652, added this pertinent statement: 'They (fiduciaries) are required to do those things which a man of reasonable intelligence and prudence would be expected to do in the management of his own affairs, but this rule, like most rules, is to be construed in the light of the conditions obtaining when it is applied.'

This standard of conduct has been applied consistently in this jurisdiction where the trustee had no personal interest in the transaction other than a reasonable *90 charge for services rendered. In each of the cases cited in which recovery against the trustee was denied, the evidence did not show the existence of any material fact which was calculated to influence the trustee adversely to the best interests of the trust estate. There was no evidence tending to produce prejudice or bias in the mind of the trustee for or against making the investment, or realizing on the investment if conditions justified such action to preserve the estate. The trustee, in accepting and managing the trust property, must keep himself in a position to form an unbiased judgment on questions affecting the property under his control. An unbiased judgment cannot be formed and a sound discretion cannot be exercised, within the meaning of the rule, if the trustee has a personal interest in the transaction or represents an interest therein adverse to the trust estate.

The circumstances, under which this $8,500 bond was executed by the maker and acquired by the trustee, are stated in a letter signed by Mrs. Spence to her attorneys **756 in this case and filed as an exhibit. The pertinent parts of this letter read:

> When Governor Trinkle placed the deed of trust for $8500.00 against my half interest in the Sand Mountain farm he brought me the deed of trust to sign and of course stated that in the circumstances we would just have to do it. He tended to all the business and I trusted him implicitly and let him tend to it without attempting to take care of any of the details. So in one sense of the word I did not know anything about it, but of course he told me what he was going to do with the money and at the time I knew that he was going to use the money to pay and satisfy the items subsequently set out by him in the letter which Mr. Walker has shown to you gentlemen and which you are at liberty to file with this statement. But Governor Trinkle did not physically place any of the $8500.00 in my hands and I did not physically have anything to do with paying off the obligations mentioned in that letter. He had me execute the note and deed of trust, constituting a lien on my half *91 of the Sand Mountain farm. He then sold the note to E. Lee Trinkle, Trustee, J. P. M. Simmerman estate, for $8500.00 in cash. I do not know whether he had before this lent $8500.00 to himself or to a third person. That was none of my business, but after placing the $8500.00 note in the trust fund or fiduciary account he then took the $8500.00 in cash - no matter from what source it had immediately come - and paid off the obligations mentioned in the letter with it as he had planned and as he had notified me in the letter, and that left me owing that note. (Italics supplied.)

> This is very similar to all the other transactions.

The letter to which Mrs. Spence refers in the above statement is a letter to her from Governor Trinkle bearing date on January 2, 1931. These letters and other evidence in the case show that Mr. Trinkle was a brother-in-law of Mrs. Ethel K. Spence. He was her confidential and financial advisor and agent, to whom the borrower confided the complete management and control of the bulk of her property. The trustee was a half owner of the 600-acre Sand Mountain farm, the one-half interest to which was given as security for the payment of trust funds loaned. He was half owner of the stock and equipment on the farm. He was the active and the exclusively managing partner of the entire farming operations. The trustee and Mrs. Spence were joint obligors on other notes and bonds totaling quite a large sum. The financial, as well as the personal, interests of the two were so entwined, one with the other, that a financial disaster to one inevitably would affect adversely the financial interests of the other.

The trustee, in making this loan, was dealing with himself as the partner and financial agent of the borrower. The inference from all the evidence is that the trustee, in making the loan, was influenced by the necessity of the borrower rather than the best interests of the trust estate. He was not in a position to form an unbiased opinion or to exercise a sound discretion as to the best interests of the trust. *92

The proceeds of this loan were expended by the trustee and not by the borrower. In his letter to Mrs. Spence, he said that $7,905 of the $8,500 was used to pay amounts 'due for various loans (not included in above) that have been made within the last year, plus back interest due on the $15,000 in the Farmers Bank that you have, over and above $5,000 that we owe jointly, of the $20,000 in the Farmers, also Yellowstone note of Trinkle Bros., and, also, the individual note of Ethel for $350.00, the individual note of Norred for $275,00, and the individual unpaid checks of Norred, for money gotten, amounting to $101.00.' The remaining sum, $595, together with a like amount advanced by Mr. Trinkle, was deposited in the bank to the credit to E. Lee Trinkle, farm account, and used by him in the operation of the farms owned by the trustee and the borrower.

Among other pertinent facts bearing on the advisability of making this loan, in the first instance, was that the maker of this obligation personally owed $60,229 and was jointly obligated with the trustee on other notes totaling at least $25,000. Her attorney, T. F. Walker, testified that the value of her real estate was less than $50,000, which was all the property she then owned except 'personal effects, and possibly some stocks that more than likely turned out to be valueless.' Hence, the maker of this bond was insolvent at the time the trustee made the loan to her. She was not gainfully employed and her income seems to have been restricted to the proceeds from the operation of a boarding house and one-half the net proceeds from the income of two farms. Any prudent man, in making **757 a loan with or without security, gives due weight to the ability of the maker to keep the interest and taxes paid, and repay the loan when due. The ability of the obligor in this instance to pay interest depended upon the successful operation of the farm by the trustee himself. Its rental value in 1940 was stated to be only $750.

An undivided interest in real estate is not an attractive security for a loan. Any one of the owners has a right at *93 any time to sue for partition and force a division or sale. The successful operation of a farm owned by two or more persons depends upon the energy, temperament and business ability of the respective owners. No prudent person would make such an investment without careful consideration of the possibility of disagreement, partition or sale.

Any valuation placed on Mrs. Spence's interest in the Sand Mountain farm would necessarily affect the interests of the owner of the other half. This owner, as stated, was the trustee himself. He was in no position to form a disinterested opinion as to the loan value of the property accepted by him as trustee to secure the payment of trust funds intrusted to his management and control. The successful operation of the Sand Mountain farm did not depend upon the maker of the $8,500 bond, but it depended upon the energy and the business capacity of the trustee himself. This is true not only of this farm but of several other enterprises in which the borrower and the lender were jointly interested.

The family ties, and the joint financial interests of the borrower and the lender in the subject matter tended to prevent the trustee from forming an unbiased judgment of the value of the security taken to secure trust funds. These ties and financial interests place the trustee in this position. His duties as a trustee required him to be free to act promptly, efficiently and vigorously, if necessary to preserve the funds under his control. On the other hand, his affection for his sister-in-law, and his own financial interests tended to induce him to indulge the debtor beyond financial safety of the trust fund. In other words, his duties as trustee were in conflict with his own personal interests, and with his natural desire to aid his sister-in-law and to act for her best interests as her financial agent. Such a position for a trustee is manifestly improper and should not receive the approval of a court of equity. 'In short, it may be laid down as a general rule, that a trustee is bound not to do anything which can place him in a position inconsistent with the interests of the trust, or which have a tendency to   *94 interfere with his duty in discharging it.' 1st Story's Eq. Ju., sec. 322.

It does not appear how much, if any, of the interest was paid by the maker of the bond. It seems that the interest was paid by the trustee himself. He stated, in his memorandum of March 30, 1938, that 'whilst all of this interest has been paid, as above set forth, a great deal of this interest has been paid by me individually (and I am holding those original notes with that interest to be repaid me when they are settled by Mrs. Spence, or by sale of her land, or when collected from other parties. The back of the notes other than the Spence notes will show how much interest is due me that I have advanced on same).'

The family connection of the parties, the fact that the trustee was the financial agent and advisor of the borrower, and the personal interests of the trustee in the proceeds of the loan and the farm given as security, make this investment a transaction which should be governed by the principles involved in those cases in which a trustee deals with himself in respect to the trust estate. This class of transactions is voidable by the beneficiary at his election, regardless of whether fraud or any advantage or inadequacy of consideration is shown by the evidence. This conclusion renders it unnecessary to discuss the evidence introduced by the general creditors of the Trinkle estate tending to show that the investment was good in 1930 when it was consummated.

In Waddy v. Grimes, 154 Va. 615, 647, 153 S.E. 807, it was held that where a beneficiary conveyed land by deed to the wife of the fiduciary, 'Equity would raise a prima facie presumption against its validity, and would cast upon the party seeking to sustain the deed the burden of proving affirmatively its compliance with equitable requisites and overcoming the presumption. *95**758 There is a distinction to be made between transactions occurring directly between a trustee and his cestui que trust, and those transactions in which the trustee deals with himself in respect to the trust estate. The latter class of transactions are voidable by the cestui que trust at his election without giving any reason or alleging any fraud, or any advantage or inadequacy of price.' Lord Ellenborough, in Thompson v. Havelock, 1 Campb. 528, 10 Revised Rep. 744, said that 'no man should be allowed to have an interest against his duty.'

It appears that the trustee made annual settlements of his account of the estate with the commissioner of accounts. In 1935 the trustee arbitrarily reduced the rate of interest from six to five per cent., and made disbursements annually thereafter at the reduced rate. These settlements were approved by the commissioner of accounts and confirmed by the trial court. However, the trustee did not furnish the commissioner with a list of the investments and the collateral held to secure payment, nor was he required by the commissioner so to do. Code, sec. 5408. Under the circumstances, confirmation of the commissioner's report by the court is not a bar to the recovery of the full legal rate of interest on this investment in this cause.

It is well to note that appellant does not impute to the trustee mala fides or fraud in this transaction. It is said in the brief: 'We have said nothing in this petition which we intended as a reflection on the character or integrity of Governor Trinkle. It is our opinion that he fully expected and intended to account to the beneficiaries of the Simmerman estate for every penny of the principal plus the interest.' Again, elsewhere in the same brief, it is stated: 'If he were alive today, we believe he would be the last person to contend otherwise.'

While the evidence does not show that Governor Trinkle personally assumed the obligation in question, as stated, the manner in which he made this loan, and his personal interest in the borrower, in the proceeds of the loan and in the *96 security given, render his estate liable, with or without proof of an express promise to pay the obligation. ...

[T]he cause remanded, with directions to the trial court to enter a decree permitting the substituted trustee to recover in accordance with the views expressed in this opinion.

---

2.   Duty of Impartiality Among Beneficiaries

In the absence of contrary indication in the trust instrument, the law presumes the settlor intended even-handed treatment and equal concern for all beneficiaries. This has obvious implications for distributions from the trust. If, for example, the trust instrument authorizes the trustee to distribute income to two beneficiaries as needed for their comfort, and if the two beneficiaries are similarly situated, then presumptively the trustee should give them roughly equal shares of the trust income. When there are different categories of beneficiaries, however – most commonly, beneficiaries receiving distributions fo trust income for life and remainder beneficiaries who take the remaining principal when the life estate holders die – then impartiality requires investment decision making aimed at balancing the competing interests, at generating substantial income while also increasing the value of the principal.

§ 64.2-765. Impartiality

If a trust has two or more beneficiaries, the trustee shall act impartially in investing, managing, and distributing the trust property, giving due regard to the beneficiaries' respective interests.

§ 64.2-785. Loyalty and impartiality

A. A trustee shall invest and manage the trust assets solely in the interest of the beneficiaries.

B. If a trust has two or more beneficiaries, the trustee shall act impartially in investing and managing the trust assets, taking into account any differing interests of the beneficiaries.

Supreme Court of Virginia.
Sturgis v. Stinson
241 Va. 531, 404 S.E.2d 56 (1991)

LACY, Justice.

... Dr. William J. Sturgis, Jr., died testate in 1986, leaving an estate valued at $1,140,462, **58 consisting of an automobile, approximately $300,000 in various stocks and bonds, and two parcels of real estate-Bush Hill Farm (the farm), valued in the estate inventory at $708,500, and a one-third undivided interest in another parcel of land with a value of $126,000. His will provided *534 that his widow, Anne Sturgis, receive all the income from his estate for her lifetime. At her death, or if she were to renounce the income, the residue of the estate was to pass to his children, Susan Sturgis Stinson and Christopher S. Sturgis (the remaindermen).

The testator named his wife and Robert C. Oliver, Jr., as co-executors. Upon the wife's election not to serve, Oliver qualified as executor of the estate. In 1989, he filed a bill of complaint stating that the income beneficiary, Mrs. Sturgis, had complained that "the income derived from the estate is insufficient based upon the value of the assets of the estate" and asked that property of the trust be sold and so reinvested as to derive greater income. The remaindermen opposed the sale of the property and maintained that the trust assets could not be sold without their consent. The executor sought the guidance of the chancellor. ...

Bush Hill Farm... constitutes approximately 75% of the corpus of the trust and, at the time of trial, had a fair market value of $1.5 million. The maximum annual net income generated by this asset and paid to Mrs. Sturgis was $1,265.99 in 1988. Mrs. Sturgis asserts that this return on the property, representing eighty-four one-thousandths of one percent of its fair market value, classifies this property as an unproductive asset and that, under general trust principles, the executor has an obligation to sell it and reinvest the proceeds. ...

Under general trust law principles, where, as here, a trust is created for successive beneficiaries, the trustee has a duty to *535 deal impartially with them. Shriners Hospitals v. Smith, 238 Va. 708, 710, 385 S.E.2d 617, 618 (1989). The parties agree that the executor's duties in relation to trust assets set out in the Restatement (Second) of Trusts embody sound and appropriate principles:

> The trustee is under a duty to the beneficiary to use reasonable care and skill to make the trust property productive. Restatement (Second) of Trusts § 181 (1959).

Unless it is otherwise provided by the terms of the trust, if property held in trust to pay the income to a beneficiary for a designated period and thereafter to pay the principal to another beneficiary produces no income or an income substantially less than the current rate of return on trust investments, and is likely to continue unproductive or under-productive, the trustee is under a duty to the beneficiary entitled to the income to sell such property within a reasonable time. Id. at § 240.

The executor and remaindermen assert that... management of the farm and other trust assets were "otherwise provided by the terms of the" will. The remaindermen argue **59 that the testator intended that the farm not be sold unless necessary to meet the needs of the income beneficiary. The executor argues that as long as the income beneficiary is receiving income sufficient to meet her needs, his discretion as to the management of trust assets should not be disturbed. In contrast, Mrs. Sturgis argues that the will places no condition or limitation on the amount of income she is to receive and contains nothing to support the inference drawn by the chancellor that the testator wished to retain the farm as a family heritage. ... Resolution of the dispute rests upon the testator's intention as reflected in the will. ... *536 ...

Paragraph Four of the will consists of three sections. The first declares that Mrs. Sturgis is to receive "[a]ll of the income of my estate, of every nature and wheresoever situate," during her lifetime. The second section of Paragraph Four provides that:

> If at any time, ... in the opinion of my Co-Executor, ... the income of my estate together with such other income available to my wife is insufficient to meet any unusual expense ... or to provide for her comfortable maintenance and welfare, then such Co-Executor may pay to my wife ... such amounts from the principal or corpus of my estate as such Co-Executor deems necessary for such purposes.

The final section of Paragraph Four provides that when Mrs. Sturgis dies or "if she should decide that she has no need for such income" the estate devolves upon Christopher Sturgis and Susan Stinson.

Paragraph Six provides in pertinent part:

> It is my will, and I direct that my Executors and their successors have, in addition to all other powers granted by law, the powers set forth in Section 64.1-57 of the Code of Virginia (1950), as in force on the date of the execution of this will, together with the right to sell, pledge, or hypothecate real estate and other property.

*537 Contrary to the argument advanced by the executor and the remaindermen, the second section of Paragraph Four imposes no limitation on the first section of that paragraph. Indeed, the second section confers a separate benefit upon the widow; in the event the income otherwise available to her "is insufficient to meet any unusual expense ... or to provide for her comfortable maintenance and welfare," the executor is empowered to invade and deplete the corpus of the trust for her benefit. Consideration of the widow's need is of concern to the executor and a precondition to his actions only for depletion of the trust corpus. The power to deplete the corpus for that purpose is irrelevant to the issues framed in this appeal.

The power of the executor to convert and reinvest corpus assets is granted by Paragraph Six, in which the executor is given the right to dispose of property and to exercise all powers and rights afforded a fiduciary under general law and as set forth in Code § 64.1-57. The will does not specify any criteria of need or other preconditions **60 for the executor's exercise of these powers. Nor is there any indication that the income beneficiary would receive anything less than all the net income, regardless of amount, and irrespective of need, generated from the executor's exercise of his investment and management authority.

This interpretation is consistent with certain actions of the executor. As he testified, he had converted a number of the stocks in the trust corpus to investments that generated more income, including some stocks which would have appreciated in value but which did not generate much income. His conversion of the trust corpus was not limited to personalty; the executor had also agreed to the sale of a portion of the real estate in which the trust held a one-third undivided interest. There is no indication in the record that the executor sought the remaindermen's consent for this sale, that the conversion was required due to Mrs. Sturgis' unusual expenses, or that the payment to Mrs. Sturgis of the income the new assets produced was based on the executor's determination of her need.

Furthermore, there is nothing in the will or the record to suggest that the executor was required to treat Bush Hill Farm in a different manner than other trust assets. Although the testator easily could have addressed the disposition of the farm, he did not. Indeed, the will does not even refer to the farm specifically. While Bush Hill Farm had been in the Sturgis family for many years, *538 neither the remaindermen, Dr. Sturgis, nor his parents had ever lived on the property. The only dwellings on the property were tenant farmers' shacks which had burned prior to Dr. Sturgis' death. This record does not reflect any connection the testator had with this piece of property which would support the conclusion that the testator intended to distinguish its treatment from that to be accorded other real or personal property in the trust.

We conclude, therefore, that the testator intended that Mrs. Sturgis, the income beneficiary, receive unconditionally all the income generated by the trust's assets. Additionally, if, in the opinion of the executor, the income from the trust and any other income available to her should become insufficient to meet her needs, the executor would be required to provide payments to her directly by depleting the corpus of the trust. Furthermore, we conclude that the testator did not intend to, and did not, direct or restrict the executor's management of the trust's assets, including Bush Hill Farm, except as provided under general law.

We have not previously addressed the duty of a fiduciary regarding the level of productivity of trust assets in circumstances where there are successive beneficiaries and no explicit instruction by the testator concerning that duty. We agree with the parties that the trust principles expressed in the Restatement and quoted above are appropriate, and we adopt them here.

Except for the directive on depletion of the corpus occasioned by Mrs. Sturgis' needs, the will contains no other directions regarding the management of the trust assets. Although the management discretion afforded a trustee under the Code of Virginia is extensive, see

Code §§ 64.1-57 and 55-253 et seq., that discretion is subject to the requirements of the "prudent man rule," Code § 26-45.1. The Restatement principles adopted above define a trustee's obligations under the "prudent man rule" regarding productivity of trust assets. These principles are applicable to the executor in this case as the return generated by Bush Hill Farm is so disproportionate to its value, the farm is rendered an unproductive asset.

In a second assignment of error, Mrs. Sturgis asserts that the chancellor erred "by failing to require the Trustee to sell unproductive trust assets and to allocate a portion of the proceeds of such sale to the income beneficiary as required by the Uniform Principal and Income Act, Va.Code §§ 55-253, et seq." That Act *539 provides that whenever any asset of a trust, real or personal, is unproductive, the income beneficiary "shall be entitled to share in the net proceeds received from [conversion **61 of] the property as delayed income." Code § 55-263(1). The term "delayed income" is defined as

> the difference between the net proceeds received from the property and the amount which, had it been placed at simple interest at the rate of five per centum per annum for the period during which the change was delayed, would have produced the net proceeds at the time of the change.... Code § 55-263(2).

The period of delay is calculated "from the time when the duty to make [a change] first arose, which shall be presumed, in the absence of evidence to the contrary, to be one year after the trustee first received the property if then unproductive, otherwise one year after it became unproductive." Code § 55-263(3). We think these principles are also applicable here. ...

RUSSELL, Justice, with whom STEPHENSON, Justice, joins, dissenting.

The principles of law that govern cases of this kind are well settled: the testator's intention, if legal and ascertainable, controls. All refinements of the law must yield to the testator's power to dispose of his property as he pleases. When this intention is ascertained, the quest is ended and all other rules become immaterial. Picot v. Picot, 237 Va. 686, 689, 379 S.E.2d 364, 366 (1989). In ascertaining the testator's intention, the court must examine the will as a whole, giving effect to all its parts if that can be done. Thomas v. Copenhaver, 235 Va. 124, 128, 365 S.E.2d 760, 763 (1988). The intention to be considered is that which is spoken by the words of the will, not an intention deduced from speculation as to what the testator would have done had he anticipated a change in the circumstances surrounding him *540 at the time of its execution.

The will of Dr. Sturgis is unambiguous and his overall intention is clear from its words. ... If she should experience unusual expenses, or if the income of his estate, together with any "other income available to [his widow]" should prove insufficient to provide for her "comfortable maintenance and welfare," then the co-executor was authorized to invade the corpus to the extent necessary, in the co-executor's discretion, to bring the widow's income up to that standard. ....

Unfortunately, the majority opinion appears to be based upon the notion that when Dr. Sturgis wrote paragraph six, he had forgotten paragraph four. The opinion considers the two provisions in isolation, rather than construing the will as a whole. ...

When Dr. Sturgis executed his will, he knew what his assets were. He knew that some parts of his estate produced substantial income, which would primarily benefit his widow, and that other parts would produce little income, but would constitute a substantial inheritance for his children. ... If he had intended that his executors convert all his assets into investments producing high income, he could easily have said so. ... **62 Land is not fungible. It is idle to speculate as to the testator's reason for retaining the farm as a part of his estate, for his children's benefit, rather than directing his executors to convert it into income-producing investments. The fact remains, however, that for his own reasons, he did so. He could have sold it during his lifetime, as his parents before him might have done, but he did not. Despite its deficiency as a producer of income, the farm was a *541 part of the estate which passed under the will and which he contemplated as one of the sources of income for his widow.

Construed according to the testator's clear intentions, the co-executor had authority to sell timber from the farm, or to sell or encumber the land, in whole or in part, as might be necessary to maintain the widow comfortably, but not otherwise. That view is reinforced by the circumstances surrounding the testator at the time of execution of his will. Mrs. Sturgis was not the mother of Dr. Sturgis' children; they were the children of a prior marriage. Mrs. Sturgis came into the marriage with income-producing assets of her own, and it was not apparent that it would ever become necessary to invade the corpus to maintain her comfortably. ...

Paragraph six does not require the executors to do anything. It certainly does not authorize them, or us, to disregard the clear intent of the testator, to treat land as if it were stocks and bonds, or to require conversion of the land into income-producing assets to the detriment of the testator's children. ...

In addition to investing trust property so as to achieve a fair balance between categories of beneficiaries, trustees must distribute income and expenses of the trust in an impartial and fair manner. The Code provides extensive guidance for this task. Omitted below are many provisions dealing with specific types of assets. What is included below is sufficient to provide a sense of the basic principles of allocation.

Article 4. Allocation of Receipts During Administration of Trust
Part 1. Receipts from Entities

§ 64.2-1009. Character of receipts

A. In this section, "entity" means a corporation, partnership, limited liability company, regulated investment company, real estate investment trust, common trust fund, or any other organization in which a trustee has an interest other than a trust or estate to which § 64.2-1010 applies, a business or activity to which § 64.2-1011 applies, or an asset-backed security to which § 64.2-1023 applies.

B. Except as otherwise provided in this section, a trustee shall allocate to income money received from an entity.

C. A trustee shall allocate the following receipts from an entity to principal:

   1. Property other than money;

   2. Money received in one distribution or a series of related distributions in exchange for part or all of a trust's interest in the entity;

   3. Money received in total or partial liquidation of the entity; and

   4. Money received from an entity that is a regulated investment company or a real estate investment trust if the money distributed is a capital gain dividend for federal income tax purposes.

D. Money is received in partial liquidation:

   1. To the extent that the entity, at or near the time of a distribution, indicates that it is a distribution in partial liquidation; or

   2. If the total amount of money and property received in a distribution or series of related distributions is greater than 20 percent of the entity's gross assets...

§ 64.2-1010. Distribution from trust or estate

A trustee shall allocate to income an amount received as a distribution of income from a trust or an estate in which the trust has an interest other than a purchased interest, and shall allocate to principal an amount received as a distribution of principal from such a trust or estate. ...

§ 64.2-1011. Business and other activities conducted by trustee

...

B. A trustee who accounts separately for a business or other activity may determine the extent to which its net cash receipts shall be retained for working capital, the acquisition or replacement of fixed assets, and other reasonably foreseeable needs of the business or activity, and the extent to which the remaining net cash receipts are accounted for as principal or income in the trust's general accounting records. ...

Part 2. Receipts Not Normally Apportioned

§ 64.2-1012. Principal receipts

A trustee shall allocate to principal:

1. To the extent not allocated to income under this chapter, assets received from a transferor during the transferor's lifetime, a decedent's estate, a trust with a terminating income interest, or a payer under a contract naming the trust or its trustee as beneficiary;

2. Money or other property received from the sale, exchange, liquidation, or change in form of a principal asset, including realized profit, subject to this article;
…

4. Proceeds of property taken by eminent domain, but a separate award made for the loss of income … is income; …

§ 64.2-1013. Rental property

… [T]he trustee shall allocate to income an amount received as rent of real or personal property, including an amount received for cancellation or renewal of a lease. An amount received as a refundable deposit, including a security deposit or a deposit that is to be applied as rent for future periods, shall be added to principal and held subject to the terms of the lease ...

§ 64.2-1014. Obligation to pay money

A. An amount received as interest, whether determined at a fixed, variable, or floating rate, on an obligation to pay money to the trustee, including an amount received as consideration for prepaying principal, shall be allocated to income...

B. A trustee shall allocate to principal an amount received from the sale, redemption, or other disposition of an obligation to pay money to the trustee more than one year after it is purchased or acquired by the trustee... If the obligation matures within one year after it is purchased or acquired by the trustee, an amount received in excess of its purchase price or its value when acquired by the trust shall be allocated to income. …

§ 64.2-1015. Insurance policies and similar

A. Except as otherwise provided in subsection B, a trustee shall allocate to principal the proceeds of a life insurance policy or other contract in which the trust or its trustee is named as beneficiary... The trustee shall allocate dividends on an insurance policy to income if the premiums on the policy are paid from income, and to principal if the premiums are paid from principal.

B. A trustee shall allocate to income proceeds of a contract that insures the trustee against loss of occupancy or other use by an income beneficiary, loss of income, or… loss of profits from a business. …

Part 3. Receipts Normally Apportioned

§ 64.2-1016. Insubstantial allocations not required

If a trustee determines that an allocation between principal and income required by § 64.2-1017-1020 or 64.2-1023 is insubstantial, the trustee may allocate the entire amount to principal... An allocation is presumed to be insubstantial if:

1. The amount of the allocation would increase or decrease net income in an accounting period, as determined before the allocation, by less than 10 percent; or

2. The value of the asset producing the receipt for which the allocation would be made is less than 10 percent of the total value of the trust's assets at the beginning of the accounting period.

§ 64.2-1017. Deferred compensation, annuities, and similar payments

... B. To the extent that a payment is characterized as interest or a dividend..., a trustee shall allocate it to income. The trustee shall allocate to principal the balance of the payment and any other payment received in the same accounting period that is not characterized as interest, a dividend, or an equivalent payment.

C. If no part of a payment is characterized as interest, a dividend, or an equivalent payment, and all or part of the payment is required to be made, a trustee shall allocate to income 10 percent of the part that is required to be made... and the balance to principal. If no part of a payment is required to be made or the payment received is the entire amount to which the trustee is entitled, the trustee shall allocate the entire payment to principal. ...

...

§ 64.2-1018. Liquidating asset

A. In this section, "liquidating asset" means an asset whose value will diminish or terminate because the asset is expected to produce receipts for a period of limited duration. The term includes a leasehold, patent, copyright, or royalty right...

B. A trustee shall allocate to income 10 percent of the receipts from a liquidating asset and the balance to principal.

Article 5. Allocation of Disbursements During Administration of Trust

§ 64.2-1024. Disbursements from income

A trustee shall make the following disbursements from income...:

1. One-half of the regular compensation of the trustee and of any person providing investment advisory or custodial services to the trustee;

2. One-half of all expenses for accountings, judicial proceedings, or other matters that involve both the income and remainder interests;

3. All of the other ordinary expenses incurred in connection with the administration, management, or preservation of trust property and the distribution of income, including interest, ordinary repairs, regularly recurring taxes assessed against principal, and expenses of a proceeding or other matter that concerns primarily the income interest; and

4. Recurring premiums on insurance covering the loss of a principal asset or the loss of income from or use of the asset.

§ 64.2-1025. Disbursements from principal

A. A trustee shall make the following disbursements from principal:

1. The remaining one-half of the disbursements described in subdivisions 1 and 2 of § 64.2-1024;

2. All of the trustee's compensation calculated on principal as a fee for acceptance, distribution, or termination, and disbursements made to prepare property for sale;

3. Payments on the principal of a trust debt;

4. Expenses of a proceeding that concerns primarily principal, including a proceeding to construe the trust or to protect the trust or its property;

5. Premiums paid on a policy of insurance not described in subdivision 4 of § 64.2-1024 of which the trust is the owner and beneficiary;

6. Estate, inheritance, and other transfer taxes, including penalties, apportioned to the trust; and

7. Disbursements related to environmental matters...

§ 64.2-1027. Transfers from income to reimburse principal

A. If a trustee makes or expects to make a principal disbursement described in this section, the trustee may transfer an appropriate amount from income to principal in one or more accounting periods to reimburse principal or to provide a reserve for future principal disbursements.

B. Principal disbursements to which subsection A applies include the following, but only to the extent that the trustee has not been and does not expect to be reimbursed by a third party:

1. An amount chargeable to income but paid from principal because it is unusually large, including extraordinary repairs;

2. A capital improvement to a principal asset, whether in the form of changes to an existing asset or the construction of a new asset, including special assessments;

3. Disbursements made to prepare property for rental, including tenant allowances, leasehold improvements, and broker's commissions;

4. Periodic payments on an obligation secured by a principal asset to the extent that the amount transferred from income to principal for depreciation is less than the periodic payments; and

5. Disbursements described in subdivision A 7 of § 64.2-1025. ...

§ 64.2-1028. Income taxes

A. A tax required to be paid by a trustee based on receipts allocated to income shall be paid from income.

B. A tax required to be paid by a trustee based on receipts allocated to principal shall be paid from principal, even if the tax is called an income tax by the taxing authority.

...

§ 64.2-1029. Adjustments between principal and income because of taxes

A. A fiduciary may make adjustments between principal and income to offset the shifting of economic interests or tax benefits between income beneficiaries and remainder beneficiaries that arise from:

1. Elections and decisions... that the fiduciary makes from time to time regarding tax matters;

2. An income tax or any other tax that is imposed upon the fiduciary or a beneficiary as a result of a transaction involving or a distribution from the estate or trust; or

3. The ownership by an estate or trust of an interest in an entity whose taxable income, whether or not distributed, is includable in the taxable income of the estate, trust, or a beneficiary. ...

***

Circuit Court of Virginia, Henrico County.
Trimmer v. Savage
89 Va. Cir. 135 (2014)

CATHERINE C. HAMMOND, Judge.

... Defendant Grace Trimmer is the grantor and beneficiary of a Trust Agreement dated April 29, 2010 ("the Trust"). Mrs. Trimmer has three adult children and several grandchildren. Petitioner is her son. Defendants Brenda Savage and Carolyn Trimmer are her daughters, and have served as Trustees for their mother ("the Trustees"). The Trust provides that upon the death of Mrs. Trimmer the remainder will be distributed to her three children. It also provides that if Petitioner still owes any money to his mother, the indebtedness will reduce his share.

At trial, the Court granted the Petition to remove the Trustees, and to appoint a Conservator for Grace Trimmer. The Trustees initially opposed this request for relief. However, on the morning of trial, they advised that opposition was withdrawn, and they consented to Paul Izzo's appointment as successor Trustee and Conservator, This was in keeping with the recommendation of Ms. Pape, the guardian ad litem appointed under Va.Code § 64.2–2003.

There remain two claims by Petitioner. First, he claims that the Trustees should reimburse the Trust for certain money it paid to Stephen Dalton, Esquire. See Va.Code § 64.2–792(B)(3). Second, he claims that his sisters should pay Petitioner's attorney's fees and costs in this action, pursuant to the Uniform Trust Code, Va.Code § 64.2–795. In the alternative he asks that Mrs. Trimmer's estate pay his attorney's fees and costs under Va.Code § 64.2–2008.

Reimbursement of Funds Paid to Mr. Dalton

In a separate action filed in 2011, William Trimmer, Jr. sued his two sisters claiming defamation. They employed Stephen Dalton, Esq., to represent them personally. In 2012 the case was tried to a jury. The jury returned a defense verdict. Brenda Savage used Trust property to pay $48,254.20 to Mr. Dalton for attorney's fees and costs. Brenda Savage also used Trust property to pay $14,391.80 to Carolyn Trimmer, to cover fees she paid to Mr. Dalton.

The Trustees admit that Trust property was used for this purpose. Their defense is that their mother and her attorney advised them to take this action. They also argue that any issue respecting the propriety of paying Mr. Dalton be addressed in another pending case. In that case a Commissioner in Chancery is examining whether the Trustees owe money to the Trust.

A trustee usually commits a breach of duty where she uses trust property for herself. Here, the Trustees testified that their mother wanted the Trustees to use Trust property to pay Mr. Dalton. They may honestly believe this, but the belief cannot justify the conduct, given the serious conflict existing between Petitioner and the Trustees while they managed the Trust.

At the time of the payments to Mr. Dalton, the children were adverse in a number of respects, which interfered with their legal duties. The Trustees owed a particular duty to their brother, because all three children have an interest in any Trust property that remains after their mother's death. The Trustees had a duty to preserve the Trust property for both the beneficiary, Mrs. Trimmer, and the remainder-men. Mason v. Jones, 67 Va. (26 Gratt.) 271, 277 (1875). This dovetails with the general duty of a trustee to serve impartially. See Va.Code § 64.2–765. "In the management of trust property, a trustee should always conduct himself with strict neutrality, favoring none of the parties, and endeavor to obtain an impartial direction in ail cases of doubt or difficulty." 19 M.J. Trusts and Trustees § 102; Parsons v. Wysor, 180 Va. 84 (1942). The payments to Mr. Dalton appear to infringe on the remainder interests, and to show favoritism.1 The Trustees will have to repay these funds to the Trust.2

Attorney's Fees

The fees of Mr. Haskins are reasonable. ... Although there was some evidence of cause to remove the Trustees and appoint a successor, the principal reason for a new Trustee was lack of cooperation among the three siblings. No one person can be held responsible for this. The fees should be paid from Mrs. Trimmer's estate under Va.Code § 64.2–2008.

In addition, Virginia has adopted a uniform act that enables trustees largely to obviate the conflict of interest between income and principal beneficiaries.

Chapter 10. Uniform Principal and Income Act
Article 1. Definitions and Fiduciary Duties

§ 64.2-1000. Definitions

In this chapter:

... "Income" means money or property that a fiduciary receives as current return from a principal asset. The term includes a portion of receipts from a sale, exchange, or liquidation of a principal asset, to the extent provided in Article 4 (§ 64.2-1009 et seq.).

"Income beneficiary" means a person to whom net income of a trust is or may be payable.

"Income interest" means the right of an income beneficiary to receive all or part of net income, whether the terms of the trust require it to be distributed or authorize it to be distributed in the trustee's discretion.

"Mandatory income interest" means the right of an income beneficiary to receive net income that the terms of the trust require the fiduciary to distribute.

"Net income" means the total receipts allocated to income during an accounting period minus the disbursements made from income during the period, plus or minus transfers under this chapter to or from income during the period. ...

"Principal" means property held in trust for distribution to a remainder beneficiary when the trust terminates.

"Remainder beneficiary" means a person entitled to receive principal when an income interest ends. ...

§ 64.2-1001. Fiduciary duties; general principles

A. In allocating receipts and disbursements to or between principal and income, and with respect to any matter within the scope of Articles 2 (§ 64.2-1004 et seq.) and 3 (§ 64.2-1006 et seq.), a fiduciary:

    1. Shall administer a trust or estate in accordance with the terms of the trust or the will, even if there is a different provision in this chapter;

2. May administer a trust or estate by the exercise of a discretionary power of administration given to the fiduciary by the terms of the trust or the will, even if the exercise of the power produces a result different from a result required or permitted by this chapter;

3. Shall administer a trust or estate in accordance with this chapter if the terms of the trust or the will do not contain a different provision or do not give the fiduciary a discretionary power of administration; and

4. Shall add a receipt or charge a disbursement to principal to the extent that the terms of the trust and this chapter do not provide a rule for allocating the receipt or disbursement to or between principal and income.

B. In exercising the power to adjust under subsection A of § 64.2-1002 or a discretionary power of administration regarding a matter within the scope of this chapter, whether granted by the terms of a trust, a will, or this chapter, a fiduciary shall administer a trust or estate impartially, based on what is fair and reasonable to all of the beneficiaries, except to the extent that the terms of the trust or the will clearly manifest an intention that the fiduciary shall or may favor one or more of the beneficiaries. A determination in accordance with this chapter is presumed to be fair and reasonable to all of the beneficiaries. ...

§ 64.2-1002. Fiduciary's power to adjust

A. A fiduciary may adjust between principal and income to the extent the fiduciary considers necessary if the fiduciary invests and manages trust assets as a prudent investor, the terms of the trust describe the amount that may or shall be distributed to a beneficiary by referring to the trust's income, and the fiduciary determines, after applying the rules in subsection A of § 64.2-1001, that the fiduciary is unable to comply with subsection B of § 64.2-1001.

B. In deciding whether and to what extent to exercise the power conferred by subsection A, a fiduciary shall consider all factors relevant to the trust and its beneficiaries, including the following factors to the extent they are relevant:

1. The nature, purpose, and expected duration of the trust;

2. The intent of the settlor;

3. The identity and circumstances of the beneficiaries;

4. The needs for liquidity, regularity of income, and preservation and appreciation of capital;

5. The assets held in the trust; the extent to which they consist of financial assets, interests in closely held enterprises, tangible and intangible personal property, or real property; the extent to which an asset is used by a beneficiary; and whether an asset was purchased by the fiduciary or received from the settlor;

6. The net amount allocated to income under the other sections of this chapter and the increase or decrease in the value of the principal assets, which the

fiduciary may estimate as to assets for which market values are not readily available;

7. Whether and to what extent the terms of the trust give the fiduciary the power to invade principal or accumulate income or prohibit the fiduciary from invading principal or accumulating income, and the extent to which the fiduciary has exercised a power from time to time to invade principal or accumulate income;

8. The actual and anticipated effect of economic conditions on principal and income and effects of inflation and deflation; and

9. The anticipated tax consequences of an adjustment.

C. A fiduciary may not make an adjustment:

1. That diminishes the income interest in a trust that requires all of the income to be paid at least annually to a spouse and for which an estate tax or gift tax marital deduction would be allowed, in whole or in part, if the fiduciary did not have the power to make the adjustment;

2. That reduces the actuarial value of the income interest in a trust to which a person transfers property with the intent to qualify for a gift tax exclusion;

3. That changes the amount payable to a beneficiary as a fixed annuity or a fixed fraction of the value of the trust assets;

4. From any amount that is permanently set aside for charitable purposes under a will or the terms of a trust unless both income and principal are so set aside;

5. If possessing or exercising the power to make an adjustment causes an individual to be treated as the owner of all or part of the trust for income tax purposes, and the individual would not be treated as the owner if the fiduciary did not possess the power to make an adjustment;

6. If possessing or exercising the power to make an adjustment causes all or part of the trust assets to be included for estate tax purposes in the estate of an individual who has the power to remove a fiduciary or appoint a fiduciary, or both, and the assets would not be included in the estate of the individual if the fiduciary did not possess the power to make an adjustment;

7. If the fiduciary is a beneficiary of the trust; or

8. If the fiduciary is not a beneficiary, but the adjustment would benefit the fiduciary directly or indirectly.

D. If subdivision C 5, 6, 7, or 8 applies to a fiduciary and there is more than one fiduciary, a cofiduciary to whom the provision does not apply may make the adjustment unless the exercise of the power by the remaining fiduciary or fiduciaries is not permitted by the terms of the trust. Any beneficiary or fiduciary may petition the circuit court for appointment of a cofiduciary who would be permitted to make an adjustment not permitted by the other fiduciary or fiduciaries.

E. A fiduciary may release the entire power conferred by subsection A or may release only the power to adjust from income to principal or the power to adjust from principal to income if the fiduciary is uncertain about whether possessing or exercising the power will cause a result described in subdivisions C 1 through 6 or subdivision C 8 or if the fiduciary determines that possessing or exercising the power will or may deprive the trust of a tax benefit or impose a tax burden not described in subsection C. The release may be permanent or for a specified period, including a period measured by the life of an individual.

F. Terms of a trust that limit the power of a fiduciary to make an adjustment between principal and income do not affect the application of this section unless it is clear from the terms of the trust that the terms are intended to deny the fiduciary the power of adjustment conferred by subsection A.

G. As used in this section and the application of this section elsewhere in this chapter, the term "trust" includes the assets under the control or management of a personal representative.

§ 64.2-1003. Total return unitrust

A. As used in this section:

... "Income trust" means a trust, created by either an inter vivos or a testamentary instrument, that directs or permits the trustee to distribute the net income of the trust to one or more persons...

"Interested distributee" means a person to whom distributions of income or principal can currently be made who has the power to remove the existing trustee and designate as successor a person who may be a "related or subordinate party"
....

"Interested trustee" means (i) an individual trustee to whom the net income or principal of the trust can currently be distributed or would be distributed if the trust were then to terminate and be distributed; (ii) any trustee who may be removed and replaced by an interested distributee; or (iii) an individual trustee whose legal obligation to support a beneficiary may be satisfied by distributions of income and principal of the trust.

"Total return unitrust" means (i) an income trust that has been converted under and meets the provisions of this section; or (ii) a grantor-created unitrust. ...

"Unitrust amount" means an amount computed as a percentage of the fair market value of the trust.

B. A trustee, other than an interested trustee, or where two persons are acting as trustees the trustee that is not an interested trustee, or where more than two persons are acting as trustee a majority of the trustees who are not an interested trustee, may, in his sole discretion and without judicial approval, (i) convert an income trust to a total return unitrust; (ii) convert a total return unitrust to an income trust;

or (iii) change the percentage used to calculate the unitrust amount or the method used to determine the fair market value of the trust if:

1. The trustee adopts a written policy for the trust providing: (i) in the case of a trust being administered as an income trust, that future distributions from the trust will be unitrust amounts rather than net income; (ii) in the case of a trust being administered as a total return unitrust, that future distributions from the trust will be net income rather than unitrust amounts; or (iii) that the percentage used to calculate the unitrust amount or the method used to determine the fair market value of the trust will be changed as stated in the policy;

2. The trustee sends notice... of his intention to take such action... to (i) the grantor of the trust, if living; (ii) ... the qualified beneficiaries of the trust...; and (iii) all persons acting as advisor or protector of the trust. ...;

3. At least one member of each class of qualified beneficiaries receiving notice under clause (ii) of subdivision 2 is (i) legally competent... or represented...; and

4. No person receiving such notice objects, by written instrument delivered to the trustee, to the proposed action of the trustee within 30 days of receipt of such notice.

C. If there is no trustee of the trust other than an interested trustee, the interested trustee or, where two or more persons are acting as trustee and are interested trustees, a majority of such interested trustees may, in his sole discretion and without judicial approval [same as in B above] ... if:

1. [same as B.1] ...;

2. The trustee appoints a disinterested person who, in his sole discretion but acting in a fiduciary capacity: (i) in the case of conversion to a total return unitrust, determines for the trustee (a) the percentage to be used to calculate the unitrust amount, (b) the method to be used in determining the fair market value of the trust, and (c) which assets, if any, are to be excluded in determining the unitrust amount; and (ii) determines for the trustee that conversion is in the best interests of the trust;

3. [same as B.2] ... ;

4. [same as B.3] ...; and

5. No person receiving such notice objects, by written instrument delivered to the trustee, to the proposed action of the trustee or the determinations of the disinterested person within 30 days of receipt of such notice.

D. If any trustee desires to convert an income trust to a total return unitrust, convert a total return unitrust to an income trust, or change the percentage used to calculate the unitrust amount or the method used to determine the fair market value of the trust but does not have the ability to or elects not to do it under the provisions of subsection B or C, the trustee may petition the circuit court... for such order as the trustee deems appropriate. In the event, however, there is only one trustee of such trust and such trustee is an interested trustee or in the event there are two or more trustees of such trust and a majority of them are interested trustees, the court, in its own discretion or on the petition of such trustee or trustees or any person interested in the trust, may appoint a disinterested person who, acting in a fiduciary capacity, shall present such information to the court as shall be necessary to enable the court to make its determinations hereunder. Any qualified beneficiary... may also petition...

E. The fair market value of the trust shall be determined at least annually, using such valuation date or dates or averages of valuation dates as are deemed appropriate. ...

F. The percentage to be used in determining the unitrust amount shall be a reasonable current return from the trust, in any event no less than three percent nor more than five percent, either as provided by the grantor in the governing instrument in the case of a grantor-created unitrust, or otherwise taking into account the intentions of the grantor of the trust as expressed in the governing instrument, the needs of the beneficiaries, general economic conditions, projected current earnings and appreciation for the trust, and projected inflation and its impact on the trust.

G. Following the conversion of an income trust to a total return unitrust, or upon the creation of a grantor-created unitrust, the trustee:

1. Shall treat the unitrust amount as if it were net income of the trust for purposes of determining the amount available, from time to time, for distribution from the trust, and the distribution of the unitrust amount shall be considered in full satisfaction of the distribution of all of the net income of the trust;

2. May allocate to trust income for each taxable year of the trust, or portion thereof:

a. Net short-term capital gain..., but only to the extent that the amount so allocated together with all other amounts allocated to trust income for such year or portion thereof does not exceed the unitrust amount for such year or portion thereof; and

b. Net long-term capital gain..., but only to the extent that the amount so allocated together with all other amounts, including amounts described in subdivision 2 a, allocated to trust income for such year, or portion thereof, does not exceed the unitrust amount for such year, or portion thereof; and

3. Shall treat the unitrust amount as if it were income of the trust for purposes of determining the amount of trustee compensation where the governing instrument directs that such compensation be based wholly or partially on income.

H. In administering a total return unitrust, the trustee may, in his sole discretion but subject to the provisions of the governing instrument, determine ... administrative matters as may be necessary or appropriate to carry out the purposes of this section.

...

J. ... [T]his section... shall be available to any trust... unless:

> 1. The governing instrument reflects an intention that the current... beneficiaries are to receive an amount other than a reasonable current return from the trust; ... or

> 3. The governing instrument expressly prohibits use of this section... A provision in the governing instrument that "The provisions of § 64.2-1003, Code of Virginia, as amended, or any corresponding provision of future law, shall not be used in the administration of this trust," or "My trustee shall not determine the distributions to the income beneficiary as a unitrust amount," or similar words reflecting such intent shall be sufficient to preclude the use of this section.

§ 64.2-701. Definitions

"Qualified beneficiary" means a living or then-existing beneficiary who... (i) is a distributee or permissible distributee of trust income or principal...

***

3.   Duty to Inform

§ 64.2-775. Duty to inform and report

A. A trustee shall keep the qualified beneficiaries of the trust reasonably informed about the administration of the trust and of the material facts necessary for them to protect their interests. Unless unreasonable under the circumstances, a trustee shall promptly respond to a beneficiary's request for information related to the administration of the trust. A trustee who fails to furnish information to a beneficiary or respond to a request for information regarding the administration of the trust in a good faith belief that to do so would be unreasonable under the circumstances or contrary to the purposes of the settlor shall not be subject to removal or other sanctions therefor.

B. A trustee:

> 1. Upon request of a beneficiary, shall promptly furnish to the beneficiary a copy of the trust instrument;

> 2. Within 60 days after accepting a trusteeship, shall notify the qualified beneficiaries of the acceptance and of the trustee's name, address, and telephone number;

> 3. Within 60 days after the date the trustee acquires knowledge of the creation of an irrevocable trust, or the date the trustee acquires knowledge that a formerly revocable trust has become irrevocable, whether by the death of the settlor or otherwise, shall notify the qualified beneficiaries of the trust's

existence, of the identity of the settlor or settlors, of the right to request a copy of the trust instrument, and of the right to a trustee's report as provided in subsection C; and

4. Shall notify the qualified beneficiaries in advance of any change in the method or rate of the trustee's compensation.

C. A trustee shall send to the distributees or permissible distributees of trust income or principal, and to other qualified or nonqualified beneficiaries who request it, at least annually and at the termination of the trust, a report of the trust property, liabilities, receipts, and disbursements, including the source and amount of the trustee's compensation, a listing of the trust assets and, if feasible, their respective market values. Upon a vacancy in a trusteeship, unless a cotrustee remains in office, a report shall be sent to the qualified beneficiaries by the former trustee. A personal representative, conservator, or guardian may send the qualified beneficiaries a report on behalf of a deceased or incapacitated trustee.

D. A beneficiary may waive the right to a trustee's report or other information otherwise required to be furnished under this section. A beneficiary, with respect to future reports and other information, may withdraw a waiver previously given.

E. Subdivisions B 2 and B 3 and subsection C apply only to an irrevocable trust created on or after the effective date of this chapter, and to a revocable trust that becomes irrevocable on or after the effective date of this chapter.

***

Supreme Court of Virginia.
Shriners Hospitals for Crippled Children v. Smith
238 Va. 708, 385 S.E.2d 617 (1989)

LACY, Justice.

... **618 On September 23, 1983, Mary L. Robertson executed an inter vivos trust, naming Noah Mack Smith (Smith) as trustee. The trust agreement provided that, during Robertson's lifetime, Smith would distribute to her the entire net income of the trust plus so much of the principal as Robertson should request. Upon Robertson's death, Smith was directed to pay all the trust income to Ethel Maxwell, Robertson's sister. Upon Maxwell's death, Smith was directed to pay all the trust income to Elizabeth Equi, Robertson's niece, if she were alive and unmarried. The agreement further provided that upon Equi's death, marriage, or cohabitation, Smith was to turn over the principal and any income to Shriners Hospitals for Crippled Children (the Hospital). Robertson died on May 17, 1984. Her will provided that her residuary estate be made part of the trust corpus and administered according to the terms of the trust.

The trust directed Smith to "furnish to the current beneficiary an accounting at least once a year...." On three occasions, the Hospital wrote to Smith requesting a copy of his annual accounting. *710 Smith never responded. Thereafter, the Hospital filed a bill of complaint on October 1, 1987, seeking an accounting from Smith. ...

The trust only instructs the trustee to account to the "current beneficiary." The Hospital is a vested remainderman under Virginia law. However, its interest is not yet that of a current beneficiary. The trust makes no direct reference to the Hospital or to a vested remainderman having the right to an accounting. Therefore, the trust itself does not provide the Hospital with the right to an accounting.

Nevertheless, ... a trustee should always conduct himself fairly and impartially, never favoring one beneficiary over another, in order to "preserve and protect the trust fund for the benefit of all interested in the distribution thereof." Patterson v. Old Dominion Trust Co., 139 Va. 246, 257, 123 S.E. 549, 552 (1924). The interest of current beneficiaries in the administration of the trust is obvious, and it is well settled in Virginia that they are entitled to an accounting by the trustee. Rinker v. Simpson, 159 Va. 612, 166 S.E. 546 (1932). Those with a vested remainder also have a present interest in the trust. Disney v. Wilson, 190 Va. 445, 455; 57 S.E.2d 144, 149 (1950). Such a present right supports a present interest in the administration of the trust assets. ...

Although this is a case of first impression in Virginia, prevailing American jurisprudence holds that a vested remainderman has standing to compel a trustee to account for his management of the trust assets. Section 172 comment c of the Restatement (Second) of Trusts (1959) states in part: *711

> The trustee may be compelled to account not only by a beneficiary presently entitled to the payment of income or principal, but also by a beneficiary who will be or may be entitled to receive income or principal in the future.

The majority of jurisdictions adhere to the rule that a vested remainderman has the right to an accounting without having to allege mismanagement or wrongdoing.

[In] Central Hanover Bank & Trust Co. (Momand), 176 Misc. 183, 26 N.Y.S.2d 924 (1941), ... contingent remaindermen sought their accounting while the creator of the trust was still alive. At this point, she had the right to demand an accounting herself and had the power to revoke the trust at any time. ... Unlike the contingent remaindermen in *Central Hanover Bank*, the Hospital has a present interest in the trust assets. Therefore, Central Hanover Bank does not apply to the case at bar.

We hold that, under general equity principles, a vested remainderman has the right to an accounting from the trustee, even though the terms of the trust do not provide for such an accounting. We believe that the benefit the vested remainderman will receive in knowing the status of the trust assets far outweighs any burden on the trustee to provide the accounting. ...

Circuit Court of Virginia, City of Norfolk.
Burton v. Dolph
89 Va. Cir. 101 (2014)

[For facts, see Section I.C above.]

… Virginia Code § 64.2–764 requires that a trustee administer the trust "solely in the interests of the beneficiaries." The allegations in the Complaint support Burton's cause of action under this provision. Paragraph 22 asserts that when the Lincoln Financial policies—which were to benefit Burton, among others—lapsed, Old Point Trust was the trustee of the Irrevocable Trusts; paragraph 24 of the Complaint alleges that Dolph was involved in the management of the Irrevocable Trusts, and thus received copies of premium and lapse notices for the Lincoln Financial policies; and paragraph 25 explains that Old Point Trust had the ability to borrow money against the face value of the Lincoln Financial policies in order to pay the premiums, but failed to do so. Burton contends that as a result of this series of actions and inactions, Old Point Trust breached its duty to administer the Irrevocable Trusts in the beneficiaries' favor. These allegations more than support Burton's claim. By purportedly taking action to deny Burton of the proceeds of the Lincoln Financial policies, Old Point Trust's actions could certainly be construed to be contrary to the interests of the beneficiaries. This claim therefore stands.

Burton's next claim within Count I implicates Virginia Code § 64.2–771, which provides that a trustee "shall take reasonable steps to take control of and protect the trust property." The allegations outlined above from paragraphs 22, 24, and 25 are sufficient to support a cause of action under this provision as well. The parties uniformly agree that the only sources for funding the Irrevocable Trusts were the respective Lincoln Financial policies. It follows that the sole piece of property that Old Point Trust had a duty to protect were these policies. The allegations in the Complaint satisfactorily state a claim that Old Point Trust failed to protect the trust property by allowing the policies to lapse. As a result, this claim also stands.

Burton's final claim in Count I originates under Virginia Code § 64.2–775, which provides that the trustee shall keep the "qualified beneficiaries of the trust reasonably informed about the administration of the trust and of the material facts necessary for them to protect their interests." Undoubtedly, knowledge of the lapse of the sole life insurance policies comprising the Irrevocable Trusts constitutes "material facts necessary for [Burton] to protect [her] interests." Id. Paragraph 27 of the Complaint plainly asserts that Old Point Trust failed to provide Burton with any notice regarding the impending lapse of the Lincoln Financial policies. As a result, Burton alleges in paragraph 29 that she was unable to pay the policy premiums herself to retain her interest in the resultant proceeds. To be sure, these allegations sufficiently support a cause of action under this statutory provision. This claim therefore stands, and the demurrer to Count I is overruled. …

Burton's next claim against Old Point Trust, contained in Count III, alleges that Old Point Trust breached its duty as trustee by failing to file a malpractice action against Dolph and by failing to file a conversion action against Hudgins Contracting and Lester Hudgins' Estate. She contends that Old Point Trust was aware of the occurrence of the malpractice and conversion, but failed to act upon this knowledge, thereby violating a duty imposed by Virginia Code § 64.2–773: "A trustee shall take reasonable steps to enforce claims of the trust and to defend claims against the trust." In its defense, Old Point Trust raises Article 9, section F(13) of the Irrevocable Trust agreements, which provides:

> "The Trustee may decline to enter into or maintain any litigation, endorse any policy payments, or take any other action representing any Trust insurance policies, until the Trustee shall have been indemnified against all expenses and liabilities involved in such action."

Old Point Trust contends that this language supersedes its duty under the statute, and as a result, it cannot be held liable for failing to enforce potential claims of the Irrevocable Trusts.

This particular issue is controlled by Virginia Code § 64.2–703. That provision dictates that in certain enumerated circumstances, the terms of the trust agreement itself will prevail over statutory provisions: "Except as otherwise provided in the terms of the trust, this chapter governs the duties and powers of a trustee, relations among trustees, and the rights and interests of a beneficiary." Va.Code § 64.2–703(A). Although section 703 lays out a number of exceptions to its general rule, enforcement of trust claims is not among them. It follows that if the terms of a trust agreement modify the statutory requirement to enforce claims of the trust imposed by section 773, the terms of the trust agreement will prevail. Accordingly, this claim turns on the interpretation of the language of Article 9, section F(13).

Burton argues that the language of that section of the Irrevocable Trust agreements should be read to mean that the trustee may merely delay filing appropriate litigation until it has been indemnified. She maintains that it should not be interpreted to give the trustee an option to institute litigation even when it is apparent that doing so would be appropriate. Moreover, Burton asserts that the intent of Article 9, section F(13) is to prevent the trustee from accumulating excessive litigation costs, thereby limiting the trustee's risk of personal liability.

While this may be true, the language of the trust provision at issue makes clear that the trustee retains the option of instituting litigation until it is indemnified against all costs and liabilities. The Complaint fails to set forth an allegation that Old Point Trust was ever indemnified in such a manner, and the Court cannot draw such an inference from Burton's existing assertions. Virginia Code § 64.2–703 directs that in this instance, the terms of the trust agreement outweigh any related statutory provisions. Therefore, although Burton may fairly argue that Old Point Trust's failure to institute malpractice and conversion actions was not reasonable, Article 9, section F(13) of the trust agreements preclude reaching that determination—the trust provision controls. As a result, the Court sustains the demurrer.

Dolph's Demurrer to Count IV of the Complaint.

In Count IV of the Complaint, Burton asserts a derivative claim on behalf of Old Point Trust (as trustee) against Dolph for malpractice. This claim is grounded in Dolph's purported failure to counsel Old Point Trust regarding the lapse of the Lincoln Financial policies. Dolph demurs, arguing as a threshold matter that this claim is improper because Virginia law does not recognize derivative claims brought by a beneficiary on behalf of a trustee. He further maintains that because Old Point Trust owed no duty to prevent the lapse of the policies, an action for malpractice is precluded. The Court overrules this demurrer.

The Plaintiff's Derivative Claims are Properly Before the Court.

The threshold issue here is whether Burton has standing to maintain this malpractice claim against Dolph on behalf of Old Point Trust. Burton frames it as a derivative claim, lodged as a result of Old Point Trust's failure to take action as trustee of the Irrevocable Trusts. In support of its stance that Burton lacks standing, Dolph relies primarily upon the Supreme Court's decision in Poage v. Bell, 35 Va. 604 (1837). Burton conversely argues that in view of enactment of the Virginia Uniform Trust Code in 2005, the publication of the Restatement (Second) of Trusts, and the distinction drawn in *Poage* between courts of law and equity, she has standing to assert these claims derivatively.

Poage involved a suit by a beneficiary against a third-party alleged to have converted trust property. Although the Court held that only the trustee could bring suit against the third party, it qualified its holding, explaining that while the trustee was the proper party to bring the action at law, the beneficiary could maintain the lawsuit in a court of equity. See *Poage*, 35 Va. at 607 ("This shows the propriety of confining the [beneficiary] to a court of equity (when that jurisdiction is proper for him) where all persons interested may be made parties ..."). Remarkably, since the Poage decision in 1837, only two cases have invoked its rule of law. See Busman v. Beeren & Barry Investments, LLC, 69 Va. Cir 375 (Fairfax 2005); Broyhill v. Bank of America, N.A., 2010 U.S. Dist. LEXIS 106766 (E.D.Va.2010). ... [R]eliance on these precedents is misguided. ... [explanation of why they are irrelevant]

Burton instead relies on the Restatement (Second) of Trusts § 282, which provides an exception to the general rule that trustees alone are competent to bring suit against third parties: "If the trustee improperly refuses or neglects to bring an action against the third person, the beneficiary can maintain a suit in equity against the trustee and the third person." Burton readily acknowledges that the Supreme Court has not officially adopted the Restatement and also concedes that it has yet to explicitly recognize a derivative cause of action as described in section 282. Nevertheless, ... the Supreme Court has relied upon the Restatement in resolving trust issues in the past, both before and after enactment of the Uniform Trust Code. See, e.g., Sturgis v. Stinson, 241 Va. 531, 535, 404 S.E.2d 56, 58 (1991); Leonard v. Counts, 221 Va. 582, 588, 272 S.E.2d 190, 195 (1980); Broaddus v.. Gresham, 181 Va. 725, 733 (1943); Carlson v. Wells, 183, 705 S.E.2d 101, 105 (2011). Certainly, this consistent reliance upon the Restatement is harmonious with section 704 of Virginia's version of the Uniform Trust Code, which provides that "[t]he common law of trusts and principles of equity" should be used to supplement the provisions of the statute. Va.Code § 64.2–704. Indeed, the Restatement is simply a compilation of common law principles that have developed over the years. Nothing in Virginia law dispels the notion that courts should look to the Restatement for guidance in deciding cases-in fact, quite the opposite is true. See Belcher v. Dandridge, 61 Va. Cir.

684, 688 (Norfolk 2002) ("[T]he Supreme Court has traditionally viewed the Restatement as persuasive authority.").

Burton's argument on this point is further bolstered by the Official Comments to the Uniform Trust Code.[8]

> [8] "The Comments provide background information (such as the origin of a rule), make important cross-references, state certain assumptions upon which the statutory language is based, explain the rationale for differentiating between default and mandatory rules, and, more generally, elaborate on the intended meaning of certain statutory provisions." John E. Donaldson & Robert T. Danforth, The Virginia Uniform Trust Code, 40 U. Rich. L.Rev. 325, 332 (2005). Indeed, regular consultation of the Comments is crucial to achieving one of the chief goals of the Uniform Trust Code: to promote uniformity in application of the statute. See id. Dependence on the Comments is especially important in view of the complexity of the statute itself, because it could not realistically have been drafted to account for every conceivable situation. Id. Undoubtedly, this concern is heightened in Virginia, where we are without the benefit of the Code's legislative history. Id. at 332–33.

Although no provisions of the Code expressly afford Burton the right to lodge a derivative claim, the Comments contemplate the existence of such a cause of action and certainly, no provision of the Code precludes it. Specifically, the Comment to Uniform Trust Code § 1004 (codified verbatim at Virginia Code § 64.2–795) acknowledges that in certain cases, litigation may be instituted by a beneficiary against a third party because the trustee has failed to do so himself. See Comment to Uniform Trust Code § 1004 ("On other occasions, the suit by the beneficiary is brought because of the trustee's failure to take action against a third party, such as to recover property properly belonging to the trust."). In support of this proposition, the Comment cites with approval section 282 of the Restatement (Second) of Trusts.

Upon consideration of the competing positions on this issue, the Court finds that Burton has standing to lodge derivative claims as a beneficiary of the Irrevocable Trusts. The only cognizable argument that the Defendant advances rests upon a Supreme Court case decided in 1837. And while *Poage* has not expressly been overruled, it has hardly been cited as authority since it was decided; furthermore, to the extent it has been relied upon, it has been so by courts whose decisions are not binding upon this one. In the Court's view, although it is persuasive authority, the Restatement more accurately reflects the current state of the law, especially after the enactment of the Virginia Uniform Trust Code.

Moreover, nothing in the Trust statute precludes derivative actions instituted by beneficiaries of a trust. In fact, the Comments to the Code acknowledge the utility in referencing the Restatement, and in particular, recognize the existence of a cause of action brought by a beneficiary under section 282. Further, the Supreme Court has time and again looked to the Restatement for instruction in deciding cases implicating trust issues, and doing so is consistent with Virginia Code § 64.2–704, which calls on common law principles to supplement the statutory provisions of the Code. In view of this landscape, the Court finds that Burton has standing to lodge her derivative claims.[9] ...

> [9] This finding is consistent with the Court's stance on Count III concerning Old Point Trust's option to enforce claims of the Irrevocable Trusts. As a practical matter, allowing a beneficiary to derivatively bring suit against a third party is prudent where the provisions of the trust agreement and statutory scheme conspire to create a situation where the trustee is under no obligation to file suit and the beneficiary lacks standing to do so.

The Complaint Supports the Cause of Action Stated in Count IV.

In Count IV, Burton alleges that Dolph committed legal malpractice through a series of actions and inactions taken with respect to the Irrevocable Trusts. ... "A cause of action for legal malpractice requires the existence of an attorney-client relationship which gives rise to a duty, breach of that duty by the defendant attorney, and that the damages claimed by the plaintiff client must have been proximately caused by the defendant attorney's breach." In this regard, an action for the professional negligence of an attorney is one for breach of contract-but for the absence of the contract, the attorney owes no duty to the client. ... The Complaint clearly alleges that an attorney-client relationship between Dolph and Old Point Trust/Irrevocable Trusts in fact existed. ... Burton also alleges that Dolph owed these clients a duty and lays out the nature of the duty. And finally, the Complaint contains sufficient allegations that Dolph breached these duties, and that in doing so, he caused damages by impairing the value of the Irrevocable Trusts. The Court consequently overrules this demurrer.

Dolph's Demurrer to Count V of the Complaint.

Dolph also demurs to Count V of the Complaint, in which he is the subject of a direct action for malpractice. Burton asserts this claim as a non-client beneficiary under Virginia Code § 55–22, arguing that she was an intended beneficiary of the attorney-client relationship between Dolph and Old Point Trust/Irrevocable Trusts. Dolph contends that the Complaint does not support Burton's claim that she was an intended beneficiary of his legal services. In particular, he maintains that Burton cannot point to the terms of any attorney-client agreement that could serve as the basis for the allegations in Count V. The Court disagrees and overrules the demurrer.

Whether a non-client third-party can bring suit against an attorney for malpractice is controlled by the Supreme Court's decision in Copenhaver v. Rogers, 238 Va. 361, 384 S.E.2d 593 (1989). In Copenhaver, the defendant law firm prepared wills for a client one year prior to her death. After the will was admitted to probate, the law firm submitted a petition to uphold trust terms that had been added to the will via codicil. The petition, however, mistakenly asked the trial court to void the trust on the ground that it had no trust term. As a result, the grandchildren of the client for whom the law firm had prepared the will-brought suit against the law firm for malpractice, claiming that the firm's actions resulted in a loss of their residuary share of the trust. Precisely like Burton does here, the plaintiffs in *Copenhaver* predicated their own standing upon a theory that they were intended third-party beneficiaries.

In dismissing the plaintiffs' claims, the Court explained that "[i]n order to proceed on the third-party beneficiary contract theory, the party claiming the benefit must show that the parties to a contract clearly and definitely intended to confer a benefit upon him." Copenhaver, 238 Va. at 367, 384 Va. at 596. Therefore, absent a showing that the party against whom liability is asserted assumed an obligation for the benefit of the third party, a cause of action under Virginia Code § 55–22 is precluded. Id. ("Put another way, a person who benefits only incidentally from a contract between others cannot sue thereon."). The Court went to great lengths to point out the difference between being the intended beneficiary of an estate—which the plaintiffs in Copenhaver were—and the intended beneficiary of a contract between an attorney and a client, which they were not. Id. Indeed, the Court wrote that only when a plaintiff could demonstrate that the clear intent of the attorney-client contract was to benefit her, could that plaintiff sue upon a theory that she was an intended third party beneficiary.10 Id.

Unlike the *Copenhaver* plaintiffs, Burton properly makes the distinction between being the beneficiary of the trust agreement and the beneficiary of the attorney-client contract between Dolph and Old Point Trust/Irrevocable Trusts. Although the assertions supporting this claim are sparing, they are sufficient to survive demurrer. Particularly, paragraph 84 of the Complaint describes the attorney-client agreement between Dolph and Old Point Trust, and asserts that as part of the agreement, Dolph agreed to "assist the Trustee in the Trustee's maximization of the benefits available to the beneficiaries." While this is the only allegation in the 106 paragraph-long Complaint that discusses the attorney-client agreement, it is enough to support Burton's assertion that the agreement "clearly and definitely intended to confer a benefit" upon her as a beneficiary of the Irrevocable Trusts. As Burton frames it, this clause can be read to mean that she was a clearly contemplated beneficiary of the attorney-client agreement at issue. On demurrer, the Court is not in a position to speculate about the truth of this allegation, nor can it even consider the likelihood of Burton being able to substantiate this claim at trial. Because it must accept the factual allegations in the Complaint as true, the Court overrules this demurrer.

Hudgins Contracting's and Lester Hudgins' Estate's Demurrer to Count VI of the Complaint.

In Count VI, Burton asserts a derivative claim of conversion against Hudgins Contracting and Lester Hudgins' Estate on behalf of Old Point Trust.12 She contends that by purchasing the Replacement Policies to supersede the Lincoln Financial Policies, these defendants acted illegally. The Defendants demur, arguing that because (i) Burton failed to allege that they ever took possession of the Lincoln Financial policies; and (ii) Burton was not entitled to immediate possession of the policies, the elements of conversion were not satisfied.

The Supreme Court has explained:

> Any distinct act of dominion wrongfully exerted over the property of another, and in denial of his rights, or inconsistent therewith, may be treated as a conversion and it is not necessary that the wrongdoer apply the property

to his own use. And when such conversion is proved, the plaintiff is entitled to recover, irrespective of good or bad faith, care or negligence, knowledge or ignorance. Universal C.I.T. Credit Corp. v. Kaplan, 198 Va. 67, 76, 92 S.E.2d 359, 365 (1956).

Further, "[a]n action for conversion can be maintained only by the person having a property interest in and entitled to the immediate possession of the item alleged to have been wrongfully converted." Economopoulos v. Kolaitis, 259 Va. 806, 814, 528 S.E.2d 714, 719 (2000). Although the Defendants assert that "[t]he general rule in the Commonwealth is that an action for conversion applies only to tangible property," Golden v. Chaplin, 79 Va. Cir. 155, 156 (Fairfax 2009), that is a misstatement of the law—indeed, the very case they cite in support of that proposition granted a plaintiff's claim for conversion of money.

Given this legal backdrop, the Court finds that Burton's claim for conversion withstands demurrer. The Complaint contains allegations that Hudgins Contracting purchased the Replacement Policies, and that the application for those policies made clear that they were intended to replace the Lincoln Financial policies, comprising the Irrevocable Trusts. Burton further asserts that Hudgins Contracting transferred ownership of the Replacement Policies to Lester Hudgins, who in turn named a separate revocable trust as beneficiary of those policies. In view of these allegations, the Complaint supports a valid cause of action for conversion. Contrary to the Defendants' contentions, Burton need not allege that the Defendants ever took possession of the Lincoln Financial policies. Instead, all Burton must allege is that they committed "[a]ny distinct act of dominion wrongfully exerted over" the property of the individual asserting the cause of action. In this instance, Burton correctly points out that because she is asserting these claims derivatively on behalf of the trustee of the Irrevocable Trusts, the property at issue is the trust property—the Lincoln Financial policies. Undoubtedly, the claims that Hudgins Contracting purchased the Replacement Policies and substituted them for the Lincoln Financial policies without the consent of the trustee are sufficient to state a cause of action for conversion. The demurrer to Count VI is therefore overruled.

Hudeins Contracting's, Dolph's, and Lester Hudgins' Estate's Demurrer to Count VII

In Count VII, Burton alleges a derivative claim of conspiracy against Hudgins Contracting, Lester Hudgins' Estate, and Dolph.13 Specifically, she asserts that these defendants collectively participated in a scheme to convert the assets of the Irrevocable Trusts. In this regard, Count VII essentially asserts a claim of conspiracy to commit the acts alleged in Count VI. ...

"A common law conspiracy consists of two or more persons combined to accomplish, by some concerted action, some criminal or unlawful purpose or some lawful purpose by a criminal or unlawful means." Commercial Business Sys. v. BellSouth Servs., 249 Va. 39, 48, 453 S.E.2d 261, 267 (1995). "However, the intra-corporate immunity doctrine, which has been adopted by the Virginia Supreme Court and the Fourth Circuit, deems multiple defendants a single entity for the purpose of analyzing a civil conspiracy claim if such defendants are employees or agents of the same entity and are acting within the scope of their employment/agency." Fox v. Deese, 234 Va. 412, 428, 362 S.E.2d 699, 708 (1987). In other words, a single entity, "[b]y definition ... cannot conspire with itself." Id. ...

[A]llegations in the... lay out a scheme in which Hudgins Contracting and Lester Hudgins acted in concert to purchase the Replacement Policies and swap them into the place of the existing Lincoln Financial Policies [and]... that Dolph participated in this scheme with the other named defendants. Read collectively, these assertions adequately state a claim for conspiracy to convert the assets of the Irrevocable Trusts. With respect to the intra-corporate immunity defense, the Complaint does not specifically allege that the conspiracy occurred within the scope of either Lester Hudgins' or Dolph's employment with Hudgins Contracting, as is required for the Defendants to avail themselves of immunity. ... [I]f further evidence establishes that the conspiracy was executed within either defendant's scope of employment with Hudgins Contracting, each may ultimately raise the defense through a vehicle other than demurrer. To do so now, however, is improper.

The Defendants' argument that the Estate of Lester Hudgins cannot be party to the conspiracy claim likewise fails. A careful reading of the Complaint reveals that the substance of the allegations in this particular claim all name Lester Hudgins himself as the liable party. The Complaint references the Estate only to the extent that it is the entity ultimately responsible for compensating the Plaintiff if she is successful at trial. Of course, this makes sense if for no other reason than that a conspiracy involving Hudgins could not have happened after he died.

The posture of the claim finds further support in the statutory scheme. Virginia Code § 8.01–25 provides for the survival of a cause of action in the event of the death of any of the litigants:

> Every cause of action whether legal or equitable, which is cognizable in the Commonwealth of Virginia, shall survive either the death of the person against whom the cause of action is or may be asserted, or the death of the person in whose favor the cause of action existed, or the death of both such persons.

The plain language of the statute makes clear that so long as a cause of action existed prior to the litigant's death, it will continue to exist afterwards. Nothing in the statute purports to alter the statute of limitations or the substance of any particular claim.

Seen in this light, Count VII simply alleges a tort against Lester Hudgins. The Plaintiff casts Hudgins, not his Estate, as the wrongdoer; the cause of action no doubt arose while Hudgins was still alive; and the Defendants have made no argument that the claim was untimely filed. Under Virginia Code § 8.01–25, Hudgins' death has no bearing on the substance of the Plaintiffs claims. That provision dictates that he is just as liable now as he would be were he still alive. The Estate is named in the Complaint only to account for this potential liability, not as a co-conspirator working to convert the assets of the Irrevocable Trusts. The Court therefore overrules the demurrer to Count VII. ...

---

4. Duty of Proper Management and Investment

Typically the first thing a trustee must do is take possession of the trust assets and arrange for them to be securely and separately maintained.

Article 8. Duties and Powers of Trustee

§ 64.2-771. Control and protection of trust property

A trustee shall take reasonable steps to take control of and protect the trust property.

§ 64.2-784. Duties at inception of trusteeship

Within a reasonable time after accepting a trusteeship or receiving trust assets, a trustee shall review the trust assets and make and implement decisions concerning the retention and disposition of assets, in order to bring the trust portfolio into compliance with the purposes, terms, distribution requirements, and other circumstances of the trust, and with the requirements of this article.

Circuit Court of Virginia, Richmond County.
Tillar v. Stump
87 Va. Cir. 43 (2013)

MELVIN R. HUGHES, JR., J.

... Plaintiff, Thomas C. Tillar, Jr., successor trustee of the Tillar Irrevocable Trust for Thomas C. Tillar and Ruth W. Tillar, has brought claims against the former and initial trustee, defendant C. Jeffrey Stump (Stump) alleging (1) breach of fiduciary duty, (2) breach of contract, (3) negligence, and (4) accountant malpractice seeking judgment in the amount of $800,000. ...

The trust was created by Thomas and Ruth Tillar, husband and wife, in November 1999. Under a provision in the trust instrument, the Tillar Irrevocable Trust..., the trust was funded with an initial $10.00, the only trust asset at the time of creation. Later, the trust received additional funds after Thomas and Ruth surrendered an original life insurance policy issued by the co-defendant, Federated Insurance Company, for its cash value. The beneficiaries of the trust are Plaintiff, who is Thomas and Ruth's son, and, Elizabeth Kennedy Tillar, daughter and Thomas' sister. At the time of the trust's creation, Stump signed on as trustee.

In January 2000, Thomas and Ruth applied for and received from Federated a twenty-five year Last Survivor Life insurance policy with a face value of $800,000. Shortly thereafter, under provisions in the trust instrument for the acquisition and maintenance of insurance policies, Thomas and Ruth gave the policy to, and it was accepted by, the trust and it became trust property. Under the trust, any proceeds of insurance are to be paid to the trust upon the death of the last survivor between Thomas and Ruth for the benefit of Thomas, Jr. and Elizabeth. By January 2001, Stump paid $80,000 in insurance premiums on the trust's behalf.

In December, 2002, Federated notified Stump that $24,983.86 was due for premiums but Stump remitted only $3,708.76, the balance remaining in the trust from the cash surrender. Following Thomas' death in December 2003, Plaintiff discovered, in 2011, that the policy had lapsed in 2009 due to lack of premium payment. After receiving Ruth Tillar's medical records, Federated declined to reinstate the $800,000 policy. Attempts to get coverage from other insurers also proved unsuccessful. Alleging that the trust "will not receive the $800,000 in life insurance proceeds upon his mother's death" for the beneficiaries ... "[a]s a consequence of the actions and omissions of the defendants ..." (Stump and the insurer), Plaintiff asserts that the trust has been "damaged and seeks a judgment in the amount of $800,000.00." ...

Plaintiff's first count alleges that Stump breached his fiduciary duty in that Stump failed to: (1) pay the insurance premiums resulting in the lapse of the policy, (2) make any informed decisions regarding the Policy, (3) inform the beneficiaries of any significant events and circumstances ... and (4) act with ordinary prudence. Under law, a trustee who "has special skills or expertise ... shall use those skills or expertise." Va.Code § 64.2–768 and "[a] trustee shall take reasonable steps to take control of and protect the trust property." Va.Code § 64.2–771. The trust instrument states that the trustee may deal with insurance policies "as the owner." Article 4 of the trust instrument lists various powers that the trustee may exercise in his "sole and absolute discretion." However, pursuant to Va.Code § 64.2–776:

> Notwithstanding the breadth of discretion granted to a trustee in the terms of the trust, including the use of such terms as "absolute," "sole," or "uncontrolled," the trustee shall exercise discretionary power in good faith and in accordance with the terms and purposes of the trust and the interests of the beneficiaries.

Stump primarily argues that Plaintiff has... failed to allege resulting damages... [Because] he would not receive the insurance proceeds until the death of his mother, who is living, plaintiff has not yet been injured and may never be, if the insured outlives the Policy's term. Stump's argument, while innovative, fails because... the Policy had some value in and of itself[3] at the time Stump is said to have allowed it to lapse, and now with the lapse the Policy has no value.[4]

[3] For example, the fair market value of the policy.

[4] ... [I]t may be inferred from Plaintiff's allegations that Stump knew or should have known that the assets in the Trust were insufficient to maintain the Policy and that Stump should have either (1) allowed the Policy to lapse without ever making a payment, and that, (2) since he did choose to fund it, he should have found an alternative way to maintain the Policy and was negligent for failing to do so.

Fiduciaries are required to do those things which a [person] of reasonable intelligence and prudence would be expected to do in the management of his own affairs. *Harris v. Citizen's Bank & Trust Co.*, 172 Va. 111,125,200 S.E. 652,657 (1939). ...

Count 2 alleges a breach of contract. A breach of a trust agreement is actionable. *Ward v. Nationsbank, N.A.*, 256 Va. 427, 507 S.E.2d 616 (1998). ... [F]ailing to notify the settlors is not a breach of the terms of the trust agreement. Pursuant to art. 11 § 4 of the Trust a trustee "shall not be required to furnish trust records ... to any individual ... that is not a beneficiary." However, failing to respond to any notices and failing to make decisions relative to benefits of the trust could be a violation of the trust agreement. For example, such an omission could violate art. 12 § 2 because the trustee "... shall not exercise any power in a manner inconsistent with the beneficiaries' right to the beneficial enjoyment of the trust property." Failing to act to save trust property may be a breach of the trust agreement. ...[5]

> [5] The trust instrument grants to the trustee the power to borrow funds to pay premiums and assign the policy as security for a loan. See Article Four Section 1.a.

Count 3 asserts a claim of negligence. Such a claim must arise from an independent duty "... [f]or the violation of certain common law and statutory duties involving the safety of persons and property, which are imposed to protect the broad interests of society." *Filak v. George*, 267 Va. 612, 618, 594 S.E.2d 610, 613 (2004). Here, Plaintiff alleges that Stump was negligent when he failed to maintain the trust property, the Policy, and that by his negligence the Policy lapsed. Stump, but for the trust agreement and the corresponding fiduciary duties, would not have had any duty to maintain the trust property. Thus it can be said that "[b]ut for the existence of the [trust agreement], [Stump] would [not] have owed any fiduciary duty to [Plaintiff]. That certain ... fiduciary duties arose by implication does not alter the result." *Augusta Mut. Ins. Co. v. Mason*, 274 Va. 199, 207, 645 S.E.2df 290, 295 (2007) (breach of agency agreement is contract, not tort, notwithstanding fiduciary duties that arose from the agreement). Thus, Stump's demurrer to Count 2 will be sustained.

In Count 4, Plaintiff alleges professional malpractice. The elements of accountant malpractice are: "(1) an accountant-client relationship giving rise to a duty; (2) the accountant breached the duty; and (3) the breach of that duty was a proximate cause of the claimed damages." *Forte v. Atkins*, 68 Va. Cir. 411, 412 (Loudoun 2005). In such a case, a duty arises, if at all, from the professional agreement. *Stanley v. Cobbe*, 83 Va. Cir. 51, 53 (Martinsville 2011) ("... the source of duty must emanate from the professional agreement.") Here, the only agreement alleged to exist is the trust agreement. A professional agreement has not been alleged. Accordingly, Stump's demurrer to Count 4 will be sustained. ...

In some cases, obtaining possession of trust property could entail taking legal action against others.

§ 64.2-774. Collecting trust property

A trustee shall take reasonable steps to compel a former trustee or other person to deliver trust property to the trustee, and to redress a breach of trust or duty known to the trustee to have been committed by a former trustee or other fiduciary.

***

In addition to collecting trust property, trustees must "earmark" it and keep it separate from their personal assets or the assets of other accounts the trustee might manage, so that there is no commingling of trust assets that could cause confusion regarding ownership that leads to loss for the trust.

§ 64.2-772. Recordkeeping and identification of trust property

A. A trustee shall keep adequate records of the administration of the trust.

B. A trustee shall keep trust property separate from the trustee's own property.

C. Except as otherwise provided in subsection D, a trustee shall cause the trust property to be designated so that the interest of the trust, to the extent feasible, appears in records maintained by a party other than a trustee or beneficiary.

D. If the trustee maintains records clearly indicating the respective interests, a trustee may invest as a whole the property of two or more separate trusts.

E. A deed or other instrument purporting to convey or transfer real or personal property to a trust instead of to the trustee or trustees of the trust shall be deemed to convey or transfer such property to the trustee or trustees as fully as if made directly to the trustee or trustees.

***

Supreme Court of Appeals of Virginia
First Nat. Bank v. Commercial Bank & Trust Co.
163 Va. 162, 175 S.E. 775 (1934)

CHINN, J., delivered the opinion of the court.

On September 14, 1929, Commercial Bank and Trust Company of Danville, and J. S. Thompson, of Pittsylvania county, qualified in the circuit court of that county as committees *167 of the estate of Mrs. Salina B. Motley, an insane person. Said committees executed bond, conditioned according to law, in the sum of $87,500 but no surety was required of them. As a result of certain litigation, on August 6, 1931, the executors of John J. Motley, the deceased husband of Mrs. Salina B. Motley, paid over to her said committees the sum of $50,000 by check... J. S. Thompson and C. L. Booth, trust officer of the Commercial Bank and Trust Company, ... deposited the [money] to the credit of the committees in the Commercial Bank and Trust Company. At the time of the deposit an ordinary deposit slip was made out by Mr. Booth, the trust officer, which did not differ in any way from the deposit slips in common use by the general depositors of the bank. This deposit was not, however, entered as a general deposit on the individual or general ledger of the bank, but was set up in the form of a receipt on a separate ledger kept by the trust department of the bank, reading as follows: 'By amount received from C. M. Mahan and E. C. Hurt, Jr., executors of the will of John J. Motley, deceased, as per decree of the Circuit Court of Pittsylvania county, Virginia, dated August 1, 1931 - $50,000.' The ledger also showed the nature of the trust was, 'as committee with J. S. Thompson for Mrs. Salina B. Motley.' ...

It also appears that on the same day disbursements were made out of the trust fund to pay money borrowed by the committees for *168 Mrs. Motley's benefit, attorney's fees allowed by the court, and other expenses, aggregating the sum of $15,180.90; and on September 14, 1931, other disbursements were made amounting to $2,673.13 leaving to the credit of said fund a net balance in the hands of the bank of $32,145.97. ...

The Commercial Bank and Trust Company closed its doors on October 17, 1931; receivers were duly appointed; and the First National Bank of Danville qualified as joint committee with J. S. Thompson in the place and stead of the closed bank. ... **777 [They] assert[ed] that they are entitled to have the assets in the hands of the receivers of the closed bank impressed with a trust in favor of their ward's estate... The special commissioner found against the claim to a preference [over creditors of the bank]... The corporation court thereupon sustained the commissioner's findings and allowed said committees only a general claim against the bank's receivers for $32,145.97, with 4% interest thereon..., and also awarded a judgment against the receivers in the sum of $500, which the court decided had been improperly properly charged against the fund by the Commercial Bank and Trust Company, co-committee, for commissions, thus making a total allowance on account of the claim of the committees of $32,645.97, with interest as aforesaid, without preference over the other creditors of the closed bank. ... *169

The right of a cestui que trust to follow his trust money or other property into the hands of the receivers of an insolvent bank is based upon rights of property. It is not based upon a debt due and owing, nor upon the ground of compensation for loss of the property or fund, but upon the fundamental principle that the funds are still the property of the cestui que trust and he is entitled to reclaim them whether in their original or some altered form. In other words, the underlying theory is that the title to the trust fund did not pass to the bank and the claimant is therefore only recovering his own.

Accordingly, it is generally held that when there is a general deposit of funds in a bank, the relation of debtor and creditor at once arises, and the money becomes the property of the bank; and in that case, the cestui que trust or other owner has no claim upon the assets of the bank superior to that of the bank's general creditors. But when the deposit is special in its nature, or is made wrongfully, or without lawful authority on the part of the trustee or other fiduciary, there is no relationship of debtor and creditor between the bank and the beneficial owner, and the title to the fund does not, therefore, pass to the bank but remains in the cestui que trust who is entitled to follow them into the hands of the receivers upon the bank's insolvency. ... *170 ...

It appears from the record that when the funds in question were placed in the bank it was understood by Mr. Thompson, the bank's co-committee, and the bank's officials that the balance remaining after making the disbursements hereinbefore mentioned was to be held by the bank only until it could be invested in securities prescribed by the statute for the investment of such funds. There was no understanding that the money should be loaned to the bank or that it should be placed on general deposit, and the receipt of the money was entered only on the trust ledger. Mr. Thompson, for his part, understood that the money was to be held by the trust department until proper investment could be found for it, and that the affairs of that department were kept separate from the other department of the bank. The money was never invested according to Mr. Thompson's understanding and as contemplated by the bank's officers when it was deposited, but immediately upon its receipt was appropriated by the bank to its own use.

Under these circumstances we do not think the bank, in the proper exercise of the trust imposed upon it, could rightly make a general deposit of the said trust fund with itself, and by commingling said funds with its own in its ordinary commercial transactions **778 change the existing fiduciary relation to that of debtor and creditor and then claim it had thereby acquired title to said fund. The bank, though authorized to act in both a fiduciary and commercial capacity, constituted but a single corporate entity. It could not *171 rightly destroy the trust relation and claim the fiduciary funds in question had become its own on the debtor and creditor theory merely by the process, figuratively speaking, of shifting such funds from one hand to the other.

As aptly said by Justice Cordoza in the case of Genesee Wesleyan Seminary v. U.S. Fidelity & Guaranty Co., 247 N.Y. 52, 159 N.E. 720, 722, 56 A.L.R. 964: 'A trust imposed by law is not to be divested at the instant of its creation and silently, as if by sleight of hand, converted into a loan.' ... In addition to being treasurer of the Seminary, Holden was likewise a private banker... When Holden collected money as treasurer of the Seminary he placed it on deposit with himself as banker. His bank became insolvent and he filed a petition in bankruptcy. ... Holden loaned to corporations in which he was a stock-holder and officer a large part of the deposits in his bank. ... [I]n discussing Holden's duties as treasurer and banker..., Justice Cordoza... said:

> We think the plaintiff's deposit should have been kept apart from others and held by the treasurer as a fund subject to a trust. Deposits in a bank or with a banker are classified often as general or special. The presumption is said to be that a deposit is general. The relation then created is that of debtor and creditor as upon any other loan. A special deposit is sometimes said to be equivalent to a bailment. It is not always of that order. Such a deposit *172 may exist where the duty of the depositary is to hold, not the identical bills or coins, but an equivalent sum, to be kept intact, however, for the use of the depositor. A bank accepting such a deposit is chargeable with the responsibility, civil or criminal, like any other trustee, if it uses for itself what was to be held in trust for someone else. The fund may not be drawn down by loans or other withdrawals below the level of the trust.

... The right on the part of the committee, exercising due care in its selection, to deposit the trust funds in another bank of discount and deposit so long as they were kept separate from their own funds cannot be denied. Neither does there seem any good reason why the Commercial Bank and Trust Company could not have deposited said fund with itself, provided, whether kept in its own vaults or in another banking institution, the same was properly earmarked according to its true ownership. These are entirely different propositions, however, from that of mingling the trust funds committed to its care with its own, and using the same in its general banking business as was done by the fiduciary bank in this case. ... *173 ...**779 ...

Our conclusion is, therefore, that the action of the bank in making a general deposit with itself of the trust funds committed to its care and appropriating them to its own use as it did, though not amounting to fraud, was wrongful and without authority on the part of the bank, and there having been no contract relation between the beneficiary and said bank with reference to the so-called deposit and use of said funds, the bank acquired no title to the same, and Mrs. Motley's representatives are, therefore, entitled to follow said funds into the hands of the receivers of the closed bank. ...

[T]he modern and prevailing doctrine is, that it is not necessary, in order to follow and recover a trust fund from the *174 receivers of an insolvent bank, to identify the specific property into which it has been converted where the fund has been mingled with the other funds of the bank. Under this doctrine it is well settled in Virginia as in nearly all jurisdictions, that the mingling of trust funds with the general funds of the fiduciary bank does not extinguish the trust, or defeat the right of the beneficiary to follow and recover the trust fund or its equivalent, but extends the trust or lien to the whole mass of money in the receivers' hands. [In] Board of Supervisors v. Prince Edward-Lunenburg County Bank, 138 Va. 333, 121 S.E. 903, 906..., Judge Sims, in delivering the opinion of the court, quotes with approval from the case of Richardson v. New Orleans Deb. Red. Co., 102 Fed. 780, in part as follows:

> If a banker takes $1,000, not his own, and mixes the sum with $10,000 of his own money, can the owner of the $1,000 reclaim it? Has he, in equity, a charge on the whole to the amount of his money which has gone into it? Formerly, it was held that he had not. The equitable right of following misapplied money, it was said, depended on identifying it, the equity attaching to the very property misapplied. Money, it was said, had no earmarks, and the tracing of the fund would fail. This view was manifestly inequitable and unjust, and so, finally, it was held that confusion by commingling does not destroy the equity, but converts it into a charge upon the entire mass, giving to the party injured by the unlawful diversion of the fund a priority of right over the other creditors of the possessor and wrongdoer

In Evans v. French, 222 Mo.App. 990, 6 S.W.(2d.) 655, 658, the court stated...: *175

> In cases where a trust fund is mingled with the general assets of the bank, and the entire fund so mingled is used in the general business of the bank, the bank cannot take advantage of its own wrong in mingling said funds,

and insist that the claimant of the trust fund show the specific fund claimed is in the hands of the commission in charge of the assets of the bank, but on account of the wrongful act of the bank in mingling such funds and thus making it impossible to trace and identify the trust fund, the entire assets of the bank will be subject to a lien in favor of the claimant of the trust fund.

We nowhere find the rule more clearly and concisely stated than in the recent case of Schumacher v. Harriett (C.C.A.) 52 Fed.(2d) 817, 818, where Judge Parker, speaking for the court, says:

> The rule is well settled that where property or funds which are the subject of a trust are used by a bank in such a way as merely to decrease its liabilities and not to augment its assets, no charge upon the assets arises in favor of the cestui que trust. (Citing authorities.) On the other hand, it is equally well settled that, where a bank acting as trustee mingles a trust fund with its other funds, the common fund resulting is **780 impressed with a trust to the amount of the trust fund which has been so commingled and lost its identity; and in such case the cestui que trust is entitled to have the trust declared and the trust fund separated from the other funds, even though the bank subsequently to the commingling may have added to and made payments from the common fund, as the presumption is that it respected the trust and did not make payment from the trust property. … *176 …

The doctrine above stated, that all withdrawals and disbursements by the bank are presumed to be as its own portion of the mixed fund, since it is presumed that the trustee acted rightfully and left the trust funds intact rather than that he violated the trust, and that any balance remaining in the common fund and passing into the hands of the receivers is presumed to include or to be a part of the trust funds and subject to the trust, is sustained by the overwhelming weight of authority. … [T]he presumption in question applies not only to the cash and cash items in the insolvent bank itself but also the credits or deposits in its favor in other banks. … "Such an item for all practical purposes differs not at all from currency. It increases the cash funds of the bank just as much as does a deposit of currency. If the bank cashes it and covers the proceeds into its vaults, the augmentation, of course, is apparent. If, however, the bank treats the cash item as its own and uses it for other banking purposes, such as payment *177 of debts or creating credits in other banks, the cash in the vaults of the bank is relieved to that extent; and, where a trust with respect to a cash item is involved, it must be presumed that the intention was that cash remaining in the vaults of the bank is to be substituted under the trust. … In the complexities of modern banking, cash, cash items, and credit balances react upon each other so rapidly that in ordinary cases it is vain to attempt to distinguish between them. … There is as little reason for distinguishing between cash, cash items, and deposits in other banks in the application of the equitable doctrine, as there would be in distinguishing between moneys kept in different vaults of the same bank." … *178 …

It appears… that there came into the hands of the receivers cash and cash items of $28,946.24 and also a net balance of cash on deposit with other banks of $10,703.77, making cash or its equivalent coming into the receivers' hands $39,650. … *179 … Mrs.

Motley… is entitled to have a trust in her favor impressed upon the entire mass of assets in the receivers' hands for the full amount of her claim, it appearing that the common fund with which it was commingled, to which the presumption of preservation attaches, was never subsequent to the commingling less than the amount of said trust fund. … Mrs. Motley's committees are entitled to recover from the receivers of the Commercial Bank and Trust Company, to be paid out of the assets of said bank in the receivers' hands, the sum of $32,145.97 with interest thereon at 6%… and also recover of the receivers the further sum of $500 representing one-half of the amount wrongfully charged against the trust estate of Mrs. Motley on account of commissions…, with interest thereon…

Traditionally the most onerous burden for trustees has been investing. The law used to reflect a narrowly conservative view of what constituted "prudent management," and even provide a limited list of permissible investments. In addition, courts would assess a trustee's prudence by looking at each transaction or investment in isolation. Modern trust law gives trustees much more extensive freedom in choice of investments, empowers trustees to achieve fairness between categories of beneficiaries by means other than changing a portfolio, and judges investment decision making by looking at the trust's entire portfolio – not each investment on its own -- to see whether it achieves an adequate diversification and balance of secure income and potential for principal growth.

Article 8. Duties and Powers of Trustee

§ 64.2-777. General powers of trustee

A. A trustee, without authorization by the court, may exercise:

1. Powers conferred by the terms of the trust; and

2. Except as limited by the terms of the trust:

a. All powers over the trust property that an unmarried competent owner has over individually owned property;

b. Any other powers appropriate to achieve the proper investment, management, and distribution of the trust property; and

c. Any other powers conferred by this chapter.

B. The exercise of a power is subject to the fiduciary duties prescribed by this article.

§ 64.2-778. Specific powers of trustee

A. Without limiting the authority conferred by § 64.2-777, a trustee may:

1. Collect trust property and accept or reject additions to the trust property from a settlor or any other person;

2. Acquire or sell property…;

3. Exchange, partition, or otherwise change the character of trust property;

4. Deposit trust money in an account in a regulated financial service institution;

5. Borrow money, with or without security, and mortgage or pledge trust property for a period within or extending beyond the duration of the trust;

6. With respect to an interest in a proprietorship, partnership, limited liability company, business trust, corporation, or other form of business or enterprise, continue the business or other enterprise and take any action that may be taken by shareholders, members, or property owners, including merging, dissolving, or otherwise changing the form of business organization or contributing additional capital;

7. With respect to stocks or other securities, exercise the rights of an absolute owner, including the right to:

a. Vote, or give proxies to vote, with or without power of substitution, or enter into or continue a voting trust agreement;

b. Hold a security in the name of a nominee or in other form without disclosure of the trust so that title may pass by delivery;

c. Pay calls, assessments, and other sums chargeable or accruing against the securities, and sell or exercise stock subscription or conversion rights; and

d. Deposit the securities with a depository or other regulated financial service institution;

8. With respect to an interest in real property, construct, or make ordinary or extraordinary repairs to, alterations to, or improvements in, buildings or other structures, demolish improvements, raze existing or erect new party walls or buildings, subdivide or develop land, dedicate land to public use or grant public or private easements, and make or vacate plats and adjust boundaries;

9. Enter into a lease for any purpose as lessor or lessee, including a lease or other arrangement for exploration and removal of natural resources, with or without the option to purchase or renew, for a period within or extending beyond the duration of the trust;

10. Grant an option involving a sale, lease, or other disposition of trust property or acquire an option for the acquisition of property, including an option exercisable beyond the duration of the trust, and exercise an option so acquired;

11. Insure the property of the trust against damage or loss and insure the trustee, the trustee's agents, and beneficiaries against liability arising from the administration of the trust;

12. Abandon or decline to administer property of no value or of insufficient value to justify its collection or continued administration;

13. With respect to possible liability for violation of environmental law:

a. Inspect or investigate property the trustee holds or has been asked to hold, or property owned or operated by an organization in which the trustee holds or has been asked to hold an interest, for the purpose of determining the application of environmental law with respect to the property;

b. Take action to prevent, abate, or otherwise remedy any actual or potential violation of any environmental law affecting property held directly or indirectly by the trustee, whether taken before or after the assertion of a claim or the initiation of governmental enforcement;

c. Decline to accept property into trust or disclaim any power with respect to property that is or may be burdened with liability for violation of environmental law;

d. Compromise claims against the trust that may be asserted for an alleged violation of environmental law; and

e. Pay the expense of any inspection, review, abatement, or remedial action to comply with environmental law;

14. Pay or contest any claim, settle a claim by or against the trust, and release, in whole or in part, a claim belonging to the trust;

15. Pay taxes, assessments, compensation of the trustee and of employees and agents of the trust, and other expenses incurred in the administration of the trust;

16. Exercise elections with respect to federal, state, and local taxes;

17. Select a mode of payment under any employee benefit or retirement plan, annuity, or life insurance payable to the trustee, exercise rights thereunder, including exercise of the right to indemnification for expenses and against liabilities, and take appropriate action to collect the proceeds;

18. Make loans out of trust property, including loans to a beneficiary on terms and conditions the trustee considers to be fair and reasonable under the circumstances, and the trustee has a lien on future distributions for repayment of those loans;

19. Pledge trust property to guarantee loans made by others to the beneficiary;

20. Appoint a trustee to act in another jurisdiction with respect to trust property located in the other jurisdiction, confer upon the appointed trustee all of the powers and duties of the appointing trustee, require that the appointed trustee furnish security, and remove any trustee so appointed;

21. Pay an amount distributable to a beneficiary who is under a legal disability or who the trustee reasonably believes is incapacitated, by paying it directly to the beneficiary or applying it for the beneficiary's benefit, or by:

a. Paying it to the beneficiary's conservator or, if the beneficiary does not have a conservator, the beneficiary's guardian;

b. Paying it to the beneficiary's custodian under the Uniform Transfers to Minors Act (§ 64.2-1900 et seq.) or custodial trustee under the Uniform Custodial Trust Act (§ 64.2-900 et seq.), and, for that purpose, creating a custodianship or custodial trust;

c. If the trustee does not know of a conservator, guardian, custodian, or custodial trustee, paying it to an adult relative or other person having legal or physical care or custody of the beneficiary, to be expended on the beneficiary's behalf; or

d. Managing it as a separate fund on the beneficiary's behalf, subject to the beneficiary's continuing right to withdraw the distribution;

22. On distribution of trust property or the division or termination of a trust, make distributions in divided or undivided interests, allocate particular assets in proportionate or disproportionate shares, value the trust property for those purposes, and adjust for resulting differences in valuation;

23. Resolve a dispute concerning the interpretation of the trust or its administration by mediation, arbitration, or other procedure for alternative dispute resolution;

24. Prosecute or defend an action, claim, or judicial proceeding in any jurisdiction to protect trust property and the trustee in the performance of the trustee's duties;

25. Sign and deliver contracts and other instruments that are useful to achieve or facilitate the exercise of the trustee's powers; and

26. On termination of the trust, exercise the powers appropriate to wind up the administration of the trust and distribute the trust property to the persons entitled to it.

...

§ 64.2-763. Duty to administer trust and invest

Upon acceptance of a trusteeship, the trustee shall administer the trust and invest trust assets in good faith, in accordance with its terms and purposes and the interests of the beneficiaries, and in accordance with this chapter. In administering, managing and investing trust assets, the trustee shall comply with the provisions of the Uniform Prudent Investor Act below) and the Uniform Principal and Income Act below).

§ 64.2-766. Prudent administration

A trustee shall administer the trust as a prudent person would, by considering the purposes, terms, distributional requirements, and other circumstances of the trust. In satisfying this standard, the trustee shall exercise reasonable care, skill, and caution.

§ 64.2-768. Trustee's skills

A trustee who has special skills or expertise, or is named trustee in reliance upon the trustee's representation that the trustee has special skills or expertise, shall use those special skills or expertise.

§ 64.2-767. Costs of administration

In administering a trust, the trustee may incur only costs that are reasonable in relation to the trust property, the purposes of the trust, and the skills of the trustee.

§ 64.2-773. Enforcement and defense of claims

A trustee shall take reasonable steps to enforce claims of the trust and to defend claims against the trust.

§ 64.2-776. Discretionary powers; tax savings

...

B. Subject to subsection D, and unless the terms of the trust expressly indicate that a rule in this subsection does not apply:

1. A person other than a settlor who is a beneficiary and trustee of a trust that confers on the trustee a power to make discretionary distributions to or for the trustee's personal benefit may exercise the power only in accordance with an ascertainable standard; and

2. A trustee may not exercise a power to make discretionary distributions to satisfy a legal obligation of support that the trustee personally owes another person.

For purposes of this subsection, "trustee" includes a person who is deemed to have any power of a trustee, whether because such person has the right to remove or replace any trustee or because a reciprocal trust or power doctrine applies.

C. A power whose exercise is limited or prohibited by subsection B may be exercised by a majority of the remaining trustees whose exercise of the power is not so limited or prohibited. If the power of all trustees is so limited or prohibited, the court may appoint a special fiduciary with authority to exercise the power.

D. Subsection B does not apply to:

1. A power held by the settlor's spouse who is the trustee of a trust for which a marital deduction, as defined in § 2056(b)(5) or 2523(e) of the Internal Revenue Code of 1986, as in effect on the effective date of this chapter, or as later amended, was previously allowed;

2. Any trust during any period that the trust may be revoked or amended by its settlor; or

3. A trust if contributions to the trust qualify for the annual exclusion under § 2503(c) of the Internal Revenue Code of 1986, as in effect on the effective date of this chapter, or as later amended.

Article 9. Uniform Prudent Investor Act

§ 64.2-781. Prudent investor rule

A. ... [A] trustee who invests and manages trust assets owes a duty to the beneficiaries of the trust to comply with the prudent investor rule set forth in this article.

B. The prudent investor rule, a default rule, may be expanded, restricted, eliminated, or otherwise altered by the provisions of a trust. A general authorization in a controlling document authorizing a trustee to invest in such assets as the trustee, in his sole discretion, may deem best, or other language purporting to expand the trustee's investment powers, shall not be construed to waive the rule of subsection A unless the controlling document expressly manifests an intention that it be waived (i) by reference to the "prudent man" or "prudent investor" rule, (ii) by reference to power of the trustee to make "speculative" investments, (iii) by an express authorization to acquire or retain a specific asset or type of asset such as a closely held business, or (iv) by other language synonymous with clause (i), (ii) or (iii). A trustee shall not be liable to a beneficiary for the trustee's good faith reliance on a waiver of the rule of subsection A.

§ 64.2-782. Standard of care; portfolio strategy; risk and return objectives

A. A trustee shall invest and manage trust assets as a prudent investor would, by considering the purposes, terms, distribution requirements, and other circumstances of the trust. In satisfying this standard, the trustee shall exercise reasonable care, skill, and caution.

B. A trustee's investment and management decisions respecting individual assets shall be evaluated not in isolation but in the context of the trust portfolio as a whole and as a part of an overall investment strategy having risk and return objectives reasonably suited to the trust.

C. Among circumstances that a trustee shall consider in investing and managing trust assets are such of the following as are relevant to the trust or its beneficiaries:

1. General economic conditions;

2. The possible effect of inflation or deflation;

3. The expected tax consequences of investment decisions or strategies;

4. The role that each investment or course of action plays within the overall trust portfolio, which may include financial assets, interests in closely held enterprises, tangible and intangible personal property, and real property;

5. The expected total return from income and the appreciation of capital;

6. Other resources of the beneficiaries;

7. Needs for liquidity, regularity of income, and preservation or appreciation of capital; and

8. An asset's special relationship or special value, if any, to the purposes of the trust or to one or more of the beneficiaries.

D. A trustee shall make a reasonable effort to verify facts relevant to the investment and management of trust assets.

E. A trustee may invest in any kind of property or type of investment consistent with the standards of this article.

F. A trustee who has special skills or expertise, or is named trustee in reliance upon the trustee's representation that the trustee has special skills or expertise, has a duty to use those special skills or expertise.

G. A trustee may hold any policies of life insurance... with no duty or need to (i) determine whether any such policy is or remains a proper investment, (ii) dispose of such policy in order to diversify the investments of the trust, or (iii) exercise policy options under any such contract not essential to the continuation of the life insurance provided by such contract. ...

§ 64.2-783. Diversification by trustee

A trustee shall diversify the investments of the trust unless the trustee reasonably determines that, because of special circumstances, the purposes of the trust are better served without diversifying.

§ 64.2-786. Investment costs

In investing and managing trust assets, a trustee may only incur costs that are appropriate and reasonable in relation to the assets, the purposes of the trust, and the skills of the trustee.

§ 64.2-787. Reviewing compliance

Compliance with the prudent investor rule is determined in light of the facts and circumstances existing at the time of a trustee's decision or action and not by hindsight.

§ 64.2-789. Language invoking standard of article

The following terms or comparable language in the provisions of a trust, unless otherwise limited or modified by language articulating the investment standard to which the trustee is to be held, authorizes any investment or strategy permitted under this article: "investments permissible by law for investment of trust funds," "legal investments," "authorized investments," "using the judgment and care under the circumstances then prevailing that persons of prudence, discretion, and intelligence exercise in the management of their own affairs, not in regard to speculation but in regard to the permanent disposition of their funds, considering the probable income as well as the probable safety of their capital," "prudent man rule," "prudent trustee rule," "prudent person rule," and "prudent investor rule."

***

For many non-institutional trustees, the management and investment duties might be, or at least seem, overwhelming. The UTC and the Uniform Prudent Investor Act authorize the trustee to delegate these functions to a substantial degree.

Article 8. Duties and Powers of Trustee

§ 64.2-769. Delegation by trustee

A. A trustee may delegate duties and powers that a prudent trustee of comparable skills could properly delegate under the circumstances. The trustee shall exercise reasonable care, skill, and caution in:

1. Selecting an agent;

2. Establishing the scope and terms of the delegation, consistent with the purposes and terms of the trust; and

3. Periodically reviewing the agent's actions in order to monitor the agent's performance and compliance with the terms of the delegation.

B. In performing a delegated function, an agent owes a duty to the trust to exercise reasonable care to comply with the terms of the delegation.

C. A trustee who complies with subsection A is not liable to the beneficiaries or to the trust for an action of the agent to whom the function was delegated.

D. By accepting a delegation of powers or duties from the trustee of a trust that is subject to the law of the Commonwealth, an agent submits to the jurisdiction of the courts of the Commonwealth.

Article 9. Uniform Prudent Investor Act

§ 64.2-788. Delegation of investment and management functions

A. A trustee may delegate investment and management functions that a prudent trustee of comparable skills could properly delegate under the circumstances. The trustee shall exercise reasonable care, skill, and caution in:

1. Selecting an agent;

2. Establishing the scope and terms of the delegation, consistent with the purposes and terms of the trust; and

3. Periodically reviewing the agent's actions in order to monitor the agent's performance and compliance with the terms of the delegation.

B. In performing a delegated function, an agent owes a duty to the trust to exercise reasonable care to comply with the terms of the delegation.

C. A trustee who complies with the requirements of subsection A is not liable to the beneficiaries or to the trust for the decisions or actions of the agent to whom the function was delegated. ...

***

In addition, § 64.2-778.1 of the UTC authorizes a trustee to create a second trust with a separate trustee to handle some portion of the trust assets.

Custodial Trusts

Chapter 9 (of the Trusts subtitle in Title 64.2 of the Virginia Code enacts the Uniform Custodial Trust Act. Instead of including the extensive statutory provisions regarding this less common form of trust, below is a useful summary of custodial trusts provided by the Uniform Law Commissioners:

Custodial Trust Act Summary

We are perfectly free to be irresponsible with the property that we accumulate. We can dissipate it, abandon it, or ignore it. Most of us choose to be more responsible, however. We tend to accumulate property for the economic security it provides ourselves and our families. It comes as a great shock, therefore, when we find that controlling and protecting it at key moments in our lives is much harder than we imagined. What happens if we become incapacitated? Guardianships and conservatorships are expensive last resorts that mean total loss of control. What happens when we die? Wills and the probate process offer some solace, but probate becomes more onerous and expensive than helpful. Extensive estate planning with its panoply of generation-skipping devices, such as trusts, is expensive and beyond the resources of most people. The search for a better way continues.

The Uniform Law Commissioners' Uniform Custodial Trust Act, promulgated in 1987, offers some needed help. Inter vivos and testamentary, discretionary trusts are too complicated to meet certain needs. But the trust form of ownership, simplified and carefully prescribed in a statute, can meet them—thus the Uniform Custodial Trust Act (UCTA).

A trust is, simply, a legal structure for organizing the ownership and management of property for its preservation on behalf of specified individuals. A trust involves three fundamental participants: a donor who puts property in a trust; a trustee who owns and manages the trust; and beneficiaries who receive the financial benefit of the trust and for whom the property is preserved. A trust arises in a trust agreement or instrument (a document) in which the donor names the trustee and beneficiaries. The donor also establishes the trustee's powers over the property and the beneficiaries' rights to principal and income in the trust instrument. The donor then transfers property to the trustee, who owns it for the benefit of the beneficiaries. The trustee is also a fiduciary, meaning that he or she is subject to special rules and standards of care when managing the trust's assets. All trusts have these characteristics, and a custodial trust is but one of a number of kinds of trusts.

The UCTA allows any person to create a custodial trust by executing a simple statement (it may be a separate document or merely a notation on an existing title document) that the property is being placed in trust under the Act. The trustee's obligations arise upon acceptance of the property. That is all that is necessary to create the trust.

The UCTA permits a kind of springing trust too—a trust that arises upon the happening of a future event. Any person can create such a trust with respect to specific property by executing a simple statement, indicating that the trust will be established upon the happening of the event.

The UCTA also allows anybody obligated to an incapacitated person, without a conservator (a conservator is a court-appointed manager of an incapacitated person's property), to establish a custodial trust into which property satisfying the obligation is placed for the incapacitated person as beneficiary. If the value of the property so placed exceeds $20,000, however, a transfer into such a trust must be approved by a court.

What distinguishes a custodial trust from other kinds of trusts? To begin with, the UCTA governs all aspects of the trust relationship, including a trustee's powers and obligations. Therefore, elaborate trust documents are not needed. Second, a custodial trust exists at the will of its beneficiaries. Any beneficiary can terminate his or her share of the trust. Third, trust beneficiaries can direct the trustee's payment of income to themselves. Fourth, the beneficiaries can direct the trustee's investment and management of the trust property. Fifth, at a beneficiary's incapacity, the trust continues as a discretionary trust, with the trustee as a full fiduciary. Therefore, no conservator needs to be appointed for the purposes of managing the trust property. Sixth, a beneficiary may direct the trustee by a simple writing to distribute the trust property in any fashion the beneficiary desires at the beneficiary's death. The writing is not a will unless the beneficiary makes it one, and the distribution is a non-probate transfer of the property.

These powers of beneficiaries distinguish a custodial trust from all other trusts. Trustees under the common law are not subject to the direction of beneficiaries. The powers of the beneficiaries in the UCTA suggest why such a trust is called "custodial" and suggest the values of a custodial trust, as well as its limitations.

A trust is custodial because the trustee's powers are limited by the beneficiaries the trustee is a custodian for the beneficiaries' interests. The trustee is a custodian until such time as a beneficiary becomes incapacitated. The custodial trust is an ideal form of ownership for anyone who wants to make sure property is properly managed before incapacity and protected afterwards. A person with property merely conveys the property to a trustee, naming himself or herself as beneficiary. While there are no questions of capacity, the beneficiary retains significant powers over the property. At incapacity, his or her appointed trustee continues to manage the property and use it for the beneficiary. If incapacity is temporary, the beneficiary reasserts his or her powers when capacity returns. If at any time a beneficiary with capacity desires to terminate the custodial trust, he or she simply terminates it.

Who will use the trust? Older people who want to make sure they control who manages their property when they are incapacitated, are the most likely users of the UCTA. People who go on long trips and who want to assure proper management while they are gone or who want protection if they become incapacitated while traveling can use a custodial trust rather than a power of attorney if it suits their needs. These are examples of people and situations for which the UCTA was created.

At the same time, people who need discretionary trusts for estate planning and tax purposes will continue to turn to traditional trust law. The control provided to beneficiaries in the UCTA and the ability to terminate a custodial trust do not make it suitable for these purposes.

The UCTA fills very particular needs of ordinary people. It should be considered strongly by any state or jurisdiction conscious of the difficulties an ordinary person has in preparing for personal incapacity and death.

C. Settlor waiver of duties

We saw at the outset of this chapter that the UTC for the most part creates default rules that a settlor may override, but there are some absolute rules not subject to waiver by settlors, including a minimal duty for trustees.

§ 64.2-703. Default and mandatory rules

...

B. The terms of a trust prevail over any provision of this chapter except: ...

2. The duty of a trustee to act in good faith and in accordance with the terms and purposes of the trust and the interests of the beneficiaries; ...

8. The effect of an exculpatory term under § 64.2-799; ...

11. The power of the court to take such action and exercise such jurisdiction as may be necessary in the interests of justice.

§ 64.2-776. Discretionary powers; tax savings

A. Notwithstanding the breadth of discretion granted to a trustee in the terms of the trust, including the use of such terms as "absolute," "sole," or "uncontrolled," the trustee shall exercise a discretionary power in good faith and in accordance with the terms and purposes of the trust and the interests of the beneficiaries. ...

§ 64.2-799. Exculpation of trustee

A. A term of a trust relieving a trustee of liability for breach of trust is unenforceable to the extent that it:

1. Relieves the trustee of liability for breach of trust committed in bad faith or with reckless indifference to the purposes of the trust or the interests of the beneficiaries; or

2. Was inserted as the result of an abuse by the trustee of a fiduciary or confidential relationship to the settlor.

B. An exculpatory term drafted or caused to be drafted by the trustee is invalid as an abuse of a fiduciary or confidential relationship unless the trustee proves that the existence and contents of the exculpatory term were adequately communicated to the settlor.

***

Supreme Court of Virginia.
Hoffman v. First Virginia Bank of Tidewater
220 Va. 834, 263 S.E.2d 402 (1980)

COCHRAN, Justice.

**404 *836 ... Helen B. Hoffman, formerly Helen C. Ballard, and other beneficiaries under the will of William P. Ballard, deceased, (collectively, the complainants, or the beneficiaries), filed their amended bill of complaint in the trial court against First Virginia Bank of Tidewater, successor to Southern Bank of Norfolk (the Trustee), serving as trustee of the marital trust established by the will for the benefit of Helen C. Ballard during her lifetime. Complainants sought to remove the Trustee and to surcharge its accounts. Copies of the will and inventory of the estate were attached to the bill of complaint as exhibits.

Complainants alleged that the marital trust comprised assets having a total value of $103,972.33, as of August 15, 1972, the date of its establishment; that various securities in the trust were sold between December 7, 1972, and January 4, 1973, and the sum of $39,575.88, being substantially all the proceeds derived therefrom and approximating 38% of the total trust assets, was invested in the securities of three real estate investment trusts (REITs); that from January, 1973 until September, 1973 the securities of all REITs declined in value; that about September, 1973 prices for REIT securities "plummeted" and by the end of that year the market for such securities had "substantially collapsed"; and that the REIT securities held by the Trustee became "substantially worthless".

Complainants alleged that First Virginia negligently failed to observe reasonable standards for prudent fiduciary investment for a trust of modest size, by failing to diversify the trust investments, by investing in speculative securities unsuitable for the trust, by failing to maintain adequate surveillance of the investments, by failing to apply available investment information and advice, and by failing to render timely accountings to the beneficiaries. The amended bill of complaint contained no allegation of fraud, bad faith, or conflict of interest on the part of the Trustee.

Complainants sought to replace First Virginia as trustee with two specified individuals as substitute trustees. Complainants also sought to surcharge First Virginia for all fees and commissions taken or accrued, and the sum of $39,575.88, with 8% interest, costs and attorney's fees, subject to credit against principal for the value of the REIT investments and to credit against interest for interest and dividends received from such investments. ... *837 ...**405 ... *839 ... **406 ...

Code s 26-45.1 provides in pertinent part as follows:

> (a) [A]n executor, administrator, trustee or other fiduciary... shall exercise the judgment of care under the circumstances then prevailing, which men of prudence, discretion and intelligence exercise in the management of their own affairs, not in regard to speculation but in regard to the permanent disposition of their funds, considering the probable income as well as the probable safety of their capital. Within the limitations of the foregoing standard..., [a fiduciary] is authorized to acquire and retain every kind of property, real, personal or mixed, and every kind of investment... which men of prudence, discretion and intelligence acquire or retain for their own account; and within the limitations of the foregoing standard, ... may retain property properly acquired, without limitation as to time and without regard to its suitability for original purchase. ... *840 ...

> (b) Nothing contained in this section shall be construed as authorizing any departure from, or variation of, the express terms or limitations set forth in any will, agreement, court order or other instrument creating or defining an executor's, administrator's, trustee's or other fiduciary's duties and powers...

This statute, first enacted in 1956 (Acts 1956, c. 660), merely incorporated the principle long established by our case law that, unless a trust instrument provides otherwise, the "prudent man rule" will be applied to the management of assets by a fiduciary. ... **407 ... The beneficiaries acknowledge that a testator may waive the "prudent man rule", but they say that Ballard did not do so. Although there was no express waiver, a waiver may arise by necessary implication *841 from the language used in the will. Therefore, we review the powers granted to the testamentary trustee by the will.

In Article V, the testator gave his executor and trustee "full discretionary powers of management . . . without being restricted to those investments authorized by statute in Virginia for the investment of trust funds . . .." This provision authorized the fiduciary to invest in assets other than those specifically listed in Code §§ 26-40 and 26-40.1 [now repealed].

The testator was especially interested in giving his executor and trustee power to retain any or all of his investments, and he exonerated the fiduciary, acting in either capacity, from liability for depreciation in the value of securities so retained. This provision was important to afford flexibility in protecting the testator's interests in the closely-held, family corporations listed in the inventory of his estate.

The powers of the trustee alone were then stated. The will authorized investment "in any type of real or personal property . . . regardless of diversification or State laws, and . . . in common stocks, unimproved real estate, non-productive items, common trust funds, investment company shares . . ..” This language, the Trustee maintains, gave it the broadest possible investment authority and waived the application of the "prudent man rule". We agree.

Having already provided that the executor and trustee could invest without being restricted to the list of legal investments under Code §§ 26-40 and 26-40.1, the testator clearly intended to grant more comprehensive powers to the trustee alone. Accordingly, he specifically waived any requirement of diversification of investments, and then removed any further restrictions upon the trustee's investment powers by eliminating the constraints of laws otherwise applicable. We cannot agree with the contention of the beneficiaries that the testator intended by these provisions only to reaffirm his waiver of the "legal list" of investments... The terminology is too broad to be construed as applying to a single investment law, embraced within the two statutes, that had already been eliminated. The language is clear and unambiguous, so that no extrinsic evidence is admissible to explain its meaning. We conclude that the testator's language must be construed as a waiver of the "prudent man rule" that had been incorporated into the statute law of the Commonwealth.

As the Trustee was authorized to invest in any kind of real or personal property, it could purchase securities of REITs. As the *842 Trustee was not required to diversify, it could purchase as many of these securities as it deemed advisable. As the Trustee was expressly authorized to retain investments as long as it deemed advisable, it was under no obligation to sell in a declining market. A prudent man might not have invested in REIT securities, or might have diversified the investments to a greater extent, or might have sold the REITS before their market value deteriorated, but the Trustee was acting pursuant to the expanded authority granted to it by the testator. **408

The broad investment powers were first conferred upon the testator's wife and brother, but later were transferred without diminution to the bank of which he was a stockholder and director. It is apparent that, in view of his close association with each of the fiduciaries named in his will and in his codicil, the testator was content to grant to them the widest possible discretionary powers in the administration of his estate. In order to impose liability, therefore, it must be alleged and proved that the fiduciary acted dishonestly or in bad faith, or abused the discretion vested in it.

The beneficiaries have not alleged fraud, dishonesty, or bad faith. In oral argument, they contended that the Trustee abused its discretion by failing to diversify. But the testator expressly authorized the Trustee not to diversify, so there was no abuse of discretion in following this authorization.

The beneficiaries insisted that the Trustee had no discretion to invest in speculative securities. However, the will authorized, without restriction, investment in any kind of security, and the express authorization to invest in nonproductive items and unimproved real estate shows an invent to permit the fiduciary in its discretion to invest in speculations. If the fiduciary did so invest, therefore, it did so pursuant to the terms of the will.

The beneficiaries argued that the Trustee negligently failed to maintain surveillance over the REIT securities and as a consequence failed to sell them when their value was declining. This was not an allegation of abuse of discretion but of negligence. But the Trustee was expressly authorized to retain, as long as it deemed advisable, any investment. We construe this authorization as sufficient to permit the Trustee to determine in its discretion the nature and extent of the surveillance required in managing the securities in its custody. A prudent man might have exercised sounder judgment in acquiring and reviewing *843 the securities in the trust account, but the testator chose to rely solely upon the judgment of his fiduciary.

We conclude that the chancellor did not err in sustaining the demurrer as to the Trustee's management of the investments. ... However, the adult beneficiaries have the right under the will at any time to file a petition in the trial court and have the Trustee replaced. ... The remedy is always available, as the Trustee acknowledged, regardless of fault on its part; the beneficiaries need not allege or prove fault. Accordingly, we well affirm the judgment of the trial court without prejudice to the rights of the beneficiaries to proceed in the trial court pursuant to the provision of the will to replace the Trustee if they be so advised.

D. Beneficiary authorization or ratification of breach

§ 64.2-800. Beneficiary's consent, release, or ratification

A trustee is not liable to a beneficiary for breach of trust if the beneficiary consented to the conduct constituting the breach, released the trustee from liability for the breach, or ratified the transaction constituting the breach, unless:

1. The consent, release, or ratification of the beneficiary was induced by improper conduct of the trustee; or

2. At the time of the consent, release, or ratification, the beneficiary did not know of the beneficiary's rights or of the material facts relating to the breach.

Chapter Six
Probate Procedure and the Role of Personal Administrator

This chapter collects Code provisions and case law dealing with more procedural aspects of estate practice, including details about the probate process and the PR's responsibilities. These rules are difficult to find interesting until one finds oneself in the position of actually having to administer an estate, being a potential heir or beneficiary who worries about someone else's handling of an estate, or explaining to a client the process that will swing into motion upon his or her death and how it could go wrong.

Article 5. Probate.

§ 64.2-443. Jurisdiction of probate of wills.

A. ... A will shall be offered for probate in the circuit court in the county or city wherein the decedent has a known place of residence...

B. Where any person has become, either voluntarily or involuntarily, a patient in a nursing home, convalescent home, or similar institution due to advanced age or impaired health, the place of legal residence of the person shall be rebuttably presumed to be the same as it was before he became a patient.

§ 64.2-444. Clerks may probate wills.

A. The clerk of any circuit court, or any duly qualified deputy of such clerk, may admit wills to probate, appoint and qualify executors, administrators, and curators of decedents... in the same manner and with like effect as the circuit court. ...

§ 64.2-445. Appeal from order of clerk.

Any person interested in the probate of the will may appeal any order entered pursuant to § 64.2-444 within six months after the entering of such an order ...

§ 64.2-446. Motion for probate; process against persons interested in probate.

A. A person offering, or intending to offer, to a circuit court or to the clerk of the circuit court a will for probate, may request that the clerk of such court summon any person interested in the probate of the will to appear to show cause why the will should not be admitted to probate. ...

C. In the absence of [such] request ..., the court... may proceed to admit or reject the will without summoning any party.

§ 64.2-447. Use of depositions.

A. The deposition of a witness who subscribed a will attesting that the will is the will of the testator, or in the case of a holographic will, a witness attesting that the will is wholly in the handwriting of the testator, may be admitted as evidence to prove the will if the witness (i) resides outside of the Commonwealth or (ii) resides in the Commonwealth but is unable to testify for any reason before the court or clerk where the will is offered. ...

B. ...[I]f probate is opposed by some person interested in the probate of the will, such person shall have the right to examine such witness.

§ 64.2-448. Complaint to impeach or establish a will; limitation of action; venue.

A. A person interested in the probate of the will... may file a complaint to impeach or establish the will within one year from the date of the order entered by the court in exercise of its original jurisdiction or after an appeal of an order entered by the clerk, or, if no appeal from an order entered by the clerk is taken, from the date of the order entered by the clerk.

B. A person interested in the probate of the will who had been proceeded against by an order of publication... may file a complaint to impeach or establish the will within two years from the date of the order entered by the court..., unless he actually appeared as a party or had been personally served with a summons to appear.

C. A person interested in the probate of the will who has not otherwise been before the court and who was a minor at the time of the order... may file a complaint to impeach or establish the will within one year after such person reaches the age of maturity or is judicially declared emancipated.

D. A person interested in the probate of the will... who was incapacitated at the time of the order ... may file a complaint to impeach or establish the will within one year after such person is restored to capacity.

E. Upon the filing of a complaint to impeach or establish the will..., the court shall order a trial by jury to ascertain whether what was offered for probate is the will of the testator. ... The court shall decide whether to admit the will to probate.

***

Supreme Court of Virginia.
Martone v. Martone
257 Va. 199, 509 S.E.2d 302 (1999)

KINSER, Justice.

... This suit was commenced on behalf of nine-year-old Stephanie Gale Martone by her **304 mother and next friend. Stephanie filed a bill in equity for issue devisavit vel non to determine which of three documents is the last will and testament of her grandfather, Dr. Alexander L. Martone. She named Dr. Martone's widow, Joan D. Martone (Mrs. Martone), Dr. Martone's children from his first marriage, his grandchildren, great-grandchildren, and all unknown or unborn issue or heirs of Dr. Martone (unknown heirs) as defendants.

Pursuant to Code § 64.1–90 [now § 64.2-448], Stephanie asserts that she is a "person interested" in the probate of her grandfather's will and that she was "not otherwise ... before the court" in a prior probate proceeding. ...*203 ... The prior probate proceeding to which Stephanie refers was commenced on June 24, 1996, when Mrs. Martone filed an application in the Circuit Court for the City of Norfolk for quasi inter partes probate of Dr. Martone's will dated March 3, 1995.[3]

> [3] Dr. Martone died on June 6, 1996.

Mrs. Martone named Dr. Martone's four adult children as parties in that proceeding. On September 6, 1996, at the request of the children, the court entered a decree converting the quasi inter partes probate to an inter partes proceeding pursuant to Code § 64.1–80. The court also ordered that all interested persons be made parties to the proceeding and that all testamentary documents of Dr. Martone be filed. In response to the court's decree, two testamentary documents dated April 10, 1991, and February 6, 1995, respectively, were filed, in addition to the March 3, 1995 will that Mrs. Martone had originally submitted for probate. However, no other persons were added as parties, nor was a guardian ad litem appointed to represent the interests of any minors or unknown heirs.

The parties to that probate proceeding submitted the issue devisavit vel non to a jury. That jury, in special interrogatories, found that Dr. Martone possessed testamentary capacity when he executed the March 1995 will and that he was not acting under the undue influence of Mrs. Martone. Accordingly, the court entered judgment on the verdict on March 14, 1997, and admitted the March 1995 will to probate. That will expressly revoked all prior wills, devised and bequeathed Dr. Martone's estate to Mrs. Martone, and named her as executor of his estate.[4]

> [4] The February 1995 document contained essentially the same provisions as the March 1995 will.

In the present case, Stephanie is a proponent of the 1991 document. In that writing, Dr. Martone devised and bequeathed his estate to his trustee, Peter W. Martone, to be administered pursuant to the terms of a trust agreement also dated April 10, 1991. The only provision in that will for his grandchildren and great-grandchildren is found in Article V(b), which states in pertinent part:

*204 Any net income collected from assets held by my Executor [Peter W. Martone] during the period of administration of my estate may, in whole or in part, in the sole discretion of the Executor, be distributed to any one or more person or persons, to **305 the permissible exclusion of any one or more of them, within a class consisting of my wife and my issue, or may be accumulated and added to the principal of my residuary estate, or may be applied by my Executor to the payment of debts, funeral expenses, administration costs and/or taxes payable out of my estate....

In Article VIII of the trust established by Dr. Martone on the same day that he executed the 1991 will, he directed that the trust property "shall be held and/or distributed as [he] shall have designated in written instructions addressed to [the trustee]...." In the same article, Dr. Martone also provided that, if he failed to leave instructions for any portion of the trust estate, the trustee shall distribute that property "to such person or persons as would inherit personal property from [Dr. Martone] in accordance with, and in the proportions provided by, the laws of the Commonwealth of Virginia as if [he] had died intestate, unmarried and owning such part or portion of the trust estate." Thus, the 1991 will and trust are the only instruments in which Dr. Martone provided for his children, grandchildren, and great-grandchildren.

In response to Stephanie's bill in equity, all the defendants (including the guardian ad litem appointed by the court for the unknown heirs), except Mrs. Martone, filed answers and cross-bills seeking the same relief as Stephanie, i.e., to have the 1991 document probated as the last will and testament of Dr. Martone. Stephanie and these cross-plaintiffs assert that Dr. Martone was acting under the undue influence of Mrs. Martone when he executed the March 1995 will. This position is the same one that Dr. Martone's children advanced in the prior probate proceeding. ...

In a decree dated December 19, 1997, the circuit court... dismissed this action. In a letter opinion, the court discussed the nature of the interest created in Dr. Martone's 1991 will for the benefit of his grandchildren and great-grandchildren: *205

[T]he grandchildren and great-grandchildren will take under the 1991 will only from the income from the estate while in the hands of the executor before he transfers the assets to the trustee. However, there is a further qualification. They will take only if the executor, in his sole discretion, decides to make such distributions, and even then he may distribute to some, but not all, in such amounts and proportions as he, in his sole discretion, deems appropriate. There is no mandate for the executor to make any distributions at all.

The court concluded that the interest that these parties may have "cannot rise above the level of a mere expectancy."

The court further determined that all the parties in the present action who were not named as parties in the prior probate proceeding were, nevertheless, fully represented in that proceeding by Dr. Martone's children. Thus, by applying the doctrines of res judicata and virtual representation, the court concluded that the grandchildren, great-grandchildren, and unknown heirs are precluded from proceeding under Code § 64.1–90 to establish the 1991 document as the last will and testament of Dr. Martone. The court likewise found that Dr. Martone's four children are barred by the doctrine of res judicata from relitigating the probate of the March 1995 will....

II.

To impeach or establish a will pursuant to Code § 64.1–90, a party must, inter alia, be a "person interested." Title 64.1 pertaining to wills and decedents' estates does not define the term "person interested" although it is used in several sections of that title. However, we believe that the term means that an individual must have a legally ascertainable, pecuniary interest, which will be impaired by probating a will or benefited by setting aside the will, and not a mere expectancy. *206 [citations to decisions in other states]; see also Fitzgibbon v. Barry, 78 Va. 755, 760 (1884) ("[I]n no case ... is it necessary to make those persons parties who are entitled 'only to future and very uncertain and contingent interests.'").

The interest that the grandchildren, great-grandchildren, and unknown heirs assert in order to qualify as a "person interested" is found in Article V(b) of Dr. Martone's 1991 will.[8]

> [8] Since all of Dr. Martone's children were living at the time of his death, Article V(b) of the 1991 will is the only provision under which his grandchildren and great-grandchildren could receive a distribution from his estate.

In that provision, Dr. Martone authorized his executor to distribute any net income from assets held during the administration of the estate to any one or more persons in a class consisting of Dr. Martone's wife and his issue.[9]

> [9] For the purposes of this case, we assume, without deciding, that the term "issue" as used in the 1991 will includes Dr. Martone's grandchildren, great-grandchildren, and unknown heirs.

However, the executor has absolute discretion in deciding whether to accumulate income and add it to the principal of the residuary estate; to apply it to the payment of debts, taxes, and other expenses of the estate; or to distribute it to members of the designated class. Even if the executor chooses to disburse income, he also has complete discretion as to the amount of any distribution and to whom it will be paid. In other words, he can disburse income to some members of the class and exclude others. We have stated that "equity will not compel or control ... [the] discretion or exercise" *207 of "a mere naked power [of disposal among the members of a class that is] purely discretionary with the donee." Daniel v. Brown, 156 Va. 563, 571, 159 S.E. 209, 211 (1931).

Thus, we conclude that the interest created by Article V(b) of the 1991 will is a mere expectancy, not a legally ascertainable right. It is, therefore, not sufficient to satisfy the requirement of a "person interested" under Code § 64.1–90 with regard to the grandchildren, great-grandchildren, and unknown heirs. Under the 1991 will, only Dr. Martone's four children are "person[s] interested." However, as already noted, they litigated their claim in the prior probate proceeding when they attempted to establish the 1991 document as Dr. Martone's last will and testament. ...

[T]he decision in Gaddess v. Norris' Ex'rs, 102 Va. 625, 46 S.E. 905 (1904), does not compel a different result. In that case, the decedent's will established a trust for his six children. The decedent directed his trustee to distribute a portion of **307 the income each year to his children during their respective lives. The will further granted a power of appointment to each child to dispose of his or her share of the trust by will in favor of any of his or her issue. If any child died without having exercised the power of appointment, his or her share passed to his or her issue. Because of the nature of the grandchildren's interests, we concluded that they had to be named as parties to a suit to construe the decedent's will. Unlike the interest in the present case, the grandchildren in Gaddess had more than a mere expectancy. Some or all of them would receive a portion of the decedent's estate either by exercise of the power of appointment or as takers in default. Id. at 630, 46 S.E. at 907.

Similarly, we held in NationsBank of Va., N.A. v. Estate of Grandy, 248 Va. 557, 560, 450 S.E.2d 140, 143 (1994), that "the interests of the potential beneficiaries [of a trust were] too remote to require the joinder of those potential beneficiaries as necessary parties." The interests of the potential beneficiaries were contingent interests that could be defeated by any future issue of Grandy, the beneficiary of the trust.

We next consider the children's contention that the circuit court erred by applying the doctrine of res judicata to dismiss their cross-bills. They argue that the court had no basis for that ruling because the record of the prior probate proceeding was not before the court, in particular, the final decree entered in that proceeding. We do not agree. *208

The same judge presided over both the instant action and the prior probate proceeding. Moreover, the court was entitled to take judicial notice of the record in that case when ruling on Mrs. Martone's demurrer since Stephanie and the cross-plaintiffs referred to the prior probate proceeding in their cross-bills. See Fleming v. Anderson, 187 Va. 788, 794–95, 48 S.E.2d 269, 272 (1948) ("[W]here the plaintiff refers to another proceeding or judgment, and specifically bases his right of action, in whole or in part, on something which appears in the record of the prior case, the court, in passing on a demurrer to the complaint, will take judicial notice of the matters appearing in the former case."). ... For these reasons, we will affirm the judgment of the circuit court.[10]

[10] Since the grandchildren, great-grandchildren, and unknown heirs are not "person[s] interested," we need not address whether they were otherwise before the court in the prior probate proceeding through "virtual representation."

Chapter 5. Personal Representatives and Administration of Estates.
Article 1. Appointment and Qualification.

§ 64.2-500. Grant of administration with the will annexed.

A. If the will does not name an executor, or the executor named refuses to accept, fails to give bond, or dies, resigns, or is removed from office, the court or clerk may grant administration with the will annexed to a person who is a residual or substantial legatee under the will,… or if such person fails to apply for administration within 30 days, to a person who would have been entitled to administration if there had been no will.

B. Administration shall not be granted to any person unless he takes the required oath and gives bond, and the court or clerk is satisfied that he is suitable and competent to perform the duties of his office. Administration shall not be granted to any person under a disability as defined in § 8.01-2 [felons, children, mentally incapacitated persons].

C. If any beneficiary of the estate objects, a spouse or parent who has been barred from all interest in the estate because of desertion or abandonment as provided under § 64.2-308 or 64.2–308.17… may not serve as an administrator of the estate.

§ 64.2-513. Effect of death, resignation, or removal of sole executor.

Upon the death, resignation, or removal of the sole surviving executor under any last will, administration of the estate of the testator not already administered may be granted, with the will annexed, to any person the court deems appropriate.

§ 64.2-502. Grant of administration of intestate estate.

A. The court or the clerk who would have jurisdiction as to the probate of a will, if there were a will, has jurisdiction to hear and determine the right of administration of the estate in the case of a person dying intestate. Administration shall be granted as follows:

1. During the first 30 days following the decedent's death, the court or the clerk may grant administration to a sole distribute…, or in the absence of a sole distributee, to any distributee… who presents written waivers of the right to qualify from all other competent distributees.

2. After 30 days have passed since the decedent's death, the court or the clerk may grant administration to the first distribute… who applies, provided, that if, during the first 30 days following the decedent's death, more than one distributee notifies the court or the clerk of an intent to qualify after the 30-day period has elapsed, the court or the clerk shall not grant administration to any distributee, or his designee, until the court or the clerk has given all such distributees an opportunity to be heard.

3. After 45 days have passed since the decedent's death, the court or the clerk may grant administration to any nonprofit charitable organization that operated as a conservator or guardian for the decedent at the time of his … However, if, during the first 45 days following the decedent's death, any distributee notifies the court or the clerk of an intent to qualify after the 45-day period has elapsed, the court or the clerk shall not grant administration to any such organization until the court or the clerk has given all such distributees an opportunity to be heard. …

4. After 60 days have passed since the decedent's death, the court or the clerk may grant administration to one or more of the creditors or to any other person...

B. When granting administration, if the court determines that it is in the best interests of a decedent's estate, the court may depart from the provisions of this section at any time and grant administration to such person as the court deems appropriate.

C. ... Admission of a will to probate... terminates any previous grant of administration.

D. The court or clerk shall not grant administration to any person unless satisfied that... such person is not under a disability as defined in § 8.01-2 or...convicted of a felony offense of (i) fraud or misrepresentation or (ii) robbery, extortion, burglary, larceny, embezzlement, fraudulent conversion, perjury, bribery, treason, or racketeering. ...

E. If any beneficiary of the estate objects, a spouse or parent who has been barred from all interest in the estate because of desertion or abandonment as provided under § 64.2-308 or 64.2–308.17... may not serve as an administrator of the estate of the deceased spouse or child.

§ 64.2-503. Oath and bond of administrator of intestate estate.

An administrator of an intestate estate shall give bond and take an oath...

§ 64.2-505. When security not required.

A. ... However, the court or clerk shall not require a personal representative to furnish security if:

    1. All distributees of a decedent's estate or all beneficiaries under the decedent's will are personal representatives of that decedent's estate..; or

    2. The will waives security of an executor nominated therein.

B. Notwithstanding subsection A, upon the motion of any person who has a pecuniary interest in an estate, the court or clerk may require the personal representative to furnish security. ...

Article 2. Nonresident Trustees.

§ 64.2-1426. Nonresident fiduciaries.

A. A natural person who is not a resident of the Commonwealth may be appointed or allowed to qualify or act as the personal representative, or trustee under a will, of any decedent, or appointed as the guardian of an infant's estate or the guardian or conservator of the property of an incapacitated person... [E]ach such nonresident shall file... consent in writing that service of process in any action or proceeding against him as personal representative, trustee under a will, conservator, or guardian, or any other notice with respect to the administration of the estate, trust, or person in his charge... may be by service upon the clerk of the court... or upon such resident of the Commonwealth and at such address as the nonresident may appoint... [W]here any nonresident qualifies, other than as a guardian of an incapacitated person, pursuant to this subsection, bond with surety shall be required in every case, unless a resident personal representative, trustee, or fiduciary qualifies at the same time or the court or clerk... waives surety...

B. A corporation shall not be appointed or allowed to qualify or act as personal representative, as trustee under a will, or as one of the personal representatives or trustees under a will of any decedent, or appointed or allowed to qualify or act as guardian of an infant, as one of the guardians of an infant, as guardian of the person or property of an incapacitated person..., or as one of the guardians or conservators, unless the corporation is authorized to do business in the Commonwealth. ...

§ 64.2-517. Exercise of discretionary powers by surviving executors or administrators with the will annexed

A. When discretionary powers are conferred upon the executors under any will and some, but not all, of the executors die, resign, or become incapable of acting, the executors or executor remaining shall continue to exercise the discretionary powers conferred by the will, unless the will expressly provides that the discretionary powers cannot be exercised by fewer than all of the original executors named in the will.

B. When discretionary powers are conferred upon the executors under any will and all of the executors or the sole executor if only one is named in the will dies, resigns, or becomes incapable of acting, the administrator with the will annexed appointed by the court shall exercise the discretionary powers conferred by the will upon the original executors or executor, unless the will expressly provides that the discretionary powers can only be exercised by the executors or executor named in the will.

***

Supreme Court of Virginia.
Bartee v. Vitocruz
288 Va. 106, 758 S.E.2d 549 (2014)

Opinion by Senior Justice ELIZABETH B. LACY.

*108 ... On January 12, 2010, Tonia Michelle Begley presented to the Emergency Department of Wellmont Lonesome Pine Hospital complaining of chest pain, anxiety and elevated blood pressure. Marissa G. Vitocruz, M.D., evaluated, treated and discharged Ms. Begley from the Emergency Department. Ms. Begley died on January 13, 2010.

On January 29, 2010, Robert Bartee and Wiley Begley qualified in the Circuit Court of Wise County, Virginia, as co-administrators of Ms. Begley's estate. On August 31, 2011, Wiley Begley died. On *109 December 22, 2011, Robert Bartee, as the "duly qualified ... **550 administrator" of Ms. Begley's estate filed a wrongful death lawsuit... alleging that Vitocruz was negligent in her medical care and treatment of Ms. Begley and that Vitocruz' negligence was the proximate cause of Ms. Begley's death.

Vitocruz filed motions to dismiss and abate the wrongful death action asserting that Bartee lacked standing to file the action without the co-administrator joining in the case. ... *110 ...

In Addison v. Jurgelsky, 281 Va. 205, 208, 704 S.E.2d 402, 404 (2011), we held that one of two co-administrators of an estate had standing to file a wrongful death action pursuant to Code § 8.01–50 and that such filing was not a nullity. However, because Code § 8.01–50 requires unity of action "whether there is one personal representative or more than one," the other co-administrator was a necessary party plaintiff to the action. Applying Code § 8.01–5, we concluded that the second co-administrator could be joined as a party plaintiff... 281 Va. at 211, 704 S.E.2d at 406. ...

Bartee argues... he..., as remaining co-administrator, had complete power and authority to maintain the wrongful death action. This **551... is an issue of first impression... Bartee relies on the doctrine of survivorship as the basis for his position, citing Virginia cases that hold where joint executors are appointed in a will that does not require joint exercise of the power, and one executor dies, the power of the office devolves on the surviving executor to exercise the power of that office. Hofheimer v. Seaboard Citizens' Nat'l Bank, 154 Va. 896, 156 S.E. 581 (1931); Shepherd v. Darling, 120 Va. 586, 91 S.E. 737 (1917); Davis v. Christian, 56 Va. (15 Gratt.) 11 (1859). ... *111 ... [O]ur review of the relevant Virginia statutes and case law addressing the powers of administrators and substitution of parties is consistent with the application of the doctrine of survivorship upon which Bartee relies in this case.

Compliance with the trial court's requirement that Bartee add Wiley Begley, the other named co-administrator, or some other co-administrator as a party plaintiff is not possible under Virginia statutory and case law. First, Wiley Begley could not be added as a necessary party plaintiff because he was deceased. Generally, if a person becomes incapable of prosecuting or defending a case due to death, the action may proceed on behalf of the decedent's estate by and through the substitution of decedent with his personal representative. Code § 8.01–56; Rule 3:17; see also Estate of James v. Peyton, 277 Va. 443, 451, 674 S.E.2d 864, 867 (2009)(holding that personal representative of estate may be substituted for deceased party defendant). However, when an executor or an administrator of an intestate's estate dies, the estate of the deceased executor or administrator, by and through the estate's personal representative, does not succeed to the interest of the executor as executor or administrator as administrator. Rather, a new administrator ... must be appointed... See also Code § 64.2–513 relating to executors. Therefore, in this case, neither Wiley Begley nor his estate, by and through its personal representative, could be joined as a necessary party for the prosecution of this wrongful death action. *112

Second, Virginia jurisprudence provides that once the administrator or administrators of an intestate's estate have been properly qualified and appointed, another administrator may not be appointed unless there is a vacancy in the office. Bolling v. D'Amato, 259 Va. 299, 303–04, 526 S.E.2d 257, 259 (2000). A vacancy in the office exists only when there is no existing qualified administrator. Id. If the office of administrator is not vacant, it follows that the powers of the office have not terminated and therefore the remaining co-administrator must have the authority to exercise the powers attached to the office.

We reached this conclusion long ago in *Davis* with regard to executors. 56 Va. (15 Gratt.) at 38. In *Davis*, we concluded that, because the office survives as long as a co-executor survives, "by parity of reason" the powers of the office survive and can be executed by the sole surviving executor unless the will specifically required joint exercise of the powers. Id. We see no reason why this same rationale **552 should not be applied to the office of administrator of an intestate estate. To do otherwise would either prevent administration of the estate or require a duly qualified administrator to submit his resignation to the court and, upon notice to the parties in interest, the court could accept the resignation and then allow another person to qualify as an administrator. Code § 64.2–610(B).2 Neither course of action is acceptable. Requiring the resignation and reappointment of a duly qualified administrator elevates form over substance, is an unnecessary use of judicial resources, would delay administration of the intestate's estate—in this case, the prosecution of the wrongful death action—and provides no benefit to any party involved. Alternatively, applying the survivorship doctrine to administrators allows the efficient use of judicial resources, continuation of the estate's administration, and is not prejudicial to any party.

Vitocruz argues, however, that the survivorship doctrine cannot be applied to administrators because in enacting Code § 64.2–517 the General Assembly limited the doctrine of survivorship to executors and administrators with the will annexed. We disagree. We cannot *113 say that the intent of the General Assembly in enacting Code § 64.2–517 was to limit the survivorship principle to co-executors. A long-standing policy distinction exists between executors and administrators. Executors are specific individuals chosen by the testator to administer the testator's estate. If co-executors are appointed, there is a presumption that the testator intended that the administration be accomplished jointly by the named individuals. Therefore, Code § 64.2–517 provides important notice to the testator that the survivorship principle will be applied unless the testator provides otherwise in the will. No such presumption of joint administration exists in the case of an intestate's estate and therefore notice to the testator afforded by Code § 64.2–517 is not relevant in the case of intestacy.

In summary,... Bartee, as a duly appointed co-administrator of the estate of Tonia Begley at the time he filed the wrongful death action against Vitocruz, had standing to file the action. Because the other co-administrator had died, there was no other necessary party who could be joined as a party plaintiff. The office of administrator of Tonia Begley's estate was not vacant and no other appointment could be made until a vacancy existed. Applying the doctrine of survivorship, the power of appointment given Bartee and Wiley Begley as co-administrators to prosecute a wrongful death action pursuant to Code § 8.01–50 could be exercised by Bartee as the sole remaining administrator. ....

The outcome in Bartee seems to depend on the rule that a court may appoint an administrator only when there is a vacancy, and this led to a sensible outcome. The court could perhaps simply have ruled that there is no requirement to appoint a replacement for a deceased administrator unless the office is entirely vacant, but in any event the court reached a sensible outcome. In an earlier case, however, Bolling v. D'Amato, 259 Va. 299, 526 S.E.2d 257 (2000), the Supreme Court invoked the same rule to produce a seemingly senseless outcome. The court invalidated a circuit court's appointment of a second administrator for an estate, which was exclusively for the purpose of having a fiduciary capable of advancing a medical malpractice claim on behalf of the estate. The circuit court had initially appointed the surviving spouse, but she did not feel capable of initiating and overseeing litigation, so she asked her son to become co-administrator. After the son was appointed and filed suit against the physician, the physician defended on the ground that the son's appointment as a co-administrator was improper. The Supreme Court agreed with the physician and said the malpractice suit must be dismissed, explaining: "To obtain joint administration in this case, Betty Chloe Bolling's appointment should first have been revoked and then the son and widow could have been appointed as joint administrators." So when there is no administrator, the court may appoint two or more as co-administrators, but if there is one in place, the court may not add any others, not even to replace a co-administrator who drops out, and not even if the one existing administrator requests appointment of another.

So that they can defend their interests, persons who could possibly receive some of a decedent's wealth are entitled to know who is managing the estate.

§ 64.2-508. Written notice of probate, qualification, and entitlement to copies of inventories, accounts, and reports to be provided to certain parties.

A. Except [if waived or sent to an agent, or if the probate estate is $5000 or less]..., a personal representative of a decedent's estate or a proponent of a decedent's will when there is no qualification shall provide written notice of qualification or probate, and notice of entitlement to copies of wills, inventories, accounts, and reports, to the following persons:

    1. The surviving spouse of the decedent, if any;

    2. All heirs at law of the decedent, whether or not there is a will;

    3. All living and ascertained beneficiaries under the will of the decedent, including those who may take under § 64.2-418 [anti-lapse rule], and beneficiaries of any trust created by the will; and

    4. All living and ascertained beneficiaries under any will of the decedent previously probated in the same court. ...

C. [specifies content of the notice] ....

***

Once appointed the PR has duties to act immediately to take care of the expenses and debts a decedent ordinarily leaves behind, and power to collect the property the decedent owned or became entitled to.

Article 3. Authority and General Duties.

§ 64.2-512. Funeral expenses.

Subject to the provisions of § 64.2-528 [giving priority to costs of administration and spousal rights], reasonable funeral and burial expenses of a decedent shall be considered an obligation of the decedent's estate...

§ 64.2-518. When personal representative may renew obligation of decedent.

A. When a decedent is obligated on any note, bond, or other obligation... the decedent's personal representative may execute... a new note, bond, or other obligation... binding upon the estate ...

C. The personal representative is not personally liable for any note, bond, or other obligation for the payment of money executed pursuant to this section.

§ 64.2-519. Suits upon judgment and contracts of decedent and actions for personal injury or wrongful death.

A personal representative may sue or be sued (i) upon any judgment for or against the decedent, (ii) upon any contract of or with the decedent, or (iii) in any action for personal injury or wrongful death against or on behalf of the estate.

***

Supreme Court of Virginia.
In re Woodley
290 Va. 482, 777 S.E.2d 560 (2015)

Opinion by Justice D. ARTHUR KELSEY.

*484 ... In 2009, a tragic school bus accident killed four-year-old Jameer Khamarie Woodley. His parents initially qualified as co-administrators of his estate, posting a $64,000 bond. Later, they qualified as co-administrators specifically "under Va.Code § 8.01–50," posting a $100 bond and filing a wrongful death suit against the Southampton County School Board and three bus drivers. A jury awarded damages to the statutory beneficiaries, including the decedent's three older brothers. Jaylon Woodley, twelve years old at the time of the verdict, was awarded $750,000. Jaleel Woodley, five years old at the time, was awarded $200,000. **562

The parents presented to the trial court two proposed irrevocable trusts to receive the funds awarded to their minor sons. The trusts would be professionally managed by an independent trust company serving as trustee. The parents would have no "ongoing rights," including the "right to control, alter, amend, or terminate [the] Trust Agreement." The agreements emphasized that the trust assets were to be used exclusively for the benefit of each minor son and not to be used without court permission as a substitute for the parents' legal duty of support. The agreements also gave the trustee the discretion to spread out over time the distribution of the assets after the sons reached the age of majority, subject to judicial review if requested by one of the sons. *486

The parents also presented the trial court with an affidavit from the proposed trustee. The trustee verified that she served as an officer in a trust company that provides professionally managed trust and investment services. The company, she stated, has been "recognized as a fiduciary by both The Bureau of Financial Institutions and The Federal Reserve." Consistent with the stated purpose of the minor beneficiaries' trust instruments, the "trust assets would typically be invested in a mixed portfolio of conservatively chosen stocks and bonds." The trust company projected a possible 7% rate of return on the trust assets.

The trial court rejected the proposed trusts and directed payment of the awards to the clerk of court. By letter, the clerk advised the parties that the funds would be deposited in a savings account at SunTrust Bank with a "current rate-of-return" of "one tenth of one percent (.10%)." ...

On appeal, the parents contend that the trial court erred when it ordered payment of the minors' wrongful death awards to the clerk of court. We agree. ... *487... **563 Under the Death by Wrongful Act Statute, the personal representative of the decedent plays a pivotal role. In this context, the personal representative includes the executor or administrator of a decedent's estate who has been qualified by a court to hold the position. See Code § 1–234. A wrongful death action may only "be brought by and in the name of the personal representative of such deceased person." Johnston Mem'l Hosp. v. Bazemore, 277 Va. 308, 312, 672 S.E.2d 858, 860 (2009). A wrongful death award "recovered in any action shall be paid to the personal representative." Code § 8.01–54(C). From the gross award, the personal representative must "pay the costs and reasonable attorney's fees," as well as "hospital, medical, and funeral expenses." Id. "The remainder of the amount recovered shall thereafter be distributed by the personal representative ... to the beneficiaries." Id.

These statutory provisions presuppose that the personal representative who receives and distributes the award does so in his capacity as a fiduciary representing the interests of the beneficiaries. See Antisdel v. Ashby, 279 Va. 42, 51, 688 S.E.2d 163, 168 (2010) (discussing the appointment of a personal representative for the purpose of wrongful death and personal injury survival actions in terms of "fiduciary power"); Wilson, 207 Va. at 1036, 154 S.E.2d at 128 (reciting the accepted principle that "in an action for wrongful death the personal representative of the deceased sues primarily as trustee for certain statutory beneficiaries and not for the general benefit of the decedent's estate"); Anderson v. Hygeia Hotel Co., 92 Va. 687, 692, 24 S.E. 269, 271 (1896) (noting that the personal representative in a wrongful death action proceeds "primarily and substantially as a trustee for [the statutory beneficiaries]"); Martin P. Burks, Common Law and

Statutory Pleading and Practice § 67, at 134 (T. Munford Boyd ed., 4th ed.1952) (stating that the personal representative in a wrongful death suit "acts, not *488 in his capacity as the general representative of the decedent's estate, but in a capacity more nearly analogous to that of a trustee for the statutory beneficiaries").

Longstanding principles outside the context of the Death by Wrongful Act Statute similarly recognize that a "personal representative of a decedent holds a position of trust and confidence." A personal representative "must exercise the highest fidelity and utmost good faith in dealing with the estate. In the discharge of his fiduciary obligations, he is required to use the same measure of care which a careful and prudent person would ordinarily use under like circumstances in his own personal affairs." Virginia Trust Co. v. Evans, 193 Va. 425, 433, 69 S.E.2d 409, 414 (1952).[7] **564

[7] A fiduciary can be held liable for violating his fiduciary duties. See, e.g., Code § 64.2–770(D) (stating that, in the context of trusts, "[t]he holder of a power to direct is liable for any loss that results from breach of a fiduciary duty"). These principles apply equally to fiduciaries serving as personal representatives who represent the interests of the statutory beneficiaries under the Virginia Death by Wrongful Act Statute.

The Death by Wrongful Act Statute directs that an award "shall be paid to the personal representative" and then specifies that the "remainder of the amount recovered shall thereafter be distributed by the personal representative" to the beneficiaries in accord with the allocation of the awards in the verdict. Code § 8.01–54(C). This statutory duty necessarily presupposes that the *489 distribution will be made in full conformity with the personal representative's fiduciary obligations. When the beneficiaries are adults, the distribution duty is purely ministerial—each adult beneficiary receives whatever he is entitled to receive. In contrast, when the beneficiaries are minors, the distribution duty requires a multitude of judgment calls by the personal representative. How and for what length of time should the funds be preserved? What type of entity should manage the funds and with what type of investment vehicle, governed by what level of risk-reward ratio?

Nothing in the Death by Wrongful Act Statute authorizes a trial court presiding over a wrongful death award to dictate proactively the specific choices that a personal representative should make on these issues. In this case, the parents sought to establish professionally managed, irrevocable trusts, to appoint a disinterested and experienced officer of a well-recognized institution to serve as trustee, to govern the trusts through trust instruments that expressly precluded any interference by the parents, and to provide for a gradual payout of the trust assets throughout the early years of their sons' adult lives. The trial court presiding over the wrongful death awards in this case had no authority to disregard the statutory command directing that the award "shall be paid" to the personal representatives. Code § 8.01–54(C).[8]

[8] We leave for another day the question whether a trial court has any supervisory power over a personal representative in a wrongful death action in circumstances in which the evidence gives rise to a reasonable suspicion that the personal representative is contemplating action that would constitute a breach of fiduciary

duty. Because nothing in this case raises such suspicions, we do not address such hypothetical situations.

Our confidence on this subject is bolstered by other provisions conspicuously present in the Code. Code § 8.01–55 authorizes a personal representative to "compromise any claim" so long as he obtains the approval or consent of the circuit court. When a settlement of a wrongful death claim involves a minor beneficiary, Code § 8.01–424(A) grants the circuit court "the power to approve and confirm" the proposed compromise. If the court approves the compromise, Code § 8.01–424(E) authorizes the court, in its discretion, to direct payment "to the parent or guardian of the minor to be held in trust for the benefit of the minor." If the court deems it appropriate, the approved trust may provide for its termination "at any time following attainment of majority." Id.

*490 The presence of specific authorization for court review and approval of wrongful death settlements involving minors contrasts sharply with the absence of any such authority over the distribution of wrongful death awards to minors.9 The reason for this could be quite simple. In some cases, like the present one, the personal representatives (parents of the deceased child) are themselves statutory beneficiaries. Allowing them to have unreviewable power to structure a global settlement on behalf of all beneficiaries (which is the norm in this type of litigation) would place their personal interests in conflict with the interests of the minor beneficiaries. No such potential conflicts of interest exist, however, when a judge or jury **565 decides by verdict the specific amounts awarded to each statutory beneficiary.

We may hypothesize policy reasons for treating wrongful death awards differently than wrongful death settlements, but our decision does not depend on such speculations. The legislature is "the author of public policy." For us, then, "the 'best indications of public policy are to be found in the enactments of the Legislature.'" "We can only administer the law as it is written." We may not extend the meaning of a statute "simply because it may seem to us that a similar policy applies, or upon the speculation that if the legislature had thought of it, very likely broader words would have been used." We acknowledge the concerns expressed by our colleague on the trial court about the risks posed by hampering judicial control over the distribution of wrongful death awards to minor *491 beneficiaries. These concerns are no doubt born of experience and a commendable sense of judicial caution. It is altogether possible, as our colleague concluded, that the legislature implicitly intended trial courts to supervise, as a matter of course, all wrongful death awards to minor beneficiaries. For us, however, "[t]he question here is not what the legislature intended to enact, but what is the meaning of that which it did enact. We must determine the legislative intent by what the statute says and not by what we think it should have said." What the legislature said is that a wrongful death award "shall be paid to the personal representative" for distribution to the beneficiaries. Code § 8.01–54(C). We presume that the legislature says what it means and means what it says. ... We reverse and enter final judgment ordering the payment of the awards to the personal representatives.

Article 4. Power With Respect to Real Estate.

§ 64.2-523. Personal representative may execute deed pursuant to written contract of decedent.

When any decedent has executed and delivered a bona fide written contract of sale, purchase option, or other agreement binding such deceased person, his heirs, personal representatives, or assigns, to convey any real property or any interest therein, his personal representatives may execute a deed and do all things necessary to effect the transfer of title to such real property or any interest therein to the purchaser upon the purchaser's full compliance with the terms and conditions of such contract, option, or agreement. Such transfer shall be as effective as if it had been made by the decedent. The contract, option, or agreement shall be attached to any deed executed by a personal representative pursuant to this section and the clerk shall record such contract, option, or agreement in the deed book. ...

***

Various code provisions guide the PR's fulfillment of duties regarding debts and expenses, which can be of intense interest to heirs or will beneficiaries whose expectancy might diminish in value as a result. Some require the probate court to assist the PR in identifying creditors.

Article 5. Liability of Personal Estate to Debts.

§ 64.2-526. What personal estate to be sold; use of proceeds.

A. Subject to [spousal rights]... and excluding personal estate that the will directs not to be sold, the personal representative shall sell such assets of the personal estate where the retention of such assets is likely to result in an impairment of value. ...

B. If, after the sale pursuant to subsection A, the personal estate is not sufficient to pay the funeral expenses, charges of administration, debts, and legacies, the personal representative shall sell so much of the remaining personal estate as is necessary to pay such obligations. In conducting such a sale, the personal representative shall give as much consideration as practicable to preserving specific bequests in the will and to [spousal rights]...

C. Unless necessary for the payment of funeral expenses, charges of administration, or debts, the personal representative shall not sell personal estate that the will directs not to be sold.

§ 64.2-528. Order in which debts and demands of decedents to be paid.

When the assets of the decedent in his personal representative's possession are not sufficient to satisfy all debts and demands against him, they shall be applied to the payment of such debts and demands in the following order:

1. Costs and expenses of administration;

2. The allowances provided [to a surviving spouse];

3. Funeral expenses not to exceed $4,000;

4. Debts and taxes with preference under federal law;

5. Medical and hospital expenses of the last illness of the decedent...;

6. Debts and taxes due the Commonwealth; ...

8. Debts and taxes due localities and municipal corporations of the Commonwealth; and

9. All other claims.

No preference shall be given in the payment of any claim over any other claim of the same class, and a claim due and payable shall not be entitled to a preference over a claim not due.

§ 64.2-529. Creditors to be paid in order of their classification; class paid ratably...

No payment shall be made to creditors of any one class until all those of the preceding class have been fully paid, and if the assets are not sufficient to pay all the creditors of any one class, the creditors of such class shall be paid ratably...

Article 6. Liability of Real Estate to Debts.

[See Chapter Three regarding priority of assets for payment of debts]

§ 64.2-534. Liability of heir or devisee for value of real estate sold and conveyed; validity of premature conveyances.

A. Any heir or devisee who sells and conveys any real estate that is an asset for the payment of a decedent's debts... is liable for the value of such real estate, with interest, to those persons entitled to be paid out of the real estate.

B. [Subsection A does not apply if] ... (i) the sale was made more than one year after the death of the decedent, (ii) the conveyance was bona fide, and (iii) at the time of such conveyance, no action has been commenced for the administration of the real estate and no reports have been filed of the debts and demands of such creditors. ...

§ 64.2-538. Lien acquired during lifetime of decedent not affected.

This article shall not affect any lien acquired during the lifetime of the decedent.

Article 9. Settlement of Accounts and Distribution.

§ 64.2-550. Proceedings for receiving proof of debts by commissioners of accounts.

A. A commissioner of accounts... shall, when requested to so do by a personal representative or any creditor, legatee, or distributee of a decedent, or may at any other time determined by the commissioner of accounts..., conduct a hearing for receiving proof of debts and demands against the decedent or the decedent's estate. The commissioner of accounts shall publish notice of the hearing ... in a newspaper published or having general circulation in the jurisdiction where the personal representative qualified. ...

B. The personal representative shall give written notice ... to any claimant of a disputed claim that is known to the personal representative ...

§ 64.2-554. When distribution may be required; refunding bond.

A personal representative shall not be compelled to pay any legacy made in the will or to distribute the estate of the decedent for six months from the date of the order conferring authority on the first executor or administrator of such decedent and, except when it is otherwise specifically provided for in the will, the personal representative shall not be compelled to make such payment or distribution until the legatee or distributee gives a bond, executed by himself or some other person, with sufficient surety, to refund a due proportion of any debts or demands subsequently proved against the decedent or the decedent's estate and of the costs of the recovery of such debts or demands. ...

§ 64.2-555. When fiduciaries are protected by refunding bonds.

If any personal representative pays any legacy made in the will or distributes any of the estate of the decedent and a proper refunding bond for what is so paid or distributed, with sufficient surety at the time it was made, is filed and recorded pursuant to § 64.2-554, such personal representative shall not be personally liable for any debt or demand against the decedent, whether it be of record or not, unless, within six months from his qualification or before such payment or distribution, he had notice of such debt or demand. However, if any creditor of the decedent establishes a debt or demand against the decedent's estate by judgment therefor or by confirmation of a report of the commissioner of accounts that allows the debt or demand, a suit may be maintained on such refunding bond, in the name of the obligee or his personal representative, for the benefit of such creditor, and a recovery shall be had thereon to the same extent that would have been had if such obligee or his personal representative had satisfied such debt or demand.

§ 64.2-556. Order to creditors to show cause against distribution of estate to legatees or distributees; liability of legatees or distributees to refund.

A. When a report of the accounts... has been filed..., the court, after six months from the qualification of the personal representative, may, on motion of the personal representative ... or... legatee or distributee of the decedent, enter an order for the creditors and all other persons interested in the estate of the decedent to show cause on the day named in the order against the payment and delivery of the estate of the decedent to his legatees or distributees. A copy of the order shall be published ... On or after the day named in the order, the court may order the payment and delivery to the legatees or distributees of the whole or a part of the money and other estate not before distributed.... However, every legatee or distributee to whom any such payment or delivery is made... may, in a suit brought against him within five years after such payment or delivery is made, be adjudged to refund a due proportion of any claims enforceable against the decedent or his estate ... and the costs of the recovery of such claim....

B. Any personal representative who has in good faith complied with the provisions of this section and has, in compliance with or, as subsequently approved by, the order of the court, paid and delivered the money or other estate in his possession to any party that the court has adjudged entitled thereto shall not be liable for any demands of creditors and all other persons. ...

Circuit Court of Virginia, Fairfax County.
Conte v. Pilsch
79 Va. Cir. 628 (2009)

JANE MARUM ROUSH, J.

... Evelyn Taylor Pilsch... on June 2, 2008 at the age of 97. In her will, Evelyn made the following bequest:

> To THOMAS E. PILSCH, if he survives me, FIVE THOUSAND DOLLARS ($5,000). In the event said beneficiary predeceases me, then said sum shall be given to his wife, MRS. EVANGELINE PILSCH.

After Evelyn's death, Mr. Conte [executor] attempted to locate the heirs. He received an email that, among other things, advised him that Thomas E. Pilsch had died. Mr. Conte apparently overlooked that email.

Mr. Conte located a Thomas E. Pilsch living in McLean, Virginia. Mr. Conte notified this Thomas E. Pilsch that he was receiving a bequest from Evelyn's estate and sent him a check for $5,000. Mr. Conte had actually located Thomas E. Pilsch, Jr., the son of the "Thomas E. Pilsch" and "Evangeline Pilsch" named in the will. Both Thomas E. Pilsch and Evangeline Pilsch predeceased Evelyn. When Mr. Conte learned that he had given the bequest to the wrong person, he demanded that the money be returned to the estate. The defendant Thomas E. Pilsch, Jr. refuses to return the $5,000. ...[1]

[1] The intended beneficiary Thomas E. Pilsch was the brother of Evelyn's late husband. The defendant is Evelyn's late husband's nephew. The anti-lapse statute, Va.Code. Ann. 64.1–64.1, does not apply in this case.

There is no question that the executor made a mistake in paying the $5,000 to the defendant Thomas E. Pilsch, Jr. The issue is whether the estate must bear the loss or whether Thomas E. Pilsch, Jr. must repay the estate. ...

The case of Lee v. Barksdale, 83 N.C.App. 368 (1986), is instructive. In that case, the testator clearly intended to divide his residuary estate into three equal shares. An error in the executor's calculations led to an unequal disbursement of the estate. The court held that "the mistake in calculation was one of fact, not of law, and plaintiff executor clearly stated a cause of action upon which relief could be granted." Id. at 376. The court relied on 31 Am.Jur.2d, Executors and Administrators, § 965, in which it is stated "[a] devisee is liable to refund money which has been paid to him by the executor under a mistake of fact, and repayment of the amount wrongfully paid may be enforced against him in a suit by the executor." Id. at 377.

*2 Virginia courts have required the return of wrongly distributed funds under the theory of unjust enrichment. In Piedmont Trust Bank v. Aetna Casualty and Surety Company, 210 Va. 396 (1969), the court held that funds mistakenly paid by an insurance company must be returned to avoid unjust enrichment to the claimant.

The defendant argues that Mr. Conte in his individual capacity should be required to reimburse the estate for the $5,000. That position does not find support in Virginia law. The Supreme Court of Virginia has held "administrators, executors and other trustees are not to be held personally responsible for any loss of the trust property or funds where there is no just imputation of *mala fides* on their part, and the fault is at most but an error of judgment, or a want of unusual sharp-sighted vigilance." Herelick v. Southern Dry Goods & Notion Co., 139 Va. 121, 130 (1924). In this case, there is no allegation or evidence that Mr. Conte acted in bad faith. He simply overlooked the email that told him that the intended beneficiary Thomas E. Pilsch had died and instead mistakenly distributed the bequest to his son Thomas E. Pilsch, Jr.. ...

ADJUDGED, ORDERED and DECREED that the ... Executor ... recover and have judgment against the defendant, Thomas E. Pilsch, Jr., in the amount of Five Thousand Dollars ($5,000.00) plus interest... together with court costs...

The probate court, clerk, or commissioner oversees the PR's fulfillment of duties. In order to do this, they must receive an inventory of assets, periodic reports of PR actions, and a final accounting.

Subtitle IV. Fiduciaries and Guardians
Part A. Fiduciaries.
Chapter 12. Commissioners of Accounts.

§ 64.2-1200. Commissioners of accounts.

A. The judges of each circuit court shall appoint as many commissioners of accounts as may be necessary to carry out the duties of that office. The commissioner of accounts shall have general supervision of all fiduciaries admitted to qualify in the court or before the clerk of the circuit court and shall make all ex parte settlements of the fiduciaries' accounts.

§ 64.2-1215. Power of commissioner of accounts to enforce the filing of inventories.

A. If any fiduciary fails to make the return required by § 64.2-1300, the commissioner of accounts shall issue, through the sheriff or other proper officer, a summons to the fiduciary requiring him to make such return. ...

B. Whenever the commissioner of accounts reports to the court that a fiduciary who is an attorney-at-law licensed to practice in the Commonwealth has failed to make the required return within 30 days after the date of service of a summons, the commissioner of accounts shall also mail a copy of his report to the Virginia State Bar.

§ 64.2-1216. Failure to account; enforcement.

[same as § 64.2-1215 for final accounting]

§ 64.2-1217. Forfeiture of fiduciary's commission.

If a fiduciary wholly fails to file an account..., the fiduciary shall receive no compensation for his services... unless allowed by the commissioner of accounts for good cause shown...

§ 64.2-1218. When fiduciaries personally liable for costs.

The costs of all proceedings against a fiduciary who fails without good cause to make the returns and exhibits required shall be paid by him personally...

Chapter 13. Inventories and Accounts.

§ 64.2-1300. Inventories to be filed with commissioners of accounts.

A. Every personal representative or curator shall, within four months after the date of the order conferring his authority, return to the commissioner of accounts an inventory of all the personal estate under his supervision and control, the decedent's interest in any multiple party account in any financial institution, all real estate over which he has the power of sale, and any other real estate that is an asset of the decedent's estate...

B. [similar provision for any "guardian of an estate, conservator, or committee"]

C. Every trustee who qualifies in the circuit court clerk's office shall, within four months after the first date that any assets are received, return to the commissioner of accounts an inventory of the real and personal estate which is under the trustee's supervision and control... [unless] not required to account under the provisions of § 64.2-1307...

D. In listing property..., the fiduciary shall place the market value on each item. The market value shall be determined as of (i) the date of death if a decedent's estate; (ii) the date assets are received by the trustee if a trust; or (iii) the date of qualification in all other cases. ...

§ 64.2-1303. Copies of inventories and accounts to be provided by personal representatives.

A. Every personal representative filing with the commissioner of accounts an inventory or account... shall, on or before the date of such filing, send a copy thereof by first-class mail to those persons to whom notice [of probate was required]... and who requested the same from the personal representative in writing. ...

§ 64.2-1304. Personal representatives.

A. Within 16 months from the date of the qualification, personal representatives shall exhibit before the commissioner of accounts a statement of all money and other property that the fiduciary has received, has become chargeable with, or has disbursed within 12 months from the date of qualification.

B. After the first account of the fiduciary has been filed and settled, the second and subsequent accounts for each succeeding 12-month period shall be due within four months from the last day of the 12-month period...

§ 64.2-1306. Testamentary trustees.

A. ... [T]estamentary trustees shall exhibit a statement of all money and other property that the fiduciary has received, has become chargeable with, or has disbursed for each calendar year before the commissioner of accounts... on an annual basis ...

§ 64.2-1307. Testamentary trustees under a will waiving accounts...

... B. If (i) the will of a decedent... contains a waiver of the obligations of the testamentary trustee nominated therein to account or (ii) the sole beneficiary of the trust also is a trustee, the trustee will not be required to file accounts with the commissioner of accounts. ...

D. Notwithstanding a waiver in the will... any... beneficiary may, at any time during the administration of the trust, demand... that the trustee settle annually with the commissioner of accounts. ...

F. ... [A]ny trustee under a will... shall be relieved of the duty to file an inventory or annual accounts... if the will of the decedent does not direct the filing of such inventory or accounts and the trustee (i) obtains the written consent of all... beneficiaries... to whom income or principal of the trust could be currently distributed...

***

The PR is a fiduciary with respect to the estate and is under duties similar to those for a trustee, including loyalty and diligent protection and prudent management of estate assets.

Chapter 14. Fiduciaries Generally.
Article 1. Appointment, Qualification, Resignation, and Removal of Fiduciaries.

§ 64.2-1415. Liability for losses by negligence or failure to make defense.

A. If any personal representative, guardian, conservator, curator, or committee, or any agent or attorney-at-law, by his negligence or improper conduct, loses any debt or other money, he shall be charged with the principal of what is so lost, and interest thereon, in like manner as if he had received such principal.

B. If any personal representative, guardian, conservator, curator, or committee pays any debt the recovery of which could be prevented by reason of illegality of consideration, lapse of time, or otherwise, knowing the facts by which the recovery could have been prevented, no credit shall be allowed to him for such payment.

§ 64.2-1416. Liability of fiduciary for actions of cofiduciary.

A. As used in this section, "fiduciary" ... shall not include trustees subject to the requirements and provisions of the Uniform Trust Code (§ 64.2-700 et seq.).

B. Any power vested in three or more fiduciaries may be exercised by a majority of the fiduciaries, but a fiduciary who has not joined in exercising a power is not liable to the beneficiaries or to others for the consequences of the exercise. A dissenting fiduciary is not liable for the consequences of an act in which he joins at the direction of the majority of the fiduciaries if he expressed his dissent in writing to any of his cofiduciaries, if the act is not of itself a patent breach of trust.

C. A fiduciary shall be answerable and accountable only for his own acts, receipts, neglects, or defaults, and not for those of any cofiduciary, ... or for any loss that does not result from his own default or negligence. ...

E. This section does not excuse a cofiduciary from liability for failing to (i) participate in the administration of trust, (ii) attempt to prevent a breach of trust, or (iii) seek advice and guidance from the circuit court in an apparently recurring situation unless otherwise expressly provided by the instrument under which the cofiduciary is acting.

***

Few reported decisions analyze the prudence of a PR's management, disposition, or investment of estate assets. The upshot of the following decision appears to be that prudence is not to be judged in hindsight but rather in terms of the reasonableness of a PR's judgment in light of the facts known at the time.

Supreme Court of Appeals of Virginia
Virginia Sur. Co. v. Hilton
181 Va. 952, 27 S.E.2d 62 (1943)

GREGORY, J., delivered the opinion of the court.

J. H. Amburgey died intestate in June, 1936, leaving surviving him his widow and five children of whom three *955 were minors. His son, B. H. Amburgey, qualified as administrator of the estate and gave bond for $3,000 with the Virginia Surety Company, Inc., as surety.

The estate consisted of a stock of merchandise which was appraised at $1,389; cash in bank, certain fixtures and other small items, all of which were appraised at the aggregate value of $2,458.50. There were several parcels of real estate.

The merchandise was sold by the administrator to his uncle for $1,389, the full appraised value. The sale was made on credit and the purchase price was to be paid at the rate of $50 per month. Monthly notes for $50 were made by the purchaser, payable to the administrator. They were endorsed by the grandfather and grandmother of the administrator who were solvent at that time.

The administrator filed his annual report on June 19, 1937, and his account as administrator **63 was settled by the commissioner of accounts. ... There was an indebtedness due by the estate to L. N. Hilton for $1,750 which was evidenced by a series of notes made by J. H. Amburgey during his lifetime. They were payable at the rate of $50 per month, ten of which were paid, leaving twenty-five unpaid, aggregating $1,250 exclusive of interest.

It was apparent that the personal property would be insufficient to pay the obligations of the estate, and therefore L. N. Hilton instituted a suit to sell the real estate of the deceased. This was done and the net amount of $335.10 realized from the sale was applied as a credit on the indebtedness due Hilton. The suit was for the sole purpose of selling the real estate of the deceased and to pay his debts. Later, the cause was referred to a commissioner of the court who restated the account. The account disclosed that the assets in the administrator's hands were still insufficient to discharge the liabilities. *956 In January, 1942, Hilton filed a supplemental bill in the cause, alleging that the administrator had been guilty of a breach of trust and had squandered the assets of the estate, and asking for a judgment against the surety for the amount which he claimed had been wasted by the administrator. ... *957 ...

There is no evidence which discloses any neglect or dereliction on [the administrator's] part relating to his management or control of the assets of the estate. The condition of his bond was that he 'shall faithfully discharge the duties of his office, post, or trust of administrator, * * *'. No breach of the bond has been proven.

As we have already stated, there came into the hands of the administrator a stock of goods which was appraised at $1,389. He sold these goods to a brother of the decedent at the appraised value on a credit of $50 per month. The purchaser gave the administrator $50 monthly notes made by him. They were endorsed by his father and mother (who were the grandparents of the administrator), both of whom appear to have been solvent at the time of the sale of the goods and of their endorsement. **64 Seven of these notes aggregating $350 were paid, leaving unpaid the remainder of them, amounting to $1,039, exclusive of interest. ... Was it such a breach of duty for the administrator to make the sale and fail to collect the $1,039 from the purchaser of the goods and his endorsers as would have justified the court in holding the surety company liable on the administrator's *958 bond? The record is meager on the point but it fails entirely to show that the administrator failed in his duty.

By Code, section 5381, (Michie), the administrator is directed to sell the goods of the decedent (except those mentioned in section 5380 which do not embrace a stock of merchandise) as soon as is convenient, giving a reasonable credit and taking good security. The purchaser and endorsers on his notes, according to the evidence, became insolvent after the sale and the notes could not be collected. One of the endorsers conveyed his property and the administrator employed counsel to institute suit against the grantee to set aside the conveyance. The suit was instituted but it was not prosecuted to a conclusion because it later became apparent that whatever could be realized by doing so would not justify the expenditure of the costs attending the conduct of such a suit.

Our conclusion is that the administrator sold the stock of goods on credit to a solvent purchaser, who supplied endorsers who were also solvent at the time of the sale. The fact that he failed in his efforts to collect the entire purchase price, without more, is not sufficient to declare him guilty of a breach of his fiduciary duties so as to charge the amount he failed to collect against the surety of his bond. Glen Falls Ind. Co. v. Wall, 163 Va. 635, 177 S.E. 901.

Under Code, section 5406, (Michie), the administrator is only chargeable with money he fails to collect through his negligence or other improper conduct. And he is not required to sue for a debt due the estate when it is apparent that the debtor is unable to pay it. Lovett v. Thomas, 81 Va. 245. ... *959 ... [T]herefore, the complainant was entitled only to his pro rata share of the proceeds of the estate as a general creditor... He was not entitled to interest after insolvency, which was shown to exist at the death of the intestate, or to attorney's fees ...

It is conceded by Virginia Surety Company that the administrator had, after the payment of the cost of administration and after the payment of the preferred debts, $902.92 or 41 per cent of the amounts due the general creditors and that the dividend going to the complainant is 41 per cent of his total claim of $1,650, which is $676.50, from which is to be deducted the admitted amount already paid him by the administrator of $408.42. There remains due the complainant $268.08 for which the appellant [the surety company] admits it is liable. By a like computation, the Virginia Surety Company also admits its liability upon the claim of Clinchfield Lumber and Supply Company. This claim was $70.52 and 41 per cent of it amounts to $28.81, for which the surety company is liable. … [A] final decree should now be rendered by this court against the Virginia Surety Company, in favor of L. N. Hilton for $268.08, and in favor of Clinchfield Lumber and Supply Company for $28.81, both to bear interest from the date of the entry of the decree by this court. The Virginia Surety Company having substantially prevailed, costs should be awarded in its favor.

Self-dealing is an inherent temptation for a PR, as it is for a trustee. One way a PR can benefit personally is by reporting the highest possible value for the total estate on the inventory submitted to the Commissioner. Valuing tangible property, personal and real, can in particular allow for subjective judgments and carefully orchestrated appraisals. Artificially high valuations can not only result in higher PR compensation but also skew the distribution of the estate to heirs or beneficiaries. Unlike many other states, Virginia does not statutorily prescribe a fixed percentage of estate value as the PR's commission, but instead directs the Commissioner of Accounts to award "reasonable" compensation, yet the Commissioner is likely to base the amount in part on the value of the estate.

§ 64.2-1208. Expenses and commissions allowed fiduciaries.

A. In stating and settling the account, the commissioner of accounts shall allow the fiduciary any reasonable expenses incurred by him and, except in cases in which it is otherwise provided, a reasonable compensation in the form of a commission on receipts or otherwise. …

***

In the following case, an executor sought to give himself a relatively high commission and also engaged in his personal capacity in a transaction with the estate.

Supreme Court of Appeals of Virginia
Virginia Trust Co. v. Evans
193 Va. 425, 69 S.E.2d 409 (1952)

SPRATLEY, J., delivered the opinion of the court.

Arthur Thomas Kelly Evans, a resident of Bath county, Virginia, departed this life testate on May 21, 1948. His will was probated on June 10, 1948. On the same day the Virginia

Trust Company named as executor in the will duly qualified as such and proceeded to administer the estate.

By his will testator made twelve specific bequests of his property, and disposed of the remainder by devising and bequeathing two-thirds to his nephew, Arthur Armitage Evans, and one-third to his nephew, George Evans. The will did not direct that any of the property be sold or not sold.

The final account of the executor showed receipt of personal property having a gross appraised value of $73,331.75. Included in the gross sum were 40 shares of Gastonia Coca-Cola Bottling Company stock, appraised at $50,000; 250 shares of Thompson-Lundmark Gold Mines, Ltd.; and 5,333-1/3 shares of Upper Canadian Mines, Ltd., both Canadian companies appraised at $8,952.92. Not included in the account were the twelve specific legacies delivered in kind to the named legatees, and about 300,000 shares of stock of twelve Canadian mining companies having little or no value.

Among the assets which came into the executor's hands were a bank balance of about $9,000 in the First National Bank of Atlanta, Georgia, a small balance in a bank in London, England, and some stocks, bonds and other property in Canada. The principal assets located in Canada were a $5,000 Dominion of Canada 3% bond, and a balance of $789.12 with the Bank of Nova Scotia. The Coca-Cola Bottling Company stock and the Canadian mining stocks were located in a safety deposit box in the Virginia Trust Company in Richmond, Virginia. The bank *427 balance in Canada, less cost of transfer to the United States, in the net sum of $732.48, was withdrawn by the executor, and the Dominion of Canada bond was sold for the net sum of $4,443.75.

According to the record, the testator's investment in the 40 shares of Coca-Cola stock was $3,000. There was no established market value for these shares, the Gastonia Coca-Cola Bottling Company being a closed corporation, with only 600 shares outstanding, of which the testator owned only one-fifteenth. During the five-year period prior to the testator's death, he had received average yearly dividends of $74 per share on this stock, that is, $2,960 annually. During the period of administration of the estate from January 1, 1949, to January 5, 1950, the executor received dividends thereon amounting to $8,400.

The executor requested the Gastonia Coca-Cola Bottling Company to furnish **411 it with information showing the value of its stock for the purpose of inventory and appraisement. A representative of the Coca-Cola Company came to Richmond, and furnished the executor with the desired information, thereupon, in consideration of the established factors, a method of appraisement was adopted which produced the value of $1,250 per share. This appraisal was discussed with agents of the Federal Bureau of Internal Revenue, and an agreement was reached to adopt that value as a fair market value of the stocks for tax purposes. This was confirmed by the United States Treasury Department, and thereafter accepted by the tax authorities of the State of Virginia.

The representative of the Coca-Cola Company advised the executor not to sell the stock of his company. The residuary legatees were informed of all of the facts and the foregoing suggestion. Promptly thereafterwards, in June, 1948, the residuary legatees requested distribution and delivery of the Coca-Cola, Thompson-Lundmark Mines, Ltd., and Upper Canadian Mines, Ltd., stock to them in kind. Distribution and delivery were accordingly made.

In the settlement of its final account before the commissioner of accounts of Bath county, the executor charged 5% commission on $73,331.75, the gross appraised value of the estate, which amount included $58,952.92, the appraised value of the stocks delivered in kind to the residuary legatees. It also charged $40.83 for interest on money advanced to the estate to pay the specific legacies before the expiration of one year after the death *428 of the testator. The commissioner refused to allow 5% commission charged on the value of the stock delivered in kind; but approved an allowance of 2 1/2%, or the sum of $1,473.82 instead of $2,947.64. He further refused to allow the interest charge on money advanced by the executor. The total commissions charged by the executor were $3,666.59 and the amount allowed by the commissioner was $2,192.77. A 5% commission was originally charged on a portion of the specific legacies delivered in kind; but upon refusal of the commissioner to approve such allowance the claim for the charge was withdrawn, and is not in issue here. The executor excepted to the actions of the commissioner...

The Virginia Trust Company specializes in the administration of trusts and estates. It is staffed by a capable personnel of trained experts and professional employees. It satisfactorily obtained by correspondence the transfer of the foreign assets to Virginia, in compliance with government regulations, without loss. It prepared and filed the necessary State and Federal returns for income, inheritance and estate tax purposes. It paid all funeral expenses, debts, all specific legacies, and delivered in kind the 40 shares of Coca-Cola stock and the Canadian mining stocks to the residuary legatees. ...

The law in Virginia regarding a fiduciary's right to compensation is stated in section 26-30, Code, 1950 [virtually identical to current § 64.2-1208]. This statute has been before this court in numerous cases. **412. It is unnecessary to review all of them. It is sufficient to refer only to those which deal with the distribution in kind of a part or the whole of the estate.

In Claycomb v. Claycomb (1854), 10 Gratt. (51 Va.) 589, the question involved was the right of the executor to a commission of 5% on the appraised value of slaves delivered in kind among the legatees as directed by the will. It was held that the executor was not entitled to such commission, the court saying: 'It was not necessary to sell any of the slaves for the payment of debts, legacies or expense of administration.' The executor was not entitled by law or by will to sell, and did not sell any of them.

In Gregory v. Parker (1891), 87 Va. 451, 12 S.E. 801, the committee of an insane person delivered in kind a registered United States bond, and charged the estate with 5% commission on the value of the bond. In refusing to allow the commission the court had this to say at page 453: 'The said United States registered bond was not due and payable, nor was it collectable of the Government. It was not perishable; and neither debts nor other necessities of Mrs. Gregory's large estate in the hands of her committee required, the sale or conversion of the said bond into money; and, in fact, there was no change in the security or investment whatever. The custody of the bond was attended with no risk or trouble, * * *.'

In Bliss v. Spencer (1919), 125 Va. 36, 61, 99 S.E. 593, 5 A.L.R. 619, the court approved the rule involved in Gregory v. Parker, supra, as well established, and sound and just in cases to which it is applicable. It there said that in reading the cases which held that a fiduciary was entitled to commissions on the appraised value of property delivered in kind to the legatees it is disclosed that in each case there was 'some peculiar circumstance' upon which the decisions turned.

In Williams v. Bond (1917), 120 Va. 678, 91 S.E. 627, we said:

> Where no compensation at all is named in the will, the rule is that the allowance shall be reasonable, being usually 5% on receipts, subject to increase or reduction of this rate under *430 peculiar circumstances. These propositions are not controverted and are well settled.

In Jones v. Virginia Trust Co. (1925), 142 Va. 229, 128 S.E. 533, this is said:

> From a very early period, beginning with the case of Granberry v. Granberry, 1 Wash. (1 Va.) 246, 1 Am.Dec. 455, to the recent case of Williams v. Bond, 120 Va. 678, a commission of five per cent upon receipts has been the measure of compensation allowed a fiduciary, except under peculiar circumstances, when the commission or compensation has been increased or reduced as the exigencies demanded. The cases on the question of compensation to fiduciaries where distribution of the estate is made in kind are not altogether in harmony. ...

> In a note to section 5425 it is said: 'Commissions are not to be allowed to the fiduciary upon the value of property belonging to the estate, and finally turned over to him in kind, unless when it was perishable, or was such property as the fiduciary might properly have sold, or bonds which he might have collected but did not, and with consent of cestui que trust paid over to him in kind as so much money.' ...

> In reviewing the cases which hold that a fiduciary is not entitled to any compensation whatever where the property bequeathed (though not specific) is delivered in kind, we think the rule laid down is too restricted to meet the requirements of modern business. On the other hand, in view of the fact that the bulk of many large estates is composed of stocks and bonds, which are preferable to money, we are of opinion that the rule laid down in Allen v. Virginia Trust Co., supra, is too liberal.

... **413 ... Jones v. Virginia Trust Co., page 241, lays down the general principles which should govern in the consideration of the issue before us.

> Inasmuch as the statute fails to lay down a hard and fast rule, we are of the opinion that the court should not do so. *431 To us, a fair construction of the statute seems to be that if the fiduciary sells property, of whatever kind, he is generally entitled to a commission of five per cent on the receipts. If he has the right to sell, but those entitled to the proceeds of sale prefer to take the property in kind, then he is generally entitled to receive five per cent

commission upon the appraised value of the property. If he is not entitled to sell the property, but must deliver in kind (except in the case of a specific legacy), he is only entitled to a reasonable compensation to be fixed by the commissioner, or court, upon the proper proof of the expense incurred, the risk taken, and the services rendered in connection with the property so delivered to those entitled thereto.

In Trotman v. Trotman (1927), 148 Va. 860, 868, Justice Holt, later Chief Justice, said that the word 'reasonable' as used in the statute 'is but another way of saying that they (commissions) are to be measured by the conscience of the court.' Proceeding, he pointed out: 'The value of the estate, the character of the work, the difficulties encountered, and the results obtained must all be remembered in reaching a judgment.'

The decisions subsequent to 1927 are not in complete harmony. A careful reading of them discloses that each turned upon some peculiar circumstances.

In Mapp v. Hickman (1935), 164 Va. 386, 180 S.E. 296, the court, considering the value of the estate and the character of the work required of the fiduciary, thought a five per centum commission on securities distributed in kind too high; but allowed full commission on receipts and one and one-half per centum on the securities delivered in kind.

In Grandy v. Grandy (1941), 177 Va. 601 and Swank v. Reherd (1943), 181 Va. 943, the principles stated in Jones v. Virginia Trust Co., are cited and approved. In each case the executor was given express authority by the will of their testator, and in each of them appeared special circumstances in connection therewith. In *Grandy*, a 5% commission was allowed because of the difficult and unusual duties required of the personal representative and the manifest intention of the testator. In *Swank*, a 5% commission was allowed 'on the appraised value of the real estate,' whether converted or not, the beneficiaries choosing to take it in kind rather than in cash. The opinion sets out considerable litigation with reference *432 to the estate and satisfactory results obtained by the executors, without going into detail as to the labors involved.

Appellant contends that the 'power to sell' and the 'right to sell' have the same meaning, and argues since it had the power to sell it was entitled to a 5% commission on the appraised value of all the property which came into its possession, regardless of its distribution in kind. This, we think, is too liberal a view. It was disapproved in Jones v. Virginia Trust Co., at page 241.

The phrases 'power to sell' and 'right to sell,' as used in the decisions do not have exactly the same meaning. The personal representative is for most purposes regarded as the owner of the legal title to the personal property of his decedent, and may dispose of it as if it were his own, except that he cannot bequeath it, nor can it be taken on execution for his debt. When sold and disposed of, the assets cannot be followed into the alienee's hands by creditors of the estate or by legatees either general or specific, except on the ground of fraud.

Generally speaking, the power of the fiduciary to sell means the authority **414 given by statute, or by the instrument creating the trust, or the capacity inherent in the functioning of the office of the fiduciary. On the other hand, the right to sell is used in the sense of doing that which is proper or correct, in adherence to duty and necessity. However that may be, compensation for the fiduciary is to be measured not solely by the power or right of the fiduciary to sell or not to sell; but as we have said by taking into consideration, 'The value of the estate, the character of the work, the difficulties encountered, and the results obtained.'

The statutory authority of the personal representative to sell assets of the estate is confined to §§ 64-143, 64-144 and 64-145, Code, 1950. Section 64-144 is broad enough to authorize the sale of stocks, bonds and other property, 'as are likely to be impaired in value by keeping.' Any further right to sell arises from the duty of the personal representative to protect and conserve the assets of the estate, or to make correct distribution to the legatees or distributees. If there be no requirement or necessity to sell, and the legatees or distributees request distribution in kind, such distribution should be made. We can see little difference in the *433 responsibilities of the executor of a solvent estate where the testator bequeaths a portion of his property in kind, and where the legatees are in accord and promptly request that the property to which they are entitled be distributed to them in kind. After all, a personal representative, after the satisfaction of funeral expenses, debts, costs of administration, and payment of specific legacies, if any, holds the remainder of the personal property in trust for the purpose of administration and distribution to the persons entitled thereto.

The personal representative of a decedent holds a position of trust and confidence. He is 'deemed a trustee, exercising a continuing trust as to legatees and distributees of his decedent's estate.' Jones v. Jones, 92 Va. 590, 598, 24 S.E. 255. He must exercise the highest fidelity and utmost good faith in dealing with the estate. In the discharge of his fiduciary obligations, he is required to use the same measure of care which a careful and prudent person would ordinarily use under like circumstances in his own personal affairs. Harris v. Citizens Bank (1939), 172 Va. 111.

Our conclusion is that the amount of compensation to which a personal representative may be entitled is dependent upon the facts of the particular case. Since it is still practically impossible to lay down a hard and fast rule because of the many factors involved, we must rely on general principles, remembering that the personal representative is entitled to a reasonable reward, commensurate with the value of his services under the attendant circumstances, the results obtained, and the responsibility assumed. In some instances 5% upon the appraised value of property coming into his hands would not be sufficient; in others it would be too much. Compensation has been refused for delinquency of duty. Section 26-19, Code of 1950; Dearing v. Walter, 179 Va. 620, 20 S.E.(2d) 483.

The allowance or refusal of compensation rests in the sound discretion of the court under the circumstances of each case. In view of the changing economic conditions of the modern world, and new legislation affecting the administration of estates of decedents, particularly with regard to taxation, we think, that in measuring the compensation of a personal representative there should also be considered the amount and character of *434 expert service required and rendered to meet current problems imposed by provisions of testator's will, or by the law, or arising out of current conditions, and the responsibilities assumed.

Nothing we have said should be understood as denying the personal representative the right to sell when authorized by statute, directed by will, or required for the security and benefit of the estate, or when necessary to effect a correct degree of distribution in kind. However, when **415 there is no reason to sell, and the legatees or distributees request distribution in kind such distribution should be made. In the latter event, the personal representative, 'except in cases in which it is otherwise provided,' is entitled to reasonable compensation in the form of a commission, or otherwise, for service rendered under the peculiar circumstances of the case.

In the case before us, there are no peculiar circumstances to require extra compensation. The transfer of the foreign assets to Virginia was accomplished without difficulty. The tax appraisals were arrived at without controversy. Negotiations between the governmental authorities, the executor, the legatees and the distributees of the estate were amicable. It was not necessary to sell the securities involved. The executor did nothing to change them or their investment. Their custody was not attended with risk or trouble, and in case of their loss or destruction they could have been reissued. The estate was unembarrassed, its transactions few and simple, and its administration easy. We, therefore, agree with the commissioner and the trial judge that, under the circumstances of this case, a total compensation of $2,192.77, including a 2 1/2% commission on the stocks delivered in kind to the residuary legatees, was reasonable and amply sufficient to cover the services and responsibilities of the executor.

We come next to one of the secondary questions.

We are told that the funeral expenses and all foreseeable obligations had been paid by June 25, 1948, at which time the executor had in hand $6,522.78. It used this cash, together with $727.22 which it advanced, to pay the specific pecuniary legacies, totaling $7,250, before the expiration of one year after testator's death. One of the residuary legatees requested or assented to such payment. Except for an unexpected physician's bill of $525, funds for which were advanced on June 28, 1948, there was no other advance of any consequence to pay debts. Advances *435 thereafter were for foreign death duties, necessary before the foreign assets could be reduced to possession, for United States income and State of Virginia inheritance taxes, and to the residuary legatees themselves.

The advances were made from day to day to keep the account in balance, taking into consideration receipts from all sources, including dividend income. The total interest on all the advances, which were not fully repaid, until October 6, 1949, was the sum of $45.55, charged at the rate of 4%. ... Interest would have accrued on the specific pecuniary legacies had they not been paid within one year after May 1, 1948, the date of testator's death. On May 21, 1949, funds were insufficient for the full payment of these legacies, even if all funds received had been retained. Some funds were necessary to be obtained through sale of assets of the estate, or from a loan, if liability for interest on the legacies and unpaid matured debts was to be avoided. The executor deferred to the wishes of the residuary legatees, withheld from sale the securities they wished to receive in kind, and delayed a sale of the Dominion of Canada 3% bond. By withholding sale of that bond until October 6, 1949, it obtained $137.50 interest which the estate would not have received had the bonds been sold one month after the qualification of the executor. By the latter action, the legatees benefited to the extent of $96.67, the difference between $137.50 and $40.83 interest charged on funds advanced by the executor. They ought not to be heard now to complain, nor should the executor be the loser by reason of its actions taken in the legatees' interest.

We do not approve of the practice of a fiduciary borrowing from himself personally at the expense of the estate, unless the manifest exigencies of the situation require him to do so in order to protect and conserve the estate. Such practice might conceivably lead to many opportunities **416 for misconduct. However, under the facts and circumstances of the present case, we are not disposed to criticize the executor, or deny it the small amount of interest claimed.

For the reasons given, we are of opinion that so much of the decree complained of as ordered the executor to pay to the *436 estate $1,472.83, excess of commissions over 2 1/2% on the appraised value of the securities delivered in kind to the residuary legatees should be approved, and so much of the said decree as refuses to allow the executor $40.83, interest upon funds advanced for the purposes stated, should be reversed. ...

Since Evans, there have been just a few reported decisions concerning disputes over a PR's commission. In the most recent, In re Estate of Cary, 37 Va. Cir. 376 (1995), a will provision contained a clause granting compensation that is "usual and customary at the time for like services rendered in like circumstances." The Circuit Court for Arlington County stated that "this provision should be construed in the light of the friendship between the men and the attorney-client relationship." Citing Evans, the court stated that "compensation is to be measured by the conscience of the court" and "the allowance of compensation to fiduciaries is in the direction of a fact-specific analysis of each case rather than the application of a general rule." It approved the Commissioner's decision to award 5% of the estate of $1.8 million.

We saw in Chapter Three a Supreme Court decision, Gaymon v. Gaymon, responding to an executor's request for "aid and guidance," based on the executor's self-interested belief that certain will language ("It is understood that in the case that Mrs. VIOLETA N. GAYMON and I have residence at the Fox Mill address at the time of my demise, she would have a life estate in the same for the remainder of her life.") was merely precatory rather than affirmatively creating a life estate for a surviving spouse. The Court found the executor's interpretation implausible. The widow then sued the executor for wasting estate assets on frivolous and self-serving litigation. From an estate worth less than a half million dollars, the executor used nearly one hundred thousand dollars for attorney fees and other expenses relating to the litigation.

The Circuit Court for Fairfax County, in Gaymon v. Gaymon, 63 Va. Cir. 264 (2003), stated that when "a fiduciary's conduct materially advances his own personal interests, the law places the burden on the fiduciary to demonstrate that his conduct was appropriate... taken within the scope of his authority,... in good faith, and comported with ordinary prudence." The court cited secondary authorities for the proposition that "aid and direction suits are permitted to seek advice and direction where necessary" and that in "cases of doubt or difficulty the expense incident to instituting and conducting such a suit... is to be borne by the estate, not by the personal representative out of his own pocket," but that "in plain cases an administrator 'is not justified in seeking, aid, direction, guidance and protection from the court," and the estate should not be charged with "this unnecessary expense, which is generally quite substantial, because such aid of a court can only be obtained in a plenary suit in equity, with all persons interested in the point of doubt regularly convened as parties." The court noted further: "Nor is it appropriate for a personal representative to appeal a decree where the chancellor's ruling does not adversely affect the interests of the estate," citing Caine v. Freier, 264 Va. 251, 257 (2002). The court therefore easily found that the expense for the appeal to the Supreme Court should be borne by the executor personally and not by the estate, and it also found that bringing the aid and direction suit in the first place was in bad faith, because manifestly aimed "to frustrate the decedent's intent to convey a life estate to Violeta Gaymon, an intent explicitly stated in the decedent's will," and not, as the executor claimed, to fulfill the decedent's wishes. It also disapproved using estate funds for seeking to force the surviving spouse to pay interest, taxes, and insurance on the property in questions, because this also "was not taken on account of an exigency in administering the estate," as there was no danger of these expenses being charged against the estate or of a foreclosure on the property adversely affecting the estate, as opposed to the beneficiaries. In short: "This was a dispute between feuding beneficiaries that should have been litigated by the parties in interest with their own funds." The court therefore ordered the executor to repay the estate for the litigation expenses, including the attorney fees, with interest. To the extent any portion of fees paid to the law firm was properly incurred for other, appropriate purposes relating to estate administration, fiduciary principles "place the burden on the executor to demonstrate which of his bills paid were rendered for services benefiting the estate." Thus, the executor would be responsible for the entire legal bill unless he could demonstrate specific amounts were for proper estate purposes. Finally, the court ruled that "William V. Gaymon's sweeping misuse of estate assets to fund attorney's fees to advance his own interests justifies his removal as executor."

Chapter 15. Investments.

§ 64.2-1500. Court orders regarding money in possession of fiduciary.

If a report... shows that money is in the possession of a fiduciary, the circuit court in which the report is filed may order that the money be invested or loaned out...

§ 64.2-1501. Time within which... to invest funds; reasonable diligence required.

A. ... [A] fiduciary shall only be required to invest in accordance with the provisions of §§ 64.2-1502 through 64.2-1506 [listing permissible investments, principally government bonds and bank savings accounts] and the Uniform

Prudent Investor Act and, if he invests in accordance with these provisions, he shall be accountable only for such interest and profits as are earned. If any funds are otherwise invested without the previous consent of the court..., the burden shall be on the... fiduciary... to show... that, after exercising reasonable diligence, he was unable to invest the funds in accordance with these provisions and that the investment made was reasonable and proper under all of the circumstances and fair to the beneficiary of the funds.

B. This section shall not be construed as altering the provisions of any will, deed, or other instrument that give the fiduciary discretion as to the rate of interest, character of security, nature or investment under the trust, or time within which the trust funds are to be loaned or invested.

***

Many testators will incorporate into their will by reference the following statutory provisions, conferring broad powers on the executor and the trustee of any testamentary trust.

§ 64.2-105. Incorporation by reference of certain powers of fiduciaries into will or trust instrument.

... B. The following powers, in addition to all other powers granted by law, may be incorporated in whole or in part in any will or trust instrument by reference to this section:

1. To keep and retain any or all investments and property, real, personal or mixed, including stock in the fiduciary, if the fiduciary is a corporation, in the same form as they are at the time the investments and property come into the custody of the fiduciary, regardless of the character of the investments and property, whether they are such as then would be authorized by law for investment by fiduciaries, or whether a disproportionately large part of the trust or estate remains invested in one or more types of property, for such time as the fiduciary deems best, and to dispose of such property by sale, exchange, or otherwise as and when such fiduciary deems advisable. ...

3. To sell, assign, exchange, transfer and convey, or otherwise dispose of, any or all of the investments and property, real, personal or mixed, that are included in, or may at any time become part of the trust or estate upon such terms and conditions as the fiduciary, in his absolute discretion, deems advisable... [T]he fiduciary has the power to make, execute, acknowledge, and deliver any and all instruments of conveyance, deeds of trust, or assignments...

5. To lease any or all of the real estate... Any lease made by the fiduciary may extend beyond the term of the trust or administration of the estate...

6. To vote any stocks, bonds, or other securities held by the fiduciary...

7. To borrow money for such periods of time and upon such terms and conditions as to rates, maturities, renewals, and security as to the fiduciary seems advisable… for the purpose of paying (i) debts, taxes, or other charges against the trust or estate or any part thereof and (ii) with prior approval of the court for any proper purpose of the trust or estate. ….

9. To compromise, adjust, arbitrate, sue on or defend, abandon, or otherwise deal with and settle claims in favor of or against the trust or estate as the fiduciary deems best, and his decision is conclusive.

10. To make distributions in cash or in kind or partly in each at valuations to be determined by the fiduciary, whose decision as to values shall be conclusive.

11. To repair, alter, improve, renovate, reconstruct, or demolish any of the buildings on the real estate held by the fiduciary and to construct such buildings and improvements thereon as the fiduciary in his discretion deems advisable.

12. To employ and compensate, out of the principal or income, or both as to the fiduciary seems proper, agents, accountants, brokers, attorneys…, tax specialists, licensed real estate brokers, licensed salesmen, and other assistants and advisors...

14. To retain any interest held by the fiduciary in any business… for any length of time… including the power to (i) participate in the conduct of such business…; (ii) participate in any incorporation, reorganization, merger, consolidation, recapitalization, or liquidation of the business; (iii) invest additional capital in, subscribe to additional stock or securities of, and loan money or credit with or without security to, such business out of the trust or estate property; …; and (viii) sell or liquidate such interest or any part thereof at any time. ...

15. To do all other acts and things not inconsistent with the provisions of the will or trust in which these powers are incorporated that the fiduciary deems necessary or desirable for the proper management of the trusts herein created, in the same manner and to the same extent as an individual could do with respect to his own property. …

17. During the minority, incapacity, or the disability of any beneficiary, and in the sole discretion of the fiduciary, to distribute income and principal…: (i) directly to the beneficiary; (ii) to a relative, friend, guardian, conservator, or committee, to be expended by such person for the education, maintenance, support, or benefit of the beneficiary; (iii) by the fiduciary expending the same for the education, maintenance, support, or benefit of the beneficiary; (iv) to an adult person or bank authorized to exercise trust powers as custodian for a minor beneficiary under the Uniform Transfers to Minors Act… [or] Uniform Custodial Trust Act ...

19. To purchase and hold life insurance policies on the life of any beneficiary...

20. To make any election… relating to… any taxes or assessments on assets or income of the estate or in connection with any fiduciary capacity...

21. To comply with environmental law:…

a. To inspect property held by the fiduciary…;

b. To take… any action necessary to… remedy any actual or threatened violation of, any environmental law…;

c. To refuse to accept property in trust if the fiduciary determines… [it] either is contaminated… or… could result in liability…;

d. To disclaim any power… that… may cause the fiduciary to incur personal liability…; and

e. To charge the cost of any inspection, review, abatement, response, cleanup, or remedial action authorized herein against the income or principal of the trust or estate. …

D. This section shall not be construed to affect the application of the standard of judgment and care as set forth in the Uniform Prudent Investor Act (§ 64.2-780 et seq.).

***

Supreme Court of Virginia.
Campbell v. Harmon
271 Va. 590, 628 S.E.2d 308 (2006)

G. STEVEN AGEE, Justice.

*593 … Margaret Stewart Little, as part of a trust agreement created during her lifetime, established the Margaret Stewart Little Marital Trust ("the Marital Trust") for the benefit of her husband, Gordon Little, *594 which took effect at her death in 1984. The following terms governed the Marital Trust's administration and distribution:

> 1. The Trustees shall pay to or for the benefit of [Gordon Little], all of the trust net income, in installments to be selected by the Trustees … provided, however, that the Trustees shall pay to [Gordon] not less than the sum of $3,000 per month …. In addition to the net income the Trustees may pay to or for the benefit of [Gordon Little] as much of the trust principal as the Trustees, in their absolute discretion, deem necessary for his support and health expenses, including, but not limited to, medical, hospital, doctors, nursing, dental and other health expenses.

Under the terms of the Marital Trust, Little was the sole income beneficiary of that trust during his lifetime and payment of the net trust income to him was a mandatory requirement of the trust. The Marital Trust further provided that upon Little's death it would terminate and any remaining trust property, "excluding undistributed income, [would] vest in and be added to the Family Trust."[2]

> [2] Neither Gordon Little nor his estate was a beneficiary of, had any interest in, or control of the Family Trust, which was also created by Margaret Stewart Little.

"The undistributed income held by the Trustees as of the date of" Little's death, however, would "be paid to the personal representative of his estate for the purposes of administration therein."

... **310 ... From 1984 until his death in June 1999, Little received certain distributions from the Trustees out of the Marital Trust. The Trustees never rendered an accounting to Little during his lifetime as to the discharge of their fiduciary duties under the Marital Trust. The record does not indicate Little formally requested an accounting. Following Little's death, his will was admitted to probate and Jerry Allen Campbell qualified as the executor of Little's estate. A provision of Little's will provides: "I grant unto my Executor all rights and powers set forth in Section 64.1–57 [now § 64.2-105] of the Code of Virginia." *595 ...

In July 2000, Campbell filed a bill of complaint to compel an accounting and other relief from the Trustees. ... Campbell sought to have the Trustees account for two events: First, for tangible personal property the Trustees "removed from Heritage Farm[3] following the death of Gordon Little," and, second, "for their administration of the Margaret Stewart Little [Marital] Trust."

[3] Until his death, Little continued operating a thoroughbred farm located in Fauquier County and known as Heritage Farm, which was an asset of the Marital Trust.

Campbell asserted that the Trustees wrongfully removed tangible personal property from Heritage Farm after Little's death that belonged to Little personally. Campbell further alleged that a "full, complete and fair accounting by the Defendant Trustees will show that moneys are due from the [Marital Trust] to the Estate of Gordon Little." ... *596 ... **311

II. ANALYSIS

... **312 ... *598 ... Code § 8.01–25 reflects the General Assembly's clear intent that: "Every cause of action whether legal or equitable, which is cognizable in the Commonwealth of Virginia, shall survive ... the death of the person in whose favor the cause of action existed ...." Assuming the trial court correctly found that Little had a cause of action for an accounting from the Trustees for their administration of the Marital Trust prior to his death, that cause of action survives Little's death under Code § 8.01–25 because it "existed" prior to his death. Contrast Rutter v. Jones, Blechman, Woltz & Kelly, P.C., 264 Va. 310, 313–14, 568 S.E.2d 693, 694–95 (2002) (claim for legal malpractice brought by decedent's personal representative did not survive because claim did not arise until after decedent's death).

Contrary to the Trustees' assertion, the broad language contained in Code § 8.01–25 making it applicable to "[e]very cause of action" is not derogated by other statutes conferring standing to personal representatives in particular situations. Indeed, the Trustees' position ignores situations where Code § 8.01–25 would not apply to preserve a cause of action, but the specific authorization to sue or be sued by a decedent's personal representative in other Code sections permits the claim.

Code § 8.01–25 only applies to causes of action "exist[ing]" prior to the decedent's death and provides that a "cause of action asserted by the decedent in his lifetime" for personal injury does not "survive," but rather can be amended as a wrongful death action under Code § 8.01–56. *599 ... Thus, Code § 8.01–56, as well as §§ 8.01–57 and 8.01–63, for example, provide the basis for a separate cause of action, wrongful death, which did not exist during the decedent's lifetime and thus could not be maintained under the aegis of Code § 8.01–25.

Moreover, to adopt the Trustees' position would render Code § 8.01–25 meaningless because the only causes of action that would survive an individual's death would be those where the decedent's personal representative is specifically granted standing to bring an action by another statute. In effect, the Trustees' position as adopted by the trial court is a judicial repeal of Code § 8.01–25. This result eviscerates the principle well-established in our jurisprudence that when "the legislature has used words of a plain and definite import[,] the courts cannot put upon them a construction which amounts to holding the legislature did not mean what it actually has expressed."

Consequently, Little's cause of action to compel an accounting from the Trustees for the administration of the Marital Trust under Code § 8.01–31 survives Little's death pursuant to Code § 8.01–25.[4]

> [4] Code § 8.01–31 states: "An accounting in equity may be had against any fiduciary or by one joint tenant, tenant in common, or coparcener for receiving more than comes to his just share or proportion, or against the personal representative of any such party."

Thus, Campbell, in his capacity as executor of Little's estate, has standing to bring an action to compel an **313 accounting by the Trustees for the administration of the Marital Trust while Little was a beneficiary of that trust.

The fact that Little's will does not expressly grant the executor of his estate authority to pursue actions under Code § 8.01–31 does not alter our analysis. In Isbell v. Flippen, 185 Va. 977, 41 S.E.2d 31 (1947), ... the Court... cited the statutory duty of personal representatives to: "administer, well and truly, the whole personal estate of his decedent." Id. (quoting Code § 5377, now [§ 64.2-514]). *600 Because "[o]ne of the primary obligations of the personal representative is to collect the assets of the estate," the personal representative had not only the authority, but most likely even the duty, to file suit to collect debts owed to the decedent's estate. Id. ("failure to proceed promptly with the collection of assets due the decedent's estate is negligence, for which the personal representative may be liable"); see also O'Brien v. O'Brien, 259 Va. 552, 557, 526 S.E.2d 1, 4 (2000). Thus, Campbell's power to seek an accounting under Code § 8.01–31 is part of his fiduciary duty and authority as executor of Little's estate.

Similarly, Campbell's standing to seek an accounting under Code §§ 8.01–25 and 8.01–31 is unaffected by the clause in Little's will granting Campbell "all rights and powers set forth in [Code §] 64.1–57." The statutory powers incorporated into a will by reference... are not the only powers possessed by an executor. As the text of Code § 64.1–57 plainly states: "The following powers, in addition to all other powers granted by law, may be incorporated in whole or in part in any will or trust instrument by reference to this section." (Emphasis added.) By incorporating the powers listed in Code § 64.1–57, a testator does not thereby exclude "all other powers granted by law" from the executor. The right to compel an accounting is such an "other power granted by law" as the foregoing discussion of Code §§ 8.01–31 and 8.01–25 reflect. Accordingly, the mere fact that Little's will incorporates Code § 64.1–57 and does not contain a specific grant of authority to the executor to seek an accounting is no barrier to Campbell exercising "all other powers granted by law." ...

Thus, the Trustees, subject to any valid defenses on the merits, none of which are before this Court, must account to Campbell for their administration of the Marital *601 Trust during Little's lifetime, including the computation and distribution of the trust net income. This accounting would include any undistributed income of the Marital Trust accrued as of the date of Little's death, as Little had a right to such income up until that time. ...

Campbell also contends he has a cause of action for an accounting from the Trustees for their alleged removal of tangible personal property purportedly belonging to Little from Heritage Farm following Little's death. ... But Code § 8.01–25 cannot apply to authorize an accounting for the tangible personal property because the **314 statute only permits survival of causes of action existing at the time of the decedent's death. Little clearly had no cause of action against the Trustees during his lifetime for the alleged removal of property that occurred after his death. As the executor's powers are derivative of Little's, Campbell acquired no standing to compel an accounting for the operation of the Marital Trust after the date of Little's death, when Little's right to an accounting had ceased. Code § 8.01–25 thus cannot be the basis for granting Campbell standing to compel an accounting for the conversion of tangible personal property that only occurred after Little's death. See Rutter, 264 Va. at 313–14, 568 S.E.2d at 694–95. ...[6]

> [6] The issue is not before us as to what rights, if any, Campbell may assert under Code § 64.1–145 or otherwise as to the claim for wrongfully removed tangible personal property and we express no opinion in that regard. [see below]

---

§ 64.2-520. Action for goods carried away, or for waste, destruction of, or damage to estate of decedent

A. Any action for damages for the taking or carrying away of any goods, or for the waste, destruction of, or damage to any estate of or by the decedent, whether such damage be direct or indirect, may be maintained by or against the decedent's personal representative.

...

C. Any action pursuant to this section shall survive pursuant to § 8.01-25.

Chapter Seven
Other Aspects of Planning for Incapacity and Death

This final chapter addresses additional ways, besides arranging for passing of wealth at death, that estate planning clients can prepare for their incapacity and death. This includes creating a durable power of attorney for management of one's wealth during incapacity (as an alternative to putting one's wealth in trust), arranging for others to care for a dependent offspring or spouse, and making in advance or delegating decisions regarding one's medical care until death and disposition of one's body after death. When an incapacitated person has not pre-arranged for a selected individual or institution to manage his or her care and finances, courts have authority to appoint someone as guardian or conservator.

I.   Powers of Attorney

Any competent adult can at any time grant a power of attorney to another competent adult simply for sake of convenience, authorizing the other person to act as an agent with respect to financial management and decision making. Traditionally, a power of attorney necessarily expired when the principal became incapacitates, because oversight of and direction to the agent were essential features of a power of attorney. Today, however, the law authorizes creating of such agency relationships that persist even after the principal becomes incapacitated, and in fact creates a presumption that any power of attorney is "durable."

Part B. Powers of Attorney..
Chapter 16. Uniform Power of Attorney Act.
Article 1. General Provisions.

§ 64.2-1600. Definitions.

… "Agent" means a person granted authority to act for a principal under a power of attorney, ...

"Durable," with respect to a power of attorney, means not terminated by the principal's incapacity. …

"Good faith" means honesty in fact.

"Incapacity" means inability of an individual to manage property or business affairs because the individual:

> 1. Has an impairment in the ability to receive and evaluate information or make or communicate decisions even with the use of technological assistance; or

2. Is missing or outside the United States and unable to return.

"Power of attorney" means a writing or other record that grants authority to an agent to act in the place of the principal, whether or not the term power of attorney is used.

"Presently exercisable general power of appointment," with respect to property or a property interest subject to a power of appointment, means power exercisable at the time in question to vest absolute ownership in the principal individually, the principal's estate, the principal's creditors, or the creditors of the principal's estate. ... The term does not include a power exercisable in a fiduciary capacity or only by will.

"Principal" means an individual who grants authority to an agent in a power of attorney. ...

§ 64.2-1601. Applicability.

This chapter applies to all powers of attorney except: ...

2. A power to make health care decisions;... and

5. A power to make arrangements for burial or disposition of remains...

§ 64.2-1602. Power of attorney is durable.

A power of attorney created under this chapter is durable unless it expressly provides that it is terminated by the incapacity of the principal.

§ 64.2-1603. Execution of power of attorney.

A power of attorney shall be signed by the principal or in the principal's conscious presence by another individual directed by the principal to sign the principal's name on the power of attorney. ...

§ 64.2-1606. Nomination of conservator or guardian...

... B. If, after a principal executes a power of attorney, a court appoints a conservator or guardian of the principal's estate or other fiduciary charged with the management of some or all of the principal's property, the agent is accountable to the fiduciary as well as to the principal. The power of attorney is not terminated and the agent's authority continues unless limited, suspended, or terminated by the court.

§ 64.2-1607. When power of attorney effective.

A. A power of attorney is effective when executed unless the principal provides in the power of attorney that it becomes effective at a future date or upon the occurrence of a future event or contingency.

B. If a power of attorney becomes effective upon the occurrence of a future event or contingency, the principal, in the power of attorney, may authorize one or more persons to determine in a writing or other record that the event or contingency has occurred.

C. If a power of attorney becomes effective upon the principal's incapacity and the principal has not authorized a person to determine whether the principal is incapacitated, or the person authorized is unable or unwilling to make the determination, the power of attorney becomes effective upon a determination... by (i) the principal's attending physician and a second physician or licensed clinical psychologist after personal examination of the principal... or (ii) an attorney-at-law, a judge, or an appropriate governmental official that the principal is incapacitated within the meaning of subdivision 1 of the definition of incapacity in § 64.2-1600. ...

§ 64.2-1608. Termination of power of attorney or agent's authority.

A. A power of attorney terminates when:

    1. The principal dies;

    2. The principal becomes incapacitated, if the power of attorney is not durable;

    3. The principal revokes the power of attorney;

    4. The power of attorney provides that it terminates;

    5. The purpose of the power of attorney is accomplished; ...

B. An agent's authority terminates when:

    1. The principal revokes the authority;

    2. The agent dies, becomes incapacitated, or resigns;

    3. Unless the power of attorney otherwise provides, an action is filed (i) for the divorce or annulment of the agent's marriage to the principal or their legal separation, (ii) by either the agent or principal for separate maintenance from the other, or (iii) by either the agent or principal for custody or visitation of a child in common with the other; or

    4. The power of attorney terminates. ...

F. The execution of a power of attorney does not revoke a power of attorney previously executed by the principal unless the subsequent power of attorney provides that the previous power of attorney is revoked or that all other powers of attorney are revoked.

§ 64.2-1609. Coagents and successor agents.

A. A principal may designate two or more persons to act as coagents. Unless the power of attorney otherwise provides, each coagent may exercise its authority independently.

B. A principal may designate one or more successor agents to act if an agent resigns, dies, becomes incapacitated, is not qualified to serve, or declines to serve. A principal may grant authority to designate one or more successor agents to an agent or other person designated by name, office, or function. ...

C. Except as otherwise provided in the power of attorney and subsection D, an agent that does not participate in or conceal a breach of fiduciary duty committed by another agent, including a predecessor agent, is not liable for the actions of the other agent.

D. An agent that has actual knowledge of a breach or imminent breach of fiduciary duty by another agent shall notify the principal and, if the principal is incapacitated, take any action reasonably appropriate in the circumstances to safeguard the principal's best interest. An agent that fails to notify the principal or take action as required by this subsection is liable for the reasonably foreseeable damages that could have been avoided if the agent had notified the principal or taken such action.

§ 64.2-1612. Agent's duties.

A. Notwithstanding provisions in the power of attorney, an agent that has accepted appointment shall:

1. Act in accordance with the principal's reasonable expectations to the extent actually known by the agent and, otherwise, in the principal's best interest;

2. Act in good faith; and

3. Act only within the scope of authority granted in the power of attorney.

B. Except as otherwise provided in the power of attorney, an agent that has accepted appointment shall:

1. Act loyally for the principal's benefit;

2. Act so as not to create a conflict of interest that impairs the agent's ability to act impartially in the principal's best interest;

3. Act with the care, competence, and diligence ordinarily exercised by agents in similar circumstances;

4. Keep a record of all receipts, disbursements, and transactions made on behalf of the principal;

5. Cooperate with a person that has authority to make health care decisions for the principal... and otherwise act in the principal's best interest; and

6. Attempt to preserve the principal's estate plan... if preserving the plan is consistent with the principal's best interest based on all relevant factors, including:

    a. The value and nature of the principal's property;

    b. The principal's foreseeable obligations and need for maintenance;

    c. Minimization of taxes...; and

d. Eligibility for a benefit, a program, or assistance under a statute or regulation.

C. An agent that acts in good faith is not liable to any beneficiary of the principal's estate plan for failure to preserve the plan.

D. An agent that acts with care, competence, and diligence for the best interest of the principal is not liable solely because the agent also benefits from the act...

E. If an agent is selected by the principal because of special skills or expertise...., the special skills or expertise shall be considered in determining whether the agent has acted with care, competence, and diligence under the circumstances.

F. Absent a breach of duty to the principal, an agent is not liable if the value of the principal's property declines. ...

§ 64.2-1613. Exoneration of agent.

A provision in a power of attorney relieving an agent of liability for breach of duty is binding on the principal and the principal's successors in interest except to the extent the provision:

1. Relieves the agent of liability for breach of duty committed dishonestly, with an improper motive, or with reckless indifference to the purposes of the power of attorney or the best interest of the principal; or

2. Was inserted as a result of an abuse of a confidential or fiduciary relationship with the principal.

§ 64.2-1614. Judicial relief.

A. ... [T]he following persons may petition a court to construe a power of attorney or review the agent's conduct, and grant appropriate relief:

1. The principal or the agent;

2. A guardian, conservator, personal representative of the estate of a deceased principal, or other fiduciary acting for the principal;

3. A person authorized to make health care decisions for the principal;

4. The principal's spouse, parent, or descendant;

5. An adult who is a brother, sister, niece, or nephew of the principal;

6. A person named as a beneficiary to receive any property, benefit, or contractual right on the principal's death or as a beneficiary of a trust created by or for the principal that has a financial interest in the principal's estate;

7. The adult protective services unit of the local department of social services for the county or city where the principal resides or is located;

8. The principal's caregiver or another person that demonstrates sufficient interest in the principal's welfare; and

9. A person asked to accept the power of attorney.

...

C. The agent may, after reasonable notice to the principal, petition the circuit court for authority to make gifts of the principal's property to the extent not inconsistent with the express terms of the power of attorney or other writing. ...

Article 2. Authority.

§ 64.2-1622. Authority that requires specific grant; grant of general authority.

A. ... [A]n agent under a power of attorney may do the following... only if the power of attorney expressly grants the agent the authority...:

1. Create, amend, revoke, or terminate an inter vivos trust;

2. Make a gift;

3. Create or change rights of survivorship;

4. Create or change a beneficiary designation;

5. Delegate authority granted under the power of attorney;

6. Waive the principal's right to be a beneficiary of a joint and survivor annuity, including a survivor benefit under a retirement plan; or

7. Exercise fiduciary powers that the principal has authority to delegate.

...

G. An act performed by an agent pursuant to a power of attorney has the same effect and inures to the benefit of and binds the principal and the principal's successors in interest as if the principal had performed the act.

H. Notwithstanding the provisions of subsection A, if a power of attorney grants to an agent authority to do all acts that a principal could do, the agent shall have the authority to make gifts in any amount of any of the principal's property to any individuals or to [charitable] organizations... in accordance with the principal's personal history of making or joining in the making of lifetime gifts. ...

§ 64.2-1624. Construction of authority generally.

Except as otherwise provided in the power of attorney, by executing a power of attorney that incorporates by reference a subject described in §§ 64.2-1625 through 64.2-1638 or that grants to an agent authority to do all acts that a principal could do pursuant to subsection C of § 64.2-1622, a principal authorizes the agent, with respect to that subject, to:

1. Demand, receive, and obtain by litigation or otherwise, money or another thing of value to which the principal is, may become, or claims to be entitled, and conserve, invest, disburse, or use anything so received or obtained for the purposes intended;

2. Contract in any manner with any person... and perform, rescind, cancel, terminate, reform, restate, release, or modify... another contract made by or on behalf of the principal;

3. Execute, acknowledge, seal, deliver, file, or record any instrument or communication...;

4. Initiate,... settle, oppose, or... compromise... a claim existing in favor of or against the principal...;

5. Seek on the principal's behalf the assistance of a court or other governmental agency to carry out an act authorized in the power of attorney;

6. Engage, compensate, and discharge an attorney, accountant,... or other advisor;
...

9. Access communications intended for... the principal...; and

10. Do any lawful act with respect to the subject and all property related to the subject.

§ 64.2-1625. Real property.

Unless the power of attorney otherwise provides, language in a power of attorney granting general authority with respect to real property authorizes the agent to:

1. ... [A]cquire or reject an interest in real property...;

2. ... [G]rant or dispose of an interest in real property...;

3. Pledge or mortgage an interest in real property... to borrow money...;

4. Release, assign, satisfy, or enforce by litigation... [any] claim to real property...;

5. Manage or conserve an interest in real property..., including:

    a. Insuring against liability or casualty or other loss;

    b. Obtaining or regaining possession...;

    c. Paying... or contesting taxes or assessments...; and

    d. Purchasing supplies, hiring assistance or labor, and making repairs or alterations...;

6. Use, develop,... remove,... or install structures or other improvements...;

8. Change the form of title...; and

9. Dedicate to public use, with or without consideration, easements or other real property...

§ 64.2-1626. Tangible personal property.

[similar to § 64.2-1625]

§ 64.2-1630. Operation of entity or business.

Subject to the terms of a document or an agreement governing an entity…, and unless the power of attorney otherwise provides, language in a power of attorney granting general authority with respect to operation of an entity or business authorizes the agent to: … [do pretty much anything the principal could do]

***

§ 64.2-1631 (Insurance and annuities), § 64.2-1632 (Estates, trusts, and other beneficial interests), and § 64.2-1633 (Claims and litigation), § 64.2-1635 (Benefits from governmental programs or civil or military service), § 64.2-1636 (Retirement plans), and § 64.2-1637 (Taxes) likewise authorize an agent to do pretty much all that the principal could do if competent. Of particular significance is a provision in § 64.2-1632(B)(8) stating that "[u]nless the power of attorney otherwise provides, language in a power of attorney granting general authority with respect to estates, trusts, and other beneficial interests authorizes the agent to… [r]eject, renounce, disclaim, release, or consent to a reduction in or modification of a share in or payment from an estate, trust, or other beneficial interest." Before enactment of this provision, a circuit court had approved of an "attorney-in-fact's" disclaiming on behalf of a surviving wife, who was elderly, incompetent, and institutionalized, her right to her husband's entire estate under his will, finding that it caused her no harm because it would just have gone to the facility or her heirs anyway, and not improved her life at all. Turner ex rel. Dove v. Bowman, 64 Va. Cir. 354 (2004).

§ 64.2-1634. Personal and family maintenance.

A. Unless the power of attorney otherwise provides, language in a power of attorney granting general authority with respect to personal and family maintenance authorizes the agent to:

1. Perform the acts necessary to maintain the customary standard of living of the principal, the principal's spouse, and the following individuals, whether living when the power of attorney is executed or later born:

a. The individuals legally entitled to be supported by the principal; and

b. The individuals whom the principal has customarily supported or indicated the intent to support;

2. Make periodic payments of child support and other family maintenance required by a court or governmental agency or an agreement to which the principal is a party;

3. Provide living quarters for the individuals described in subdivision 1…

4. Provide normal domestic help, usual vacations and travel expenses, and funds for shelter, clothing, food, appropriate education, including

postsecondary and vocational education, and other current living costs for the individuals described in subdivision 1;

5. Pay expenses for necessary health care and custodial care on behalf of the individuals described in subdivision 1; ...

7. Continue any provision made by the principal for automobiles or other means of transportation, including registering, licensing, insuring, and replacing them, for the individuals described in subdivision 1;

8. Maintain credit and debit accounts for the convenience of the individuals described in subdivision 1 and open new accounts; and

9. Continue payments incidental to the membership or affiliation of the principal in a religious institution, club, society, order, or other organization or to continue contributions to those organizations. ...

§ 64.2-1638. Gifts.

...

B. Unless the power of attorney otherwise provides, language in a power of attorney granting general authority with respect to gifts authorizes the agent only to:

1. Make outright to, or for the benefit of, a person a gift of any of the principal's property... in an amount per donee not to exceed the annual dollar limits of the federal gift tax exclusion under Internal Revenue Code 26 U.S.C. § 2503 (b)...

C. An agent may make a gift of the principal's property only as the agent determines is consistent with the principal's objectives if actually known by the agent and, if unknown, as the agent determines is consistent with the principal's best interest based on all relevant factors, including:

1. The value and nature of the principal's property;

2. The principal's foreseeable obligations and need for maintenance;

3. Minimization of taxes, including income, estate, inheritance, generation-skipping transfer, and gift taxes;

4. Eligibility for a benefit, a program, or assistance under a statute or regulation; and

5. The principal's personal history of making or joining in making gifts.

***

There is precisely one Virginia court decision interpreting this state's enactment of the Uniform Power of Attorney Act.

Circuit Court of Virginia, Fairfax County.
Inova Health Systems Services, Inc. v. Bainbridge
81 Va. Cir. 39 (2010)

LESLIE M. ALDEN, Circuit Court Judge.

... Inova Health Systems Services, Inc. t/a Commonwealth Care Center seek[s] a judgment against Susan Bainbridge for care provided by Inova to Betty M. Callicotte–Meier. ...

On or about June 14, 2004, Ms. Callicotte–Meier was admitted to Inova's Commonwealth Care Center as a resident. Inova's Commonwealth Care Center is a nursing facility which provides long-term care to its residents. According to Inova, Ms. Callicotte–Meier was admitted pursuant to an Admissions Agreement executed on June 14, 2004. The recitals of the Agreement state that the Agreement is between Inova, the Responsible Party, and the Resident. The recitals also list Ms. Callicotte–Meier as both the Responsible Party and the Resident.

However, the Agreement was not signed by Ms. Callicotte–Meier. The Agreement was signed by Ms. Bainbridge who signed on the signature line titled Responsible Party. Ms. Bainbridge signed the Agreement on July 22, 2004 more than a month after Ms. Callicotte–Meier was admitted. It appears that, on July 7, 2004, Ms. Bainbridge was appointed Ms. Callicotte–Meier's General Power of Attorney ("POA"). The POA indicates that, at the time the POA was executed, Ms. Callicotte–Meier was unable to sign the POA and gave verbal consent in the presence of two witnesses.

The Agreement requires the Responsible Party and the Resident to use the Resident's income to pay Inova for the Resident's care. The Agreement further requires the Resident to appoint the Responsible Party as a Special POA to preserve the Resident's income and to promptly pay Inova; however, no Special POA was executed here.[1]

> [1] Although the Agreement requires the Resident to appoint the Responsible Party POA pursuant to a Special POA to preserve the Resident's income and pay Inova, Ms. Bainbridge was appointed pursuant to a General POA which did not provide specific directions to preserve income or provide payment to Inova. It is not clear whether appointing Ms. Bainbridge pursuant to a Special POA would alter the Court's analysis.

Finally, the Agreement requires the Responsible Party to assist Inova in obtaining Medicaid for the Resident by providing the necessary financial information.

Ms. Callicotte–Meier resided at Inova's Commonwealth Care Center from June 14, 2004 through the date of her discharge on March 11, 2005. From November 2004 through March 11, 2005, Medicaid covered the cost of Ms. Callicotte–Meier's care. However, from July 2004 through September 2004, the cost of Ms. Callicotte–Meier's care was not covered by either her private insurance or Medicaid, so Ms. Callicotte–Meier was required to make payments from her own income. From July 2004 to September 2004, only one payment of $1,000 was made leaving a balance of $23,782.33.

During this time, Inova claims that Ms. Bainbridge was in control of Ms. Callicotte–Meier's finances and wrote numerous checks to herself and her friend instead of using Ms. Callicotte–Meier's income to pay for her care at the Inova. In addition, Inova claims that Ms. Bainbridge failed to assist Inova in obtaining Medicaid for Ms. Callicotte–Meier by not providing the required financial information. After being unable to obtain Ms. Callicotte–Meier's financial information from Ms. Bainbridge, on December 21, 2004, an employee of Inova took Ms. Callicotte–Meier to the bank to obtain the necessary paperwork. At that time, the bank informed Ms. Callicotte–Meier that Ms. Bainbridge had closed her savings account and taken the balance of $2,351.44 as a cash withdrawal. After returning to Inova, Ms. Callicotte–Meier executed a Power of Attorney Revocation revoking Ms. Bainbridge's authority as POA.

Ms. Callicotte–Meier was eventually able to obtain Medicaid which covered the cost of her care retroactive to November 2004. However, Inova never received payment for the $23,782.33 owed for July 2004 to September 2004. Ms. Callicotte–Meier passed away in August 2008, and Ms. Bainbridge qualified as adminstratrix of Ms. Callicotte–Meier's estate. Although Inova attempted to recover the amount owed from Ms. Callicotte–Meier's estate, the Commissioner of Accounts concluded that Ms. Callicotte–Meier's estate was insolvent.

Being unable to collect the balance due from Ms. Callicotte–Meier's estate, on March 5, 2009, Inova filed a Complaint against Ms. Bainbridge for breach of the Agreement in the amount of $23,782.33. Inova claims that, as the Responsible Party, Ms. Bainbridge had an independent contractual duty to use Ms. Callicotte–Meier's income to pay for her care and to assist Inova in obtaining Medicaid for Ms. Callicotte–Meier. Ms. Bainbridge filed an Answer, pro se, denying that she owed Inova for Ms. Callicotte–Meier's care. ...

Legal Analysis

Inova's claim against Ms. Bainbridge rests upon the contention that, even though Ms. Bambridge was Ms. Callicotte–Meier's agent, Ms. Bainbridge personally obligated herself to perform under the Agreement when she signed the Agreement on the signature line labeled Responsible Party. ....

I. Agency

[T]he general rule is that, "[w]here an agent makes a full disclosure of the fact of his agency, and the name of his principal, and contracts only as the agent of the named principal, he incurs no personal responsibility." Richmond U.P.R. Co. v. New York S.B.R. Co., 95 Va. 386, 395, 28 S.E. 573, 575 (1897). There are circumstances where an agent of a disclosed principal may personally bind himself such as where the agent enters into an independent, collateral agreement Harriss, Magill & Co. v. John H. Rodgers & Co., 143 Va. 815, 829, 129 S.E. 513, 517 (1925). However, "the presumption is that [an agent] intends to bind only his principal, and the burden of proof is upon him who undertakes to establish the agent's personal liability." Richmond U.P.R. Co., 95 Va. at 395, 28 S.E. at 575. …

Inova contends that Ms. Bainbridge obligated herself to pay Inova from Ms. Callicotte–Meier's income and to assist Inova in obtaining Medicaid for Ms. Callicotte–Meier. To prevail under the common law principles of agency cited above, Inova has the burden of proving that Ms. Bainbridge intended to bind herself. However, under the facts of this case, Inova cannot meet its burden.

There is no dispute that, at the time Ms. Bainbridge signed the Agreement, she was Ms. Callicotte–Meier's agent pursuant to a POA. There is also no dispute that, at the time Ms. Bainbridge signed the Agreement, Inova knew Ms. Bainbridge was Ms. Callicotte–Meier's POA. Entering into the Agreement was within the scope of Ms. Bainbridge's authority pursuant to the General POA. The Agreement was entered into for Ms. Callicotte–Meier's benefit and her benefit alone. Moreover, Ms. Callicotte–Meier did not sign the Agreement herself, presumably, because she was physically unable to do so which is why she also had to give verbal permission to execute the POA. Therefore, without Ms. Bainbridge's signature, Inova would not have had written contract with Ms. Callicotte–Meier. Finally, the Agreement identifies the two parties to the Agreement: Inova as Center and Ms. Callicotte–Meier as Resident and Responsible Party. The facts point to one conclusion: Ms. Bainbridge signed the Agreement as the agent and on behalf of Ms. Callicotte–Meier with no intention to personally bind herself.

Although the Agreement appears to contemplate a three-party contract between Inova, the Resident, and the Responsible Party, the Agreement in this case lists Ms. Callicotte–Meier as both Resident and Responsible Party. Inova focuses on the fact that Ms. Bainbridge signed on the signature line titled Responsible Party instead of the line titled Resident as evidence that Ms. Bainbridge personally assumed the duties of the Responsible Party. However, this argument is unpersuasive. The Agreement clearly lists Ms. Callicotte–Meier as the Responsible Party and the Court must read the Agreement as written. TM Delmarva Power, L.L.C. v. NCP of Virginia, L.L.C., 263 Va. 116, 119, 557 S.E.2d 199, 200 (2002). If the parties intended that Ms. Bainbridge be the Responsible Party, the parties would have listed her as the Responsible Party. To the extent there is any ambiguity, it must be construed against Inova as the drafter of the Agreement. Martin & Martin, Inc. v. Bradley Enterprises, Inc., 256 Va. 288, 291, 504 S.E.2d 849, 851 (1998).

Inova also focuses a great deal on Ms. Bainbridge's alleged misappropriation of over $8,000 of Ms. Callicotte–Meier's income while Ms. Bainbridge was POA. Although Ms. Bainbridge claims that all these charges were for legitimate costs incurred or services rendered for the care of Ms. Callicotte–Meier's cat, Spunky, the Court agrees that these expenses are extremely large and highly suspicious. Unfortunately, this Court cannot take action upon Ms. Bainbridge's alleged self-dealing because Inova is without standing to raise the issue. As Ms. Callicotte–Meier's POA, Ms. Bainbridge owed a fiduciary duty to Ms. Callicotte–Meier. Va.Code § 26–85. Even assuming that Ms. Bainbridge breached that duty by misappropriating Ms. Callicotte–Meier's income to her own personal use, only Ms. Callicotte–Meier or an individual identified in Virginia Code § 26–87 [now § 64.2-1614] has standing to bring such a claim against Ms. Bainbridge. Va.Code § 26–87.

Therefore under the common law and the facts of this case, Ms. Bainbridge could not be found liable because she was acting as an agent of a disclosed principal when she signed the Agreement with Inova. Still, Inova claims that the provisions of Social Security Act and Virginia Code § 32.1–138.3 require a different outcome.

II. Social Security Act

Inova concedes that the Responsible Party provisions of the Agreement are "unusual." However, Inova argues that the form and substance of these provisions are allowed and even dictated by the Social Security Act. As a nursing facility that accepts patients eligible for Medicaid, Inova is governed by certain provisions of the Social Security Act... Specifically, 42 USCS § 1396r(c)(5)(A)(ii) provides that a nursing facility must "not require a third party guarantee of payment to the facility as a condition of admission (or expedited admission) to, or continued stay in, the facility." However, the statute does allow a facility to require "an individual, who has legal access to a resident's income or resources available to pay for care in the facility, to sign a contract (without incurring personal financial liability) to provide payment from the resident's income or resources for such care." 42 USCS § 1396r(c)(5)(B)(ii). ...

It is clear from language in 42 USCS § 1396r that Congress did not want nursing homes to force others not in privity, such as a resident's family member, to assume personal financial responsibility for the care of the resident. See also 104 H. Rpt. 651 (stating that purpose was to prevent financial exploitation of residents and their families). Furthermore, even though 42 USCS § 1396r(c)(5)(B)(ii) allows a nursing facility to require a person with legal access to a resident's funds to sign an admission agreement, the statute is equally clear that a person does so without incurring personal liability. See also 56 FR 48826 (when such a person signs an admission agreement, "the person providing the guarantee assumes no personal liability"). ...

The fact that a defendant at some point had access to the resident's income does not change the fact that plaintiff is seeking a judgment to be paid from the defendant's personal assets. ...

Although it may seem unusual that Congress would allow a nursing home to require an individual to sign an admission agreement but not give the nursing home recourse if that individual failed to make payments, it is not for this Court to create such a remedy. If Congress wanted to create a remedy, it could have done so expressly, and if that were the case, Congress certainly would not have included the express language "without incurring personal liability."

Even if the prohibition on third-party personal liability was not clear from the plain language of the statute, Virginia law would require this Court to strictly construe the statute. As discussed previously, Ms. Bainbridge could not be found liable under the common law because she was acting as the agent of a disclosed principal. Therefore any statute that would allow such liability is in derogation of the common law. ... Therefore, this Court must conclude that "without incurring personal liability" means no personal liability.

III. Virginia Code § 32.1–138.3

... Virginia Code § 32.1–138.3 mimics, in part, the language of 42 USCS § 1396r and provides:

> Any facility certified under Title XVIII or XTX of the United States Social Security Act shall not require a third party guarantee of payment to the facility as a condition of admission or of expedited admission to, or continued stay in, the facility. This section shall not be construed to prevent a facility from requiring an individual who has legal access to a resident's income or resources which are available to pay for care in the facility to sign a contract without incurring personal financial liability except for breach of the duty to provide payment from the resident's income or resources for such care.

The language of the Virginia statute is almost identical to the federal statutes with the exception of the final clause regarding a "duty to provide payment from the resident's income or resources for such care." Va.Code § 32.1–138.3. Given Congress's clear prohibition on third-party personal liability, there is a conflict between the federal statutes and the Virginia Code.

The Supremacy Clause of the United States Constitution ... gives rise to the doctrine of federal preemption of conflicting state law. ... [C]ompliance with both state and federal law is impossible. Because the Virginia Code appears to allow personal liability where the federal law prohibits it, it is impossible for any court granting relief under the Virginia Code, by finding someone personally liable, to be in compliance with the federal law. Therefore, to the extent that Virginia Code § 32.1–138.3 allows an individual, who has legal access to a resident's income and who signs an admissions contract, to be held personally liable, the Virginia Code is preempted by 42 USCS § 1396r(c)(5)(B)(ii).[4]

> [4] Notwithstanding the conflict between the federal statute and the Virginia Code, Ms. Bainbridge could not be held personally liable under the facts of this case because she signed the Agreement as an agent and she received no benefit for assuming personal liability.

Accordingly, the Court finds that Ms. Bainbridge is not liable for breach of contract or liable for the outstanding debt owed to Invoa for Ms. Callicotte–Meier's care.

II.   Guardians and Conservators for an Incapacitated Adult

For more extensive assistance and decision making than a holder of a power of attorney typically provides, the law authorizes courts to appoint guardians (for personal care) and conservators (for financial management) for incapacitated adults. Proceedings to accomplish this can be quite difficult emotionally for family members, and those who petition might not have entirely disinterested motives (or might be suspected by the alleged incompetent person to have impure motives).

Part D. Guardianship of Incapacitated Persons.
Chapter 20. Guardianship and Conservatorship.
Article 1. Appointment.

§ 64.2-2000. Definitions.

… "Conservator" means a person appointed by the court who is responsible for managing the estate and financial affairs of an incapacitated person …

"Guardian" means a person appointed by the court who is responsible for the personal affairs of an incapacitated person, including responsibility for making decisions regarding the person's support, care, health, safety, habilitation, education, therapeutic treatment, and, if not inconsistent with an order of involuntary admission, residence. …

"Incapacitated person" means an adult who has been found by a court to be incapable of receiving and evaluating information effectively or responding to people, events, or environments to such an extent that the individual lacks the capacity to (i) meet the essential requirements for his health, care, safety, or therapeutic needs without the assistance or protection of a guardian or (ii) manage property or financial affairs or provide for his support or for the support of his legal dependents without the assistance or protection of a conservator. A finding that the individual displays poor judgment alone shall not be considered sufficient evidence that the individual is an incapacitated person within the meaning of this definition. …

§ 64.2-2001. Filing of petition; jurisdiction; instructions to be provided.

A. A petition for the appointment of a guardian or conservator shall be filed with the circuit court of the county or city in which the respondent is a resident or… resided immediately prior to becoming a patient, voluntarily or involuntarily, in a hospital… or a resident in a nursing facility or nursing home, convalescent home, assisted living facility...

§ 64.2-2002. Who may file petition; contents.

A. Any person may file a petition for the appointment of a guardian, a conservator, or both.

...

§ 64.2-2003. Appointment of guardian ad litem.

A. ... [T]he court shall appoint a guardian ad litem to represent the interests of the respondent. ...

§ 64.2-2004. Notice of hearing; jurisdictional.

...

D. The notice to the respondent shall include a brief statement in at least 14-point type of the purpose of the proceedings and shall inform the respondent of the right to be represented by counsel... and to a hearing... Additionally, the notice shall include the following statement in conspicuous, bold print.

WARNING

AT THE HEARING YOU MAY LOSE MANY OF YOUR RIGHTS. A GUARDIAN MAY BE APPOINTED TO MAKE PERSONAL DECISIONS FOR YOU. A CONSERVATOR MAY BE APPOINTED TO MAKE DECISIONS CONCERNING YOUR PROPERTY AND FINANCES. THE APPOINTMENT MAY AFFECT CONTROL OF HOW YOU SPEND YOUR MONEY, HOW YOUR PROPERTY IS MANAGED AND CONTROLLED, WHO MAKES YOUR MEDICAL DECISIONS, WHERE YOU LIVE, WHETHER YOU ARE ALLOWED TO VOTE, AND OTHER IMPORTANT RIGHTS.

...

§ 64.2-2005. Evaluation report.

A. A report evaluating the condition of the respondent... shall be prepared by one or more licensed physicians or psychologists...

B. The report... shall contain...:

1. A description of the nature, type, and extent of the respondent's incapacity, including the respondent's specific functional impairments;

2. A diagnosis or assessment of the respondent's mental and physical condition, including... an evaluation of the respondent's ability to learn self-care skills, adaptive behavior, and social skills and a prognosis for improvement...

§ 64.2-2006. Counsel for respondent.

... If the respondent is not represented by counsel, the court may appoint legal counsel... upon request of the respondent or the guardian ad litem, if the court determines that counsel is needed to protect the respondent's interest. Counsel appointed by the court shall be paid a fee that is fixed by the court to be taxed as part of the costs of the proceeding. A health care provider shall disclose or make available to the attorney, upon request, any information, records, and reports concerning the respondent that the attorney determines necessary...

§ 64.2-2007. Hearing on petition to appoint.

A. The respondent is entitled to a jury trial upon request, and may compel the attendance of witnesses, present evidence on his own behalf, and confront and cross-examine witnesses. ...

C. In determining the need for a guardian or a conservator and the powers and duties of any guardian or conservator, if needed, consideration shall be given to the following factors: (i) the limitations of the respondent; (ii) the development of the respondent's maximum self-reliance and independence; (iii) the availability of less restrictive alternatives, including advance directives and durable powers of attorney; (iv) the extent to which it is necessary to protect the respondent from neglect, exploitation, or abuse; (v) the actions needed to be taken by the guardian or conservator; (vi) the suitability of the proposed guardian or conservator; and (vii) the best interests of the respondent.

D. If, after considering the evidence presented at the hearing, the court or jury determines on the basis of clear and convincing evidence that the respondent is incapacitated and in need of a guardian or conservator, the court shall appoint a suitable person, who may be the spouse of the respondent, to be the guardian or the conservator or both, giving due deference to the wishes of the respondent. ...

§ 64.2-2008. Fees and costs.

A. ... The court may require the petitioner to pay or reimburse all or some of the respondent's reasonable costs and fees and any other costs incurred under this chapter if the court finds that the petitioner initiated a proceeding under this chapter that was in bad faith or not for the benefit of the respondent. ...

§ 64.2-2009. Court order of appointment; limited guardianship and conservatorship.

A. The court's order appointing a guardian or conservator shall... define the powers and duties of the guardian or conservator so as to permit the incapacitated person to care for himself and manage property to the extent he is capable;... specify the legal disabilities, if any, of the person in connection with the finding of incapacity...

B. The court may appoint a limited guardian for an incapacitated person who is capable of addressing some of the essential requirements for his care for the limited purpose of medical decision making, decisions about place of residency, or other specific decisions regarding his personal affairs. The court may appoint a limited conservator for an incapacitated person who is capable of managing some of his property and financial affairs for limited purposes that are specified in the order. ...

D. A guardian need not be appointed for a person who has appointed an agent under an advance directive... unless the court determines that the agent is not acting in accordance with the wishes of the principal or there is a need for decision making outside the purview of the advance directive. A conservator need not be appointed for a person who has appointed an agent under a durable power of attorney, unless the court determines... that the agent is not acting in the best interests of the principal or there is a need for decision making outside the purview of the durable power of attorney...

***

A recent Supreme Court illustrates how the consequences of coming under a guardianship can differ depending on whether it is a full or limited guardianship.

Supreme Court of Virginia.
Lopez-Rosario v. Habib
291 Va. 293, 785 S.E.2d 214 (2016)

Opinion by Justice S. BERNARD GOODWYN.

*295 ... Kenia L. Lopez–Rosario (Lopez–Rosario) is an adult with several physical and cognitive disabilities. On May 13, 2010, Lopez–Rosario's parents, Kenia I.R. Lopez and Israel Lopez petitioned the Circuit Court of Loudoun County to appoint them as Lopez–Rosario's co-guardians. The petition stated that Lopez–Rosario "is an incapacitated individual as defined by Virginia Code Ann. § 37.2–1000 and Article II Section 1 of the Constitution of Virginia." It added that Lopez–Rosario requires extensive care on a daily basis and is cared for by her mother full time.

A psychologist's report filed with the petition stated, "Kenia functions at about the level of a six year old child. Estimated intellectual functioning is in the range of mild mental retardation. She cannot understand spoken speech, but can understand and communicate in ASL [(American Sign Language)], though at the level of a young child." The report stated that Lopez–Rosario's "[cognitive] condition is permanent and expected to remain stable."

The circuit court held, and its order stated, that Lopez–Rosario's "best interests shall be met by appointing co-guardians for her personal decisions, including decisions relating to her health, safety, treatment and care." ... *296 ... **215... [1]

> [1] According to the report attached to the petition for appointment of guardians, the petition "arose from a requirement of NCMC [(Children's National Medical Center)] that someone have legal responsibility for making the decision to permit Kenia's recent orthopedic surgery. That situation was handled satisfactorily via a temporary guardianship, but, going forward, Kenia needs someone who can make any such decisions in the future."

Subsequently, Lopez–Rosario had surgery to remove her gallbladder. The surgeon, Christine Habib, M.D., allegedly made an error that injured Lopez–Rosario. On March 7, 2014, Lopez–Rosario filed suit against Dr. Habib and her employer, Virginia Surgery Associates, alleging that Dr. Habib's negligence caused her injury. Lopez–Rosario filed suit in her own name and without indication that she was under a guardianship. The defendants filed a plea in bar/motion to dismiss, arguing that because her parents had been appointed as her guardians, Lopez–Rosario could not file suit under her own name. Lopez–Rosario opposed the plea in bar/motion to dismiss, arguing that the guardianship was limited to medical decisions and did not include matters such as filing lawsuits. ...

ANALYSIS

... *297 ... If a fiduciary is appointed for a ward, the ward loses the ability to file suit in his or her own name. Code § 64.2–2025 states, in relevant part,

> Subject to any conditions or limitations set forth in the order appointing the fiduciary, the fiduciary shall prosecute or defend all actions or suits to which the incapacitated person is a party at the time of qualification of the fiduciary and all such actions or suits subsequently instituted after 10 days' notice of the pendency of the action or suit.

Further, we held in Cook v. Radford Community Hospital, 260 Va. 443, 451, 536 S.E.2d 906, 910 (2000), that pursuant to a previous version of Code § 64.2–2025, "the ward does not have standing to sue in his or her own name" if a fiduciary has been appointed on his or her behalf..., implying that a guardian was a fiduciary. Id. at 446–47 & n. 2, 451, 536 S.E.2d at 907 & n. 2, 910. Correspondingly, Code § 64.2–2019(A) provides that "[a] guardian stands in a fiduciary relationship to the incapacitated person for whom he was appointed guardian." Thus, a guardian is a fiduciary for purposes of Code § 64.2–2025. **216

In this case, the guardianship order appointed the parents as "co-guardians" of Lopez–Rosario. The term "Guardian" as used in the Code "means a person appointed by the court who is responsible for the personal affairs of an incapacitated person, including *298 responsibility for making decisions regarding the person's support, care, health, safety, habilitation, education, therapeutic treatment, and, if not inconsistent with an order of involuntary admission, residence." Code § 64.2–2000.

However, Code § 64.2–2009 allows for the creation of a guardianship for a limited purpose. ... Thus, while the Code and our precedent in Cook show that the appointment of a guardian for the full range of statutory purposes removes from the ward the ability to file suit in his or her own name, it is possible for a guardianship to be limited in nature, such that the guardian does not have authority over legal decisions. Therefore, we must determine whether the circuit court erred in ruling that the parents' guardianship over Lopez–Rosario was as broad as the statutes authorize rather than being limited such that it did not provide the parents authority to make legal decisions on behalf of Lopez–Rosario. ...

Given that the psychologist's report states that the petition was filed to enable the parents to make medical decisions for Lopez–Rosario and that *299 Children's National Medical

Center paid the fees and costs associated with obtaining the guardianship order, it appears that the immediate purpose for filing for a guardianship was to enable Lopez–Rosario's parents to make medical decisions on her behalf. However, the language of the order is controlling in this case. See Temple v. Mary Washington Hospital, 288 Va. 134, 141, 762 S.E.2d 751, 754 (2014) ("This Court has stated on numerous occasions.... that trial courts speak only through their written orders and that such orders are presumed to reflect accurately what transpired.").

The circuit court's order states that Lopez–Rosario was "deemed incapacitated and unable to care for her person and estate" and that her "incapacity is expected to be permanent." It gave the parents authority to make decisions for Lopez–Rosario regarding "support care, health, safety, habilitation, therapeutic treatment and residence of Kenia L. Lopez–Rosario."

Code § 64.2–2000 states that a "Guardian" is "responsible for the personal affairs of an incapacitated person, including responsibility for making decisions regarding the person's support, care, health, safety, habilitation, education, therapeutic treatment, and, if not inconsistent with an order of involuntary admission, residence." The guardianship order noted Lopez–Rosario's incapacity and gave the parents authority in each area listed in the definition of "Guardian" under Code § 64.2–2000.4 The order did not specify any **217 limitations on the parents' guardianship, effectively granting them all of the authority that a court may vest in a guardian. Thus, the parents are Lopez–Rosario's full guardians, not limited ones.

As guardians, the parents were Lopez–Rosario's fiduciaries. Code § 64.2–2019(A). Thus, pursuant to Code § 64.2–2025, the parents had the authority and obligation to prosecute lawsuits on *300 Lopez–Rosario's behalf. Therefore, in accordance with our prior decision in Cook, 260 Va. at 451, 536 S.E.2d at 910, Lopez–Rosario lacked standing to file suit in her own name. ...

---

§ 64.2-2011. Qualification of guardian or conservator...

A. A guardian or conservator appointed in the court order shall qualify before the clerk upon the following:

> 1. Subscribing to an oath promising to faithfully perform the duties of the office...;

> 2. Posting of bond, but no surety shall be required on the bond of the guardian, and the conservator's bond may be with or without surety, as ordered by the court...

C. A conservator shall have all powers granted pursuant to § 64.2-2021 as are necessary and proper for the performance of his duties in accordance with this chapter, subject to the limitations that are prescribed in the order. ...

§ 64.2-2012. Petition for restoration, modification, or termination; effects.

A. Upon petition by the incapacitated person, the guardian or conservator, or any other person or upon motion of the court, the court may (i) declare the incapacitated person restored to capacity; (ii) modify the type of appointment or the areas of protection, management, or assistance previously granted or require a new bond; (iii) terminate the guardianship or conservatorship; (iv) order removal of the guardian or conservator...; or (v) order other appropriate relief. ...

§ 64.2-2013. Standby guardianship or conservatorship for incapacitated persons.

... B. On petition of one or both parents, one or more children, or the legal guardian of an incapacitated person..., the court may appoint a standby guardian or a standby conservator, or both, of the incapacitated person. ...

C. The standby fiduciary shall be authorized without further proceedings to assume the duties of his office immediately upon the death or adjudication of incapacity of the last surviving of the parents or children of the incapacitated person or of his legal guardian...

Article 2. Powers, Duties, and Liabilities.

§ 64.2-2019. Duties and powers of guardian.

A. A guardian stands in a fiduciary relationship to the incapacitated person for whom he was appointed guardian and may be held personally liable for a breach of any fiduciary duty to the incapacitated person. A guardian shall not be liable for the acts of the incapacitated person unless the guardian is personally negligent. A guardian shall not be required to expend personal funds on behalf of the incapacitated person.

B. A guardian's duties and authority shall not extend to decisions addressed in a valid advance directive or durable power of attorney previously executed by the incapacitated person. ...

C. A guardian shall maintain sufficient contact with the incapacitated person to know of his capabilities, limitations, needs, and opportunities. The guardian shall visit the incapacitated person as often as necessary.

D. A guardian shall be required to seek prior court authorization to change the incapacitated person's residence to another state, to terminate or consent to a termination of the person's parental rights, or to initiate a change in the person's marital status.

E. A guardian shall, to the extent feasible, encourage the incapacitated person to participate in decisions, to act on his own behalf, and to develop or regain the capacity to manage personal affairs. A guardian, in making decisions, shall consider the expressed desires and personal values of the incapacitated person to the extent known and shall otherwise act in the incapacitated person's best interest and exercise reasonable care, diligence, and prudence. A guardian shall not unreasonably restrict an incapacitated person's ability to communicate with, visit, or interact with other persons with whom the incapacitated person has an established relationship. ...

§ 64.2-2020. Annual reports by guardians.

A. A guardian shall file an annual report... with the local department of social services...

B. The report to the local department of social services shall include:

1. A description of the current mental, physical, and social condition of the incapacitated person;

2. A description of the person's living arrangements during the reported period;

3. The medical, educational, vocational, and other professional services provided to the person and the guardian's opinion as to the adequacy of the person's care;

4. A statement of the frequency and nature of the guardian's visits with and activities on behalf of the person;

5. A statement of whether the guardian agrees with the current treatment or habilitation plan;

6. A recommendation as to the need for continued guardianship, any recommended changes in the scope of the guardianship, and any other information useful in the opinion of the guardian...

§ 64.2-2021. General duties and liabilities of conservator.

A. At all times the conservator shall exercise reasonable care, diligence, and prudence and shall act in the best interest of the incapacitated person. To the extent known to him, a conservator shall consider the expressed desires and personal values of the incapacitated person. ...

C. A conservator shall, to the extent feasible, encourage the incapacitated person to participate in decisions, to act on his own behalf, and to develop or regain the capacity to manage the estate and his financial affairs. A conservator also shall consider the size of the estate, the probable duration of the conservatorship, the incapacitated person's accustomed manner of living, other resources known to the conservator to be available, and the recommendations of the guardian.

D. A conservator stands in a fiduciary relationship to the incapacitated person for whom he was appointed conservator and may be held personally liable for a breach of any fiduciary duty. ...

§ 64.2-2022. Management powers and duties of conservator.

A. A conservator, in managing the estate, shall have the powers set forth in § 64.2-105 ... as well as the following powers...:

6. To initiate a proceeding (i) to revoke a power of attorney... (ii) to make an augmented estate election...,or (iii) to make an election to take a family allowance, exempt property, or a homestead allowance...; and
7. To borrow money... for any purpose...

§ 64.2-2023. Estate planning.

A. ... [T]he court may for good cause shown authorize a conservator to (i) make gifts from income and principal of the incapacitated person's estate not necessary for the incapacitated person's maintenance to those persons to whom the incapacitated person would, in the judgment of the court, have made gifts if he had been of sound mind, (ii) disclaim property..., or (iii) create a revocable or irrevocable trust on behalf of an incapacitated person with terms approved by the court or transfer assets of an incapacitated person or an incapacitated person's estate to a trust.

B. In a proceeding under this section, a guardian ad litem shall be appointed to represent the interest of the incapacitated person. ... [T]he beneficiaries and intestate heirs shall be deemed possessed of inchoate property rights. ...

C. The court shall... consider[] (i) the size and composition of the estate; (ii) the nature and probable duration of the incapacity; (iii) the effect of the gifts, disclaimers, trusts, or transfers on the estate's financial ability to meet the incapacitated person's foreseeable health, medical care, and maintenance needs; (iv) the incapacitated person's estate plan and the effect of the gifts, disclaimers, trusts, or transfers on the estate plan; (v) prior patterns of assistance or gifts to the proposed donees; (vi) the tax effect of the proposed gifts, disclaimers, trusts, or transfers; (vii) the effect of any transfer of assets or disclaimer on the establishment or retention of eligibility for medical assistance services;... and (ix) other factors that the court may deem relevant. ...

E. If the gifts by the conservator... do not exceed $150 to each donee in a calendar year and do not exceed a total of $750 in a calendar year, the conservator may make such gifts without a hearing under this section, the appointment of a guardian ad litem, or giving notice to any person. ...

F. The conservator may... execut[e] a preneed funeral contract...

G. A conservator may exercise the incapacitated person's power to revoke or amend a trust ... with the approval of the court for good cause shown, unless the trust instrument expressly provides otherwise.

***

A circuit was called on to address an aspect of estate planning not mentioned in § 64.2-2023 – that is, whether a conservator, or a person under a conservatorship, may change the beneficiary designation on a non-probate transfer.

Circuit Court of Virginia.
Minnesota Life Ins. Co. v. Brown
86 Va. Cir. 68 (2012)

MARY JANE HALL, Judge.

… The issue presented by this case is one on which Virginia case law or statutory authority offers little guidance: whether a duly-appointed conservator for an incapacitated person may revoke a beneficiary designation for her ward's life insurance benefits and designate a different beneficiary. … The following chronology of events has been established by the evidence:

1. Edward Brown, Sr. ("Brown"), father of Ja'Sahn Brown, married Beverly Brown in 2003.

2. On March 5, 2003, Brown designated Beverly Brown as the beneficiary of his Virginia Retirement System life insurance policy, issued by Minnesota Life Insurance Company.

3. On November 19, 2005, Brown suffered an anoxic brain injury which rendered him mentally and physically incapacitated. He was hospitalized for several months and initially unable to walk, speak, eat without a feeding tube, or care for himself at all.

4. On February 16, 2006, Beverly Brown was appointed guardian and conservator for Brown. A number of incidents followed almost immediately, giving rise to substantial concern by Brown's family that Beverly Brown was abusing and/or neglecting her husband and his medical needs and controlling his finances with no accounting. Ja'Sahn Brown initiated contact with the guardian ad litem for redress.

5. On April 28, 2006, as a result of alleged abuse and neglect, Beverly Brown was removed as guardian/conservator and Jewish Family Services (JFS) was appointed in her place.

6. On June 19, 2007, Ja'Sahn Brown was appointed guardian/conservator for her father, replacing Jewish Family Services in that role. Brown moved in with Ja'Sahn Brown, who cared for him and supported him for the next four years until his death.

7. Through 2008, as Brown received occupational therapy, speech therapy, and physical therapy, his condition gradually improved to the level where he could exercise certain tasks on his own. He regained the ability to walk, to eat independently, and to speak.

8. Beverly Brown did not visit her husband from 2008 until his death.

9. In January or February of 2010, as part of the process to effect her father's retirement from the Indian Creek Correctional Center, Ja'Sahn Brown asked her father whether he wanted any benefits to be left to Beverly Brown; and he told her that he did not.

10. On February 9, 2010, Ja'Sahn Brown executed a Designation of Beneficiary form for her father's Minnesota Life policy, revoking his prior designation and designating herself as the beneficiary. She signed the form in her capacity as "guardian and conservator for Edward V. Brown, Sr."

11. Brown passed away on September 28, 2011.

12. On September 29, 2011, Ja'Sahn Brown executed an Irrevocable Assignment and Power of attorney, assigning to Beach Funeral and Cremation Services, Inc. the right to be paid from the Minnesota Life insurance policy for her father's funeral expenses. Beach Funeral subsequently assigned its right to be paid from this policy to Beta Capital Corporation. By the terms of this assignment, Beta Capital is requesting an award of the original amount of $8,140.06 plus costs, attorney's fees, and interest from the interpleaded funds.

13. By Order dated May 21, 2012, Minnesota Life properly interpleaded the sum of $66,238.08 with the Clerk of this Court.

LEGAL ANALYSIS

Virginia Code § 64.2–2009 gives the Court jurisdiction to define the powers of guardians and conservators upon appointment with the goal of "permit[ting] the incapacitated person to care for himself and manage property to the extent he is capable." In this case, the Court granted Ja'Sahn Brown those powers defined by statute under Va.Code §§ 37.2–1000 et seq. (now codified as Va.Code §§ 64.2–2000 et seq.). Va.Code § 64.2–2021 requires that the conservator "shall exercise reasonable care, diligence, and prudence and shall act in the best interest of the incapacitated person. To the extent known to him, a conservator shall consider the expressed desires and personal values of the incapacitated person." Va.Code § 64.2–2022 sets out the duties and powers of a conservator and enumerates the powers such a person may exercise without prior authorization of the court. These powers include the ability to "execute and deliver all instruments and to take all other actions that will serve in the best interests of the incapacitated person." Va.Code § 64.2–2022(A)(5).

Beverly Brown claims that Ja'Sahn Brown's modification of the beneficiary designation lacks validity because a guardian or conservator may not make such a change for a person who has no capacity to do it himself. In support of her position, Beverly Brown cites Shands v. Shands, 175 Va. 156, 7 S.E.2d 112 (1940) and Bryson v. Turnbull, 194 Va. 528, 74 S.E.2d 180 (1953). In *Shands*, the Court held only that a guardian appointed to manage the property of an incompetent person must return that property to the incapacitated owner upon restoration of capacity of the owner. 175 Va. at 160. The specific question at issue here, whether a guardian may dispose of the incapacitated person's property contrary to previous direction, was not addressed.

Bryson is much more factually similar to the instant case. In *Bryson*, the testator had become mentally incapacitated after executing a will; and she was appointed a guardian who allowed timber to be removed from her property. The question for the Court was whether the proceeds of the timber should pass as realty to the beneficiaries who were to inherit the real property, or as personalty to different beneficiaries. Ruling that the timber proceeds must pass as realty, the Court used language that supports Beverly Brown's position herein: "Under these circumstances the intent [the testator] exercised when she made her will was never changed. The opportunity to change her intentions was denied her. The intervention of mental incompetency demands this conclusion." Bryson, 194 Va. at 533. The Court expressly held, "Neither the committee nor the court can rewrite the will or change the beneficiaries named therein ... The will cannot be revoked or modified." Id. at 537–38.

Read in isolation, that holding indeed suggests that a guardian or conservator must not be permitted to change her ward's beneficiary after the onset of mental incapacity. The *Bryson* Court did not address, however, whether the incapacitated person had stated any desire about the disposition of the property. The opinion reveals nothing about the nature of her incapacity. It does not refer to any evidence offered about her desire or her ability to express any desire.

The current statute, not applicable in *Bryson*, does contemplate that a conservator will heed the wishes her ward expresses during the conservatorship. As one recent case has held,

> The appointment of a guardian/conservator... and a determination that the ward is incapacitated does not, in itself, mean the ward is incapable of making any decisions. In fact, Code § 37.2–1020(E) requires the guardian, to the extent feasible, to encourage the ward to participate in decisions. The guardian shall consider the expressed desires and personal values of the ward. Thus, the legislature envisioned that some incapacitated persons have the ability to make decisions and to consider their own needs and interests. Andrews v. Creacey, 56 Va.App. 606, 621, 696 S.E.2d 218, 225 (Va.Ct.App.2010).

In order to be found incapacitated, thus requiring appointment of a conservator, a Court need find only that the individual lacks capacity to "manage property or financial affairs or provide for his support" without a conservator's assistance. Va.Code § 64.2–2000.

The most instructive case cited to the Court is Parish v. Parish, 281 Va. 191, 704 S.E.2d 99 (2011), where the Court approved a will made by a testator who was under a guardianship at the time: "The mere fact that one is under a conservatorship is not an adjudication of insanity and does not create a presumption of incapacity." Id. at 198. The Court relied upon Thomason v. Carlton, 221 Va. 845, 852, 276 S.E.2d 171, 175 (1981):

> Neither sickness nor impaired intellect is sufficient, standing alone, to render a will invalid. If at the time of its execution the testatrix was capable of recollecting her property, the natural objects of her bounty and their claims upon her, knew the business about which she was engaged and how she wished to dispose of her property, that is sufficient.

If an incapacitated person may have sufficient capacity to make a will, it follows that he may likewise have sufficient capacity to direct a change in his life insurance beneficiary designation. Both are testamentary decisions that take effect at death. Arguing against the application of *Parish*, Beverly Brown argues that the evidential support for the testator's capacity in that case was far stronger than what has been presented in support of Brown's capacity. In *Parish*, the proponent of the will offered testimony from a paralegal and a witness present when the testator signed the will, both of whom were satisfied that he'd known what he was doing. He presented the testimony of a treating physician and a social worker who saw the testator regularly, the attorney in the conservatorship, and two family members, all of whom confirmed his ability to make a will. All of this testimony was offered to rebut the testimony of the testator's son (the contestant of the will), his daughter-in-law, and a treating neurologist, who opined that the testator was not competent to make a will. See *Parish*, 281 Va. at 200–201.

While it is unquestionably true that the Parish trial judge had much more evidence of the testator's capacity at the time he made his will than has been presented to this Court regarding Brown's capacity, the Parish holding was not conditioned upon the type or the amount of evidence offered. It held only that capacity must be proven by a preponderance of the evidence.

The only witness about Brown's stated desire that Beverly Brown should not receive benefits came from Ja'Sahn Brown. That evidence, while not overwhelming, was not controverted. It was generally corroborated by the testimony of family members who described meaningful conversations with Brown that they had had during the period of Ja'Sahn Brown's conservatorship. No other specific evidence that Brown intended to withdraw any financial benefit from Beverly Brown was offered, but the general testimony that he could express his wishes to a limited degree, that he was fond of his daughter and wanted to remain with her, and that he did not wish to see or go back to Beverly Brown, all corroborates Ja'Sahn Brown's testimony. Although the Parish holding rested upon much stronger evidence in support of capacity than is present in the instant case, Parish also had evidence on both sides of the capacity issue. In contrast, Beverly Brown offered no evidence whatever either that her husband lacked the capacity to make a change to his designation or that he in fact gave no such instruction to his daughter. Beverly Brown offered no testimony at all.

Therefore, while fully acknowledging that Ja'Sahn Brown would have improved her position with more evidence along the type, that the prevailing party in Parish offered, the evidence that she did submit about her father's capacity and his wish to change his beneficiary, was not controverted. That Brown should prefer to confer a benefit on his daughter who took him in and cared for him during his last four years of life, rather than on a spouse of just a few years who was removed as guardian for malfeasance and who had no contact with him for his last three years, is a conclusion that was supported by a preponderance of the evidence. The Court therefore finds that Ja'Sahn Brown revoked the beneficiary designation because her father desired and directed that she do so.

Beta Capital Corporation, which seeks to uphold the validity of the revocation, advances the argument that a guardian/conservator may change an insurance beneficiary designation for an incapacitated person with his or her substituted judgment as a matter of law. The Court does not reach that issue, because the Court finds that Brown intended to change his beneficiary and sufficiently communicated that instruction to Ja'Sahn Brown.

The Court upholds the validity of the revocation of Beverly Brown as the designated beneficiary and directs that the insurance proceeds be distributed to Beta Capital Corporation in the amount of $8,140.86 plus attorney's fees of $2,713.35, plus interest at the rate of 6% per annum from September 28, 2011.1 The balance of the insurance proceeds is to be distributed to Ja'Sahn Brown. …

A conservator or guardian is entitled to compensation.

§ 64.2-1208. Expenses and commissions allowed fiduciaries.

A.   [T]he commissioner of accounts shall allow the fiduciary any reasonable expenses incurred by him and, except in cases in which it is otherwise provided, a reasonable compensation in the form of a commission on receipts or otherwise. Unless otherwise provided by the court, any guardian appointed… shall also be allowed reasonable compensation for his services.

***

In In re Estate of Clark, 85 Va. Cir. 143 (2012), the Circuit Court for Fairfax County faulted a law firm that was serving as a guardian for charging a lawyer's-fee rate for all time spent, including much time that was spent on non-legal work. The court stated: "While it is reasonable for a Guardian to hire an attorney to help advise the Guardian as to the proper, legal course of action, and such decisions require legal expertise and would qualify as legal work, the attorney Guardian is permitted to charge a reasonable rate for legal services. Beyond this type of work involving legal skill, the reasonable rate that the Guardian may charge is the rate commensurate with the rate being charged in the marketplace for similar skills or tasks."

III.   Guardians, Conservators, and Custodians for a Client's Children

Younger clients who have minor children, or grandparents who have custody of young grandchildren, should consider naming someone in their will as guardian of the child in case of the client's incapacity or death. Absent such designation, if a child is left with no caretaker, the court will appoint a guardian. Even when a child is in a parent's custody, a guardian of the property might be needed if the child receives a large amount of wealth from some decedent's estate.

Part C. Guardianship of Minor..
Chapter 17. Appointment of Guardian.

§ 64.2-1700. Natural guardians.

The parents of an unmarried minor child are the joint natural guardians of the person of such child with equal legal powers and legal rights with regard to such child, provided that the parents are living together, are respectively competent to transact their own business, and are not otherwise unsuitable. Upon the death of either parent, the survivor shall be the natural guardian of the person of such child. If either parent has abandoned the family, the other parent shall be the natural guardian of the person of such child.

§ 64.2-1701. Testamentary guardians.

A. Every parent may by will appoint (i) a guardian of the person of his minor child and (ii) a guardian for the estate bequeathed or devised by the parent to his minor child for such time during the minor's infancy as the parent directs. A guardian of a minor's estate shall have custody and control of the estate committed to his care. A guardian of the person of a minor other than a parent is not entitled to custody of the person of the minor so long as either of the minor's parents is living and such parent is a fit and proper person to have custody of the minor. ...

§ 64.2-1702. Appointment of guardians.

The circuit court... may appoint a guardian for the estate of the minor and may appoint a guardian for the person of the minor unless a guardian has been appointed   for   the   minor   pursuant   to   §   64.2-1701.

§ 64.2-1703. Nomination of guardians.

A. A minor who is at least 14 years old may... nominate his own guardian for the estate or person of the minor, who shall be appointed if the court or clerk find that the guardian nominated is suitable and competent. ...

B. In no case shall any person not related to the minor be appointed guardian until 30 days have elapsed since the death or disqualification of any natural or testamentary guardians and the minor's next of kin have had an opportunity to petition the court for appointment ..

§ 64.2-1704. Guardian's bond.

Before any person may be appointed the guardian for the estate of a minor, the person... shall take an oath that he will faithfully perform the duties of his office to the best of his judgment and give his bond in an amount at least equal to the value of the minor's personal estate coming under his control... unless it is waived.... [by the court] or... by the testator's will. ...

Chapter 18. Custody and Care of Ward and Estate.

§ 64.2-1800. Custody, care, and education of ward; ward's estate.

Unless a guardian of the person of a minor is appointed..., a guardian of a minor's estate... shall have custody of his ward. The guardian of a minor's estate... shall provide for the minor's health, education, maintenance, and support from the income of the minor's estate and, if income is not sufficient, from the corpus of the minor's estate.

§ 64.2-1801. Parental duty of support.

Notwithstanding... § 64.2-1800, a guardian of a minor's estate shall not make any distribution of income or corpus of the minor's estate to or for the benefit of a ward who has a living parent... except to the extent that the distribution is authorized by (i) the deed, will, or other instrument under which the estate is derived or (ii) the circuit court, upon a finding that (a) the parent is unable to completely fulfill the parental duty of supporting the minor, (b) the parent cannot for some reason be required to provide such support, or (c) a proposed distribution is beyond the scope of parental duty of support in the circumstances of a specific case. ...

§ 64.2-1803. Termination of guardianship.

Unless the guardian of a minor's estate dies, is removed, or resigns the guardianship, the guardian shall continue in office until the minor attains the age of majority or, in the case of testamentary guardianship, until the termination of the period set forth in the testator's will. At the expiration of the guardianship, the guardian shall deliver and pay all the estate and money in his possession, or with which he is chargeable, to the person entitled to receive such estate and money.

§ 64.2-1804. Powers of courts over guardians.

The circuit courts may... remove any guardian for neglect or breach of trust and appoint another guardian for the ward, and make any order for the custody, health, maintenance, education, and support of a ward and the management, disbursement, preservation, and investment of the ward's estate.

§ 64.2-1805. Powers of guardian.

A. ... [A] guardian of a ward's estate shall have the powers set forth in § 64.2-105 [above] ... A guardian of a ward's estate shall also have the following powers:

1. To ratify or reject a contract entered into by the ward;

2. To pay any sum distributable for the benefit of the ward by paying the sum directly to the ward, to the provider of goods and services that have been furnished to the ward..., or to a ward's custodian...;

3. To maintain life, health, casualty, and liability insurance for the benefit of the ward;...

6. To initiate a proceeding to seek a divorce or to make an augmented estate election...; and

7. To borrow money... [and] pledge such portion of the ward's personal estate, and real estate... as may be required to secure such loan...

***

Someone who wishes to confer wealth on a minor through a will, non-probate instrument, or lifetime gift might identify an adult to hold and manage the wealth for the minor.

Chapter 19. Virginia Uniform Transfers to Minors Act.

§ 64.2-1900. Definitions.

… "Conservator" means a person appointed or qualified by a court to act as… guardian of a minor's property or… authorized to perform substantially the same functions. …

"Member of the minor's family" means the minor's parent, stepparent, spouse, grandparent, brother, sister, uncle, or aunt, whether of the whole or half blood or by adoption. …

§ 64.2-1902. Nomination of custodian.

A. A person having the right to designate the recipient of property transferable upon the occurrence of a future event may revocably nominate a custodian to receive the property for a minor beneficiary upon the occurrence of the event by naming the custodian followed in substance by the words: "as custodian for .... (name of minor) under the Virginia Uniform Transfers to Minors Act."
…

§ 64.2-1903. Transfer by gift or exercise of power of appointment.

A person may make a transfer by irrevocable gift to, or the irrevocable exercise of a power of appointment in favor of, a custodian for the benefit of a minor...

§ 64.2-1904. Transfer authorized by will or trust.

… If the testator or settlor has not nominated a custodian… or all persons so nominated as custodian die before the transfer or are unable, decline, or are ineligible to serve, the personal representative or the trustee shall designate the custodian from among those eligible to serve as custodian for property of that kind under subsection A of § 64.2-1908.

§ 64.2-1905. Other transfer by fiduciary.

A. … [A] personal representative or trustee may make an irrevocable transfer to an adult or trust company as custodian for the benefit of a minor pursuant to § 64.2-1908 in the absence of a will or under a will or trust that does not contain an authorization to do so.

B. [same authorization for a conservator to make a transfer] …

§ 64.2-1906. Transfer by obligor.

A. ... [A] person not subject to § 64.2-1904 or who holds property of or owes a liquidated debt to a minor not having a conservator may make an irrevocable transfer to a custodian for the benefit of the minor pursuant to § 64.2-1908.

B. If a person having the right to do so under § 64.2-1902 has nominated a custodian under that section to receive the custodial property, the transfer shall be made to that person.

C. If no custodian has been nominated... a transfer under this section may be made to an adult member of the minor's family or to a trust company unless the property exceeds $25,000 in value, in which event the transfer may be made if authorized by the court.

§ 64.2-1908. Manner of creating custodial property and effecting transfer; designation of initial custodian; control.

A. Custodial property is created and a transfer is made whenever: ... [the transferor registers the property] in the name of the transferor, an adult other than the transferor, or a trust company, followed in substance by the words: "as custodian for _____ (name of minor) under the Virginia Uniform Transfers to Minors Act"; or ... [delivers or assigns the property with a writing] to an adult other than the transferor or to a trust company... "as custodian for _____ (name of minor) under the Virginia Uniform Transfers to Minors Act." ...

B. An instrument in the following form satisfies the requirements...

TRANSFER UNDER VIRGINIA UNIFORM TRANSFERS TO MINORS ACT

I, _____ (name of transferor or name and representative capacity if a fiduciary) hereby transfer to _____ (name of custodian), as custodian for _____ (name of minor) under the Virginia Uniform Transfers to Minors Act, the following: (insert a description of the custodial property sufficient to identify it).

Dated: _____

_____
(Signature)

_____ (name of custodian) acknowledges receipt of the property described above as custodian for the minor named above under the Virginia Uniform Transfers to Minors Act.

Dated: _____

_____
Signature of Custodian)

...

§ 64.2-1910. Validity and effect of transfer.

A. The validity of a transfer made in a manner prescribed in this chapter is not affected by... [d]esignation of an ineligible custodian or... [d]eath or incapacity of a person nominated under § 64.2-1902 or designated under § 64.2-1908 as custodian or the disclaimer of the office by that person.

B. A transfer made pursuant to § 64.2-1908 is irrevocable, and the custodial property is indefeasibly vested in the minor, but the custodian has all the rights, powers, duties, and authority provided in this chapter and neither the minor nor the minor's legal representative has any right, power, duty, or authority with respect to the custodial property except as provided in this chapter.

C. By making a transfer, the transferor incorporates in the disposition all the provisions of this chapter...

§ 64.2-1911. Care of custodial property; duties of custodian.

A. A custodian shall take control of custodial property, register or record title to custodial property, if appropriate, and collect, hold, manage, invest, and reinvest custodial property.

B. In dealing with custodial property, a custodian shall observe the standard of care set forth in the Uniform Prudent Investor Act... However, a custodian, in the custodian's discretion and without liability to the minor or the minor's estate, may retain any custodial property received from a transferor. ...

E. A custodian shall keep records of all transactions... and shall make them available for inspection... by a parent or legal representative of the minor or by the minor if the minor has attained the age of 14 years.

§ 64.2-1912. Powers of custodian.

A custodian, acting in a custodial capacity, has all the rights, powers, and authority over custodial property that unmarried adult owners have over their own property...

§ 64.2-1913. Use of custodial property.

A. A custodian may deliver or pay to the minor or expend for the minor's benefit so much of the custodial property as the custodian considers advisable... without regard to (i) the duty or ability... of any other person to support the minor or (ii) any other income or property of the minor which may be... available for that purpose.

B. At any time a custodian may, without court order, transfer all or part of the custodial property to a qualified minor's trust. ...

C. On petition of an interested person or the minor if the minor has attained the age of 14 years, the court may order the custodian to deliver or pay to the minor or expend for the minor's benefit so much of the custodial property as the court considers advisable...

§ 64.2-1914. Custodian's expenses, compensation, and bond.

A. A custodian is entitled to reimbursement from custodial property for reasonable expenses incurred in the performance of the custodian's duties.

B. A custodian, other than one who is a transferor under § 64.2-1903, has a noncumulative election... to charge reasonable compensation....

§ 64.2-1917. Renunciation, resignation, death, or removal of custodian...

... F. A transferor,... an adult member of the minor's family, a guardian of the person of the minor, the conservator of the minor, or the minor, if the minor has attained the age of 14 years, may petition the court to (i) remove the custodian for cause and to designate a successor custodian... or (ii) require the custodian to give appropriate bond.

§ 64.2-1919. Termination of custodianship.

The custodian shall transfer the custodial property to the minor... upon the... minor's attainment of 18 years of age...

IV.   Health Care and End of Life Decisions

An important consideration in clients' financial planning is the cost associated with declining health and incapacity. In addition, clients ideally should make decisions while competent about what sort of care they wish to receive if and when they do become incapacitated or who they would wish to make such decisions for them.

A. Government Assistance With Health and Dependent Care

Medicare is a state-administered (though partly federally-funded) program that provides persons 65 or older, without regard to wealth or income, with no-cost coverage for short-term stays in a hospital or nursing facility. Other aspects of Medicare operate like a subsidized health care plan, charging monthly premiums and covering doctors' services, outpatient care, medical supplies, preventive services, and prescription drugs.

More important to end-of-life planning for most people is the state-administered (but partly federally-funded) Medicaid program, which was created to ensure proper medical and institutional for people who are poor. For persons entering a nursing home, Medicaid will begin paying the bills only after a client's assets have dissipated to a low level. The rules for qualification are complicated, contained in an enormous manual available at the website for Virginia's Department of Medical Assistance Services http://dmasva.dmas.virginia.gov/Content_pgs/rcp-elmanual.aspx.

There are two related aims clients typically have that can be in tension with each other when it comes to Medicaid eligibility: 1) They want to pass on some of their wealth to loved ones, but 2) They do not want to be in a situation in which they cannot afford the care they need but they cannot yet qualify for Medicaid because they have transferred to loved ones wealth they could have used for their care. The law does not permit a wealthy person to give away all their wealth to others and then ask for the government to pay for their stay in a nursing home; it presumes that people should use nearly all of their own wealth to pay for their own care before they ask the government to help them (even though they likely have been paying taxes into the Medicaid fund throughout their adult lives). The rules for qualification and coverage vary to some degree by state.

In Virginia, persons who are age 65 or older, blind, or disabled are eligible for Medicaid if their income (including Social Security benefits, pensions, wages, interest, dividends, etc.) is three times the level of the Supplemental Security Income (SSI) amount for an individual ($2,199 for 2015) or less and if their "countable resources" are at or below a certain low level ($2,000 for a single person). Countable resources include everything a person owns that could be converted to cash and that are not currently needed for daily living, so would include bank accounts, stocks, bonds, cash value of some life insurance policies, and other property "that does not adjoin your home." Initially excluded from resources for persons entering a care facility, just in case they might return home, are their "home and adjoining property." The exclusion last for six months or for as long as a spouse or dependent child remains living in the home. Permanently excluded are the value of burial plots, life estates, and most tangible personal property (car, furniture, jewelry). So can a person just about to enter a nursing home simply transfer all his or her wealth to family members and immediately apply for Medicaid? There are two reasons not to do this.

One reason not to give away the farm is that many of the better nursing homes pick and choose whom they admit as residents, and they tend to disfavor applicants who are on Medicaid from the outset, because Medicaid will only pay them a limited amount, an amount that is typically less than the facility's normal charge – that is, what they charge "private pay" residents. So at least in some locations, if you want admission to the nicest facility, you will likely need to be in a financial position to offer the facility private pay for at least a couple of years. A couple of years at the average nice nursing home costs a couple of hundred thousand dollars. Persons who are indigent when they first seek to enter a nursing home are likely to be stuck with "the county home."

The second reason is that the Medicaid program has "look back" rules, designed precisely to prevent wealthy people from making themselves eligible for government assistance, that treat an applicant as still owning any wealth they transferred during a particular period of time prior to applying. In Virginia, this is five years. So gifts to one's children of a quarter million dollars in assets immediately before entering a nursing home will result in one's being ineligible for Medicaid for as long as that quarter million dollars would have covered the cost of the nursing home. (Or if it were a million dollars, ineligibility would be for five years, the full-length of the look back period, given that a million dollar would pay for more than five years of care in any but the toniest of nursing homes.)

The rules for elibility are far more complicated than this brief summary could convey. The paradox for people who want to engage in "Medicaid planning" is that lawyers are ethically constrained in assisting clients to do this – that is, artificially to create eligibility for a government benefit. And the irony is that, to the extent affluence correlates with educational level or intellectual ability, more affluent people will be more able than less affluent people to create an artificial need for government assistance – in other words, will be better able to preserve their wealth for family members instead of paying their own way in a nursing home, if they can comprehend the complex rules without the assistance of a lawyer.

B. Health Care Decision Making

Advance planning for health care decision making in the event of incapacity can take the form of specifying one's wishes as to what should be done in certain circumstances or of appointing another person to make decisions on one's behalf. Virginia law combines these two approaches in a document called an "advance directive" and specifies the requirements for the directive to be effective. An advance directive can also provide instructions regarding donation of organs or one's entire body, for medical care or research purposes, upon one's death. In the absence of an effective advance directive or health care proxy, the Code establishes a priority list for choosing someone to make surrogate medical decisions for an incompetent persons.

Title 54.1. Professions and Occupations
Subtitle III. Professions and Occupations Regulated by Boards Within the
Department of Health Professions
Chapter 29. Medicine and Other Healing Arts
Article 8. Health Care Decisions Act

§ 54.1-2982. Definitions

… "Capacity reviewer" means a licensed physician or clinical psychologist who is qualified by training or experience to assess whether a person is capable or incapable of making an informed decision. …

"Durable Do Not Resuscitate Order" means a written physician's order… to withhold cardiopulmonary resuscitation from a particular patient in the event of cardiac or respiratory arrest. For purposes of this article, cardiopulmonary resuscitation shall include cardiac compression, endotracheal intubation and other advanced airway management, artificial ventilation, and defibrillation and related procedures. …

"Health care" means the furnishing of services to any individual for the purpose of preventing, alleviating, curing, or healing human illness, injury or physical disability, including but not limited to, medications; surgery; blood transfusions; chemotherapy; radiation therapy; admission to a hospital, nursing home, assisted living facility, or other health care facility; psychiatric or other mental health treatment; and life-prolonging procedures and palliative care.

"Incapable of making an informed decision" means the inability of an adult patient, because of mental illness, intellectual disability, or any other mental or physical disorder that precludes communication or impairs judgment, to make an informed decision about providing, continuing, withholding or withdrawing a specific health care treatment or course of treatment because he is unable to understand the nature, extent or probable consequences of the proposed health care decision, or to make a rational evaluation of the risks and benefits of alternatives to that decision. ...

"Patient care consulting committee" means a committee duly organized by a facility licensed to provide health care..., or a hospital or nursing home... owned or operated by an agency of the Commonwealth that is exempt from licensure..., to consult on health care issues only... Each patient care consulting committee shall consist of five individuals, including at least one physician, one person licensed or holding a multistate licensure privilege... to practice professional nursing, and one individual responsible for the provision of social services to patients of the facility. At least one committee member shall have experience in clinical ethics and at least two committee members shall have no employment or contractual relationship with the facility or any involvement in the management, operations, or governance of the facility, other than serving on the patient care consulting committee. ...

"Persistent vegetative state" means a condition caused by injury, disease or illness in which a patient has suffered a loss of consciousness, with no behavioral evidence of self-awareness or awareness of surroundings in a learned manner, other than reflex activity of muscles and nerves for low level conditioned response, and from which, to a reasonable degree of medical probability, there can be no recovery. ...

"Terminal condition" means a condition caused by injury, disease or illness from which, to a reasonable degree of medical probability a patient cannot recover and (i) the patient's death is imminent or (ii) the patient is in a persistent vegetative state.

§ 54.1-2983. Procedure for making advance directive; notice to physician

Any adult capable of making an informed decision may, at any time, make a written advance directive to address any or all forms of health care in the event the declarant is later determined to be incapable of making an informed decision. A written advance directive shall be signed by the declarant in the presence of two subscribing witnesses and may (i) specify the health care the declarant does or does not authorize; (ii) appoint an agent to make health care decisions for the declarant; and (iii) specify an anatomical gift, after the declarant's death, of all of the declarant's body or an organ, tissue or eye donation... A written advance directive may be submitted to the Advance Health Care Directive Registry...

Further, any adult capable of making an informed decision who has been diagnosed by his attending physician as being in a terminal condition may make an oral advance directive (i) directing the specific health care the declarant does or does not authorize in the event the declarant is incapable of making an informed decision, and (ii) appointing an agent to make health care decisions for the declarant under the circumstances stated in the advance directive if the declarant should be determined to be incapable of making an informed decision. An oral advance directive shall be made in the presence of the attending physician and two witnesses.

An advance directive may authorize an agent to take any lawful actions necessary to carry out the declarant's decisions, including, but not limited to, granting releases of liability to medical providers, releasing medical records, and making decisions regarding who may visit the patient.

It shall be the responsibility of the declarant to provide for notification to his attending physician that an advance directive has been made. ... In the event the declarant is comatose, incapacitated or otherwise mentally or physically incapable of communication, any other person may notify the physician of the existence of an advance directive... An attending physician who is so notified shall promptly make the advance directive... a part of the declarant's medical records.

§ 54.1-2983.2. Capacity; required determinations

A. Every adult shall be presumed to be capable of making an informed decision unless he is determined to be incapable of making an informed decision in accordance with this article. A determination that a patient is incapable of making an informed decision may apply to a particular health care decision, to a specified set of health care decisions, or to all health care decisions. No person shall be deemed incapable of making an informed decision based solely on a particular clinical diagnosis.

B. Prior to providing, continuing, withholding, or withdrawing health care pursuant to an authorization that has been obtained or will be sought pursuant to this article..., the attending physician shall certify in writing upon personal examination of the patient that the patient is incapable of making an informed decision regarding health care and shall obtain written certification from a capacity reviewer that, based upon a personal examination of the patient, the patient is incapable of making an informed decision. ...

D. A single physician may, at any time, upon personal evaluation, determine that a patient who has previously been determined to be incapable of making an informed decision is now capable of making an informed decision...

§ 54.1-2984. Suggested form of written advance directives

An advance directive executed pursuant to this article may, but need not, be in the following form:

ADVANCE MEDICAL DIRECTIVE

I, _____, willingly and voluntarily make known my wishes in the event that I am incapable of making an informed decision, as follows:

I understand that my advance directive may include the selection of an agent as well as set forth my choices regarding health care.

The term "health care" means [copied from § 54.1-2982].

The phrase "incapable of making an informed decision" means [copied from § 54.1-2982].

The determination that I am incapable of making an informed decision shall be made by... [copied from § 54.1-2983.2].

If, at any time, I am determined to be incapable of making an informed decision, I shall be notified...

(SELECT ANY OR ALL OF THE OPTIONS BELOW.)

OPTION I: APPOINTMENT OF AGENT (CROSS THROUGH OPTIONS I AND II BELOW IF YOU DO NOT WANT TO APPOINT AN AGENT TO MAKE HEALTH CARE DECISIONS FOR YOU.)

I hereby appoint _____ (primary agent), of _____ (address and telephone number), as my agent to make health care decisions on my behalf as authorized in this document. If _____ (primary agent) is not reasonably available or is unable or unwilling to act as my agent, then I appoint _____ (successor agent), of _____ (address and telephone number), to serve in that capacity.

I hereby grant to my agent, named above, full power and authority to make health care decisions on my behalf as described below whenever I have been determined to be incapable of making an informed decision. My agent's authority hereunder is effective as long as I am incapable of making an informed decision.

In exercising the power to make health care decisions on my behalf, my agent shall follow my desires and preferences as stated in this document or as otherwise known to my agent. My agent shall be guided by my medical diagnosis and prognosis and any information provided by my physicians as to the intrusiveness, pain, risks, and side effects associated with treatment or nontreatment. My agent shall not make any decision regarding my health care which he knows, or upon reasonable inquiry ought to know, is contrary to my religious beliefs or my basic values, whether expressed orally or in writing. If my agent cannot determine what health care choice I would have made on my own behalf, then my agent shall make a choice for me based upon what he believes to be in my best interests.

OPTION II: POWERS OF MY AGENT (CROSS THROUGH ANY
LANGUAGE YOU DO NOT WANT AND ADD ANY LANGUAGE YOU
DO WANT.)

The powers of my agent shall include the following:

A. To consent to or refuse or withdraw consent to any type of health care, treatment, surgical procedure, diagnostic procedure, medication and the use of mechanical or other procedures that affect any bodily function, including, but not limited to, artificial respiration, artificially administered nutrition and hydration, and cardiopulmonary resuscitation. This authorization specifically includes the power to consent to the administration of dosages of pain-relieving medication in excess of recommended dosages in an amount sufficient to relieve pain, even if such medication carries the risk of addiction or of inadvertently hastening my death;

B. To request, receive, and review any information, verbal or written, regarding my physical or mental health, including but not limited to, medical and hospital records, and to consent to the disclosure of this information;

C. To employ and discharge my health care providers;

D. To authorize my admission to or discharge (including transfer to another facility) from any hospital, hospice, nursing home, assisted living facility or other medical care facility. If I have authorized admission to a health care facility for treatment of mental illness, that authority is stated elsewhere in this advance directive;

E. To authorize my admission to a health care facility for the treatment of mental illness for no more than 10 calendar days provided I do not protest the admission and a physician on the staff of or designated by the proposed admitting facility examines me and states in writing that I have a mental illness and I am incapable of making an informed decision about my admission, and that I need treatment in the facility; and to authorize my discharge (including transfer to another facility) from the facility;

F. To authorize my admission to a health care facility for the treatment of mental illness for no more than 10 calendar days, even over my protest, if a physician on the staff of or designated by the proposed admitting facility examines me and states in writing that I have a mental illness and I am incapable of making an informed decision about my admission, and that I need treatment in the facility; and to authorize my discharge (including transfer to another facility) from the facility. [My physician or licensed clinical psychologist hereby attests that I am capable of making an informed decision and that I understand the consequences of this provision of my advance directive: _____];

G. To authorize the specific types of health care identified in this advance directive [specify cross-reference to other sections of directive] even over my protest. [My physician or licensed clinical psychologist hereby attests that I am capable of making an informed decision and that I understand the consequences of this provision of my advance directive: _____];

H. To continue to serve as my agent even in the event that I protest the agent's authority after I have been determined to be incapable of making an informed decision;

I. To authorize my participation in any health care study approved by an institutional review board or research review committee according to applicable federal or state law that offers the prospect of direct therapeutic benefit to me;

J. To authorize my participation in any health care study approved by an institutional review board or research review committee pursuant to applicable federal or state law that aims to increase scientific understanding of any condition that I may have or otherwise to promote human well-being, even though it offers no prospect of direct benefit to me;

K. To make decisions regarding visitation during any time that I am admitted to any health care facility, consistent with the following directions: _____; and

L. To take any lawful actions that may be necessary to carry out these decisions, including the granting of releases of liability to medical providers. Further, my agent shall not be liable for the costs of health care pursuant to his authorization, based solely on that authorization.

OPTION III: HEALTH CARE INSTRUCTIONS

(CROSS THROUGH PARAGRAPHS A AND/OR B IF YOU DO NOT WANT TO GIVE ADDITIONAL SPECIFIC INSTRUCTIONS.)

A. I specifically direct that I receive the following health care if it is medically appropriate under the circumstances as determined by my attending physician: _____.

B. I specifically direct that the following health care not be provided to me under the following circumstances (you may specify that certain health care not be provided under any circumstances): _____.

OPTION IV: END OF LIFE INSTRUCTIONS

(CROSS THROUGH THIS OPTION IF YOU DO NOT WANT TO GIVE INSTRUCTIONS IN CASE YOU HAVE A TERMINAL CONDITION.)

If at any time my attending physician should determine that I have a terminal condition where the application of life-prolonging procedures-- including artificial respiration, cardiopulmonary resuscitation, artificially administered nutrition, and artificially administered hydration--would serve only to artificially prolong the dying process, I direct that such procedures be withheld or withdrawn, and that I be permitted to die naturally with only the administration of medication or the performance of any medical procedure deemed necessary to provide me with comfort care or to alleviate pain.

OPTION: LIFE-PROLONGING PROCEDURES DURING PREGNANCY. (If you wish to provide additional instructions or modifications to instructions you have already given regarding life-prolonging procedures that will apply if you are pregnant at the time your attending physician determines that you have a terminal condition, you may do so here.)

If I am pregnant when my attending physician determines that I have a terminal condition, my decision concerning life-prolonging procedures shall be modified as follows:

OPTION: OTHER DIRECTIONS ABOUT LIFE-PROLONGING PROCEDURES. (If you wish to provide your own directions, or if you wish to add to the directions you have given above, you may do so here. If you wish to give specific instructions regarding certain life-prolonging procedures, such as artificial respiration, cardiopulmonary resuscitation, artificially administered nutrition, and artificially administered hydration, this is where you should write them.) I direct that:

OPTION: My other instructions regarding my care if I have a terminal condition are as follows:

In the absence of my ability to give directions regarding the use of such life-prolonging procedures, it is my intention that this advance directive shall be honored by my family and physician as the final expression of my legal right to refuse health care and acceptance of the consequences of such refusal.

OPTION V: APPOINTMENT OF AN AGENT TO MAKE AN ANATOMICAL GIFT OR ORGAN, TISSUE OR EYE DONATION (CROSS THROUGH IF YOU DO NOT WANT TO APPOINT AN AGENT TO MAKE AN ANATOMICAL GIFT OR ANY ORGAN, TISSUE OR EYE DONATION FOR YOU.)

Upon my death, I direct that an anatomical gift of all of my body or certain organ, tissue or eye donations may be made pursuant to Article 2 (§ 32.1-289.2 et seq.) of Chapter 8 of Title 32.1 and in accordance with my directions, if any. I hereby appoint _____ as my agent, of _____ (address and telephone number), to make any such anatomical gift or organ, tissue or eye donation following my death. I further direct that: _____ (declarant's directions concerning anatomical gift or organ, tissue or eye donation).

This advance directive shall not terminate in the event of my disability.

AFFIRMATION AND RIGHT TO REVOKE: By signing below, I indicate that I am emotionally and mentally capable of making this advance directive and that I understand the purpose and effect of this document. I understand I may revoke all or any part of this document at any time (i) with a signed, dated writing; (ii) by physical cancellation or destruction of this advance directive by myself or by directing someone else to destroy it in my presence; or (iii) by my oral expression of intent to revoke.

(Date)
        (Signature of Declarant)

The declarant signed the foregoing advance directive in my presence.

(Witness)

(Witness)

§ 54.1-2985. Revocation of an advance directive

A. An advance directive may be revoked at any time by the declarant who is capable of understanding the nature and consequences of his actions (i) by a signed, dated writing; (ii) by physical cancellation or destruction of the advance directive by the declarant or another in his presence and at his direction; or (iii) by oral expression of intent to revoke. A declarant may make a partial revocation of his advance directive... Any such revocation shall be effective when communicated to the attending physician. ..

B. If an advance directive has been submitted to the Advance Health Care Directive Registry ..., any revocation of such directive shall also be notarized before being submitted to the Department of Health for removal from the registry. However, failure to notify the Department of Health of the revocation of a document filed with the registry shall not affect the validity of the revocation, as long as it meets the requirements of subsection A.

§ 54.1-2986. Procedure in absence of an advance directive; procedure for advance directive without agent; no presumption; persons who may authorize health care for patients incapable of informed decisions

A. Whenever a patient is determined to be incapable of making an informed decision and (i) has not made an advance directive in accordance with this article or (ii) has made an advance directive in accordance with this article that does not indicate his wishes with respect to the health care at issue and does not appoint an agent, the attending physician may, upon compliance with the provisions of this section, provide, continue, withhold or withdraw health care upon the authorization of any of the following persons, in the specified order of priority, if the physician is not aware of any available, willing and capable person in a higher class:

1. A guardian for the patient. ...; or

2. The patient's spouse except where a divorce action has been filed...; or

3. An adult child of the patient; or

4. A parent of the patient; or

5. An adult brother or sister of the patient; or

6. Any other relative of the patient in the descending order of blood relationship; or

7. Except in cases in which the proposed treatment recommendation involves the withholding... a life-prolonging procedure, any adult, except any director, employee, or agent of a health care provider currently involved in the care of the patient, who (i) has exhibited special care and concern for the patient and (ii) is familiar with the patient's religious beliefs and basic values and any preferences previously expressed by the patient regarding health care, to the extent that they are known. ...

If two or more of the persons listed in the same class in subdivisions A 3 through A 7 with equal decision-making priority inform the attending physician that they disagree as to a particular health care decision, the attending physician may rely on the authorization of a majority of the reasonably available members of that class.

B. Regardless of the absence of an advance directive, if the patient has expressed his intent to be an organ donor in any written document, no person noted in this section shall revoke, or in any way hinder, such organ donation.

§ 54.1-2986.1. Duties and authority of agent or person identified in § 54.1-2986

A. If the declarant appoints an agent in an advance directive, that agent shall have (i) the authority to make health care decisions for the declarant as specified in the advance directive if the declarant is determined to be incapable of making an informed decision and (ii) decision-making priority over any person identified in §

54.1-2986. In no case shall the agent refuse or fail to honor the declarant's wishes in relation to anatomical gifts or organ, tissue or eye donation. Decisions to restrict visitation of the patient may be made by an agent only if the declarant has expressly included provisions for visitation in his advance directive; such visitation decisions shall be subject to physician orders and policies of the institution to which the declarant is admitted. No person authorized to make decisions for a patient under § 54.1-2986 shall have authority to restrict visitation of the patient.

B. Any agent or person authorized to make health care decisions pursuant to this article shall (i) undertake a good faith effort to ascertain the risks and benefits of, and alternatives to any proposed health care, (ii) make a good faith effort to ascertain the religious values, basic values, and previously expressed preferences of the patient, and (iii) to the extent possible, base his decisions on the beliefs, values, and preferences of the patient, or if they are unknown, on the patient's best interests.

§ 54.1-2986.2. Health care decisions in the event of patient protest

A. Except as provided in subsection B or C, the provisions of this article shall not authorize providing, continuing, withholding or withdrawing health care if the patient's attending physician knows that such action is protested by the patient.

B. A patient's agent may make a health care decision over the protest of a patient who is incapable of making an informed decision if:

1. The patient's advance directive explicitly authorizes the patient's agent to make the health care decision at issue, even over the patient's later protest, and the patient's attending physician or licensed clinical psychologist attested in writing at the time the advance directive was made that the patient was capable of making an informed decision and understood the consequences of the provision;

2. The decision does not involve withholding or withdrawing life-prolonging procedures; and

3. The health care that is to be provided, continued, withheld or withdrawn is determined and documented by the patient's attending physician to be medically appropriate and is otherwise permitted by law.

C. In cases in which a patient has not explicitly authorized his agent to make the health care decision at issue over the patient's later protest, a patient's agent or person authorized to make decisions pursuant to § 54.1-2986 may make a decision over the protest of a patient who is incapable of making an informed decision if:

1. The decision does not involve withholding or withdrawing life-prolonging procedures;

2. The decision does not involve (i) admission to a facility as defined in § 37.2-100 or (ii) treatment or care that is subject to regulations adopted pursuant to § 37.2-400;

3. The health care decision is based, to the extent known, on the patient's religious beliefs and basic values and on any preferences previously expressed by the patient in an advance directive or otherwise regarding such health care or, if they are unknown, is in the patient's best interests;

4. The health care that is to be provided, continued, withheld, or withdrawn has been determined and documented by the patient's attending physician to be medically appropriate and is otherwise permitted by law; and

5. The health care that is to be provided, continued, withheld, or withdrawn has been affirmed and documented as being ethically acceptable by the health care facility's patient care consulting committee, if one exists, or otherwise by two physicians not currently involved in the patient's care or in the determination of the patient's capacity to make health care decisions.

D. A patient's protest shall not revoke the patient's advance directive unless it meets the requirements of § 54.1-2985.

E. If a patient protests the authority of a named agent or any person authorized to make health care decisions by § 54.1-2986, except for the patient's guardian, the protested individual shall have no authority under this article to make health care decisions on his behalf unless the patient's advance directive explicitly confers continuing authority on his agent, even over his later protest. If the protested individual is denied authority under this subsection, authority to make health care decisions shall be determined by any other provisions of the patient's advance directive, or in accordance with § 54.1-2986 or in accordance with any other provision of law.

§ 54.1-2987.1. Durable Do Not Resuscitate Orders

A. A Durable Do Not Resuscitate Order may be issued by a physician for his patient with whom he has a bona fide physician/patient relationship…, and only with the consent of the patient or, if the patient is a minor or is otherwise incapable of making an informed decision regarding consent for such an order, upon the request of and with the consent of the person authorized to consent on the patient's behalf.

B. If a patient is able to, and does, express to a health care provider or practitioner the desire to be resuscitated in the event of cardiac or respiratory arrest, such expression shall revoke the provider's or practitioner's authority to follow a Durable Do Not Resuscitate Order. In no case shall any person other than the patient have authority to revoke a Durable Do Not Resuscitate Order executed upon the request of and with the consent of the patient himself.

If the patient is a minor or is otherwise incapable of making an informed decision and the Durable Do Not Resuscitate Order was issued upon the request of and with the consent of the person authorized to consent on the patient's behalf, then the expression by said authorized person to a health care provider or practitioner of the desire that the patient be resuscitated shall so revoke the provider's or practitioner's authority to follow a Durable Do Not Resuscitate Order. ...

§ 54.1-2990. Medically unnecessary health care not required...

A. Nothing in this article shall be construed to require a physician to prescribe or render health care to a patient that the physician determines to be medically or ethically inappropriate. However, in such a case, if the physician's determination is contrary to the request of the patient, the terms of a patient's advance directive, the decision of an agent or person authorized to make decisions..., or a Durable Do Not Resuscitate Order, the physician shall make a reasonable effort to inform the patient or the patient's agent or person with decision-making authority... If the conflict remains unresolved, the physician shall make a reasonable effort to transfer the patient to another physician...

D. Nothing in this article shall be construed to condone, authorize or approve mercy killing or euthanasia, or to permit any affirmative or deliberate act or omission to end life other than to permit the natural process of dying.

§ 54.1-2991. Effect of declaration; suicide; insurance...

The withholding or withdrawal of life-prolonging procedures in accordance with the provisions of this article shall not, for any purpose, constitute a suicide. Nor shall the making of an advance directive pursuant to this article affect the sale, procurement or issuance of any policy of life insurance, nor shall the making of an advance directive or the issuance of a Durable Do Not Resuscitate Order pursuant to this article be deemed to modify the terms of an existing policy of life insurance. No policy of life insurance shall be legally impaired or invalidated by the withholding or withdrawal of life-prolonging procedures from an insured patient in accordance with this article, notwithstanding any term of the policy to the contrary. A person shall not be required to make an advance directive... as a condition for being insured...

***

The emphasis in this article of Title 54.1 is on designating a person to act as ongoing agent for an incapacitated individual, and defining the scope of the agent's authority. Another Title of the Virginia Code, though, Title 37.2, which used to contain the statutory provisions regarding guardianship and conservatorship, contains a chapter entitled Judicial Authorization of Treatment that empowers a court to order medical interventions in the absence of a private proxy consent. A case that ended at the Court of Appeals tested the limits of the court's power.

Court of Appeals of Virginia.
Cavuoto v. Buchanan County Dept. of Social Services
44 Va.App. 326, 605 S.E.2d 287 (2004)

FELTON, Judge.

Linda Cavuoto (appellant) appeals that portion of the judgment of the Circuit Court of Buchanan County requiring her to undergo medical examination and evaluation at the University of Virginia Medical Center. ....

*328 Appellant is a fifty-one-year-old woman suffering from morbid obesity and depression. She had been disabled for some three years when she moved with her husband to Virginia. She had been bedridden for more **288 than two years. The Buchanan County Department of Social Services (DSS) became involved with appellant in November 2002 after determining she was in need of adult protective services.

Following a fire in the house in which appellant and her husband resided, DSS obtained an emergency court order on December 3, 2003, committing appellant involuntarily to Heritage Hall, a nursing home.[2]

> [2] Pursuant to Code §§ 63.2–1608 and –1609, a court may order involuntary adult protective services through an emergency order "if an adult lacks the capacity to consent to receive adult protective services." Code § 63.2–1608(A).

On December 9, 2003, the trial court extended the temporary order for an additional five days.

On December 15, 2003, DSS filed a Petition for Treatment and Detention pursuant to Code § 37.1–134.21 seeking a court order authorizing placement of appellant in a nursing home to provide her with care and treatment. DSS asserted that appellant was incapable of making informed health care decisions because of her depression and was incapable of properly caring for herself. DSS also asserted that appellant had been uncooperative while she was a patient at Heritage Hall.

Caroline Thompson Schleifer, a licensed professional counselor, testified as to the results of a psychosocial evaluation of appellant she conducted on December 5, 2003 at Heritage Hall. Based on her evaluation of appellant, she opined that appellant understood the purpose of *329 the evaluation and provided pertinent information regarding her medical history. Appellant informed Schleifer of her history of depression and of treatment she received prior to moving to Virginia. Schleifer noted that appellant expressed suicidal thoughts and feelings of "helplessness and hopelessness" as a result of her deteriorating health and financial circumstances. Although she testified that appellant suffered "from depression brought on by major life stressors," Schleifer opined that appellant's depression did not impair her ability to make informed decisions concerning her health. She advised the trial court that appellant needed additional evaluation at a more comprehensive medical center; that Heritage Hall was not meeting all of appellant's medical needs; and that "[appellant] may be a good candidate for going to the University of Virginia and having a complete orthopedic and diagnostic work up with regard to [her medical condition]."

After hearing the evidence, the trial court found "that despite her depression, appellant is capable of making informed health care decisions." It ordered her released to her husband's care from the nursing home, where she had been confined pursuant to the emergency protective order. Nevertheless, relying on Schleifer's recommendation of the need for further evaluation and her opinion that Heritage Hall could not meet appellant's needs, the trial court ordered appellant to undergo a comprehensive examination and evaluation to address her depression and obesity and that DSS schedule an appointment at the University of Virginia Medical Center for that purpose.

ANALYSIS

On appeal, appellant... argues that because the trial court found that she was capable of making informed health care decisions, it lacked authority pursuant to Code § 37.1–134.21 to order her to undergo the medical examination and evaluation. ...*330 ...

In general, a mentally competent adult has the right to refuse medical treatment. **289 See Cruzan v. Director, Missouri Dept. of Health, 497 U.S. 261, 262, 110 S.Ct. 2841, 2843, 111 L.Ed.2d 224 (1990) (recognizing the Fourteenth Amendment guarantee of the right to refuse medical treatment) (citing Jacobson v. Massachusetts, 197 U.S. 11, 24–30, 25 S.Ct. 358, 360–63, 49 L.Ed. 643 (1905) (balancing an individual's liberty interest in declining an unwanted smallpox vaccine against the State's interest in preventing disease)).

> No right is held more sacred, or is more carefully guarded, by the common law, than the right of every individual to the possession and control of his own person, free from all restraint or interference of others, unless by clear and unquestionable authority of law. United States v. Charters, 829 F.2d 479, 490–91 (4th Cir.1987). [4]
>
> [4] The right to be free of undesired physical touching originates in early law, including the English common law, and "is reflected in the tort of battery which protects the individual against even the slightest unconsented touching." Charters, 829 F.2d at 490 (citing W. Keeton, et al. Prosser and Keeton on The Law of Torts § 9 p. 39 (5th ed.1984)); see Pugsley v. Privette, 220 Va. 892, 263 S.E.2d 69 (1980) (holding that physician's performing surgery without a patient's informed consent constitutes battery).

However, this fundamental liberty interest must be balanced with the State's interests in protecting persons who cannot make informed health decisions, either because they are incapable of making such decisions or incapable of communicating such decisions. Cruzan, 497 U.S. at 262, 110 S.Ct. at 2843.

In enacting Code § 37.1–134.21, "[t]he General Assembly provided for involuntary medical treatment in very limited circumstances, where such treatment is determined to be in the best interests of a person who is unable to give an informed consent to treatment." *331 Mullins v. Commonwealth, 39 Va.App. 728, 732, 576 S.E.2d 770, 771–72 (2003) (emphasis added). "Code § 37.1–134.21 describes the procedures to be followed and the findings a court is to make prior to authorizing such treatment." Id. Code § 37.1–134.21(A) provides that the court may order

[t]he provision, withholding or withdrawal of a specific treatment or course of treatment for a mental or physical disorder, if it finds upon clear and convincing evidence that (i) the person is either incapable of making an informed decision on his own behalf or is incapable of communicating such a decision due to a physical or mental disorder and (ii) the proposed action is in the best interest of the person.

Code § 37.1–134.21(H) requires the trial court to make specific findings as to an individual's capability to make informed health decisions before it can compel medical treatment without that person's consent. Before ordering an individual to undergo a comprehensive medical evaluation, the trial court must determine:

1. That there is no legally authorized person available to give consent [for her];

2. That [appellant] is incapable either of making an informed decision regarding a specific treatment or course of treatment or is physically or mentally incapable of communicating such a decision;

3. That [appellant] is unlikely to become capable of making an informed decision or of communicating an informed decision with the time required for decision; and

4. That the proposed course of treatment is in the best interest of [appellant]....

In terms of making informed health care decisions under Code § 37.1–134.21, we make no distinction between a medical evaluation or examination[5] on the one hand, and medical *332 treatment[6] on the other, both of which may involve intrusive procedures.

[5] Medical "examination" is defined as the "inspection, palpation, auscultation, percussion, or other means of investigation, especially for diagnosing disease, qualified according to the methods employed as physical examination, radiologic examination, diagnostic imaging examination, or cystoscopic examination." Dorland's Illustrated Medical Dictionary 630 (29th ed.2000).

[6] Medical "treatment" is defined as "the management and care of a patient for the purpose of combating disease or disorder." Dorland's at 1868.

**290 ... In reviewing a trial court's order for involuntary medical care..., "'we are bound by the trial court's findings of historical fact unless 'plainly wrong' or without evidence to support them.'" Mullins, 39 Va.App. at 732, 576 S.E.2d at 772. ... [T]he trial court concluded that a comprehensive medical examination and evaluation at the University of Virginia Medical Center was in appellant's best interest, explaining that she had "to lose weight to get better." It further stated that

[A]s part of the treatment order the Court is going to order that you go to the University of Virginia for this comprehensive examination. If it takes a day, fine; if it's [sic] take a week, fine; if it takes a month, fine. I want this comprehensive evaluation.

While the trial court's determination of the need for a comprehensive medical examination is well founded, it is not enough that the examination be in appellant's best interests. Code § 37.1–134.21(H) specifically provides that the trial court must find "[t]hat the person who is the subject of the petition *333 is incapable either of making an informed decision regarding a specific treatment or course of treatment or is physically or mentally incapable of communicating such a decision."[7]

> [7] Compare with definition of "incapacitated person" in Code § 37.1–134.6 [now § 64.2-2000 (""Incapacitated person" means an adult who has been found by a court to be incapable of receiving and evaluating information effectively or responding to people, events, or environments to such an extent that the individual lacks the capacity to (i) meet the essential requirements for his health, care, safety, or therapeutic needs without the assistance or protection of a guardian or (ii) manage property or financial affairs or provide for his support or for the support of his legal dependents without the assistance or protection of a conservator. A finding that the individual displays poor judgment alone shall not be considered sufficient evidence that the individual is an incapacitated person within the meaning of this definition. A finding that a person is incapacitated shall be construed as a finding that the person is "mentally incompetent" as that term is used in Article II, Section 1 of the Constitution of Virginia and Title 24.2 unless the court order entered pursuant to this chapter specifically provides otherwise.")] and the provisions of Code § 37.1–134.14 [now § 64.2-2009 (authorizing appointment of a guardian or conservator)].

Here, the trial court explicitly found that "despite her depression, [appellant was] capable of making informed health care decisions...."

DSS concedes on brief that the trial court failed to make the required finding pursuant to Code § 37.1–134.2(H). It contends, however, that the trial court had authority to order appellant to undergo the comprehensive medical examination under its general equity jurisdiction.

We find no authority for the proposition advanced by DSS. The authority of the trial court to order medical treatment is defined by the statute, not by the broader principles of equity. "The rule is well established in Virginia that when the legislature has enacted a comprehensive statutory scheme that encompasses a matter that was not formerly within the purview of the common law, a court, when exercising the jurisdiction conferred under that statutory scheme, may not proceed in derogation of the statutory scheme." Willis v. Gamez, 20 Va.App. 75, 82, 455 S.E.2d 274, 278 (1995). To grant courts such authority under general equity powers would eviscerate the narrowly drawn statutory scheme balancing the Commonwealth's interests in protecting its citizens with the individual's constitutionally protected liberty interest against compelled medical procedures. Absent a finding... that appellant was incapable of making an informed health care decision or communicating that decision, the trial court lacked authority, over her objection, to order her confined for an indefinite period to undergo a comprehensive health examination and evaluation. ... *334 ...

We, therefore,... vacate that portion of the judgment ... ordering appellant to "attend the comprehensive evaluation at the University of Virginia Medical Center..."

C.   Disposition of the Body

We end with perhaps the most grim of decisions a client or family member might make.

Title 54.1. Professions and Occupations
Subtitle III. Professions and Occupations Regulated by Boards Within the
Department of Health Professions
Chapter 28. Funeral Services
Article 5. Preneed Funeral Contracts

§ 54.1-2825. Person to make arrangements for funeral and disposition of remains

A. Any person may designate in a signed and notarized writing, which has been accepted in writing by the person so designated, an individual who shall make arrangements and be otherwise responsible for his funeral and the disposition of his remains, including cremation, interment, entombment, or memorialization, or some combination thereof, upon his death. Such designee shall have priority over all persons otherwise entitled to make such arrangements, provided that a copy of the signed and notarized writing is provided to the funeral service establishment and to the cemetery, if any, no later than 48 hours after the funeral service establishment has received the remains. ...

Article 1. Board of Funeral Directors and Embalmers

§ 54.1-2807.01. When next of kin disagree

A. In the absence of a designation under § 54.1-2825, when there is a disagreement among a decedent's next of kin concerning the arrangements for his funeral or the disposition of his remains, any of the next of kin may petition the circuit court where the decedent resided at the time of his death to determine which of the next of kin shall have the authority to make arrangements for the decedent's funeral or the disposition of his remains. The court may require notice to and the convening of such of the next of kin as it deems proper.

B. In determining the matter before it, the court shall consider the expressed wishes, if any, of the decedent, the legal and factual relationship between or among the disputing next of kin and between each of the disputing next of kin and the decedent, and any other factor the court considers relevant to determine who should be authorized to make the arrangements for the decedent's funeral or the disposition of his remains.

§ 54.1-2800. Definitions

"Next of kin" means any of the following persons, regardless of the relationship to the decedent: any person designated to make arrangements for the disposition of the decedent's remains upon his death pursuant to § 54.1-2825, the legal spouse, child aged 18 years or older, parent of a decedent aged 18 years or older, custodial parent or noncustodial parent of a decedent younger than 18 years of age, siblings over 18 years of age, guardian of minor child, guardian of minor siblings, maternal grandparents, paternal grandparents, maternal siblings over 18 years of age and paternal siblings over 18 years of age, or any other relative in the descending order of blood relationship.

§ 54.1-2807.02. Absence of next of kin

In the absence of a next of kin, a person designated to make arrangements for the decedent's burial or the disposition of his remains pursuant to § 54.1-2825, an agent named in an advance directive pursuant to § 54.1-2984, or any guardian appointed pursuant to Chapter 20 (§ 64.2-2000 et seq.) of Title 64.2 who may exercise the powers conferred in the order of appointment or by § 64.2-2019, or upon the failure or refusal of such next of kin, designated person, agent, or guardian to accept responsibility for the disposition of the decedent, then any other person 18 years of age or older who is able to provide positive identification of the deceased and is willing to pay for the costs associated with the disposition of the decedent's remains shall be authorized to make arrangements for such disposition of the decedent's remains. ...

Supreme Court of Virginia.
Grisso v. Nolen
262 Va. 688, 554 S.E.2d 91 (2001)

Opinion by Justice LAWRENCE L. KOONTZ, JR.

... Dillard Lawson Nolen and Lorraine Chitwood Nolen were married in 1955. The couple had one child, Sandra Nolen Grisso. Dillard Nolen and Lorraine Nolen were divorced in 1993, but continued to cohabit intermittently for the next six years until Lorraine's death on August 4, 1999. Lorraine Nolen died intestate and left no written instructions concerning the disposition of her body. Grisso, as her mother's next of *691 kin and sole heir, had her mother's **93 body interred at Sandy Ridge Baptist Church in Franklin County.

On January 7, 2000, Dillard Nolen filed a petition... seeking an order to have Lorraine Nolen's body disinterred and reburied in one of two adjoining burial plots at Franklin Memorial Park in Franklin County. ... Dillard alleged that Lorraine had "at all times indicated her desire to be buried in Franklin Memorial Park," and for that reason in 1998 he had purchased the two burial plots and a headstone engraved with his name and that of his former spouse. Dillard also alleged that he had purchased a pre-paid funeral service contract for Lorraine in 1993 prior to the couple's divorce. He further alleged that Grisso had been estranged from both her parents "for a long period of time." ... *692 ...

[T]his appeal is limited to the question of standing... [T]he evidence was **94 in conflict regarding whether Lorraine Nolen had expressed a wish to be buried at Franklin Memorial Park. There was evidence that following the couple's divorce and a subsequent violent confrontation between her husband and daughter, Lorraine had expressed a vehement desire not to be buried next to her husband, but she did not expressly state where she would prefer to be buried. However, there was evidence that, during one period when the couple had reconciled, Lorraine had accompanied her former husband to Franklin Memorial Park when he purchased the burial plots and headstone. There was also evidence that she later told several relatives and friends that she would be buried in Franklin Memorial Park next to her former husband. Although Dillard Nolen had attempted to have his former wife "make somebody power of attorney" because Grisso was "liable to bury [her] anywhere," Lorraine declined to make such an *693 election. There was no dispute that the relationship between Dillard Nolen and Grisso was strained beyond the point of foreseeable reconciliation. ...

DISCUSSION

... Lorraine Nolen made no testamentary provision regarding her desired final resting place and did not "make arrangements for [her] burial or the disposition of [her] remains" in accordance with Code § 54.1–2825. Under such circumstances, there also can be no dispute that upon her death, the proper determination of the place of her burial rested with her personal representative, her surviving spouse, or her next of kin. Goldman v. Mollen, 168 Va. 345, 354, 191 S.E. 627, 631 (1937) Thus, Grisso, as her *694 mother's next of kin, was vested with the authority to determine the place of her mother's burial.[2]

> [2] Although the record is not clear on this point, it would appear that Grisso also qualified as the personal representative of her mother's estate. Certainly, as next of kin and sole heir, she would have been the preferred person to so qualify. Code § 64.1–118 [now § 64.2-502].

By contrast, it is apparent that Dillard Nolen had no authority to arrange for the disposition of his former wife's body upon her death. He was not authorized to make such arrangements by a designation made pursuant to Code § 54.1–2825, and he was not a person entitled to preferential appointment as the personal representative of Lorraine Nolen's estate under Code § 64.1–118. Dillard Nolen was not Lorraine Nolen's "surviving spouse" as contemplated in *Goldman*, nor was he among Lorraine Nolen's "next of kin" as that term is defined with reference to who may make such arrangements because he was not the "legal spouse" of the decedent at the time of her death. See Code § 54.1–2800. **95

For these reasons, beyond question Lorraine Nolen's body was properly buried at Sandy Ridge Baptist Church, notwithstanding the subsequent revelation that her wish may have been to have her body buried at Franklin Memorial Park. This is particularly true in light of the fact that no challenge to the selection of the place of burial at Sandy Ridge Baptist Church was raised prior to the burial there, and no assertion is made that Grisso knowingly selected that place of burial against her mother's wish. It is in this factual context that we consider the issue of Dillard Nolen's standing to petition for disinterment and reburial of his ex-wife's body. Our focus is on whether he had a sufficient legal interest in Lorraine Nolen's wish regarding her final resting place so as to permit the court to invoke its equity authority to grant his petition. ...

Dillard Nolen contends that he had standing because the suit was not adversarial in nature, but was brought "in rem" in order to permit the court to determine and give effect to Lorraine Nolen's wish regarding her final resting place. ... We cannot agree with this novel premise regarding standing to invoke the authority of the court in equity to *695 consider such a weighty and sensitive matter as whether to allow the disinterment of a body from a proper grave.

There can be no question of the authority of the court in equity to authorize the disinterment of a body for reburial in another place. See, e.g., Grinnan v. Fredericksburg Lodge, 118 Va. 588, 592, 88 S.E. 79, 80 (1916). Among other reasons, this authority is necessary in order to give effect to the principle, based upon a long-standing societal belief in the sanctity of giving effect to a decedent's wishes, that "the expressed wish of one, as to his final resting place, shall, so far as it is possible, be carried out." Goldman, 168 Va. at 356, 191 S.E. at 632 (citation omitted).

However, that authority must be tempered by the principle, based upon an equally long-standing societal belief in the sanctity of graves, that "[i]nterments once made should not be disturbed except for good cause." Id. at 355, 191 S.E. at 631. Indeed, even where the party seeking disinterment was also the party responsible for selecting the initial gravesite, courts will not allow a violation of the final place of interment without good cause. See, e.g., Dougherty v. Mercantile–Safe Deposit and Trust Company, 282 Md. 617, 387 A.2d 244, 246–47 (1978). ...

[T]he circumstances of the couple's thirty-eight year marriage and continued periods of cohabitation following their divorce are insufficient to confer upon Dillard Nolen any cognizable interest or legal standing with respect to matters concerning his former wife. See, e.g., Gloth v. Gloth, 154 Va. 511, 535, 153 S.E. 879, 886 (1930) (following divorce "the marriage bond is completely severed"). One of the principal effects of a decree of divorce is to sever the property interests of the two parties including the extinguishing of all contingent property rights of one spouse to the property of the other. Code § 20–111. Similarly, to the extent that the authority to determine the disposition of a decedent's remains is a quasi-property right of a surviving spouse, Goldman, 168 Va. at 354, 191 S.E. at 631, that right would not survive the entry of a divorce decree. Cf. Vaughan v. Vaughan, 294 Mass. 164, 200 N.E. 912, 913–14 (1936) (holding that wife had standing to seek disinterment where death of husband occurred prior to entry of decree of divorce).

In short, under the specific facts of this case, Dillard was a legal stranger to Lorraine as the result of a divorce decree. As such, and notwithstanding what evidence he might have regarding Lorraine Nolen's wish as to the final resting place of her *696 body, he had no cognizable interest in the place of her burial and, thus, no standing to seek the disinterment of her body for reburial. ...   **96 ... For these reasons, we... enter final judgment dismissing the petition for disinterment and reburial.

CPSIA information can be obtained at www.ICGtesting.com
Printed in the USA
BVOW03*1938100816
458111BV00008B/7/P